D0274151

Chambers factfinder

Chambers

CHAMBERS
An imprint of Chambers Harrap Publishers Ltd
7 Hopetoun Crescent
Edinburgh, EH7 4AY

www.chambers.co.uk

This third edition published by Chambers Harrap Publishers Ltd 2008
Previous editions published 2004, 2006

A CIP catalogue record for this book is available from the British Library.

ISBN 978 0550 10290 4

Image credits

Star images, p10
Copyright © 2005 by Houghton Mifflin Company. Adapted and reproduced by permission from *The American Heritage Student Science Dictionary.*

Cloud images, pp36–7
Copyright © 2005 by Houghton Mifflin Company. Reproduced by permission from *The American Heritage Student Science Dictionary.*

Electromagnetic spectrum image, p381
Copyright © 2005 by Houghton Mifflin Company. Reproduced by permission from *The American Heritage Student Science Dictionary.*

Muscles diagram, p390
Copyright © www.arttoday.com

Designed and typeset by Chambers Harrap Publishers Ltd, Edinburgh
Typeset in Zurich BT
Printed and bound by Legoprint, Italy

Contributors

Editor

Katie Brooks

Contributors

Ian Brookes

Hilary Marsden

Alison Pickering

Colin Salter

Patrick White

Publishing Manager

Hazel Norris

Data Management

Ruth O'Donovan

Prepress

Becky Pickard

Introduction

Since its first publication in 2004, *Chambers Factfinder* has become a key part of the Chambers range of reference books. This third edition continues the tradition of being entertaining as well as informative and reliable, and is packed with up-to-date facts and figures for knowledge-seekers of all ages.

The material contained in *Chambers Factfinder* has been specially chosen for its relevance, including some information often marginalized elsewhere but that is nevertheless valuable for quizzes, crosswords, puzzles and settling arguments. A 'one-stop' approach has been taken, with careful and intuitive grouping of material ensuring that all the data on a particular subject can be found in a single place. There are 28 major subject areas, within which are clearly labelled individual subsections, arranged so as to take the user on a journey from the furthest realms of the universe to our own planet and the world around us, and then on to the world's people and the diverse fields of human culture and achievement.

Information is presented simply in tables and lists for clarity, aided by maps, diagrams, pie charts, pictures and boxes; introductory information is distinguished by background tints. Detailed contents listings at the front of the book and a handy index at the back ensure that specific facts are easy to find. However, the book is equally suited for browsing. Amusing 'fascinating fact' boxes are dotted throughout the text, ensuring that the book is a delight to dip into; some provide interesting supplementary details on a subject, while others contain quirky, intriguing snippets of information.

Chambers Factfinder has been specially designed to be accessible, user-friendly and full of the information that really matters. Whether you are hoping to win a pub quiz, trying to complete a school project or just browsing for fun, this book will fit the bill.

ABBREVIATIONS

a	acre(s)
abbrev	abbreviations
AD	Anno Domini
AU	astronomical units
BBC	British Broadcasting Corporation
BC	Before Christ
bu	bushel(s)
C	Celsius (Centigrade)
c	century
c.	circa
cc	cubic centimetre(s)
CIS	Commonwealth of Independent States
cl	centilitre(s)
cm	centimetre(s)
Co	company
cu	cubic
cwt	hundredweight(s)
dB	decibel(s)
DC	District of Columbia
dm	decimetre(s)
E	east
e	estimate
eg	for example (*exempli gratia*)
etc	and so on (*et cetera*)
EU	European Union
F	Fahrenheit
fl oz	fluid ounce(s)
ft	foot (feet)
g	gram(s)
gal	gallon(s)
GB	gigabyte(s)
ha	hectare(s)
hl	hectolitre(s)
ie	that is (*id est*)
in	inch(es)
ISO	International Organization for Standardization
IVR	International Vehicle Registration
K	Kelvin
KB	kilobyte(s)
kg	kilogram(s)
km	kilometre(s)
kph	kilometre(s) per hour
kW	kilowatt(s)
l	litre(s)
lb	pound(s)
lbm	pound(s) mass
m	metre(s)
MB	megabyte(s)
mg	milligram(s)
mi	mile(s)
ml	millilitre(s)
mm	millimetre(s)
MP	Member of Parliament
Mt	Mount
N	north
n/a	not applicable
NASA	National Aeronautics and Space Administration
no	number
oz	ounce(s)
pk	peck(s)
pop	population
p(p)	page(s)
Prot	Protestant
pt	pint(s)
qt	quart(s)
RC	Roman Catholic
S	south
sec	second(s)
SI	Système International (d'Unités)
sq	square
SS	saints
St	Saint
st	stone(s)
TV	television
UK	United Kingdom
UN	United Nations
US	United States
USA	United States of America
USSR	Union of Soviet Socialist Republics
UT	Unified Team
v	versus
W	west
yd	yard(s)
ZIP	zone improvement plan

Months are abbreviated to the first three letters (26 Nov 1976)

Additional abbreviations can be found under individual sections in the text; for example, currency abbreviations are listed under **ECONOMICS**.

Contents

CONTENTS

HUMAN GEOGRAPHY

CONTENTS

POLITICS, LAW AND ORDER

ANCIENT GREECE AND ROME

RELIGIONS, BELIEFS AND FOLKLORE

CONTENTS

TIME

SCIENCE

HUMAN BODY

MATHEMATICS

ECONOMICS

MEASUREMENT, CONVERSION AND SIZE

INVENTIONS, DISCOVERIES AND FIRSTS

ARCHITECTURE AND ENGINEERING

SOCIETY AND LEARNING

LITERATURE

ART

CONTENTS

FILM

MUSIC

FOOD AND DRINK

LANGUAGE

COMMUNICATION

TRANSPORT

SPORTS, COMPETITIONS AND GAMES

THE SOLAR SYSTEM

SUN

Age	4.6 billion–4.7 billion years	**Predicted total lifespan**	10 billion years
Distance from Earth (mean)	150 million km/93 million mi	**Surface area**	6 087 billion sq km/2 350 billion sq mi
Diameter	1 392 500km/864 950mi		
Mass	1.989×10^{30}kg/ 4.385×10^{30}lb	**Volume**	1.4122×10^{18} cu km/ 3.388×10^{17} cu mi
Luminosity	3.83×10^{27} kW	**Density (mean)**	1.409g/cu cm/87.96 lb/cu ft
Temperature (core)	15 million K/15 million°C/ 27 million°F	**Surface gravity**	2.740×10^{4}cm/sq sec/ 10 787in/sq sec
Rotation	26.8 days (of solar equator, as seen from Earth)	**Temperature (surface)**	5 770K/5 500°C/10 000°F

Composition of the Sun's photosphere

Element	% weight
Hydrogen	73.46
Helium	24.85
Oxygen	0.77
Carbon	0.29
Iron	0.16
Neon	0.12
Nitrogen	0.09
Silicon	0.07
Magnesium	0.05
Sulphur	0.04
Others	0.10

Exploding Energy

The Sun's energy comes from nuclear fusion. It consumes hundreds of millions of tonnes of hydrogen every second, which reactions convert into helium. This generates as much energy every second as almost 91 billion tonnes, or 100 billion tons, of TNT exploding.

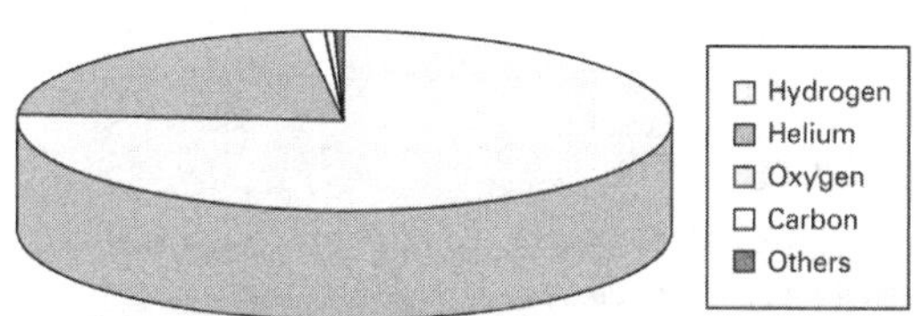

Inside the Sun

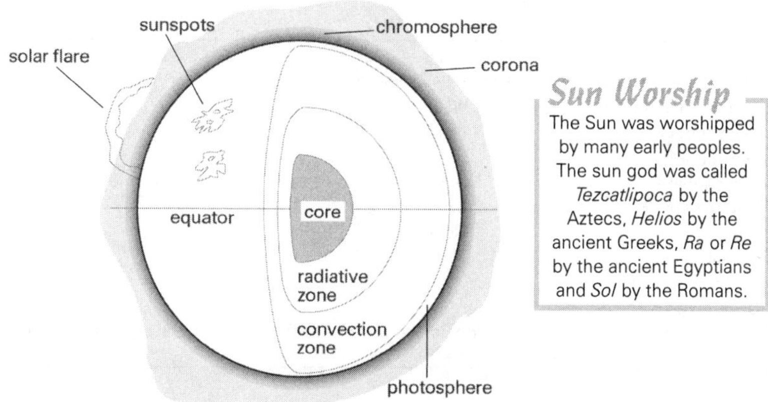

Sun Worship

The Sun was worshipped by many early peoples. The sun god was called *Tezcatlipoca* by the Aztecs, *Helios* by the ancient Greeks, *Ra* or *Re* by the ancient Egyptians and *Sol* by the Romans.

SOLAR SYSTEM

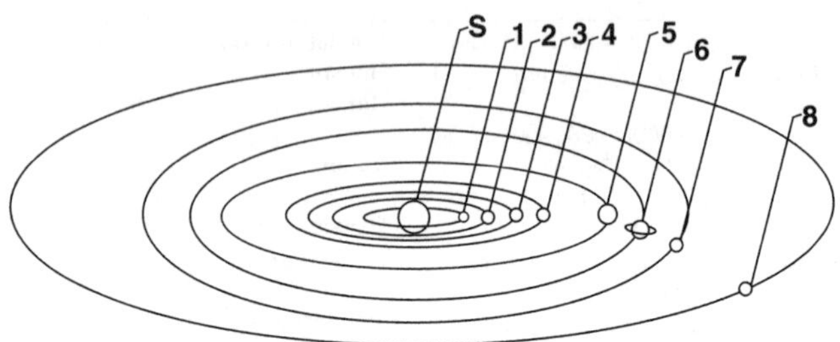

S = Sun
1 = Mercury
2 = Venus
3 = Earth
4 = Mars
5 = Jupiter
6 = Saturn
7 = Uranus
8 = Neptune

Note: Pluto is no longer officially a planet; see **Dwarf planets** later in this section

Wandering Stars

Planet comes from the Greek word *planētēs*, meaning *wanderer*. Planets were known by the ancient Greeks as *astéres planêtai*, or *wandering stars*, because it was believed that they meandered about the skies.

PLANETS

For satellites, the first figure gives the total number. The names of the major satellites are listed with those closest to the planet first; the year of discovery is given in parentheses. See **Dwarf Planets** for information on Pluto, and see separate section **The Earth** for information on the Earth.

Mercury

Diameter at equator	4878km/3031mi
Maximum distance from the Sun	69.4 million km/43 million mi
Minimum distance from the Sun	46.8 million km/29 million mi
Length of year	88 days
Length of day	58 days 16 hours
Atmosphere	Almost none; traces of oxygen, sodium, and helium
Surface gravity	370cm/sq sec/146in/sq sec
Rings	None
Satellites	None

Discovered
Known in prehistory; named after the Roman god of merchants, the messenger of the gods, possibly because of its fast movement.

Polar Planet

In 1991 radar observations indicated that Mercury may have water ice at its north and south poles.

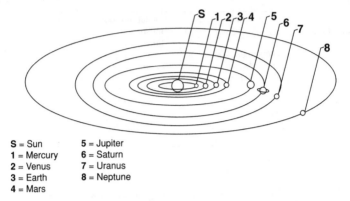

Venus

Diameter at equator	12 104km/7 521mi
Maximum distance from the Sun	109 million km/67.6 million mi
Minimum distance from the Sun	107.6 million km/66.7 million mi
Length of year	224.7 days
Length of day	243 days
Atmosphere	Mainly carbon dioxide and nitrogen; clouds of sulphuric acid
Surface gravity	887cm/sq sec/349in/sq sec
Rings	None
Satellites	None

Discovered

Known in prehistory; named after the Roman goddess of love, because of its brightness. Most of its surface features are named after female figures.

Sultry Venus

Venus has an extreme greenhouse effect due to the high concentrations of carbon dioxide in its atmosphere. Temperatures on the surface are hot enough to melt lead.

Earth

see separate section **The Earth**

Mars

Diameter at equator	6 794km/4 222mi
Maximum distance from the Sun	249.2 million km/154.5 million mi
Minimum distance from the Sun	207.3 million km/128.5 million mi
Length of year	687 days
Length of day	24 hours 37 minutes 23 seconds
Atmosphere	Carbon dioxide, nitrogen, argon
Surface gravity	371cm/sq sec/146in/sq sec
Rings	None
Satellites	2: Phobos (1877), Deimos (1877)

Discovered

Known in prehistory; named after the Roman god of war, because of its red colour.

Volcanic Mars

Mars is home to the largest volcano in the solar system, Olympus Mons. It is 624km/374mi in diameter, 25km/16mi high and has a crater 80km/50mi wide.

Jupiter

Diameter at equator	142 800km/88 700mi
Maximum distance from the Sun	817.4 million km/506.8 million mi
Minimum distance from the Sun	741.6 million km/459.8 million mi
Length of year	11.86 years
Length of day	9 hours 50 minutes 30 seconds
Atmosphere	Mainly hydrogen and helium
Surface gravity	2312cm/sq sec/910in/sq sec
Rings	Yes
Satellites	Almost 60: Io (1610), Europa (1610), Ganymede (1610) and Callisto (1610)

Discovered

Known in prehistory; named after the Roman god of the sky and its attributes (Sun, Moon, thunder, rain, etc).

Almost a Star

Jupiter is a proto-star. If it had been 50–100 times more massive, hydrogen fusion in its interior would have caused it to shine like our Sun.

Saturn

Diameter at equator	120 536km/74 900mi
Maximum distance from the Sun	1.5 billion km/937.6 million mi
Minimum distance from the Sun	1.3 billion km/834.6 million mi
Length of year	29.46 years
Length of day	10 hours 14 minutes
Atmosphere	Mainly hydrogen and helium
Surface gravity	896cm/sq sec/353in/sq sec
Rings	Yes
Satellites	At least 30: Mimas (1789), Enceladus (1789), Tethys (1684), Dione (1684), Rhea (1672), Titan (1655), Hyperion (1848), Iapetus (1671)

Discovered

Known in prehistory; named after the Roman god of fertility and agriculture.

Titanic Aliens

Saturn's largest moon, Titan, is a little bigger than the planet Mercury. Scientists think there is a chance that the organic compounds in its atmosphere may indicate the presence of some form of life.

Uranus

Diameter at equator	51 118km/31 765mi
Maximum distance from the Sun	3 billion km/1.8 billion mi
Minimum distance from the Sun	2.7 billion km/1.7 billion mi
Length of year	84.01 years
Length of day	16–28 hours[1]
Atmosphere	Hydrogen, helium, methane
Surface gravity	869cm/sq sec/342in/sq sec
Rings	Yes
Satellites	At least 20: Ariel (1851), Umbriel (1851), Miranda (1948), Titania (1787), Oberon (1787)

Discovered

1781; its discoverer, William Herschel, wanted to name it *Georgium Sidus* ('the Georgian planet') after the reigning British monarch, but the name Uranus came into more common use in around 1850. In Greek mythology Uranus was the god of the heavens.

[1] *Different latitudes rotate at different speeds.*

Catastrophic Collision

Uranus orbits the Sun 'on its side' – that is, with its poles pointing toward the Sun. This may be the result of a catastrophic collision with a huge body such as a minor planet or asteroid.

Neptune

Diameter at equator	49 492km/30 754mi
Maximum distance from the Sun	4.5 billion km/2.8 billion mi
Minimum distance from the Sun	4.4 billion km/2.7 billion mi
Length of year	164.79 years
Length of day	18–20 hours[1]
Atmosphere	Methane, hydrogen, helium
Surface gravity	1 100cm/sq sec/433in/sq sec
Rings	Yes
Satellites	11: Proteus (1989), Triton (1846), Nereid (1949)

Discovered

First observed by German astronomer Johann Galle in 1846.

[1] *Different latitudes rotate at different speeds.*

Planetary Prediction

Neptune was the first planet to be discovered by mathematical calculations, rather than by observation. In the mid-19th century, astronomers noticed that Uranus, then thought to be the outermost planet, was not always quite where they had thought it would be, and realised that there must be another planet affecting its orbit. French astronomer Urbain Leverrier and English astronomer John Couch Adams independently calculated where the extra planet must be, allowing Johann Galle to find it.

DWARF PLANETS

Until recently, Pluto was described as being the ninth and outermost planet of the solar system. However, in 2006 the International Astronomical Union (IAU) transferred Pluto into the new category of 'dwarf planet' along with two other celestial objects. Dwarf planets are like planets in that they orbit the Sun and are massive enough to be nearly spherical in shape, but unlike planets they do not have a clear neighbourhood around their orbit.

Dwarf planet	Region	Diameter
Ceres	Asteroid belt	975 × 909km
Eris	Scattered disc	2 400 ± 100km
Pluto	Kuiper belt	2 306 ± 20km

The Naming of Pluto

Pluto was discovered in 1930 by the US astronomer Clyde Tombaugh and was named for the god of the underworld from Greek and Roman mythology. The name was proposed by an eleven-year-old British girl, Venetia Burney, whose grandfather passed on her suggestion to a friend who was Professor of Astronomy at the University of Oxford. The professor sent a telegram to the Lowell Observatory, where Tombaugh was working, and the name 'Pluto' was chosen unanimously in a ballot of the observatory's members. The largest of Pluto's satellites, Charon, was named for another figure of the underworld, the ferryman of the spirits of the dead in Greek mythology.

MOON

Diameter	3 476km/2 160mi
Average distance from Earth	384 467km/238 908mi
Orbital period	27.32 days
Age	Approx 4.6 billion years
Atmosphere	Trace elements only; water ice has, however, been detected at the poles
Mean surface temperature	107°C/225°F (day), –153°C/–245°F (night)
Surface gravity	162cm/sq sec/64in/sq sec
Mass	7.3483×10^{22}kg/16.2×10^{22}lb
Density	3.341g/cu cm/208.572 lb/cu ft

Moon Mystery

No one knows for certain where the Moon comes from. The most probable theory suggests that a body approximately the size of Mars once hit the Earth, and the Moon is part of the debris from that collision. Others suggest that it may originally have been part of the Earth that broke away, or perhaps that it was separate and just happened to be caught by the Earth's gravity, or even that it formed gradually in orbit over time.

Lunar seas

The Romans thought that the dark areas visible on the surface of the Moon were lunar 'maria', seas. Modern astronomy has shown instead that they are dry plains filled with volcanic rocks. However, how they formed is still unclear.

Latin name	English name	Latin name	English name
Lacus Mortis	Lake of Death	Mare Serenitatis	Sea of Serenity
Lacus Somniorum	Lake of Dreams	Mare Smythii	Smyth's Sea
Mare Australe	Southern Sea	Mare Spumans	Foaming Sea
Mare Crisium	Sea of Crises	Mare Tranquillitatis	Sea of Tranquillity
Mare Fecunditatis	Sea of Fertility	Mare Undarum	Sea of Waves
Mare Frigoris	Sea of Cold	Mare Vaporum	Sea of Vapours
Mare Humboldtianum	Humboldt's Sea	Oceanus Procellarum	Ocean of Storms
Mare Humorum	Sea of Moisture	Palus Epidemiarum	Marsh of Epidemics
Mare Imbrium	Sea of Showers	Palus Nebularum	Marsh of Mists
Mare Ingenii[1]	Sea of Geniuses	Palus Putredinis	Marsh of Decay
Mare Marginis	Marginal Sea	Palus Somnii	Marsh of Sleep
Mare Moscoviense[1]	Moscow Sea	Sinus Aestuum	Bay of Heats
Mare Nectaris	Sea of Nectar	Sinus Iridum	Bay of Rainbows
Mare Nubium	Sea of Clouds	Sinus Medii	Central Bay
Mare Orientale[1]	Eastern Sea	Sinus Roris	Bay of Dew

[1] *On the far side of the Moon.*

Phases of the Moon

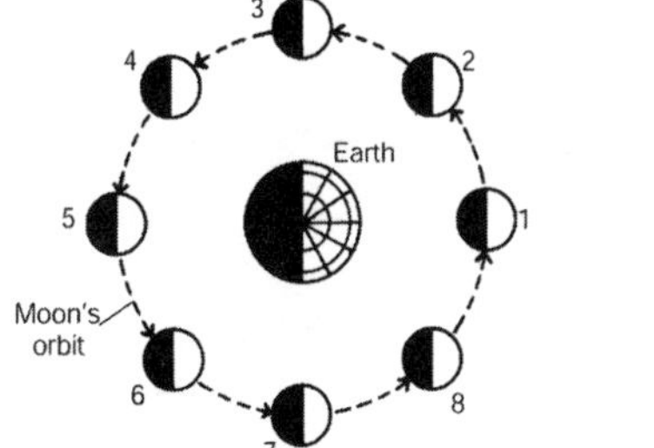

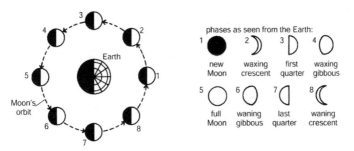

phases as seen from the Earth:

1 new Moon
2 waxing crescent
3 first quarter
4 waxing gibbous
5 full Moon
6 waning gibbous
7 last quarter
8 waning crescent

Tidal Power

The gravitational forces between the Moon and Earth mean that the Earth pulls on the Moon and keeps it in orbit. However, the Moon also has a smaller pull on the Earth; this is enough to change the height of the seas and oceans by several metres as the Moon's position changes, creating tides. Even the Earth's crust is deformed very slightly, although only by a few centimetres.

THE UNIVERSE

STARS

The constellations

A constellation is composed of stars which form a group as seen from the Earth. There are 88 constellations in total.

Latin name	English name	Latin name	English name
Andromeda	Andromeda	Lacerta	Lizard
Antlia	Air Pump	Leo	Lion
Apus	Bird of Paradise	Leo Minor	Little Lion
Aquarius	Water Bearer	Lepus	Hare
Aquila	Eagle	Libra	Scales
Ara	Altar	Lupus	Wolf
Aries	Ram	Lynx	Lynx
Auriga	Charioteer	Lyra	Harp
Boötes	Herdsman	Mensa	Table
Caelum	Chisel	Microscopium	Microscope
Camelopardalis	Giraffe	Monoceros	Unicorn
Cancer	Crab	Musca	Fly
Canes Venatici	Hunting Dogs	Norma	Level
Canis Major	Great Dog	Octans	Octant
Canis Minor	Little Dog	Ophiuchus	Serpent Bearer
Capricornus	Sea Goat	Orion	Orion
Carina	Keel	Pavo	Peacock
Cassiopeia	Cassiopeia	Pegasus	Winged Horse
Centaurus	Centaur	Perseus	Perseus
Cepheus	Cepheus	Phoenix	Phoenix
Cetus	Whale	Pictor	Easel
Chamaeleon	Chameleon	Pisces	Fishes
Circinus	Compasses	Piscis Austrinus	Southern Fish
Columba	Dove	Puppis	Ship's Stern
Coma Berenices	Berenice's Hair	Pyxis	Mariner's Compass
Corona Australis	Southern Crown	Reticulum	Net
Corona Borealis	Northern Crown	Sagitta	Arrow
Corvus	Crow	Sagittarius	Archer
Crater	Cup	Scorpius	Scorpion
Crux	Southern Cross	Sculptor	Sculptor
Cygnus	Swan	Scutum	Shield
Delphinus	Dolphin	Serpens	Serpent
Dorado	Swordfish	Sextans	Sextant
Draco	Dragon	Taurus	Bull
Equuleus	Little Horse	Telescopium	Telescope
Eridanus	River Eridanus	Triangulum	Triangle
Fornax	Furnace	Triangulum Australe	Southern Triangle
Gemini	Twins	Tucana	Toucan
Grus	Crane	Ursa Major	Great Bear
Hercules	Hercules	Ursa Minor	Little Bear
Horologium	Clock	Vela	Sails
Hydra	Sea Serpent	Virgo	Virgin
Hydrus	Water Snake	Volans	Flying Fish
Indus	Indian	Vulpecula	Fox

Twinkle, Twinkle, Little Star

Because stars are so far away, starlight has to travel a great distance to reach Earth, and stars appear only as tiny points of light in the sky. They twinkle because of rapid changes in their brightness caused by moving air in the atmosphere through which their light rays pass. The scientific word for twinkling is *scintillation*. Planets are nearer to us, meaning that they appear larger in the sky and their light is stronger and less susceptible to atmospheric turbulence, so they don't twinkle.

Brightest stars

The apparent brightness of a star is represented by a number called its magnitude. The larger the number, the fainter the star. The faintest stars visible to the naked eye are slightly fainter than magnitude six. Only approximately 6,000 of the billions of stars in the sky are visible to the naked eye. The table lists the ten brightest stars visible from the Earth (excluding our own star, the Sun).

Star name	Distance (light years)	Apparent magnitude	Absolute magnitude
Sirius A	8.6	−1.46	+1.4
Canopus	98	−0.72	−8.5
Arcturus	36	−0.06	−0.3
Alpha Centauri A	4.3	−0.01	+4.4
Vega	26.5	+0.04	+0.5
Capella	45	+0.05	−0.7
Rigel	900	+0.14	−6.8
Procyon A	11.2	+0.37	+2.6
Betelgeuse	520	+0.41	−5.5
Achernar	118	+0.51	−1.0

Nearest stars

The star of our own solar system, the Sun, is excluded.

Star name	Distance (light years)	Apparent magnitude	Absolute magnitude
Proxima Centauri	4.3	+11.05	+15.5
Alpha Centauri A	4.3	−0.01	+4.4
Alpha Centauri B	4.3	+1.33	+5.7
Barnard's Star	5.9	+9.54	+13.3
Wolf 359	7.6	+13.53	+16.7
Lalande 21 185	8.1	+7.50	+10.5
Sirius A	8.6	−1.46	+1.4
Sirius B	8.6	+8.68	+11.6
Luyten 726 8A	8.9	+12.45	+15.3
UV 726 8B	8.9	+12.95	+15.3

Biggest and Brightest Star

The Pistol Star is the largest and most powerful star known. Astronomers think it is approximately 100 times bigger than our Sun, and 10 million times brighter – it emits as much energy in just a few seconds as our Sun does in a whole year. The Pistol Star is only approximately 25,000 light years away from us, but it is hidden behind huge clouds of space dust, so despite its brightness isn't visible from the Earth.

Star life cycle

A star is a sphere of matter held together entirely by its own gravitational field, generating energy by means of nuclear fusion reactions deep in its interior. Stars shine as a result of the heat and light energy generated by these reactions. A star will go through several different stages during its lifetime, which can be billions of years.

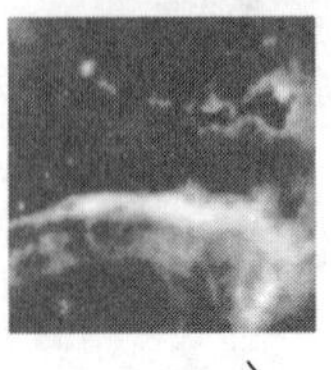

nebula

A cloud of gas and dust. As this matter contracts under gravity, the beginnings of the star are created.

As well as *white dwarf* and *black dwarf* stars, astronomers think that there may also be *brown dwarfs*, very large planets just below the critical mass needed to ignite a stellar nuclear reaction in their own interiors and turn them into stars.

main-sequence star

Eventually the star stops contracting and nuclear fusion reactions begin. The main reaction converts hydrogen into helium. The star begins to shine. Stars spend most of their life at this stage, during which their temperature and brightness will barely change. Our Sun is a main-sequence star.

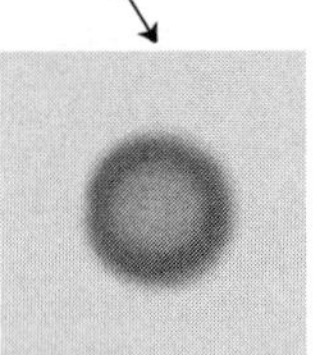

red giant

Eventually reactions in the star's core stop as all the hydrogen is exhausted. The star expands, and swells up greatly. It becomes cooler but brighter.

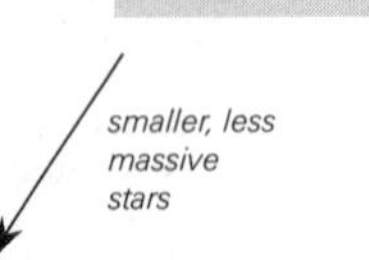

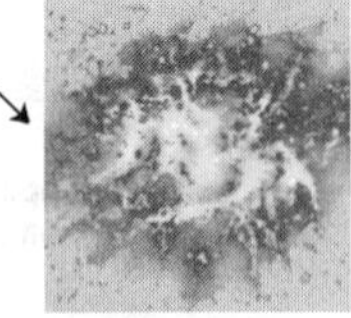

supernova

The star explodes, radiating enormous amounts of energy into space. But the core of the star can collapse under its own gravitational field.

white dwarf

The star implodes, collapsing into a small, very dense body. It is nearing the end of its life. The remains may eventually cool into a *black dwarf*, which no longer emits visible light.

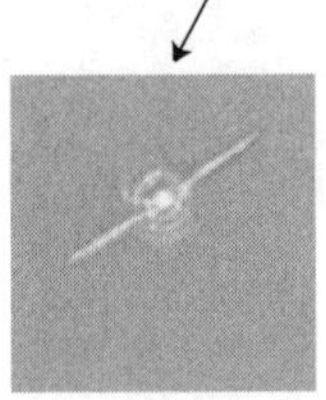

neutron star

If a star has insufficient gravity to collapse entirely, it will become a tiny body, a mass of neutrons only a few miles across, but of very high density.

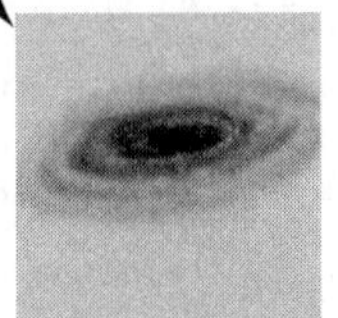

black hole

The core collapses in on itself to the point where its gravity is so strong that nothing, not even light, can escape.

COMETS

Origin

Short-period comets, those which take less than 200 years to orbit the Sun, come from the Kuiper Belt, a large ring of icy bodies orbiting the Sun just beyond Neptune.

Long-period comets take much longer to orbit the Sun (up to 30 million years) and originate in the Oort cloud, a cloud of frozen comet nuclei approximately 100 000 astronomical units[1] away from the Sun. It is estimated that the Oort cloud contains approximately 10 trillion (10 000 000 000 000) comets.

Number

Over 850 recorded to date; approximately ten new comets are discovered each year.

Size, structure and movement

The solid nucleus of a comet is usually several kilometres in diameter, but may be several hundred kilometres; it consists of ice, dust and solid particles like a large, dirty snowball. When the comet passes close to the Sun, a cloud of gas and dust is ejected from the nucleus, forming a huge head or coma, many thousands of kilometres in diameter. The radiations from the Sun elongate the gas and dust to form one or more tails, often extending millions of kilometres in space. These tails point away from the Sun, but as the comet recedes, the tail will decrease in length until the comet returns to its latent dirty snowball state.

Selected comets

The date given is the year in which the comet was first seen.

Halley: 240 BC, 76.1 year orbit
Tycho: 1577, orbit not known
Kirch[2]: 1680, 8 814 year orbit
De Chéseaux: 1744, orbit not known
Lexell: 1770, 5.6 year orbit
Encke: 1786, 3.3 year orbit
Flauergues: 1811, 3 094 year orbit
Pons-Winnecke: 1819, 6.34 year orbit
Great Comet: 1843, 512.6 year orbit
Donati: 1858, 1 950 year orbit
Tebbutt: 1861, 409.1 year orbit
Swift-Tuttle: 1862, 125 year orbit
Cruls: 1882, 758.4 year orbit
Wolf: 1884, 8.4 year orbit
Morehouse: 1908, orbit not known
Daylight Comet: 1910, orbit not known
Schwassmann-Wachmann 1: 1925, 15 year orbit
Arend-Roland: 1957, orbit not known
Mrkos: 1957, orbit not known
Humason: 1961, 3 000 year orbit
Seki-Lines: 1962, orbit not known
Ikeya-Seki: 1965, 880 year orbit
Tago-Sato-Kosaka: 1969, 420 000 year orbit
Bennett: 1970, 1 680 year orbit
Kohoutek: 1973, 75 000 year orbit
West: 1975, 500 000 year orbit
IRAS-Araki-Alcock: 1983, orbit not known
Hale-Bopp: 1995, 2 400 year orbit
Hyakutake: 1996, 18 000 year orbit

[1] *One astronomical unit is equal to the mean distance between the Earth and the Sun.*
[2] *Kirch is also known as Newton.*

Halley's Comet

One of the best-known and brightest comets is Halley's comet. First recorded in 240 BC, when it was seen over China, the comet is visible from Earth approximately every 76 years. Most famously it was visible during the Battle of Hastings in 1066, an event depicted in the Bayeux Tapestry. The comet was named after the English astronomer Edmond Halley (1656–1742), who successfully predicted the years in which it would return. Halley's comet was last seen in 1986, and will not be visible from Earth again until 2061.

ASTEROIDS AND METEORS

Annual meteor showers

Meteors appear to radiate from the named star region.

Shower	Dates	Maximum activity
Quadrantids	1–6 Jan	3–4 Jan
Lyrids	19–25 Apr	22 Apr
Alpha-Scorpiids	20 Apr–19 May	28 Apr–10 May
Eta Aquariids	1–8 May	5 May
Delta Aquariids	15 Jul–10 Aug	28 Jul–5 Aug
Perseids	27 Jul–17 Aug	11–14 Aug
Orionids	15–25 Oct	21 Oct
Taurids	25 Oct–25 Nov	4–14 Nov
Leonids	14–20 Nov	17–18 Nov
Geminids	8–14 Dec	13–14 Dec
Ursids	19–24 Dec	22–23 Dec

Falling Stars

On the night of 16–17 Nov 1966, the Leonids put on a spectacular display between western North America and the eastern USSR. It is estimated that there were approximately 2,300 meteors every minute.

Meteoroids and meteorites

Origin
Interplanetary; some may originate from the Asteroid Belt, others may have cometary origins.

Average composition
Rocky and/or metallic.

Average size
From a few micrometres to many metres or even kilometres; smaller meteoroids that burn up in the Earth's atmosphere are known popularly as 'shooting stars'; larger meteoroids that reach the Earth's surface are scientifically termed meteorites.

Speed
Meteoroids can enter the Earth's atmosphere at speeds of up to 70km/sec, or 45mi/sec. They normally burn up at a height of approximately 100km/60mi.

First recorded human injury from a meteorite
Mrs Hewlett Hodges of Sylacauga, Alabama, USA, was badly bruised by a 3.5kg/8lb meteorite which fell on her home on 30 Nov 1954.

Heaviest known meteorite
A meteorite found in Grootfontein, Namibia, in 1920 weighed 60 tonnes/59 tons. It was composed of nickel-rich iron and was almost 3m/9.8ft wide.

Asteroids

Origin
The Asteroid Belt orbiting the Sun between Mars and Jupiter. This region may contain millions of asteroids.

Number of catalogued asteroids
Approx 20 000.

Largest asteroid
Ceres (1801); 940km/584mi in diameter.

Average composition
Metallic rock with possible addition of water ice.

First landing on an asteroid
2001, on the asteroid Eros, by the unmanned NEAR Shoemaker spacecraft.

ECLIPSES

Solar eclipses

The eclipse begins in the first country named. In an annular eclipse, the apparent size of the Moon is too small for a total eclipse and a bright ring of Sun remains visible. Eclipse data is given for the years 2003–13.

Date	Type of eclipse	Visibility path
31 May 2003	Annular	Iceland, Greenland (Denmark), Scotland (UK)
23 Nov 2003	Total	Antarctica
8 Apr 2005	Annular/Total	Pacific Ocean, Panama, Venezuela
3 Oct 2005	Annular	Atlantic Ocean, Spain, Libya, Indian Ocean
29 Mar 2006	Total	Atlantic Ocean, Libya, Turkey, Russia
22 Sep 2006	Annular	Guyana, Atlantic Ocean, Indian Ocean
7 Feb 2008	Annular	Antarctica
1 Aug 2008	Total	Arctic, Siberia (Russia), China
26 Jan 2009	Annular	southern Atlantic Ocean, Indian Ocean, Borneo (Indonesia)
22 Jul 2009	Total	India, China, Pacific Ocean
15 Jan 2010	Annular	Africa, Indian Ocean, China
11 Jul 2010	Total	Pacific Ocean, southern Chile
20–21 May 2012	Annular	China, northern Pacific Ocean, North America
13 Nov 2012	Total	northern Australia, Pacific Ocean
9–10 May 2013	Annular	Australia, Pacific Ocean
3 Nov 2013	Total	Atlantic Ocean, central Africa, Ethiopia

Total eclipse

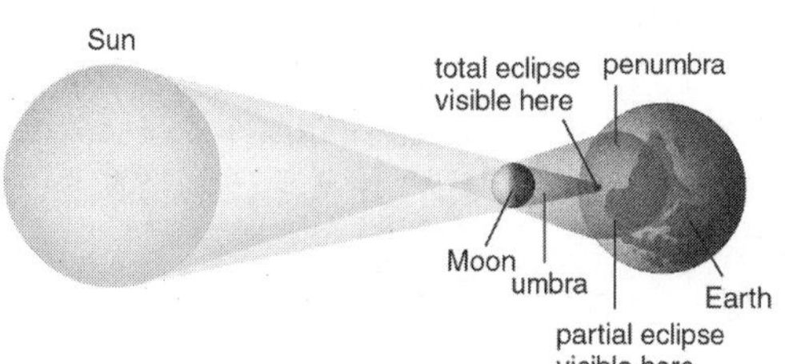

Lunar eclipses

Eclipse data is given for the years 2001–11.

Date	Type of eclipse	Time of mid-eclipse (UT[1])	Where visible
9 Jan 2001	Total	20.22	Europe, Asia, Africa
5 Jul 2001	Partial	14.57	Asia, Australia, Pacific Ocean
16 May 2003	Total	03.41	Americas, Europe, Africa
9 Nov 2003	Total	01.20	Americas, Europe, Africa, western Asia
4 May 2004	Total	20.32	Europe, Africa, Asia
28 Oct 2004	Total	03.05	Americas, Europe, Africa
17 Oct 2005	Partial	12.05	eastern Asia, Pacific Ocean, North America
7 Sep 2006	Partial	18.53	Australia, Asia, eastern Africa
3 Mar 2007	Total	23.22	Europe, Asia, Africa
28 Aug 2007	Total	10.39	Australia, Pacific Ocean, part of North America
21 Feb 2008	Total	03.27	Americas, Europe, Africa
16 Aug 2008	Partial	21.12	Europe, Africa, western Asia
31 Dec 2009	Partial	19.23	Asia, Africa, Europe
26 Jun 2010	Partial	11.39	Pacific Rim
21 Dec 2010	Total	08.17	North and South America
15 Jun 2011	Total	20.12	Asia, Africa, Europe
10 Dec 2011	Total	14.32	Pacific Ocean, Australia. eastern Asia

[1] *Universal Time, equivalent to Greenwich Mean Time (GMT).*

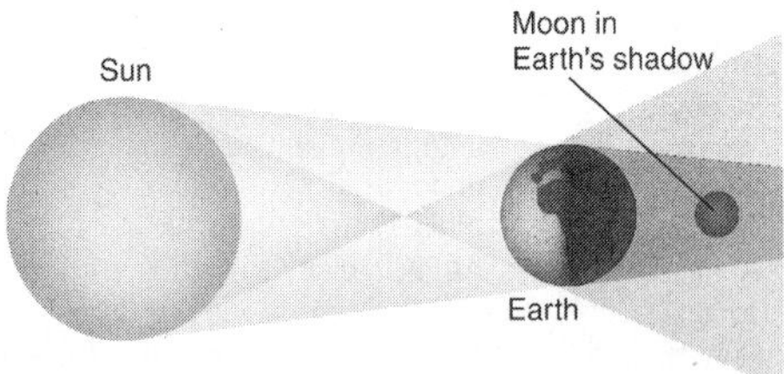

Moon-Eating Monsters

Eclipses were viewed with great fear in many ancient cultures. It was believed that the Sun or Moon was being attacked and swallowed up by a huge monster or demon, often a dragon. People would make as much noise and commotion as possible during the eclipse to scare the savage beast away and return the Sun or Moon to them safely.

Astronomy and Space Exploration

ASTRONOMERS ROYAL

Astronomer Royal is an honorary title awarded to a distinguished British astronomer. Until 1972, the director of the Royal Observatory at Greenwich automatically became the Astronomer Royal, but the two posts have since been separate.

Dates	Astronomer Royal	Dates	Astronomer Royal
1675–1719	John Flamsteed	1910–33	Sir Frank Dyson
1720–42	Edmond Halley	1933–55	Sir Harold Spencer Jones
1742–62	James Bradley	1956–71	Sir Richard Woolley
1762–4	Nathaniel Bliss	1972–82	Sir Martin Ryle
1765–1811	Nevil Maskelyne	1982–90	Sir Francis Graham-Smith
1811–35	John Pond	1991–5	Sir Arnold Wolfendale
1835–81	Sir George Airy	1995–	Sir Martin Rees
1881–1910	Sir William Christie		

Royal Raven Poo

The first Astronomer Royal, John Flamsteed, worked from the Tower of London until the building of the Royal Observatory at Greenwich was completed. Conditions at the Tower were not ideal for astronomy, however. The Tower's famous ravens found Flamsteed's telescopes to be excellent perches, and the unhappy astronomer had trouble gazing at the stars with his telescopes splattered with raven poo.

SPACE FIRSTS

Date	Event
4 Oct 1957	**First satellite** to orbit the Earth, Sputnik 1, is launched by the USSR.
3 Nov 1957	USSR's Sputnik 2 mission puts the **first living creature**, a dog called Laika, into space; Laika dies soon after launch from overheating and stress.
2 Jan 1959	USSR's Luna 1 mission **escapes Earth gravity**.
14 Sep 1959	USSR's Luna 2 mission makes a **lunar impact**.
4 Oct 1959	USSR's Luna 3 mission is launched and takes a **photo of the far side of the Moon**.
12 Aug 1960	**First communications satellite**, ECHO 1, is launched by the USA.
31 Jan 1961	**First 'chimponaut'**, a chimpanzee called Ham, enters space as part of the US Mercury programme. He survives. Previously monkeys, pigs, bears and mice had been used.
12 Apr 1961	Yuri Gagarin becomes the **first man in space**, making one orbit of the Earth aboard the USSR's Vostok 1 spacecraft. More than 400 people have since followed him.
20 Feb 1962	John Glenn becomes the **first American** to orbit the Earth.
16 Jun 1963	Valentina Tereshkova becomes the **first woman** in space aboard the USSR's Vostok 6 spacecraft.
18 Mar 1965	Alexei Leonov of the USSR's Voskhod 2 mission makes the **first spacewalk**.
1 Mar 1966	USSR robotic spacecraft Venera 3 lands on **Venus**.

SPACE FIRSTS

Date	Event
30 May 1966	US spacecraft Surveyor 1 makes a soft landing on the **Moon**.
21–27 Dec 1968	Astronauts from the USA's Apollo 8 make the **first manned orbit** of the Moon (10 orbits).
20 Jul 1969	**First men set foot on the Moon**, landing at the Sea of Tranquillity; they are the USA's Apollo 11 crew members Neil Armstrong and Buzz Aldrin. Michael Collins remains on board the spacecraft.
19 Apr 1971	Salyut 1, the world's **first space station**, is launched by the USSR.
27 Nov 1971	Robotic probe from the USSR's Mars 2 mission makes the first crash landing on **Mars**.
3 Mar 1972	USA's Pioneer 10 spacecraft is launched; it later makes a Jupiter flyby, crosses Pluto's orbit and becomes the **first man-made object to escape the solar system**.
17 Jul 1975	Apollo (USA) and Soyuz (USSR) **spacecraft dock in space**.
20 Jul 1976	USA's Viking 1 spacecraft conducts operations on the surface of **Mars**.
12 Apr 1981	USA commences **space shuttle flights**.
19 Feb 1986	Main module of Mir, the **first space station designed for semi-permanent orbit**, is launched by the USSR.
13 Mar 1986	Robotic probe Giotto, launched by the European Space Agency, has a close-up rendezvous with **Halley's comet**.
24 Apr 1990	Hubble Space Telescope, the **first optical space-based telescope**, is launched.
2 Dec 1990	**First passenger pays to go into space** aboard a Russian Soyuz TM11 flight.
18 May 1991	Helen Sharman becomes the **first British person** in space with the Soyuz TM12 mission.
31 Oct 2000	**International Space Station** receives its first residents, from the USA, Russia, Europe, Canada and Japan.
28 Apr 2001	**First space tourist** visits the International Space Station.
21 Jun 2004	SpaceShipOne becomes the **first private manned spacecraft** to fly into space, reaching 100km/62mi above the Earth. Its pilot, Mike Melvill, becomes the **first commercial astronaut**.

Astronomy Gastronomy

During the eight days of the Apollo 11 mission in 1969, the astronauts had a choice of two meals. NASA says that 'Meal A was bacon squares, peaches, sugar cookie cubes, coffee and pineapple-grapefruit drink. Meal B included beef stew, cream of chicken soup, date fruitcake, grape punch and orange drink'.

MOON LANDINGS

Mission	Launch	Duration (hours:minutes)	Crew
Apollo 11	16–24 Jul 1969	195:18	Neil A Armstrong, Michael Collins, Edwin E 'Buzz' Aldrin, Jr
On 20 Jul the first human beings land on the Moon, at the Sea of Tranquillity. Scientific instruments are deployed and 20kg/44lbs of moon rock brought back to Earth.			
Apollo 12	14–24 Nov 1969	244:36	Charles 'Pete' Conrad, Jr, Richard F Gordon, Jr, Alan L Bean
The second landing is made on 19 Nov at the Ocean of Storms. Geological studies are undertaken and parts of the unmanned Surveyor 3 craft retrieved.			
Apollo 14	31 Jan–9 Feb 1971	216:02	Alan B Shepard, Jr, Stuart A Roosa, Edgar D Mitchell
The third mission lands on 5 Feb in the Fra Mauro area, the area scheduled for the failed Apollo 13 mission (see below). The first golf shot on the Moon is played by Alan Shepard.			
Apollo 15	26 Jul–7 Aug 1971	295:12	David R Scott, James B Irwin, Alfred M Worden
On 30 Jul the fourth landing takes place. The Lunar Roving Vehicle is used for the first time. Improved spacesuits give astronauts the longest stay so far, at almost 67 hours.			
Apollo 16	16–27 Apr 1972	265:51	John W Young, Charles M Duke, Jr, Thomas K Mattingly II
The fifth Moon landing is made on 20 Apr in the Descartes Highlands area. The first studies of lunar highland geology are undertaken.			
Apollo 17	7–19 Dec 1972	301:52	Eugene A Cernan, Ronald E Evans, Harrison H 'Jack' Schmitt
The final and longest of the Apollo missions touches down successfully on 11 Dec in the Taurus–Littrow highlands and valley area. Harrison Schmitt is the first scientist–astronaut to walk on the Moon.			

Note: Apollo 13 (11–17 Apr 1970) was to have been the third Moon landing. Carrying James A Lovell, Jr, John L Swigert, Jr and Fred W Haise, Jr, the mission had to be aborted without landing on the Moon after an explosion in an oxygen tank. The mission lasted 142 hours and 54 minutes.

One Small Step

At 4:18pm (US Eastern Daylight Time) on 20 Jul 1969, the Apollo 11 lunar module touched down for the first time on the surface of the Moon and commander Neil Armstrong reported that 'the Eagle has landed'. At 10:56pm Armstrong stepped, left foot first, onto the Moon and declared 'That's one small step for a man, one giant leap for mankind'. He said the Moon has 'a stark beauty all its own'. The astronauts later spoke to the President in the White House, in what Nixon described as 'the most historic telephone call ever made', and left a plaque stating 'Here men from the planet Earth first set foot on the Moon. July 1969 AD. We came in peace for all mankind.'

SPACE RECORDS

Most time spent in space (total)	Russian cosmonaut Sergei Krikalev spent a total of 803 days 9 hours 39 minutes in space between Nov 1988 and Oct 2005.
Most time spent in space (consecutive)	Russian cosmonaut and physician Valeri Polyakov spent 437 days 17 hours 38 minutes aboard the Mir Space Station between Jan 1994 and Mar 1995.
Most space flights	US astronaut Jerry Ross completed his seventh space mission in Apr 2002. He shares the record with fellow US astronaut Franklin Chang-Diaz, who completed his seventh space mission in Jun 2002.
First space walk	Russian cosmonaut Alexei Leonov made the first spacewalk from Voskhod 2 on 18 Mar 1965.
Longest space walk	US astronauts Susan Helms and Jim Voss both spent 8 hours 56 minutes in space outside the International Space Station on 11 Mar 2001.
Longest space shuttle flight	The space shuttle Columbia, with a crew of five, completed a mission of 17 days 15 hours 53 minutes between 19 Nov and 7 Dec 1996.
Shortest manned space flight	US astronaut Alan Shepard, aboard a Mercury–Redstone rocket, made a sub-orbital flight lasting 15 minutes 28 seconds on 5 May 1961.
Longest time spent on the surface of the Moon	During the Apollo 17 lunar mission (7–19 Dec 1972), the crew spent 74 hours 59 minutes on the Moon's surface.
Longest time spent in orbit around the Moon	During the Apollo 17 lunar mission (7–19 Dec 1972), Ronald E Evans spent 147 hours 41 minutes in orbit around the Moon.
Man-made object furthest from Earth	On 17 Feb 1998 Voyager 1, launched on 5 Sep 1977, became the most remote man-made object in the universe in its journey towards interstellar regions. None of the more recent probes launched to date will catch it up.
Fastest spacecraft speed	The Helios space probes, launched in 1974 and 1976, reached speeds of 252 800kph/158 000mph as they orbited the Sun.
Oldest person in space	John Glenn, aged 77, went into space aboard the space shuttle Discovery on 15 Jan 1998. On 20 Feb 1962 he had become the first American to orbit the Earth.
Most isolated space traveller	During the USA's Apollo 15 lunar mission between 30 Jul and 1 Aug 1971, Alfred M Worden stayed in orbit around the Moon while his fellow crew members explored its surface, and travelled 3 596.4km/2 234.75mi from the nearest human being.

Out of This World

Dennis Tito, a US businessman, became the first 'space tourist' in 2001. He reportedly paid the Russian space administration $20 million, the equivalent of £14 million, to visit the International Space Station. Tito described the experience as 'paradise'. South African millionaire Mark Shuttleworth became the second space tourist in 2002, and US businessman Gregory Olsen was the third to visit the space station in 2005.

THE EARTH

There are no universally agreed estimates of many of the natural phenomena given in this section. Surveys make use of different criteria for identifying natural boundaries, and use different techniques of measurement. The estimated sizes of continents, oceans, seas, deserts and rivers are particularly subject to variation.

EARTH

Age	4.6 billion years
Distance from Sun (mean)	150 million km/93 million mi
Surface area	510 069 120 sq km/196 938 800 sq mi
Mass	5976×10^{24}kg/13175×10^{24}lb
Surface gravity	980cm/sq sec/386in/sq sec
Land surface (approximate)	148 million sq km/57 million sq mi (approx 29% of total area)
Water surface (approximate)	361.6 million sq km/140 million sq mi (approx 71% of total area)
Circumference (equator)	40 076km/24 902mi
Circumference (meridian)	40 000km/24 860mi
Diameter (equator)	12 757km/7 927mi
Diameter (meridian)	12 714km/7 900mi
Period of axial rotation	23 hours 56 minutes 4.0966 seconds
Temperature at core	4 500°C/8 100°F

Ice Kingdom

Ice permanently covers approximately 10% of the land surface of the Earth, with the majority of the ice cover at the South Pole. But there have been several great ice ages in the past, when a much larger part of the Earth's surface was covered with ice. The most famous, commonly known as 'the Ice Age', was during the Pleistocene period from approximately 2 million years ago to approximately 10,000 years ago.

Composition of the Earth's crust

Element	% weight
Oxygen	46.60
Silicon	27.72
Aluminium	8.13
Iron	5.00
Calcium	3.63
Sodium	2.83
Potassium	2.59
Magnesium	2.09
Others	1.41

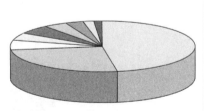

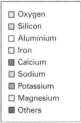

Oxygen
Silicon
Aluminium
Iron
Calcium
Sodium
Potassium
Magnesium
Others

Structure of the Earth

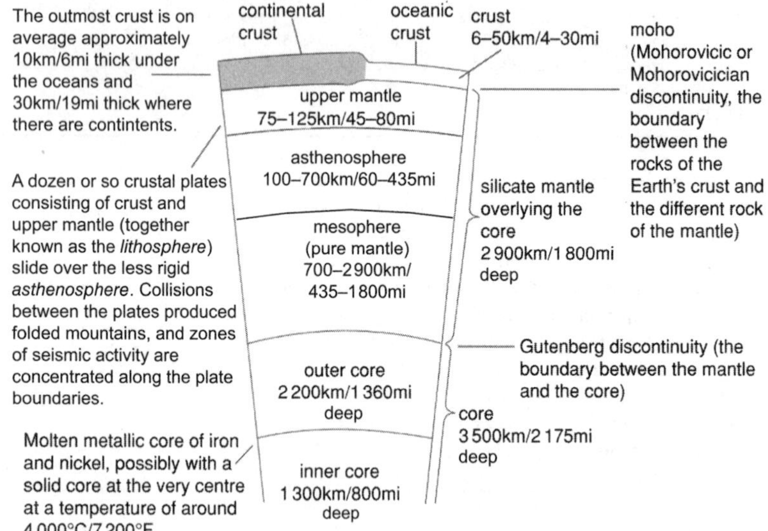

The outmost crust is on average approximately 10km/6mi thick under the oceans and 30km/19mi thick where there are contintents.
continental crust
oceanic crust
crust 6–50km/4–30mi
moho (Mohorovicic or Mohorovicician discontinuity, the boundary between the rocks of the Earth's crust and the different rock of the mantle)
upper mantle 75–125km/45–80mi
asthenosphere 100–700km/60–435mi
A dozen or so crustal plates consisting of crust and upper mantle (together known as the *lithosphere*) slide over the less rigid *asthenosphere*. Collisions between the plates produced folded mountains, and zones of seismic activity are concentrated along the plate boundaries.
silicate mantle overlying the core 2 900km/1 800mi deep
mesophere (pure mantle) 700–2900km/ 435–1800mi
Gutenberg discontinuity (the boundary between the mantle and the core)
outer core 2 200km/1 360mi deep
core 3 500km/2 175mi deep
Molten metallic core of iron and nickel, possibly with a solid core at the very centre at a temperature of around 4 000°C/7 200°F
inner core 1 300km/800mi deep

Atmosphere

The Earth's atmosphere is composed of air, generally containing 78% nitrogen, 21% oxygen and 1% argon, together with carbon dioxide, hydrogen, ozone and methane, and traces of the other rare gases. The amount of water vapour present depends on the temperature and humidity.

Gas	% volume
Nitrogen	78.1
Oxygen	20.95
Argon	0.934
Carbon dioxide	0.031
Neon	0.00182
Helium	0.00052
Methane	0.0002
Krypton	0.00011
Hydrogen	0.00005
Nitrous oxide	0.00005
Ozone	0.00004
Xenon	0.000009

Nitrogen
Oxygen
Argon
Carbon dioxide
Others

The atmosphere is divided into several layers.

Thermosphere

Air is very 'thin' (at low density) and atmospheric pressure is only a millionth of a billionth of that at sea level. Temperature increases with height, and may reach 2,000°C/3,600°F. Composed of the *ionosphere*, which reflects radio waves back to Earth enabling signals to be transmitted around the curved surface of the Earth, the *ionopause* transitional layer, and the *exosphere*, the outermost layer of the Earth's atmosphere, approximately 500km/300mi above the surface, from which light gases can escape into space.

Mesopause

Transitional layer between the mesosphere and the thermosphere, approximately 80–85km/50–55mi above the surface. The minimum atmospheric temperature, approximately –100°C/–150°F occurs in this layer, and atmospheric pressure is 100,000 times lower than at sea level.

Mesosphere

Middle atmosphere, up to approximately 85km/55mi above the surface. Temperature decreases with height.

Stratopause

Transitional layer, approximately 50–55km/30–35mi above the surface. The temperature is approximately 0°C/32°F.

Stratosphere

Contains very few clouds. Aircraft usually fly in this layer above the weather disturbances in the troposphere. Temperatures increase with height, and typical pressure is only a hundredth of that on the surface. Also includes the *ozone layer*, approximately 20–40km/12–25mi above the surface.

Tropopause

Transitional layer, approximately 10km/6mi above the surface. The temperature is approximately –60°C/–80°F.

Troposphere

Lower part of the atmosphere, from the surface up to a height varying from approximately 9km/5mi at the poles to 17km/10mi at the equator. Contains almost all of the clouds. Temperature decreases with height.

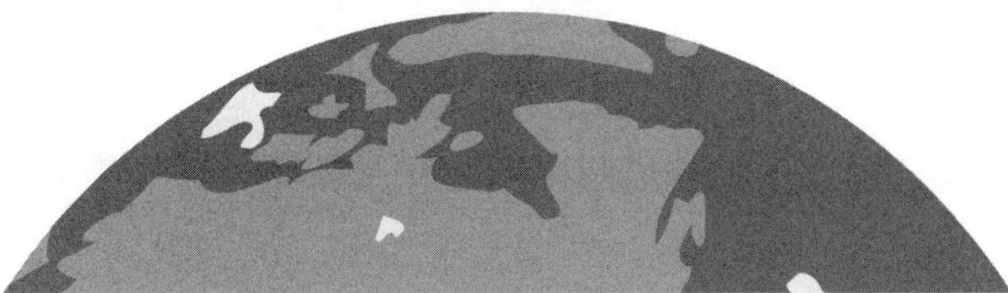

Note: Diagram not to scale.

EARTHQUAKE SEVERITY MEASUREMENT

Modified Mercalli intensity scale (1956 revision)

The Mercalli scale measures the intensity of earthquake shocks in terms of the damage they cause. It was named after the Italian geologist Giuseppe Mercalli (1850–1914).

Intensity value / description

I Not felt; marginal and long-period effects of large earthquakes.

II Felt by persons at rest, on upper floors or favourably placed.

III Felt indoors; hanging objects swing; vibration like passing of light trucks; duration estimated; may not be recognized as an earthquake.

IV Hanging objects swing; vibration like passing of heavy trucks, or sensation of a jolt like a heavy ball striking the walls; standing cars rock; windows, dishes, doors rattle; glasses clink; crockery clashes; in the upper range of IV, wooden walls and frames creak.

V Felt outdoors; direction estimated; sleepers awoken; liquids disturbed, some spilled; small unstable objects displaced or upset; doors swing, close, open; shutters, pictures move; pendulum clocks stop, start, change rate.

VI Felt by all; many frightened and run outdoors; persons walk unsteadily; windows, dishes, glassware break; knick-knacks, books, etc, fall off shelves; pictures fall off walls; furniture moves or overturns; weak plaster and masonry D crack; small bells ring (church, school); trees, bushes shake visibly, or heard to rustle.

VII Difficult to stand; noticed by drivers; hanging objects quiver; furniture breaks; damage to masonry D, including cracks; weak chimneys broken at roof line; fall of plaster, loose bricks, stones, tiles, cornices, also unbraced parapets and architectural ornaments; some cracks in masonry C; waves on ponds, water turbid with mud; small slides and caving in along sand or gravel banks; large bells ring; concrete irrigation ditches damaged.

VIII Steering of cars affected; damage to masonry C and partial collapse; some damage to masonry B; none to masonry A; fall of stucco and some masonry walls; twisting, fall of chimneys, factory stacks, monuments, towers, elevated tanks; frame houses move on foundations if not bolted down; loose panel walls thrown out; decayed piling broken off; branches broken from trees; changes in flow or temperature of springs and wells; cracks in wet ground and on steep slopes.

IX General panic; masonry D destroyed; masonry C heavily damaged, sometimes with complete collapse; masonry B seriously damaged; general damage to foundations; frame structures, if not bolted, shift off foundations; frames racked; serious damage to reservoirs; underground pipes break; conspicuous cracks in ground; in alluviated areas sand and mud ejected, earthquake fountains, sand craters.

X Most masonry and frame structures destroyed with their foundations; some well-built wooden structures and bridges destroyed; serious damage to dams, dykes, embankments; large landslides; water thrown on banks of canals, rivers, lakes, etc; sand and mud shifted horizontally on beaches and flat land; rails bent slightly.

XI Rails bent greatly; underground pipelines completely out of service.

XII Damage nearly total; large rock masses displaced; lines of sight and level distorted; objects thrown into the air.

Notes: Masonry types

A Good workmanship, mortar and design; reinforced, especially laterally, and bound together using steel, concrete, etc; designed to resist lateral forces.

B Good workmanship and mortar; reinforced, but not designed in detail to resist lateral forces.

C Ordinary workmanship and mortar; no extreme weakness like failing to tie in at corners, but neither reinforced nor designed against horizontal forces.

D Weak materials, such as adobe; poor mortar; low standards of workmanship; weak horizontally.

Richter scale

The Richter scale measures earthquake magnitude in terms of seismic energy released. It is logarithmic; a quake of magnitude 2 is barely perceptible, 5 is rather strong, and those over 7 are very strong. It was devised by US seismologist Dr Charles F Richter (1900–85).

Magnitude	Relative amount of energy released
1	1
2	31
3	960
4	30 000
5	920 000
6	29 million
7	890 million
8	28 billion
9	850 billion

Whole Lotta Shakin'

The strongest earthquake ever recorded struck Chile on 22 May 1960, and measured 9.5 on the Richter Scale. Since 1900 there have only been three other earthquakes measuring 9 or above on the Richter Scale: Kamchatka, Russia (1952; 9.0), Alaska, USA (1964; 9.2) and coastal Sumatra, Indonesia (2004; 9.0).

CONTINENTS

A continent is any of the seven main land masses of the world, namely Africa, Antarctica, Asia, Australia and Oceania, Europe, North America and South America. A continent's area also includes the submerged continental shelf around the edge of the exposed land mass.

Continent	Area	Percentage of total land mass	Lowest point below sea level	Highest elevation
Africa	30 293 000 sq km/ 11 696 000 sq mi	20.2%	Lake Assal, Djibouti –156m/–512ft	Mt Kilimanjaro, Tanzania 5 895m/19 340ft
Antarctica	13 975 000 sq km/ 5 396 000 sq mi	9.3%	Bently sub-glacial trench –2 538m/ –8 327ft	Vinson Massif 5 140m/16 864ft
Asia	44 493 000 sq km/ 17 179 000 sq mi	29.6%	Dead Sea, Israel/ Jordan/West Bank –400m/–1 312ft	Mt Everest, China/Nepal 8 850m/29 035ft
Australia and Oceania[1]	8 945 000 sq km/ 3 454 000 sq mi	5.9%	Lake Eyre, Australia –15m/–49ft	Puncak Jaya, Indonesia 5 030m/16 503ft
Europe[2]	10 245 000 sq km/ 3 956 000 sq mi	6.8%	Caspian Sea, Iran/ Russia/Turkmenistan/ Kazakhstan/Azerbaijan –29m/–94ft	Mt Elbrus, Russia 5 642m/18 510ft
North America	24 454 000 sq km/ 9 442 000 sq mi	16.3%	Death Valley, California, USA –86m/–282ft	Mt McKinley, Alaska, USA 6 194m/20 322ft
South America	17 838 000 sq km/ 6 887 000 sq mi	11.9%	Península Valdés, Argentina –40m/–131ft	Aconcagua, Argentina 6 960m/22 835ft

[1] *The land mass of Australia plus the wider continental area.*
[2] *Including the former western USSR.*

Continental drift

Continental drift is the theory that the continents were formed as a result of the breaking up of a single land mass into several smaller land masses, which slowly drifted apart across the Earth's surface. Arrows indicate the direction of drift.

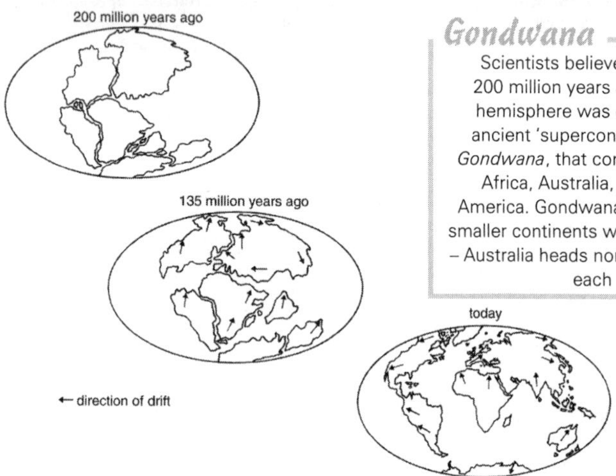

Gondwana

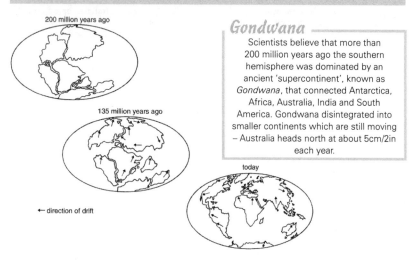

Scientists believe that more than 200 million years ago the southern hemisphere was dominated by an ancient 'supercontinent', known as *Gondwana*, that connected Antarctica, Africa, Australia, India and South America. Gondwana disintegrated into smaller continents which are still moving – Australia heads north at about 5cm/2in each year.

OCEANS

Water covers approximately 71% of the Earth's surface. Four oceans were traditionally recognized, with the International Hydrographic Organization (IHO) officially delimiting a fifth, the Southern Ocean, in 2000. However, the Atlantic Ocean and the Pacific Ocean are often divided (by the equator) into the North Atlantic and South Atlantic, and the North Pacific and South Pacific, leading to the recognition of seven oceans.

Ocean	Area	Average depth	Greatest depth
Arctic	14 056 000 sq km/ 5 427 021 sq mi	1 330m/4 400ft	Molloy Deep 5680m/18 635ft
Atlantic	76 762 000 sq km/ 29 637 808 sq mi	3 700m/12 100ft	Puerto Rico Trench 8648m/28 372ft
Indian	68 556 000 sq km/ 26 469 471 sq mi	3 900m/12 800ft	Java Trench 7 725m/25 344ft
Pacific	155 557 000 sq km/ 60 060 557 sq mi	4 300m/14 100ft	Mariana Trench 11 040m/36 220ft
Southern	20 327 000 sq km/ 7 848 254 sq mi	4 500m/14 800ft	South Sandwich Trench 7 235m/23 737ft

Water, Water, Everywhere

The Pacific Ocean alone covers approximately 28% of the Earth's surface, making this single ocean bigger than all the land mass of the Earth.

MAJOR OCEAN TRENCHES

Ocean trenches are long, narrow, steep-sided depressions in an ocean floor. They are commonly found running parallel to a continent. There are more than 20 in total; the majority are found in the Pacific Ocean.

Trench	Ocean	Greatest depth
Cayman	Atlantic	7686m/25216ft
Japan	Pacific	8513m/27929ft
Java	Indian	7725m/25344ft
Kermadec	Pacific	10047m/32962ft
Kuril	Pacific	10542m/34587ft
Mariana (Marianas)	Pacific	11040m/36220ft
Middle America	Pacific	6669m/21880ft
Nansei Shoto (Ryukyu)	Pacific	7507m/24629ft
Palau	Pacific	7986m/26200ft
Peru-Chile (Atacama)	Pacific	8065m/26460ft
Philippine (Mindanao)	Pacific	10539m/34578ft
Puerto Rico	Atlantic	8648m/28372ft
Romanche	Atlantic	7758m/25453ft
South Sandwich	Southern	7235m/23737ft
Tonga	Pacific	10882m/35702ft
Yap (West Caroline)	Pacific	8527m/27976ft

Note: Other major trenches include the Aleutian, the Izu Bonin and the Bougainville, all in the Pacific Ocean.

LARGEST SEAS

Oceans are excluded.

Sea	Area[1]
Coral Sea	4791000 sq km/1850000 sq mi
Arabian Sea	3863000 sq km/1492000 sq mi
South China (Nan) Sea	3685000 sq km/1423000 sq mi
Caribbean Sea	2718000 sq km/1050000 sq mi
Mediterranean Sea	2516000 sq km/971000 sq mi
Bering Sea	2304000 sq km/890000 sq mi
Bay of Bengal	2172000 sq km/839000 sq mi
Sea of Okhotsk	1590000 sq km/614000 sq mi
Gulf of Mexico	1543000 sq km/596000 sq mi
Gulf of Guinea	1533000 sq km/592000 sq mi
Barents Sea	1405000 sq km/542000 sq mi
Norwegian Sea	1383000 sq km/534000 sq mi
Gulf of Alaska	1327000 sq km/512000 sq mi
Hudson Bay	1232000 sq km/476000 sq mi
Greenland Sea	1205000 sq km/465000 sq mi
Arafura Sea	1037000 sq km/400000 sq mi
Philippine Sea	1036000 sq km/400000 sq mi
Sea of Japan (East Sea)	978000 sq km/378000 sq mi
East Siberian Sea	901000 sq km/348000 sq mi
Kara Sea	883000 sq km/341000 sq mi
East China Sea	664000 sq km/256000 sq mi

LARGEST ISLANDS

Sea	Area[1]
Andaman Sea	565 000 sq km/218 000 sq mi
North Sea	520 000 sq km/201 000 sq mi
Black Sea	508 000 sq km/196 000 sq mi
Red Sea	453 000 sq km/175 000 sq mi
Baltic Sea	414 000 sq km/160 000 sq mi
Persian Gulf	239 000 sq km/92 000 sq mi
St Lawrence Gulf	238 000 sq km/92 000 sq mi

[1] *Areas are rounded to the nearest 1,000 sq km/sq mi.*

Seven Seas

The term 'Seven Seas' is frequently used to refer to all the seas and oceans of the world. There are many suggestions as to the seas it specifically refers to, but it is commonly thought to refer to the oceans: Arctic, Antarctic, North Atlantic, South Atlantic, North Pacific, South Pacific and Indian Ocean.

LARGEST ISLANDS

Island	Area[1]
Australia[2]	7 692 300 sq km/2 970 000 sq mi
Greenland	2 175 600 sq km/840 000 sq mi
New Guinea	790 000 sq km/305 000 sq mi
Borneo	737 000 sq km/285 000 sq mi
Madagascar	587 000 sq km/226 600 sq mi
Baffin	507 000 sq km/195 800 sq mi
Sumatra	425 000 sq km/164 100 sq mi
Honshu (Hondo)	228 000 sq km/88 000 sq mi
Great Britain	219 000 sq km/84 600 sq mi
Victoria, Canada	217 300 sq km/83 900 sq mi
Ellesmere, Canada	196 000 sq km/75 700 sq mi
Celebes	174 000 sq km/67 200 sq mi
South Island, New Zealand	151 000 sq km/58 300 sq mi
Java	129 000 sq km/49 800 sq mi
North Island, New Zealand	114 000 sq km/44 000 sq mi
Cuba	110 900 sq km/42 800 sq mi
Newfoundland	109 000 sq km/42 100 sq mi
Luzon	105 000 sq km/40 500 sq mi
Iceland	103 000 sq km/39 800 sq mi
Mindanao	94 600 sq km/36 500 sq mi
Novaya Zemlya (two islands)	90 600 sq km/35 000 sq mi
Ireland	84 100 sq km/32 500 sq mi
Hokkaido	78 500 sq km/30 300 sq mi
Hispaniola	77 200 sq km/29 800 sq mi
Sakhalin	75 100 sq km/29 000 sq mi
Tierra del Fuego	71 200 sq km/27 500 sq mi

[1] *Areas are rounded to the nearest 100 sq km/sq mi.*
[2] *Sometimes discounted, as a continent.*

LARGEST LAKES

Lake	Location	Area[1]
Caspian Sea	Iran/Russia/Turkmenistan/ Kazakhstan/Azerbaijan	371 000 sq km/143 240 sq mi[2]
Superior	USA/Canada	82 260 sq km/31 760 sq mi[3]
Aral Sea	Uzbekistan/Kazakhstan	64 500 sq km/24 900 sq mi[2]
Victoria	east Africa	62 940 sq km/24 300 sq mi
Huron	USA/Canada	59 580 sq km/23 000 sq mi[3]
Michigan	USA	58 020 sq km/22 400 sq mi
Tanganyika	east Africa	32 000 sq km/12 360 sq mi
Baikal	Russia	31 500 sq km/12 160 sq mi
Great Bear	Canada	31 330 sq km/12 100 sq mi
Great Slave	Canada	28 570 sq km/11 030 sq mi
Erie	USA/Canada	25 710 sq km/9 930 sq mi[3]
Winnipeg	Canada	24 390 sq km/9 420 sq mi
Malawi/Nyasa	east Africa	22 490 sq km/8 680 sq mi
Ontario	USA/Canada	19 270 sq km/7 440 sq mi[3]
Ladoga	Russia	18 130 sq km/7 000 sq mi
Balkhash	Kazakhstan	17 000–22 000 sq km/6 560–8 490 sq mi[2]
Maracaibo	Venezuela	13 010 sq km/5 020 sq mi[4]
Patos	Brazil	10 140 sq km/3 920 sq mi[4]
Chad	west Africa	10 000–26 000 sq km/3 860–10 040 sq mi
Onega	Russia	9 800 sq km/3 780 sq mi
Rudolf	east Africa	9 100 sq km/3 510 sq mi
Eyre	Australia	8 800 sq km/3 400 sq mi[4]
Titicaca	Peru/Bolivia	8 300 sq km/3 200 sq mi

Note: The Caspian and Aral Seas, being entirely surrounded by land, are classified as lakes.
[1] *Areas are rounded to the nearest 10 sq km/sq mi.*
[2] *Salt lakes.*
[3] *Average of areas given by Canada and USA.*
[4] *Salt lagoons.*

GREAT LAKES

A group of five interconnected lakes, covering more than 244,000 sq km/94,000 sq mi, which separate eastern Canada from the USA. They contain approximately one-fifth of the Earth's fresh surface water.

Great Lake	Location	Area	Volume
Superior	USA/Canada	82 260 sq km/31 760 sq mi[1]	12 100 cu km/2 900 cu mi
Huron	USA/Canada	59 580 sq km/23 000 sq mi[1]	3 540 cu km/850 cu mi
Michigan	USA	58 020 sq km/22 400 sq mi	4 920 cu km/1 180 cu mi
Erie	USA/Canada	25 710 sq km/9 930 sq mi[1]	484 cu km/116 cu mi
Ontario	USA/Canada	19 270 sq km/7 440 sq mi[1]	1 640 cu km/393 cu mi

[1] *Average of areas given by Canada and USA.*

Lovely Lake

Lake Ontario's name is said to come from an Iroquois word meaning 'beautiful lake'.

LONGEST RIVERS

River	Outflow	Length[1]
Nile–Kagera–Ruvuvu–Ruvusu–Luvironza	Mediterranean Sea (Egypt)	6690km/4160mi
Amazon–Ucayali–Tambo–Ene–Apurimac	Atlantic Ocean (Brazil)	6570km/4080mi
Mississippi–Missouri– Jefferson–Beaverhead–Red Rock	Gulf of Mexico (USA)	6020km/3740mi
Chang Jiang (Yangtze)	East China Sea (China)	5980km/3720mi
Yenisey–Angara–Selenga–Ider	Kara Sea (Russia)	5870km/3650mi
Amur–Argun–Kerulen	Tartar Strait (Russia)	5780km/3590mi
Ob–Irtysh	Gulf of Ob, Kara Sea (Russia)	5410km/3360mi
Plata–Parana–Grande	Atlantic Ocean (Argentina/Uruguay)	4880km/3030mi
Huang He (Yellow)	Yellow Sea (China)	4840km/3010mi
Congo–Lualaba	South Atlantic Ocean (Angola/ Democratic Republic of the Congo)	4630km/2880mi
Lena	Laptev Sea (Russia)	4400km/2730mi
Mackenzie–Slave–Peace–Finlay	Beaufort Sea (Canada)	4240km/2630mi
Mekong	South China Sea (Vietnam)	4180km/2600mi
Niger	Gulf of Guinea (Nigeria)	4100km/2550mi

[1] *Lengths are given to the nearest 10km/mi, and include the river plus tributaries comprising the longest watercourse.*

HIGHEST WATERFALLS

The ten waterfalls with the greatest total height are listed.

Waterfall	Total height	Height of tallest drop	Location
Angel Falls	979m/3212ft	807m/2648ft	Venezuela
Tugela Falls	948m/3110ft	411m/1350ft	South Africa
Tres Hermanas (Three Sisters)	914m/3000ft	—	Peru
Olo'upena Falls	900m/2953ft	—	Hawaii, USA
Vinnufossen	860m/2822ft	420m/1378ft	Norway
Baläifossen	850m/2788ft	452m/1482ft	Norway
Pu'uka'oku Falls	840m/2756ft	—	Hawaii, USA
Browne Falls	836m/2744ft	244m/800ft	New Zealand
Strupenfossen	820m/2690ft	—	Norway
Ramnefjellsfossen (Utigardsfossen)	818m/2685ft	600m/1968ft	Norway

Niagara Falls

Almost 170,000 cu m/6 million cu ft of water per minute crashes over Niagara Falls, on the US–Canadian border. But it isn't just water that has gone over the Falls. The first person to make the 52m/170ft drop over the Horseshoe Falls in a barrel was 63-year-old Annie Taylor, who pioneered the trip on 24 Oct 1901. She has been followed by 15 others in various contraptions, some of whom have perished. The only person to survive without any protection was Kirk Jones of Michigan, who took the plunge on 21 Oct 2003.

DEEPEST CAVES

Cave	Location	Depth
Jean Bernard	France	1 494m/4 902ft
Snezhnaya	Georgia	1 340m/4 396ft
Puertas de Illamina	Spain	1 338m/4 390ft
Pierre-Saint-Martin	France	1 321m/4 334ft
Sistema Huautla	Mexico	1 240m/4 068ft
Berger	France	1 198m/3 930ft
Vqerdi	Spain	1 195m/3 921ft
Dachstein-Mammuthöhle	Austria	1 174m/3 852ft
Zitu	Spain	1 139m/3 737ft
Badalona	Spain	1 130m/3 707ft
Batmanhöhle	Austria	1 105m/3 625ft
Schneeloch	Austria	1 101m/3 612ft
G E S Malaga	Spain	1 070m/3 510ft
Lamprechtsofen	Austria	1 024m/3 360ft

LARGEST DESERTS

Desert	Location	Area[1]
Sahara	north Africa	8 600 000 sq km/3 320 000 sq mi
Arabian	south-west Asia	2 330 000 sq km/900 000 sq mi
Gobi	Mongolia and north-east China	1 166 000 sq km/450 000 sq mi
Patagonian	Argentina	673 000 sq km/260 000 sq mi
Great Victoria	south-west Australia	647 000 sq km/250 000 sq mi
Great Basin	south-west USA	492 000 sq km/190 000 sq mi
Chihuahuan	Mexico	450 000 sq km/174 000 sq mi
Great Sandy	north-west Australia	400 000 sq km/154 000 sq mi
Sonoran	south-west USA	310 000 sq km/120 000 sq mi
Kyzyl Kum	Kazakhstan	300 000 sq km/116 000 sq mi
Takla Makan	northern China	270 000 sq km/104 000 sq mi
Kalahari	south-west Africa	260 000 sq km/100 000 sq mi
Kara Kum	Turkmenistan	260 000 sq km/100 000 sq mi
Kavir	Iran	260 000 sq km/100 000 sq mi
Syrian	Saudi Arabia/Jordan/Syria/Iraq	260 000 sq km/100 000 sq mi
Nubian	Sudan	260 000 sq km/100 000 sq mi
Thar	India/Pakistan	200 000 sq km/77 000 sq mi
Ust'-Urt	Kazakhstan	160 000 sq km/62 000 sq mi
Bet-Pak-Dala	southern Kazakhstan	155 000 sq km/60 000 sq mi
Simpson	central Australia	145 000 sq km/56 000 sq mi
Dzungaria	China	142 000 sq km/55 000 sq mi
Atacama	Chile	140 000 sq km/54 000 sq mi
Namib	south-east Africa	134 000 sq km/52 000 sq mi
Sturt	south-east Australia	130 000 sq km/50 000 sq mi
Bolson de Mapimi	Mexico	130 000 sq km/50 000 sq mi
Ordos	China	130 000 sq km/50 000 sq mi
Alashan	China	116 000 sq km/45 000 sq mi

[1] *Desert areas are very approximate, because clear physical boundaries may not occur.*

HIGHEST MOUNTAINS

Mountain[1]	Location	Height[2]
Everest	China/Nepal	8850m/29040ft
K2 (Qogir)	Jammu-Kashmir[3]/China	8610m/28250ft
Kanchenjunga	India/Nepal	8590m/28170ft
Lhotse	China/Nepal	8500m/27890ft
Kangchenjunga South Peak	India/Nepal	8470m/27800ft
Makalu I	China/Nepal	8470m/27800ft
Kangchenjunga West Peak	India/Nepal	8420m/27620ft
Lhotse East Peak	China/Nepal	8380m/27500ft
Dhaulagiri	Nepal	8170m/26810ft
Cho Oyu	China/Nepal	8150m/26750ft
Manaslu	Nepal	8130m/26660ft
Nanga Parbat	Kashmir-Jammu[3]	8130m/26660ft
Annapurna I	Nepal	8080m/26500ft
Gasherbrum I	Kashmir-Jammu[3]	8070m/26470ft
Broad Peak I	Kashmir-Jammu[3]	8050m/26400ft
Gasherbrum II	Kashmir-Jammu[3]	8030m/26360ft
Gosainthan	China	8010m/26290ft
Broad Peak Central	Kashmir-Jammu[3]	8000m/26250ft
Gasherbrum III	Kashmir-Jammu[3]	7950m/26090ft
Annapurna II	Nepal	7940m/26040ft
Nanda Devi	India	7820m/25660ft
Rakaposhi	Kashmir[3]	7790m/25560ft
Kamet	India	7760m/25450ft
Ulugh Muztagh	China (Tibet)	7720m/25340ft
Tirichmir	Pakistan	7690m/25230ft
Muz Tag Ata	China	7550m/24760ft
Peak Ismoili Somoni	Tajikistan	7500m/24590ft
Pobedy Peak	China/Kyrgyzstan	7440m/24410ft
Aconcagua	Argentina	6960m/22830ft
Ojos del Salado[4]	Argentina/Chile	6910m/22660ft

[1] *Mt and similar designations have not been included in the name.*
[2] *Heights are given to the nearest 10m/ft.*
[3] *Kashmir-Jammu is a disputed region on the border of India and Pakistan.*
[4] *Ojos del Salado is the world's highest volcano.*

LONGEST MOUNTAIN RANGES

Mountain ranges longer than 3,000km/1,900mi are given.

Mountains	Location	Length[1]
Andes	South America	7200km/4500mi
Rocky Mountains	North America	4800km/3000mi
Himalayas–Karakoram–Hindu Kush	Asia	3800km/2400mi
Great Dividing Range	Australia	3600km/2250mi
Trans-Antarctic Mountains	Antarctica	3500km/2200mi
Atlantic Coast Range South	America	3000km/1900mi

[1] *Lengths are given to the nearest 100km/mi.*

Mighty Mountain

The peak of Mauna Kea, Hawaii, USA, reaches 4,205m/13,796ft above sea level. However, the base of the mountain is the seabed of the Pacific Ocean, and its full height from foot to summit is a mighty 10,205m/33,480ft – higher than Mt Everest.

PHYSICAL EXTREMES

Highest mountain	Mt Everest, China/Nepal	8850m/29 035ft
Longest mountain range	Andes, South America	7200km/4500mi
Highest cliffs	Near Molokai, Hawaii, USA	1010m/3300ft
Lowest point on Earth	Dead Sea, Israel/Jordan/West Bank (Palestine)	400m/1312ft below sea level
Deepest cave	Jean Bernard, France	1494m/4902ft
Largest cave	Sarawak Chamber (Lubang Nasib Bagus), Malaysia	700m/2300ft long by 70m/230ft high by average 300m/985ft wide
Largest ocean	Pacific Ocean	155 557 000 sq km/ 60 060 557 sq mi
Deepest point in the ocean	Challenger Deep, Mariana Trench, Pacific Ocean	11 040m/36 220ft
Highest tides	Minas Basin, Bay of Fundy, Canada	16m/53ft difference between high and low tide
Largest sea	Coral Sea	4 791 000 sq km/1 850 000 sq mi
Largest lake	Caspian Sea, Iran/Russia/ Turkmenistan/Kazakhstan/ Azerbaijan	371 000 sq km/143 240 sq mi
Deepest lake	Lake Baikal, Russia	1637m/5371ft
Highest lake	In crater of Licancábur volcano, Chile/Bolivia	5930m/19455ft
Highest navigable lake	Titicaca, Peru/Bolivia	3810m/12500ft
Saltiest lake	Don Juan Pond, Antarctica	40.2% salt by weight *(the Dead Sea has 23.1% and the ocean just 3.38%)*
Longest river	River Nile, Africa	6690km/4160mi
Highest waterfall (total height)	Angel Falls, Venezuela	979m/3212ft
Largest island	Australia[1]	7 692 300 sq km/2 970 000 sq mi
Largest desert	Sahara, north Africa	8 600 000 sq km/3 320 000 sq mi
Largest glacier	Lambert Glacier, Antarctica	1 000 000 sq km/386 102 sq mi

[1] *Sometimes discounted, as a continent.*

Mt Everest

Sir George Everest (1790–1866) was a Welsh military engineer. He became Surveyor-General of India in 1830 and completed a trigonometrical survey of the Indian subcontinent in 1841, being knighted in 1861. Mt Everest was named after him in 1865. Interestingly, Everest himself would not have recognized the modern pronunciation *ev-uh-rest*. He pronounced the name *eve-rest*.

NATIONAL PARKS (UK)

England and Wales

The National Parks and Access to the Countryside Act (1949) provided for the creation of National Parks in England and Wales. The Environment Act (1995) states their purpose as 'a) conserving and enhancing the natural beauty, wildlife and cultural heritage of the areas, and b) promoting opportunities for the understanding and enjoyment of the special qualities of those areas by the public'.

National Park	Year designated (order)	Area	Terrain
Brecon Beacons	1957 (10th)	1 351 sq km/522 sq mi	Mountains/valleys
Broads	1989 (11th)	303 sq km/117 sq mi	Waterways/fens
Dartmoor	1951 (4th)	954 sq km/368 sq mi	Moorland
Exmoor	1954 (8th)	693 sq km/268 sq mi	Moorland/coastline
Lake District	1951 (2nd)	2 292 sq km/885 sq mi	Mountains/valleys/ glaciated lakes
New Forest	2005 (12th)	580 sq km/224 sq mi	Woodland/heath
Northumberland	1956 (9th)	1 049 sq km/405 sq mi	Hills
North York Moors	1952 (6th)	1 432 sq km/554 sq mi	Woodland/moorland
Peak District	1951 (1st)	1 438 sq km/555 sq mi	Moorland/dales
Pembrokeshire Coast	1952 (5th)	620 sq km/239 sq mi	Cliffs/islands/ moorland
Snowdonia	1951 (3rd)	2 142 sq km/827 sq mi	Mountains/valleys
Yorkshire Dales	1954 (7th)	1 769 sq km/682 sq mi	Dales

Note: The South Downs are currently in the process of being designated as a National Park.

Scotland

The National Parks (Scotland) Act (2000) provided for the creation of National Parks in Scotland. The Act states their purpose as being 'a) to conserve and enhance the natural and cultural heritage of the area, b) to promote sustainable use of the natural resources of the area, c) to promote understanding and enjoyment (including enjoyment in the form of recreation) of the special qualities of the area by the public, and d) to promote sustainable economic and social development of the area's communities'.

National Park	Year established (order)	Area	Terrain
Cairngorms	2003 (2nd)	3 800 sq km/1 467 sq mi	Mountains/moorland
Loch Lomond and The Trossachs	2002 (1st)	1 865 sq km/720 sq mi	Mountains/valleys/ lochs

High Places

England's highest mountain is Scafell Pike in the Lake District at 978m/3,209ft, the highest mountain in Wales is Snowdon at 1,085m/3,560ft, and Slieve Donard at 852m/2,795ft is Northern Ireland's highest point. All three are dwarfed by Scotland's highest mountain: Ben Nevis reaches a mighty 1,343m/4,406ft, but it is still a mere pimple compared to the world's highest peaks.

BEAUFORT SCALE

Beaufort number	Wind name	m/sec	Windspeed kph	Windspeed mph	Observable wind characteristics	Sea disturbance number	Average wave height m	Average wave height ft	Observable sea characteristics
0	Calm	1	<1	<1	Smoke rises vertically	0	0	0	Sea like a mirror
1	Light air	1	1–5	1–3	Wind direction shown by smoke drift, but not by wind vanes	0	0	0	Ripples like scales, without foam crests
2	Light breeze	2	6–11	4–7	Wind felt on face; leaves rustle; vanes moved by wind	1	0.3	0–1	More definite wavelets, but crests do not break
3	Gentle breeze	4	12–19	8–12	Leaves and small twigs in constant motion; wind extends light flag	2	0.3–0.6	1–2	Large wavelets; crests begin to break; scattered white horses
4	Moderate breeze	7	20–28	13–18	Raises dust, loose paper; small branches moved	3	0.6–1.2	2–4	Small waves become longer; fairly frequent white horses
5	Fresh breeze	10	29–38	19–24	Small trees in leaf begin to sway; crested wavelets on inland waters	4	1.2–2.4	4–8	Moderate waves with a more definite long form; many white horses; some spray possible
6	Strong breeze	12	39–49	25–31	Large branches in motion; difficult to use umbrellas; whistling heard in telegraph wires	5	2.4–4	8–13	Large waves form; more extensive white foam crests; some spray probable
7	Near gale	15	50–61	32–38	Whole trees in motion; inconvenience walking against wind	6	4–6	13–20	Sea heaps up; streaks of white foam blown along
8	Gale	18	62–74	39–46	Breaks twigs off trees; impedes progress	6	4–6	13–20	Moderately high waves of greater length; well-marked streaks of foam
9	Strong gale	20	75–8	47–54	Slight structural damage occurs	6	4–6	13–20	High waves; dense streaks of foam; sea begins to roll; spray affects visibility
10	Storm	26	89–102	55–63	Trees uprooted; considerable damage occurs	7	6–9	20–30	Very high waves with long overhanging crests; dense streaks of foam blown along; generally white appearance of surface; heavy rolling
11	Violent storm	30	103–117	64–72	Widespread damage	8	9–14	30–45	Exceptionally high waves; long white patches of foam; poor visibility; ships lost to view behind waves
12–17	Hurricane	≥30	≥118	≥73		9	>14	>45	Air filled with foam and spray; sea completely white; very poor visibility

WIND

A *cyclone* is a circulation of winds in the atmosphere which rotates anticlockwise round a depression in the northern hemisphere and clockwise in the southern hemisphere.

A *hurricane* is a rotating windstorm originating over tropical oceans, with winds in excess of 119kph/74mph. Hurricanes may be up to 645km/400mi wide, and can move forwards at up to 48kph/30mph, travelling up to 4,830km/3,000mi before becoming exhausted. Hurricanes occur between Jul and Oct in the northern hemisphere and between Nov and Mar in the southern hemisphere. They are named by the National Hurricane Center, USA, in alphabetical sequence as they occur each year. Since 1978 names given have been alternately male/female. In the Pacific they are known as *typhoons*, and in the Indian Ocean as *tropical cyclones*.

A *tornado* is a column of air rotating rapidly around a very low pressure centre.

Tremendous Tornado

The largest tornado ever recorded struck northern Oklahoma, USA, in May 1999. It measured 1,600m/5,250ft in diameter.

WIND CHILL TEMPERATURE INDEX

Exposed skin cools more rapidly when exposed to wind than at the same temperature in still conditions. This means that people feel colder on a windy day than they would on a still day at the same temperature. The wind chill temperature index takes account of the temperature and the wind speed to produce the equivalent temperature experienced. Wind chill cannot be calculated accurately at temperatures above 10°C.

To convert Celsius to Fahrenheit, multiply by 9, divide by 5 and then add 32.

To convert km/h to mph, multiply by 0.6214; to convert km/h to knots, multiply by 0.5399.

Wind speed (km/h)	Outside temperature (°C)											
Calm	**5**	**0**	**–5**	**–10**	**–15**	**–20**	**–25**	**–30**	**–35**	**–40**	**–45**	**–50**
5	4	–2	–7	–13	–19	–24	–30	–36	–41	–47	–53	–58
10	3	–3	–9	–15	–21	–27	–33	–39	–45	–51	–57	–63
15	2	–4	–11	–17	–23	–29	–35	–41	–48	–54	–60	–66
20	1	–5	–12	–18	–24	–30	–37	–43	–49	–56	–62	–68
25	1	–6	–12	–19	–25	–32	–38	–44	–51	–57	–64	–70
30	0	–6	–13	–20	–26	–33	–39	–46	–52	–59	–65	–72
35	0	–7	–14	–20	–27	–33	–40	–47	–53	–60	–66	–73
40	–1	–7	–14	–21	–27	–34	–41	–48	–54	–61	–68	–74
50	–1	–8	–15	–22	–29	–35	–42	–49	–56	–63	–69	–76
60	–2	–9	–16	–23	–30	–36	–43	–50	–57	–64	–71	–78
70	–2	–9	–16	–23	–30	–37	–44	–51	–58	–65	–72	–80
80	–3	–10	–17	–24	–31	–38	–45	–52	–60	–67	–74	–81

Data source: US National Weather Service, Wind Chill Temperature Index (2001 revision).

WEATHER AND CLIMATE EXTREMES

Hottest place	Dallol, Ethiopia, at 34.4°C/93.9°F (annual mean temperature).
Highest recorded temperature in the shade	58°C/136.4°F at Al'Aziziyah, Libya, on 13 Sep 1922.
Coldest place	Plateau Station, Antarctica, at –56.6°C/–69.8°F (annual mean temperature).
Coldest recorded temperature	–89.2°C/–128.6°F at Vostok, Antarctica, on 21 Jul 1983.
Greatest temperature range	Verkhoyansk, Siberia, Russia, where temperatures can range from –68°C/–90.4°F to 37°C/98°F, a difference of 105°C/221°F.
Driest place	Atacama desert near Calama, Chile, where no rainfall was recorded in over 400 years to 1972. Today, the desert's average annual rainfall is just 0.1mm/0.0039in.
Most rain to fall in 24 hours	1 870mm/74in which fell on Cilaos, Réunion, in the Indian Ocean, on 15–16 Mar 1952.
Most intense rainfall	38.1mm/1.8in which fell in one minute at Basse Terre, Guadeloupe, Caribbean on 26 Nov 1970.
Most rainy days in a year	Mt Wai'ale'ale, Kauai, Hawaii, USA, has an average of 350 days of rain each year.
Wettest place	Mawsynram, Meghalaya State, India, where the annual average rainfall is 11 870mm/467in; in Tutunendo, Colombia, the annual average rainfall is 11 770mm/464in.
Least amount of sunshine	North and South Poles, where the sun does not rise for 182 days of winter.
Greatest amount of sunshine	Yuma, Arizona, USA, with a mean average of 4 055 hours of sun per year, or 91% of the possible hours of sunshine.
Greatest amount of snow to fall in a year	31 102mm/1 225in, at Paradise, Mt Rainier, Washington, USA, in 1971–2.
Greatest amount of snow to fall in a day	193cm/76in at Silver Lake, Colorado on 14 Apr 1921.
Highest recorded surface wind speed	371.75kph/231mph, at Mt Washington, New Hampshire, USA, on 12 Apr 1934.
Most days of thunder in a year	Tororo, Uganda, had an average of 251 days of thunder per year between 1967 and 1976.
Most hail in a year	Kericho, Kenya, has an average of 132 days of hail each year.
Heaviest hailstones	On 14 Apr 1986 hailstones weighing up to 1kg/2.2 lb fell in Gopalganj, Bangladesh, killing 92 people. On 5 Sep 1958 a hailstone weighing 142g/5oz fell at Horsham, West Sussex, the largest hailstone ever recorded in the UK.

Stormy Weather

Just one thunderstorm can produce 500 million litres, or 110 million gallons, of rain.

CLOUDS

Clouds are formed by the condensation or freezing of water vapour on minute particles in the atmosphere when air masses move upward as a result of convection currents, unstable conditions, etc, and in so doing cool rapidly. Clouds are usually classified into ten main types according to their height and shape.

Meteorologists use feet to measure cloud height; to convert to metres, multiply by 0.3048.

The Language of Clouds

The scientific study of clouds is called *nephology*, from the Greek word for cloud, *nephos*. The names of cloud types come from Latin: *cirrus* means a tuft or curl, *cumulus* means a heap, *stratus* means something spread out, *alto* means high and *nimbus* was the word for a rain-cloud.

Low clouds

The base of low clouds is usually surface–7,000ft.

Stratus (St)
Cloud base: usually surface–1,500ft.
Colour: usually grey.

Cumulonimbus (Cb)
Cloud base: usually 1,000–5,000ft.
Colour: white above with dark underside.

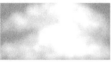

Cumulus (Cu)
Cloud base: usually 1,200–6,000ft.
Colour: white in sunlight but dark underside.

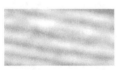

Stratocumulus (Sc)
Cloud base: usually 1,200–7,000ft.
Colour: grey or white, with shading.

Medium clouds

The base of medium clouds is usually 7,000–17,000ft, although nimbostratus may be much lower.

Nimbostratus (Ns)
Cloud base: usually 1,500–10,000ft.
Colour: dark grey.

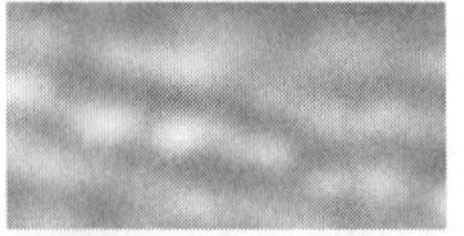

Altocumulus (Ac)
Cloud base: usually 7,000–17,000ft.
Colour: grey or white, with shading.

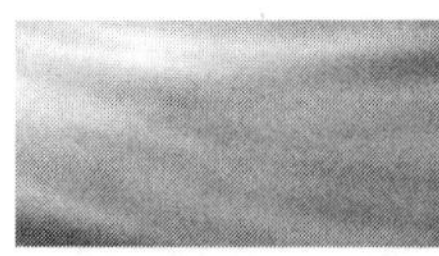

Altostratus (As)
Cloud base: usually 8,000–17,000ft.
Colour: greyish or bluish.

High clouds

The base of high clouds is usually 17,000–35,000ft. High clouds are composed of ice crystals.

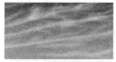

Cirrus (Ci)
Cloud base: usually 17,000–35,000ft.
Colour: white.

Cirrocumulus (Cc)
Cloud base: usually 17,000–35,000ft.
Colour: white.

Cirrostratus (Cs)
Cloud base: usually 17,000–35,000ft.
Colour: white.

On Cloud Nine

Someone who is extremely pleased or happy has long been described as being 'on cloud nine'. The phrase is thought to come from the classification system used by the old US Weather Bureau, which divided clouds into nine types: 'cloud nine' was the dramatic cumulonimbus, towering many kilometres into the sky. Hence to be on cloud nine was to be magnificently high up.

ICEBERGS

Icebergs can pose a significant hazard to shipping and as a result are reported, tracked and monitored. They are divided into two shape categories: tabular, those with a flat top and steep vertical sides, and non-tabular, which is subdivided into groups including pinnacled, domed, drydocked and wedged.

Iceberg	**Height[1] (above water)**	**Length**
growler	<1m	<5m
bergybit	1–4m	5–14m
small	5–15m	15–60m
medium	16–45m	61–120m
large	46–75m	121–200m
very large	>75m	>200m

[1] *To convert metres to feet, multiply by 3.2808.*

SHIPPING FORECAST AREAS

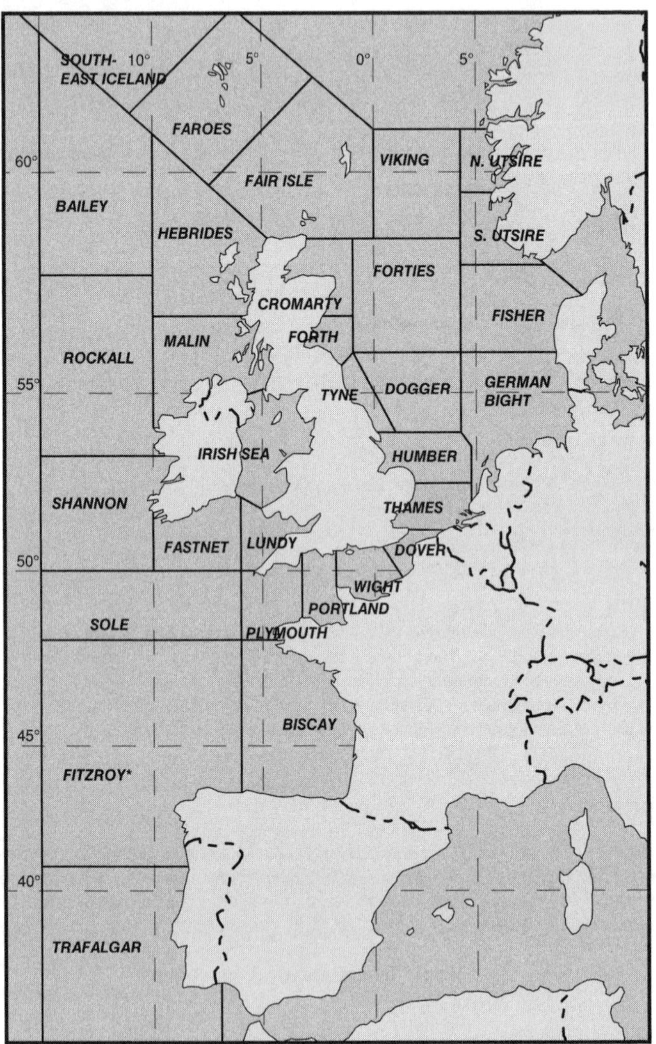

* *Formerly Finisterre (renamed 2002)* *Reproduced with data supplied by the Met Office.*

Roaring Forties

The 'Roaring Forties' is a sailors' term referring to the tract of stormy west winds and high seas south of 40°S latitude. There is also the 'Furious Fifties', a similarly turbulent stretch of ocean.

POINTS OF THE COMPASS

Naming the 32 compass points in order, in either or both directions, is called 'boxing the compass'.

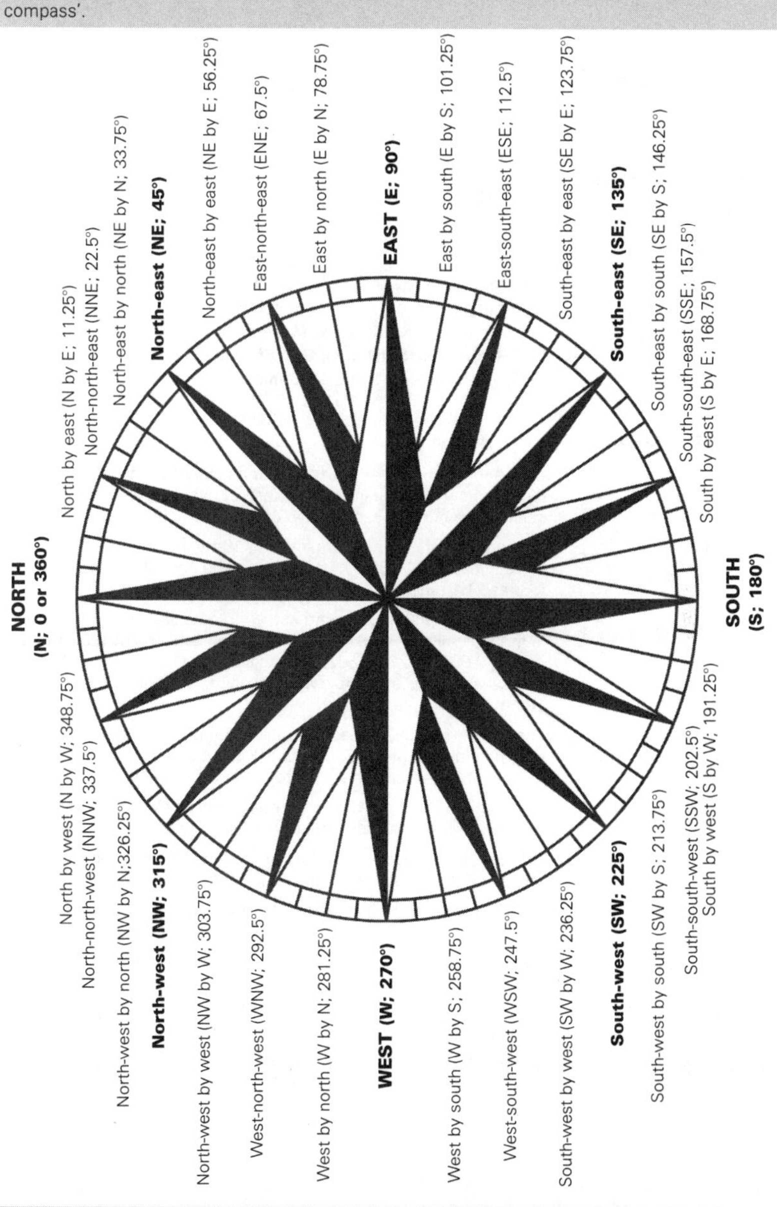

CLASSIFICATION

There are seven major levels of classification in taxonomy.

kingdom
phylum (plural **phyla**)
class
order
family
genus (plural **general**)
species

MRS GREN

Scientists identify seven characteristics of living things, which can be remembered by the acronym MRS GREN: **M**ovement, **R**espiration, **S**ensitivity, **G**rowth, **R**eproduction, **E**xcretion, **N**utrition.

FISH RECORDS

Fastest	Over short distances, the sailfish can reach a speed of 110kph/68mph; however marlins are the fastest over longer distances, and can reach a burst speed of 68–80kph/40–50mph.
Largest	The whale shark is said to reach over 18m/59ft, with the largest on record being 12.65m/41ft 6in, weighing an estimated 21.5 tonnes/21.1 tons.
Smallest	The dwarf pygmy goby, found in the streams and rivers of Luzon in the Philippines, measures 7.5–9.9mm/0.3–0.4in and weighs 4–5mg/0.00014–0.00018oz. The smallest fish found in British waters is the Guillet's goby, which reaches a maximum length of 24mm/0.95in.
Largest predatory	The great white shark reaches an average of 4.3–4.6m/14–15ft in length, and a weight of 520–770kg/1 150–1 700 lb. There are some reports of larger specimens up to 10m/33ft.
Most widespread	The distribution of the bristlemouths of genus *Cyclothone* is worldwide with the exception of the Arctic.
Most restricted	The devil's-hole pupfish inhabits only a small area of water above a rock shelf in a spring-fed pool in Ash Meadows, Nevada, USA.
Deepest dweller	In 1970 a brotulid *Bassogigas profundissimus* was recovered from a depth of 8 299m/27 230ft, making it the deepest living vertebrate.
Longest lived	Some specimens of the sturgeon are thought to be over 80 years old.
Shortest lived	Tooth carp of the suborder *Cyprinodontidae* live for only 8 months in the wild.
Most eggs	The ocean sunfish can lay up to 30 million eggs at a time. Each egg measures approximately 1.3mm/0.05in in diameter.

BIRD RECORDS

Largest	The ostrich can reach 2.75m/9ft in height and 156kg/345 lb in weight.
Smallest	The bee hummingbird of Cuba is under 6cm/2.4in long and weighs 3g/0.1oz.
Highest flier	Ruppell's griffon, a vulture, has been measured at 11 275m/36 991ft above sea level.
Fastest flier	The peregrine falcon can dive through the air at speeds up to 185kph/115mph. The fastest bird in level flight is the eider duck, which can reach 80kph/50mph.
Fastest animal on two legs	The ostrich can maintain a speed of 50kph/31mph for 15 minutes or more, and it may reach 65–70kph/40–43mph in short bursts, for example when escaping from predators.
Greatest wingspan	The wandering albatross can reach 3.65m/12ft.
Heaviest flying bird	The great bustard and the kori bustard both weigh up to 18kg/40 lb, with swans not far behind at approximately 16kg/35 lb.
Heaviest bird of prey	The Andean condor can reach 9–12kg/20–27 lb.
Deepest diver	The emperor penguin can reach a depth of 265m/870ft. The great northern diver or loon can dive to approximately 80m/262ft – deeper than any other flying bird.
Furthest migrator	The arctic tern travels up to 36 000km/22 400mi each year, flying from the Arctic to the Antarctic and back again.
Most abundant	Africa's red-billed quelea is the most numerous wild bird, with an estimated population of approximately 1.5 billion. The domestic chicken is the most abundant of all birds, numbering over 4 billion.
Largest egg	The ostrich lays the largest egg, with the heaviest specimen on record weighing 2.35kg/5 lb 2oz.

Feathered Friends

The greatest number of feathers ever counted on a bird was 25,216, on a swan.

MAMMAL RECORDS

Largest	The blue whale, up to 30m/98ft long and weighing up to 150 tonnes/148 tons, is the largest known mammal. The largest land mammal is the male African elephant, standing up to 3.3m/11ft at the shoulder and weighing up to 7 tonnes/6.89 tons.
Tallest	The giraffe stands up to 5.5m/18ft high.
Smallest	The pygmy white-toothed shrew, also called the Etruscan shrew, has a body approximately 5cm/2in long and weighs up to 2.5g/0.1oz. Some bats weigh even less.
Longest lived	Bowhead whales may be the oldest living mammals, with some specimens estimated at 177 to 245 years old at death. The next oldest are fin whales, at 114 years, and blue whales, at 110 years.
Loudest	Blue whales and fin whales can make calls that have been measured at 188 decibels and can travel for hundreds of kilometres through water.

Fastest on land The cheetah can reach 100kph/62mph, but only in short bursts. The pronghorn can maintain speeds of 50kph/31mph for several kilometres.

Largest land carnivore The Kodiak bear averages 2.4m/7.8ft in length and can weigh 680kg/1 500 lb.

Most prolific breeder A North American meadow mouse can produce up to 17 litters in a single year (4–9 babies per litter).

Longest gestation period The Asiatic elephant has the longest pregnancy, at 650–760 days.

Most widespread Humans are the most widely distributed mammals, closely followed by the house mouse, which has accompanied humans to all parts of the world.

Monkey Around

The wonderful world of monkeys includes the sun-tailed monkey, purple-faced leaf monkey, greater white-nosed monkey, red-bellied monkey, yellow-tailed woolly monkey, moustached monkey, black-bearded saki, bald-faced saki, owl-faced monkey and red-handed howler.

AMPHIBIAN RECORDS

Largest The Chinese giant salamander can grow up to 1.8m/5ft 11in long.

Smallest The world's smallest amphibian is the frog *Eleutherodactylus limbatus* of Cuba, which is only 8.51mm/0.33–0.47in long when it reaches adulthood.

Largest frog The goliath frog can weigh up to 3.25kg/7.16 lb, and reach 32cm/12.6in in length.

Longest lived The Japanese giant salamander, *Andrias japonicus*, has reached 55 years in captivity.

REPTILE RECORDS

Largest The estuarine or saltwater crocodile, which lives throughout tropical regions in Asia and the Pacific, can grow to over 7m/23ft long, although some eyewitness reports suggest crocodiles up to 10m/33ft in length.

Longest snake The reticulated python of south-east Asia grows to an average of 6m/20ft, but the greatest length on record is 10m/32ft 9.5in.

Largest snake The largest snake is probably the anaconda, which may not grow as long as the reticulated python but is thicker and heavier. Specimens have been known to reach 249kg/550 lb.

Smallest lizard Two lizards are considered to be the smallest in the world: *Sphaerodactylus ariasiae* and the *Sphaerodactylus parthenopion*, which both measure an average of 16mm/0.6in.

Longest lived tortoise Tortoises can reach ages of more than 100 years. The oldest specimen on record is a Madagascar giant tortoise that reputedly lived to 188 years, dying in 1965.

INSECT RECORDS

Longest	The stick insect *Pharnacia serratipes*, living in Indonesia, can grow to 33cm/13in long.
Most massive	Females of the goliath beetle of the Congo in Africa can grow to 100g/0.25 lb and are around the same size as a clenched fist.
Greatest wingspan	The white witch moth, living in the rainforests of South and Central America, has a wingspan of up to 36cm/14in.
Fastest flying	Some dragonflies can fly at speeds of up to 75kmph/45mph.
Largest egg	The Malaysian stick insect lays eggs around 1.3cm/0.5in long, the size of a large jelly bean. Other insects lay even larger eggs, but these are cases containing a number of individual eggs.
Loudest	The African cicada produces a call that registers up to 106.7 decibels.
Shortest lived	Mayflies live for as little as an hour as adults with wings, although they may previously have lived for 2–3 years as nymphs in bodies of water.

SPIDER RECORDS

Largest	Male goliath bird-eating spiders, found in some rainforest regions of South America, can grow to have a leg span of 28cm/11in.
Smallest	Among the smallest spiders in the world are symphytognathid spiders from central Africa. Adult individuals reach an average of 0.5mm/0.02in across.
Largest web	The golden orb web spider, living in tropical areas worldwide, makes webs which can extend to 6m/19ft 8in in height and 2m/6ft 7in in width.

WORM RECORDS

Longest	The bootlace worm can reach 40m/131ft.
Longest tapeworm	The human tapeworm can grow as long as 15m/49ft 2in.

CRUSTACEAN RECORDS

Largest	The Japanese spider crab can achieve a claw span of 3m/9ft 10in.
Heaviest	The American or North Atlantic lobster can weigh up to 20.14kg/44 lb 6oz.
Lightest	Water fleas are the smallest crustaceans, weighing as little as 0.00025g/0.0000088oz.

MOLLUSC RECORDS

Largest cephalopod	The giant squid has been measured up to 18m/59ft in length and 900kg/1 980 lb in weight. It has never been observed in the wild and scientists have so far relied on measuring dead specimens.
Largest snail	The African giant snail is the largest land gastropod. The biggest specimen on record was 39.3cm/15.5in long and weighed 900g/2 lb.
Largest bivalve	The giant clam can measure more than 1.4–1.5m/4ft 7in–4ft 11in across and weigh up to 295kg/650 lb.

JELLYFISH RECORDS

Largest	The Arctic giant jellyfish is reckoned to be the largest, with a body diameter of up to 2.2m/7ft 3in and a tentacle length of 35m/115ft.
Smallest	Polyp forms of various species of jellyfish may measure only around 1mm/0.039in across.

Venomous Jelly

The jellyfish with the deadliest venom is the box jellyfish, *Chironex fleckeri*. Also known as the sea wasp, it is found in the coastal waters of northern Australia from Nov to May. The 'bell' of the jellyfish can reach 30cm/12in across, while each of the sixty thick stinging tentacles trail up to 3m/10ft behind it; the translucent jellyfish is often almost impossible to spot in the water. Each one carries enough poison to kill 60 human adults; the venom not only attacks the nerves and heart but also destroys the skin, causing intense and excruciating pain before an agonizing death.

PLANT AND FUNGUS RECORDS

Largest living tree	The largest tree in terms of mass is the giant sequoia. The largest individual specimen is the 'General Sherman' in Sequoia National Park, California, USA, and is 83.82m/275ft tall. It is more than 10 times as massive as a blue whale.
Tallest living tree	The tallest tree is the coast redwood. The tallest individual specimen is the 'Stratosphere Giant' in the Humboldt Redwoods State Park, California, USA, and is 112.6m/369ft 4.8in tall.
Most massive plant	The largest individual plant in terms of mass so far discovered is a group of quaking aspen trees growing in the Wasatch Mountains, Utah, USA. Its roots extend over an area of 43ha/106 acres.
Oldest living tree	The tree that lives longest is estimated to be the bristlecone pine. The oldest individual yet found is named 'Methuselah' and grows in the White Mountains on the California–Nevada border in the USA. It is reckoned to be 4767 years old.
Fastest growing plant	Bamboo can grow faster than any other plant, at up to 91cm/3ft per day.
Largest flower	The parasitic *Rafflesia arnoldi*, which grows on cissus vines in the south-east Asian rainforest, has the largest flowers. They can measure up to 91cm/3ft in width, with a weight of 11kg/24lb.
Largest leaf	The largest leaves of any plant belong to the raffia palm of the Mascarene Islands, Indian Ocean, and the Amazonian bamboo palm of South America and Africa; both measure up to 20m/65ft 7in in length.
Largest seed	The giant fan palm, known as the double coconut or coco de mer, produces the largest seed, weighing up to 20kg/44lb.
Longest root	Winter rye has been shown to have one of the most extensive yet tightly-packed root systems of any plant, with a single specimen producing 622.8km/387mi of roots in only 0.051 cu m/1.8 cu ft of soil.
Largest fungus	A fungus known as the honey mushroom can extend over hundreds of hectares. The largest individual fungus of this type is thought to grow in the Malheur National Forest in the Blue Mountains of eastern Oregon, USA, and covers around 820ha/2028 acres.

MOST POISONOUS ANIMALS

Deadliest snake	The hook-nosed sea snake of seas and coastal waters in the Middle East, Asia and Australasia may be the world's deadliest snake. Its venom is 60 times more poisonous than a rattlesnake's.
Snake with most venom	The inland taipan, or fierce snake, of central Australia can deliver the greatest amount of venom per bite; 110mg/0.0038oz has been recorded, although 44mg/0.0015oz is more common. It is thought to be the most venomous land snake.
Snake responsible for most deaths	Russell's viper lives in habitats worldwide and is notably aggressive, with a deadly venom. It has probably killed more people than any other snake.
Most poisonous fish	The puffer fish of the Indian and Pacific oceans and Red Sea secretes a deadly poison that is present in its blood, organs and skin. A dose of less than 0.1g/0.004oz is sufficient to kill an adult human.
Most poisonous frog	The golden poison dart frog, living in western Colombia, secretes a poison which is the most toxic of any known land animal. Just 1g/0.035oz of it could kill 100000 people.

MOST POISONOUS PLANTS AND FUNGI

Most poisonous in the world	The seeds of the castor bean plant, the source of castor oil, are highly toxic. Just 1mg/0.00004oz of their main toxin, ricin, can be enough to kill a human adult. Ricin is considered internationally to be a chemical and biological weapon.
Most poisonous in Europe	Monkshood, also called wolfsbane, may be Europe's most poisonous plant. It was formerly used in traps to kill wolves.
Most poisonous in the USA	Western water hemlock is often cited as the most poisonous plant in the USA, and is a particular hazard to livestock. Small amounts of it are sufficient to kill a horse.
Most poisonous edible fruit	The pith surrounding the ackee fruit is commonly cooked and eaten in Jamaica. The unripe pith, however, can be highly toxic, and may lead to serious illness, coma and death if ingested.
Most poisonous fungus	The death cap is the cause of most fatal poisonings from fungi. Whitish in colour, it is often mistaken for an edible mushroom.

ANIMAL AGES

Animal	Average age reached in captivity (years)	Animal	Average age reached in captivity (years)
bear	15–30	horse	20–25
camel	12	kangaroo	4–7
cat	10–12	lion	10–15
chimpanzee	20	monkey	12–15
cow	9–15	mouse	3
dog	10–12	pig	10
elephant	30–40	pigeon	10–12
fox	7–10	rabbit	5–8
giraffe	10	rhinoceros	15–20
goat	8	sheep	12
gorilla	20	squirrel	8–10
guinea pig	4	tiger	16
hippopotamus	25–30	zebra	15

CLOSE SEASONS (UK)

The close season is the time of the year when it is illegal to kill certain game or fish. Dates given are inclusive; for birds, the first dates refer to England, Scotland and Wales and the second to Northern Ireland, while for deer the first dates refer to England, Wales and Northern Ireland, the second to Scotland. Where only one set of dates is given the close season is the same across the UK.

Fish

Close season dates vary locally, according to bylaws, species of fish and type of water (lake, river, canal, etc).

Birds

Capercailzie	1 Feb–30 Sep	Woodcock	1 Feb–30 Sep; 1 Feb–30 Sep
Partridge	2 Feb–31 Aug; 1 Feb–31 Aug	Grouse[1]	11 Dec–11 Aug; 1 Dec–11 Aug
Pheasant	2 Feb–30 Sep; 1 Feb–30 Sep	Black game[2]	11 Dec–19 Aug[3]
Common snipe	1 Feb–11 Aug; 1 Feb–31 Aug		

[1] *Includes red grouse and ptarmigan.*
[2] *Black grouse.*
[3] *To 31 Aug in Somerset, Devon and the New Forest.*

Deer

Female		*Male*	
Red deer	1 Mar–31 Oct; 16 Feb–20 Oct	Red deer	1 May–31 Jul; 21 Oct–30 Jun
Fallow deer	1 Mar–31 Oct; 16 Feb–20 Oct	Fallow deer	1 May–31 Jul
Sika deer	1 Mar–31 Oct; 16 Feb–20 Oct	Sika deer	1 May–31 Jul; 21 Oct–30 Jun
Roe deer	1 Mar–31 Oct; 1 Apr–20 Oct	Roe deer	1 Nov–31 Mar; 21 Oct–31 Mar

Note: There is no statutory close season for muntjak or Chinese water deer.

COUNTRIES A–Z

Introduction

Information given in this section is subject to frequent change.

Names of countries and cities

The official name of the country is given in English. Where appropriate the short form of the local name is given first, followed by the long form. English names of capital cities are given first, followed by the local name(s). Any notable names by which a country has been previously known in the 20c are listed with relevant dates.

Area

Area figures are for land mass only and exclude territorial waters (eg Kiribati covers approx 3 million sq km/1.2 million sq mi but land area is only 717 sq km/277 sq mi).

Chief towns

If no chief towns are given the country is too small or sparsely populated to have major settlements.

Population

Unless otherwise indicated, population statistics are mid-2007 estimates from the CIA World Factbook; figures are rounded to the nearest thousand.

Nationality

Nationality gives the usual adjective form; exceptions are clearly marked.

Time zone

No allowance is made for Daylight Saving Time.

Currency

The three-letter ISO currency code is given alongside any commonly used abbreviations.

Country codes

Country codes are from the official ISO list.

Climate

Temperature figures are given in degrees Celsius. To convert to Fahrenheit multiply by 9, divide by 5 and add 32.

National holidays

The first part of each listing gives the holidays that occur on fixed dates. Most dates are accompanied by an indication of the purpose of the day, eg Independence = Independence Day; dates which have no gloss are either fixed dates within the Christian calendar (for which see below) or bank holidays. The second part of the listing gives holidays whose dates vary, usually depending on religious factors. The most common of these are given in abbreviated form (see list below).

Where national holidays last for more than one day, the number of days devoted to the holiday is shown in parentheses. The listings do not include holidays that affect only certain parts of a country, half-day holidays or Sundays.

The following fixed dates are shown without gloss:

Jan 1	New Year's Day
Jan 6	Epiphany
Mar 21	Novrus (Persian New Year; various spellings)
May 1	Labour Day (often known by a different name, such as Workers' Day)
Aug 15	Assumption of Our Lady
Nov 1	All Saints' Day
Nov 2	All Souls' Day
Dec 8	Immaculate Conception
Dec 24	Christmas Eve
Dec 25	Christmas Day
Dec 26	Boxing Day/St Stephen's Day
Dec 31	New Year's Eve

COUNTRIES A–Z

The following abbreviations are used for variable religious feast days:

A	Ascension Thursday
Ad	Id-ul-Adha (also found with other spellings, especially Eid-ul-Adha; various names relating to this occasion are used in different countries, such as Tabaski, Id el-Kebir, Hari Raja Haji). May last from two to ten days, depending on the country or region.
Ar	Arafa
As	Ashora (found with various spellings)
C	Carnival (immediately before Christian Lent, unless specified)
CC	Corpus Christi
D	Diwali/Deepavali
EM	Easter Monday
ER	End of Ramadan (known generally as Id/Eid-ul-Fitr, but various names relating to this occasion are used in different countries, such as Karite, Hari Raja Puasa). May last from two to ten days, depending on the country or region.
ES	Easter Sunday
GF	Good Friday
HS	Holy Saturday
HT	Holy Thursday
NY	New Year
PA	Prophet's Ascension (known generally as Laylat al-Miraj in various forms and spellings)
PB	Prophet's Birthday (known generally as Maul-id-al-Nabi in various forms and spellings)
R	First day of Ramadan
WM	Whit Monday

Dependencies

Dependencies and other territories are listed by type then alphabetically.

Political leaders

Countries and organizations are listed alphabetically, with former or alternative names also given. Rulers are named chronologically since 1900 or (for new nations) since independence. For some major English-speaking nations, relevant details are also given of pre-20c rulers, along with a note of any political affiliation. Relevant details are also given of pre-20c rulers for some major monarchies, and other useful information, for example dynasties, is also included where appropriate. The list does not distinguish successive terms of office by a single ruler. Listings are complete to Jan 2008.

There is no universally agreed way of transliterating proper names in non-Roman alphabets; variations from the spellings given are therefore to be expected, especially in the case of Arabic rulers. Minor variations in the titles adopted by heads of state, or in the name of an administration, are not given; these occur most notably in countries under military rule.

ABU DHABI *see* UNITED ARAB EMIRATES

see UNITED ARAB EMIRATES

AFGHANISTAN

Official name	Islamic Republic of Afghanistan
Local name	Afqânestân (Dari), Afğānistān (Pashto)
Former name	*as listed below under Political leaders*
Independence	1919
Area	647 497 sq km/249 934 sq mi
Capital	Kabul; Kābul, Kābol
Chief towns	Herat, Kandahar
Population	31 890 000 (2007e)
Nationality	Afghan
Languages	Dari, Pashto
Ethnic groups	Pashtun 42%, Tajik 27%, Hazara 9%, Uzbek 9%, others 13%
Religions	Islam 99% (Sunni 84%, Shia 15%), others 1%
Time zone	GMT +4.5
Currency	1 Afghani (Af/AFN) = 100 puls
Telephone	+93
Internet	.af
Country code	AFG

Location
A republic in south-central Asia, bounded to the north by Turkmenistan, Uzbekistan and Tajikistan; to the extreme north-east by China and the disputed area of Jammu and Kashmir; to the east and south by Pakistan; and to the west by Iran.

Physical description
Landlocked and mountainous, centred on the Hindu Kush system which reaches over 7 000m/23 000ft in centre and north-east; highest point is Nowshak (7 485m/24 557ft); north-west is the fertile valley of Herat; arid uplands in south; desert in south-west.

Climate
Continental climate with winter severity increased by altitude; summers are warm everywhere except on the highest peaks; protected from summer monsoons by the southern mountains; lower levels have a desert or semi-arid climate.

National holidays
Feb 15 (Liberation), Mar 21, Apr 28 (Revolution), May 1, Aug 19 (National); Ad (3), As, ER (3), PB; Mt Arafat (Feb).

Political leaders

Afghan Empire

Monarch

1881–1901	Abdur Rahman Khan
1901–19	Habibullah Khan
1919–29	Amanullah Khan
1929	Habibullah Ghazi
1929–33	Nadir Shah
1933–73	Zahir Shah

Republic of Afghanistan

President

1973–8	Mohammad Daoud Khan

Democratic Republic of Afghanistan

President of Revolutionary Council

1978–9	Nour Mohammad Taraki
1979	Hafizullah Amin

Soviet invasion

1979–86	Babrak Karmal
1986–7	Haji Mohammad Chamkani *Acting*
1987–92	Mohammad Najibullah
1992	Sebghatullah Mojaddedi *Acting*

General Secretary

1978–86	*As President*
1986–92	Mohammad Najibullah

Prime Minister

1929–46	Sardar Mohammad Hashim Khan
1946–53	Shah Mahmoud Khan Ghazi
1953–63	Mohammad Daoud
1963–5	Mohammad Yousef
1965–7	Mohammad Hashim Maiwandwal
1967–71	Nour Ahmad Etemadi
1972–3	Mohammad Mousa Shafiq
1973–9	*As President*
1979–81	Babrak Karmal
1981–8	Sultan Ali Keshtmand

Republic of Afghanistan

1988–9	Mohammad Hasan Sharq
1989–90	Sultan Ali Keshtmand
1990–2	Fazal Haq Khaliqyar
1992–3	Abdul Sabour Fareed
1993–6	Gulbuddin Hekmatyar

Islamic State of Afghanistan

President

1992–2001	Burhanuddin Rabbani[1]

Chairman of Interim Government

2001–2	Hamid Karzai

Islamic Republic of Afghanistan[2]

President

2002–	Hamid Karzai

[1]*Ousted by the Taliban in 1996, but remained titular head of state; Taliban de facto rulers 1996–2001.*
[2]*Islamic Transitional State of Afghanistan until 2004.*

AJMAN *see* UNITED ARAB EMIRATES

ALBANIA

Official name	Republic of Albania
Local name	Shqipëria; Republika e Shqipërisë
Former name	Kingdom of Albania (1928–39), People's Republic of Albania (1946–76), People's Socialist Republic of Albania (until 1991)
Independence	1912
Area	28748 sq km/11097 sq mi
Capital	Tirana; Tiranë
Chief towns	Shkodër, Durrës, Vlorë, Korçë, Elbasan
Population	3600000 (2007e)
Nationality	Albanian
Languages	Albanian
Ethnic groups	Albanian 95%, Greek 3%, others 2%
Religions	Islam 70% (Sunni), Christianity 30% (Orthodox 20%, RC 10%)
Time zone	GMT +1
Currency	1 Lek (plural Lekë) (Lk/ALL) = 100 qindarka
Telephone	+355
Internet	.al
Country code	ALB

Location

A republic in the western part of the Balkan Peninsula, bounded to the north by Montenegro and Serbia; to the east by Macedonia; to the south-east by Greece; and to the west by the Adriatic Sea.

Physical description

Mountainous, relatively inaccessible and untravelled; highest point is Maja e Korabit (Golem Korab; 2753m/9032ft) on the Macedonian border; northern Albanian Alps rise to 2692m/8832ft; 50% of the population live in 25% of the area (the low-lying west).

Climate

A Mediterranean-type climate: hot and dry on the plains in summer (average Jul temperature 24–25°C); winters are mild and damp (average Jan temperature 8–9°C), but often severe in the mountains.

National holidays

Jan 1, 2, Mar 14 (Summer), 21, May 1, Oct 19 (Mother Theresa), Nov 28 (Independence), 29 (Liberation), Dec 25; Ad, EM (Orthodox), ER, GF (Orthodox).

Political leaders

Monarch

1928–39	Zog I (Ahmed Zogu)
1939–44	*Italian rule*

President

1944–85	Enver Hoxha
1985–92	Ramiz Alia
1992–7	Sali Berisha
1997–2002	Rexhep Mejdani
2002–7	Alfred Moisiu
2007–	Bamir Topi

Prime Minister

1914	Turhan Pashë Permëti
1914	Esad Toptani
1914–18	Abdullah Rushdi
1918–20	Turhan Pashë Permëti
1920	Sulejman Deluina
1920–1	Iljaz Bej Vrioni
1921	Pandeli Evangeli
1921	Xhafer Ypi
1921–2	Omer Vrioni
1922–4	Ahmed Zogu
1924	Iljaz Bej Vrioni
1924–5	Fan Noli
1925–8	Ahmed Zogu
1928–30	Koço Kota
1930–5	Pandeli Evangeli
1935–6	Mehdi Frashëri
1936–9	Koço Kota
1939–41	Shefqet Verlaci
1941–3	Mustafa Merlika-Kruja
1943	Eqrem Libohova
1943	Maliq Bushati
1943	Eqrem Libohova
1943	*Provisional Executive Committee* (Ibrahim Biçakçlu)
1943	*Council of Regents* (Mehdi Frashëri)
1943–4	Rexhep Mitrovica
1944	Fiori Dine
1944–54	Enver Hoxha
1954–81	Mehmed Shehu
1981–91	Adil Carcani
1991	Ylli Buffi
1991	Fatos Nano
1991–2	Vilson Ahmeti
1992–7	Aleksander Meksi
1997	Bashkim Fino
1997–8	Fatos Nano
1998–9	Pandeli Majko
1999–2002	Ilir Meta
2002	Pandeli Majko
2002–5	Fatos Nano
2005–	Sali Berisha

ALGERIA

Official name	People's Democratic Republic of Algeria
Local name	Al-Jazā'ir; Al-Jumh-uriyya al-Jazā'iriyya ad-Dimuqratiyya ash-Sha'biyya (Arabic), Algérie; République Algérienne Démocratique et Populaire (French)
Independence	1962
Area	2460500 sq km/949753 sq mi
Capital	Algiers; Alger, El Djazâir, Al-Jazā'ir
Chief towns	Constantine, Oran, Skikda, Annaba, Mostaganem, Blida, Tlemcen
Population	33333000 (2007e)
Nationality	Algerian
Languages	Arabic, Tamazight; French is also spoken
Ethnic groups	Arab-Berber 99%, European 1%
Religions	Islam 99% (Sunni), others 1%
Time zone	GMT +1
Currency	1 Algerian Dinar (AD, DA/DZD) = 100 centimes
Telephone	+213
Internet	.dz
Country code	DZA

Location

A republic in North Africa, crossed by the Tropic of Cancer in the south; bounded to the north by the Mediterranean Sea; to the north-east by Tunisia; to the east by Libya; to the south-east by Niger; to the south-west by Western Sahara, Mauritania and Mali; and to the west by Morocco.

Physical description

From the Mediterranean coast, where 91% of the population are located on the narrow coastal plain, the mountains rise to the Atlas Saharien; the Sahara Desert lies to the south; the Hoggar Mountains in the far south rise to 2918m/9573ft at Mt Tahat.

Climate

Typical Mediterranean climate on the north coast; snow on the higher ground; Algiers, representative of the coastal region, has average maximum daily temperatures of 15–29°C; elsewhere an essentially rainless Saharan climate.

National holidays

Jan 1, May 1, Jun 19 (Revolutionary Readjustment), Jul 5 (Independence), Nov 1 (Revolution); Ad (2), As, ER (2), NY (Muslim), PB.

Political leaders

President

1962–5	Ahmed Ben Bella
1965–78	Houari Boumédienne
1979–92	Chandli Benjedid
1992	*High Commission of State: Chair* Mohamed Boudiaf
1992–4	Ali Kafi
1994–9	Liamine Zeroual
1999–	Abdelaziz Bouteflika

Prime Minister

1962–3	Ahmed Ben Bella
1963–79	*No Prime Minister*
1979–84	Mohamed Ben Ahmed Abdelghani
1984–8	Abdelhamid Brahimi
1988–9	Kasdi Merbah
1989–91	Mouloud Hamrouche
1991–2	Sid Ahmed Ghozali
1992–3	Belaid Abdessalam
1993–4	Redha Malek
1994–5	Mokdad Sifi
1995–8	Ahmed Ouyahia
1998–9	Ismail Hamdani
1999–2000	Ahmed Benbitour
2000–3	Ali Benflis
2003–6	Ahmed Ouyahia
2006–	Abdelaziz Belkhadem

AMERICAN SAMOA *see* UNITED STATES OF AMERICA

see UNITED STATES OF AMERICA

ANDORRA

Official name	Principality of Andorra; also sometimes known as The Valleys of Andorra
Local name	Andorra; Principat d'Andorra
Area	468 sq km/181 sq mi
Capital	Andorra la Vella; Andorra la Vieja (Spanish), Andorre la Vielle (French), Andorra la Vella (Catalan)
Population	72 000 (2007e)
Nationality	Andorran
Languages	Catalan; French and Spanish are also spoken
Ethnic groups	Spanish 43%, Andorran 33%, Portuguese 11%, French 7%, others 6%
Religions	Christianity 95% (RC 94%, Prot 1%), none/unaffiliated 5%
Time zone	GMT +1
Currency	1 Euro (€/EUR) = 100 cents
Telephone	+376
Internet	.ad
Country code	AND

Location

A semi-independent neutral state in the central Pyrenees between France and Spain.

Physical description

A small, mountainous country, reaching 2 947m/9 669ft at Coma Pedrosa, occupying two valleys (del Norte and del Orient) of the River Valira.

Climate

Winters are cold but dry and sunny; the midsummer months are slightly drier than spring and autumn.

National holidays

Jan 1, 6, Mar 14 (Constitution), May 1, 25, Jun 24 (St John), Aug 15, Sep 8 (National), Nov 1, 4 (St Charles), Dec 8, 25, 26, 31; A, EM, GF, WM.

Political leaders

There are two heads of state, called Co-Princes: the President of France (see entry for France) and the Bishop of Urgell, Spain (Joan Enric Vives i Sicília since 2003).

President of the Executive Council

1982–4	Óscar Ribas Reig
1984–90	Josep Pintat Solens
1990–4	Óscar Ribas Reig
1994–2005	Marc Forné Molné
2005–	Albert Pintat Santolària

In the High Pyrenees

Andorra, nestled among the mountains of the eastern Pyrenees, proudly claims to be Europe's highest inhabited country. The lowest point is a still-respectable 840m/2,756ft above sea level, while the highest mountain, Coma Pedrosa, reaches a sizeable 2,947m/9,669ft. Andorra manages to pack 65 peaks that reach higher than 2,500m/8,202ft into just 468 sq km/181 sq mi of land.

ANGOLA

Official name	Republic of Angola
Local name	Angola; República de Angola
Former name	People's Republic of Angola (until 1992)
Independence	1975
Area	1 245 790 sq km/480 875 sq mi
Capital	Luanda
Chief towns	Huambo, Benguela, Lobito, Namibe (Moçâmedes), Cabinda, Malanje, Lubango
Population	12 264 000 (2007e)
Nationality	Angolan
Languages	Portuguese; many Bantu languages are also spoken
Ethnic groups	Ovimbundu 37%, Kimbundu 25%, Bakongo 13%, others 25%
Religions	Christianity 53% (RC 38%, Prot 15%), traditional beliefs 47%
Time zone	GMT +1
Currency	1 Kwanza (Kzrl/AOA) = 100 lwei
Telephone	+244
Internet	.ao
Country code	AGO

Location

A republic in south-west Africa, bounded to the north by Democratic Republic of the Congo; to the east by Zambia; to the south by Namibia; and to the west by the southern Atlantic Ocean; the separate province of Cabinda is enclosed by Congo and Democratic Republic of the Congo, and bounded to the west by the southern Atlantic Ocean.

Physical description

A narrow coastal plain, widening in the north towards the Congo Delta; high plateau inland with an average elevation of 1 200m/3 937ft; highest point is Serro Môco (2 619m/8 592ft); numerous rivers rise in the plateau but few are navigable for any length.

Climate

Mostly a tropical plateau climate; a single wet season Oct–Mar and a long dry season; average daily temperatures of 24–29°C in upland region; temperature and rainfall much reduced on the coast, which is semi-desert as far north as Luanda.

National holidays

Jan 1, 4 (Martyrs of the Colonial Repression), Feb 4 (Beginning of the Armed Struggle), Mar 8 (Women), April 4 (Peace and Reconciliation), May 1, 25 (Africa), Jun 1 (Children), Sep 17 (Nation's Founder/National Hero), Nov 2, 11 (Independence), Dec 25; GF, EM.

Political leaders

President

1975–9	Antonio Agostinho Neto
1979–	José Eduardo dos Santos

Prime Minister

1975–8	Lopo do Nasciemento
1978–91	*No Prime Minister*
1991–2	Fernando José de França van Dúnem
1992–6	Marcolino José Carlos Moco Santos
1996–97	Fernando José de França van Dúnem
1999–2002	*No Prime Minister*
2002–	Fernando dos Santos

ANGUILLA; **ANTARCTIC TERRITORY, BRITISH** *see* **UNITED KINGDOM**

ANTIGUA AND BARBUDA

Official name	State of Antigua and Barbuda
Local name	Antigua and Barbuda
Independence	1981
Area	442 sq km/171 sq mi
Capital	St John's
Chief towns	Codrington (on Barbuda)
Population	69 000 (2007e)
Nationality	Antiguan, Barbudan
Languages	English
Ethnic groups	African descent 92%, British 4%, others 4%
Religions	Christianity 96% (Prot 87%, RC 9%), Rastafarianism 1%, none/unaffiliated 1%, others 2%
Time zone	GMT –4
Currency	1 East Caribbean Dollar (EC$/XCD) = 100 cents
Telephone	+1 268
Internet	.ag
Country code	ATG

Location

An independent group of three islands in the Leeward group of the Lesser Antilles in the eastern Caribbean Sea: Antigua, Barbuda and the uninhabited Redonda.

Physical description

The western part of Antigua rises to 402m/1 319ft at Boggy Peak; Barbuda is a flat, coral island reaching only 44m/144ft at its highest point, with a large lagoon on its western side.

Climate

Tropical, with temperatures ranging from 24°C in Jan to 27°C in Aug–Sep.

National holidays

Jan 1, Nov 1 (Independence), Dec 9 (National Heroes), 25, 26; EM, GF, WM, Labour (1st Mon in May), Caricom (1st Mon in Jul), Emancipation (1st Mon and Tue in Aug).

Political leaders

Head of State: British monarch, represented by Governor General (Louise Lake-Tack since 2007).

Prime Minister

1981–94 Vere Cornwall Bird
1994–2004 Lester Bryant Bird
2004– Baldwin Spencer

Kings of Redonda

Although uninhabited and covering barely 1 sq km/0.4 sq mi, the tiny island of Redonda is claimed as a sovereign state by several self-styled 'kings'. The monarchy was supposedly instituted in 1865 by one Matthew Dowdy Shiell, a Caribbean trader who proclaimed himself king of the island to celebrate the birth of his first son. While the following two 'kings' were commonly acknowledged, thereafter the succession to the title 'King of Redonda' has been hotly disputed and jealously defended. Today, the two principal rivals – both with a national anthem, and both quick to denounce the other as an impudent impostor – are the British King Leo I and the Antiguan King Bob.

ARGENTINA

Official name	Argentine Republic
Local name	Argentina; República Argentina
Independence	1816
Area	2766890 sq km/1068296 sq mi
Capital	Buenos Aires
Chief towns	Córdoba, Rosario, Mendoza, La Plata, Mar del Plata, San Miguel de Tucumán
Population	40302000 (2007e)
Nationality	Argentine, Argentinian
Languages	Spanish
Ethnic groups	European (mostly Spanish and Italian) 97%, mestizo, Amerindian and others 3%
Religions	Christianity 94% (RC 92% (less than 20% practising), Prot 2%), Judaism 2%, others 4%
Time zone	GMT –3
Currency	1 Argentine Peso ($/ARS) = 100 centavos
Telephone	+54
Internet	.ar
Country code	ARG

Location

A republic in south-eastern South America, crossed by the Tropic of Capricorn in the north; bounded to the north by Bolivia and Paraguay; to the north-east by Brazil and Uruguay; to the south-east by the southern Atlantic Ocean; and to the west and south by Chile.

Physical description

The Andes stretch the entire length, north to south, forming the boundary with Chile; the highest peak is Aconcagua (6960m/22835ft); the *pampa*, a grassy, treeless plain is to the east, with uneven, arid steppes to the south.

Climate

Most of Argentina lies in the rainshadow of the Andes; temperatures range from tropical to moderately cool (average annual temperature 16°C at Buenos Aires), with some desert; the south is directly influenced by strong prevailing westerlies.

National holidays

Jan 1, Apr 2 (Veterans'/Malvinas), May 1, 25 (National), Jul 9 (National Independence), Dec 8, 25; GF, National Flag (Belgrano) (3rd Mon in Jun), Death of General San Martín (3rd Mon in Aug), Columbus (2nd Mon in Oct).

Silver Country

The name *Argentina* comes from the Latin word *argentum*, meaning 'silver'. When Spanish explorers first reached the area in the early 16c the local people gave them silver gifts, and they returned home with tales of a mountain supposedly composed of silver. The main river estuary was christened *Río de la Plata*, or 'River of Silver'.

Political leaders

President

1898–1904	Julio Argentino Roca	1928–30	Hipólito Yrigoyen
1904–6	Manuel Quintana	1930–2	José Félix Uriburu
1906–10	José Figueroa Alcorta	1932–8	Augustin Pedro Justo
1910–14	Roque Sáenz Peña	1938–40	Roberto M Ortiz
1914–16	Victorino de la Plaza	1940–3	Ramón S Castillo
1916–22	Hipólito Yrigoyen	1943–4	Pedro P Ramírez
1922–8	Marcelo T de Alvear	1944–6	Edelmiro J Farrell

1946–55	Juan Perón	1981	*Military Junta* (Roberto Eduardo Viola)
1955–8	Eduardo Lonardi	1981–2	*Military Junta* (Leopoldo Galtieri)
1958–62	Arturo Frondizi	1982–3	Reynaldo Bignone
1962–3	José María Guido	1983–8	Raúl Alfonsín
1963–6	Arturo Illia	1988–99	Carlos Saúl Menem
1966–70	Juan Carlos Ongania	1999–2001	Fernando de la Rúa
1970–1	Roberto Marcelo Levingston	2001	*Three Interim Presidents*
1971–3	Alejandro Agustin Lanusse	2002–3	Eduardo Duhalde
1973	Héctor J Cámpora	2003–7	Nestor Kirchner
1973–4	Juan Perón	2007–	Cristina Fernández de Kirchner
1974–6	Martínez de Perón		
1976–81	*Military Junta* (Jorge Rafaél Videla)		

ARMENIA

Official name	Republic of Armenia
Local name	Hayastan; Hayastany Hanrapetoutyun
Former name	Transcaucasian Soviet Federated Socialist Republic (with Azerbaijan and Georgia, 1922–36), Armenian Soviet Socialist Republic (1920–2, 1936–90), within the Union of Soviet Socialist Republics (USSR; 1922–91)
Independence	1991
Area	29800 sq km/11500 sq mi
Capital	Yerevan; Erevan
Chief towns	Vanadzor, Gyumri
Population	2972000 (2007e)
Nationality	Armenian
Languages	Armenian; Russian is also widely spoken
Ethnic groups	Armenian 98%, Azeri 1%, Russian and others 1%
Religions	Christianity 99% (Orthodox 95%, other 4%), others 1%
Time zone	GMT +4
Currency	1 Dram (Drm/AMD) = 100 lumas
Telephone	+374
Internet	.am
Country code	ARM

Location

A republic in southern Transcaucasia, bounded to the north by Georgia; to the east and south-west by Azerbaijan; to the south by Iran; and to the west by Turkey.

Physical description

Mountainous, rising to 4090m/13418ft at Mt Aragats in the west; largest lake is Sevan.

Climate

Dry and cold in the summer, cold in the winter.

National holidays

Jan 1, 2, 6 (Armenian Orthodox Christmas), Mar 8 (Women), Apr 7 (Motherhood and Beauty), 24 (Genocide Memorial), May 9 (Victory and Peace), 28 (Declaration of First Armenian Republic, 1918), Jul 5 (Constitution), Sep 21 (Independence), Dec 7 (Earthquake Memorial), 31; GF.

Political leaders

President

1991–8	Levon Ter-Petrossian
1998–	Robert Kocharyan

Prime Minister

1991–2	Gagik Haroutunian
1992–3	Khosrov Haroutunian
1993–6	Hrand Bagratian
1996–7	Armen Sarkissian
1997–8	Robert Kocharyan
1998–9	Armen Darbinian
1999	Vazgen Sarkissian
1999–2000	Aram Sarkissian
2000–7	Andranik Markarian
2007–	Serzh Sarkissian

ARUBA *see* **NETHERLANDS, THE**

AUSTRALIA

Official name	Commonwealth of Australia
Local name	Australia
Independence	1901
Area	7 682 300 sq km/2 966 136 sq mi
Capital	Canberra
Chief towns	Melbourne, Brisbane, Perth, Adelaide, Sydney
Population	20 434 000 (2007e)
Nationality	Australian
Languages	English; Aboriginal languages are also spoken
Ethnic groups	European 81%, Chinese 2%, Aboriginal and others 17%
Religions	Christianity 66% (RC 26%, Prot 20%, other 20%), others 5%, unspecified 13%, none 15%
Time zone	GMT +8/10.5
Currency	1 Australian Dollar ($A/AUD) = 100 cents
Telephone	+61
Internet	.au
Country code	AUS

Location

An independent country, entirely in the southern hemisphere, crossed by the Tropic of Capricorn; separated from Indonesia, East Timor and Papua New Guinea to the north by the Timor Sea, Arafura Sea and Torres Strait; to the east is the Pacific Ocean and Tasman Sea; to the south the Southern Ocean; and to the west the Indian Ocean.

Physical description

The largest island and the smallest continent in the world; consists largely of plains and plateaux; the West Australian plateau occupies nearly half the whole area; most of the plateau is desert; Great Dividing Range parallel to the eastern seaboard rises to 2 228m/7 310ft at Mt Kosciusko (Australia's highest point); the island of Tasmania lies to the south; fertile land is limited to the coastal east and south-east and to a small part of the south-west, and the population is concentrated in these two regions.

Climate

Half the country has a rainfall variability of more than 30%, with many areas experiencing prolonged drought; Darwin's average daily temperature is 26–34°C in Nov and 19–31°C in Jul; Melbourne's average daily temperature is 6–13°C in Jul and 14–26°C in Jan–Feb.

National holidays

Jan 1, 26 (Australia), Apr 25 (Anzac), Dec 25, 26; Queen's Birthday (Jun, *except Western Australia, Sept/Oct*), EM, GF, HS; *additional days vary between states*.

Australian states and territories

Name	Population (2006)[1]	Area	Capital
Australian Capital Territory (ACT)	336400	2432 sq km/939 sq mi	Canberra
New South Wales (NSW)	6854800	801427 sq km/309431 sq mi	Sydney
Northern Territory (NT)	212600	1346200 sq km/519768 sq mi	Darwin
Queensland (QLD)	4132000	1732700 sq km/668995 sq mi	Brisbane
South Australia (SA)	1575700	984376 sq km/380070 sq mi	Adelaide
Tasmania (TAS)	491700	68331 sq km/26383 sq mi	Hobart
Victoria (VIC)	5165400	227600 sq km/87876 sq mi	Melbourne
Western Australia (WA)	2081000	2525500 sq km/975096 sq mi	Perth

[1] *Population figures are from the Australian Bureau of Statistics.*

Overseas territories

Norfolk Island

Location	An island in the south-western Pacific Ocean, lying 1488km/925mi north-east of Sydney, eastern Australia.		
Area	35 sq km/14 sq mi	**Internet**	.nf
Capital	Kingston	**Country code**	NFK
Population	2114 (2007e)		

Heard and McDonald Islands

Location	An island group comprising Heard Island, Shag Island and the McDonald Islands in the Southern Ocean, approximately 4000km/2500mi south-west of Fremantle, western Australia.		
Area	412 sq km/159 sq mi	**Internet**	.hm
Population	uninhabited	**Country code**	HMD

Christmas Island

Location	An island in the Indian Ocean, approximately 360km/224mi south of the Indonesian island of Java.		
Area	135 sq km/52 sq mi	**Internet**	.cx
Capital	The Settlement	**Country code**	CXR
Population	1402 (2007e)		

Cocos (Keeling) Islands

Location	Two separate groups of atolls in the Indian Ocean, 3685km/2290mi west of Darwin, northern Australia, comprising 27 islands; the main islands are West Island and Home Island.		
Area	14.2 sq km/5.5 sq mi	**Internet**	.cc
Capital	West Island	**Country code**	CCK
Population	596 (2007e)		

Note: Australia also possesses the uninhabited Ashmore and Cartier Islands in the Indian Ocean and the Coral Sea Islands in the Coral Sea north-east of Australia.

Political leaders

Head of State: British monarch, represented by Governor General (Michael Jeffery since 2003).

Prime Minister

1901–3	Edmund Barton *Prot*	1939–41	Robert Gordon Menzies *Un*
1903–4	Alfred Deakin *Prot*	1941	Arthur William Fadden *Co*
1904	John Christian Watson *Lab*	1941–5	John Joseph Curtin *Lab*
1904–5	George Houston Reid *Free*	1945	Francis Michael Forde *Lab*
1905–8	Alfred Deakin *Prot*	1945–9	Joseph Benedict Chifley *Lab*
1908–9	Andrew Fisher *Lab*	1949–66	Robert Gordon Menzies *Lib*
1909–10	Alfred Deakin *Fus*	1966–7	Harold Edward Holt *Lib*
1910–13	Andrew Fisher *Lab*	1967–8	John McEwen *Co*
1913–14	Joseph Cook *Lib*	1968–71	John Grey Gorton *Lib*
1914–15	Andrew Fisher *Lab*	1971–2	William McMahon *Lib*
1915–17	William Morris Hughes *Nat Lab*	1972–5	Edward Gough Whitlam *Lab*
1917–23	William Morris Hughes *Nat*	1975–83	John Malcolm Fraser *Lib*
1923–9	Stanley Melbourne Bruce *Nat*	1983–91	Robert James Lee Hawke *Lab*
1929–32	James Henry Scullin *Lab*	1991–6	Paul Keating *Lab*
1932–9	Joseph Aloysius Lyons *Un*	1996–2007	John Howard *Lib*
1939	Earle Christmas Page *Co*	2007–	Kevin Rudd *Lab*

Co = Country; Con = Conservative; Free = Free Trade; Fus = Fusion; Lab = Labor; Lib = Liberal; Nat = Nationalist; Nat Lab = National Labor; Prot = Protectionist; Un = United

AUSTRIA

Official name	Republic of Austria
Local name	Österreich; Republik Österreich
Former name	formerly part of Austria–Hungary (until 1918)
Independence	1955
Area	83 854 sq km/32 368 sq mi
Capital	Vienna; Wien
Chief towns	Graz, Linz, Salzburg, Innsbruck, Klagenfurt
Population	8 200 000 (2007e)
Nationality	Austrian
Languages	German
Ethnic groups	Austrian 91%, former Yugoslavs 4%, others 5%
Religions	Christianity 79% (RC 74%, Prot 5%), Islam 4%, none/unaffiliated 14%, others 3%
Time zone	GMT +1
Currency	1 Euro (€/EUR) = 100 cents
Telephone	+43
Internet	.at
Country code	AUT

Location

A republic in central Europe, bounded to the north-west by Germany; to the north by the Czech Republic; to the north-east by Slovakia; to the south-east by Hungary; to the south by Slovenia and Italy; and to the west by Switzerland and Liechtenstein.

Physical description

Situated at the eastern end of the Alps, the country is almost entirely mountainous; highest point is Grossglockner, at 3797m/12 457ft; most of the country is in the drainage basin of the River Danube.

Climate
Three climatic regions: the Alps (often sunny in winter but cloudy in summer); the Danube valley and the Vienna basin (the driest region); and the south-east, a region of heavy thunderstorms; most rain in summer; winters are cold.

National holidays
Jan 1, 6, May 1, Aug 15, Oct 26 (National), Nov 1, Dec 8, 25, 26; A, CC, EM, WM.

Political leaders

Monarch (Habsburg Dynasty)

1440–93	Frederick III
1493–1519	Maximilian I
1519–58	Karl V
1558–64	Ferdinand I
1564–76	Maximilian II
1576–1612	Rudolf II
1612–19	Matthias
1619–37	Ferdinand II
1637–57	Ferdinand III
1658–1705	Leopold I
1705–11	Josef I
1711–40	Karl VI
1740–2	*Interregnum*
1742–5	Karl VII
1745–65	Franz I
1765–90	Josef II
1790–2	Leopold II
1792–1835	Franz II
1835–48	Ferdinand I
1848–1916	Franz Josef
1916–18	Karl I

President

1918–20	Karl Sätz
1920–8	Michael Hainisch
1928–38	Wilhelm Miklas
1938–45	*German rule*
1945–50	Karl Renner
1950–7	Theodor Körner
1957–65	Adolf Schärf
1965–74	Franz Jonas
1974–86	Rudolf Kirchschläger
1986–92	Kurt Waldheim
1992–2004	Thomas Klestil
2004–	Heinz Fischer

Chancellor

1918–20	Karl Renner
1920–1	Michael Mayr
1921–2	Johann Schober
1922	Walter Breisky
1922	Johann Schober
1922–4	Ignaz Seipel
1924–6	Rudolph Ramek
1926–9	Ignaz Seipel
1929–30	Ernst Streeruwitz
1930	Johann Schober
1930	Carl Vaugoin
1930–1	Otto Ender
1931–2	Karl Buresch
1932–4	Engelbert Dollfus
1934–8	Kurt von Schuschnigg
1938–45	*German rule*
1945	Karl Renner
1945–53	Leopold Figl
1953–61	Julius Raab
1961–4	Alfons Gorbach
1964–70	Josef Klaus
1970–83	Bruno Kreisky
1983–6	Fred Sinowatz
1986–97	Franz Vranitzky
1997–2000	Viktor Klima
2000–6	Wolfgang Schüssel
2006–	Alfred Gusenbauer

AZERBAIJAN

Official name	Azerbaijani Republic
Local name	Azərbaycan Respublikası
Former name	Azerbaijan People's Republic (1918–20), Transcaucasian Soviet Federated Socialist Republic (with Armenia and Georgia, 1922–36), Azerbaijan Soviet Socialist Republic (1920–2, 1936–90), within the Union of Soviet Socialist Republics (USSR; 1922–91)
Independence	1991
Area	86 600 sq km/33 428 sq mi
Capital	Baku; Bakı
Chief towns	Gäncä, Sumqayit
Population	8 120 000 (2007e)
Nationality	Azerbaijani
Languages	Azeri
Ethnic groups	Azeri 91%, Dagestani 2%, Russian 2%, Armenian 1%, others 4%
Religions	Islam 93% (Shia), Christianity 5% (Orthodox), others 2%
Time zone	GMT +4
Currency	1 New Manat (AZM) = 100 gopik
Telephone	+994
Internet	.az
Country code	AZE

Location

A republic in eastern Transcaucasia, bounded to the north by Georgia and Russia; to the east by the Caspian Sea; to the south by Iran; and to the west by Armenia, which splits the country from its enclave in the south-west.

Physical description

Crossed by the Greater Caucasus in the north and the Lesser Caucasus in the south-west; they are separated by the plain of River Kura; the highest peak is Mt Bazar-Dyuzi (4480m/14 698ft) in the north-east; 10.5% of total area is forested.

Climate

Continental; hot in summer, cold in winter.

National holidays

Jan 1, 20 (Memorial), Mar 8 (Women), 21–25, May 9 (Victory), 28 (Republic), Jun 15 (National Salvation), 26 (Armed Forces), Oct 18 (Independence), Nov 12 (Constitution), 17 (National Revival), Dec 31 (Azerbaijani Solidarity); Ad (2), EM, ER (2), GF.

Political leaders

President

1991–2	Ayaz Mutalibov	1993–2003	Heydar Aliyev
1992	Yakub Mamedov *Acting*	2003–	Ilham Aliyev
1992–3	Abul Faz Elchibey		

Prime Minister

1991–2	Hassan Hasanov	1993–4	Surat Guseinov
1992	Feirus Mustafayev *Acting*	1994–6	Fuad Kuliyev
1992–3	Rakhim Guseinov	1996–2003	Artur Rasizade
1993	Ali Masimov *Acting*	2003	Ilham Aliyev
1993	Panakh Guseinov	2003–	Artur Rasizade

Azeri Proverbs

Azerbaijan's many proverbs, known as 'father's words', include 'it's impossible to hold two watermelons in one hand' and 'don't tie garlic on your head if you don't have a headache'.

AZORES *see* PORTUGAL

see PORTUGAL

THE BAHAMAS

Official name	Commonwealth of the Bahamas
Local name	Bahamas
Independence	1973
Area	13934 sq km/5379 sq mi
Capital	Nassau
Chief towns	Freeport
Population	306000 (2007e)
Nationality	Bahamian
Languages	English
Ethnic groups	black 85%, white 12%, Asian and Hispanic 3%
Religions	Christianity 96% (Prot and others 83%, RC 13%), none/unaffiliated 3%, others 1%
Time zone	GMT –5
Currency	1 Bahamian Dollar (BA$, B$/BSD) = 100 cents
Telephone	+1242
Internet	.bs
Country code	BHS

Location

An independent country lying south-east of the coast of the US state of Florida in the northern Atlantic Ocean. The Tropic of Cancer crosses the Exuma Islands and Long Island.

Physical description

An archipelago of approximately 700 low-lying islands and over 2000 cays; the coralline limestone islands of the Bahamas comprise the two oceanic banks of Little Bahama and Great Bahama; the highest point on the low-lying islands, Mt Alvernia on Cat Island, is only 63m/207ft above sea level.

Climate

Subtropical, with average temperatures of 21°C in winter and 27°C in summer; hurricanes are frequent in Jun–Nov.

National holidays

Jan 1, Jul 10 (Independence), Oct 12 (National Heroes), Dec 25, 26; EM, GF, WM; Labour (1st Mon in Jun), Emancipation (1st Fri in Aug).

Political leaders

Head of State: British monarch, represented by Governor General (Arthur D Hanna since 2006).

Prime Minister

1973–92	Lynden O Pindling
1992–2002	Hubert A Ingraham
2002–7	Perry Christie
2007–	Hubert A Ingraham

Islands of the Shallow Seas

The Bahamas were first discovered by Europeans when Christopher Columbus arrived in 1492. The sailors were supposedly struck by the depth of the surrounding waters, and remarked '*baja mar*' – the Spanish for 'low water' or, loosely, 'shallow seas' – inadvertently christening the islands.

BAHRAIN

Official name	Kingdom of Bahrain
Local name	Al-Bahrayn; Mamlakat al-Bahrayn
Former name	State of Bahrain (until 2002)
Independence	1971
Area	678 sq km/262 sq mi
Capital	Manama; Al Manāmah
Chief towns	Al Muharraq
Population	709 000 (2007e)
Nationality	Bahraini
Languages	Arabic
Ethnic groups	Bahraini 63%, Asian 13%, other Arab 10%, Iranian 8%, others 6%
Religions	Islam 81% (of whom Shia 60%, Sunni 40%), Christian 9%, others 10%
Time zone	GMT +3
Currency	1 Bahrain Dinar (BD/BHD) = 1 000 fils
Telephone	+973
Internet	.bh
Country code	BHR

Location
A monarchy in the Arabian Gulf, midway between the Qatar Peninsula and mainland Saudi Arabia; a causeway (25km/16mi in length) connects Bahrain to Saudi Arabia.

Physical description
A group of 35 islands; the island of Bahrain is approximately 48km/30mi long and 13–16km/8–10mi wide; highest point is Jabal Dukhan (135m/443ft); largely bare and infertile, though helped by many major drainage schemes since 1973.

Climate
Cool north/north-east winds, with a little rain in Dec–Mar; rest of the year dominated by either a moist north-east wind (the *Shamal*) or the hot, sand-bearing *Qaws* from the south; average temperature 36°C in summer, 19°C in Jan.

National holidays
Jan 1, Dec 16–17 (National), 19 (Mt Arafat); Ad (3), As, ER (3), NY (Muslim), PB.

Political leaders

Emir
1971–99 Isa bin Salman Al-Khalifah
1999–2002 Hamad bin Isa Al-Khalifah

Monarch
2002– Hamad bin Isa Al-Khalifah

Prime Minister
1970– Khalifah bin Salman Al-Khalifah

Land of Immortality

In the third millennium BC Bahrain was known as *Dilmun*, and was described in an ancient tale as the 'land of immortality' where the 'flower of eternal youth' might be found. The later name *Bahrain* comes from Arabic and means 'two seas'.

BALEARIC ISLANDS *see* SPAIN

BANGLADESH

Official name	People's Republic of Bangladesh
Local name	Gana Prajatantri Bangladesh
Former name	Part of the Indian states of Bengal (until 1905) and East Bengal (until 1947), then part of Pakistan as East Pakistan (until 1971)
Independence	1971
Area	143 998 sq km/55 583 sq mi
Capital	Dhaka (formerly known as Dacca)
Chief towns	Chittagong, Khulna, Narayanganj
Population	150 448 000 (2007e)
Nationality	Bangladeshi
Languages	Bangla (Bengali); English is the second language
Ethnic groups	Bengali 98%, others 2%
Religions	Islam 83% (mostly Sunni), Hinduism 16%, others 1%
Time zone	GMT +6
Currency	1 Taka (TK/BDT) = 100 poisha
Telephone	+880
Internet	.bd
Country code	BGD

Location
A republic in southern Asia, crossed by the Tropic of Cancer; bounded to the north, east and west by India; to the south-east by Myanmar; and to the south by the Bay of Bengal.

Physical description
Mainly a vast, low-lying alluvial plain, cut by a network of rivers and marshes; main rivers (including the Ganges and the Brahmaputra) join in the south to form the world's largest delta; frequent flooding; highest point is Keokradong (1 230m/4 035ft).

Climate
Tropical monsoon climate; hot season in Mar–Jun with heavy thunderstorms; very humid, with higher temperatures inland; main rainy season is Jun–Sep; cyclones in the Bay of Bengal cause widespread flooding of coastal areas.

National holidays
Feb 21 (Shaheed Dibash/International Mother Language), Mar 26 (Independence), May 1, Nov 7 (National Revolution and Solidarity), Dec 16 (Victory), 25; Ad (3), As, ER (3), NY (Bengali), NY (Muslim), PA (Shab-e-Barat), PB; Buddha Purnima (Apr/May), Durga Puja (Dashami), Jamatul Wida, Janmashtami, Shab-e-Qadr.

Political leaders

President

1971–2	Sayed Nazrul Islam *Acting*
1972	Mujibur Rahman
1972–3	Abu Saeed Chowdhury
1973–5	Mohammad Mohammadullah
1975	Mujibur Rahman
1975	Khondaker Mushtaq Ahmad
1975–7	Abu Saadat Mohammad Sayem
1977–81	Zia Ur-Rahman
1981–2	Abdus Sattar
1982–3	Abdul Fazal Mohammad Ahsanuddin Chowdhury
1983–90	Hossain Mohammad Ershad
1990–1	Shehabuddin Ahmed *Acting*
1991–6	Abdur Rahman Biswas
1996–2001	Shehabuddin Ahmed
2001–2	A Q M Badruddoza Chowdhury
2002–	Iajuddin Ahmed

Prime Minister

1971–2	Tajuddin Ahmed
1972–5	Mujibur Rahman
1975	Mohammad Monsur Ali
1975–9	*Martial Law*
1979–82	Mohammad Azizur Rahman
1982–4	*Martial Law*

1984–5	Ataur Rahman Khan
1986–8	Mizanur Rahman Chowdhury
1988–90	Kazi Zafar Ahmed
1991–6	Khaleda Zia
1996	Mohammad Habibur Rahman
1996–2001	Sheikh Hasina Wajed
2001–6	Khaleda Zia
2006–	*No Prime Minister owing to constitutional crisis; president-appointed government until elections in 2008*

Water Lilies and Jackfruit

The national symbol of Bangladesh is the water lily, known in Bangla as the *shapla*, and the national fruit is the huge and distinctive jackfruit, called *kathal*. The little magpie robin, or *doel*, is the national bird. Bangladesh's national sport is *kabaddi*, a version of tag played barefoot by two teams of seven.

BARBADOS

Official name	Barbados
Local name	Barbados
Independence	1966
Area	430 sq km/166 sq mi
Capital	Bridgetown
Chief towns	Speightstown
Population	281 000 (2007e)
Nationality	Barbadian or Bajan (informal)
Languages	English
Ethnic groups	black 80%, white 4%, Asian and others 16%
Religions	Christianity 71% (Prot and others 67%, RC 4%), none/unaffiliated 17%, others 12%
Time zone	GMT –4
Currency	1 Barbados Dollar (BD$/BBD) = 100 cents
Telephone	+1246
Internet	.bb
Country code	BRB

Location

An independent state and the most easterly of the Caribbean Islands, situated in the northern Atlantic Ocean to the north of Guyana.

Physical description

A small, triangular island, 32km/20mi long (north-west to south-east); it rises to 340m/1 115ft at Mt Hillaby and is ringed by a coral reef.

Climate

Tropical, with an average annual temperature of 27°C.

National holidays

Jan 1, 21 (Errol Barrow), Apr 28 (National Heroes), May 1, Aug 1 (Emancipation), Nov 30 (Independence), Dec 25, 26; EM, GF, WM, Kadooment (Aug).

Political leaders

Head of State: British monarch, represented by Governor General (Sir Clifford Husbands since 1996).

Prime Minister

1966–76	Errol Walton Barrow
1976–85	J M G (Tom) Adams
1985–6	H Bernard St John
1986–7	Errol Walton Barrow
1987–94	L Erskine Sandiford
1994–2008	Owen Arthur
2008–	David Thompson

Bearded Ones

Bearded fig trees (*Ficus citrifolia*) used to be common in Barbados. When the Portuguese explorer Pedro a Campos visited in 1536, he named the island *Los Barbados*, meaning 'the bearded ones', in recognition of these trees. The tree is still featured on the national coat of arms, along with the national flower, the Pride of Barbados. The coat of arms also features a dolphin, a pelican, sugar cane and the motto 'Pride and Industry'. The national flag's ultramarine stripes represent the sea and sky and the golden centre represents the island's beautiful beaches. It also features the trident of Neptune, the ancient sea god.

BARBUDA *see* ANTIGUA AND BARBUDA

BELARUS

Official name	Republic of Belarus
Local name	Belarus; Respublika Belarus
Former name	Belorussian People's Republic (1918–19), Byelorussian or Belorussian Soviet Socialist Republic (until 1991), within the Union of Soviet Socialist Republics (USSR; 1922–91); sometimes also formerly known as Byelorussia, Belorussia, Byelarus or White Russia
Independence	1991
Area	207 600 sq km/80 134 sq mi
Capital	Minsk
Chief towns	Gomel, Vitebsk, Mogilev, Bobruysk, Grodno, Brest
Population	9 725 000 (2007e)
Nationality	Belarussian
Languages	Belarussian, Russian
Ethnic groups	Belarussian 81%, Russian 11%, Polish 4%, Ukrainian 3%, others 1%
Religions	Christianity 72% (Orthodox 60%, RC 8%, Prot 4%), others 28% (including Islam and Judaism)
Time zone	GMT +2
Currency	1 Belarussian Rouble (BR/BYR) = 100 kopeks
Telephone	+375
Internet	.by
Country code	BLR

Location

A republic in eastern Europe, bounded to the north by Latvia; to the north and east by Russia; to the south by Ukraine; to the west by Poland; and to the north-west by Lithuania.

Physical description

Largely flat, with low hills in the north-west rising to 345m/1 132ft at Dzyarzhynskaya Hara; approximately 11 000 lakes; one-third of the country is covered by forests.

Climate

Mild winters and cool summers.

National holidays

Jan 1, 7 (Orthodox Christmas), Mar 8 (Women), 15 (Constitution), May 1, 9 (Victory), Jul 3 (Independence), Nov 2 (Remembrance), Dec 25; EM, ES (Orthodox), GF.

Political leaders

Chair of Supreme Soviet

1991–4	Stanislav Shushkevich	1994–6	Mecheslav Grib

President

1994–	Alexander Lukashenko

Prime Minister

1990–4	Vyacheslav Kebich
1994–6	Mikhail Chigir
1996–2000	Sergei Ling
2000–1	Uladzimir Yarmoshyn
2001–3	Gennady Vasilyevich Novitsky
2003–	Sergey Sidorsky

BELAU *see* PALAU

BELGIUM

Official name	Kingdom of Belgium
Local name	Belgique; Royaume de Belgique (French), België; Koninkrijk België (Flemish), Belgien; Königreich Belgien (German)
Independence	1830
Area	32 545 sq km/12 562 sq mi
Capital	Brussels; Bruxelles (French), Brussel (Flemish), Brüssel (German)
Chief towns	Antwerp, Ghent, Charleroi, Liège, Bruges, Namur, Mons
Population	10 392 000 (2007e)
Nationality	Belgian
Languages	Flemish (Dutch), French, German (mainly on the eastern border); Brussels is officially a bilingual city (French and Flemish)
Ethnic groups	Fleming 58%, Walloon 31%, others 11%
Religions	Christianity 85% (RC 75%, Prot 10%), Islam 2%, none/unaffiliated 10%, others 3%
Time zone	GMT +1
Currency	1 Euro (€/EUR) = 100 cents
Telephone	+32
Internet	.be
Country code	BEL

Location

A kingdom in north-western Europe, bounded to the north by the Netherlands; to the east by Germany; to the south-east by Luxembourg; to the south by France; and to the north-west by the North Sea.

Physical description

Mostly low-lying fertile agricultural land, with some hills in the south-east (Ardennes); highest point is Signal de Botrange (694m/2 277ft); low-lying dune-fringed coastline; main rivers drain across the Dutch border and are linked by a network of canals.

Climate

Cool and temperate with strong maritime influences.

National holidays

Jan 1, May 1, Jul 21 (Independence), Aug 15, Nov 1, 11 (Armistice), Dec 25; A, EM, ES, WM, Pentecost (2); *also community holidays in Jul (Flemish), Sep (French), Nov (German)*.

Political leaders

Belgium became an independent kingdom in 1831. A national congress elected Prince Leopold of Saxe-Coburg as king.

Monarch

1831–65	Léopold I
1865–1909	Léopold II
1909–34	Albert I
1934–51	Léopold III
1944–50	Prince Charles *Regent*
1950–93	Baudouin *Regent 1950–2*
1993–	Albert II

Prime Minister

1899–1907	Paul de Smet de Nayer
1907–8	Jules de Trooz
1908–11	Frans Schollaert
1911–18	Charles de Broqueville
1918	Gerhard Cooreman
1918–20	Léon Delacroix
1920–1	Henri Carton de Wiart
1921–5	Georges Theunis
1925	Alois van de Vyvere
1925–6	Prosper Poullet
1926–31	Henri Jaspar
1931–2	Jules Renkin
1932–4	Charles de Broqueville
1934–5	Georges Theunis
1935–7	Paul van Zeeland
1937–8	Paul Émile Janson
1938–9	Paul Spaak
1939–45	Hubert Pierlot
1945–6	Achille van Acker
1946	Paul Spaak
1946	Achille van Acker
1946–7	Camille Huysmans
1947–9	Paul Spaak
1949–50	Gaston Eyskens
1950	Jean Pierre Duvieusart
1950–2	Joseph Pholien
1952–4	Jean van Houtte
1954–8	Achille van Acker
1958–61	Gaston Eyskens
1961–5	Théodore Lefèvre
1965–6	Pierre Harmel
1966–8	Paul Vanden Boeynants
1968–73	Gaston Eyskens
1973–4	Edmond Leburton
1974–8	Léo Tindemans
1978	Paul Vanden Boeynants
1979–81	Wilfried Martens
1981	Marc Eyskens
1981–91	Wilfried Martens
1992–9	Jean-Luc Dehaene
1999–	Guy Verhofstadt

BELIZE

Official name	Belize
Local name	Belize
Former name	British Honduras (until 1973)
Independence	1981
Area	22963 sq km/8864 sq mi
Capital	Belmopan
Chief towns	Belize City, Dangriga, Punta Gorda, San Ignacio
Population	294000 (2007e)
Nationality	Belizean
Languages	English; Spanish and local Mayan, Carib and Creole languages are also spoken
Ethnic groups	mestizo 49%, Creole 25%, Maya 11%, Garifuna 6%, others 9%
Religions	Christianity 92% (RC 62%, Prot 30%), none/unaffiliated 2%, others 6%
Time zone	GMT –6
Currency	1 Belizean Dollar (BZ$/BZD) = 100 cents
Telephone	+501
Internet	.bz
Country code	BLZ

Location

An independent state in Central America, bounded to the north by Mexico; to the east by the Caribbean Sea; and to the south and west by Guatemala.

Physical description

An extensive coastal plain, swampy in the north, more fertile in the south; Maya Mountains extend almost to the east coast, rising to 1120m/3674ft at Victoria Peak; inner coastal waters are protected by the world's second longest barrier reef.

Climate
Generally subtropical but tempered by trade winds; coastal temperatures vary between 10°C and 36°C, with a greater range in the mountains; variable rainfall; dry season in Feb–May; hurricanes can cause severe damage.

National holidays
Jan 1, Mar 9 (Baron Bliss), May 1, 24 (Commonwealth), Sep 10 (St George's Caye), 21 (Independence), Oct 12 (Columbus), Nov 19 (Garifuna Settlement), Dec 25, 26; EM, GF, HS.

Political leaders

Head of State: British Monarch, represented by Governor General (Sir Colville Young since 1993).

Prime Minister

1981–4	George Price	1993–8	Manuel Esquivel
1985–9	Manuel Esquivel	1998–2008	Said Musa
1989–93	George Price	2008–	Dean Barrow

Flourishing in the Shade

The national motto of Belize is *Sub Umbra Florero*, which means 'Under the shade I flourish'. Belize's national tree is the mahogany and its national flower is the black orchid. The colourful keel-billed toucan is the national bird.

BENIN

Official name	Republic of Benin
Local name	Bénin; République du Bénin
Former name	Dahomey (until 1975); People's Republic of Benin (1975–90)
Independence	1960
Area	112 622 sq km/43 472 sq mi
Capital	Porto Novo (administrative and constitutional) and Cotonou (economic and seat of government)
Chief towns	Ouidah, Abomey, Kandi, Parakou, Natitingou
Population	8 078 000 (2007e)
Nationality	Beninese
Languages	French; local languages are also spoken
Ethnic groups	Fon 39%, Bariba 21%, Yoruba 10%, others 30%
Religions	traditional beliefs 50%, Christianity 30% (mostly RC), Islam 20%
Time zone	GMT +1
Currency	1 CFA Franc (CFAFr/XOF) = 100 centimes
Telephone	+229
Internet	.bj
Country code	BEN

Location
A republic in West Africa, bounded to the north by Niger; to the east by Nigeria; to the south by the Bight of Benin in the Gulf of Guinea; to the west by Togo; and to the north-west by Burkina Faso.

Physical description
Rises from a 100km/62mi sandy coast with lagoons, to low-lying plains, then to a savanna plateau at approximately 400m/1 300ft; the Atakora Mountains rise to over 500m/1 640ft in the north-west; highest point is Mt Sokbaro (658m/2 159ft); several rivers.

Climate
Tropical climate, with three zones; south has rain throughout year, especially during the 'Guinea Monsoon' (May–Oct); centre has two rainy seasons (peaks in May–Jun and Oct); north has one (Jul–Sep).

National holidays
Jan 1, 10 (Traditional), May 1, Aug 1 (Independence), 15, Nov 1, Dec 25; A, Ad, EM, ER, PB, WM.

Political leaders

Dahomey

President

1960–3	Hubert Coutoucou Maga
1963–4	Christophe Soglo
1964–5	Sourou Migan Apithy
1965	Justin Tométin Ahomadegbé
1965	Tairou Congacou
1965–7	Christophe Soglo
1967–8	Alphonse Amadou Alley
1968–9	Émile Derlin Zinsou
1969–70	*Presidential Committee* (Maurice Kouandété)
1970–2	*Presidential Committee* (Hubert Coutoucou Maga)
1972–5	Mathieu Kérékou

Prime Minister

1958–9	Sourou Migan Apithy
1959–60	Hubert Coutoucou Maga
1960–4	*As President*
1964–5	Justin Tométin Ahomadegbé
1965–7	*As President*
1967–8	Maurice Kouandété
1968–75	*As President*

People's Republic of Benin

President and Prime Minister

1975–90	Mathieu (from 1980, sometimes called Ahmed) Kérékou

Republic of Benin

President

1990–1	Mathieu Kérékou
1991–6	Nicéphore Soglo
1996–2006	Mathieu Kérékou
2006–	Yayi Boni

Prime Minister

1990–1	Nicéphore Soglo
1991–6	*As President*
1996–8	Adrien Houngbedgi
1998	*Post abolished*

Beliefs from Benin

The religion of Voudun or Voudou (commonly known as Voodoo) is thought to have its origins in the traditional beliefs of the Yoruba and Fon tribes of Benin. The name means 'spirit', and practitioners use divination or spirit possession to communicate with the dead (*lemo*) or with powerful protective spirits. Voudun is now an officially recognized religion in Benin.

BERMUDA *see* **UNITED KINGDOM**

BHUTAN

Official name	Kingdom of Bhutan
Local name	Druk Yul
Area	46 600 sq km/18 000 sq mi
Capital	Thimphu
Chief towns	Phuntsholing
Population	2 329 000 (2007e)
Nationality	Bhutanese
Languages	Dzongkha
Ethnic groups	Bhote 50%, Nepalese 35%, others 15%
Religions	Buddhism 73%, Hinduism 22%, Islam 5%
Time zone	GMT +6
Currency	1 Ngultrum (Nu/BTN) = 100 chetrum; the Indian rupee is also used.
Telephone	+975
Internet	.bt
Country code	BTN

Location
A state in the eastern Himalayas, bounded to the north by China and to the south by India.

Physical description
High peaks of the east Himalayas, reaching over 7 000m/22 966ft in the north; highest point is Kula Kangri (7 553m/24 780ft); forested mountain ridges with fertile valleys descend to low foothills in the south; many rivers flow to meet the River Brahmaputra.

Climate
Permanent snowfields and glaciers in the mountains; subtropical forest in the south; torrential rain is common.

National holidays
Feb 21 (Birthday of Fifth King), May 2 (Birthday of Third King), Jun 2 (Coronation of Fourth King), Nov 11–13 (Birthday of Fourth King), Dec 17 (National); NY (Buddhist), *about nine other Buddhist holidays*.

Political leaders

Monarch (Druk Gyalpo)

1907–26	Uggyen Wangchuk
1926–52	Jigme Wangchuk
1952–72	Jigme Dorji Wangchuk
1972–2006	Jigme Singye Wangchuk
2006–	Jigme Khesar Namgyal Wangchuk

Prime Minister

1952–64	Jigme Palden Dorji
1964	Lhendup Dorji *Acting*
1964–98	*No Prime Minister*
1998–99	Lyonpo Jigme Yozer Thinley
1999–2000	Lyonpo Sangye Ngedup
2000–1	Lyonpo Yeshey Zimba
2001–2	Lyonpo Khandu Wangchuk
2002–3	Lyonpo Kinzang Dorji
2003–4	Lyonpo Jigme Thinley
2004–5	Lyonpo Yeshey Zimba
2005–6	Sangay Ngedup
2006–7	Khandu Wangchuk
2007–	Kinzang Dorji (*Acting*)

Land of the Thunder Dragon

The name Bhutan is thought to come from the Sanskrit word *Bhu-uttan*, meaning 'high land'. However, the Bhutanese people call their country *Druk Yul*, meaning 'Land of the Thunder Dragon'.

BOLIVIA

Official name	Republic of Bolivia
Local name	Bolivia; República de Bolivia
Independence	1825
Area	1 098 580 sq km/424 052 sq mi
Capital	La Paz (administrative) and Sucre (official and legislative)
Chief towns	Cochabamba, El Alto, Oruro, Potosí, Santa Cruz
Population	9 119 000 (2007e)
Nationality	Bolivian
Languages	Spanish, Quechua, Ayamará
Ethnic groups	mestizo 30%, Quechua 30%, Aymará 25%, European 10%, others 5%
Religions	Christianity 97% (RC 92%, Prot 5%), Baha'i 3%
Time zone	GMT –4
Currency	1 Boliviano ($b/BOB) = 100 centavos
Telephone	+591
Internet	.bo
Country code	BOL

Location

A republic in western South America, bounded to the north and east by Brazil; to the south-east by Paraguay; to the south by Argentina; to the south-west by Chile; and to the west by Peru.

Physical description

Bounded to the west by the Andes, rising to 6 542m/21 463ft at Nevado Sajama; flat 400km/250mi Altiplano Plateau in the east which lies at 3 600m/11 811ft above sea level; major lakes are Titicaca on the Peruvian border and Poopó; several rivers.

Climate

Varies, according to altitude; humid and tropical in the lowlands, cold and semi-arid in the mountains.

National holidays

Jan 1, May 1, Aug 6 (Independence), Nov 1, Dec 25; C, CC, GF.

Highest Capital

La Paz is the highest capital city in the world, with an altitude of 3,665m/12,024ft. However, it is itself dwarfed by Mt Illimani, which at 6,402m/21,004ft towers above the city to the south-east. La Paz was founded in 1548 by the Spanish.

Political leaders

President

1899–1904	José Manuel Pando
1904–9	Ismael Montes
1909–13	Heliodoro Villazón
1913–17	Ismael Montes
1917–20	José N Gutiérrez Guerra
1920–5	Bautista Saavedra
1925–6	José Cabina Villanueva
1926–30	Hernando Siles
1930	Roberto Hinojusa *President of Revolutionaries*
1930–1	Carlos Blanco Galindo
1931–4	Daniel Salamanca
1934–6	José Luis Tejado Sorzano
1936–7	David Toro
1937–9	Germán Busch
1939–40	Carlos Quintanilla *Provisional*
1940–3	Enrique Peñaranda y del Castillo
1943–6	Gualberto Villaroel
1946	Nestor Guillen
1946–7	Tomas Monje Gutiérrez
1947–9	Enrique Hertzog
1949–51	Mamerto Urriolagoitía
1951–2	Hugo Ballivián
1952	Hernán Siles Suazo
1952–6	Víctor Paz Estenssoro
1956–60	Hernán Siles Suazo
1960–4	Víctor Paz Estenssoro
1964–5	René Barrientos Ortuño
1965–6	René Barrientos Ortuño *and* Alfredo Ovando Candía

1966	Alfredo Ovando Candía
1966–9	René Barrientos Ortuño
1969	Luis Adolfo Siles Salinas
1969–70	Alfredo Ovando Candía
1970	Rogelio Mirando
1970–1	Juan José Torres Gonzales
1971–8	Hugo Banzer Suárez
1978	Juan Pereda Asbún
1978–9	*Military Junta* (David Padilla Arericiba)
1979	Walter Guevara Arze
1979–80	Lydia Gueiler Tejada
1980–1	*Military Junta* (Luis García Meza)
1981–2	*Military Junta* (Celso Torrelio Villa)
1982	Guido Vildoso Calderón
1982–5	Hernán Siles Suazo
1985–9	Víctor Paz Estenssoro
1989–93	Jaime Paz Zamora
1993–7	Gonzalo Sánchez de Lozada
1997–2001	Hugo Bánzer Suárez
2001–2	Jorge Quiroga Ramírez
2002–3	Gonzalo Sánchez de Lozada
2003–5	Carlos Mesa
2005–6	Eduardo Rodríguez *Acting*
2006–	Evo Morales

BOSNIA AND HERZEGOVINA

Official name	Republic of Bosnia and Herzegovina; sometimes also known as Bosnia-Herzegovina
Local name	Bosna i Hercegovina; Republika Bosna i Hercegovina
Former name	formerly part of the Kingdom of Serbs, Croats and Slovenes (until 1929), Kingdom of Yugoslavia (1929–41), Federal People's Republic of Yugoslavia (1945–63), Socialist Federal People's Republic of Yugoslavia (1963–92)
Independence	1992
Area	51 129 sq km/19 736 sq mi
Capital	Sarajevo
Chief towns	Banja Luka, Zenica, Tuzla, Mostar
Population	4 552 000 (2007e)
Nationality	Bosnian, Herzegovinian
Languages	Bosnian, Serbian, Croatian
Ethnic groups	Bosniak 48%, Serb 37%, Croat 14%, others 1%
Religions	Christianity 46% (Orthodox 31%, RC 15%), Islam 40%, others 14%
Time zone	GMT +1
Currency	1 Convertible Mark (KM/BAM) = 100 pfennige
Telephone	+387
Internet	.ba
Country code	BIH

Location

A republic in central Europe; bounded to the north and west by Croatia; to the east by Serbia; and to the south-east by Montenegro.

Physical description

Mountainous and includes part of the Dinaric Alps; highest point is Maglic (2 386m/7 828ft); it is noted for its limestone gorges.

Climate

Continental, with hot summers and cold winters.

National holidays

Jan 1, May 1–2; *much religious and regional variation, including:* Jan 2, 6–7 (Christmas), 9 (Republic), 14–15 (Orthodox NY), 19 (Epiphany), 27 (St Sava), Mar 1 (Independence), May 1–2, Jun 28 (St Vitus), Aug 15, Nov 1, 25 (Statehood), Dec 25; Ad, EM, ER, ES, GF, HS, PB.

Political leaders

See **Yugoslavia** for political leaders prior to 1991–2.

Republic

Chairman of the Presidency

1990–8	Alija Izetbegović
1998–9	Živko Radišić
1999–2000	Ante Jelavić
2000	Alija Izetbegović
2000–1	Živko Radišić
2001–2	Jozo Križanović
2002	Beriz Belkić
2002–3	Mirko Šarović; Borislav Paravac; Dragan Čović
2004–6	Sulejman Tihić; Borislav Paravac; Ivo Miro Jović
2006–	Nebojša Radmanović; Željko Komšić; Haris Silajdžić

Note: Tripartite presidency (one Serb, one Muslim, one Croat) rotating every eight months since 2002.

Prime Minister

1990–2	Jure Pelivan
1992–3	Mile Akmadzic
1993–6	Haris Silajdžić
1996–7	Hasan Muratović
1997–9	Boro Bosic *co-Prime Minister*
1997–2000	Haris Silajdžić *co-Prime Minister*
1999–2000	Svetozar Mihajlović *co-Prime Minister*
2000	Spasoje Tusevljak
2000–1	Martin Raguz
2001	Božidar Matić
2001–2	Zlatko Lagumdzija
2002	Dragan Mikerević
2002–7	Adnan Terzić
2007–	Nikola Špirić

Federation[1]

President

1994–7	Krešimir Zubak
1997	Vladimir Šoljić
1997–8	Ejup Ganić
1999–2000	Ivo Andrić-Lužanski
2000–1	Ejup Ganić
2001–2	Karlo Filipović
2002–3	Safet Halilović
2003–6	Niko Lozančić
2006–	Borjana Krišto

Prime Minister

1994–6	Haris Silajdžić
1996	Izudin Kapetanović
1996–2001	Edhem Bicakcić
2001	Dragan Čović *Acting*
2001–3	Alija Behmen
2003–7	Ahmet Hadžipašić
2007–	Nedžad Branković

Republika Srpska[2]

President

1992–6	Radovan Karadžić
1996–8	Biljana Plavšic
1998–9	Nikola Poplašen
2000–2	Mirko Šarović
2002–6	Dragan Čović
2006–7	Milan Jelic
2007–	Rajko Kuzmanović

Prime Minister

1992–3	Branko Djeric
1993–4	Vladimir Lukic
1994–5	Dusan Kozic
1995–6	Rajko Kasagic
1996–8	Gojko Kličković
1998–2001	Milorad Dodik
2001–3	Mladen Ivanić
2003–5	Dragan Mikerević
2005–6	Pero Bukejlović
2006–7	Milorad Dodik

[1]*Bosniac–Croat Federation.* [2]*Bosnian Serb Republic.*

BOTSWANA

Official name	Republic of Botswana
Local name	Botswana
Former name	Bechuanaland (until 1966)
Independence	1966
Area	582 096 sq km/224 689 sq mi
Capital	Gaborone
Chief towns	Francistown, Lobatse, Selebi-Phikwe, Orapa, Jwaneng
Population	1 815 000 (2007e)
Nationality	Motswana (singular noun), Batswana (plural noun), Tswana (adjective)
Languages	Setswana, English
Ethnic groups	Tswana (Setswana) 79%, Kalanga 11%, Basarwa 3%, others 7%
Religions	Christianity 72%, traditional beliefs 6%, others 1%, none/unaffiliated 21%
Time zone	GMT +2
Currency	1 Pula (P, Pu/BWP) = 100 thebe
Telephone	+267
Internet	.bw
Country code	BWA

Location

A republic in southern Africa, crossed by the Tropic of Capricorn; bounded to the north and west by Namibia; to the north by Zambia; to the east by Zimbabwe; and to the south by South Africa.

Physical description

Kalahari desert covers 84% of the land, at an average elevation of approximately 1 100m/3 609ft; most people live in the fertile east, bordered by the River Limpopo; highest point is Otse Mountain (1 491m/4 892ft); rich Okavango River delta in the north-west.

Climate

Largely subtropical, increasingly arid in the south and west; rainfall in the north and east falls almost totally in summer (Oct–Apr); average maximum daily temperatures 23–32°C; annual rainfall is erratic in the Kalahari Desert.

National holidays

Jan 1, May 1, Jul 1 (Sir Seretse Khama), 15–16 (President), Sep 30 (Botswana), Dec 25, 26; A, EM, GF, HS.

Political leaders

President

1966–80	Seretse Khama
1980–98	Ketumile Masire
1998–	Festus Mogae

Kalahari Country

The Kalahari desert covers 84% of Botswana. Known as 'Kgalagadi' in the Setswana language, the desert landscape varies from sand dunes and salt pans to mile upon mile of scrubland and stunted trees. The Central Kalahari Game Reserve covers 52,800 sq km/20,400 sq mi – an area larger than Switzerland.

BOUVET ISLAND *see* NORWAY

BRAZIL

Official name	Federative Republic of Brazil
Local name	Brasil; República Federativa do Brasil
Independence	1822
Area	8 511 965 sq km/3 285 618 sq mi
Capital	Brasília
Chief towns	São Paulo, Rio de Janeiro, Belo Horizonte, Recife, Salvador
Population	190 010 000 (2007e)
Nationality	Brazilian
Languages	Portuguese
Ethnic groups	white 54%, mixed 38%, black 6%, others 2%
Religions	Christianity 89% (RC 74% (nominal), Prot 15%), Spiritualism 1%, others 2%, none/unaffiliated 8%
Time zone	GMT –2/5
Currency	1 Real (R$/BRL) = 100 centavos
Telephone	+55
Internet	.br
Country code	BRA

Location

A republic in eastern and central South America, crossed by the Equator in the north and the Tropic of Capricorn in the south-east; bounded to the north-west by Colombia; to the north by Venezuela, Guyana, Suriname and French Guiana; to the east by the Atlantic Ocean; to the south by Uruguay; to the south-west by Argentina and Paraguay; and to the west by Peru and Bolivia.

Physical description

The low-lying Amazon basin in the north is drained by rivers that carry one fifth of the earth's running water; the highest peak is Pico da Neblina (3014m/9888ft) in the south; 30% of the population live on a narrow coastal strip approximately 100km/62mi wide.

Climate

Almost entirely tropical; the Amazon basin has no dry season, with average midday temperatures of 27–32°C; long droughts in the north-east with daily temperatures 21–36°C; hot and tropical on the coast; seasonal, temperate climate in the far south.

National holidays

Jan 1, Apr 21 (Tiradentes), May 1, Sep 7 (Independence), Oct 12 (Our Lady of Aparecida), Nov 2, 15 (Republic), Dec 24, 25, 31; C (3), CC, ES, GF; *much local variation*.

Political leaders

President

1898–1902	Manuel Ferraz de Campos Sales
1902–6	Francisco de Paula Rodrigues Alves
1906–9	Alfonso Pena
1909–10	Nilo Peçanha
1910–14	Hermes Rodrigues da Fonseca
1914–18	Venceslau Brás Pereira Gomes
1918–19	Francisco de Paula Rodrigues Alves
1919–22	Epitácio Pessoa
1922–6	Artur da Silva Bernardes
1926–30	Washington Luís Pereira de Sousa
1930–45	Getúlio Dorneles Vargas
1945–51	Eurico Gaspar Dutra
1951–4	Getúlio Dorneles Vargas
1954–5	João Café Filho
1955	Carlos Coimbra da Luz
1955–6	Nereu de Oliveira Ramos
1956–61	Juscelino Kubitschek de Oliveira
1961	Jânio da Silva Quadros
1961–3	João Belchior Marques Goulart
1963	Pascoal Ranieri Mazilli
1963–4	João Belchior Marques Goulart
1964	Pascoal Ranieri Mazilli
1964–7	Humberto de Alencar Castelo Branco
1967–9	Artur da Costa e Silva
1969–74	Emílio Garrastazu Médici

1974–9	Ernesto Geisel	1990–2	Fernando Collor de Mello
1979–85	João Baptista de Oliveira Figueiredo	1992–4	Itamar Franco
1985–90	José Sarney	1994–2002	Fernando Henrique Cardoso
		2003–	Luiz Inacio 'Lula' da Silva

South American Giant

Brazil is the largest country in South America, and covers almost half the total area of the continent. It is crossed by both the Equator and the Tropic of Capricorn, has North Atlantic and South Atlantic coasts, and borders every other South American country except Ecuador and Chile.

BRITISH ANTARCTIC TERRITORY *see* UNITED KINGDOM

BRITISH INDIAN OCEAN TERRITORY *see* UNITED KINGDOM

BRITISH VIRGIN ISLANDS *see* UNITED KINGDOM

BRUNEI DARUSSALAM

Official name	State of Brunei, Abode of Peace
Local name	Brunei; Negara Brunei Darussalam
Independence	1984
Area	5765 sq km/2225 sq mi
Capital	Bandar Seri Begawan
Chief towns	Kuala Belait, Seria, Muara, Bangar, Pekan Tutong
Population	375000 (2007e)
Nationality	Bruneian
Languages	Malay; English and Chinese are widely spoken
Ethnic groups	Malay 67%, Chinese 15%, indigenous 6%, others 12%
Religions	Islam 67%, Buddhism 13%, Christianity 10%, traditional beliefs and others 10%
Time zone	GMT +8
Currency	1 Brunei Dollar (B$/BND) = 100 cents
Telephone	+673
Internet	.bn
Country code	BRN

Location

A state on the north-west coast of Borneo, south-eastern Asia, bounded by the South China Sea in the north-west, and on all other sides by Malaysia's Sarawak and Sabah states.

Physical description

Swampy coastal plain rising through foothills to a mountainous region on the Malaysian border; highest point is Bukit Pagon (1850m/6098ft); 75% is equatorial rainforest; the Limbang River Valley in Sarawak divides the state into two.

Climate

Tropical climate, with high temperatures and humidity, and no marked seasons; average daily temperature 24–30°C; rainfall in the interior is twice as high as on the coast.

National holidays

Jan 1, Feb 23 (National), May 31 (Armed Forces), Jul 15 (Sultan's Birthday), Dec 25; Ad, ER (2), NY (Chinese), NY (Muslim), PA, PB, R, Revelation of the Koran.

Political leaders

Monarch (Sultan)

1967– Muda Hassanal Bolkiah Mu'izzadin Waddaulah

The Royal Umbrella

The red national crest of Brunei Darussalam is a striking feature in the centre of the state's yellow, white and black flag. The crest was developed from ancient royal symbols, and each element has a particular significance. At the top are the *bendera*, a small pennant, and the *payung ubor-ubor*, or royal umbrella, symbolizing the monarchy. Beneath is the *sayap*, two wings each with four feathers that represent the 'protection of justice, tranquillity, prosperity and peace', followed by the *bulan*, the crescent symbol of Islam, with the state's motto: 'always in service with God's guidance'. Finally, on each side of the crest is a *tangan* or *kimhap*, an outstretched hand, which the government explains as representing their 'pledge to promote welfare, peace and prosperity'. Beneath the crest is a scroll inscribed with the name Brunei Darussalam.

BULGARIA

Official name	Republic of Bulgaria
Local name	Bălgarija; Republika Bălgarija
Former name	*as listed below under Political leaders*
Independence	1908
Area	110912 sq km/42812 sq mi
Capital	Sofia; Sofija
Chief towns	Plovdiv, Varna, Ruse, Burgas, Stara Zagora, Pleven
Population	7323000 (2007e)
Nationality	Bulgarian
Languages	Bulgarian
Ethnic groups	Bulgarian 84%, Turk 9%, Roma 2%, others 2%
Religions	Christianity 84% (Orthodox 83%, other 1%), Islam 12%, others 4%
Time zone	GMT +2
Currency	1 Lev (Lv/BGN) = 100 stotinki
Telephone	+359
Internet	.bg
Country code	BGR

Location

A republic in south-eastern Europe, bounded to the north by Romania; to the east by the Black Sea; to the south-east by Turkey; to the south by Greece; to the south-west by Macedonia; and to the west by Serbia.

Physical description

Traversed west to east by the Balkan Mountains, rising to over 2000m/6562ft; Rhodope Mountains in the south-west rise to nearly 3000m/9842ft; highest point is Musala (2925m/9596ft); comparatively narrow lowlands stretch south from the River Danube.

Climate

Largely continental, with hot summers and cold winters, but to the south the climate is increasingly Mediterranean; winters are slightly warmer on the Black Sea coast.

National holidays
Jan 1, Mar 3 (National), May 1, 6 (St George/Army), 24 (Slavonic Script and Bulgarian Culture), Sep 6 (Unification), 22 (Independence), Dec 24, 25, 26; EM, ES (Orthodox) .

Political leaders

Tsardom of Bulgaria

Monarch

1887–1908 Ferdinand *Prince*
1908–18 Ferdinand I
1918–43 Boris III
1943–6 Simeon II

People's Republic of Bulgaria

President

1946–7 Vasil Kolarov
1947–50 Mincho Naichev
1950–8 Georgi Damianov
1958–64 Dimitro Ganev
1964–71 Georgi Traikov
1971–89 Todor Zhivkov
1989–90 Petar Mladenov

Premier

1946–9 Georgi Dimitrov
1949–50 Vasil Kolarov
1950–6 Vulko Chervenkov
1956–62 Anton Yugov
1962–71 Todor Zhivkov
1971–81 Stanko Todorov
1981–6 Grisha Filipov
1986–90 Georgy Atanasov
1990 Andrei Lukanov
1990–1 Dimitur Popov

First Secretary

1946–53 Vulko Chervenkov
1953–89 Todor Zhivkov
1989–90 Petar Mladenov
1990 Alexander Lilov

Republic of Bulgaria

President

1990–7 Zhelyu Zhelev
1997–2002 Petar Stoyanov
2002– Georgi Parvanov

Prime Minister

1991–2 Filip Dimitrov
1992–4 Lyuben Berov
1994–5 Renate Indzhova *Acting*
1995–7 Zhan Videnov
1997 Stefan Sofiyanski *Acting*
1997–2001 Ivan Kostov
2001–5 Simeon Saxe-Coburg Gotha (Simeon II)
2005– Sergei Stanishev

Return of the King

King Simeon II went into exile in 1946 when Bulgaria became a republic, and lived in Spain for more than 50 years. After the fall of communism he returned to Bulgaria and in 2001 was elected Prime Minister, becoming the first eastern European former monarch to return to power.

BURKINA FASO

Official name	Burkina Faso
Local name	Burkina Faso
Former name	Upper Volta (until 1984)
Independence	1960
Area	274 540 sq km/105 972 sq mi
Capital	Ouagadougou
Chief towns	Bobo-Dioulasso, Koudougou, Ouahigouya, Tenkodogo
Population	14 326 000 (2007e)
Nationality	Burkinabé
Languages	French; many local languages are also spoken
Ethnic groups	Mossi 45%, Mande 10%, Fulani 9%, Bobo 7%, others 29%
Religions	Islam 50%, traditional beliefs 40%, Christianity (mostly RC) 10%
Time zone	GMT
Currency	1 CFA Franc (CFAFr/XOF) = 100 centimes
Telephone	+226
Internet	.bf
Country code	BFA

Location

A republic in West Africa, bounded to the north and north-west by Mali; to the east by Niger; to the south-east by Benin; to the south by Togo and Ghana; and to the south-west by Côte d'Ivoire.

Physical description

Low-lying plateau, falling away to the south; highest point is Tena Kourou (749m/2 457ft); many rivers (tributaries of the Volta or Niger) are unnavigable in the dry season; wooded savannas in the south; semi-desert in the north.

Climate

Tropical climate; average temperature 27°C in the dry season (Dec–May); rainy season (Jun–Oct), with violent storms (Aug); the *harmattan* wind blows from the north-east (Dec–Mar); rainfall decreases from south to north.

National holidays

Jan 1, 3 (Revolution), Mar 8 (Women), May 1, Aug 5 (Independence), 15, Nov 1, Dec 11 (National), 25; A, Ad, EM, ER, PB.

Land of Honest Men

Previously known as Upper Volta, after the upper reaches of the River Volta, Burkina Faso was renamed in 1984 by the politician Thomas Sankara (1950–87). The new name came from the local languages and means 'Land of Honest Men' or 'Land of Upright Men'.

Political leaders

Upper Volta

President

1960–6 Maurice Yaméogo
1966–80 Sangoulé Lamizana
1980 Saye Zerbo
1982–3 Jean-Baptiste Ouedraogo *Chairman of People's Salvation Council*
1983–4 Thomas Sankara *Chairman of National Revolutionary Council*

Burkina Faso

President

1984–7	Thomas Sankara *Chairman*
1987–	Blaise Compaoré

Prime Minister

1992–4	Youssouf Ouedraogo
1994–6	Roch Christian Kaboré
1996–2000	Kadré Désiré Ouedraogo
2000–7	Paramanga Ernest Yonli
2007–	Tertius Zongo

BURMA *see* **MYANMAR**

BURUNDI

Official name	Republic of Burundi
Local name	Burundi; République du Burundi (French), Republika y'UBurundi (Kirundi)
Former name	Urundi, as part of Ruanda-Urundi (with Rwanda, until 1962), Kingdom of Burundi (1962–6)
Independence	1962
Area	27 834 sq km/10 744 sq mi
Capital	Bujumbura
Chief towns	Bubanza, Ngozi, Muyinga, Muramvya, Gitega, Bururi, Rutana
Population	8 390 000 (2007e)
Nationality	Burundian
Languages	French, Kirundi; Swahili is also spoken
Ethnic groups	Hutu 85%, Tutsi 14%, others 1%
Religions	Christianity 67% (RC 62%, Prot 5%), traditional beliefs 23%, Islam 10%
Time zone	GMT +2
Currency	1 Burundi Franc (BuFr, FBu/BIF) = 100 centimes
Telephone	+257
Internet	.bi
Country code	BDI

Location

A republic in central Africa, bounded to the north by Rwanda; to the east and south by Tanzania; to the south-west by Lake Tanganyika; and to the west by Democratic Republic of the Congo.

Physical description

Lies across the Nile–Congo watershed; bounded to the west by the narrow River Ruizi plain and Lake Tanganyika; River Akanyaru forms northern border; interior plateau at average height of approximately 1 500m/4 921ft; highest point is Mt Heha (2 670m/8 760ft).

Climate

Equatorial climate, varying with altitude and season; moderately wet, except during the dry season (Jun–Sep).

National holidays

Jan 1, Feb 5 (Unity), May 1, Jul 1 (Independence), Aug 15, Oct 13 (Rwagasore's Assassination), 21 (Ndadaye's Assassination), Nov 1, Dec 25; A, ER.

African Switzerland

Burundi's government has dubbed the country 'the heart of Africa', an 'African Switzerland', the 'country of the thousand and one hills' and the 'country of eternal spring'.

Political leaders

Monarch

1962–6	Mwambutsa IV
1966	Ntare V

President

1966–77	Michel Micombero
1977–87	Jean-Baptiste Bagaza
1987–93	*Military Junta* (Pierre Buyoya)
1993	Melchior Ndadaye
1994	Cyprien Ntaryamira
1994–6	Sylvestre Ntibantunganya
1996–2003	Pierre Buyoya
2003–5	Domitien Ndayizeye
2005–	Pierre Nkurunziza

Prime Minister

1961	Joseph Cimpaye
1961	Louis Rwagasore
1962–3	André Muhirwa
1963–4	Pierre Ngendandumwe
1964–5	Albin Nyamoya
1965	Pierre Ngendandumwe
1965	Pie Masumbuko *Acting*
1965	Joseph Bamina
1965–6	Léopold Biha
1966–76	Michel Micombero
1976–8	Edouard Nzambimana
1978–87	*No Prime Minister*
1987–8	Pierre Buyoya
1988–93	Adrien Sibomana
1993–4	Sylvie Kinigi
1994–5	Anatole Kanyenkiko
1995–6	Antoine Nduwayo
1996–8	Pascal-Firmin Ndimira
1998–	*No Prime Minister*

CAICOS ISLANDS *see* **UNITED KINGDOM**

CAMBODIA

Official name	Kingdom of Cambodia
Local name	Kâmpuchéa; Preăh Réaché 'Anachâkr Kâmpuchéa
Former name	formerly part of Indochina (until 1953), Kingdom of Cambodia (1953–70), Khmer Republic (1970–6), Democratic Kampuchea (1976–9), People's Republic of Kampuchea (1979–89), State of Cambodia (1989–93)
Independence	1953
Area	181 035 sq km/69 880 sq mi
Capital	Phnom Penh; Phnum Pénh
Chief towns	Battambang, Kâmpŏng Som, Kâmpŏng Chhnăng
Population	13 996 000 (2007e)
Nationality	Cambodian
Languages	Khmer; French is also widely spoken
Ethnic groups	Khmer 90%, Vietnamese 5%, Chinese 1%, others 4%
Religions	Buddhism 95%, Islam 2%, others 3%
Time zone	GMT +7
Currency	1 Riel (CRI/KHR) = 100 sen
Telephone	+855
Internet	.kh
Country code	KHM

Location

A republic in south-east Asia, bounded to the north-west by Thailand; to the north by Laos; to the east by Vietnam; and to the south and south-west by the Gulf of Thailand.

CAMBODIA

Physical description

Surrounds the Tonlé Sap (lake) on the Cambodian Plain, which is crossed by the floodplain of the Mekong River; Cardamom Mountains stretch 160km/100mi across the Thailand border, rising to 1813m/5948ft at Phnom Aural.

Climate

Tropical monsoon climate, with a wet season in May–Sep; heavy rainfall in the south-western mountains; high temperatures in the lowland region throughout the year.

National holidays

Jan 1, 7 (Victory over Genocide), Mar 8 (Women), May 1, 13–15 (King's Birthday), Jun 18 (Queen Mother's Birthday), Sep 24 (Constitution), Oct 29 (Coronation), 30 (late King Sihanouk's Birthday) (3), Nov 9 (Independence), Dec 10 (Human Rights); Cambodian NY (Apr) (3), Meak Bochea (Feb), Pchum Ben (Sep) (3), Royal Ploughing Ceremony (May), Visaka Bochea (May), Water/Moon Festival (Nov) (3).

Political leaders

Monarch

1941–55 Norodom Sihanouk II
1955–60 Norodom Suramarit

Head of State

1960–70 Prince Norodom Sihanouk

Khmer Republic Head of State

1970–2 Cheng Heng *Acting*
1972–5 Lon Nol
1975–6 Prince Norodom Sihanouk
1976–81 Khieu Samphan
1981–91 Heng Samrin

President of Government in exile (until 1991)

1970–5 Prince Norodom Sihanouk
1982–93 Prince Norodom Sihanouk

Monarch

1993–2004 King Norodom Sihanouk
2004– King Norodom Sihamoni

Prime Minister

1945–6 Son Ngoc Thanh
1946–8 Prince Monireth
1948–9 Son Ngoc Thanh
1949–51 Prince Monipong
1951 Son Ngoc Thanh
1951–2 Huy Kanthoul
1952–3 Norodom Sihanouk II
1953 Samdech Penn Nouth
1953–4 Chan Nak
1954–5 Leng Ngeth
1955–6 Prince Norodom Sihanouk
1956 Oum Chheang Sun
1956 Prince Norodom Sihanouk
1956 Khim Tit
1956 Prince Norodom Sihanouk
1956 Sam Yun
1956–7 Prince Norodom Sihanouk
1957–8 Sim Var
1958 Ek Yi Oun
1958 Samdech Penn Nouth *Acting*
1958 Sim Var
1958–60 Prince Norodom Sihanouk
1960–1 Pho Proung
1961 Samdech Penn Nouth
1961–3 Prince Norodom Sihanouk
1963–6 Prince Norodom Kantol
1966–7 Lon Nol
1967–8 Prince Norodom Sihanouk
1968–9 Samdech Penn Nouth
1969–72 Lon Nol

Khmer Republic Prime Minister

1972 Sisovath Sivik Matak
1972 Son Ngoc Thanh
1972–3 Hang Thun Hak
1973 In Tam
1973–5 Long Boret
1975–6 Samdech Penn Nouth

1976–9	Pol Pot	1981–5	Chan Si
1979–81	Khieu Samphan	1985–93	Hun Sen

Prime Minister (Government in exile until 1991)

1970–3	Samdech Penn Nouth	1997	Ung Huot *First Prime Minister* Hun Sen *Second Prime Minister*
1982–91	Son Sann	1998–	Hun Sen
1993–7	Norodom Ranariddh *First Prime Minister* Hun Sen *Second Prime Minister*		

CAMEROON

Official name	Republic of Cameroon
Local name	Cameroun; République du Cameroun
Former name	Kamerun (until 1919), French Cameroon (until 1960) and British Cameroon (until 1961, when south part joined new Republic of Cameroon, north part joined Nigeria), Federal Republic of Cameroon (1961–72), United Republic of Cameroon (1972–84)
Independence	1960
Area	475 439 sq km/183 519 sq mi
Capital	Yaoundé
Chief towns	Douala
Population	18 060 000 (2007e)
Nationality	Cameroonian
Languages	French, English; many local languages are also spoken
Ethnic groups	Fang 21%, Bamileke and Bamum 19%, Douala, Luanda and Bassa 15%, Fulani 10%, others 35%
Religions	Christianity 40%, traditional beliefs 40%, Islam 20%
Time zone	GMT +1
Currency	1 CFA Franc (CFAFr/XAF) = 100 centimes
Telephone	+237
Internet	.cm
Country code	CMR

Location

A republic in West Africa, bounded to the north-west by Nigeria; to the north-east by Chad; to the east by the Central African Republic; to the south-east by Congo; to the south by Gabon and Equatorial Guinea; and to the west by the Gulf of Guinea.

Physical description

Equatorial forest on the coastal plain rising to a central plateau of over 1 300m/4 265ft; west is forested and mountainous; active volcano Mt Cameroon (4 070m/13 352ft) is the highest peak in West Africa; savanna and semi-desert towards Lake Chad.

Climate

North has a wet season in Apr–Sep, dry the rest of the year; northern plains are semi-arid; equatorial south has rain throughout the year, with two wet seasons and two dry seasons; maximum daily temperatures in the south average 27–30°C.

National holidays

Jan 1, Feb 11 (Youth), May 1, 20 (National), Aug 15, Dec 25; A, Ad, ER, ES, GF.

Political leaders

President

1960–82	Ahmadou Ahidjo
1982–	Paul Biya

Prime Minister

1960	Ahmadou Ahidjo
1960–1	Charles Assalé
1961–75	*No Prime Minister*
1975–82	Paul Biya
1982–3	Bello Bouba Maigari
1983–4	Luc Ayang
1984–91	*No Prime Minister*
1991–2	Sadou Hayatou
1992–6	Simon Achidi Achu
1996–2004	Peter Mafany Musonge
2004–	Ephraïm Inoni

Prawn River

In 1472 the Portuguese sailor Fernando Po sailed up the River Wouri in Douala. He was amazed at the number of prawns in the river, and so named the place *Rio dos Camarões*, or 'River of Prawns'. From *camarões* the name Cameroon evolved.

CANADA

Official name	Canada
Local name	Canada
Area	9970610 sq km/3848655 sq mi
Capital	Ottawa
Chief towns	Calgary, Edmonton, Montréal, Québec, Toronto, Vancouver, Victoria, Winnipeg
Population	33390000 (2007e)
Nationality	Canadian
Languages	English, French
Ethnic groups	British origin 28%, mixed 26%, French origin 23%, other European 15%, Amerindian 2%, others 6%
Religions	Christianity 70% (RC 43%, Prot 23%, other 4%), Islam 2%, others/unaffiliated 12%, none 16%
Time zone	GMT –3.5/8
Currency	1 Canadian Dollar (C$, Can$/CAD) = 100 cents
Telephone	+1
Internet	.ca
Country code	CAN

Location

An independent country in North America, bounded to the north-west by the US state of Alaska; to the north by the Arctic Ocean, Beaufort Sea and Baffin Bay; to the north-east by the Davis Strait; to the east by the Labrador Sea and the Atlantic Ocean; to the south by the United States of America; and to the west by the Pacific Ocean.

Physical description

North-east is dominated by the Canadian Shield; mountains of Nova Scotia and New Brunswick in the east; fertile lowlands in south Québec and Ontario; flat prairie country south and west of the Shield, stretching to the Western Cordillera, which includes the Rocky, Cassiar and Mackenzie mountains; Coast Mountains flank a rugged, heavily-indented coastline, rising to 5950m/19520ft at Mt Logan (highest peak); approximately 45% is forested; Great Lakes in south-east Ontario.

Climate

North coast is permanently ice-bound or obstructed by ice floes, except for Hudson Bay (frozen for approximately 9 months each year); cold air from the Arctic sweeps south and east in winter and spring; mild winters and warm summers on the west coast and some inland valleys of British Columbia; winter temperatures on the Atlantic shores are warmer than those of the interior, but summer temperatures are lower; much of the southern interior has warm summers and long, cold winters.

National holidays
Jan 1, Jul 1 (Canada), Nov 11 (Remembrance), Dec 25, 26; EM, GF, Labour (1st Mon in Sep), Thanksgiving (2nd Mon in Oct), Victoria (Mon preceding May 25).

Misdirected Names

Canada gained its name when early 16c explorers were directed by local indigenous people to the nearest village: *kanata* was the Huron-Iroquois word for 'settlement'. The explorers later used *kanata* to refer to the whole of the local area, and then to the larger region, and finally to everywhere north of the St Lawrence River. By the 1700s the name referred to a vast swathe of the continent.

Provinces of Canada

Name	Population (2006e)[1]	Area	Capital
Alberta (AB)	3375800	661848 sq km/ 255472 sq mi	Edmonton
British Columbia (BC)	4310500	944735 sq km/ 364667 sq mi	Victoria
Manitoba (MB)	1177800	647797 sq km/ 250050 sq mi	Winnipeg
New Brunswick (NB)	749200	72908 sq km/ 28142 sq mi	Fredericton
Newfoundland and Labrador (NL)	509700	405212 sq km/ 156412 sq mi	St John's
Northwest Territories (NT)	41900	1346106 sq km/ 519597 sq mi	Yellowknife
Nova Scotia (NS)	934400	55284 sq km/ 21340 sq mi	Halifax
Nunavut (NU)	30800	2093190 sq km/ 807971 sq mi	Iqaluit
Ontario (ON)	12687000	1076395 sq km/ 415488 sq mi	Toronto
Prince Edward Island (PE)	138500	5660 sq km/ 2185 sq mi	Charlottetown
Québec (QC)	7651500	1542056 sq km/ 595234 sq mi	Québec City
Saskatchewan (SK)	985400	651036 sq km/ 251300 sq mi	Regina
Yukon Territory (YT)	31200	482443 sq km/ 186223 sq mi	Whitehorse

[1] *Population figures are from Statistics Canada.*

Political leaders

Head of State: British monarch, represented by Governor General (Michaelle Jean since 2005).

Prime Minister

1867–73	John A Macdonald *Con*	1891–2	John J C Abbot *Con*
1873–8	Alexander Mackenzie *Lib*	1892–4	John S D Thompson *Con*
1878–91	John A Macdonald *Con*	1894–6	Mackenzie Bowell *Con*

1896	Charles Tupper *Con*
1896–1911	Wilfrid Laurier *Lib*
1911–20	Robert Borden *Con/Un*
1920–1	Arthur Meighen *Un/Con*
1921–6	William Lyon Mackenzie King *Lib*
1926	Arthur Meighen *Con*
1926–30	William Lyon Mackenzie King *Lib*
1930–5	Richard Bedford Bennett *Con*
1935–48	William Lyon Mackenzie King *Lib*
1948–57	Louis St Laurent *Lib*
1957–63	John George Diefenbaker *Con*
1963–8	Lester Bowles Pearson *Lib*
1968–79	Pierre Elliott Trudeau *Lib*
1979–80	Joseph Clark *Con*
1980–4	Pierre Elliott Trudeau *Lib*
1984	John Turner *Lib*
1984–93	Brian Mulroney *Con*
1993	Kim Campbell *Con*
1993–2004	Jean Chrétien *Lib*
2004–6	Paul Martin *Lib*
2006–	Stephen Harper *Con*

Con = Conservative; Un = Unionist; Lib = Liberal

Long and Winding Road

The Trans-Canada Highway is the world's longest national highway. It runs 7,821km/4,860mi from St John's in Newfoundland and Labrador to Victoria in British Columbia.

Maple Leaves

The maple tree is the national tree of Canada, and the maple leaf its internationally recognized symbol. Ten species of maple tree grow in Canada: the *bigleaf*, *black*, *Douglas*, *Manitoba*, *mountain*, *red*, *silver*, *striped*, *sugar* and *vine maple*.

CANARY ISLANDS *see* SPAIN

CAPE VERDE

Official name	Republic of Cape Verde
Local name	Cabo Verde; República de Cabo Verde
Independence	1975
Area	4 033 sq km/1 557 sq mi
Capital	Praia
Chief towns	Mindelo
Population	424 000 (2007e)
Nationality	Cape Verdean
Languages	Portuguese; Crioulo, a Creole language blending Portuguese and West African words, is spoken widely
Ethnic groups	mestizo 71%, African 28%, European 1%
Religions	Christianity 98% (RC), others 1%, none/unaffiliated 1%
Time zone	GMT –1
Currency	1 Cape Verde Escudo (CVEsc/CVE) = 100 centavos
Telephone	+238
Internet	.cv
Country code	CPV

Location
An island group in the Atlantic Ocean off the coast of West Africa.

Physical description
Islands are of volcanic origin, mostly mountainous; highest peak is Pico do Cano (2 829m/9 281ft), an active volcano on Fogo Island; coastal plains are semi-desert; savanna or thin forest lies on the mountains; fine, sandy beaches on most islands.

Climate
Located at the northern limit of the tropical rain belt; low and unreliable rainfall mainly in Aug and Sep; cooler and damper in the uplands; severe drought can occur; tropical heat; average temperatures at Praia range between 21°C (Jan) and 27°C (Oct).

National holidays
Jan 1, 20 (National Heroes), May 1, Jul 5 (Independence), Aug 15, Nov 1, Dec 25; *some religious and regional variation*.

Political leaders

President

1975–91	Arístides Pereira
1991–2001	Antonio Mascarenhas Monteiro
2001–	Pedro Pires

Prime Minister

1975–91	Pedro Pires
1991–2000	Carlos Wahnon Veiga
2000–1	António Gualberto do Rosário
2001–	José Maria Neves

Black Sands
Cape Verde is renowned for its black sand beaches, such as that at Faja d'Agua on the small island of Brava. The black volcanic sand is rich in minerals, and is reputed to have beneficial medicinal qualities.

CAYMAN ISLANDS *see* UNITED KINGDOM

CENTRAL AFRICAN REPUBLIC

Official name	Central African Republic (CAR)
Local name	République Centrafricaine (French), Ködörösêse tî Bêafrîka (Sango)
Former name	Ubangi Shari (until 1958), Central African Republic (1958–76), Central African Empire (1976–9)
Independence	1960
Area	622 984 sq km/240 534 sq mi
Capital	Bangui
Chief towns	Berbérati, Bouar, Bossangoa
Population	4 369 000 (2007e)
Nationality	Central African
Languages	French, Sango
Ethnic groups	Baya 33%, Banda 27%, Mandjia 13%, Sara 10%, Mboum 7%, others 10%
Religions	Christianity 50% (Prot 25%, RC 25%), traditional beliefs 35%, Islam 15%
Time zone	GMT +1
Currency	1 CFA Franc (CFAFr/XAF) = 100 centimes
Telephone	+236
Internet	.cf
Country code	CAF

Location
A republic in central Africa, bounded to the north-west by Chad; to the north-east by Sudan; to the south by Democratic Republic of the Congo and Congo; and to the west by Cameroon.

Physical description
On a plateau forming the watershed between the Chad and Congo river basins; highest ground is in the north-east (Massif des Bongos) and north-west; highest point is Mont Ngaoui (1 420m/4 659ft).

Climate
Single rainy season in the north between May and Sep; more equatorial climate in the south; average temperatures at Bangui are 24–27°C.

National holidays
Jan 1, Mar 29 (Death of President Boganda), May 1, Jun 1 (Prayer), Aug 13 (Independence), 15, Nov 1, Dec 1 (National), 25; A, EM.

Political leaders

President

1960–6	David Dacko
1966–79	Jean-Bédel Bokassa (*from 1977, Emperor Bokassa I*)
1981–93	André Kolingba
1993–2003	Ange-Félix Patasse
2003–	François Bozizé

Prime Minister

1991–2	Edouard Frank
1992–3	Thimothée Malendoma
1993	Enoch Derant Lakoué
1993–5	Jean-Luc Mandaba
1995–6	Gabriel Koyambounou
1996–7	Jean-Paul Ngoupandé
1997–9	Michel Gbezera-Bria
1999–2001	Anicet Georges Dologuélé
2001–3	Martin Ziguélé
2003	Abel Goumba
2003–5	Célestin Gaombalet
2005–8	Élie Doté
2008–	Faustin-Archange Touadéra

CHAD

Official name	Republic of Chad
Local name	Tchad; République du Tchad
Independence	1960
Area	1 284 640 sq km/495 871 sq mi
Capital	N'Djamena (also Ndjamena)
Chief towns	Moundou, Sarh, Abéché
Population	9 886 000 (2007e)
Nationality	Chadian
Languages	French, Arabic; many local languages are also spoken
Ethnic groups	Arab 26%, Sara 25%, Teda 18%, others 31%
Religions	Islam 51%, Christianity 35%, traditional beliefs 7%, others 7%
Time zone	GMT +1
Currency	1 CFA Franc (CFAFr/XAF) = 100 centimes
Telephone	+235
Internet	.td
Country code	TCD

Location
A republic in north central Africa, bounded to the north by Libya; to the east by Sudan; to the south by Central African Republic; and to the west by Cameroon, Nigeria and Niger. The Tropic of Cancer passes the northern tip.

Physical description
A mostly arid, semi-desert plateau at the edge of the Sahara Desert; Lake Chad lies in the south-west; Tibesti Mountains rise to 3415m/11 204ft at Emi Koussi; vegetation is generally desert scrub or steppe; most people live in the tropical south.

Climate
Moderately wet in the south between May and Oct, but dry for the rest of the year; hot and arid north is almost rainless; central plain is hot and dry, with a brief rainy season during Jun–Sep.

National holidays
Jan 1, May 1, Aug 11 (Independence), Nov 1, 28 (Republic), Dec 1 (Liberty and Democracy), 25; Ad, EM, ER, PB.

Political leaders

President

1960–75	François Tombalbaye	1979	Mohammed Shawwa
1975–9	*Supreme Military Council* (Félix Malloum)	1979–82	Goukouni Oueddi
1979	Goukouni Oueddi	1982–90	Hissène Habré
		1990–	Idriss Déby

Prime Minister

1991–2	Jean Alingue Bawoyeu	1999–2002	Negoum Yamassoum
1992–3	Joseph Yodemane	2002–3	Haroun Kabadi
1993	Fidèle Moungar	2003–5	Moussa Faki Mahamat
1993–5	Delwa Kassiré Koumakoye	2005–7	Pascal Yoadimnadji
1995–7	Koibla Djimasta	2007–	Nourradine Delwa Kassiré Coumakoye
1997–9	Nassour Ouaidou Guelendouksia		

CHANNEL ISLANDS *see* UNITED KINGDOM

CHILE

Official name	Republic of Chile
Local name	Chile; República de Chile
Independence	1818
Area	756 626 sq km/292 058 sq mi
Capital	Santiago
Chief towns	Valparaíso, Concepción, Talcahuano, Antofagasta, Viña del Mar
Population	16 285 000 (2007e)
Nationality	Chilean
Languages	Spanish
Ethnic groups	mestizo 95%, Amerindian 3%, others 2%
Religions	Christianity 99% (RC 89%, Prot 10%), others 1%
Time zone	GMT –4
Currency	1 Chilean Peso (Ch$/CLP) = 100 centavos
Telephone	+56
Internet	.cl
Country code	CHL

Location

A republic in south-western South America, crossed by the Tropic of Capricorn in the north; bounded to the north by Peru and Bolivia; to the east by Argentina; and to the west by the Pacific Ocean.

Physical description

Narrow coastal belt, backed by Andean mountains rising in the north to 6 723m/22 057ft at Llullaillaco; highest point is Ojos del Salado (6 910m/22 660ft); lower mountains in the centre and south; fertile central valley; Atacama Desert lies in the far north-west.

Climate

Highly varied (spans 37° of latitude; altitudes from the Andean peaks to the coastal plain); extreme aridity in the Atacama Desert; cold, wet and windy in the far south; Mediterranean climate in centre, with warm, wet winters and dry summers.

National holidays

Jan 1, May 1, 21 (Navy), Jun 29 (SS Peter and Paul), Jul 16 (Our Lady of Carmen), Aug 15, Sep 18 (Independence), 19 (Army), Oct 12 (Columbus), Nov 1, Dec 8, 25; GF, HS.

Political leaders

President

1900–1	Federico Errázuriz Echaurren
1901	Aníbal Zañartu *Vice President*
1901–3	Germán Riesco
1903	Ramón Barros Luco *Vice President*
1903–6	Germán Riesco
1906–10	Pedro Montt
1910	Ismael Tocornal *Vice President*
1910	Elías Fernández Albano *Vice President*
1910	Emiliano Figueroa Larraín *Vice President*
1910–15	Ramón Barros Luco
1915–20	Juan Luis Sanfuentes
1920–4	Arturo Alessandri
1924–5	*Military Juntas*
1925	Arturo Alessandri
1925	Luis Barros Borgoño *Vice President*
1925–7	Emiliano Figueroa
1927–31	Carlos Ibáñez
1931	Pedro Opaso Letelier *Vice President*
1931	Juan Esteban Montero *Vice President*
1931	Manuel Trucco Franzani *Vice President*
1931–2	Juan Esteban Montero
1932	*Military Juntas*
1932	Carlos G Dávila *Provisional*
1932	Bartolomé Blanche *Provisional*
1932	Abraham Oyanedel *Vice President*
1932–8	Arturo Alessandri Palma
1938–41	Pedro Aguirre Cerda
1941–2	Jerónimo Méndez Arancibia *Vice President*
1942–6	Juan Antonio Ríos Morales
1946–52	Gabriel González Videla
1952–8	Carlos Ibáñez del Campo
1958–64	Jorge Alessandri Rodríguez
1964–70	Eduardo Frei Montalva
1970–3	Salvador Allende Gossens
1973–90	Augusto Pinochet Ugarte
1990–3	Patricio Aylwin Azócar
1993–9	Eduardo Frei Ruíz-Tagle
2000–6	Ricardo Lagos Escobar
2006–	Michelle Bachelet

CHINA

Official name	People's Republic of China (PRC)
Local name	Zhong Guo; Zhonghua Renmin Gongheguo
Area	9 597 000 sq km/3 704 000 sq mi
Capital	Beijing (formerly known as Peking)
Chief towns	Shanghai, Tianjin, Shenyang, Wuhan, Guangzhou
Population	1 321 852 000 (2007e)
Nationality	Chinese
Languages	standard Chinese (Putong-hua) or Mandarin, also Yue (Cantonese), Wu, Minbei, Minnan, Xiang, Gan, Hakka; minority languages
Ethnic groups	Han 92%, others 8%
Religions	Chinese folk religion 20%, Buddhism 8%, Christianity 5% (Prot 4%, RC 1%), Islam 2%, others 6%, none/unaffiliated 59%
Time zone	GMT +8
Currency	1 Yuan ($, Y/CNY) or Renminbi (RMBY) = 10 jiao = 100 fen
Telephone	+86
Internet	.cn
Country code	CHN

Location

A state in central and eastern Asia, crossed by the Tropic of Cancer in the south; bounded to the north-west by Kyrgyzstan and Kazakhstan; to the north by Mongolia and Russia; to the east by North Korea, the Yellow Sea and the East China Sea; to the south by the South China Sea, Vietnam, Laos, Myanmar, India, Bhutan and Nepal; and to the west by India, the disputed region of Jammu and Kashmir, Pakistan, Afghanistan and Tajikistan.

Physical description

Over two-thirds is upland, mountain and plateau; highest mountains are in the west, where the Tibetan Plateau rises to an average altitude of 4 000m/13 123ft; highest point is Mt Everest 8 850m/29 035ft; land descends to desert or semi-desert in Sinkiang and Inner Mongolia; broad fertile plains of Manchuria in the north-east and the densely forested Changpai Shan uplands; fertile southern plains and east coast are heavily populated.

Climate

Varied, with seven zones: (1) north-east has cold winters, with strong north winds and warm, humid summers; in Manchuria, the rivers are frozen for four to six months each year, and snow lies for 100–150 days; (2) centre has warm and humid summers, sometimes typhoons or tropical cyclones on the coast; (3) south, partly within the tropics, is the wettest area in summer; frequent typhoons (especially during Jul–Oct); (4) south-west has summer temperatures moderated by altitude, winters are mild with little rain; summers are wet on the mountains; (5) Tibet autonomous region, a high plateau surrounded by mountains, has severe winters with frequent light snow and hard frost, summers are warm, but nights are cold; (6) Xinjiang and the western interior has an arid desert climate with cold winters; (7) Inner Mongolia has an extreme continental-type climate, with cold winters and warm summers, and strong winds in winter and spring.

National holidays

Jan 1, May 1–3, Oct 1–3 (National); Spring Festival/Chinese NY (3) (Jan/Feb); *also, local holidays and holidays observed by certain groups*.

Special Administrative Regions

Hong Kong (HK)

Location	Comprises the Kowloon/New Territories peninsula and more than 200 islands in the South China Sea.		
Local name	Xianggang; Xianggang Tebie Xingzhengqu	**Population**	6 980 000 (2007e)
		Internet	.hk
Area	16 sq km/6 sq mi	**Country code**	HGK

Macao

Location	Macao peninsula is linked by bridge and causeway to two islands in the South China Sea.		
Local name	Aomen; Aomen Tebie Xingzhengqu; Macau (Portuguese)	**Population**	457 000 (2007e)
		Internet	.mo
		Country code	MAC
Area	1 067 sq km/412 sq mi		

Note: China also occupies the Paracel Islands in the South China Sea.

Political leaders

Dynasties

c.22c–18c BC	Xia
c.18c–12c BC	Shang or Yin
c.1122/1066–771 BC	Western Chou
771–256 BC	Eastern Chou
403–222 BC	Warring States Period
222–206 BC	Qin (Ch'in)
206 BC–AD 9	Western ('Former') Han
AD 8–23	Interregnum (Wang Mang)
AD 25–220	Eastern Han
AD 220–280	Three Kingdoms Period
AD 265–317	Western Jin (Chin)
AD 317–420	Eastern Jin (Chin)
AD 420–589	Southern Dynasties
581–618	Sui
618–907	Tang
907–960	Five Dynasties and Ten Kingdoms Period
960–1279	Song (Sung)
1122–1234	Jin (Jurchen)
1279–1368	Yuan (Mongol)
1368–1644	Ming
1644–1911	Qing (Manchu)

Qing (Manchu) dynasty

Emperor

1875–1908	Guangxu (Kuang-hsü)
1908–12	Xuantong (Hsüan-t'ung)

Prime Minister

1901–3	Ronglu (Jung-lu)
1903–11	Prince Qing (Ch'ing)
1912	Lu Zhengxiang (Lu Cheng-hsiang)
1912	Yuan Shikai (Yüan Shih-k'ai)

Republic of China

President

1912	Sun Yat-sen (Sun Yixian) *Provisional*
1912–16	Yuan Shikai (Yüan Shih-k'ai)
1916–17	Li Yuanhong (Li Yüan-hung)
1917–18	Feng Guozhang (Feng Kuo-chang)
1918–22	Xu Shichang (Hsü Shih-ch'ang)
1921–5	Sun Yat-sen (Sun Yixian) *Canton Administration*
1922–3	Li Yuanhong (Li Yüan-hung)
1923–4	Cao Kun (Ts'ao K'un)
1924–6	Duan Qirui (Tuan Ch'i-jui)
1926–7	*Civil Disorder*
1927–8	Zhang Zuolin (Chang Tso-lin)
1928–31	Chiang K'ai-shek (Jiang Jieshi)
1931–2	Cheng Minxu (Ch'eng Ming-hsü) *Acting*
1932–43	Lin Sen (Lin Sen)
1940–4	Wang Jingwei (Wang Ching-wei) *in Japanese-occupied territory*
1943–9	Chiang K'ai-shek (Jiang Jieshi)
1945–9	*Civil War*
1949	Li Zongren (Li Tsung-jen)

Premier

1912	Tang Shaoyi (T'ang Shao-i)
1912–13	Zhao Bingjun (Chao Ping-chün)
1912–13	Xiong Xiling (Hsiung Hsi-ling)
1914	Sun Baoyi (Sun Pao-chi)
1915–16	*no Premier*
1916–17	Duan Qirui (Tuan Ch'i-jui)
1917–18	Wang Shizhen (Wang Shih-chen)
1918	Duan Qirui (Tuan Ch'i-jui)
1918–19	Qian Nengxun (Ch'ien Neng-hsün)
1919	Gong Xinzhan (Kung Hsin-chan)
1919–20	Jin Yunpeng (Chin Yün-p'eng)
1920	Sa Zhenbing (Sa Chen-ping)
1920–1	Jin Yunpeng (Chin Yün-p'eng)
1921–2	Liang Shiyi (Liang Shih-i)
1922	Zhou Ziqi (Chow Tzu-ch'i) *Acting*
1922	Yan Huiqing (Yen Hui-ch'ing)
1922	Wang Chonghui (Wang Ch'ung- hui)
1922–3	Wang Daxie (Wang Ta-hsieh)
1923	Zhang Shaozeng (Chang Shao-ts'eng)
1923–4	Gao Lingwei (Kao Ling-wei)
1924	Sun Baoyi (Sun Pao-ch'i)
1924	Gu Weijun (Ku Wei-chün) *Acting*
1924	Yan Huiqing (Yen Hui-ch'ing)
1924–5	Huang Fu (Huang Fu) *Acting*
1925	Duan Qirui (Tuan Ch'i-jui)
1925–6	Xu Shiying (Hsü Shih-ying)
1926	Jia Deyao (Chia Te-yao)
1926	Hu Weide (Hu Wei-te)
1926	Yan Huiqing (Yen Hui-ch'ing)
1926	Du Xigui (Tu Hsi-kuei)
1926–7	Gu Weijun (Ku Wei-chün)
1927	*Civil Disorder*

President of the Executive Council

1928–30	Tan Yankai (T'an Yen-k'ai)
1930	T V Soong (Sung Tzu-wen) *Acting*
1930	Wang Jingwei (Wang Ching-wei)
1930–1	Chiang K'ai-shek (Jiang Jieshi)
1931–2	Sun Fo (Sun Fo)
1932–5	Wang Jingwei (Wang Ching-wei)
1935–7	Chiang K'ai-shek (Jiang Jieshi)
1937–8	Wang Chonghui (Wang Ch'ung-hui) *Acting*
1938–9	Kong Xiangxi (K'ung Hsiang-hsi)
1939–44	Chiang K'ai-shek (Jiang Jieshi)
1944–7	T V Soong (Sung Tzu-wen)
1945–9	*Civil War*
1948	Wang Wenhao (Wong Wen-hao)
1948–9	Sun Fo (Sun Fo)
1949	He Yingqin (Ho Ying-ch'in)
1949	Yan Xishan (Yen Hsi-shan)

People's Republic of China

President

1949–59	Mao Zedong (Mao Tse-tung)	1978–83	Ye Jianying
1959–68	Liu Shaoqi	1983–8	Li Xiannian
1968–75	Dong Biwu	1988–93	Yang Shangkun
1975–6	Zhu De	1993–2003	Jiang Zemin
1976–8	Sung Qingling	2003–	Hu Jintao

Premier/Prime Minister

1949–76	Zhou Enlai (Chou En-lai)	1987–98	Li Peng
1976–80	Hua Guofeng	1998–2003	Zhu Rongji
1980–7	Zhao Ziyang	2003–	Wen Jiabao

Chairman of the Communist Party

1935–76	Mao Zedong (Mao Tse-tung)
1976–81	Hua Guofeng
1981–2	Hu Yaobang

General Secretary of the Communist Party

1982–7	Hu Yaobang
1987–9	Zhao Ziyang
1989–2002	Jiang Zemin
2002–	Hu Jintao

Note: Names are listed only in Pinyin transliterations for recent leaders.

Red for Go

The colour red is associated with the Communist party in China. During the Cultural Revolution (1966–76) it was reported that some over-zealous revolutionaries wanted the red traffic light to mean 'go', to symbolize the forward-thinking nature of the Communist regime.

CHINA, REPUBLIC OF; CHINESE TAIPEI *see* TAIWAN

CHRISTMAS ISLAND; COCOS ISLANDS *see* AUSTRALIA

COLOMBIA

Official name	Republic of Colombia
Local name	Colombia; República de Colombia
Independence	1810 (declared), 1819 (full)
Area	1 140 105 sq km/440 080 sq mi
Capital	Bogotá; Santa Fé de Bogotá
Chief towns	Medellín, Cali, Barranquilla
Population	44 380 000 (2007e)
Nationality	Colombian
Languages	Spanish
Ethnic groups	mestizo 58%, white 20%, mulatto 14%, black 4%, mixed black and Amerindian 3%, Amerindian 1%
Religions	Christianity 90% (RC), others 10%
Time zone	GMT –5
Currency	1 Colombian Peso (Col$/COP) = 100 centavos
Telephone	+57
Internet	.co
Country code	COL

Location

A republic in north-western South America, crossed by the Equator in the south; bounded to the north-west by Panama; to the north by the Caribbean Sea; to the east by Venezuela; to the south-east by Brazil; to the south by Ecuador and Peru; and to the west by the Pacific Ocean.

Physical description

Caribbean and Pacific coastlines, with several islands; Andes run north to south, branching into three dividing narrow coastal plains from forested Amazon basin lowlands; highest peaks are Pico Cristóbal Colón and Pico Simón Bolívar (both 5775m/18947ft) and Nevado del Huila (5750m/18864ft).

Climate

Hot and humid coastal plains in the north-west and west; drier period on the Caribbean coast (Dec–Apr); in the Andes rainfall is even throughout the year; hot and humid tropical lowlands in the east.

National holidays

Jan 1, 6, Mar 19 (St Joseph), May 1, Jun 29 (SS Peter and Paul), Jul 20 (Independence), Aug 7 (Battle of Boyacá), 15, Oct 12 (Columbus), Nov 1, 11 (Independence of Cartagena), Dec 8, 25; A, CC, GF, HT, Sacred Heart (Jun).

Political leaders

President

1900–4	José Manuel Marroquín *Vice President*
1904–9	Rafael Reyes
1909–10	Ramón González Valencia
1910–14	Carlos E Restrepo
1914–18	José Vicente Concha
1918–21	Marco Fidel Suárez
1921–2	Jorge Holguín *President Designate*
1922–6	Pedro Nel Ospina
1926–30	Miguel Abadía Méndez
1930–4	Enrique Olaya Herrera
1934–8	Alfonso López
1938–42	Eduardo Santos
1942–5	Alfonso López
1945–6	Alberto Lleras Camargo *President Designate*
1946–50	Mariano Ospina Pérez
1950–3	Laureano Gómez
1953–7	Gustavo Rojas Pinilla
1957	*Military Junta*
1958–62	Alberto Lleras Camargo
1962–6	Guillermo León Valencia
1966–70	Carlos Lleras Restrepo
1970–4	Misael Pastrana Borrero
1974–8	Alfonso López Michelsen
1978–82	Julio César Turbay Ayala
1982–6	Belisario Betancur
1986–90	Virgilio Barco Vargas
1990–4	César Gaviria Trujillo
1994–8	Ernesto Samper Pizano
1998–2002	Andrés Pastrana Arango
2002–	Álvaro Uribe Vélez

Orchids and Condors

The national flower of Colombia is the orchid, while the national tree is the wax palm, which only grows in the Colombian Andes and is the world's tallest palm tree, reaching up to 70m/230ft. The mighty condor is the national bird, a creature of great historical and cultural significance for the people. It lives high in the Andes and is known as the 'eternal bird' for its long lifespan.

COMOROS

Official name	Union of the Comoros
Local name	Comores; Union des Comores
Former name	Federal Islamic Republic of the Comoros (until 2001)
Independence	1975
Area	1 862 sq km/719 sq mi
Capital	Moroni; Môrônï
Population	711 000 (2007e)
Nationality	Comoran
Languages	French, Arabic; Shikomoro, or Comoran, a local Arabic-Swahili dialect, is also spoken
Ethnic groups	Comorian 97%, others 3%
Religions	Islam 98% (Sunni), Christianity 2% (RC)
Time zone	GMT +3
Currency	1 Comoran Franc (KMF) = 100 centimes
Telephone	+269
Internet	.km
Country code	COM

Location

An island group at the northern end of the Mozambique Channel in the Indian Ocean, between Mozambique and Madagascar.

Physical description

Three volcanic islands, Grand Comore (Njazídja), Anjouan (Nzwani) and Mohéli (Mwali); interiors vary from steep mountains to low hills; highest point is the active volcano Le Karthala (2 360m/7 743ft) on Grand Comore.

Climate

Tropical; May–Oct is the dry season and Nov–Apr is the hot, humid season; average temperatures are 20°C in Jul and 28°C in Nov.

National holidays

Jan 1, Mar 18 (Cheikh al-Maarouf), May 1, Jul 6 (National), Nov 26 (Cheikh al-Maarouf's Death); Ad (2), ER (3), NY (Muslim), PA, PB.

Political leaders

President

1976–78	Ali Soilih
1978–89	Ahmed Abdallah Abderemane
1989–96	Said Mohammed Djohar
1996–8	Mohammed Taki Abdoulkarim
1998–9	Tadjiddine Ben Said Massounde *Interim*
1999–2002	Azali Assoumani
2002	Hamada Madi Boléro *Interim*
2002–6	Azali Assoumani
2006–	Ahmed Abdallah Sambi

Prime Minister

1976–8	Abdallah Mohammed
1978–82	Salim Ben Ali
1982–4	Ali Mroudjae
1984–92	*No Prime Minister*
1992	Mohammed Taki Abdoulkarim
1993	Ibrahim Abdermane Halidi
1993	Said Ali Mohammed
1993–4	Ahmed Ben Cheikh Attoumane
1994	Mohammed Abdou Madi
1994–5	Halifa Houmadi
1995–6	Caambi el-Yachourtu
1996	Tadjiddine Ben Said Massounde
1996–7	Ahmed Abdou
1997–8	Nourdine Bourhane
1998–9	Abbas Djoussouf
1999–2000	Bianrifi Tarmidi
2000–2	Hamada Madi Boléro
2002–	*No Prime Minister*

CONGO

Official name	Republic of Congo; also sometimes known as Congo (Brazzaville) or Congo-Brazzaville
Local name	Congo; République du Congo
Former name	Middle Congo (until 1960), Republic of Congo (1960–70), People's Republic of Congo (1970–92)
Independence	1960
Area	341 945 sq km/131 990 sq mi
Capital	Brazzaville
Chief towns	Pointe-Noire, Loubomo, Nkayi
Population	3 801 000 (2007e)
Nationality	Congolese, Congo
Languages	French, Kikongo, Lingala
Ethnic groups	Kongo 49%, Sangha 20%, Teke 17%, Mbosi 11%, others 3%
Religions	Christianity 50% (RC), traditional beliefs 48%, Islam 2%
Time zone	GMT +1
Currency	1 CFA Franc (CFAFr/XAF) = 100 centimes
Telephone	+242
Internet	.cg
Country code	COG

Location
A west central African republic, crossed by the Equator, bounded to the north-west by Cameroon; to the north by the Central African Republic; to the east and south by Democratic Republic of the Congo; to the south-west by the Angolan province of Cabinda and the southern Atlantic Ocean; and to the west by Gabon.

Physical description
Short Atlantic coastline fringes a broad mangrove plain that rises inland to mountains reaching 900m/2 953ft; River Congo flows south-west to the coast; Monts de la Lékéti reach 1 040m/3 412ft; mainly covered by dense grassland, mangrove and forest.

Climate
Hot, humid, equatorial climate; rainfall decreases near the Atlantic coast and in the south; temperatures vary little, with average daily maximum temperatures at Brazzaville 28–33°C; dry season is Jun–Sep.

National holidays
Jan 1, May 1, Jun 10 (Reconciliation), Aug 15 (Independence), Nov 1, Dec 25; A, EM, WM.

Political leaders

President

1960–3	Abbé Fulbert Youlou	1969–77	Marien Ngouabi
1963–8	Alphonse Massemba-Debat	1977–9	Joachim Yhomby Opango
1968	Marien Ngouabi	1979–92	Denis Sassou-Nguesso
1968	Alphonse Massemba-Debat	1992–7	Pascal Lissouba
1968–9	Alfred Raoul	1997–	Denis Sassou-Nguesso

Prime Minister

1958	Jacques Opangault	1973–5	Henri Lopès
1958–60	Fulbert Youlou	1975–84	Louis Sylvain Goma
1960–3	*No Prime Minister*	1984–9	Ange-Édouard Poungui
1963–6	Pascal Lissouba	1989–90	Alphonse Poaty-Souchlaty
1966–8	Ambroise Noumazalaye	1990–1	Pierre Moussa *Acting*
1968–9	Alfred Raoul	1991	Louis Sylvain Goma
1969–73	*No Prime Minister*	1991–2	André Milongo

1992	Stéphane Maurice Bongho-Nouarra
1992–3	Claude Antoine Dacosta
1993–6	Joachim Yhombi-Opango
1996–7	Charles David Ganao
1997	Bernard Kolelas
1997–2005	*No Prime Minister*
2005–	Isidore Mvouba

Free French

During World War II Brazzaville served as the headquarters of the Free French forces led by General Charles de Gaulle. In the film *Casablanca* (1942), Rick and Captain Louis Renault head for the Free French garrison in Brazzaville at the end of the film and at the start of 'a beautiful friendship'.

CONGO, DEMOCRATIC REPUBLIC OF THE

Official name	Democratic Republic of the Congo (DR Congo, DRC or DROC); also sometimes known as Congo (Kinshasa) or Congo-Kinshasa
Local name	Congo; République Démocratique du Congo
Former name	Congo Free State (until 1908), Belgian Congo (until 1960), Republic of the Congo (1960–4), Democratic Republic of Congo (1964–71), Zaïre (1971–97)
Independence	1960
Area	2343950 sq km/904765 sq mi
Capital	Kinshasa
Chief towns	Lubumbashi, Kisangani, Mbuji-Mayi, Kananga
Population	65751000 (2007e)
Nationality	Congolese, Congo
Languages	French, Kikongo, Lingala
Ethnic groups	Bantu and Hamitic 44%, others 56%
Religions	Christianity 70% (RC 50%, Prot 20%), Islam 10%, others and traditional beliefs 20%
Time zone	GMT +1/2
Currency	1 Congolese Franc (CF/CDF) = 100 centimes
Telephone	+243
Internet	.cd
Country code	COD

Location

A central African republic, crossed by the Equator; bounded to the north by the Central African Republic; to the north-east by Sudan; to the east by Uganda, Rwanda, Burundi and Tanzania; to the south-east by Zambia; to the south-west by Angola; and to the west by Congo and the Atlantic Ocean.

Physical description

Rises in the east from a low-lying basin to a densely-forested plateau; Ruwenzori Mountains in the north-east rise to 5110m/16765ft at Pic Marguerite on Mt Ngaliema (Mt Stanley); chain of lakes in the Rift Valley; short 43km/27mi Atlantic coastline.

Climate

Hot and humid equatorial climate; average maximum daily temperatures range between 28°C and 31°C.

National holidays

Jan 1, 4 (Martyrs of Independence), 16–17 (National Heroes), May 1, 17 (National Liberation), Jun 30 (Independence), Aug 1 (Parents), Dec 25.

Political leaders

President

1960–5	Joseph Kasavubu	1997–2001	Laurent Kabila
1965–97	Mobutu Sese Seko (*formerly* Joseph Mobutu)	2001–	Joseph Kabila

Prime Minister

1960	Patrice Lumumba	1988	Sambura Pida Nbagui
1960	Joseph Ileo	1988–90	Léon Kengo Wa Dondo
1960–1	*College of Commissioners*	1990–1	Lunda Bululu
1961	Joseph Ileo	1991	Mulumba Lukeji
1961–4	Cyrille Adoula	1991	Etienne Tshisekedi
1964–5	Moïse Tshombe	1991	Bernardin Mungul Diaka
1965	Evariste Kimba	1991–2	Karl I Bond
1965–6	Mulamba Nyungu wa Kadima	1992–3	Etienne Tshisekedi
1966–77	*As President*	1993–4	Faustin Birindwa
1977–80	Mpinga Kasenga	1994–7	Léon Kengo Wa Dondo
1980	Bo-Boliko Lokonga Monse Mihambu	1997	Etienne Tshisekedi
1980–1	Nguza Karl I Bond	1997	Likulia Bolongo
1981–3	Nsinga Udjuu	1997–2007	*No Prime Minister*
1983–6	Léon Kengo Wa Dondo	2007–	Antoine Gizenga
1986–8	*No Prime Minister*		

Mighty River

The River Congo is the second longest river in Africa, and the tenth longest in the world, at a massive 4,630km/2,880mi. It rises as the River Lualaba, crosses the Equator and becomes known as the River Congo, then flows in an arc across central Africa. The first European discovery of the river mouth was in 1482, but its extent was appreciated only in the 19c, with explorations by Stanley, Livingstone and others.

COOK ISLANDS *see* NEW ZEALAND

COSTA RICA

Official name	Republic of Costa Rica
Local name	Costa Rica; República de Costa Rica
Independence	1821
Area	51 022 sq km/19 694 sq mi
Capital	San José
Chief towns	Cartago, Heredia, Liberia, Puntarenas, Limón
Population	4 134 000 (2007e)
Nationality	Costa Rican
Languages	Spanish
Ethnic groups	white and mestizo 94%, black and mulatto 3%, Amerindian 1%, Chinese 1%, others 1%
Religions	Christianity 91% (RC 76%, Prot 14%), others 6%, none 3%
Time zone	GMT –6
Currency	1 Costa Rican Colón (CR₡/CRC) = 100 céntimos
Telephone	+506
Internet	.cr
Country code	CRI

Location
A republic in Central America, bounded to the north by Nicaragua; to the east by the Caribbean; to the south-east by Panama; and to the west by the Pacific Ocean.

Physical description
A series of volcanic ridges form the backbone (some volcanoes active); highest peak is Chirripó Grande (3819m/12529ft); central plateau lies at an altitude of 800–1400m/2600–4600ft; swampy near the coast, with tropical forest inland; some lowland savanna.

Climate
Tropical climate, with a small temperature range and abundant rainfall; more temperate in the central uplands; dry season is Dec–May; average annual temperature is 26–28°C.

National holidays
Jan 1, Apr 11 (Juan Santamaría), May 1, Jul 25 (Guanacaste), Aug 2 (Lady of the Angels), 15 (Mothers), Sep 15 (Independence), Oct 15 (Columbus), Dec 25; ES, GF, HS, HT.

Political leaders

President

1894–1902	Rafael Yglesias y Castro
1902–6	Ascención Esquivel Ibarra
1906–10	Cleto González Víquez
1910–12	Ricardo Jiménez Oreamuno
1912–14	Cleto González Víquez
1914–17	Alfredo González Flores
1917–19	Federico Tinoco Granados
1919	Julio Acosta García
1919–20	Juan Bautista Quiros
1920–4	Julio Acosta García
1924–8	Ricardo Jiménez Oreamuno
1928–32	Cleto González Víquez
1932–6	Ricardo Jiménez Oreamuno
1936–40	León Cortés Castro
1940–4	Rafael Ángel Calderón Guardia
1944–8	Teodoro Picado Michalski
1948	Santos Léon Herrera
1948–9	*Civil Junta* (José Figueres Ferrer)
1949–52	Otilio Ulate Blanco
1952–3	Alberto Oreamuno Flores
1953–8	José Figueres Ferrer
1958–62	Mario Echandi Jiménez
1962–6	Francisco José Orlich Bolmarcich
1966–70	José Joaquín Trejos Fernández
1970–4	José Figueres Ferrer
1974–8	Daniel Oduber Quirós
1978–82	Rodrigo Carazo Odio
1982–6	Luis Alberto Monge Álvarez
1986–90	Oscar Arias Sánchez
1990–4	Rafael Ángel Calderón Fournier
1994–8	José Maria Figueres Olsen
1998–2002	Miguel Angel Rodríguez Echevarría
2002–6	Abel Pacheco de la Espriella
2006–	Oscar Arias Sánchez

Pacifists on the Pacific

Costa Rica is one of very few countries not to have an army. The military was abolished in 1948, and the government claims to have since invested the money saved into improving the quality of life and living standards of its people. But what Costa Rica lacks in military muscle, it makes up for in wildlife; the country estimates that it covers just 0.03% of the Earth's land surface, but contains approximately 6% of the world's biodiversity.

CÔTE D'IVOIRE

Official name	Republic of Côte d'Ivoire
Local name	Côte d'Ivoire; République de la Côte d'Ivoire
Former name	Ivory Coast (until 1986)
Independence	1960
Area	320 633 sq km/123 764 sq mi
Capital	Yamoussoukro (official) and Abidjan (administrative and economic)
Chief towns	Bouaké, Daloa, Man, Korhogo, Gagnoa
Population	18 013 000 (2007e)
Nationality	Ivorian
Languages	French; many local languages are also spoken
Ethnic groups	Akan 40%, Kru 17%, Voltaic 15%, Malinke 15%, Southern Mande 11%, others 2%
Religions	Christianity 38%, Islam 35%, traditional beliefs 27%
Time zone	GMT
Currency	1 CFA Franc (CFAFr/XOF) = 100 centimes
Telephone	+225
Internet	.ci
Country code	CIV

Location

A republic in West Africa, bounded to the north-west by Guinea; to the north by Mali and Burkina Faso; to the east by Ghana; to the south by the Gulf of Guinea; and to the west by Liberia.

Physical description

Sandy beaches and lagoons, backed by a broad forest-covered coastal plain; land rises towards savanna at 300–350m/980–1 150ft; Mt Nimba massif in the north-west reaches 1 752m/5 748ft (highest point); rivers generally flow north to south.

Climate

Tropical, varying with distance from the coast; rainfall decreases towards the north; average temperatures are 25–27°C.

National holidays

Jan 1, May 1, Aug 7 (Independence), 15, Nov 1, 15 (Peace), Dec 7 (Houphouët–Boigny), 25; A, Ad, EM, ER, PB, WM; Revelation of Koran.

Political leaders

President

1960–93	Félix Houphouët-Boigny	1999–2000	Robert Guëi
1993–9	Henri Konan-Bédié	2000–	Laurent Gbagbo

Prime Minister

1958–9	Auguste Denise	2000	Seydou Diarra
1959–60	Félix Houphouët-Boigny	2000–3	Pascal Affi N'Guessan
1960–90	*No Prime Minister*	2003–5	Seydou Diarra
1990–3	Alassane Dramane Ouattara	2005–7	Charles Konan Banny
1993–9	Daniel Kablan Duncan	2007–	Guillaume Kigbafori Soro
1999	Robert Guëi		

Cocoa Kings

Côte d'Ivoire is the world's largest producer of cocoa. In 2003–4 it produced approximately 1.4 million tonnes/1,382,800 tons of cocoa beans, dwarfing its nearest competitor, Ghana, which produced only 736,000 tonnes/724,300 tons.

CROATIA

Official name	Republic of Croatia
Local name	Hrvatska; Republika Hrvatska
Former name	formerly part of Kingdom of Serbs, Croats and Slovenes (until 1929), Kingdom of Yugoslavia (1929–41), Independent State of Croatia (1941–45), Federal People's Republic of Yugoslavia (1945–63), Socialist Federal People's Republic of Yugoslavia (1963–91)
Independence	1991
Area	56 538 sq km/21 824 sq mi
Capital	Zagreb
Chief towns	Rijeka, Cakovec, Split, Zadar
Population	4 493 000 (2007e)
Nationality	Croatian
Languages	Croatian
Ethnic groups	Croat 90%, Serb 4%, others 6%
Religions	Christianity 93% (RC 88%, Orthodox 5%), Islam 1%, others 6%
Time zone	GMT +1
Currency	1 Kuna (Kn/HRK) = 100 lipa
Telephone	+385
Internet	.hr
Country code	HRV

Location

A republic in central Europe, bounded to the north by Slovenia; to the north-east by Hungary; to the east by Serbia; to the south-east by Bosnia and Herzegovina; and to the south-west by the Adriatic Sea and Montenegro.

Physical description

Mountainous, with islands on the Adriatic coast; highest point is Dinara (1 831m/6 007ft); inland terrain includes fertile plains.

Climate

Continental; hot summers and cold winters.

National holidays

Jan 1, 6, May 1, Jun 22 (Anti-fascism), 25 (Statehood), Aug 5 (Victory and Thanksgiving), 15, Oct 8 (Independence), Nov 1, Dec 25, 26; CC, EM, ES.

Political leaders

See **Yugoslavia** for political leaders prior to 1991–2.

President

1992–9	Franjo Tudjman
1999–2000	Vlatko Pavletić *Acting*
2000	Zlatko Tomčić *Acting*
2000–	Stjepan Mesić

Prime Minister

1990	Stjepan Mesić
1990–1	Josip Manolić
1991–2	Franjo Gregurić
1992–3	Hrvoje Šarinić
1993–5	Nikica Valentić
1995–2000	Zlatko Mateša
2000–3	Ivica Račan
2003–	Ivo Sanader

CUBA

Official name	Republic of Cuba
Local name	Cuba; República de Cuba
Independence	1902
Area	110 860 sq km/42 792 sq mi
Capital	Havana; La Habana
Chief towns	Santiago de Cuba, Camagüey, Holguín, Santa Clara, Guantánamo
Population	11 394 000 (2007e)
Nationality	Cuban
Languages	Spanish
Ethnic groups	mulatto 51%, white 37%, black 11%, Chinese 1%
Religions	traditional beliefs 54%, Christianity 46% (RC 40%, Prot 6%)
Time zone	GMT –5
Currency	1 Cuban Peso (Cub$/CUP) = 100 centavos
Telephone	+53
Internet	.cu
Country code	CUB

Location
An island republic lying between the Gulf of Mexico and the Caribbean Sea, south of the US state of Florida.

Physical description
An archipelago, comprising the island of Cuba, Isla de la Juventud and approximately 1 600 islets and cays; heavily indented coastline; highest peak is Pico Turquino (2 005m/6 578ft); mostly flat, with wide, fertile valleys and plains.

Climate
Subtropical, warm and humid; average annual temperature is 25°C; dry season is Nov–Apr; hurricanes usually occur between Jun and Nov.

National holidays
Jan 1 (Liberation), May 1, Jul 25–27 (Revolution), Oct 10 (War of Independence), Dec 25.

Political leaders

President

1902–6	Tomas Estrada Palma
1906–9	*US rule*
1909–13	José Miguel Gómez
1913–21	Mario García Menocal
1921–5	Alfredo Zayas y Alfonso
1925–33	Gerardo Machado y Morales
1933	Carlos Manuel de Céspedes
1933–4	Ramón Grau San Martín
1934–5	Carlos Mendieta
1935–6	José A Barnet y Vinagres
1936	Miguel Mariano Gómez y Arias
1936–40	Federico Laredo Bru
1940–4	Fulgencio Batista
1944–8	Ramón Grau San Martín
1948–52	Carlos Prío Socarrás
1952–9	Fulgencio Batista
1959	Manuel Urrutia
1959–76	Osvaldo Dorticós Torrado
1959–76	Fidel Castro Ruz *Prime Minister and First Secretary*
1976–	Fidel Castro Ruz *President*
2006–	Raul Castro Ruz *Acting President owing to Fidel Castro's ill health*

Chatty Castro

Cuban President Fidel Castro holds the world record for the longest continuous speech at the United Nations. On 26 Sep 1960 Castro's speech denouncing imperialism and colonialism lasted an exhausting four and a half hours. He prefaced the speech by assuring those present that he would endeavour to be brief.

CYPRUS

Official name	Republic of Cyprus
Local name	Kipros; Kypriaki Dimokratía (Greek), Kibris; Kibris Çumhuriyeti (Turkish)
Independence	1960
Area	9251 sq km/3571 sq mi
Capital	Nicosia; Lefkosía (Greek), Lefkoşa (Turkish)
Chief towns	Larnaca, Limassol, Kyrenia; Famagusta (formerly the chief port) is under Turkish occupation and has been declared closed by the Cyprus government
Population	788 000 (2007e)
Nationality	Cypriot
Languages	Greek, Turkish, with English widely spoken
Ethnic groups	Greek 77%, Turkish 18%, others 5%
Religions	Christianity 78% (Orthodox), Islam 18%, others 4%
Time zone	GMT +2
Currency	1 Euro (€/EUR) = 100 cents; Turkish lira are used in the northern part under Turkish occupation
Telephone	+357
Internet	.cy
Country code	CYP

Location
An island republic in the eastern Mediterranean Sea, south of Turkey and west of Syria.

Physical description
Kyrenia Mountains extend along the north coast; forest-covered Troüdos Mountains in the south-west rise to 1951m/6401ft at Mt Olympus; fertile plain across the island centre; indented coastline with several long, sandy beaches.

Climate
Typical Mediterranean climate with hot, dry summers and warm, wet winters; average daily temperatures (Jul–Aug) 22–29°C; winters are mild (average temperature 4°C in the mountains, 10°C on the plain); snow on higher land in winter.

National holidays
Jan 1, 6, Mar 25 (Greek National), Apr 1 (Greek Cypriot National), May 1, Aug 15, Oct 1 (Independence), 28 (Greek National Ochi), Dec 24, 25, 26; EM (Orthodox), GF (Orthodox); Green Monday (Feb/Mar), Kataklysmos (May/Jun).

Note: Turkey has occupied the northern third of Cyprus since 1974. It declared this area to be the Turkish Federated State of Cyprus in 1975 and the Turkish Republic of Northern Cyprus in 1983; the state is recognized only by Turkey. It has been led by Rauf Denktaş (from inception to 2005) and Mehmet Ali Talat (since 2005).

Political leaders

President

1960–77	Archbishop Makarios III
1977–88	Spyros Kyprianou
1988–93	Georgios Vassiliou
1993–2003	Glafcos Clerides
2003–	Tassos Papadopoulos

CZECH REPUBLIC

Official name	Czech Republic
Local name	České Republiky, Česká Republika, Cesko
Former name	formerly part of Czechoslovakia (until 1993)
Independence	1993
Area	78864 sq km/30441 sq mi
Capital	Prague; Praha
Chief towns	Brno, Plzen, Ostrava, Olomouc
Population	10229000 (2007e)
Nationality	Czech
Languages	Czech
Ethnic groups	Czech 90%, Moravian 4%, Slovak 2%, others 4%
Religions	Christianity 29% (RC 27%, Prot 2%), unspecified 9%, none/unaffiliated 59%
Time zone	GMT +1
Currency	1 Koruna (Kč/CZK) = 100 haléřú
Telephone	+420
Internet	.cz
Country code	CZE

Location

A republic in central Europe, bounded to the north and west by Germany; to the north and east by Poland; to the south-east by Slovakia; and to the south by Austria.

Physical description

Bohemia and West Moravia are separated from East Moravia and Slovakia by the River Morava valley; western range of the Carpathians rise in the east; highest point is Sněžka(1602m/5256ft); many lakes and rivers; richly wooded.

Climate

Continental, with warm, humid summers and cold, dry winters.

National holidays

Jan 1, May 1, 8 (Liberation), Jul 5 (SS Cyril and Methodius), 6 (Martyrdom of Jan Hus), Sep 28 (Statehood), Oct 28 (Independence), Nov 17 (Freedom and Democracy), Dec 24, 25, 26; EM.

Political leaders

Czechoslovakia

President

1918–35 Tomáš Garrigue Masaryk
1935–8 Edvard Beneš
1938 Emil Hácha
1938–45 Edvard Beneš *President in Exile (German Occupation)*
1939–45 Emil Hácha *State President (German Occupation)*
1939–45 Jozef Tiso *Slovak Republic President (German Occupation)*
1945–8 Edvard Beneš
1948–53 Klement Gottwald
1953–7 Antonín Zápotocký
1957–68 Antonín Novotný
1968–75 Ludvík Svoboda
1975–89 Gustáv Husák
1989–93 Václav Havel

Prime Minister

1918–19 Karel Kramář
1919–20 Vlastimil Tusar
1920–1 Jan Černý
1921–2 Edvard Beneš
1922–6 Antonín Švehla
1926 Jan Černý
1926–9 Antonín Švehla
1929–32 František Udržal
1932–5 Jan Malypetr
1935–8 Milan Hodža

1938	Jan Syrový
1938–9	Rudolf Beran
1940–5	Jan Šrámek *in exile*
1945–6	Zdeněk Fierlinger
1946–8	Klement Gottwald
1948–53	Antonín Zápotocký
1953–63	Viliám Široký
1963–8	Josef Lenárt
1968–70	Oldřich Černik
1970–88	Lubomír Štrougal
1988–9	Ladislav Adamec
1989–92	Marian Calfa
1992	Jan Strasky

First Secretary of the Communist Party

1948–52	Rudolf Slánsky
1953–68	Antonín Novotný
1968–9	Alexander Dubček
1969–87	Gustáv Husák
1987–9	Miloš Jakeš
1989	Karel Urbánek
1989–93	Ladislav Adamec

In 1993 Czechoslovakia divided into two separate states, the Czech Republic and **Slovakia** (see separate entry).

Czech Republic

President

1993–2003	Václav Havel
2003–	Václav Klaus

Prime Minister

1993–7	Václav Klaus
1997–8	Josef Tosovsky
1998–2002	Miloš Zeman
2002–4	Vladimír Špidla
2004–5	Stanislav Gross
2005–6	Jirí Paroubek
2006–	Mirek Topolánek

DENMARK

Official name	Kingdom of Denmark
Local name	Danmark; Kongeriget Danmark; also sometimes known as Rigsfællesskabet, the United Kingdom of Denmark, including the Faroe Islands and Greenland
Area	43 076 sq km/16 627 sq mi
Capital	Copenhagen; København
Chief towns	Århus, Odense, Ålborg, Esbjerg, Randers, Kolding
Population	5 468 000 (2007e)
Nationality	Dane, Danish
Languages	Danish
Ethnic groups	Danish 96%, Faroese and Inuit 1%, others 3%
Religions	Christianity 84% (Prot 83%, RC 1%), Islam 4%, unaffiliated 7%, unspecified/others 1%, none 4%
Time zone	GMT +1
Currency	1 Danish Krone (Dkr/DKK) = 100 øre
Telephone	+45
Internet	.dk
Country code	DNK

DENMARK

Location
A kingdom in northern Europe, comprising most of the Jutland Peninsula, bounded to the south by Germany, and more than 400 islands in the Baltic Sea and the North Sea.

Physical description
The smallest of the Scandinavian countries; uniformly low-lying; highest point (Ejer Bavnehøj) is only 173m/567ft; no large rivers and few lakes; shoreline is indented by many lagoons and fjords, the largest of which is Lim Fjord.

Climate
Much modified by the Gulf Stream, giving cold and cloudy winters, and warm, sunny summers.

National holidays
Jan 1, Jun 5 (Constitution), Dec 24, 25, 26; A, EM, GF, HT, WM, General Prayer (Apr/May).

Danish self-governing territories

Faroe Islands

Location	The group of 18 islands and smaller islets lying between the Shetland Islands and Iceland, and subject to the Danish crown. Also spelt Faeroe Islands.		
Local name	Føroyar (Faroese)/Færøerne (Danish)	**Population**	47 000 (2007e)
		Internet	.fo
Area	1 399 sq km/540 sq mi	**Country code**	FRO
Capital	Tórshavn (1999e)		

Sheep Islands

The local name for the Faroes is *Føroyar*, which comes from an old Norse word meaning 'Sheep Islands'.

Greenland

Location	The second-largest island in the world (after Australia), lying north-east of North America in the North Atlantic and Arctic oceans; autonomous with limited self-government but subject to the Danish crown.		
Local name	Kalaallit Nunaat (Inuit)/ Grønland (Danish)	**Population**	56 000 (2007e)
		Internet	.gl
Area	2 175 600 sq km/839 780 sq mi	**Country code**	GRL
Capital	Nuuk (Inuit), Godthåb (Danish)		

Glacier to Iceberg

The world's most active glacier is found at Ilulissat on Greenland's west coast. 'Ilulissat' means 'the icebergs' and the town lies on a fjord full of bergs created by the glacier. Moving at 25–30m/80–100ft a day, the glacier 'calves' across a 10km/6mi long front and produces 20 million tons of ice every 24 hours.

Political leaders

Monarch

1448–81	Kristian I	1746–66	Frederik V
1481–1513	Johan	1766–1808	Kristian VII
1513–23	Kristian II	1808–39	Frederik VI
1523–34	Frederik I	1839–48	Kristian VIII
1534–59	Kristian III	1848–63	Frederik VII
1559–88	Frederik II	1863–1906	Kristian IX
1588–1648	Kristian IV	1906–12	Frederik VIII
1648–70	Frederik III	1912–47	Kristian X
1670–99	Kristian V	1947–72	Frederik IX
1699–1730	Frederik IV	1972–	Margrethe II
1730–46	Kristian VI		

Prime Minister

1900–1	Hannibal Sehested	1945	Wilhelm Buhl
1901–5	J H Deuntzer	1945–7	Knud Kristensen
1905–8	J C Christensen	1947–50	Hans Hedtoft
1908–9	Niels Neergaard	1950–3	Erik Eriksen
1909	Ludvig Holstein-Ledreborg	1953–5	Hans Hedtoft
1909–10	C Th Zahle	1955–60	Hans Christian Hansen
1910–13	Klaus Berntsen	1960–2	Viggo Kampmann
1913–20	C Th Zahle	1962–8	Jens Otto Krag
1920	Otto Liebe	1968–71	Hilmar Baunsgaard
1920	M P Friis	1971–2	Jens Otto Krag
1920–4	Niels Neergaard	1972–3	Anker Jørgensen
1924–6	Thorvald Stauning	1973–5	Poul Hartling
1926–9	Thomas Madsen-Mygdal	1975–82	Anker Jørgensen
1929–42	Thorvald Stauning	1982–93	Poul Schlüter
1942	Wilhelm Buhl	1993–2001	Poul Nyrup Rasmussen
1942–3	Erik Scavenius	2001–	Anders Fogh Rasmussen
1943–5	*No government*		

DJIBOUTI

Official name	Republic of Djibouti
Local name	Djibouti; République de Djibouti (French), Jumhūriyya Jibūt (Arabic)
Former name	French Somaliland (until 1967), French Territory of the Afars and Issas (1966–77)
Independence	1977
Area	23 310 sq km/8 998 sq mi
Capital	Djibouti; Djīboûtï
Chief towns	Tadjoura, Dikhil, Obock, Ali-Sabieh
Population	496 000 (2007e)
Nationality	Djiboutian
Languages	Arabic, French
Ethnic groups	Issa 60%, Afar 35%, Arab and others 5%
Religions	Islam 94% (Sunni), Christianity 6% (RC 4%, Prot 2%)
Time zone	GMT +3
Currency	1 Djibouti Franc (DF, DjFr/DJF) = 100 centimes
Telephone	+253
Internet	.dj
Country code	DJI

Location

A republic in north-east Africa, bounded to the north by Eritrea and the Gulf of Aden; to the east by Somalia; and to the west and south by Ethiopia.

Physical description

A series of plateaux dropping down from mountains to flat low-lying rocky desert; 350km/220mi of fertile coastal strip around the Gulf of Tadjoura, which juts deep into the country; highest point, Moussa Ali, rises to 2020m/6627ft in the north.

Climate

Semi-arid with a hot season (May–Sep); very hot on coastal plains, maximum average daily temperature dropping below 30°C for only three months (Dec–Feb); slightly lower temperatures in the interior highlands.

National holidays

Jan 1, May 1, Jun 27–28 (National), Dec 25; Ad (2), ER (2), NY (Muslim), PA, PB.

Political leaders

President

1977–99	Hassan Gouled Aptidon
1999–	Ismaïl Omar Guelleh

Prime Minister

1977–8	Abdallah Mohammed Kamil
1978–2001	Barkat Gourad Hamadou
2001–	Dileïta Mohamed Dileïta

Low-Lying Lake

Djibouti's Lake Assal is the lowest point in Africa, at –156m/–512ft. It lies in a rift valley, separated from the Gulf of Tadjoura that leads into the Gulf of Aden only by rocks made of ancient lava flows. These form a natural barrier and stop the lake being flooded by the salt waters of the Gulf.

DOMINICA

Official name	Commonwealth of Dominica
Local name	Dominica
Independence	1978
Area	751 sq km/290 sq mi
Capital	Roseau
Chief towns	Portsmouth, Grand Bay
Population	72 000 (2007e)
Nationality	Dominican
Languages	English; French Creole is also spoken
Ethnic groups	African/mixed African-European 97%, Amerindian 2%, others 1%
Religions	Christianity 92% (RC 77%, Prot 15%), others 6%, none 2%
Time zone	GMT –4
Currency	1 East Caribbean Dollar (EC$/XCD) = 100 cents
Telephone	+1767
Internet	.dm
Country code	DMA

Location

An independent island republic located in the Windward Islands, in the east Caribbean Sea.

Physical description

Roughly rectangular in shape, with a deeply-indented coastline; approximately 50km/30mi long and 26km/16mi wide, rising to 1447m/4747ft at Morne Diablotin; volcanic origin, with many fumaroles and sulphur springs; forestry covers 67% of its area.

Climate

Warm and humid; average monthly temperatures are 26–32°C; subject to hurricanes.

National holidays

Jan 1, Nov 3 (Independence), 4 (Community Service), Dec 25, 26; C (2), EM, GF, WM, Emancipation (1st Mon in Aug), Labour (1st Mon in May).

Political leaders

President

1978–9	Louis Cools-Lartigue *Interim*	1983–93	Clarence Augustus Seignoret
1979–80	Frederick Degazon[1]	1993–8	Crispin Anselm Sorhaindo
1979–80	Jenner Armour *Acting*	1998–2003	Vernon Shaw
1980–3	Aurelius Marie	2003–	Nicholas Liverpool

Prime Minister

1978–9	Patrick Roland John	2000	Rosie Douglas
1979–80	Oliver Seraphine	2000–4	Pierre Charles
1980–95	Mary Eugenia Charles	2004–	Roosevelt Skerrit
1995–2000	Edison James		

[1] *Left Dominica Jun 1979 but did not officially resign until Feb 1980.*

Tall is Her Body

Dominica was first inhabited by the Igneri tribe from Orinoco c.3000 BC. Four thousand years later it was colonized by the Kalinago people, who christened the island *Wai tukubuli*, meaning 'tall is her body' in their Carib language.

DOMINICAN REPUBLIC

Official name	Dominican Republic (DR)
Local name	República Dominicana
Independence	1844
Area	48442 sq km/18699 sq mi
Capital	Santo Domingo
Chief towns	Santiago, La Vega, San Juan, San Francisco de Macorís, La Romana
Population	9366000 (2007e)
Nationality	Dominican
Languages	Spanish
Ethnic groups	mulatto 73%, white 16%, black 11%
Religions	Christianity 95% (RC), others 5%
Time zone	GMT –4
Currency	1 Dominican Republic Peso (RD$, DR$/DOP) = 100 centavos
Telephone	+1809
Internet	.do
Country code	DOM

Location

A republic in the West Indies, comprising the eastern two-thirds of the island of Hispaniola in the Caribbean Sea, and bounded by Haiti to the west.

DOMINICAN REPUBLIC

Physical description

Crossed by the Cordillera Central, a heavily-wooded range with many peaks over 3000m/9840ft; Pico Duarte (3175m/10417ft) is the highest peak in the Caribbean; Lake Enriquillo lies in a broad valley in the south-west; wide coastal plain to the east.

Climate

Tropical maritime with a rainy season from May to Nov; average temperature at Santo Domingo ranges between 24°C (Jan) and 27°C (Jul); hurricanes may occur in Jun–Nov.

National holidays

Jan 1, 6, 21 (Our Lady of Altagracia), 26 (Duarte), Feb 27 (Independence), May 1, Sep 24 (Our Lady of Mercedes), Dec 25; CC, GF; Constitution Day (Nov), Restoration Day (Aug).

Political leaders

President

1899–1902	Juan Isidro Jiménez
1902–3	Horacio Vásquez
1903	Alejandro Wos y Gil
1903–4	Juan Isidro Jiménez
1904–6	Carlos Morales
1906–11	Ramon Cáceres
1911–12	Eladio Victoria
1912–13	Adolfo Nouel y Bobadilla
1913–14	José Bordas y Valdés
1914	Ramon Báez
1914–16	Juan Isidro Jiménez
1916–22	*US occupation* (Francisco Henríquez y Carrajal)
1922–4	*US occupation* (Juan Batista Vicini Burgos)
1924–30	Horacio Vásquez
1930	Rafael Estrella Urena
1930–8	Rafael Leónidas Trujillo y Molina
1938–40	Jacinto Bienvenudo Peynado
1940–2	Manuel de Jesus Troncoso de la Concha
1942–52	Rafael Leónidas Trujillo y Molina
1952–60	Hector Bienvenido Trujillo
1960–2	Joaquín Videla Balaguer
1962	Rafael Bonnelly
1962	*Military Junta* (Huberto Bogaert)
1962–3	Rafael Bonnelly
1963	Juan Bosch Gavino
1963	*Military Junta* (Emilio de los Santos)
1963–5	Donald Reid Cabral
1965	*Civil War*
1965	Elias Wessin y Wessin
1965	Antonio Imbert Barreras
1965	Francisco Caamaño Deñó
1965–6	Héctor Garcia Godoy Cáceres
1966–78	Joaquín Videla Balaguer
1978–82	Antonio Guzmán Fernández
1982–6	Salvador Jorge Blanco
1986–96	Joaquín Videla Balaguer
1996–2000	Leonel Fernández Reyna
2000–4	Hipólito Mejía
2004–	Leonel Fernández Reyna

Hispaniola

The Dominican Republic comprises the east of the island of Hispaniola, an island first discovered by Europeans when Christopher Columbus visited it in 1492. It became the first Spanish colony in the Caribbean under the name Santo Domingo. The name Hispaniola is derived from *La Isla Española*, 'the Spanish island'.

DUBAI *see* **UNITED ARAB EMIRATES**

EAST TIMOR

Official name	Democratic Republic of East Timor
Local name	Timor-Leste; República Democrática de Timor-Leste (Portuguese), Timor Lorosa'e; Republika Demokratika Timor Lorosa'e (Tetum)
Former names	Portuguese Timor (until 1975), part of Indonesia (1976–2002)
Independence	2002
Area	14874 sq km/5743 sq mi
Capital	Dili
Chief towns	Baucau, Pante Macassar
Population	1085000 (2007e)
Nationality	Timorese
Languages	Portuguese, Tetum; English and Indonesian are also spoken
Ethnic groups	Malayo-Polynesian, Papuan
Religions	Christianity 93% (RC 90%, Prot 3%), Islam 4%, others 3%
Time zone	GMT +8
Currency	1 US Dollar ($/USD) = 100 cents
Telephone	+670
Internet	.tp
Country code	TLS

Location

A republic in south-east Asia, comprising the eastern half of the island of Timor and bounded by Indonesia to the west; also includes the enclave of Oecusse in the west of the island; separated from Australia by the Timor Sea.

Physical description

Mountainous, with numerous rivers; highest peak is Tata Mailau (2950m/9678ft); also includes the smaller islands of Pulau Atauro and Jaco.

Climate

Hot and humid equatorial climate; dry season (Jun–Sep), rainy season (Dec–Mar); average temperature is 27°C on the coast, falling inland and with altitude.

National holidays

Jan 1, May 1, 20 (Independence Restoration), Aug 30 (Popular Consultation), Nov 1, 2, 12 (Youth), 28 (Independence), Dec 7 (Heroes), 8, 25; Ad, CC, ER, GF.

Political leaders

President

2002–7	Xanana Gusmão
2007–	José Ramos-Horta

Prime Minister

2002–6	Mari Alkatiri
2006–7	José Ramos-Horta
2007–	Xanana Gusmão

A New Country

East Timor gained its independence on 20 May 2002, becoming the first new nation of the 21st century. It became a member of the United Nations the same year.

ECUADOR

Official name	Republic of Ecuador
Local name	Ecuador; República del Ecuador
Independence	1822
Area	270699 sq km/104490 sq mi
Capital	Quito
Chief towns	Guayaquil, Cuenca, Riobamba, Esmeraldas
Population	13756000 (2007e)
Nationality	Ecuadorean or Ecuadorian
Languages	Spanish; Quechua is also spoken
Ethnic groups	mestizo 65%, Amerindian 25%, white 7%, black 3%
Religions	Christianity 96% (RC 94%, Prot 2%), others 4%
Time zone	GMT –5
Currency	1 US Dollar ($, US$/USD) = 100 cents
Telephone	+593
Internet	.ec
Country code	ECU

Location

A republic in north-west South America, crossed by the Equator; bounded to the north by Colombia; to the south and east by Peru; and to the west by the Pacific Ocean; also includes the Galápagos Islands.

Physical description

Coastal plain in west; Andean uplands in the centre, three main ranges which include Cotopaxi (5896m/19344ft), the world's highest active volcano; highest point is Mt Chimborazo (6267m/20560ft); forested alluvial plains in east; frequent earthquakes; the Galápagos Islands include six main volcanic islands.

Climate

Hot and humid coast, rain throughout the year (especially Dec–Apr); temperatures are much reduced by altitude; Quito has warm days and chilly nights, with frequent heavy rain in the afternoon; hot and wet equatorial climate in the east.

National holidays

Jan 1, May 1, 24 (Battle of Pichincha), Aug 10 (Independence), Oct 9 (Independence of Guayaquil), Nov 2, 3 (Independence of Cuenca), Dec 25; C (2), GF; *also unofficial and local holidays*.

Political leaders

President

1895–1901	Eloy Alfaro
1901–5	Leónides Plaza Gutiérrez
1905–6	Lizardo García
1906–11	Eloy Alfaro
1911	Emilio Estrada
1911–12	Carlos Freile Zaldumbide
1912–16	Leónides Plaza Gutiérrez
1916–20	Alfredo Baquerizo Moreno
1920–4	José Luis Tamayo
1924–5	Gonzálo S Córdova
1925–6	*Military Juntas*
1926–31	Isidro Ayora
1931–2	*Four Acting Presidents*
1932–3	Juan de Dios Martínez Mera
1933–4	Abelardo Montalvo
1934–5	José María Velasco Ibarra
1935	Antonio Pons
1935–7	Federico Páez
1937–8	Alberto Enríquez Gallo
1938	Manuel María Borrero
1938–9	Aurelio Mosquera Narváez
1939–40	Julio Enrique Moreno
1940–4	Carlos Alberto Arroya del Río
1944–7	José María Velasco Ibarra
1947	Carlos Mancheno
1947–8	Carlos Julio Arosemena Tola
1948–52	Galo Plaza Lasso
1952–6	José María Velasco Ibarra
1956–60	Camilo Ponce Enríquez
1960–1	José María Velasco Ibarra
1961–3	Carlos Julio Arosemena Monroy
1963–6	*Military Junta*

1966	Clemente Yerovi Indaburu	1996–7	Abdalá Bucaram Ortiz
1966–8	Otto Arosemena Gómez	1997	Rosalia Arteaga *Acting*
1968–72	José María Velasco Ibarra	1997–8	Fabián Alarcón Rivero
1972–6	Guillermo Rodríguez Lara	1998–2000	Jamil Mahuad Witt
1976–9	*Military Junta*	2000–3	Gustavo Noboa Bejerano
1979–81	Jaime Roldós Aguilera	2003–5	Lucio Gutiérrez
1981–4	Oswaldo Hurtado Larrea	2005–7	Alfredo Palacio
1984–8	León Febres Cordero	2007–	Rafael Correa
1988–92	Rodrigo Borja Cevallos		
1992–6	Sixto Durán Ballén		

Incas and Volcanoes

Quito sits at an altitude of 2,850m/9,350ft at the foot of Guagua Pichincha, an active volcano prone to showering the city with clouds of ash. Quito was an Inca capital, but was destroyed by followers of the Inca leader Atahualpa when it became clear that it would be captured by the Spanish in the early 1530s. It was refounded in 1534.

EGYPT

Official name	Arab Republic of Egypt
Local name	Misr; Al-Jumhūriyya al-Mişriyya al-'Arabiyya
Former name	formerly part of the United Arab Republic, with Syria (1958–61; name retained until 1971)
Independence	1922
Area	1 001 449 sq km/386 559 sq mi
Capital	Cairo; El Qāhirah
Chief towns	Alexandria, Port Said, Aswan, Suez, El Gîza
Population	80 335 000 (2007e)
Nationality	Egyptian
Languages	Arabic
Ethnic groups	Eastern Hamitic 91%, others 9%
Religions	Islam 90% (mostly Sunni), Christianity 10% (mostly Coptic)
Time zone	GMT +2
Currency	1 Egyptian Pound (£E, LE/EGP) = 100 piastres
Telephone	+20
Internet	.eg
Country code	EGY

Location

A republic in north-east Africa, crossed by the Tropic of Cancer in the south; bounded to the north by the Mediterranean Sea; to the north-east by Israel; to the east by the Red Sea; to the south by Sudan; and to the west by Libya.

Physical description

River Nile flows north, dammed to create Lake Nasser; huge delta north of Cairo; Western Desert covers over two-thirds of the country; highest point is Gebel Katherîna (2 637m/8 651ft); 90% of the population live on the Nile floodplain (approximately 3% of the country's area).

Climate

Mainly desert, except for an 80km/50mi wide Mediterranean coastal fringe; very hot on the coast when the dust-laden *khamsin* wind blows north from the Sahara (Mar–Jun).

National holidays

Jan 7 (Coptic Christmas), Apr 25 (Sinai Liberation), May 1, Jul 23 (Revolution), Oct 6 (Armed Forces); Ad (3), EM (Coptic), ER (2), NY (Muslim), PB.

Political leaders

Khedive

1895–1914	Abbas Helmi II

Sultan

1914–17	Hussein Kamel
1917–22	Ahmed Fouad

Kingdom of Egypt

Monarch

1922–36	Fouad I
1936–7	Farouk *Trusteeship*
1937–52	Farouk I

Republic of Egypt

President

1953–4	Mohammed Najib
1954–70	Gamal Abdel Nasser
1970–81	Mohammed Anwar El-Sadat
1981–	Mohammed Hosni Mubarak

Prime Minister

1895–1908	Mustafa Fahmy
1908–10	Butros Ghali
1910–14	Mohammed Said
1914–19	Hussein Rushdi
1919	Mohammed Said
1919–20	Yousuf Wahba
1920–1	Mohammed Tewfiq Nazim
1921–2	Adli Yegen
1922	Abdel Khaliq Tharwat
1922–3	Mohammed Tewfiq Nazim
1923–4	Yehia Ibrahim
1924	Saad Zaghloul
1924–6	Ahmed Zaywan
1926–7	Adli Yegen
1927–8	Abdel Khaliq Tharwat
1928	Mustafa An-Nahass
1928–9	Mohammed Mahmoud
1929–30	Adli Yegen
1930	Mustafa An-Nahass
1930–3	Ismail Sidqi
1933–4	Abdel Fattah Yahya
1934–6	Mohammed Tewfiq Nazim
1936	Ali Maher
1936–7	Mustafa An-Nahass
1937–9	Mohammed Mahmoud
1939–40	Ali Maher
1940	Hassan Sabri
1940–2	Hussein Sirry
1942–4	Mustafa An-Nahass
1944–5	Ahmed Maher
1945–6	Mahmoud Fahmy El-Nuqrashi
1946	Ismail Sidqi
1946–8	Mahmoud Fahmy El-Nuqrashi
1948–9	Ibrahim Abdel Hadi
1949–50	Hussein Sirry
1950–2	Mustafa An-Nahass
1952	Ali Maher
1952	Najib El-Hilali
1952	Hussein Sirry
1952	Najib El-Hilali
1952	Ali Maher
1952–4	Mohammed Najib
1954	Gamal Abdel Nasser
1954	Mohammed Najib
1954–62	Gamal Abdel Nasser
1958–61	*United Arab Republic*
1962–5	Ali Sabri
1965–6	Zakariya Mohyi Ed-Din
1966–7	Mohammed Sidqi Soliman
1967–70	Gamal Abdel Nasser
1970–2	Mahmoud Fawzi
1972–3	Aziz Sidki
1973–4	Mohammed Anwar El-Sadat
1974–5	Abdel Aziz Hijazy
1975–8	Mamdouh Salem
1978–80	Mustafa Khalil
1980–1	Mohammed Anwar El-Sadat
1981–2	Mohammed Hosni Mubarak
1982–4	Fouad Monyi Ed-Din
1984	Kamal Hassan Ali
1985–6	Ali Lotfi
1986–96	Atif Sidqi
1996–1999	Ahmed Kamal Al-Ganzouri
1999–2004	Atef Muhammed Ebeid
2004–	Ahmed Nazif

Ancient Egyptian dynasties

All dates are BC.

c.3100–2890	I	*Early Dynastic Period*
c.2890–2686	II	(First use of stone in building; hieroglyphic script developed.)
c.2686–2613	III	*Old Kingdom*
c.2613–2494	IV	(The age of the great pyramid builders. Longest reign in history: Pepi II, 90 years.)
c.2494–2345	V	
c.2345–2181	VI	
c.2181–2173	VII	*First Intermediate Period*
c.2173–2160	VIII	(Social order upset; few monuments built.)
c.2160–2130	IX	
c.2130–2040	X	
c.2133–1991	XI	
1991–1786	XII	*Middle Kingdom*
1786–1633	XIII	(Golden age of art and craftsmanship.)
1786–c.1603	XIV	*Second Intermediate Period*
1674–1567	XV	(Country divided into principalities.)
c.1684–1567	XVI	
c.1660–1567	XVII	
1567–1320	XVIII	*New Kingdom*
1320–1200	XIX	(Began with colonial expansion, ended in divided rule.)
1200–1085	XX	
1085–945	XXI	*Third Intermediate Period*
945–745	XXII	(Revival of prosperity and restoration of cults.)
745–718	XXIII	
718–715	XXIV	
715–668	XXV	
664–525	XXVI	*Late Period*
525–404	XXVII	(Completion of Nile–Red Sea canal. Alexander the Great reached Alexandria in 332 BC.)
404–399	XXVIII	
399–380	XXIX	
380–343	XXX	
343–332	XXXI	

see also **EGYPTIAN GODS** *under* **RELIGIONS, BELIEFS AND FOLKLORE** *and* **SEVEN WONDERS OF THE WORLD** *under* **ANCIENT GREECE AND ROME**

ÉIRE *see* **IRELAND**

EL SALVADOR

Official name	Republic of El Salvador
Local name	El Salvador; República de El Salvador
Independence	1841
Area	21 476 sq km/8 290 sq mi
Capital	San Salvador
Chief towns	Santa Ana, San Miguel, Mejicanos
Population	6 948 000 (2007e)
Nationality	Salvadoran
Languages	Spanish
Ethnic groups	mestizo 90%, white 9%, Amerindian 1%
Religions	Christianity 82% (RC 57%, Prot 25%), unaffiliated 17%, others 1%
Time zone	GMT –6
Currency	1 US Dollar ($, US$/USD) = 100 cents
Telephone	+503
Internet	.sv
Country code	SLV

Location
A republic in Central America, bounded to the north and east by Honduras; to the south by the Pacific Ocean; and to the west by Guatemala.

Physical description
Two volcanic ranges running east to west; highest volcano is Santa Ana (Ilamatepec) at 2 362m/7 749ft; terrain ranges from a narrow coastal belt in the south through upland valleys and plateaux to mountains in the north; highest point is Cerro El Pital (2 730m/8 957ft); many volcanic lakes; earthquakes are common.

Climate
Varies greatly with altitude; hot and tropical on the coastal lowlands; single rainy season (May–Oct); temperate uplands; average annual temperature at San Salvador is 23°C.

National holidays
Jan 1, May 1, Aug 4–6 (Patronal festivals), Sep 15 (Independence), Nov 2, Dec 25; ES, GF, HS, HT; *some local variation; public and private sector holidays may differ*.

Political leaders

President

1899–1903	Tomás Regalado
1903–7	Pedro José Escalon
1907–11	Fernando Figueroa
1911–13	Manuel Enrique Araujo
1913–14	Carlos Meléndez *President Designate*
1914–15	Alfonso Quiñónez Molina *President Designate*
1915–18	Carlos Meléndez
1918–19	Alfonso Quiñónez Molina *Vice President*
1919–23	Jorge Meléndez
1923–7	Alfonso Quiñónez Molina
1927–31	Pio Romero Bosque
1931	Arturo Araujo
1931	*Military Administration*
1931–4	Maximiliano H Martinez *Vice President*
1934–5	Andrés I Menéndez *Provisional*
1935–44	Maximiliano H Martinez
1944	Andrés I Menéndez *Vice President*
1944–5	Osmin Aguirre y Salinas *Provisional*
1945–8	Salvador Castaneda Castro
1948–50	*Revolutionary Council*
1950–6	Oscar Osorio
1956–60	José María Lemus
1960–1	*Military Junta*
1961–2	*Civil-Military Administration*
1962	Rodolfo Eusebio Cordón *Provisional*
1962–7	Julio Adalberto Rivera
1967–72	Fidel Sánchez Hernández

1972–7	Arturo Armando Molina	1984–9	José Napoleón Duarte
1977–9	Carlos Humberto Romero	1989–94	Alfredo Cristiani
1979–82	*Military Juntas*	1994–9	Armando Calderón Sol
1982–4	*Government of National Unanimity* (Alvaro Magaña)	1999–2004	Francisco Flores Perez
		2004–	Elias Antonio Saca

ENGLAND *see* UNITED KINGDOM

EQUATORIAL GUINEA

Official name	Republic of Equatorial Guinea
Local name	Guinea Ecuatorial; República de Guinea Ecuatorial
Former name	Spanish Guinea (until 1968)
Independence	1968
Area	26016 sq km/10042 sq mi
Capital	Malabo
Chief towns	Bata and Evinayong on the mainland, Luba and Riaba on Bioko
Population	551000 (2007e)
Nationality	Equatorial Guinean or Equatoguinean
Languages	Spanish, French; pidgin English and Fang are also spoken
Ethnic groups	Fang 82%, Bubi 11%, Ndowe 4%, others 3%
Religions	Christianity 93% (RC 87%, Prot 6%), traditional beliefs 5%, Islam 1%, none/unaffiliated 1%
Time zone	GMT +1
Currency	1 CFA Franc (CFAFr/XAF) = 100 centimes
Telephone	+240
Internet	.gq
Country code	GNQ

Location
A republic in western central Africa, comprising a mainland area (Río Muni), bounded to the north by Cameroon; to the east and south by Gabon; and to the west by the Gulf of Guinea; and several islands (notably Bioko and Annobón) in the Gulf of Guinea.

Physical description
Mainland rises sharply from a narrow coast of mangrove swamps towards the heavily-forested African plateau; Bioko Island, about 160km/100mi north-west of the mainland, is of volcanic origin, rising to 3007m/9865ft at Pico de Basilé.

Climate
Hot and humid equatorial; average maximum daily temperature is 29–32°C.

National holidays
Jan 1, May 1, Jun 5 (President's Birthday), Aug 3 (Armed Forces), Oct 12 (Independence), Dec 8, 25; CC, GF, Constitution (Aug).

Political leaders

President

1968–79	Francisco Macias Nguema
1979–	Teodoro Obiang Nguema Mbasogo

Prime Minister

1963–8	Bonifacio Ondó Edu	1996–2001	Ángel Serafín Seriche Dougan
1968–82	*No Prime Minister*	2001–4	Cándido Muatetema Rivas
1982–92	Cristino Seriche Bioko	2004–6	Miguel Abia Biteo Boricó
1992–6	Silestre Siale Bileka	2006–	Ricardo Mangue Obama Nfubea

Misleading Monicker

Despite its name, mainland Equatorial Guinea is not in fact crossed by the Equator. However, the Equator does pass between the mainland and one of its islands, Annobón.

ERITREA

Official name	State of Eritrea
Local name	Hagere Eretra, al-Dawla al-Iritra
Former name	formerly part of Ethiopia (until 1993)
Independence	1993
Area	121 320 sq km/46 841 sq mi
Capital	Asmara; Asmera
Chief towns	Assab, Massawa, Keren, Tessenai
Population	4 906 000 (2007e)
Nationality	Eritrean
Languages	Arabic, Tigrinya
Ethnic groups	Tigrinya 50%, Tigrean 35%, Afar 4%, Saho 3%, Kunama 3%, others 5%
Religions	Islam 60% (Sunni), Christianity 37% (Coptic etc 32%, RC 5%), others 3%
Time zone	GMT +3
Currency	1 Nakfa (Nfa/ERN) = 100 cents
Telephone	+291
Internet	.er
Country code	ERI

Location

A country in north-east Africa, bounded to the north and west by Sudan; to the north-east by the Red Sea; to the south-east by Djibouti; and to the south by Ethiopia.

Physical description

Low-lying coastline stretching 1 000km/620mi along the Red Sea, rising to an inland plateau; highest point is Soira (3 018m/9 901ft).

Climate

Hot and dry along the Red Sea desert coast; cooler and wetter in the central highlands; semi-arid in the western hills and lowlands.

National holidays

Jan 1, 19 (Coptic Epiphany), Feb 10 (Fenkil), May 24 (Independence/Liberation), Jun 20 (Martyrs), Sep 1 (Revolution); *much religious and regional variation, often including:* Jan 7 (Coptic Christmas), Mar 8 (Women), May 1, Sep 27 (Feast of the Cross); Ad, ER, ES (Coptic), GF (Coptic), NY (Coptic), NY (Muslim), PB.

Political leaders

President

1993– Isaias Afewerki

ESTONIA

Official name	Republic of Estonia
Local name	Eesti; Eesti Vabariik (Estonian), Estonskaya (Russian)
Former name	Estonian Soviet Socialist Republic (1940–90), within the Union of Soviet Socialist Republics (USSR; 1940–91)
Independence	1991
Area	45 100 sq km/17 409 sq mi
Capital	Tallinn
Chief towns	Tartu, Narva, Kohtla-Järve, Pärnu
Population	1 316 000 (2007e)
Nationality	Estonian
Languages	Estonian
Ethnic groups	Estonian 68%, Russian 26%, Ukrainian 2%, Belarussian 1%, Finnish 1%, others 2%
Religions	Christianity 28% (Lutheran Prot 14%, Orthodox 13%, other 1%), unaffiliated 34%, others/unspecified 32%, none 6%
Time zone	GMT +2
Currency	1 Kroon (KR/EEK) = 100 sents
Telephone	+372
Internet	.ee
Country code	EST

Location

A republic in north-eastern Europe, bounded to the north by the Gulf of Finland; to the east by Russia; to the south by Latvia; and to the west by the Baltic Sea.

Physical description

Over 1 500 lakes in a fairly flat terrain; highest point is Suur Munamagi (318m/1 043ft); there are many islands on the coast, notably Saaremaa, Hiiumaa and Muhu; 36% of the area is forested.

Climate

Cool summers, wet winters.

National holidays

Jan 1, Feb 24 (Independence), May 1, Jun 23 (Victory), 24 (St John/Midsummer), Aug 20 (Restoration of Independence), Dec 25, 26; GF, Whit Sunday.

Political leaders

President

1990–2	Arnold Rüütel
1992–2001	Lennart Meri
2001–6	Arnold Rüütel
2006–	Toomas Hendrik Ilves

Prime Minister

1990–2	Edgar Savisaar
1992	Tiit Vähi
1992–4	Mart Laar
1994–5	Andres Tarand
1995–7	Tiit Vähi
1997–9	Mart Siimann
1999–2002	Mart Laar
2002–3	Siim Kallas
2003–5	Juhan Parts
2005–	Andrus Ansip

ETHIOPIA

Official name	Federal Democratic Republic of Ethiopia
Local name	Ityopya; Ya'Ityopya Federalawi Dimokrasyawi Repeblik
Former name	Abyssinia (until 1936), part of Italian East Africa (1936–41), People's Democratic Republic of Ethiopia (1987–91)
Area	1 128 497 sq km/435 600 sq mi
Capital	Addis Ababa; Ādīs Ābeba, Addis Abeba
Chief towns	Dire Dawa, Harer
Population	76 512 000 (2007e)
Nationality	Ethiopian
Languages	Amharic; 70 local languages are also spoken
Ethnic groups	Oromo 40%, Amhara and Tigrean 32%, Sidamo 9%, Shankella 6%, Somali 6%, others 7%
Religions	Islam 47%, Christianity 36% (Coptic), traditional beliefs 12%, others 5%
Time zone	GMT +3
Currency	1 Ethiopian Birr (EB/ETB) = 100 cents
Telephone	+251
Internet	.et
Country code	ETH

Location

A republic in north-east Africa, bounded to the north by Djibouti and Eritrea; to the east and south-east by Somalia; to the south by Kenya; and to the west and south-west by Sudan.

Physical description

Dominated by a mountainous central plateau; split diagonally by the Great Rift Valley; highest point is Ras Dashen (4 620m/15 157ft); plateau is crossed east to west by the Blue Nile, which has its source in Lake Tana; north and east are relatively low-lying; in the north-east the Danakil Depression dips to 116m/381ft below sea level; the country is landlocked, having lost about 10% of its territory and all of its Red Sea coastline when the former province of Eritrea gained its independence in 1993.

Climate

Tropical, moderated by higher altitudes; distinct wet season (Apr–Sep); temperatures warm, but rarely hot all year round; hot, semi-arid north-east and south-east lowlands; severe droughts in the 1980s caused widespread famine.

National holidays

Jan 7 (Coptic Christmas), 19 (Coptic Epiphany), Mar 2 (Victory of Adowa), May 1, 5 (Patriots), 28 (Downfall of the Dergue), Sep 12 (Coptic NY), 28 (Finding of the True Cross); Ad, ER, ES (Coptic), GF (Coptic), PB.

Political leaders

Monarch

1889–1911 Menelik II
1911–16 Lij Iyasu (Joshua)
1916–28 Zawditu
1928–74 Haile Selassie *Emperor from 1930*

Chairman of Provisional Military Administrative Council

1974–7 Teferi Benti
1977–87 Mengistu Haile Mariam

President

1987–91 Mengistu Haile Mariam
1991 Tesfaye Gebre Kidan *Acting*
1991–5 Meles Zenawi
1995–2001 Negasso Gidada
2001– Girma Wolde-Giorgis

Prime Minister

1987–9	Fikre Selassie Wogderess	1991–5	Tamirat Layne *Acting*
1989–91	Haile Yimenu *Acting*	1995–	Meles Zenawi
1991	Tesfaye Dinka *Acting*		

FALKLAND ISLANDS *see* UNITED KINGDOM

FAROE ISLANDS *see* DENMARK

FIJI

Official name	Republic of the Fiji Islands
Local name	Matanitu Ko Viti
Former name	Republic of Fiji (1987–98)
Independence	1970
Area	18 333 sq km/7 076 sq mi
Capital	Suva
Chief towns	Lautoka, Ba, Labasa, Nadi, Nausori
Population	919 000 (2007e)
Nationality	Fijian
Languages	Fijian, Hindi
Ethnic groups	Fijian 55%, Indian 37%, others 8%
Religions	Christianity 46% (Prot 37%, mainly Methodist, RC 9%), Hinduism 38%, Islam 8%, Sikhism 1%, others 7%
Time zone	GMT +12
Currency	1 Fiji Dollar (F$/FJD) = 100 cents
Telephone	+679
Internet	.fj
Country code	FJI

Location
An independent republic in the south-west Pacific Ocean.

Physical description
A Melanesian island group of 844 islands and islets, of which approximately 100 are permanently inhabited; larger islands are generally mountainous; highest peak, Tomaniivi, is on Viti Levu (1 324m/4 348ft); smaller islands consist of limestone, with little vegetation; extensive coral reef (Great Sea Reef) stretches for 500km/300mi along western fringe.

Climate
Winds are variable in the wet season between Nov and Apr, with tropical cyclonic storms likely; temperatures average 23–27°C; humidity on the windward slopes averages 74%.

National holidays
Jan 1, Dec 25, 26; D, EM, GF, HS, PB; Fiji (Oct), Queen's Birthday (Jun), Ratu Sir Lala Sukuna (May), Youth and Commonwealth (Mar).

Political leaders

Head of State until 1987: British monarch, represented by Governor General.

Governor General

1970–3	Robert Sidney Foster	1987	*Military Administration* (Sitiveni Rabuka)
1973–83	George Cakobau		
1983–7	Penaia Ganilau		

President

1987–93	Penaia Ganilau	2000–	Ratu Josefa Iloilo *Interim President until 2001*
1993–2000	Kamisese Mara		
2000	*Interim Military Government* (Frank Bainimarama)		

Prime Minister

1970–87	Kamisese Mara	2000	Epeli Nailatika *Interim*
1987	Timoci Bavadra	2000–1	Laisenia Qarase
1987–92	Kamisese Mara	2001	Tevita Momoedonu
1992–9	Sitiveni Rabuka	2001–6	Laisenia Qarase
1999–2000	Mahendra Chaudhry	2006–7	Jona Senilagakali *Interim*
2000	Tevita Momoedonu *Acting*	2007–	Frank Bainimarama *Interim*

Whales' Teeth

One of the national symbols of Fiji is the *tabua*, a whale's tooth. Historically very rare, the tabua is of supreme importance in Fijian traditions. Highly prized in ceremonies, it is regarded as a symbol of peace, understanding and love.

FINLAND

Official name	Republic of Finland
Local name	Suomi; Suomen Tasavalta (Finnish), Republiken Finland (Swedish)
Independence	1917
Area	338 145 sq km/130 524 sq mi
Capital	Helsinki (Finnish), Helsingfors (Swedish)
Chief towns	Tampere, Turku, Espoo, Vantaa
Population	5 238 000 (2007e)
Nationality	Finnish
Languages	Finnish, Swedish
Ethnic groups	Finnish 93%, Swedish 6%, others 1%
Religions	Christianity 86% (Prot 84%, Orthodox 1%, other 1%), none/unaffiliated 14%
Time zone	GMT +2
Currency	1 Euro (€/EUR) = 100 cents
Telephone	+358
Internet	.fi
Country code	FIN

Location

A republic in northern Europe, bounded to the north by Norway; to the east by Russia; to the south by the Gulf of Finland; and to the west by the Gulf of Bothnia and Sweden.

Physical description

A low-lying glaciated plateau; over one-third of the country is north of the Arctic Circle; highest peak is Halti (1 328m/4 356ft); over 60 000 shallow lakes in the south-east; Saaristomeri archipelago has over 17 000 islands; 65% is forest and 10% water.

Climate

Northern location is ameliorated by the Baltic Sea; western winds bring warm air currents in summer; Eurasian winds bring cold spells in winter and heatwaves in summer; during summer the sun stays above the horizon for over 70 days.

National holidays

Jan 1, 6, May 1, Nov 1, Dec 6 (Independence), 25, 26; A, EM, ES, GF, Midsummer Day (Jun), Whit Sunday (May/Jun).

Political leaders

Finland was under Swedish control from the 13c until it was ceded to Russia in 1809. Russian rulers then assumed the title of Grand Duke of Finland. In 1917 it became an independent monarchy. However in Nov 1918, after initially accepting the throne the previous month, Landgrave Frederick Charles of Hesse, the brother-in-law of the German Emperor Wilhelm II, withdrew his acceptance because of the Armistice and the ensuing abdication of Wilhelm II. The previous regent remained in power until a Republic was declared in Jul 1919.

Monarch

1918	Dr Pehr Evind Svinhufvud *Regent*
1918	Landgrave Frederick Charles of Hesse *(withdrew acceptance)*
1918–19	Dr Pehr Evind Svinhufvud *Regent*

President

1919–25	Kaarlo Ståhlberg
1925–31	Lauri Relander
1931–7	Pehr Svinhufvud
1937–40	Kyösti Kallio
1940–4	Risto Ryti
1944–6	C G E Mannerheim
1946–56	Juho Paasikivi
1956–82	Urho Kekkonen
1982–94	Mauno Koivisto
1994–2000	Martti Ahtisaari
2000–	Tarja Halonen

Prime Minister

1917–18	Pehr Svinhufvud
1918	Juho Paasikivi
1918–19	Lauri Ingman
1919	Kaarlo Castrén
1919–20	Juho Vennola
1920–1	Rafael Erich
1921–2	Juho Vennola
1922	Aino Cajander
1922–4	Kyösti Kallio
1924	Aino Cajander
1924–5	Lauri Ingman
1925	Antti Tulenheimo
1925–6	Kyösti Kallio
1926–7	Väinö Tanner
1927–8	Juho Sunila
1928–9	Oskari Mantere
1929–30	Kyösti Kallio
1930–1	Pehr Svinhufvud
1931–2	Juhu Sunila
1932–6	Toivo Kivimäki
1936–7	Kyösti Kallio
1937–9	Aino Cajander
1939–41	Risto Ryti
1941–3	Johann Rangell
1943–4	Edwin Linkomies
1944	Andreas Hackzell
1944	Urho Castrén
1944–5	Juho Paasikivi
1946–8	Mauno Pekkala
1948–50	Karl Fagerholm
1950–3	Urho Kekkonen
1953–4	Sakari Tuomioja
1954	Ralf Törngren
1954–6	Urho Kekkonen
1956–7	Karl Fagerholm
1957	Väinö Sukselainen
1957–8	Rainer von Fieandt
1958	Reino Kuuskoski
1958–9	Karl Fagerholm
1959–61	Väinö Sukselainen
1961–2	Martti Miettunen
1962–3	Ahti Karjalainen
1963–4	Reino Lehto
1964–6	Johannes Virolainen
1966–8	Rafael Paasio
1968–70	Mauno Koivisto
1970	Teuvo Aura
1970–1	Ahti Karjalainen
1971–2	Teuvo Aura
1972	Rafael Paasio
1972–5	Kalevi Sorsa
1975	Keijo Liinamaa
1975–7	Martti Miettunen
1977–9	Kalevi Sorsa
1979–82	Mauno Koivisto
1982–7	Kalevi Sorsa

1987–91	Harri Holkeri	2003	Anneli Jäätteenmäki
1991–5	Esko Aho	2003–	Matti Vanhanen
1995–2003	Paavo Lipponen		

Curious Contests

Finland hosts some of the world's strangest competitions. The most famous is perhaps the Wife Carrying World Championships, which take place annually in Sonkajärvi. Contestants must carry a woman (although not necessarily their own wife) over a 253m/830ft track, with the fastest couple winning the wife's weight in beer. But while this contest is believed to have its roots in a traditional Finnish custom, some of the other competitions are of rather more recent vintage. The World Air Guitar Championships take place in Oulu, and the Mobile Phone Throwing World Championships in Savonlinna; both attract thousands of spectators and media attention from around the world.

FRANCE

Official name	French Republic
Local name	France; République Française
Area	551 000 sq km/213 000 sq mi
Capital	Paris
Chief towns	Marseilles, Lyons, Toulouse, Nice, Strasbourg
Population	60 876 000 (2007e)
Nationality	French
Languages	French
Ethnic groups	European, with North African, German, Indochinese and Basque minorities
Religions	Christianity 88% (RC 86%, Prot 2%), Islam 7%, Judaism 1%, none/unaffiliated 4%
Time zone	GMT +1
Currency	1 Euro (€/EUR) = 100 cents
Telephone	+33
Internet	.fr
Country code	FRA

Location

A republic in western Europe, bounded to the north-west by the English Channel; to the north-east by Belgium, Luxembourg and Germany; to the east by Germany, Switzerland, Italy and Monaco; to the south by the Mediterranean Sea, Spain and Andorra; and to the west by the Bay of Biscay; also includes the island of Corsica in the Mediterranean Sea.

Physical description

A country of low and medium-sized hills and plateaux deeply cut by rivers; bounded to the south and east by large mountain ranges; the Alps rise to 4 807m/15 771ft at Mont Blanc (the highest point) in the east, and the Pyrenees lie to the south; many major rivers.

Climate

South has a Mediterranean climate, with warm, moist winters and hot, dry summers; climate is maritime in the north-west; east has a continental climate.

National holidays

Jan 1, May 1, 8 (Victory), Jul 14 (Bastille), Aug 15, Nov 1, 11 (Armistice), Dec 25; A, EM, WM.

Overseas departments

French Guiana

Location	Situated on the north-eastern coast of South America, it is bounded to the west by Suriname; to the east and south by Brazil; and to the north by the Atlantic Ocean.		
Local name	Guyane	**Population**	199 000 (2006e)
Area	90 909 sq km/35 091 sq mi	**Internet**	.gf
Capital	Cayenne	**Country code**	GUF

Guadeloupe

Location	A group of five islands in the central Lesser Antilles, in the east Caribbean Sea.		
Local name	Guadeloupe	**Population**	453 000 (2006e)
Area	1 704 sq km/658 sq mi	**Internet**	.gp
Capital	Basse-Terre	**Country code**	GLP

Martinique

Location	An island in the Windward group of the Lesser Antilles, in the east Caribbean Sea, between Dominica and St Lucia.		
Local name	Martinique	**Population**	436 000 (2006e)
Area	1 079 sq km/416 sq mi	**Internet**	.mq
Capital	Fort-de-France	**Country code**	MTQ

Réunion

Location	An island in the Indian Ocean, to the east of Madagascar.		
Local name	Réunion	**Population**	787 000 (2006e)
Area	2 510 sq km/969 sq mi	**Internet**	.re
Capital	St Denis	**Country code**	REU

Overseas territories

French Polynesia

Location	An island grouping of five scattered archipelagoes in the south-east Pacific Ocean, between the Cook Islands in the west and the Pitcairn Islands in the east.		
Local name	Polynésie Française	**Population**	279 000 (2007e)
Area	3 941 sq km/1 521 sq mi	**Internet**	.pf
Capital	Papeete	**Country code**	PYF

New Caledonia

Location	A group of islands in the south-west Pacific Ocean, 1 100km/680mi east of Australia.		
Local name	Nouvelle-Calédonie	**Population**	222 000 (2007e)
Area	18 575 sq km/7 170 sq mi	**Internet**	.nc
Capital	Nouméa	**Country code**	NCL

French Southern and Antarctic Territories

Location	A group of islands in the southern Indian Ocean and Adélie Land in Antarctica.		
Local name	Terres australes et antarctiques françaises	**Population**	Scientific staff only
		Internet	.tf
Area	507781 sq km/196003 sq mi	**Country code**	ATF

Wallis and Futuna Islands

Location	An island grouping (consisting principally of Wallis Island (Uvéa), Futuna and Alofi) in the south-central Pacific Ocean, lying north-east of Fiji.		
Local name	Îles de Wallis et Futuna	**Population**	16000 (2007e)
Area	274 sq km/106 sq mi	**Internet**	.wf
Capital	Mata-Utui; Matâ'utu	**Country code**	WLF

DOM-TOM

French overseas departments and territories are collectively known as the *DOM-TOM*, *Départements d'outre-mer* and *Territoires d'outre-mer*. In contrast, the mainland of France is often known as *l'Hexagone*, a reference to its roughly hexagonal shape.

Territorial collectivities

Mayotte

Location	A small island group of volcanic origin, east of Comoros, in the west Indian Ocean.		
Local name	Mayotte	**Population**	209000 (2007e)
Area	374 sq km/144 sq mi	**Internet**	.yt
Capital	Mamoudzou	**Country code**	MYT

St Barthelémy

Location	A small island in the Pacific Ocean, north-west of Guadeloupe and east of Puerto Rico.		
Local name	St-Barthelémy	**Population**	6900 (1999)
Area	21 sq km/8 sq mi	**Internet**	.bl
Capital	Gustavia	**Country code**	BLM

St Martin

Location	The northern half of the island of St Martin in the Pacific Ocean, north-west of Guadeloupe and south-east of Puerto Rico.		
Local name	St-Martin	**Population**	33100 (2004)
Area	54.4 sq km/21 sq mi	**Internet**	.mf
Capital	Marigot	**Country code**	MAF

St Pierre and Miquelon

Location	Two islands in the North Atlantic Ocean, south of Newfoundland (Canada).		
Local name	St-Pierre-et-Miquelon	**Population**	7000 (2007e)
Area	240 sq km/93 sq mi	**Internet**	.pm
Capital	St Pierre	**Country code**	SPM

Note: France also possesses Bassas da India, Europa Island, the Glorioso Islands, Juan de Nova and Tromelin Island in the Indian Ocean and Clipperton Island in the Pacific Ocean, all largely uninhabited.

Political leaders

Monarch

987–996	Hugh Capet
996–1031	Robert II
1031–60	Henry I
1060–1108	Philip I
1108–37	Louis VI
1137–80	Louis VII
1180–1223	Philip II Augustus
1223–6	Louis VIII
1226–70	Louis IX
1270–85	Philip III
1285–1314	Philip IV
1314–16	Louis X
1316	John I
1316–22	Philip V
1322–8	Charles IV
1328–50	Philip VI
1350–64	John II
1364–80	Charles V
1380–1422	Charles VI
1422–61	Charles VII
1461–83	Louis XI
1483–98	Charles VIII
1498–1515	Louis XII
1515–47	Francis I
1547–59	Henry II
1559–60	Francis II
1560–74	Charles IX
1574–89	Henry III
1589–1610	Henry IV (of Navarre)
1610–43	Louis XIII
1643–1715	Louis XIV
1715–74	Louis XV
1774–92	Louis XVI
1793–1804	*Republic*
1804–14	*Empire* (Napoleon Bonaparte)
1814–24	Louis XVIII
1824–30	Charles X
1830–48	Louis-Philippe
1848	*monarchy dissolved*

Royal Nicknames

Derogatory nicknames for early French kings include the *Bald* (Charles I, 823–77), the *Fat* (Charles II, 839–88) and the *Simple* (Charles III, 879–929). But they weren't all bad. There was also the *Fair* (Charles IV, 1294–1328), the *Wise* (Charles V, 1338–80), the *Victorious* (Charles VII, 1403–61), the *Affable* (Charles VIII, 1470–98), the *Well-Beloved* (Louis XV, 1710–74) and, of course, the *Sun King* himself, Louis XIV (1638–1715).

Third Republic

President

1899–1906	Emile Loubet
1906–13	Armand Fallières
1913–20	Raymond Poincaré
1920	Paul Deschanel
1920–4	Alexandre Millerand
1924–31	Gaston Doumergue
1931–2	Paul Doumer
1932–40	Albert Lebrun

Prime Minister

1899–1902	Pierre Waldeck-Rousseau
1902–5	Emile Combes
1905–6	Maurice Rouvier
1906	Jean Sarrien
1906–9	Georges Clemenceau
1909–11	Aristide Briand
1911	Ernest Monis
1911–12	Joseph Caillaux
1912–13	Raymond Poincaré
1913	Aristide Briand
1913	Jean Louis Barthou
1913–14	Gaston Doumergue
1914	Alexandre Ribot
1914–15	René Viviani
1915–17	Aristide Briand
1917	Alexandre Ribot
1917	Paul Painlevé
1917–20	Georges Clemenceau
1920	Alexandre Millerand
1920–1	Georges Leygues
1921–2	Aristide Briand
1922–4	Raymond Poincaré
1924	Frédéric François-Marsal
1924–5	Édouard Herriot
1925	Paul Painlevé
1925–6	Aristide Briand
1926	Édouard Herriot
1926–9	Raymond Poincaré
1929	Aristide Briand
1929–30	André Tardieu
1930	Camille Chautemps
1930	André Tardieu
1930–1	Théodore Steeg
1931–2	Pierre Laval
1932	André Tardieu
1932	Édouard Herriot
1932–3	Joseph Paul-Boncour
1933	Édouard Daladier
1933	Albert Sarrault
1933–4	Camille Chautemps
1934	Édouard Daladier
1934	Gaston Doumergue
1934–5	Pierre-Étienne Flandin
1935	Fernand Bouisson
1935–6	Pierre Laval
1936	Albert Sarrault
1936–7	Léon Blum
1937–8	Camille Chautemps
1938	Léon Blum
1938–40	Édouard Daladier
1940	Paul Reynaud
1940	Philippe Pétain

Vichy Government

President and Prime Minister

1940–4	Philippe Pétain

Provisional Government of the French Republic

President and Prime Minister

1944–6	Charles de Gaulle
1946	Félix Gouin
1946	Georges Bidault

Fourth Republic

President

1947–54	Vincent Auriol
1954–8	René Coty

Prime Minister

1946–7	Léon Blum
1947	Paul Ramadier
1947–8	Robert Schuman
1948	André Marie
1948	Robert Schuman
1948–9	Henri Queuille
1949–50	Georges Bidault
1950	Henri Queuille
1950–1	René Pleven
1951	Henri Queuille
1951–2	René Pleven
1952	Edgar Faure
1952–3	Antoine Pinay
1953	René Mayer
1953–4	Joseph Laniel
1954–5	Pierre Mendès-France
1955–6	Edgar Faure
1956–7	Guy Mollet

1957	Maurice Bourgès-Maunoury	1958	Pierre Pfimlin
1957–8	Félix Gaillard	1958–9	Charles de Gaulle

Fifth Republic

President

1958–69	Charles de Gaulle	1981–95	François Mitterrand
1969–74	Georges Pompidou	1995–2007	Jacques Chirac
1974–81	Valéry Giscard d'Estaing	2007–	Nicolas Sarkozy

Prime Minister

1959–62	Michel Debré	1988–91	Michel Rocard
1962–8	Georges Pompidou	1991–2	Édith Cresson
1968–9	Maurice Couve de Murville	1992–3	Pierre Bérégovoy
1969–72	Jacques Chaban Delmas	1993–5	Édouard Balladur
1972–4	Pierre Mesmer	1995–7	Alain Juppé
1974–6	Jacques Chirac	1997–2002	Lionel Jospin
1976–81	Raymond Barre	2002–5	Jean-Pierre Raffarin
1981–4	Pierre Mauroy	2005–7	Dominique de Villepin
1984–6	Laurent Fabius	2007–	François Fillon
1986–8	Jacques Chirac		

FRENCH GUIANA; FRENCH POLYNESIA; FRENCH SOUTHERN AND ANTARCTIC TERRITORIES *see* FRANCE

FUJAIRAH *see* UNITED ARAB EMIRATES

GABON

Official name	Gabonese Republic
Local name	Gabon; République Gabonaise
Former name	French West Africa (1910–60)
Independence	1960
Area	267 667 sq km/103 319 sq mi
Capital	Libreville
Chief towns	Lambaréné, Franceville, Port Gentil
Population	1 455 000 (2007e)
Nationality	Gabonese
Languages	French; local languages are widely spoken
Ethnic groups	Bantu tribes (Fang, Bapounou, Nzebi and Obamba are the main groupings) 89%, other Africans and Europeans 11%
Religions	Christianity 73%, Islam 12%, traditional beliefs 10%, unaffiliated 5%
Time zone	GMT +1
Currency	1 CFA Franc (CFAFr/XAF) = 100 centimes
Telephone	+241
Internet	.ga
Country code	GAB

Location
A republic in west Africa, crossed by the Equator, bounded to the north by Equatorial Guinea and Cameroon; to the east and south by Congo; and to the west by the Atlantic Ocean.

Physical description
On the Equator for 880km/550mi west to east; lagoons and estuaries on the coast; land rises towards the African central plateau, cut by several rivers, notably the Ogooué; highest point is Mont Iboundji (1 575m/5 167ft).

Climate
Typical equatorial climate, hot, wet and humid; Libreville has an average maximum daily temperature of 33–37°C.

National holidays
Jan 1, Apr 17 (Women), May 1, Aug 15, 16–17 (Independence), Nov 1, Dec 25; Ad, EM, ER, WM.

Political leaders

President

1960–7	Léon M'ba
1967–	Omar (*to 1973* Bernard-Albert) Bongo

Prime Minister

1960–75	*As President*
1975–90	Léon Mébiame (Mébiane)
1991–3	Casimir Oyé M'ba
1993–8	Paulin Obame-Nguema
1999–2006	Jean-François Ntoutoume-Emane
2006–	Jean Eyeghe Ndong

Hooded Cloak

The name Gabon is thought to come from the Portuguese word *gabão*, meaning a hooded cloak with sleeves, coined in reference to the shape of the coast and river estuary by Portuguese explorers in the late 15c.

THE GAMBIA

Official name	Republic of the Gambia
Local name	Gambia
Former name	Senegambia (with Senegal, 1982–9)
Independence	1965
Area	10 402 sq km/4 015 sq mi
Capital	Banjul
Chief towns	Serrekunda, Brikama, Bakau, Georgetown
Population	1 688 000 (2007e)
Nationality	Gambian
Languages	English; Mandinka, Fula and Wolof are also spoken
Ethnic groups	Mandinka 42%, Fulani 18%, Wolof 16%, Dyola 10%, Serahuli 9%, non-African 1%, others 4%
Religions	Islam 90%, Christianity 9%, traditional beliefs 1%
Time zone	GMT
Currency	1 Dalasi (D/GMD) = 100 butut
Telephone	+220
Internet	.gm
Country code	GMB

Location
A republic situated in west Africa, bounded by the Atlantic Ocean in the west and on all other sides by Senegal.

Physical description
A strip of land stretching 322km/200mi east to west along the River Gambia; flat country, not rising above 90m/295ft.

Climate
Tropical; rainy season Jun–Sep with rainfall decreasing inland; high humidity in the wet season with high night temperatures; average temperatures range from 23°C (Jan) to 27°C (Jul), rising inland to over 40°C.

National holidays
Jan 1, Feb 18 (Independence), May 1, Jul 22 (Revolution), Aug 15, Dec 25; Ad, As, EM, ER, GF, PB.

Political leaders

President

1965–94	Dawda Kairaba Jawara
1994–	Yahya Jammeh *Head of military junta 1994–6*

GAZA STRIP *see* PALESTINIAN AUTONOMOUS AREAS *under* ISRAEL

GEORGIA

Official name	Georgia
Local name	Sak'art'velos Respublikis
Former name	Georgian Democratic Republic (1918–21), Transcaucasian Soviet Federated Socialist Republic (with Armenia and Azerbaijan, 1922–36), Georgian Soviet Socialist Republic (1936–90), within the Union of Soviet Socialist Republics (USSR; 1922–91)
Independence	1991
Area	69 700 sq km/26 900 sq mi
Capital	T'bilisi or Tbilisi; also sometimes called Tiflis
Chief towns	Kutaisi, Rustavi, Batumi, Sukhumi, Poti
Population	4 646 000 (2007e)
Nationality	Georgian
Languages	Georgian, Russian; Abkhazia is an official language in that province
Ethnic groups	Georgian 84%, Azeri 6%, Armenian 6%, Russian 1%, others 3%
Religions	Christianity 84% (Georgian Orthodox 65%, Russian Orthodox 10%, Armenian Orthodox 8%, RC 1%), Islam 10%, others 1%, none 5%
Time zone	GMT +3
Currency	1 Lari (GEL) = 100 tetri
Telephone	+995
Internet	.ge
Country code	GEO

Location
A republic in central and western Transcaucasia, bounded to the north by Russia; to the east by Azerbaijan; to the south by Armenia; to the south-west by Turkey; and to the west by the Black Sea.

Physical description
Contains the Greater Caucasus in the north and the Lesser Caucasus in the south; forest covers approximately 39% of the land; highest point is Mt Shkhara (5 608m/18 399ft).

Climate
Subtropical, warm and humid in the west; continental in the east with hot summers and cold winters.

National holidays
Jan 1–2, 7 (Orthodox Christmas), 19 (Orthodox Epiphany), Mar 3 (Mothers), 8 (Women), Apr 9 (Independence Restoration), May 9 (Victory), 12 (St Andrew), 26 (Independence), Aug 28 (Orthodox Assumption), Oct 14 (Svetitskhovloba), Nov 23 (St George); ES, EM, GF, HS (all Orthodox).

Political leaders

President

1991–2	Zviad Gamsakhurdia
1992	*Military Council*
1992–2003	Eduard Shevardnadze
2003–4	Nino Burjanadze *Acting*
2004–	Mikhail Saakashvili

Prime Minister

1990–1	Tengiz Sigua
1991	Murman Omanidze *Acting*
1991–2	Bessarion Gugushvili
1992–3	Tengiz Sigua
1993	Eduard Shevardnadze *Acting*
1993–5	Otar Patsatsia

State Minister

1995–8	Niko Lekishvili
1998–2000	Vazha Lordkipanidze
2000–1	Giorgi Arsenishvili
2001–3	Avtandil Jorbenadze
2003–5	Zurab Zhvania
2005	Mikhail Saakashvili *Acting*
2005–7	Zurab Noghaideli
2007–	Lado Gurgenidze

Mkhedruli ABC

The Georgian language has its own unique alphabet, called Mkhedruli, which has been in use since the eleventh century. Each letter of this alphabet corresponds to a sound in the language. While the Georgian language was threatened during the Soviet era, today it is protected; there are a number of official state organizations devoted to its promotion and preservation.

GEORGIA, SOUTH *see* UNITED KINGDOM

GERMANY

Official name	Federal Republic of Germany
Local name	Deutschland; Bundesrepublik Deutschland
Former name	*as listed below under Political leaders*
Area	357 868 sq km/138 137 sq mi
Capital	Berlin
Chief towns	Bonn, Hamburg, Munich, Cologne, Essen, Leipzig, Frankfurt (am Main)
Population	82 401 000 (2007e)
Nationality	German
Languages	German; Sorbian (a Slavic language) is spoken by a few
Ethnic groups	German 92%, Turkish 2%, others 6%
Religions	Christianity 68% (Prot 34%, RC 34%), Islam 4%, others and unaffiliated 28%
Time zone	GMT +1
Currency	1 Euro (€/EUR) = 100 cents
Telephone	+49
Internet	.de
Country code	DEU

Location

An independent republic in central Europe, bounded to the north by the North Sea, Denmark and the Baltic Sea; to the east by Poland and the Czech Republic; to the south-east and south by Austria; to the south-west by Switzerland; and to the west by France, Luxembourg, Belgium and the Netherlands.

Physical description
Baltic coastline is backed by a fertile low-lying plain, low hills, and many glacial lakes; central uplands include the Black Forest; land rises in the south in several ranges, notably the Bavarian Alps; highest peak is the Zugspitze (2962m/9717ft); many major rivers.

Climate
Winters are mild but stormy in the north-west; elsewhere, the climate is continental (more temperate in the east); average winter temperatures 2°C (north) to –3°C (south); average summer temperature 16°C (north), slightly higher in the south.

National holidays
Jan 1, May 1, Oct 3 (German Unity), Dec 25, 26; A, EM, GF, WM; *much regional variation*.

German Feast

The German authorities estimate that there are over 550 sources of natural mineral water in Germany, and more than 1,200 breweries that produce over 5,000 different beers. German bakers have come up with more than 300 kinds of bread and over 1,200 types of biscuit and cake.

Political leaders

German Empire

Modern Germany was united under Prussia in 1871.

Emperor

1871–88	Wilhelm I
1888	Friedrich
1888–1918	Wilhelm II *abdicated 1918*

Chancellor

1909–17	Theobald von Bethmann Hollweg
1917	Georg Michaelis
1917–18	Georg Graf von Hertling
1918	Prince Max von Baden
1918	Friedrich Ebert

German Republic

President

1919–25	Friedrich Ebert
1925–34	Paul von Hindenburg

Reich Chancellor

1919	Philipp Scheidemann
1919–20	Gustav Bauer
1920	Hermann Müller
1920–1	Konstantin Fehrenbach
1921–2	Karl Joseph Wirth
1922–3	Wilhelm Cuno
1923	Gustav Stresemann
1923–4	Wilhelm Marx
1925–6	Hans Luther
1926–8	Wilhelm Marx
1928–30	Hermann Müller
1930–2	Heinrich Brüning
1932	Franz von Papen
1932–3	Kurt von Schleicher
1933	Adolf Hitler

Chancellor and Führer

1933–45	Adolf Hitler *Führer from 1934*
1945	Karl Dünitz

Allied Occupation

1945–9	*Military Governors*

German Democratic Republic (East Germany)

President

1949–60	Wilhelm Pieck

Chairman of the Council of State

1960–73	Walter Ernst Karl Ulbricht
1973–6	Willi Stoph
1976–89	Erich Honecker
1989	Egon Krenz
1989–90	Gregor Gysi *General Secretary as Chairman*

Premier

1949–64	Otto Grotewohl
1964–73	Willi Stoph
1973–6	Horst Sindermann
1976–89	Willi Stoph
1989–90	Hans Modrow
1990	Lothar de Maizière

German Federal Republic (West Germany)

President

1949–59	Theodor Heuss
1959–69	Heinrich Lübke
1969–74	Gustav Heinemann
1974–9	Walter Scheel
1979–84	Karl Carstens
1984–90	Richard von Weizsäcker

Chancellor

1949–63	Konrad Adenauer
1963–6	Ludwig Erhard
1966–9	Kurt Georg Kiesinger
1969–74	Willy Brandt
1974–82	Helmut Schmidt
1982–90	Helmut Kohl

Germany

President

1990–4	Richard von Weizsäcker
1994–9	Roman Herzog
1999–2004	Johannes Rau
2004–	Horst Köhler

Chancellor

1990–8	Helmut Kohl
1998–2005	Gerhard Schröder
2005–	Angela Merkel

Canine Luxury Tax

German dog owners have to pay an annual tax for their pooches. The tax is known as Hundesteuer – literally 'dog licence fee' – and started in Germany around 1810 under the assumption that someone who could afford to own an animal as a pet could also afford to pay a tax on it. The tax amount varies throughout the country; in Berlin the cost is €150 per year.

GHANA

Official name	Republic of Ghana
Local name	Ghana
Former name	British Gold Coast and British Togoland (until 1957)
Independence	1957
Area	238686 sq km/92133 sq mi
Capital	Accra
Chief towns	Sekondi-Takoradi, Kumasi, Tamale
Population	22931000 (2007e)
Nationality	Ghanaian
Languages	English; almost 50 African languages are also spoken
Ethnic groups	African 98% (of whom Akan 44%, Mossi 16%, Ewe 13%, Ga-Adangame 8%, Gurma 3%, Yoruba 1%), others 2%
Religions	Christianity 63%, traditional beliefs 21%, Islam 16%
Time zone	GMT
Currency	1 Cedi (₵/GHS) = 100 pesewas
Telephone	+233
Internet	.gh
Country code	GHA

Location

A republic in West Africa, bounded to the north by Burkina Faso; to the east by Togo; to the south by the Gulf of Guinea; and to the west by Côte d'Ivoire.

Physical description

Coastline of sand bars and lagoons; low-lying plains inland, leading to the Ashanti plateau in the west and the River Volta basin in the east, dammed to form Lake Volta; mountains rise in the east to 885m/2904ft at Afadjato.

Climate

Tropical climate, including a warm, dry coastal belt in the south-east, a hot, humid south-west corner, and hot, dry savanna in the north.

National holidays

Jan 1, Mar 6 (Independence), May 1, 25 (Africa), Jul 1 (Republic), Dec 25, 26, 31 (Revolution); Ad, EM, ER, GF; National Farmers (Dec).

Political leaders

President

1960–6 Kwame Nkrumah

Chairman of National Liberation Council

1966–9 Joseph Arthur Ankrah
1969 Akwasi Amankwa Afrifa
1969–70 *Presidential Committee*

President

1970–2 Edward Akufo-Addo

Chairman

1972–8 *National Redemption Council* (Ignatius Kuti Acheampong)
1978–9 *Supreme Military Council* (Fred W Akuffo)
1979 *Armed Forces Revolutionary Council* (Jerry John Rawlings)

President

1979–81 Hilla Limann

Chairman of Provisional National Defence Council

1981–2001	Jerry John Rawlings *President from 1992*

President

2001–	John Kufuor

Prime Minister

1960–9	*As President*	1972–8	*As President*
1969–72	Kufi Abrefa Busia	1978–	*No Prime Minister*

GIBRALTAR *see* UNITED KINGDOM

GREECE

Official name	Hellenic Republic
Local name	Ellas, Ellada; Elliniki Dimokratia
Former name	Kingdom of Greece (until 1924 and 1935–73), Republic of Greece (until 1935)
Independence	1832
Area	131 957 sq km/50 935 sq mi
Capital	Athens; Athína
Chief towns	Thessaloniki, Patras, Heraklion, Volos, Larisa, Piraieus
Population	10 706 000 (2007e)
Nationality	Greek
Languages	Greek
Ethnic groups	Greek 98%, Turkish and others 2%
Religions	Christianity 98% (Orthodox), Islam 1%, others 1%
Time zone	GMT +2
Currency	1 Euro (€/EUR) = 100 cents
Telephone	+30
Internet	.gr
Country code	GRC

Location

A republic in south-eastern Europe, occupying the southern part of the Balkan Peninsula and numerous islands in the Aegean and Ionian seas; bounded to the north by Albania and Macedonia; to the north-east by Bulgaria and to the east by Turkey.

Physical description

A large area of mainland, including the Peloponnese peninsula in the south, linked to the rest of the mainland by the narrow Isthmus of Corinth; over 6 000 islands, notably Crete, Euboea, Lesbos, Rhodes, Chios, Cephalonia, Lemnos, Samos, Naxos and Corfu; nearly 80% is mountainous or hilly; highest point is Mt Olympus (2 917m/9 570ft); several rivers and smaller lakes.

Climate

Mediterranean on the coast and islands, with mild, rainy winters and hot, dry summers; rainfall occurs almost entirely in the winter months.

National holidays

Jan 1, 6, Mar 25 (Independence), May 1, Aug 15, Oct 28 (Ochi), Dec 25, 26; EM, ES, GF, HS, WM, Shrove Monday (all Orthodox).

Political leaders

Monarch

1832–62	Otto of Bavaria	1920–2	Constantine I
1863–1913	George I	1922–3	George II
1913–17	Constantine I	1923–4	Paul Koundouriotis *Regent*
1917–20	Alexander		

President

1924–6	Paul Koundouriotis
1926	Theodore Pangalos
1926–9	Paul Koundouriotis
1929–35	Alexander T Zaïmis

Monarch

1935	George Kondylis *Regent*
1935–47	George II
1947–64	Paul
1964–7	Constantine II
1967–73	*Military Junta*
1973	George Papadopoulos *Regent*

President

1973	George Papadopoulos
1973–4	Phaedon Gizikis
1974–5	Michael Stasinopoulos
1975–80	Constantine Tsatsos
1980–5	Constantine Karamanlis
1985–90	Christos Sartzetakis
1990–5	Constantine Karamanlis
1995–2005	Constantine Stephanopoulos
2005–	Karolos Papoulias

Prime Minister

1899–1901	George Theotokis
1901–2	Alexander T Zaïmis
1902–3	Theodore Deligiannis
1903	George Theotokis
1903	Demetrius G Rallis
1903–4	George Theotokis
1904–5	Theodore Deligiannis
1905	Demetrius G Rallis
1905–9	George Theotokis
1909	Demetrius G Rallis
1909–10	Kyriakoulis P Mavromichalis
1910	Stephen N Dragoumis
1910–15	Eleftherios K Venizelos
1915	Demetrius P Gounaris
1915	Eleftherios K Venizelos
1915	Alexander T Zaïmis
1915–16	Stephen Skouloudis
1916	Alexander T Zaïmis
1916	Nicholas P Kalogeropoulos
1916–17	Spyridon Lambros
1917	Alexander T Zaïmis
1917–20	Eleftherios K Venizelos
1920–1	Demetrius G Rallis
1921	Nicholas P Kalogeropoulos
1921–2	Demetrius P Gounaris
1922	Nicholas Stratos
1922	Peter E Protopapadakis
1922	Nicholas Triandaphyllakos
1922	Sortirios Krokidas
1922	Alexander T Zaïmis
1922–3	Stylianos Gonatas
1924	Eleftherios K Venizelos
1924	George Kaphandaris
1924	Alexander Papanastasiou
1924	Themistocles Sophoulis
1924–5	Andreas Michalakopoulos
1925–6	Alexander N Chatzikyriakos
1926	Theodore Pangalos
1926	Athanasius Eftaxias
1926	George Kondylis
1926–8	Alexander T Zaïmis
1928–32	Eleftherios K Venizelos
1932	Alexander Papanastasiou
1932	Eleftherios K Venizelos
1932–3	Panagiotis Tsaldaris
1933	Eleftherios K Venizelos
1933	Nicholas Plastiras
1933	Alexander Othonaos
1933–5	Panagiotis Tsaldaris
1935	George Kondylis
1935–6	Constantine Demertzis
1936–41	John Metaxas
1941	Alexander Koryzis
1941	George II *Chairman of Ministers*
1941	*German Occupation* (Emmanuel Tsouderos)
1941–2	George Tsolakoglou
1942–3	Constantine Logothetopoulos
1943–4	John Rallis
1941–4	Emmanuel Tsouderos *Government in exile*
1944	Sophocles Venizelos *Government in exile*
1944–5	George Papandreou *Government in exile*
1945	Nicholas Plastiras
1945	Peter Voulgaris
1945	Damaskinos, Archbishop of Athens
1945	Panagiotis Kanellopoulos
1945–6	Themistocles Sophoulis

1946	Panagiotis Politzas
1946–7	Constantine Tsaldaris
1947	Demetrius Maximos
1947	Constantine Tsaldaris
1947–9	Themistocles Sophoulis
1949–50	Alexander Diomedes
1950	John Theotokis
1950	Sophocles Venizelos
1950	Nicholas Plastiras
1950–1	Sophocles Venizelos
1951	Nicholas Plastiras
1952	Demetrius Kiusopoulos
1952–5	Alexander Papagos
1955	Stephen C Stefanopoulos
1955–8	Constantine Karamanlis
1958	Constantine Georgakopoulos
1958–61	Constantine Karamanlis
1961	Constantine Dovas
1961–3	Constantine Karamanlis
1963	Panagiotis Pipinellis
1963	Stylianos Mavromichalis
1963	George Papandreou
1963–4	John Parskevopoulos
1964–5	George Papandreou
1965	George Athanasiadis-Novas
1965	Elias Tsirimokos
1965–6	Stephen C Stefanopoulos
1966–7	John Paraskevopoulos
1967	Panagiotis Kanellopoulos
1967–74	*Military Junta*
1967	Constantine Kollias
1967–73	George Papadopoulos
1973	Spyridon Markezinis
1973–4	Adamantios Androutsopoulos
1974–80	Constantine Karamanlis
1980–1	George Rallis
1981–9	Andreas Papandreou
1989	Tzannis Tzannetakis
1989–90	Xenofon Zolotas
1990–3	Constantine Mitsotakis
1993–6	Andreas Papandreou
1996–2004	Kostas Simitis
2004–	Kostas Karamanlis

Greek Islands

Greece includes around 6,000 islands, but just 227 are inhabited.

GREENLAND *see* DENMARK

GRENADA

Official name	State of Grenada
Local name	Grenada
Independence	1974
Area	344 sq km/133 sq mi
Capital	St George's
Chief towns	Gouyave, Victoria, Grenville
Population	90 000 (2007e)
Nationality	Grenadian or Grenadan
Languages	English
Ethnic groups	African descent 82%, mixed 13%, European and East Indian 5%
Religions	Christianity 100% (RC 53%, Prot 47%)
Time zone	GMT –4
Currency	1 East Caribbean Dollar (EC$/XCD) = 100 cents
Telephone	+1473
Internet	.gd
Country code	GRD

Location

An independent country of the West Indies, the most southerly of the Windward Islands in the eastern Caribbean Sea, comprising the main island of Grenada and the South Grenadines.

Physical description

Main island of Grenada is 34km/21mi long and 19km/12mi wide, of volcanic origin, with a ridge of mountains along its entire length; highest point is Mt St Catherine, which rises to 843m/2 766ft.

Climate

Subtropical; the average annual temperature is 23°C.

National holidays

Jan 1, Feb 7 (Independence), May 1, Aug 6 (Emancipation), Oct 25 (Thanksgiving), Dec 25, 26; C (Aug) (2), CC, EM, GF, WM.

Political leaders

Head of State: British monarch, represented by Governor General (Sir Daniel Williams since 1996).

Prime Minister

1974–9	Eric M Gairy
1979–83	Maurice Bishop
1983–4	Nicholas Brathwaite *Chairman of Interim Council*
1984–9	Herbert A Blaize
1989–90	Ben Jones
1990–5	Nicholas Brathwaite
1995–	Keith Mitchell

GRENADINES *see* ST VINCENT AND THE GRENADINES

GUADELOUPE *see* FRANCE

GUAM *see* UNITED STATES OF AMERICA

GUATEMALA

Official name	Republic of Guatemala
Local name	Guatemala; República de Guatemala
Independence	1839
Area	108 889 sq km/42 031 sq mi
Capital	Guatemala City; La Ciudad de Guatemala
Chief towns	Quetzaltenango, Escuintla, Antigua, Mazatenango
Population	12 728 000 (2007e)
Nationality	Guatemalan
Languages	Spanish; many indigenous languages are also spoken
Ethnic groups	mestizo (Ladino) and European 59%, Amerindian 40%, others 1%
Religions	Christianity 95% (RC 73%, Prot 22%), traditional beliefs (Mayan) 5%
Time zone	GMT –6
Currency	1 Quetzal (Q/GTQ) = 100 centavos
Telephone	+502
Internet	.gt
Country code	GTM

Location

A republic in central America, bounded to the north and west by Mexico; to the east by Belize and the Caribbean Sea; to the south-east by Honduras and El Salvador; and to the south-west by the Caribbean Sea.

GUATEMALA

Physical description
Over two-thirds mountainous with large forests; narrow Pacific coastal plain; highlands rise to 2500–3000m/8200–9840ft, with volcanoes on the southern edge; highest point is Tajumulco (4220m/13845ft); low undulating tableland in north.

Climate
Humid and tropical in the lowlands and on the Caribbean coast; rainy season from May to Oct; higher rainfall on exposed slopes; Guatemala City average temperatures are 17°C (Jan) and 21°C (Jul); subject to severe hurricanes and earthquakes.

National holidays
Jan 1, May 1, Jun 30 (Army), Sep 15 (Independence), Oct 20 (Revolution), Nov 1, Dec 25, 31; ES, GF, HS, HT (*date varies locally*).

Political leaders

President

1898–1920	Manuel Estrada Cabrera
1920–2	Carlos Herrera y Luna
1922–6	José María Orellana
1926–30	Lázaro Chacón
1930	Baudillo Palma
1930–1	Manuel María Orellana
1931	José María Reyna Andrade
1931–44	Jorge Ubico Castañeda
1944	Federico Ponce Vaidez
1944–5	Jacobo Arbenz Guzmán
1945–51	Juan José Arévalo
1951–4	Jacobo Arbenz Guzmán
1954	*Military Junta* (Carlos Díaz)
1954	Elfego J Monzón
1954–7	Carlos Castillo Armas
1957	*Military Junta* (Oscar Mendoza Azurdia)
1957	Luis Arturo Gonzélez López
1957–8	*Military Junta* (Guillermo Flores Avendaño)
1958–63	Miguel Ydígoras Fuentes
1963–6	*Military Junta* (Enrique Peralta Azurdia)
1966–70	Julio César Méndez Montenegro
1970–4	Carlos Araña Osorio
1974–8	Kyell Eugenio Laugerua García
1978–82	Romeo Lucas García
1982	Angel Aníbal Guevara
1982–3	Efraín Rios Montt
1983–6	Oscar Humberto Mejía Victores
1986–91	Marco Vinicio Cerezo Arévalo
1991–3	Jorge Serrano Elias
1993–6	Ramiro de León Carpio
1996–2000	Álvaro Arzú Irigoyen
2000–4	Alfonso Portillo Cabrera
2004–8	Óscar Berger Perdomo
2008–	Álvaro Colom Caballeros

Resplendent Quetzal

The national bird of Guatemala is the quetzal, also known as the resplendent trogon. The quetzal has beautiful shimmering golden-green feathers, a crimson breast and brilliant iridescent tail feathers that may be up to 90cm/3ft long. It is steeped in myth and folklore, linked to the ancient Aztec god *Quetzalcoatl* and associated with freedom and liberty. The quetzal is immensely symbolic in Guatemala and has not only given its name to the national currency and to the major town of Quetzaltenango, but is depicted on the flag and the coat of arms and has appeared on postage stamps.

GUIANA, FRENCH *see* FRANCE

GUINEA

Official name	Republic of Guinea
Local name	Guinée; République de Guinée
Former name	French Guinea (until 1958), Republic of Guinea (1958–79), People's Revolutionary Republic of Guinea (1979–84)
Independence	1958
Area	246 048 sq km/94 974 sq mi
Capital	Conakry
Chief towns	Kankan, Kindia, Labé
Population	9 948 000 (2007e)
Nationality	Guinean
Languages	French is the official language; eight local languages are also widely spoken
Ethnic groups	Peulh 40%, Malinke 30%, Soussou 20%, others 10%
Religions	Islam 85%, Christianity 8%, traditional beliefs 7%
Time zone	GMT
Currency	1 Guinea Franc (GFr/GNF) = 100 centimes
Telephone	+224
Internet	.gn
Country code	GIN

Location

A republic in West Africa, bounded to the north-west by Guinea-Bissau; to the north by Senegal and Mali; to the east by Côte d'Ivoire; to the south by Liberia and Sierra Leone; and to the south-west by the Atlantic Ocean.

Physical description

Coastal mangrove forests, rising to a forested and cultivated narrow coastal plain; massif beyond at approximately 900m/2 952ft; highest point is Mt Nimba (1 752m/5 748ft); savanna plains in the east; forested Guinea Highlands in the south rise above 1 000m/3 280ft.

Climate

Tropical climate (wet season May–Oct); average temperature in the dry season on the coast is 32°C, dropping to 23°C in the wet season; cooler inland.

National holidays

Jan 1, Apr 3 (Second Republic), May 1, 25 (Africa), Aug 15, Oct 2 (Independence), Nov 1, Dec 25; Ad, EM, ER, PB.

Political leaders

President

1961–84	Ahmed Sékou Touré
1984–	Lansana Conté

Prime Minister

1958–72	Ahmed Sékou Touré
1972–84	Louis Lansana Beavogui
1984–5	Diarra Traoré
1985–96	*No Prime Minister*
1996–9	Sidia Touré
1999–2004	Lamine Sidime
2004	François Lonseny Fall
2004–6	Cellou Dalein Diallo
2006–7	*No Prime Minister*
2007–	Lansana Kouyaté

Local Languages

Although French is the official language of Guinea, the government estimates that only 15–20% of the country's people speak it. Instead, most people speak one of eight major national languages, of which the most important are Soussou, Malinke, Kissi, Peulh, Toma and Guerze.

GUINEA-BISSAU

Official name	Republic of Guinea-Bissau
Local name	Guiné-Bissau; República da Guiné-Bissau
Former name	Portuguese Guinea (1952–74)
Independence	1973 (proclaimed), 1974 (recognized)
Area	36 260 sq km/14 000 sq mi
Capital	Bissau
Chief towns	Bafatá, Bolama, Mansôa
Population	1 473 000 (2007e)
Nationality	Guinea-Bissauan
Languages	Portuguese, Guinean Creole (Crioulo); many African languages are also spoken
Ethnic groups	Balante 30%, Fulani 20%, Malinke 14%, Mandyako 13%, Pepel 7%, other African 15%, others 1%
Religions	traditional beliefs 50%, Islam 45%, Christianity 5%
Time zone	GMT
Currency	1 CFA Franc (CFAFr/XOF) = 100 centimes
Telephone	+245
Internet	.gw
Country code	GNB

Location

A republic in West Africa, bounded to the north by Senegal; to the east and south-east by Guinea; and to the south-west by the Atlantic Ocean.

Physical description

Indented coast with islands (including the heavily-forested Bijagós Archipelago) and mangrove-lined estuaries, backed by forested coastal plains; low-lying, with savanna-covered plateaux in the south and east, rising to 310m/1 017ft.

Climate

Tropical climate with a wet season (Jun–Oct); average annual temperature range at Bissau is 24–27°C.

National holidays

Jan 1, 20 (Heroes), Mar 8 (Women), May 1, Aug 3 (Pidjiguiti), Sep 24 (National), Nov 14 (Readjustment Movement), Dec 25; Ad, ER.

Political leaders

President

1974–80	Luis de Almeida Cabral
1980–4	*Revolutionary Council* (João Bernardo Vieira)
1984–99	João Bernardo Vieira
1999–2000	Malai Bacai Sanhá *Interim*
2000–3	Kumba Yalla
2003	Veríssimo Correia Seabra *Interim*
2003–5	Henrique Rosa *Interim*
2005–	João Bernardo Vieira

Prime Minister

1992–4	Carlos Correia
1994–7	Manuel Saturnino da Costa
1997–8	Carlos Correia
1998–2000	Francisco Fadul
2000–1	Caetano N'Tchama
2001	Faustino Imbali
2001–2	Alamara Nhassé
2002–3	Mário Pires
2003–4	Artur Sanhá
2004–5	Carlos Gomes Júnior
2005–7	Aristides Gomes
2007–	Martinho N'Dafa Cabi

GUYANA

Official name	Co-operative Republic of Guyana
Local name	Guyana
Former name	British Guiana (until 1966)
Independence	1966
Area	214969 sq km/82978 sq mi
Capital	Georgetown
Chief towns	Linden, New Amsterdam
Population	769000 (2007e)
Nationality	Guyanese
Languages	English; Hindi, Urdu and local dialects are also spoken
Ethnic groups	East Indian 50%, black 36%, Amerindian 7%, white, Chinese and mixed 7%
Religions	Christianity 57% (Prot 49%, RC 8%), Hinduism 28%, Islam 7%, unaffiliated 4%, others 2%, none 2%
Time zone	GMT –4
Currency	1 Guyana Dollar (G$/GYD) = 100 cents
Telephone	+592
Internet	.gy
Country code	GUY

Location

A republic on the northern coast of South America, bounded to the north by the Atlantic Ocean; to the east by Suriname; to the south by Brazil; and to the west by Venezuela.

Physical description

Inland forest covers approximately 85% of the land area; grass-covered savanna in the hinterland; coastal plain, below sea level at high tide, is protected by sea defences, canals and dams; highest peak is Mt Roraima (2810m/9219ft) in the Pakaraima Mountains.

Climate

Equatorial climate in the lowlands, hot, wet, with constant high humidity; temperatures of 23–34°C in coastal lowlands with two seasons of high rainfall (May–Jul, Nov–Jan); lower temperatures on the high plateau inland.

National holidays

Jan 1, Feb 23 (Republic), May 1, 5 (Indian Heritage), 26 (Independence), Jul 3 (Caricom), Aug 1 (Freedom), Dec 25, 26; Ad, D, EM, ER, GF, PB; Phagwah (Mar).

Political leaders

President

1970	Edward A Luckhoo	1992–7	Cheddi Bharrat Jagan
1970–80	Arthur Chung	1997	Samuel Hinds
1980–5	Linden Forbes Sampson Burnham	1997–9	Janet Jagan
1985–92	Hugh Desmond Hoyte	1999–	Bharrat Jagdeo

Prime Minister

1966–85	Linden Forbes Sampson Burnham	1997	Janet Jagan
1985–92	Hamilton Green	1997–	Samuel Hinds
1992–7	Samuel Hinds		

Land of Many Waters

The Atlantic Ocean pounds the coastline of northern Guyana and the country is criss-crossed by many rivers. Guyana also boasts the world's longest single-drop waterfall, Kaieteur Falls, where the Potaro River plunges 226m/741ft in one leap before continuing downward for another 231m/759ft. The name *Guyana* is believed to come from an Amerindian word meaning 'land of many waters'.

HAITI

Official name	Republic of Haiti
Local name	Haïti; République d'Haïti
Independence	1804
Area	27 750 sq km/10 712 sq mi
Capital	Port-au-Prince
Chief towns	Port-de-Paix, Cap-Haïtien, Gonaïves, Les Cayes, Jacmel, Jérémie
Population	8 706 000 (2007e)
Nationality	Haitian
Languages	French, Creole
Ethnic groups	black 95%, mulatto and white 5%
Religions	Christianity 96% (RC 80%, Prot 16%), others 3%, none/unaffiliated 1% *Note: Around half the population practises voodoo*
Time zone	GMT –5
Currency	1 Gourde (G, Gde/HTG) = 100 centimes
Telephone	+509
Internet	.ht
Country code	HTI

Location

A republic in the West Indies, comprising the western third of the island of Hispaniola in the Caribbean Sea and bounded by the Dominican Republic to the east; also includes the islands of Gonâve off the west coast and Tortue off the north coast.

Physical description

Consists of two mountainous peninsulas separated by a deep structural depression; to the east is the Massif de la Selle, with Haiti's highest peak, La Selle (2680m/8792ft).

Climate

Tropical maritime; average monthly temperatures range from 24°C to 29°C; the wet season is May–Sep; hurricanes are common.

National holidays

Jan 1 (Independence), 2 (Founders), Apr 14 (Pan-American), May 1, 18 (Flag and University), Aug 15, Oct 17 (Death of Dessalines), 24 (United Nations), Nov 1, 2, 18 (Battle of Vertières), Dec 25; A, C, CC, GF.

Political leaders

President

1896–1902	P A Tirésias Simon Lam
1902	Boisrond Canal
1902–8	Alexis Nord
1908–11	Antoine Simon
1911–12	Michel Cincinnatus Leconte
1912–13	Tancrède Auguste
1913–14	Michael Oreste
1914	Oreste Zamor
1914–15	Joseph Davilmare Théodore
1915	Jean Velbrun-Guillaume
1915–22	Philippe Sudre Dartiguenave
1922–30	Joseph Louis Bornó
1930	Étienne Roy
1930–41	Sténio Joseph Vincent
1941–6	Élie Lescot
1946	*Military Junta* (Frank Lavaud)
1946–50	Dumarsais Estimé
1950	*Military Junta* (Frank Lavaud)
1950–6	Paul E Magloire
1956–7	François Sylvain
1957	*Military Junta*
1957	Léon Cantave
1957	Daniel Fignolé
1957	Antoine Kebreau
1957–71	François Duvalier ('Papa Doc')
1971–86	Jean-Claude Duvalier ('Baby Doc')
1986–8	Henri Namphy
1988	Leslie Manigat
1988	Henri Namphy
1988–90	Prosper Avril
1990–1	Ertha Pascal-Trouillot
1991	Jean-Bertrand Aristide

1991	Raoul Cédras	1994–6	Jean-Bertrand Aristide
1991–2	Joseph Nérette	1996–2000	René Préval
1992–3	Marc-Louis Bazin	2000–4	Jean-Bertrand Aristide
1993–4	Jean-Bertrand Aristide	2004–6	Boniface Alexandre *Interim*
1994	Émile Jonassaint	2006–	René Préval

Prime Minister

1988	Martial Célestin	1995–6	Claudette Werleigh
1988–91	*No Prime Minister*	1996–7	Rosny Smarth
1991	René Préval	1998–2001	Jacques-Édouard Alexis
1991–2	Jean-Jacques Honorat *Interim*	2001–2	Jean-Marie Cherestal
1992–3	Marc Bazin	2002–4	Yvon Neptune
1993–4	Robert Malval	2004–6	Gérard Latortue *Interim*
1994–5	Smarck Michel	2006–	Jacques-Édouard Alexis

Slave Revolution

The Haitian Revolution of 1791–1804 was the only successful slave revolution in the New World. It created the world's first black-led republic, and meant that Haiti became the first Caribbean state to achieve independence. The revolution began in Aug 1791 with a slave revolt led by Toussaint L'Ouverture and culminated in the independence of Haiti in 1804 when a slave named Dessalines proclaimed himself Emperor of the independent country.

HEARD AND MACDONALD ISLANDS *see* AUSTRALIA

HERZEGOVINA *see* BOSNIA AND HERZEGOVINA

HOLLAND *see* THE NETHERLANDS

HOLY SEE *see* VATICAN

HONDURAS

Official name	Republic of Honduras
Local name	Honduras; República de Honduras
Independence	1821 (from Spain), 1838 (as sovereign state)
Area	112 088 sq km/43 266 sq mi
Capital	Tegucigalpa
Chief towns	San Pedro Sula, Choluteca, La Ceiba, El Progreso
Population	7 484 000 (2007e)
Nationality	Honduran
Languages	Spanish; English is also spoken
Ethnic groups	mestizo 90%, Amerindian 7%, black 2%, white 1%
Religions	Christianity 100% (RC 80%, Prot 20%)
Time zone	GMT –6
Currency	1 Lempira (L, La/HNL) = 100 centavos
Telephone	+504
Internet	.hn
Country code	HND

HONDURAS

Location

A republic in Central America, bounded to the north by the Caribbean Sea; to the south-east by Nicaragua; to the south by the Pacific Ocean; to the south-west by El Salvador; and to the west by Guatemala; also comprises the Bay Islands in the Caribbean Sea and a group of nearly 300 islands in the Gulf of Fonseca.

Physical description

Southern coastal lands are separated from those of the Caribbean by mountains running north-west to south-east; southern plateau rises to 2870m/9416ft at Cerro Las Minas; Laguna Caratasca lies in the extreme north-east.

Climate

Tropical climate in coastal areas, temperate in the centre and west; two wet seasons in upland areas (May–Jul, Sep–Oct); variable temperatures in the interior, 15–24°C; on the coastal plains the average temperature is 30°C.

National holidays

Jan 1, Apr 14 (Americas), May 1, Sep 15 (Independence), Oct 3 (Morozán), 12 (Columbus), 21 (Army), Dec 25; ES, GF, HS, HT.

Political leaders

President

1900–3	Terencio Sierra
1903	Juan Angel Arias
1903–7	Manuel Bonilla Chirinos
1907–11	Miguel R Dávila
1912–15	Manuel Bonilla Chirinos
1915–20	Francisco Bertrand
1920–4	Rafael López Gutiérrez
1924–5	Vicente Tosta Carrasco
1925–8	Miguel Paz Barahona
1929–32	Vicente Mejía Clindres
1932–49	Tiburcio Carías Andino
1949–54	Juan Manuel Gálvez

Head of State

1954–6	Julio Lozano Diaz
1956–7	*Military Junta*

President

1958–63	José Ramón Villeda Morales

Head of State

1963–5	Oswaldo López Arellano

President

1965–71	Oswaldo López Arellano
1971–2	Ramón Ernesto Cruz

Head of State

1972–5	Oswaldo López Arellano
1975–8	Juan Alberto Melgar Castro
1978–82	Policarpo Paz García

President

1982–6	Roberto Suazo Córdova
1986–9	José Azcona Hoyo
1989–93	Rafael Leonardo Callejas
1993–7	Carlos Roberto Reina
1997–2002	Carlos Roberto Flores Facussé
2002–6	Ricardo Maduro
2006–	Manuel Zelaya Rosales

Deep Blue Sea

Christopher Columbus arrived on the Caribbean coast of Honduras in 1502. He is reported to have exclaimed at how deep the coastal waters were, thus naming the country: *honduras* is the Spanish word for 'depths'. This was not the first time that Columbus's comments on the sea had resulted in a country name that would still be used 500 years later (see the fact box at **the Bahamas**).

HONG KONG *see* **CHINA**

HUNGARY

Official name	Republic of Hungary
Local name	Magyarorszag; Magyar Küztársaság
Former name	formerly part of Austria-Hungary (until 1918), Hungarian People's Republic (1918, 1919, 1949–89), Hungarian Soviet Republic (1919), Hungarian State (1919–20, 1944–6), Hungarian Kingdom (1920–44), Hungarian Republic (1946–9)
Independence	1918
Area	93 030 sq km/35 910 sq mi
Capital	Budapest
Chief towns	Debrecen, Miskolc, Szeged, Pécs, Györ
Population	9 956 000 (2007e)
Nationality	Hungarian
Languages	Magyar (Hungarian)
Ethnic groups	Magyar 92%, Roma 2%, others 6%
Religions	Christianity 75% (RC 52%, Prot 19%, other 4%), others 11%, none/unaffiliated 14%
Time zone	GMT +1
Currency	1 Forint (Ft/HUF) = 100 fillér
Telephone	+36
Internet	.hu
Country code	HUN

Location

A republic in central Europe, bounded to the north by Slovakia; to the east by Ukraine and Romania; to the south by Serbia and Croatia; and to the west by Slovenia and Austria.

Physical description

Drained by the River Danube and its tributaries (flowing north to south); frequent flooding; low spur of the Alps in the west, separating the Little Hungarian Plain from the Transdanubian downlands; highest peak is Kékes (1 014m/3 327ft).

Climate

Fairly extreme continental climate with a marked difference between summer and winter; wettest in spring and early summer; winters are cold and the Danube sometimes freezes over for long periods; frequent fog in settled winter weather.

National holidays

Jan 1, Mar 15 (Revolution), May 1, Aug 20 (National/St Stephen), Oct 23 (Republic), Nov 1, Dec 25, 26; EM, ES, WM, Whit Sunday.

Political leaders

Monarch

1900–16	Franz Josef I
1916–18	Karl IV

President

1919	Mihály Károlyi
1919	*Revolutionary Governing Council* (Sándor Garbai)
1920–44	Miklós Horthy *Regent*
1944–5	*Provisional National Assembly*
1946–8	Zoltán Tildy
1948–50	Árpád Szakasits
1950–2	Sándor Rónai
1952–67	István Dobi
1967–87	Pál Losonczi
1987–8	Károly Németh
1988–9	Brunó Ferenc Straub
1989–90	Mátyás Szúrüs
1990–2000	Árpád Göncz
2000–5	Ferenc Mádl
2005–	László Sólyom

Premier

1899–1903	Kálmán Széll
1903	Károly Khuen-Héderváry
1903–5	István Tisza
1905–6	Géza Fejérváry
1906–10	Sándor Wekerle
1910–12	Károly Khuen-Héderváry
1912–13	Lázló Lukács
1913–17	István Tisza
1917	Móric Esterházy
1917–18	Sándor Wekerle
1918–19	Mihály Károlyi
1919	Dénes Berinkey
1919	*Revolutionary Governing Council*
1919	Gyula Peidl
1919	István Friedrich
1919–20	Károly Huszár
1920	Sándor Simonyi-Semadam
1920–1	Pál Teleki
1921–31	István Bethlen
1931–2	Gyula Károlyi
1932–6	Gyula Gömbös
1936–8	Kálman Darányi
1938–9	Béla Imrédy
1939–41	Pál Teleki
1941–2	Lázló Bárdossy
1942–4	Miklós Kállay
1944	Döme Sztójay
1944	Géza Lakatos
1944	Ferenc Szálasi
1944–5	*Provisional National Assembly* (Béla Dálnoki Miklós)
1945–6	Zoltán Tildy
1946–7	Ferenc Nagy
1947–8	Lajos Dinnyés
1948–52	István Dobi
1952–3	Mátyás Rákosi
1953–5	Imre Nagy
1955–6	András Hegedüs
1956	Imre Nagy
1956–8	János Kádár
1958–61	Ferenc Münnich
1961–5	János Kádár
1965–7	Gyula Kállai
1967–75	Jenö Fock
1975–87	György Lázár
1987–8	Károly Grosz
1988–90	Miklás Németh
1990–3	József Antall
1993–4	Péter Boross
1994–8	Gyula Horn
1998–2002	Viktor Orban
2002–4	Peter Medgyessy
2004–	Ferenc Gyurcsány

First Secretary

1949–56	Mátyás Rákosi
1956	Ernö Gerö
1956–88	János Kádár
1988–90	Károly Grosz

ICELAND

Official name	Republic of Iceland
Local name	Ísland; Lyđveldiđ Ísland
Former name	formerly part of Denmark (to 1918), Kingdom of Iceland (1918–44)
Independence	1944
Area	103 000 sq km/40 000 sq mi
Capital	Reykjavík
Chief towns	Akureyri, Húsavík, Akranes, Keflavík, Ísafjördur
Population	302 000 (2007e)
Nationality	Icelandic
Languages	Icelandic
Ethnic groups	Icelandic 94%, Danish 1%, others 5%
Religions	Christianity 94% (Prot 90%, RC 2%, other 2%), none/unaffiliated 6%
Time zone	GMT
Currency	1 Króna (IKr/ISK) = 100 aurar
Telephone	+354
Internet	.is
Country code	ISL

Location

An island state lying between the northern Atlantic Ocean and the Arctic Ocean, south-east of Greenland and 900km/550mi west of Norway across the Norwegian Sea.

Physical description

A volcanic island, with several active volcanoes; heavily indented coastline, with many long fjords; high ridges rise to 2119m/6952ft at Hvannadalshnúkur; large snowfields and glaciers cover much of the land area.

Climate

Changeable climate, with relatively mild winters; average daily temperatures are minimum –2°C (Jan), maximum 14°C (Jul–Aug); Reykjavík is generally ice-free throughout the year; summers are cool and cloudy.

National holidays

Jan 1, May 1, Jun 17 (National), Aug 6 (Commerce), Dec 25, 26; A, EM, ES, GF, HT, WM, Whit Sunday, First Day of Summer (Apr).

Political leaders

President

1944–52	Sveinn Björnsson
1952–68	Ásgeir Ásgeirsson
1968–80	Kristján Eldjárn
1980–96	Vigdís Finnbogadóttir
1996–	Ólafur Ragnar Grimsson

Prime Minister

1900–1	C Goos
1901–4	P A Alberti
1904–9	Hannes Hafstein
1909–11	Björn Jónsson
1911–12	Kristján Jónsson
1912–14	Hannes Hafstein
1914–15	Sigurður Eggerz
1915–17	Einar Arnórsson
1917–22	Jón Magnússon
1922–4	Sigurður Eggerz
1924–6	Jón Magnússon
1926–7	John þorláksson
1927–32	Tryggvi þórhallsson
1932–4	Ásgeir Ásgeirsson
1934–42	Hermann Jónasson
1942	Ólafur Thors
1942–4	Björn þórðarsson
1944–7	Ólafur Thors
1947–9	Stefán Jóhann Stefánsson
1949–50	Ólafur Thors
1950–3	Steingrímur Steinþórsson
1953–6	Ólafur Thors
1956–8	Hermann Jónasson
1958–9	Emil Jónsson
1959–61	Ólafur Thors
1961	Bjarni Benediktsson
1961–3	Ólafur Thors
1963–70	Bjarni Benediktsson
1970–1	Jóhann Hafstein
1971–4	Ólafur Jóhannesson
1974–8	Geir Hallgrímsson
1978–9	Ólafur Jóhannesson
1979	Benedikt Gröndal
1980–3	Gunnar Thoroddsen
1983–7	Steingrímur Hermannsson
1987–8	Thorsteinn Pálsson
1988–91	Steingrímur Hermannsson
1991–2004	Davíd Oddsson
2004–6	Halldór Ásgrímsson
2006–	Geir Hilmar Haarde

Geysers Galore

Iceland is famous for geysers – springs that periodically spout hot water and steam into the air. The most well-known is *Geysir*, meaning 'the gusher', which was first recorded in the year 1294 and from which the term *geyser* is derived. Others include *Strokkur* ('the churn'), *Smiður* ('the carpenter'), *Fata* ('the bucket') and *Óperrishola* ('the rainmaker').

INDIA

Official name	Republic of India
Local name	Bhāat (Hindi)
Independence	1947
Area	3287590 sq km/1269338 sq mi
Capital	New Delhi; Nī Dillī
Chief towns[1]	Ahmadabad, Bangalore, Chennai, Hyderabad, Jaipur, Kanpur, Kolkata, Lucknow, Mumbai, Nagpur, Poona
Population	1129866000 (2007e)
Nationality	Indian
Languages	Hindi, English and 17 others
Ethnic groups	Indo-Aryan 72%, Dravidian 25%, others 3%
Religions	Hinduism 81%, Islam 13% (Sunni), Sikhism 2%, Christianity 2%, others and unspecified 2%
Time zone	GMT +5.5
Currency	1 Indian Rupee (Re, Rs/INR) = 100 paise
Telephone	+91
Internet	.in
Country code	IND

Location

A federal republic in southern Asia, crossed by the Tropic of Cancer; bounded to the north-west by Pakistan and the disputed region of Jammu and Kashmir; to the north by China, Nepal and Bhutan; to the east by Myanmar and Bangladesh; to the south-east by the Bay of Bengal; and to the south-west by the Arabian Sea.

Physical description

The second largest state in Asia, bordered to the north by the Himalayas; highest peaks are over 7000m/22966ft; Kanchenjunga (8598m/28298ft) on the Nepalese border is the highest point; central river plains to the south (including the Ganges and Brahmaputra); best agricultural land is in the east; plateau in the southern peninsula; Thar Desert in the north-west is bordered by semi-desert; coastal plains are important areas of rice cultivation.

Climate

Dominated by the Asiatic monsoon; rains come from the south-west (Jun–Oct); rainfall decreases (Dec–Feb) with winds from the north, followed by drought until Mar or May; temperatures in the mountains vary greatly with altitude; desert conditions in the extreme west; south of the plateau is tropical, even in the cool season; west coast is subject to rain throughout the year, with high humidity in the south; cyclones and storms on the south-east coast (especially Oct–Dec), with high temperatures and humidity during the monsoon season.

National holidays

Jan 26 (Republic), Aug 15 (Independence), Oct 2 (Mahatma Gandhi's Birthday) *all India; each state has its own holidays, but the most widely observed include:* Dec 25, Ad, D, ER, GF, NY (Muslim), PB; Buddha Purnima (Apr/May), Dussehra (Sep/Oct), Guru Nanak's Birth (Nov), Maha Shivaratri (Feb), Mahavir Jayanti (Feb/Mar), Ram Navami (Mar).

[1] *India has renamed several of its cities and states in recent years, reverting to pre-colonial names. Thus, Bombay is now known as Mumbai, Calcutta as Kolkata and Madras as Chennai. Other such changes may follow.*

Political leaders

President

1950–62	Rajendra Prasad
1962–7	Sarvepalli Radhakrishnan
1967–9	Zakir Husain
1969	Varahagiri Venkatagiri *Acting*
1969	Mohammed Hidayatullah *Acting*
1969–74	Varahagiri Venkatagiri
1974–7	Fakhruddin Ali Ahmed
1977	B D Jatti *Acting*

1977–82	Neelam Sanjiva Reddy	1997–2002	Kocheril Raman Narayanan
1982–7	Giani Zail Singh	2002–7	A P J Abdul Kalam
1987–92	Ramaswami Venkataraman	2007–	Pratibha Patil
1992–7	Shankar Dayal Sharma		

Prime Minister

1947–64	Jawaharlal Nehru	1989–90	Vishwanath Pratap Singh
1964	Gulzari Lal Nanda *Acting*	1990–1	Chandra Shekhar
1964–6	Lal Bahadur Shastri	1991–6	P V Narasimha Rao
1966	Gulzari Lal Nanda *Acting*	1996	Atal Behari Vajpayee
1966–77	Indira Gandhi	1996–7	H D Deve Gowda
1977–9	Morarji Desai	1997	Inder Kumar Gujral
1979–80	Charan Singh	1998–2004	Atal Behari Vajpayee
1980–4	Indira Gandhi	2004–	Manmohan Singh
1984–9	Rajiv Gandhi		

INDONESIA

Official name	Republic of Indonesia
Local name	Indonesia; Republik Indonesia
Former name	Netherlands East Indies, Dutch East Indies (until 1949), Republic of the United States of Indonesia (1949–50)
Independence	1945 (declared), 1949
Area	1 906 240 sq km/735 809 sq mi
Capital	Jakarta
Chief towns	Jayapura, Bandung, Semarang, Surabaya, Medan, Palembang
Population	234 694 000 (2007e)
Nationality	Indonesian
Languages	Bahasa Indonesia; English, Dutch and Javanese are also widely spoken, and 300 regional languages
Ethnic groups	Javanese 45%, Sundanese 14%, coastal Malays 7%, Madurese 7%, others 27%
Religions	Islam 88%, Christianity 8%, Hinduism 2%, Buddhism 1%, others 1%
Time zone	GMT +7/9
Currency	1 Rupiah (Rp/IDR) = 100 sen
Telephone	+62
Internet	.id
Country code	IDN

Location

A republic in south-east Asia, bounded to the north of the island of Borneo by Malaysia; to the east of the island of Timor by East Timor; and to the east of the island of New Guinea by Papua New Guinea; the Indian Ocean lies to the west; the Java Sea, Banda Sea, Arafura Sea and Timor Sea surround some of its islands; the Pacific Ocean lies to the north. The Equator passes through several islands including Sumatra and Borneo.

Physical description

The world's largest island group; five main islands and 30 smaller archipelagoes totalling 13 677 islands and islets, of which approximately 6 000 are inhabited; over 100 volcanic peaks on Java, of which 15 are active; highest point is Puncak Jaya (5 030m/16 503ft).

Climate

Hot and humid equatorial climate; dry season (Jun–Sep), rainy season (Dec–Mar), apart from the Moluccas (Jun–Sep); average temperature is 27°C on island coasts, falling inland and with altitude.

National holidays
Jan 1, Aug 17 (Independence), Dec 25; A, Ad, ER (2), ES, GF, NY (Chinese), NY (Muslim), NY (Hindu), PA, PB, Waisak (May/Jun).

Political leaders

President

1945–9	Ahmed Sukarno	1999–2001	Abdurrahman Wahid
1949–66	Ahmed Sukarno	2001–4	Megawati Sukarnoputri
1966–98	T N J Suharto	2004–	Susilo Bambang Yudhoyono
1998–9	B J Habibie		

Prime Minister

1945	R A A Wiranatakusumah	1952–3	Dr Wilopo
1945–7	Sutan Sjahrir	1953–5	Ali Sastroamidjojo
1947–8	Amir Sjarifuddin	1955–6	Burhanuddin Harahap
1948	Mohammed Hatta	1956–7	Ali Sastroamidjojo
1948–9	Sjarifuddin Prawiraranegara	1957–9	Raden Haji Djuanda Kurtawidjaja
1949	Susanto Tirtoprodjo	1959–63	Ahmed Sukarno
1949	Mohammed Hatta	1963–6	S E Subandrio
1950	Dr Halim	1966–	*No Prime Minister*
1950–1	Mohammed Natsir		
1951–2	Sukiman Wirjosandjojo		

IRAN

Official name	Islamic Republic of Iran
Local name	Îrân; Jomhûri-ye-Eslâmi-ye-Îrân
Former name	Persia (until 1935)
Independence	1925
Area	1 648 000 sq km/636 128 sq mi
Capital	Tehran; Tehrān
Chief towns	Mashhad, Isfahan, Tabriz, Shiraz, Abadan
Population	65 397 000 (2007e)
Nationality	Iranian
Languages	Farsi (Persian), with several minority languages spoken
Ethnic groups	Persian 51%, Azeri 24%, Gilaki and Mazandarani 8%, Kurdish 7%, others 10%
Religions	Islam 98% (Shia 89%, Sunni 9%), others 2%
Time zone	GMT +3.5
Currency	1 Iranian Rial (Rls/IRR) = 100 dinars
Telephone	+98
Internet	.ir
Country code	IRN

Location
A republic in south-west Asia, bounded to the north by Armenia, Azerbaijan, the Caspian Sea and Turkmenistan; to the east by Afghanistan and Pakistan; to the south by the Gulf of Oman and the Arabian Gulf; to the south-west by Iraq; and to the north-west by Turkey.

Physical description
A vast arid central plateau, average elevation 1 200m/3 936ft, with many salt and sand basins; rimmed by mountain ranges that drop to narrow coastal lowlands; Elburz Mountains in the north rise to 5 670m/18 602ft at Mt Damavand.

Climate
Mainly a desert climate; average temperatures at Tehran are 2°C (Jan), 29°C (Jul); Caspian coast is wetter than interior; hot and humid around Arabian Gulf; frequent earthquakes.

National holidays
Feb 11 (Islamic Revolution), Mar 20 (Oil Nationalization), 21–24, Apr 1 (Islamic Republic), 2 (Nature), Jun 4 (Imam Khomeini's Death), 5 (Khordad Revolt); Ad, As, ER, PA, PB, Eid Ghadir, Tassua, Arbain, Death of the Prophet, Martyrdom of Fatima, Imam Ali's Birthday, Imam Mahdi's Birthday, Martyrdom of Imam Ali, Martyrdom of Imam Sadeq, Imam Reza's Birthday.

Political leaders

Shah

1896–1907	Muzaffar Ad-Din
1907–9	Mohammed Ali
1909–25	Ahmad Mirza
1925–41	Mohammed Reza Khan
1941–79	Mohammed Reza Pahlavi

Leader of the Islamic Republic

1979–89	Ayatollah Ruhollah Khomeini
1989–	Ayatollah Sayyed Ali Khamenei

President

1980–1	Abolhassan Bani-Sadr
1981	Mohammed Ali Rajai
1981–9	Sayyed Ali Khamenei
1989–97	Ali Akbar Hashemi Rafsanjani
1997–2005	Mohammad Khatami
2005–	Mahmoud Ahmadinejad

Prime Minister

1979	Shahpur Bakhtiar
1979–80	Mehdi Bazargan
1980–1	Mohammed Ali Rajai
1981	Mohammed Javad Bahonar
1981	Mohammed Reza Mahdavi-Kani
1981–9	Mir Hossein Moussavi

IRAQ

Official name	Republic of Iraq
Local name	Al-Jumhūriyya al-'Iraqiyya
Former name	part of the Ottoman Empire (until 1916), State of Iraq (1920–21), Iraqi Kingdom (1921–32), Kingdom of Iraq (1932–58)
Independence	1932
Area	434 925 sq km/167 881 sq mi
Capital	Baghdad
Chief towns	Basra, Kirkuk, Mosul
Population	27 500 000 (2007e)
Nationality	Iraqi
Languages	Arabic; Kurdish is also spoken
Ethnic groups	Arab 77%, Kurdish 18%, Turkmen, Assyrian and others 5%
Religions	Islam 97% (Shia 62%, Sunni 35%), Christianity and others 3%
Time zone	GMT +3
Currency	1 New Iraqi Dinar (ID/IQD) = 1 000 fils
Telephone	+964
Internet	.iq
Country code	IRQ

Location
A republic in western Asia, bounded to the north by Turkey; to the east by Iran; to the south-east by Kuwait and the Arabian Gulf; to the south by Saudi Arabia; to the west by Jordan; and to the north-west by Syria.

IRAQ

Physical description

Largely comprises the vast alluvial tract of the Tigris–Euphrates lowland; the rivers join about 190km/118mi from the Arabian Gulf; lowland has swamp vegetation; mountains in the north-east rise to over 3000m/9840ft; highest point is Haji Ibrahim (3600m/11810ft); desert in other areas.

Climate

Mainly arid; summers are very hot and dry; winters are often cold; average temperatures at Baghdad are 10°C (Jan) and 35°C (Jul); rainfall is highest in the north-east.

National holidays

Jan 1, May 1, Jul 14 (Republic), 17 (Republic); Ad (4), ER (2), NY (Muslim), PB.

Between the Rivers

The area corresponding to modern-day Iraq was known to the Ancient Greeks as Mesopotamia, from the Greek for 'between the rivers'. It was named for the Tigris and the Euphrates, two large rivers that flow through the region.

Political leaders

Monarch

1921–33 Faisal I
1933–9 Ghazi I
1939–58 Faisal II (*Regent* 1939–53, Abdul Illah)

Commander of the National Forces

1958–63 Abdul Karim Qassem

Head of Council of State

1958–63 Mohammed Najib Ar-Rubai

President

1963–6 Abd as-Salam Arif
1966–8 Abd ar-Rahman Arif
1968–79 Ahmad Hassan al-Bakr
1979–2003 Saddam Hussein
2003–4 *US-controlled transitional administration*
2004–5 Ghazi Yawer *Interim*
2005– Jalal Talabani *Interim President until 2006*

Prime Minister

1958–63 Abdul Karim Qassem
1963 Ahmad Hassan al-Bakr
1963–5 Tahir Yahya
1965 Arif Abd ar-Razzaq
1965–6 Abd ar-Rahman al-Bazzaz
1966–7 Naji Talib
1967 Abd ar-Rahman Arif
1967–8 Tahir Yahya
1968 Abd ar-Razzaq an-Naif
1968–79 Ahmad Hassan al-Bakr
1979–91 Saddam Hussein
1991 Sadun Hammadi
1991–3 Mohammed Hamzah az-Zubaydi
1993–4 Ahmad Hussein Khudayir as-Samarrai
1994–2003 Saddam Hussein[1]
2003–4 *US-controlled transitional administration*
2004–5 Iyad Allawi *Interim*
2005–6 Ibrahim Jaafari *Interim*
2006– Nouri Jawad al-Maliki

[1] *Overthrown by a US-led military coalition.*

IRELAND

Official name	Ireland
Local name	Éire
Independence	1921 (treaty), 1922 (Irish Free State)
Area	70282 sq km/27129 sq mi
Capital	Dublin; Baile Átha Cliath
Chief towns	Cork, Limerick, Waterford, Galway, Drogheda, Dundalk, Sligo
Population	4109000 (2007e)
Nationality	Irish
Languages	Irish, English; the Irish Gaelic-speaking areas, mostly in the west, are known as the *Gaeltacht*
Ethnic groups	Irish 95%, others 5%
Religions	Christianity 93% (RC 88%, Prot 3%, other 2%), others and unspecified 4%, none 3%
Time zone	GMT
Currency	1 Euro (€/EUR) = 100 cents
Telephone	+353
Internet	.ie
Country code	IRL

Location

A republic occupying all but north-eastern Ireland, separated from Great Britain by the Irish Sea and St George's Channel, and bounded to the north-east by Northern Ireland, part of the United Kingdom.

Physical description

Mountainous landscapes in the west with quartzite peaks weathered into conical mountains; highest point is Carrantuohill (1041m/3415ft); mountains in the south create a landscape of ridges and valleys; eastern lowlands drained by slow-moving rivers.

Climate

Mild and equable, with few extremes of temperature; rainfall is heaviest in the west.

National holidays

Jan 1, Mar 17 (St Patrick), Dec 25, 26; EM, GF, 1st Mon in May, 1st Mon in Jun, 1st Mon in Aug, last Mon in Oct public holidays.

Political leaders

Governor General

1922–7	Timothy Michael Healy
1927–32	James McNeill
1932–6	Donald Buckley
1936–7	Frank Fahy *and* Éamon de Valera *Acting heads of state*

President

1937–8	*Presidential Commission*
1938–45	Douglas Hyde
1945–59	Sean Thomas O'Kelly
1959–73	Éamon de Valera
1973–4	Erskine H Childers
1974–6	Carroll Daly
1976–90	Patrick J Hillery
1990–7	Mary Robinson
1997–	Mary McAleese

Prime Minister

1919–21	Éamon de Valera
1922	Arthur Griffiths
1922–32	William Cosgrave
1932–48	Éamon de Valera
1948–51	John Aloysius Costello
1951–4	Éamon de Valera
1954–7	John Aloysius Costello
1957–9	Éamon de Valera
1959–66	Sean Lemass
1966–73	John Lynch

1973–7	Liam Cosgrave	1987–92	Charles Haughey
1977–9	John Lynch	1992–4	Albert Reynolds
1979–82	Charles Haughey	1994–7	John Bruton
1982–7	Garrett Fitzgerald	1997–	Bertie Ahern

IRELAND, NORTHERN; ISLE OF MAN *see* UNITED KINGDOM

ISRAEL

Official name	State of Israel
Local name	Medinat Yisra'el, Dawlat Israqā'īl
Independence	1948
Area	20 770 sq km/8 017 sq mi
Capital[1]	Tel Aviv-Jaffa
Chief towns	Jerusalem, Haifa, Beersheba, Acre, Holon
Population	6 427 000 (2007e)
Nationality	Israeli
Languages	Hebrew, Arabic
Ethnic groups	Israel-born Jewish 51%, Jewish, born elsewhere 25%, Arab and others 24%
Religions	Judaism 76%, Islam 16%, Druze 2%, Christianity 2%, unspecified 4%
Time zone	GMT +2
Currency	1 New Israeli Shekel[2] (NIS/ILS) = 100 agorot
Telephone	+972
Internet	.il
Country code	ISR

Location

A republic in the Middle East, bounded to the north by Lebanon; to the north-east by Syria; to the east by Jordan; to the south-west by Egypt; and to the west by the Mediterranean Sea.

Physical description

Extends 420km/260mi north to south; narrow coastal plain; mountainous interior, rising to 1 208m/3 963ft at Mt Meron; drops below sea level in the Jordan–Red Sea Rift Valley; Negev Desert in the south occupies approximately 60% of the country's area.

Climate

Typically Mediterranean in the north and centre, with hot, dry summers and warm, wet winters; average temperatures at Tel Aviv-Jaffa are 14°C (Jan) to 27°C (Jul); rainfall is heavier inland, with occasional snow; low rainfall in Negev Desert.

National holidays

Rosh Hashanah (Jewish NY; Sep/Oct), Yom Kippur (Sep/Oct), Sukkot (Sep/Oct), Simhat Torah (Oct), Purim (Feb/Mar), Passover (Mar/Apr), Independence (Apr/May), Shavuot (May/Jun); *Israel's national holidays have fixed dates in the Jewish calendar; for example Chanukah begins on 25 Kislev.*

[1] *Israel claims Jerusalem as its capital, but this is not recognized internationally.*
[2] *Also sometimes transliterated as sheqel.*

Political leaders

President

1948–52	Chaim Weizmann	1983–93	Chaim Herzog
1952–63	Itzhak Ben-Zvi	1993–2000	Ezer Weizman
1963–73	Zalman Shazar	2000–7	Moshe Katsav
1973–8	Ephraim Katzair	2007–	Shimon Peres
1978–83	Yitzhak Navon		

Prime Minister

1948–53	David Ben-Gurion
1954–5	Moshe Sharett
1955–63	David Ben-Gurion
1963–9	Levi Eshkol
1969–74	Golda Meir
1974–7	Yitzhak Rabin
1977–83	Menachem Begin
1983–4	Yitzhak Shamir
1984–8	Shimon Peres
1988–92	Yitzhak Shamir
1992–5	Yitzhak Rabin
1995–6	Shimon Peres *Acting*
1996–9	Binyamin Netanyahu
1999–2001	Ehud Barak
2001–6	Ariel Sharon
2005–	Ehud Olmert *Interim Prime Minister until 2006*

Palestinian Autonomous Areas

Local name	Palestine; Qita Ghazzah (Gaza Strip), Daffah al-Gharbiyah (West Bank)
Former name	Palestine (under British mandate 1920–48)
Area[1]	6231 sq km/2406 sq mi (total)
Capital[2]	Gaza City
Chief towns	Nablus, Hebron, Jericho, Ramallah, Bethlehem (West Bank); Khan Yunis, Rafah (Gaza Strip)
Population	3918000 (2007e)
Nationality	Palestinian
Languages	Arabic; Hebrew, English
Ethnic groups	Palestinian Arab and other 83%, Jewish 17% (West Bank); Palestinian Arab and other 99.4%, Jewish 0.6% (Gaza Strip)
Religions	Islam 75% (Sunni), Jewish 17%, Christian and other 8% (West Bank); Islam (Sunni) 98.7%, Christian 0.7%, Jewish 0.6% (Gaza Strip)
Time zone	GMT +2
Currency	1 Jordanian Dinar (JD) = 1000 fils, 1 New Israeli Shekel[3] (NIS/ILS) = 100 agorot
Telephone	+970
Internet	.ps
Country code	PSE

Location

A disputed territory in the Middle East. It comprises the Gaza Strip, bordering the Mediterranean Sea to the west, Egypt to the south-west and otherwise surrounded by Israel; and the West Bank, a region separated from Jordan to the west by the River Jordan and the Dead Sea and otherwise surrounded by Israel.

Physical description

Gaza Strip is a low-lying, sandy coastal plain; highest point is Abu 'Awdah (105m/344ft); West Bank has a mountainous interior, dropping to below sea level (–400m/–1312ft) at the Dead Sea; highest point is Tall Asur (1022m/3353ft).

Climate

Typically Mediterranean temperate climate, with hot, dry summers and warm, wet winters.

[1]*412 sq km/159 sq mi is fully autonomous (352 sq km/136 sq mi Gaza Strip and 60 sq km/23 sq mi Jericho area of West Bank); 5819 sq km/2247 sq mi is partially autonomous (West Bank).*
[2]*Palestine claims East Jerusalem as its capital, but this is under Israeli occupation; Gaza City is the administrative capital.*
[3]*Also sometimes transliterated as sheqel.*

Ancient Jericho

The West Bank city of Jericho is the site of the world's earliest known town, continuously occupied from c.9000 BC–1850 BC.

Political leaders

The West Bank was administered by Jordan until Israel took control after the Six Day War in 1967; Jordan's claims were ceded to the Palestine Liberation Organization (PLO) in 1974 and its legal and administrative links were cut in 1988. The Gaza Strip was administered by Egypt from 1949 until it was lost to the Israelis in 1967; the Israeli military administered it until 1994. In 1993 negotiations between Israel and the PLO resulted in a 'Declaration of Principles on Interim Self Government Arrangements' concerning Palestinian self-rule in the occupied territories, and in May 1994 a transitional period of self-rule began in the Gaza Strip and the Jericho area of the West Bank under the Palestinian National Authority.

Leader of the Palestinian National Authority

1994–2004 Yasser Arafat
2004 Ahmed Qureia *Acting for Arafat*
2004 Rauhi Fattouh *Acting*
2005– Mahmoud Abbas (Abu Mazen)

Prime Minister

2003 Mahmoud Abbas (Abu Mazen)
2003–6 Ahmed Qureia (Abu Ala)
2006–7 Ismail Haniyeh
2007– Salam Khaled Abdallah Fayyad *Interim*

ITALY

Official name	Italian Republic
Local name	Italia; Repubblica Italiana
Former name	*as listed below under Political leaders*
Area	301 225 sq km/116 273 sq mi
Capital	Rome; Roma
Chief towns	Milan, Turin, Genoa, Naples, Bologna, Palermo, Florence, Venice
Population	58 148 000 (2007e)
Nationality	Italian
Languages	Italian; German, French and Slovene are also spoken in some parts
Ethnic groups	Italian 94%, others 6%
Religions	Christianity 83% (mostly RC), Islam 1%, unaffiliated 14%, others 2%
Time zone	GMT +1
Currency	1 Euro (€/EUR) = 100 cents
Telephone	+39
Internet	.it
Country code	ITA

Location

A republic in southern central Europe, bounded to the north-west by France; to the north by Switzerland and Austria; to the north-east by Slovenia; the south is surrounded by the Adriatic, Ionian, Tyrrhenian and Mediterranean seas.

Physical description

Peninsula extends approximately 800km/500mi south-east; Alps in the north form an arc, with the highest peaks along the Swiss–French frontier at Mont Blanc (Monte Bianco; 4807m/15771ft) and the Matterhorn (4477m/14688ft); broad, fertile Lombardo–Venetian plain; several lakes at the foot of the Alps; three active volcanoes: Mt Etna (3323m/10902ft), Vesuvius (1277m/4190ft) and Stromboli (926m/3038ft); also includes Sicily, Sardinia and some smaller islands; it completely encloses San Marino.

Climate

Great variation; north has hot, sunny summers and short, cold winters; higher areas are cold, wet, often snowy; coastal regions have a Mediterranean climate (warm, wet winters and hot, dry summers); long hours of summer sunshine in the extreme south.

National holidays

Jan 1, 6, Apr 25 (Liberation), May 1, Jun 2 (National), Aug 15, Nov 1, Dec 8, 25, 26; EM; *much local variation*.

Political leaders

Kingdom of Italy

Monarch

1861–78	Victor-Emmanuel II
1878–1900	Humbert I
1900–46	Victor-Emmanuel III
1946	Humbert II

Prime Minister

1900–1	Giuseppe Saracco
1901–3	Giuseppe Zanardelli
1903–5	Giovanni Giolitti
1905–6	Alessandro Fortis
1906	Sydney Sonnino
1906–9	Giovanni Giolitti
1909–10	Sydney Sonnino
1910–11	Luigi Luzzatti
1911–14	Giovanni Giolitti
1914–16	Antonio Salandra
1916–17	Paolo Boselli
1917–19	Vittorio Emanuele Orlando
1919–20	Francesco Saverio Nitti
1920–1	Giovanni Giolitti
1921–2	Ivanoe Bonomi
1922	Luigi Facta
1922–43	Benito Mussolini
1943–4	Pietro Badoglio
1944–5	Ivanoe Bonomi
1945	Ferrucio Parri
1945	Alcide de Gasperi

Italian Republic

President

1946–8	Enrico de Nicola
1948–55	Luigi Einaudi
1955–62	Giovanni Gronchi
1962–4	Antonio Segni
1964–71	Giuseppe Saragat
1971–8	Giovanni Leone
1978–85	Alessandro Pertini
1985–92	Francesco Cossiga
1992–9	Oscar Luigi Scalfaro
1999–2006	Carlo Azeglio Ciampi
2006–	Giorgio Napolitano

Prime Minister

1946–53	Alcide de Gasperi
1953–4	Giuseppe Pella
1954	Amintore Fanfani
1954–5	Mario Scelba
1955–7	Antonio Segni
1957–8	Adone Zoli
1958–9	Amintore Fanfani
1959–60	Antonio Segni
1960	Fernando Tambroni
1960–3	Amintore Fanfani
1963	Giovanni Leone
1963–8	Aldo Moro
1968	Giovanni Leone
1968–70	Mariano Rumor
1970–2	Emilio Colombo
1972–4	Giulio Andreotti
1974–6	Aldo Moro
1976–8	Giulio Andreotti
1979–80	Francisco Cossiga
1980–1	Arnaldo Forlani
1981–2	Giovanni Spadolini
1982–3	Amintore Fanfani
1983–7	Bettino Craxi
1987	Amintore Fanfani
1987–8	Giovanni Goria
1988–9	Ciriaco de Mita
1989–92	Giulio Andreotti
1992–3	Giuliano Amato
1993–4	Carlo Azeglio Ciampi
1994	Silvio Berlusconi

1995–6	Lamberto Dini	2000–1	Giuliano Amato
1996–8	Romano Prodi	2001–6	Silvio Berlusconi
1998–2000	Massimo D'Alema	2006–	Romano Prodi

IVORY COAST *see* CÔTE D'IVOIRE

JAMAICA

Official name	Jamaica
Local name	Jamaica
Independence	1962
Area	10 957 sq km/4 229 sq mi
Capital	Kingston
Chief towns	Montego Bay, Spanish Town
Population	2 780 000 (2007e)
Nationality	Jamaican
Languages	English; Jamaican Creole is also spoken
Ethnic groups	black 91%, mixed 7%, East Indian 1%, others 1%
Religions	Christianity 66% (Prot 64% (about half Church of God), RC 2%), Rastafarianism 1%, unaffiliated 21%, others 12%
Time zone	GMT –5
Currency	1 Jamaican Dollar (J$/JMD) = 100 cents
Telephone	+1876
Internet	.jm
Country code	JAM

Location
An island country in the West Indies in the Caribbean Sea.

Physical description
The third-largest island in the Caribbean Sea with a maximum length of 234km/145mi; mountainous and rugged particularly in the east, where the Blue Mountains rise to 2 256m/7 401ft at Blue Mountain Peak; more than 100 small rivers.

Climate
Humid and tropical climate at sea level, more temperate at higher altitudes; coastal temperatures range from 21°C to 34°C; virtually no rainfall on the south and south-west plains; lies within the hurricane belt.

National holidays
Jan 1, May 23 (Labour), Aug 1 (Emancipation), 6 (Independence), Oct 21 (National Heroes), Dec 25, 26; Ash Wednesday, EM, GF.

Political leaders

Head of State: British monarch, represented by Governor General (Kenneth Hall since 2006).

Prime Minister

1962–7	William Alexander Bustamante	1989–92	Michael Norman Manley
1967	Donald Burns Sangster	1992–2006	Percival James Patterson
1967–72	Hugh Lawson Shearer	2006–7	Portia Simpson Miller
1972–80	Michael Norman Manley	2007–	Bruce Golding
1980–9	Edward Phillip George Seaga		

JAN MAYEN ISLAND *see* NORWAY

JAPAN

Official name	Japan
Local name	Nihon
Area	381 945 sq km/147 431 sq mi
Capital	Tokyo; Tōkyō, Tôkyô
Chief towns	Yokohama, Osaka, Nagoya, Sapporo, Kyoto, Kobe
Population	127 433 000 (2007e)
Nationality	Japanese
Languages	Japanese
Ethnic groups	Japanese 99%, others 1%
Religions	Shintoism and Buddhism 84%, Christianity 1%, others 15%
Time zone	GMT +9
Currency	1 Yen (Y, ¥/JPY) = 100 sen
Telephone	+81
Internet	.jp
Country code	JPN

Location

An island state off the east coast of Asia, comprising the four large islands of Hokkaido (the northernmost island), Honshu (the largest island), Kyushu and Shikoku (in the south-west), and many small islands; the country tails off to the south into the Ryukyu chain of volcanic islands, of which Okinawa is the largest.

Physical description

Consists mainly of steep mountains with many volcanoes; Hokkaido has a central range rising to over 2 000m/6 562ft, falling to coastal uplands and plains; Honshu comprises parallel arcs of mountains bounded by narrow coastal plains and includes Mt Fuji (3 776m/12 388ft), Japan's highest point; heavily populated Kanto plain lies in the east; frequent earthquakes.

Climate

Oceanic climate, influenced by the Asian monsoon; short, warm summers, and severe winters with heavy snow in the north; average daily temperature at Akita (north Honshu) ranges from –5°C to 2°C (Jan), 19°C to 28°C (Aug); variable winter weather throughout; typhoons occur in summer and early autumn; mild, almost subtropical winters with light rainfall in south Honshu, Shikoku and Kyushu; summer heat is often oppressive.

National holidays

Jan 1, Feb 11 (National Foundation), Apr 29 (Showa), May 3 (Constitution), 4 (Greenery), 5 (Children), Sep 15 (Respect for the Aged), Nov 3 (Culture), 23 (Labour Thanksgiving), Dec 23 (Emperor's Birthday); Autumnal Equinox (Sep), Coming-of-Age (2nd Mon in Jan), Marine Day (Jul), Fitness (2nd Mon in Oct), Vernal Equinox (Mar); *government and banks* Jan 2, 3, Dec 31.

Political leaders

Emperor

660–585 BC	Jimmu[1]
581–549 BC	Suizei[1]
549–511 BC	Annei[1]
510–477 BC	Itoku[1]
475–393 BC	Kosho[1]
392–291 BC	Koan[1]
290–215 BC	Korei[1]
214–158 BC	Kogen[1]
158–98 BC	Kaika[1]
97–30 BC	Sujin[1]
29 BC–AD 70	Suinin[1]
AD 71–130	Keiko[1]
AD 131–190	Seimu[1]
AD 192–200	Chuai[1]
AD 270–310	Ojin[2]
AD 313–399	Nintoku[2]
AD 400–405	Richu[2]
AD 406–410	Hanzei[2]
AD 412–453	Ingyo[2]
AD 453–456	Anko[2]

AD 456–479	Yuryaku[2]
AD 480–484	Seinei[2]
AD 485–487	Kenzo[2]
AD 488–498	Ninken[2]
AD 498–506	Buretsu[2]
507–531	Keitai[2]
531–535	Ankan[2]
535–539	Senka[2]
539–571	Kimmei
572–585	Bidatsu
585–587	Yomei
587–592	Sushun
592–628	Suiko *(Empress)*
629–641	Jomei
642–645	Kogyoku *(Empress)*[3]
645–654	Kotuko
655–661	Saimei *(Empress)*[3]
662–671	Tenji
671–672	Kobun
673–686	Temmu
686–697	Jito *(Empress)*
697–707	Mommu
707–715	Gemmei *(Empress)*
715–724	Gensho *(Empress)*
724–749	Shomu
749–758	Koken *(Empress)*[4]
758–764	Junnin
764–770	Shotoku *(Empress)*[4]
770–781	Konin
781–806	Kammu
806–809	Heizei
809–823	Saga
823–833	Junna
833–850	Nimmyo
850–858	Montoku
858–876	Seiwa
876–884	Yozei
884–887	Koko
887–897	Uda
897–930	Daigo
930–946	Suzaku
946–967	Murakami
967–969	Reizei
969–984	En-yu
984–986	Kazan
986–1011	Ichijo
1011–16	Sanjo
1016–36	Go-Ichijo
1036–45	Go-Suzaku
1045–68	Go-Reizei
1068–72	Go-Sanjo
1072–86	Shirakawa
1086–1107	Horikawa
1107–23	Toba
1123–41	Sutoku
1141–55	Konoe
1155–8	Go-Shirakawa
1158–65	Nijo
1165–8	Rokujo
1168–80	Takakura
1180–3	Antoku
1183–98	Go-Toba
1198–1210	Tsuchimikado
1210–21	Juntoku
1221	Chukyo
1221–32	Go-Horikawa
1232–42	Shijo
1242–6	Go-Saga
1246–59	Go-Fukakusa
1259–74	Kameyama
1274–87	Go-Uda
1287–98	Fushimi
1298–1301	Go-Fushimi
1301–8	Go-Nijo
1308–18	Hanazono
1318–39	Go-Daigo
1339–68	Go-Murakami
1368–83	Chokei
1383–92	Go-Kameyama

Northern Court

1331–3	Kogon
1336–48	Komyo
1348–51	Suko
1352–71	Go-Kogon
1371–82	Go-Enyu
1382–1412	Go-Komatsu
1412–28	Shoko
1428–64	Go-Hanazono
1464–1500	Go-Tsuchimikado
1500–26	Go Kashiwabara
1526–57	Go-Nara
1557–86	Ogimachi
1586–1611	Go-Yozei
1611–29	Go-Mizuno-o
1629–43	Meisho *(Empress)*
1643–54	Go-Komyo
1654–63	Go-Sai
1663–87	Reigen
1687–1709	Higashiyama
1709–35	Nakamikado

1735–47	Sakuramachi	1846–66	Komei
1747–62	Momozono	1867–1912	Mutsuhito (Meiji Era)
1762–70	Go-Sakuramachi *(Empress)*	1912–26	Yoshihito (Taisho Era)
1770–9	Go-Momozono	1926–89	Hirohito (Showa Era)
1779–1817	Kokaku	1989–	Akihito (Heisei Era)
1817–46	Ninko		

Prime Minister

1900–1	Hirobumi Ito	1945	Naruhiko Higashikuni
1901–6	Taro Katsura	1945–6	Kijuro Shidehara
1906–8	Kimmochi Saionji	1946–7	Shigeru Yoshida
1908–11	Taro Katsura	1947–8	Tetsu Katayama
1911–12	Kimmochi Saionji	1948	Hitoshi Ashida
1912–13	Taro Katsura	1948–54	Shigeru Yoshida
1913–14	Gonnohyoe Yamamoto	1954–6	Ichiro Hatoyama
1914–16	Shigenobu Okuma	1956–7	Tanzan Ishibashi
1916–18	Masatake Terauchi	1957–60	Nobusuke Kishi
1918–21	Takashi Hara	1960–4	Hayato Ikeda
1921–2	Korekiyo Takahashi	1964–72	Eisaku Sato
1922–3	Tomosaburo Kato	1972–4	Kakuei Tanaka
1923–4	Gonnohyoe Yamamoto	1974–6	Takeo Miki
1924	Keigo Kiyoura	1976–8	Takeo Fukuda
1924–6	Takaaki Kato	1978–80	Masayoshi Ohira
1926–7	Reijiro Wakatsuki	1980–2	Zenko Suzuki
1927–9	Giichi Tanaka	1982–7	Yasuhiro Nakasone
1929–31	Osachi Hamaguchi	1987–9	Noburu Takeshita
1931	Reijiro Wakatsuki	1989	Sasuke Uno
1931–2	Tsuyoshi Inukai	1989–91	Toshiki Kaifu
1932–4	Makoto Saito	1991–93	Kiichi Miyazawa
1934–6	Keisuke Okada	1993	Morihiro Hosokawa
1936–7	Koki Hirota	1994	Tsutoma Hata
1937	Senjuro Hayashi	1994–6	Tomiichi Murayama
1937–9	Fumimaro Konoe	1996–8	Ryutaro Hashimoto
1939	Kiichiro Hiranuma	1998–2000	Keizo Obuchi
1939–40	Nobuyuki Abe	2000	Mikio Aoki *Acting*
1940	Mitsumasa Yonai	2000–1	Yoshiro Mori
1940–1	Fumimaro Konoe	2001–6	Junichiro Koizumi
1941–4	Hideki Tojo	2006–7	Shinzo Abe
1944–5	Kuniaki Koiso	2007–	Yasuo Fukuda
1945	Kantaro Suzuki		

[1] *The first 14 emperors (to Chuai) are regarded as legendary.*
[2] *The regnal dates for the 15th to the 28th emperor (Senka), taken from the early Japanese chronicle, 'Nihon shoki', are not considered to be authentic.*
[3] *Same empress although reigns have different names.*
[4] *Same empress although reigns have different names.*

Growing Old Gracefully

Japan has the highest life expectancy in the world, at an average of 81.9 years. By 2050, life expectancy at birth for the Japanese is forecast to rise to 88.3 years. In 2003 the Japanese government announced that the country has more than 20,000 centenarians.

JORDAN

Official name	Hashemite Kingdom of Jordan
Local name	Al'Urdunn; Al-Mamlaka al-Urdunniyya al-Hashimiyya
Former name	Emirate of Transjordan (until 1946), Hashemite Kingdom of Transjordan (1946–9)
Independence	1946
Area	89 213 sq km/34 445 sq mi
Capital	Amman; 'Ammān
Chief towns	Irbid, Zarqa, Salt, Karak, Aqaba
Population	6 053 000 (2007e)
Nationality	Jordanian
Languages	Arabic
Ethnic groups	Arab 98%, others 2%
Religions	Islam 92% (Sunni), Christianity 6%, others 2%
Time zone	GMT +2
Currency	1 Jordanian Dinar (JD/JOD) = 1 000 fils
Telephone	+962
Internet	.jo
Country code	JOR

Location
A kingdom in the Middle East, bounded to the north by Syria; to the north-east by Iraq; to the east and south by Saudi Arabia; and to the west by Israel.

Physical description
Divided by the Red Sea–Jordan rift valley; lowest point is –400m/–1 312ft at the Dead Sea; sides of the rift rise through undulating hills; Syrian desert in the east, sandy in the south, hard and rocky further north; highest point is Jabal Rum (1 754m/5 755ft).

Climate
Desert covers approximately 90% of the country; summers are uniformly hot and sunny; typically Mediterranean climate elsewhere, with hot, dry summers and cool, wet winters; temperatures at Amman are 7°C (Jan), 25°C (Jul).

National holidays
Jan 1, May 1, 25 (Independence), Dec 25; Ad (4), ER (3), NY (Muslim), PB.

Political leaders

Monarch

1921–51	Abdullah I ibn Hussein
1951–2	Talal I
1952–99	Hussein ibn Talal
1999–	Abdullah II ibn Hussein

Prime Minister

1921	Rashid Tali
1921	Muzhir Ar-Raslan
1921–3	Rida Ar-Riqabi
1923	Muzhir Ar-Raslan
1923–4	Hassan Khalid
1924–33	Rida Ar-Riqabi
1933–8	Ibrahim Hashim
1938–44	Taufiq Abul-Huda
1944–5	Samir Ar-Rifai
1945–7	Ibrahim Hashim
1947–50	Taufiq Abul-Huda
1950	Said Al-Mufti
1950–1	Samir Ar-Rifai
1951–3	Taufiq Abul-Huda
1953–4	Fauzi Al-Mulqi
1954–5	Taufiq Abul-Huda
1955	Said Al-Mufti
1955	Hazza Al-Majali
1955–6	Ibrahim Hashim
1956	Samir Ar-Rifai
1956	Said Al-Mufti
1956	Ibrahim Hashim
1956–7	Suleiman Nabulsi
1957	Hussein Fakhri Al-Khalidi

1957–8	Ibrahim Hashim
1958	Nuri Pasha Al-Said
1958–9	Samir Ar-Rifai
1959–60	Hazza Al-Majali
1960–2	Bahjat Talhuni
1962–3	Wasfi At-Tall
1963	Samir Ar-Rifai
1963–4	Sharif Hussein Bin Nasir
1964–5	Bahjat Talhuni
1965–7	Wasfi At-Tall
1967	Sharif Hussein Bin Nasir
1967	Saad Jumaa
1967–9	Bahjat Talhuni
1969	Abdul Munem Rifai
1969–70	Bahjat Talhuni
1970	Abdul Munem Rifai
1970	*Military Junta* (Mohammed Daud)
1970	Mohamed Ahmed Tugan
1970–1	Wasfi At-Tall
1971–3	Ahmad Lozi
1973–6	Zeid Rifai
1976–9	Mudar Badran
1979–80	Sharif Abdul Hamid Sharaf
1980	Kassem Rimawi
1980–4	Mudar Badran
1984–5	Ahmad Ubayat
1985–9	Zeid Ar-Rifai
1989	Sharif Zaid ibn Shaker
1989–91	Mudar Badran
1991	Taher Al-Masri
1991–3	Sharif Zaid ibn Shaker
1993–5	Abdel Salam Al-Majali
1995–7	Abdul Karim Kabariti
1997–8	Abdel Salam Al-Majali
1998–9	Fayez Tarawneh
1999–2000	Abdul Raouf Rawabdeh
2000–3	Ali Abu Al-Ragheb
2003–5	Faisal Al-Fayez
2005	Adnan Badran
2005–7	Marouf al-Bakhet
2007–	Nader Dahabi

KAMPUCHEA *see* CAMBODIA

KAZAKHSTAN

Official name	Republic of Kazakhstan
Local name	Qazaqstan Respūblīkasy
Former name	Kazakh Soviet Socialist Republic (until 1991), within the Union of Soviet Socialist Republics (USSR; 1922–91)
Independence	1991
Area	2717300 sq km/1048878 sq mi
Capital	Astana
Chief towns	Karaganda, Semipalatinsk, Chimkent, Petropavlovsk
Population	15285000 (2007e)
Nationality	Kazakhstani
Languages	Kazakh; Russian is also widely spoken
Ethnic groups	Kazakh 53%, Russian 30%, Ukrainian 4%, Uzbek 3%, German 2%, others 8%
Religions	Islam 47%, Christianity 46% (Orthodox 44%, Prot 2%), others 7%
Time zone	GMT +4/6
Currency	1 Tenge (KZT) = 100 tiyn
Telephone	+7
Internet	.kz
Country code	KAZ

Location

A republic in western Asia, bounded to the north by Russia; to the east by China; to the south by Kyrgyzstan, Uzbekistan and Turkmenistan; and to the west by the Caspian Sea.

Physical description

Steppeland in the north gives way to desert in the south; mountain ranges in the east and south-east; highest point is Khan Tengri (6995m/22949ft) in the Tien Shan mountains; largest lake is Lake Balkhash; Aral Sea lies on the south border with Uzbekistan.

Climate
Continental; hot summers and cold winters.

National holidays
Jan 1, 2, 7 (Orthodox Christmas), Mar 8 (Women), 22 (Novrus), May 1 (Unity), 9 (Victory), Aug 30 (Constitution), Oct 25 (Republic), Dec 16 (Independence); Ad.

Political leaders

President

1991–	Nursultan Nazarbayev

Prime Minister

1991–4	Sergei Tereshchenko	2002–3	Imangali Tasmagambetov
1994–7	Akezhan Kazhageldin	2003–7	Daniyal Akhmetov
1997–9	Nurlan Balgimbayev	2007–	Karim Masimov
1999–2002	Kasymzhomart Tokaev		

KEELING ISLANDS *see* AUSTRALIA

KENYA

Official name	Republic of Kenya
Local name	Jamhuri ya Kenya
Former name	British East Africa Protectorate (until 1920)
Independence	1963
Area	564 162 sq km/217 766 sq mi
Capital	Nairobi
Chief towns	Mombasa, Kisumu, Nakuru, Malindi
Population	36 914 000 (2007e)
Nationality	Kenyan
Languages	English and Swahili, with many tribal languages spoken
Ethnic groups	Kikuyu 22%, Luhya 14%, Luo 13%, Kalenjin 12%, Kamba 11%, other African 27%, others 1%
Religions	Christianity 78% (Prot 45%, RC 33%), traditional beliefs 10%, Islam 10%, others 2%
Time zone	GMT +3
Currency	1 Kenyan Shilling (Ksh/KES) = 100 cents
Telephone	+254
Internet	.ke
Country code	KEN

Location
A republic in East Africa, crossed by the Equator; bounded to the north by Ethiopia; to the north-east by Somalia; to the east by the Indian Ocean; to the south by Tanzania; to the west by Uganda and Lake Victoria; and to the north-west by Sudan.

Physical description
Highest point is Mt Kenya (5 200m/17 060ft); Great Rift Valley in the west runs north to south; dry, arid semi-desert in the north; largest body of water is Lake Turkana in the north; Chalbi Desert lies south-east of the lake.

Climate
Tropical climate on the coast, with high temperatures and humidity; in Mombasa the average daily temperatures are 27–31°C; annual rainfall decreases from south to the far north; frost and snow lie in the high mountains.

National holidays
Jan 1, May 1, Jun 1 (Madaraka), Oct 10 (Moi), 20 (Kenyatta), Dec 12 (Independence), 25, 26; EM, ER, GF.

Political leaders

President

1963–78	Mzee Jomo Kenyatta
1978–2002	Daniel arap Moi
2002–	Mwai Kibaki

KIRIBATI

Official name	Republic of Kiribati
Local name	Kiribati; Ribaberikin Kiribati
Former name	Gilbert Islands, as part of the Gilbert and Ellice Islands (until 1979)
Independence	1979
Area	811 sq km/313 sq mi
Capital	Tarawa
Population	108 000 (2007e)
Nationality	I-Kiribati
Languages	English, I-Kiribati
Ethnic groups	Micronesian 99%, others 1%
Religions	Christianity 92% (RC 52%, Prot 40%), others 8%
Time zone	GMT +12/14
Currency	1 Australian Dollar ($A/AUD) = 100 cents
Telephone	+686
Internet	.ki
Country code	KIR

Location

An island republic in the central Pacific Ocean; the Equator passes between islands.

Physical description

A group of 33 low-lying coral islands scattered over approximately 3 million sq km/1.2 million sq mi of the central Pacific Ocean; islands seldom rise to more than 4m/13ft and usually consist of a reef enclosing a lagoon; Banaba, a solid coral outcrop with a fringing reef, rises to 87m/285ft.

Climate

Maritime equatorial climate in the central islands; islands further north and south are tropical; average annual temperature is 27°C; rainy season from Nov to Apr; some islands suffer from periodic drought.

National holidays

Jan 1, Mar 5 (Women), Apr 27 (Health), Jul 9, 10, 11 (Gospel), 12–13 (Independence), Aug 6 (Youth), Dec 10 (Human Rights), 25, 26; GF, EM; *length of holidays varies locally*.

It's a Date

The International Date Line runs through the middle of Kiribati, meaning that the time difference between its easternmost and westernmost islands should be 24 hours. However, in 1995 the government 'bent' the Date Line to make the date the same everywhere, moving the line hundreds of kilometres east in a bulge big enough to include all the islands.

Political leaders

President

1979–82	Ieremia T Tabai
1982–3	*Council of State* (Rota Onorio)
1983–91	Ieremia T Tabai
1991–4	Teatao Teannaki
1994	*Council of State* (Tekire Tameura/ Ata Teaotai)
1994–2003	Teburoro Tito
2003	*Council of State* (Tion Otang)
2003–	Anote Tong

KOREA, NORTH

Official name	Democratic People's Republic of Korea (DPRK)
Local name	Chosun; Chosun Minchu-chui In'min Kongwa-guk
Independence	1948
Area	122 098 sq km/47 130 sq mi
Capital	Pyongyang; P'yŏngyang
Chief towns	Chongjin, Sinuiju, Wonsan, Kaesong
Population	23 302 000 (2007e)
Nationality	North Korean
Languages	Korean
Ethnic groups	Korean 100%
Religions	traditional beliefs 16%, Chondogyo 14%, Buddhism 2%, Christianity 1%, none/unaffiliated 67%
Time zone	GMT +9
Currency	1 Won (NKW/KPW) = 100 chon
Telephone	+850
Internet	.kp
Country code	PRK

Location

A state in eastern Asia, comprising the northern half of the Korean Peninsula, bounded to the north by China; to the north-east by Russia; to the east by the Sea of Japan (the East Sea); to the south by South Korea, from which it is separated by a demilitarized zone; and to the west by Korea Bay.

Physical description

On a high plateau occupying the north of a mountainous peninsula which projects south-east from China; many areas rise to over 2 000m/6 562ft; highest point is Mt Paektu (2 744m/9 003ft); lower mountains in the south descend to coastal plains.

Climate

Temperate, with warm summers and severely cold winters; rivers freeze for 3–4 months, and ice blocks harbours; daily temperatures at Pyongyang in the west range from –3°C to –13°C (Jan), and from 20°C to 29°C (Jul–Aug).

National holidays

Jan 1, Feb 16–17 (Kim Jong-il's Birthday), Apr 15 (Kim Il-sung's Birthday), 25 (Army), May 1, Jul 27 (Victory), Aug 15 (Liberation), Sep 9 (National), Oct 10 (Foundation of the Workers' Party), Dec 27 (Constitution); Harvest Moon Festival (Sep/Oct), Spring Festival (Jun).

Political leaders

President

1948–57 Kim Doo-bong
1957–72 Choi Yong-kun
1972–94 Kim Il-sung
1994–7 *Position vacant*
1998– Kim Il-sung (deceased) *Eternal President*

Chairman of National Defence Commission

1993– Kim Jong-il

Prime Minister

1948–76 Kim Il-sung
1976–7 Park Sung-chul
1977–84 Li Jong-ok
1984–6 Kang Song-san
1986–8 Yi Kun-mo
1988–92 Yon Hyong-muk
1992–7 Kang Song-san
1997–2003 Hong Song-nam
2003–7 Pak Pong-ju
2007– Kim Yong-il

KOREA, SOUTH

Official name	Republic of Korea (ROK)
Local name	Hanguk; Dae-han-min-guk
Independence	1948
Area	98 913 sq km/38 180 sq mi
Capital[1]	Seoul; Sŏul
Chief towns	Inchon, Pusan, Taegu
Population	49 045 000 (2007e)
Nationality	South Korean
Languages	Korean
Ethnic groups	Korean 100%
Religions	Christianity 29% (Prot 18%, RC 11%), Buddhism 23%, unaffiliated 47%, others 1%
Time zone	GMT +9
Currency	1 Won (W/KRW) = 100 jeon
Telephone	+82
Internet	.kr
Country code	KOR

Location

A republic in eastern Asia, comprising the southern half of the Korean Peninsula and about 3 000 islands off its west and south coasts, bounded to the north by North Korea, from which it is separated by a demilitarized zone; to the east by the Sea of Japan (the East Sea); to the south by the Korean Strait; and to the west by the Yellow Sea.

Physical description

Taebaek Sanmaek Range runs north to south along the east coast, reaching heights of over 900m/2 953ft; it descends through a series of ridges to broad, undulating coastal lowlands; highest peak is Halla-san (1 950m/6 398ft) on the island of Cheju-do.

Climate

Extreme continental climate, with cold winters and hot summers; typhoons possible in the wettest months (Jun–Sep); average daily temperatures at Seoul range from –9°C to 0°C (Jan), 22°C to 31°C (Aug).

National holidays

Jan 1, Mar 1 (Independence Movement), May 5 (Children), Jun 6 (Memorial), Jul 17 (Constitution), Aug 15 (Independence), Oct 3 (National Foundation), Dec 25; NY (Korean) (Jan/Feb) (3), Lord Buddha's Birthday (May), Harvest Moon Festival (Sep/Oct) (3).

[1] *In 2004 plans were announced to transfer the capital to the Yeongi-Kongju area by 2012; whether this will be put into effect remains uncertain.*

Political leaders

President

1948–60	Syngman Rhee
1960	Ho Chong *Acting*
1960	Kwak Sang-hun *Acting*
1960	Ho Chong *Acting*
1960–3	Yun Po-sun
1963–79	Park Chung-hee
1979–80	Choi Kyu-hah
1980	Park Choong-hoon *Acting*
1980–8	Chun Doo-hwan
1988–93	Roh Tae-woo
1993–7	Kim Young-sam
1997–2003	Kim Dae-jung
2003–8	Roh Moo-hyun
2008–	Lee Myung-bak

Prime Minister

1948–50	Lee Pom-sok
1950	Shin Song-mo *Acting*
1950–1	John M Chang
1951–2	Ho Chong *Acting*
1952	Lee Yun-yong *Acting*
1952	Chang Taek-sang
1952–4	Paik Too-chin
1954–6	Pyon Yong-tae
1956–60	Syngman Rhee
1960	Ho Chong
1960–1	John M Chang
1961	Chang To-yong
1961–2	Song Yo-chan
1962–3	Kim Hyun-chul
1963–4	Choe Tu-son
1964–70	Chung Il-kwon
1970–1	Paik Too-chin
1971–5	Kim Jong-pil
1975–9	Choi Kyu-hah
1979–80	Shin Hyun-hwak
1980	Park Choong-hoon *Acting*
1980–2	Nam Duck-woo
1982	Yoo Chang-soon
1982–3	Kim Sang-hyup
1983–5	Chin Lee-chong
1985–8	Lho Shin-yong
1988	Lee Hyun-jae
1988–90	Kang Young-hoon
1990–1	Ro Jai-bong
1991–2	Chung Won-shik
1992–3	Hyun Soong-jong
1993	Hwang In-sung
1993–4	Lee Hoi-chang
1994	Lee Yung-duck
1994–5	Yi Hong-ku
1995–7	Lee Soo-sung
1997–8	Koh Kun
1998–2000	Kim Jong-pil
2000	Park Tae-joon
2000	Lee Hun-jai *Acting*
2000–2	Lee Han-dong
2002–3	Kim Suk-soo
2003–4	Ko Kun
2004–6	Lee Hae-chan
2006–7	Han Myung-sook
2007–	Han Duck-soo

KOSOVO *see* SERBIA

KUWAIT

Official name	State of Kuwait
Local name	Dawlat al-Kuwayt
Independence	1961
Area	17 818 sq km/6 878 sq mi
Capital	Kuwait City; Al Kuwayt
Chief towns	Shuwaikh, Mina al Ahmadi
Population	2 505 000 (2007e)
Nationality	Kuwaiti
Languages	Arabic; English is also widely spoken
Ethnic groups	Kuwaiti 45%, other Arab 35%, South Asian 9%, Iranian 4%, others 7%
Religions	Islam 85% (Sunni 60%, Shia 25%), others 15%
Time zone	GMT +3
Currency	1 Kuwaiti Dinar (KD/KWD) = 1 000 fils
Telephone	+965
Internet	.kw
Country code	KWT

Location

An independent state at the head of the Arabian Gulf, bounded to the north and west by Iraq; to the east by the Arabian Gulf; and to the south by Saudi Arabia.

Physical description

Consists of the mainland and nine offshore islands; terrain is flat or gently undulating, rising in the south-west to 271m/889ft; Wadi al Batin runs along the western border with Iraq; terrain is generally stony with sparse vegetation.

Climate

Hot, dry climate; summer temperatures are very high, often above 45°C (Jul–Aug); winter daytime temperatures often exceed 20°C; humidity is generally high; sandstorms are common throughout the year.

National holidays

Jan 1, Feb 25 (National), 26 (Liberation); Mt Arafat, Ad (3), ER (2/3), NY (Muslim), PA, PB.

Political leaders

Emir

Family name: Al-Sabah

1896–1915	Mubarak
1915–17	Jaber II
1917–21	Salem Al-Mubarak
1921–50	Ahmed Al-Jaber
1950–65	Abdallah Al-Salem
1965–77	Sabah Al-Salem
1978–2006	Jaber Al-Ahmed Al-Jaber
2006	Saad Al-Abdallah Al-Salem *Abdicated*
2006–	Sabah Al-Ahmed Al-Jaber Al-Sabah

Prime Minister

1962–3	Jaber Al-Ahmed Al-Jaber Al-Sabah
1963–5	Sabah Al-Salem Al-Sabah
1965–78	Jaber Al-Ahmed Al-Jaber Al-Sabah
1978–2003	Saad Al-Abdallah Al-Salem Al-Sabah
2003–6	Sabah Al-Ahmed Al-Jaber Al-Sabah
2006–	Nasser Al-Mohammad Al-Ahmed Al-Sabah

KYRGYZSTAN

Official name	Kyrgyz Republic
Local name	Kyrgyz Respublikasy
Former name	Kyrgyz Soviet Socialist Republic (until 1990), within the Union of Soviet Socialist Republics (USSR; 1922–91)
Independence	1991
Area	198 500 sq km/76 621 sq mi
Capital	Bishkek; Biškek
Chief towns	Osh, Przhevalsk, Kyzyl-Kiya
Population	5 284 000 (2007e)
Nationality	Kyrgyz
Languages	Kyrgyz, Russian
Ethnic groups	Kyrgyz 67%, Uzbek 14%, Russian 11%, Ukrainian 1%, others 7%
Religions	Islam 75%, Christianity 20% (Orthodox), others 5%
Time zone	GMT +5
Currency	1 Som (Kgs/KGS) = 100 tyjyn[1]
Telephone	+996
Internet	.kg
Country code	KGZ

Location

A republic in central Asia, bounded to the north by Kazakhstan; to the south-east by China; to the south by Tajikistan; and to the west by Uzbekistan.

Physical description

Largely occupied by the Tien Shan Mountains; highest point is Pobedy Peak (7 439m/24 406ft); Lake Issyk-Kul is the largest lake.

Climate

Varies according to location; sub-tropical in the south-west, dry in the north and west, continental to polar in the mountainous east.

National holidays

Jan 1, 7 (Orthodox Christmas), Feb 23 (Defenders), Mar 8 (Women), 21, 24 (National Revolution), May 1, 5 (Constitution), 9 (Victory), Aug 31 (Independence), Nov 7 (Social Revolution); Ad, ER.

[1] *Also sometimes transliterated as tyin or tyiyn.*

Political leaders

President

1991–2005	Askar Akayev
2005–	Kurmanbek Bakiyev

Prime Minister

1991	Nasirdin Isanov
1991–2	Andrey Andreyevich Yordan *Acting*
1992–3	Tursunbek Chyngyshev
1993–8	Apas Jumagulov
1998	Kubanychbek Djumaliyev
1998	Boris Silayev *Acting*
1998–9	Jumabek Ibraimov
1999	Boris Silayev *Acting*
1999–2000	Amangeldy Muraliyev
2000–2	Kurmanbek Bakiyev
2002–5	Nikolai Tanayev
2005	Kurmanbek Bakiyev
2005	Medetbek Kerimkulov *Acting*
2005–7	Feliks Kulov
2007	Azim Isabekov
2007	Almazbek Atambeyev
2007	Iskenderbek Aidaraliyev
2007–	Igor Vitalevic Chudinov

Yurts in the Sun

The national flag of Kyrgyzstan has a red background, symbolizing courage and audacity. In its centre is a golden sun, representing peace and wealth. Within the sun is a *tunduk*, the roof of a yurt, symbolizing home within the big wide world.

LAOS

Official name	Lao People's Democratic Republic
Local name	Lao; Sathalanalat Paxathipatai Paxaxôn Lao
Former name	Kingdom of Laos (1945–75)
Independence	1949
Area	236 800 sq km/91 405 sq mi
Capital	Vientiane; Viangchan
Chief towns	Luang Prabang, Pakse, Savannakhét
Population	6 522 000 (2007e)
Nationality	Lao or Laotian
Languages	Lao
Ethnic groups	Lao 52%, Khmu 11%, Phuthai 10%, Hmong 7%, ethnic Vietnamese/Chinese 1%, others 19%
Religions	Buddhism 60%, traditional beliefs and other faiths 40%
Time zone	GMT +7
Currency	1 New Kip (Kp/LAK) = 100 at
Telephone	+856
Internet	.la
Country code	LAO

Location

A republic in south-east Asia, bounded to the north by China; to the east by Vietnam; to the south by Cambodia; and to the west by Thailand and Myanmar.

Physical description
On the Indochinese Peninsula; dense jungle and rugged mountains in the east; highest point is Phu Bia (2820m/9252ft); Mekong River flows north-west–south-east, following much of the west frontier with Thailand.

Climate
Monsoonal with heavy rain in May–Sep; hot and dry Feb–Apr; average annual temperatures in Vientiane are 14–34°C.

National holidays
Jan 1, 20 (Army), Mar 8 (Women), 22 (People's Party), May 1, Jun 1 (Children), Aug 13 (Free Laos), Oct 12 (Liberation), Dec 2 (National); NY (Chinese) (Jan/Feb), NY (Lao) (Apr) (3), Bouk Khao Pansa (Sep/Oct), Khao Pansa (Jul), Vesak (May).

Political leaders

Monarch

1904–59	Sisavang Vong
1959–75	Savang Vatthana

President

1975–87	Souphanouvong
1987–91	Phoumi Vongvichit
1991–2	Kaysone Phomvihane
1992–8	Nouhak Phoumsavan
1998–2006	Khamtai Siphandon
2006–	Choummaly Sayasone

Prime Minister

1951–4	Souvanna Phouma
1954–6	Katay Don Sasorith
1956–8	Souvanna Phouma
1958–9	Phoui Sahanikone
1959–60	Sunthone Patthamavong
1960	Kou Abhay
1960	Somsanith
1960	Souvana Phouma
1960	Sunthone Patthamavong
1960	Quinim Pholsena
1960–2	Boun Oum Na Champassac
1962–75	Souvanna Phouma
1975–91	Kaysone Phomvihane
1991–8	Khamtai Siphandon
1998–2001	Sisavath Keobounphan
2001–6	Boungnang Vorachit
2006–	Bouasone Bouphavanh

LATVIA

Official name	Republic of Latvia
Local name	Latvija; Latvijas Republika
Former name	Latvian Soviet Socialist Republic (1940–90), within the Union of Soviet Socialist Republics (USSR; 1940–91)
Independence	1991
Area	63 700 sq km/24 600 sq mi
Capital	Riga; Rīga
Chief towns	Daugavpils, Liepaja
Population	2 260 000 (2007e)
Nationality	Latvian
Languages	Latvian
Ethnic groups	Latvian 57%, Russian 30%, Belarussian 4%, Ukrainian 3%, others 6%
Religions	Christianity 58% (Prot 36% (Lutheran), RC 22%), other, unaffiliated and none 42%
Time zone	GMT +2
Currency	1 Lat (Ls/LVL) = 100 santims
Telephone	+371
Internet	.lv
Country code	LVA

Location

A republic in north-eastern Europe, bounded to the north-west by the Gulf of Riga; to the north by Estonia; to the east by Russia; to the south-east by Belarus; to the south by Lithuania; and to the west by the Baltic Sea.

Physical description

A flat, glaciated area; north-west coast is indented by the Gulf of Riga; highest point is Gaizinkalns (312m/1 024ft); over 40% is forested.

Climate

Moderate winters; cool, rainy summers.

National holidays

Jan 1, May 1, 4 (Independence Restoration), Jun 23 (Ligo/Midsummer's Eve), 24 (Jani/St John), Nov 18 (Independence), Dec 25, 26, 31; EM, ES, GF.

Political leaders

President

1990–3	Anatolijs Gorbunovs	1999–7	Vaira Vike-Freiberga
1993–9	Guntis Ulmanis	2007–	Valdis Zatlers

Prime Minister

1990–3	Ivars Godmanis	1999–2000	Andris Skele
1993–4	Valdis Birkavs	2000–2	Andris Berzins
1994–5	Maris Gailis	2002–4	Einars Repse
1995–7	Andris Skele	2004	Indulis Emsis
1997–8	Guntars Krasts	2004–7	Aigars Kalvitis
1998–9	Vilis Kristopans	2007–	Ivars Godmanis

Crocodile Dundee?

In the small village of Dundaga, north-east of Riga, is a huge statue of a crocodile. It commemorates local man Arvids von Blumenfelds, who emigrated to Australia in the 1940s and lived in the outback. It is said that the film *Crocodile Dundee* (1986) was inspired by his exploits.

LEBANON

Official name	Republic of Lebanon
Local name	Al-Lubnān; Al-Jumhūriyya al-Lubnaniyya (Arabic), Liban; République Libanaise (French)
Independence	1943
Area	10452 sq km/4034 sq mi
Capital	Beirut; Bayrūt
Chief towns	Tripoli, Saida, Zahle
Population	3925000 (2007e)
Nationality	Lebanese
Languages	Arabic, French; English and Armenian are also spoken
Ethnic groups	Arab 95%, Armenian 4%, others 1%
Religions	Islam 60%, Christianity 39%, others 1%
Time zone	GMT +2
Currency	1 Lebanese Pound (LL, L£/LBP) = 100 piastres
Telephone	+961
Internet	.lb
Country code	LBN

Location
A republic on the eastern coast of the Mediterranean Sea, bounded to the north and east by Syria, and to the south by Israel.

Physical description
Narrow Mediterranean coastal plain rises to the Lebanon Mountains, which extend along most of the country; peaks include the Qornet es-Sauda (3090m/10137ft); arid eastern slopes fall to the fertile El Beqaa plateau; Anti-Lebanon range lies in the east.

Climate
Mediterranean, varying with altitude, with hot, dry summers and warm, moist winters; average temperatures at Beirut are 13–27°C; much cooler and drier in the Beqaa valley and irrigation is essential.

National holidays
Jan 1, 6 (Armenian Christmas), Feb 9 (St Maron), May 1, 6 (Martyrs), 13 (Resistance and Liberation), Aug 15, Nov 22 (Independence), Dec 25; Ad (2), As, ER (2), GF (Orthodox), GF (Western), NY (Muslim), PB.

Political leaders

President

1943–52	Bishara Al-Khoury
1952–8	Camille Shamoun
1958–64	Fouad Shehab
1964–70	Charle Hilo
1970–6	Suleiman Frenjieh
1976–82	Elias Sarkis
1982	Bashir Gemayel
1982–8	Amin Gemayel
1988–9	*No President*
1989	René Muawad
1989–98	Elias Hrawi
1998–2007	Émile Lahoud
2007–	Fouad Siniora *Acting*

Prime Minister

1943	Riad Solh
1943–4	Henry Pharaon
1944–5	Riad Solh
1945	Abdul Hamid Karame
1945–6	Sami Solh
1946	Saadi Munla
1946–51	Riad Solh
1951	Hussein Oweini
1951–2	Abdullah Yafi
1952	Sami Solh
1952	Nazem Accari
1952	Saeb Salam
1952	Fouad Chehab
1952–3	Khaled Chehab
1953	Saeb Salam
1953–5	Abdullah Yafi
1955	Sami Solh
1955–6	Rashid Karami
1956	Abdullah Yafi
1956–8	Sami Solh
1958–60	Rashid Karami
1960	Ahmad Daouq
1960–1	Saeb Salam
1961–4	Rashid Karami
1964–5	Hussein Oweini
1965–6	Rashid Karami
1966	Abdullah Yafi
1966–8	Rashid Karami
1968–9	Abdullah Yafi
1969–70	Rashid Karami
1970–3	Saeb Salam
1973	Amin al-Hafez
1973–4	Takieddine Solh
1974–5	Rashid Solh
1975	Noureddin Rifai
1975–6	Rashid Karami
1976–80	Selim al-Hoss
1980	Takieddine Solh
1980–4	Chafiq al-Wazan
1984–8	Rashid Karami
1988–90	Michel Aoun/Selim al-Hoss
1990–2	Umar Karami
1992–8	Rafiq al-Hariri
1998–2000	Selim al-Hoss
2000–4	Rafiq al-Hariri
2004–5	Umar Karami
2005	Najib Mikati
2005–	Fouad Siniora

LESOTHO

Official name	Kingdom of Lesotho
Local name	Lesotho; Mmuso wa Lesotho
Former name	Basutoland (until 1966)
Independence	1966
Area	30 460 sq km/11 758 sq mi
Capital	Maseru
Chief towns	Mafeteng, Quthing
Population	2 125 000 (2007e)
Nationality	Mosotho (singular), Basotho (plural)
Languages	Sesotho, English; Zulu and Xhosa are also spoken
Ethnic groups	Sotho 99%, others 1%
Religions	Christianity 90% (RC 45%, Prot 45%), others 10%
Time zone	GMT +2
Currency	1 Loti (plural Maloti) (M, LSM/LSL) = 100 lisente; the South African Rand is also used
Telephone	+266
Internet	.ls
Country code	LSO

Location
An African kingdom completely bounded by South Africa.

Physical description
Drakensberg Mountains in north-east and east include the highest peak, Thabana Ntlenyana (3482m/11 424ft); Mulati Mountains running south to west form a steep escarpment; population mainly lives west of the highlands at altitude of 1 500–1 800m/4 920–5 900ft.

Climate
Mild, dry winters; warm summer season is Oct–Apr; lowland summer maximum temperature is 32°C, winter minimum is 7°C.

National holidays
Jan 1, Mar 11 (Moshoeshoe), May 1, 25 (Africa/Heroes), Jul 17 (King's Birthday), Oct 4 (Independence), Dec 25, 26; A, EM, GF.

Political leaders

Monarch
1966–70 Moshoeshoe II

Head of State
1970 Leabua Jonathan

Monarch
1970 'MaMohato Lerotholi *Queen Regent*
1970–90 Moshoeshoe II
1990 'MaMohato Lerotholi *Queen Regent*
1990–5 Letsie III
1995–6 Moshoeshoe II
1996 'MaMohato Lerotholi *Queen Regent*
1996– Letsie III

Prime Minister
1966–86 Leabua Jonathan

Chairman of Military Council
1986–91 Justin Metsing Lekhanya
1991–3 Elias Tutsoane Ramaema

Prime Minister

1993–4	Ntsu Mokhehle
1994	Hae Phoofolo *Interim*
1994–8	Ntsu Mokhehle
1998–	Bethuel Pakalitha Mosisili

LIBERIA

Official name	Republic of Liberia
Local name	Liberia
Independence	1847
Area	111 370 sq km/42 999 sq mi
Capital	Monrovia
Chief towns	Harper, Greenville, Buchanan, Robertsport
Population	3 196 000 (2007e)
Nationality	Liberian
Languages	English; many local languages are also spoken
Ethnic groups	African 95% (includes Kpelle, Bassa, Grebo, Gio, Kru, Mano), Americo-Liberian 2.5%, Congo people 2.5%
Religions	Christianity 40%, traditional beliefs 40%, Islam 20%
Time zone	GMT
Currency	1 Liberian Dollar (L$/LRD) = 100 cents
Telephone	+231
Internet	.lr
Country code	LBR

Location

A republic in West Africa, bounded to the north-west by Sierra Leone; to the north by Guinea; to the east by Côte d'Ivoire; and to the south by the Atlantic Ocean.

Physical description

Low coastal belt with lagoons, beaches, and mangrove marshes; rolling plateau (500–800m/1 640–2 624ft) with grasslands and forest; land rises inland to mountains; highest point is Mt Wuteve (1 380m/4 528ft); rivers cut south-west down through the plateau.

Climate

Equatorial climate, with high temperatures and abundant rainfall; rainfall declines from south to north; high humidity during the rainy season (Apr–Sep), especially on the coast.

National holidays

Jan 1, Feb 11 (Armed Forces), Mar 15 (J J Roberts' Birthday), Apr 12 (Redemption), May 14 (National Unification), 25 (Africa), Jul 26 (Independence), Aug 24 (National Flag), Nov 29 (President Tubman's Birthday), Dec 25; Decoration (Mar), National Fast and Prayer (Apr), Thanksgiving (Nov).

Political leaders

President

1900–4	Garretson Wilmot Gibson
1904–12	Arthur Barclay
1912–20	Daniel Edward Howard
1920–30	Charles Dunbar Burgess King
1930–43	Edwin J Barclay
1943–71	William V S Tubman
1971–80	William Richard Tolbert

Chairman of People's Redemption Council

1980–6	Samuel K Doe

President

1986–90	Samuel K Doe
1991–4	Amos Sawyer *Interim*

Chairman of Council of State

1994–5	David Kpormakor
1995–6	Wilton Sankawulo
1996–7	Ruth Perry

President

1997–2003	Charles Taylor	2003–6	Gyude Bryant *Transitional*
2003	Moses Zeh Blah *Interim*[1]	2006–	Ellen Johnson-Sirleaf

[1] *Charles Taylor went into exile in Aug 2003; Moses Zeh Blah handed power to a transitional government in Oct 2003.*

LIBYA

Official name	Great Socialist People's Libyan Arab Jamahiriya
Local name	Lībyā; Al-Jamāhīriyya Al-'Arabiyya Al-Lībiyya Ash-Sha'biyya Al-Ishtirākiyya
Former name	United Libyan Kingdom (1951–63), Libyan Kingdom (1963–9), Libyan Arab Republic (1969–77)
Independence	1951
Area	1 758 610 sq km/678 823 sq mi
Capital	Tripoli; Tarābulus
Chief towns	Misratah, Benghazi, Tobruk
Population	6 037 000 (2007e)
Nationality	Libyan
Languages	Arabic
Ethnic groups	Arab and Berber 97%, others 3%
Religions	Islam 97% (Sunni), others 3%
Time zone	GMT +2
Currency	1 Libyan Dinar (LD/LYD) = 1 000 dirhams
Telephone	+218
Internet	.ly
Country code	LBY

Location

A state in North Africa, crossed by the Tropic of Cancer in the south; bounded to the north-west by Tunisia; to the north by the Mediterranean Sea; to the east by Egypt; to the south-east by Sudan; to the south by Chad; to the south-west by Niger; and to the west by Algeria.

Physical description

Mainly low-lying Saharan desert or semi-desert; land rises in the south to over 2 000m/6 561ft in the Tibesti Massif; highest point, Pic Bette (2 286m/7 500ft), lies on the Chad frontier; surface water is limited to infrequent oases.

Climate

Mediterranean climate on the coast; Tripoli, representative of the coastal region, has average maximum daily temperatures of 16–30°C; temperatures in the south are over 40°C for three months of the year.

National holidays

Mar 2 (Jamahiriya/Declaration), 28 (British Evacuation), Jun 11 (US Evacuation), Sep 1 (Revolution), Oct 7 (Italian Evacuation), 26 (Memorial), Dec 24 (Independence); Ad (2), As, ER (3), NY (Muslim), PA, PB.

Political leaders

Monarch

1951–69 Idris I (Sidi Muhammad Idris Al-Mahdi As-Sanusi)

Chairman of Revolutionary Command Council

1969–77 Muammar Al-Gaddafi

General Secretary of the General People's Congress

1977–9	Muammar Al-Gaddafi	1984–90	Mifta al-Usta Umar
1979–81	Abdul Ati Al-Ubaidi	1990–2	Abdul Razzaq as-Sawsa
1981–4	Muhammad Az-Zaruq Rajab	1992–	Zintani Muhammad az-Zintani

Leader of the Revolution

1979–	Muammar Al-Gaddafi

Prime Minister

1951–4	Mahmud al-Muntasir	1965–7	Hussein Mazzek
1954	Muhammad Sakizli	1967	Abdul Qadir al-Badri
1954–7	Mustafa Ben Halim	1967–8	Abdul Hamid al-Bakkoush
1957–60	Abdul Majid Kubar	1968–9	Wanis al-Qaddafi
1960–3	Muhammad Osman Said	1969–70	Mahmud Sulayman al-Maghribi
1963–4	Mohieddin Fikini	1972–7	Abdul Salam Jalloud
1964–5	Mahmud al-Muntasir		

General Secretary of the General People's Committee

1977–9	Abdul Ati al-Ubaidi	1994–7	Abdul Majid al-Qaud
1979–84	Jadallah Azzuz at-Talhi	1997–2000	Muhammad Ahmad al-Mangoush
1984–6	Muhammad az-Zaruq Rajab	2000–3	Mubarak Abdallah al-Shamikh
1986–7	Jadallah Azzuz at-Talhi	2003–6	Shukri Muhammad Ghanim
1987–90	Umar Mustafa al-Muntasir	2006–	Al-Baghdadi Ali al-Mahmudi
1990–4	Abu Zayd Umar Durda		

LIECHTENSTEIN

Official name	Principality of Liechtenstein
Local name	Liechtenstein; Fürstentum Liechtenstein
Independence	1719 (part of Holy Roman Empire to 1806)
Area	160 sq km/62 sq mi
Capital	Vaduz
Chief towns	Schaan, Triesen, Balzers
Population	34 000 (2007e)
Nationality	Liechtensteiner, Liechtenstein
Languages	German, spoken in the form of an Alemannic dialect
Ethnic groups	Liechtensteiner 86%, Italian, Turkish and others 14%
Religions	Christianity 83% (RC 76%, Prot 7%), others 6%, unknown 11%
Time zone	GMT +1
Currency	1 Swiss Franc (SFr, SwF/CHF) = 100 centimes = 100 rappen
Telephone	+423
Internet	.li
Country code	LIE

Location

An independent principality in central Europe, bounded by Austria to the east and Switzerland to the west.

Physical description

Bounded to the west by the River Rhine, its valley occupying approximately 40% of the country; much of the rest consists of forested mountains, rising to 2 599m/8 527ft in the Grauspitz.

Climate

Mild, influenced by a warm south wind (the *Föhn*); average maximum temperature of 20–28°C in summer.

National holidays

Jan 1, 6, Feb 2 (Candlemas), Mar 19 (St Joseph), May 1, Aug 15 (National), Sep 8 (Nativity of Our Lady), Nov 1, Dec 8, 25, 26; A, CC, EM, ES, WM, Whit Sunday.

Political leaders

Prince

1858–1929	Johann II
1929–38	Franz von Paula
1938–89	Franz Josef II
1989–	Hans Adam II

Prime Minister

1928–45	Franz Josef Hoop
1945–62	Alexander Friek
1962–70	Gérard Batliner
1970–4	Alfred J Hilbe
1974–8	Walter Kieber
1978–93	Hans Brunhart
1993	Markus Büchel
1993–2001	Mario Frick
2001–	Otmar Hasler

LITHUANIA

Official name	Republic of Lithuania
Local name	Lietuva; Lietuvos Respublika
Former name	Lithuanian Soviet Socialist Republic (1940–90), within the Union of Soviet Socialist Republics (USSR; 1940–91)
Independence	1990 (declared), 1991 (recognized)
Area	65 200 sq km/25 167 sq mi
Capital	Vilnius
Chief towns	Kaunas, Klaipėda, Šiauliai
Population	3 575 000 (2007e)
Nationality	Lithuanian
Languages	Lithuanian
Ethnic groups	Lithuanian 83%, Polish 7%, Russian 6%, others 4%
Religions	Christianity 85% (RC 79%, Russian Orthodox 4%, Prot 2%), others and unspecified 5%, none 10%
Time zone	GMT +2
Currency	1 Litas (Lt/LTL) = 100 centas
Telephone	+370
Internet	.lt
Country code	LTU

Location

A republic in north-eastern Europe, bounded to the north by Latvia; to the east and south by Belarus; to the south-west by Poland and the Kaliningrad region of Russia; and to the west by the Baltic Sea.

Physical description

Glaciated plains cover much of the area; highest point is Juozapine Hill (294m/965ft).

Climate

Varies between maritime and continental; wet, with moderate winters and summers.

National holidays

Jan 1, Feb 16 (Independence), Mar 11 (Independence Restoration), May 1, 6 (Mothers), Jun 24 (St John), Jul 6 (Coronation of Mindaugus), Aug 15, Nov 1, Dec 25, 26; EM, ES, Easter Tuesday; Mother's Day (1st Mon in May).

Political leaders

President

1990–3	Vytautas Landsbergis	2003–4	Rolandas Paksas
1993–8	Algirdas Brazauskas	2004	Arturas Paulauskas *Acting*
1998–2003	Valdas Adamkus	2004–	Valdas Adamkus

Prime Minister

1990–1	Kazimiera Prunskienë	1999	Irena Degutienë *Acting*
1991	Albertas Simenas	1999	Rolandas Paksas
1991–2	Gediminas Vagnorius	1999	Irena Degutienë *Acting*
1992	Aleksandras Abisala	1999–2000	Andrius Kubilius
1992–3	Bronislovas Lubys	2000–1	Rolandas Paksas
1993–6	Adolfas Slezevicius	2001	Eugenijus Gentvilas *Acting*
1996	Laurynas Stankevicius	2001–6	Algirdas Brazauskas
1996–9	Gediminas Vagnorius	2006–	Gediminas Kirkilas

Amber was known as 'Lithuania's gold' and was collected and traded for centuries.

LUXEMBOURG

Official name	Grand Duchy of Luxembourg
Local name	Luxembourg; Grand-Duché de Luxembourg (French), Luxemburg; Grossherzogtum Luxemburg (German), Lëtzebuerg; Groussherzogtom Lëtzebuerg (Lëtzebuergesch)
Independence	1867
Area	2586 sq km/998 sq mi
Capital	Luxembourg; Luxembourg (French), Luxemburg (German), Lëtzebuerg (Lëtzebuergesch)
Chief towns	Esch-sur-Alzette, Dudelange, Differdange
Population	480000 (2007e)
Nationality	Luxembourger, Luxembourg
Languages	French, German, Lëtzebuergesch
Ethnic groups	Luxembourger 60%, Portuguese 15%, French 5%, Italian 4%, Belgian 4%, German 2%, others 10%
Religions	Christianity 90% (mostly RC), Islam 2%, others and none 8%
Time zone	GMT +1
Currency	1 Euro (€/EUR) = 100 cents
Telephone	+352
Internet	.lu
Country code	LUX

Location
An independent constitutional monarchy in north-western Europe, bounded to the north-east and east by Germany; to the south by France; and to the north-west and west by Belgium.

Physical description
Divided into two natural regions: Ösling in the north (wooded, hilly land) and flatter, more fertile Gutland; highest point is Buurgplaatz (559m/1833ft); water resources developed by canalization of the River Mosel, hydroelectric dams on the River Our and reservoirs on the River Sûre.

Climate
Drier and sunnier in the south, but winters can be severe; summers and autumns are warm enough for cultivation of vines in the sheltered Mosel Valley.

National holidays
Jan 1, May 1, Jun 23 (National), Aug 15, Nov 1, Dec 25, 26; A, EM, WM.

Political leaders

Grand Dukes and Duchesses

1890–1905	Adolf of Nassau
1905–12	William IV
1912–19	Marie Adelaide
1919–64	Charlotte (*in exile* 1940–4)
1964–2000	Jean
2000–	Henri

Prime Minister

1889–1915	Paul Eyschen
1915	Mathias Mongenast
1915–16	Hubert Loutsch
1916–17	Victor Thorn
1917–18	Léon Kaufmann
1918–25	Emil Reuter
1925–6	Pierre Prum
1926–37	Joseph Bech
1937–53	Pierre Dupong (*in exile* 1940–4)
1953–8	Joseph Bech
1958–9	Pierre Frieden
1959–69	Pierre Werner
1969–79	Gaston Thorn
1979–84	Pierre Werner
1984–95	Jacques Santer
1995–	Jean-Claude Juncker

Grand Cuisine

Luxembourg has more Michelin-starred restaurants per square mile than any other country in the world.

MACAO *see* CHINA

MACEDONIA

Official name	Former Yugoslav Republic of Macedonia (FYRM or FYR Macedonia; *international name*); Republic of Macedonia (*local name*)
Local name	Makedonija; Republika Makedonija, Poranesna Jugoslovenska Republika Makedonija
Former name	formerly part of Kingdom of Serbs, Croats and Slovenes (until 1929), Kingdom of Yugoslavia (1929–41), Federal People's Republic of Yugoslavia (1945–63), Socialist Federal People's Republic of Yugoslavia (1963–91)
Independence	1991
Area	25 713 sq km/9 925 sq mi
Capital	Skopje
Chief towns	Bitola, Gostivar, Tetovo, Kumanovo
Population	2 056 000 (2007e)
Nationality	Macedonian
Languages	Macedonian, Albanian
Ethnic groups	Macedonian 64%, Albanian 25%, Turkish 4%, others 7%
Religions	Christianity 65% (Orthodox), Islam 33%, others 2%
Time zone	GMT +1
Currency	1 Denar (D, den/MKD) = 100 deni
Telephone	+389
Internet	.mk
Country code	MKD

Location
A republic in southern Europe, bounded to the north by Serbia; to the east by Bulgaria; to the south by Greece; and to the west by Albania.

Physical description
Mountainous, covered with deep basins and valleys; bisected by the River Vardar; highest point is Golem Korab (Maja e Korabit; 2 753m/9 032ft) on the Albanian border.

Climate
Cold winters and warm, dry summers.

National holidays
Jan 1, 2, 7 (Orthodox Christmas), May 1, 24 (SS Cyril and Methodius), Aug 2 (Ilinden/National), Sep 8 (Independence), Oct 11 (Anti-fascism), 23 (Revolution), Dec 8 (St Kliment Ohridski); EM (Orthodox), ER, ES (Orthodox); *various other holidays designated for specific religious and ethnic groups*.

Political leaders

See **Yugoslavia** for political leaders prior to 1991–2.

President

1991–5	Kiro Gligorov	1999–2004	Boris Trajkovski
1995–8	Stojan Andov *Acting*	2004	Ljupco Jordanovski *Interim*
1998–9	Kiro Gligorov	2004–	Branko Crvenkovski

Prime Minister

1991–2	Branko Crvenkovski	2002–4	Branko Crvenkovski
1992–6	Petar Gosev	2004	Hari Kostov
1996–8	Branko Crvenkovski	2004–6	Vlado Buckovski
1998–2002	Ljubco Georgievski	2006–	Nikola Gruesvski

MADAGASCAR

Official name	Republic of Madagascar
Local name	Madagasikara; Repoblikan'i Madagasikara (Malagasy), Madagascar; République du Madagascar (French)
Former name	Malagasy Republic (1958–75), Democratic Republic of Madagascar (until 1992)
Independence	1960
Area	587 040 sq km/226 656 sq mi
Capital	Antananarivo
Chief towns	Toamasina, Mahajanga, Fianarantsoa, Antsiranana, Toliara
Population	19 449 000 (2007e)
Nationality	Malagasy
Languages	Malagasy, French
Ethnic groups	Merina 26%, Betsimisaraka 16%, Betsileo 12%, Tsimihety 7%, Sakalava 7%, others 32%
Religions	Christianity 50%, traditional beliefs 40%, Islam 10%
Time zone	GMT +3
Currency	1 Ariary (A/MGA) = 5 Iraimbilanja
Telephone	+261
Internet	.mg
Country code	MDG

Location
An island republic in the Indian Ocean, crossed by the Tropic of Capricorn in the south, separated from Mozambique by the Mozambique Channel.

Physical description
Ridge of mountains runs north to south, rising to 2 876m/9 436ft at Maromokotra; cliffs to the east drop down to a coastal plain through tropical forest; a terraced descent to the west through savanna to the coast, which is heavily indented in the north.

Climate
Temperate climate in the highlands; tropical coastal region.

National holidays
Jan 1, Mar 29 (Martyrs), May 1, Jun 26 (Independence), Aug 15, Nov 1, Dec 25; A, EM, WM.

Political leaders

President

1960–72	Philibert Tsiranana	1975–93	Didier Ratsiraka
1972–5	Gabriel Ramanantsoa	1993–7	Albert Zafy
1975	Richard Ratsimandrava	1997–2002	Didier Ratsiraka
1975	Gilles Andriamahazo	2002–	Marc Ravalomanana

Prime Minister

1960–75	*As President*	1995–6	Emmanuel Rakotovahiny
1975–6	Joël Rakotomala	1996–7	Norbert Ratsirahonana
1976–7	Justin Rakotoriaina	1997–8	Paskal Rakotmavo
1977–88	Désiré Rakotoarijaona	1998–2002	Tantely Andrianarivo
1988–91	Victor Ramahatra	2002–7	Jacques Sylla
1991–3	Guy Willy Razanamasy	2007–	Charles Rabemananjara
1993–5	Francisque Ravony		

MADEIRA *see* PORTUGAL

MALAWI

Official name	Republic of Malawi
Local name	Dziko la Malawi
Former name	Nyasaland (until 1964), part of the Federation of Rhodesia and Nyasaland (1953–63)
Independence	1964
Area	118 484 sq km/45 735 sq mi
Capital	Lilongwe
Chief towns	Blantyre, Zomba, Limbe, Salima
Population	13 603 000 (2007e)
Nationality	Malawian
Languages	English, Chichewa
Ethnic groups	Maravi 59%, Lomwe 20%, Yao 13%, Ngoni 6%, others 2%
Religions	Christianity 70%, Islam 20% (Sunni), others 10%
Time zone	GMT +2
Currency	1 Kwacha (MK/MWK) = 100 tambala
Telephone	+265
Internet	.mw
Country code	MWI

Location
A republic in south-eastern Africa, bounded to the north by Tanzania; to the east by Lake Nyasa (Lake Malawi); to the south-west and south-east by Mozambique; and to the west by Zambia.

Physical description
Crossed north to south by the Great Rift Valley in which lies Africa's third-largest lake, Lake Nyasa (Lake Malawi); high plateaux on either side (900–1 200m/2 950–3 937ft); highlands in the south rise to 3 000m/9 840ft at Sapitwa Peak on Mt Mulanje.

Climate
Tropical climate in the south, with high year-round temperatures, 28–37°C; more moderate temperatures in centre; higher rainfall in the mountains overlooking Lake Nyasa.

National holidays
Jan 1, 15 (Chilembwe), Mar 3 (Martyrs), May 1, Jun 14 (Freedom), Jul 6 (Independence), Dec 25, 26; EM, ER, GF, Mothers (2nd Mon in Oct).

Political leaders

President

1966–94	Hastings Kamuzu Banda
1994–2004	Bakili Muluzi
2004–	Bingu wa Mutharika

Get By in Chichewa

The Chichewa word for *hello* is *moni*, and *how are you?* is *muli bwanji?* Other useful words include *madzi* for *water*, *chakudya* for *food* and *chimbudzi* for *toilet*. If you hear a shout of *mkango*, it is either time to grab your camera or run for your life – it means *lion*.

MALAYSIA

Official name	Federation of Malaysia
Local name	Malaysia
Independence	1957
Area	329 749 sq km/127 283 sq mi
Capital	Kuala Lumpur (official) and Putrajaya (administrative and seat of government)
Chief towns	George Town, Ipoh, Malacca, Johor Baharu, Kuching, Kota Kinabalu
Population	24 821 000 (2007e)
Nationality	Malaysian
Languages	Bahasa Malaysia (Malay); Chinese, English, Tamil and local languages are also spoken
Ethnic groups	Malay 50%, Chinese 24%, indigenous people 11%, Indian 7%, others 8%
Religions	Islam 60%, Buddhism 19%, Christianity 9%, Hinduism 6%, traditional Chinese religions 3%, others 3%
Time zone	GMT +8
Currency	1 Malaysian Ringgit (dollar) (M$/MYR) = 100 cents
Telephone	+60
Internet	.my
Country code	MYS

Location
An independent federation of states in south-east Asia, including mainland peninsular Malaysia, bounded to the north by Thailand and linked by a causeway to Singapore in the south; also includes the northern part of the island of Borneo, bounded to the south by Indonesia and completely surrounding Brunei Darussalam.

Physical description
Mainland peninsula (700km/435mi long) of mountains with narrow coastal plains; mostly tropical rainforest and mangrove swamp; Sarawak has a narrow, swampy coastal belt and mountainous interior; Sabah has a deeply indented coastline and narrow coastal plain, rising sharply into mountains reaching 4094m/13 431ft at Mt Kinabalu, Malaysia's highest peak.

Climate
Tropical climate, with highest temperatures in coastal areas; strongly influenced by monsoon winds; high humidity.

National holidays
Jan 1 (*most states*), May 1, Jun 2 (Head of State's Birthday), Aug 31 (National), Dec 25; Ad, D (*most states*), ER (2), NY (Chinese) (Jan/Feb) (2), NY (Muslim), PB, Wesak (May); *regional variations*.

Political leaders

Head of State (Yang di-Pertuan Agong)

1957–63	Abdul Rahman
1963–5	Syed Putra Jamalullah
1965–70	Ismail Nasiruddin Shah
1970–5	Abdul Halim Muadzam Shah
1975–9	Yahya Petra Ibrahim
1979–84	Haji Ahmad Shah Al-Mustain Billah
1984–9	Mahmood Iskandar Shah
1989–94	Azlan Muhibuddin Shah
1994–9	Jaafar Ibni Abdul Rahman
1999–2001	Salehuddin Abdul Aziz Shah
2001	Mizal Zainal Abidin *Acting*
2001–6	Syed Sirajuddin Syed Putra Jamalullail
2006–	Mizan Zainal Abidin ibn al-Marhum

Prime Minister

1957–70	Abdul Rahman Putra Al-Haj
1970–6	Abdul Razak bin Hussein
1976–9	Haji Hussein bin Onn
1979–97	Mahathir bin Mohamad
1997	Anwar Ibrahim *Acting*
1997–2003	Mahathir bin Mohamad
2003–	Abdullah Ahmad Badawi

Malaysian Mud

The name of Malaysia's capital city, *Kuala Lumpur*, comes from Malay words meaning 'muddy estuary'.

MALDIVES

Official name	Republic of Maldives
Local name	Dhivehi Raajje; Dhivehi Rājjē Jumhūriyyā
Former name	Maldive Islands
Independence	1965
Area	300 sq km/120 sq mi
Capital	Malé; Daviyani
Population	369 000 (2007e)
Nationality	Maldivian
Languages	Dhivehi; English is spoken widely
Ethnic groups	Maldivian (mixture of South Indian, Sinhalese and Arab) with African minorities
Religions	Islam 100% (Sunni)
Time zone	GMT +5
Currency	1 Rufiyaa (MRf, Rf/MVR) = 100 laarees
Telephone	+960
Internet	.mv
Country code	MDV

Location
An archipelago republic in the Indian Ocean; the Equator passes between islands.

Physical description
Small, low-lying islands, no more than 1.8m/6ft above sea level, with sandy beaches fringed with coconut palms. Of the 1 190 islands, spread over 26 coral atolls, fewer than 200 are inhabited; Fua Mulaku Island is the largest island, while Huvadhoo Atoll is the largest atoll.

Climate

Generally warm and humid; affected by south-west monsoons from Apr to Oct; average daily temperature is 22°C.

National holidays

Jan 1, Jul 26 (Independence), Nov 3 (Victory), 11 (Republic); Ad, ER, NY (Muslim), PB, R; Embracing of Islam (Apr) (2), Haj (Dec), National (Mar/Apr).

Political leaders

Monarch (Sultan)

1954–68 Mohammed Farid Didi

President

1968–78 Ibrahim Nasir
1978– Maumoon Abdul Gayoom

Maldives in the Dictionary

The Maldives have contributed just one word to the English language: *atoll*, meaning a coral island with a circular belt of coral enclosing a central lagoon. The language of the Maldives, Dhivehi, is unusual in that it has no word for *hello* or *goodbye*. *Kihineh* is used instead of *hello*, meaning *how are you?*, while *dhanee!* or *I'm going!* is often used instead of *goodbye*.

MALI

Official name	Republic of Mali
Local name	Mali; République du Mali
Former name	French Sudan (until 1959), Mali Federation (until 1960)
Independence	1960
Area	1 240 192 sq km/478 714 sq mi
Capital	Bamako
Chief towns	Ségou, Mopti, Sikasso, Kayes, Gao, Timbuktu
Population	11 995 000 (2007e)
Nationality	Malian
Languages	French; Bambara and other local languages are spoken widely
Ethnic groups	Mande 50% (includes Bambara, Malinke, Soninke), Peul 17%, Voltaic 12%, Songhai 6%, Tuareg and Moor 10%, others 5%
Religions	Islam 90% (mostly Sunni), traditional beliefs 9%, Christianity 1%
Time zone	GMT
Currency	1 CFA Franc (CFAFr/XOF) = 100 centimes
Telephone	+223
Internet	.ml
Country code	MLI

Location

A republic in West Africa, crossed by the Tropic of Cancer in the north; bounded to the north-west by Mauritania; to the north-east by Algeria; to the east by Niger; to the south-east by Burkina Faso; to the south by Côte d'Ivoire; to the south-west by Guinea; and to the west by Senegal.

Physical description

On the fringe of the Sahara; lower part of the Hoggar massif is located in the north; arid plains between 300m/984ft and 500m/1 640ft; featureless desert land in the north with sand dunes; highest point is Hombori Tondo (1 155m/3 789ft); mainly savanna in the south.

Climate
Hot, dry climate with rainfall increasing from north to south; in the south the rainfall season lasts for five months (Jun–Oct); almost no annual average rainfall in the Saharan north.

National holidays
Jan 1, 20 (Armed Forces), Mar 26 (Martyrs), May 1, 25 (Africa), Sep 22 (Independence), Dec 25; Ad, EM, ER, PB, Prophet's Baptism.

Political leaders

President

1960–8	Modibo Keita
1968–91	Moussa Traoré[1]
1991–2	Amadou Toumani Touré[2]
1992–2002	Alpha Oumar Konaré
2002–	Amadou Toumani Touré

Prime Minister

1986–88	Mamadou Dembelé
1988–91	*No Prime Minister*
1991–2	Soumana Sacko
1992–3	Younoussi Touré
1993–4	Abdoulaye Sekou Sow
1994–2000	Ibrahim Boubacar Keita
2000–2	Mande Sidibe
2002–4	Ahmed Mohamed ag Hamani
2004–7	Ousmane Issoufi Maïga
2007–	Modibo Sidibé

[1] *Chairman of Military Committee for the National Liberation until 1969; Head of State until 1979; President from 1979.*
[2] *Chairman of Military Committee for the Salvation of the People.*

MALTA

Official name	Republic of Malta
Local name	Malta; Repubblika ta' Malta
Independence	1964
Area	316 sq km/122 sq mi
Capital	Valletta
Chief towns	Sliema, Birkirkara, Qormi, Rabat, Victoria
Population	402 000 (2007e)
Nationality	Maltese
Languages	English, Maltese; there are many Arabic words in the local vocabulary
Ethnic groups	Maltese 98%, British 2%
Religions	Christianity 98% (RC), others 1%, none/unaffiliated 1%
Time zone	GMT +1
Currency	1 Euro (€/EUR) = 100 cents
Telephone	+356
Internet	.mt
Country code	MLT

Location
An archipelago republic in the central Mediterranean Sea.

Physical description
Generally low-lying, rising to 253m/830ft; no rivers or mountains; well-indented coastline.

Climate
Dry summers and mild winters; average daily winter temperature is 13°C.

National holidays
Jan 1, Feb 10 (St Paul's Shipwreck), Mar 19 (St Joseph), 31 (Freedom), May 1, Jun 7 (Sette Giugno), 29 (SS Peter and Paul), Aug 15, Sep 8 (Our Lady of Victories), 21 (Independence), Dec 8, 13 (Republic), 25; GF.

Political leaders

President

1974–6	Anthony Mamo	1989–94	Vincent Tabone
1976–81	Anton Buttigieg	1994–9	Ugo Mifsud Bonnici
1981–2	Albert Hyzler *Acting*	1999–2004	Guido de Marco
1982–7	Agatha Barbara	2004–	Edward Fenech-Adami
1987–9	Paul Xuereb *Acting*		

Prime Minister

1962–71	G Borg Olivier	1996–8	Alfred Sant
1971–84	Dom Mintoff	1998–2004	Edward Fenech-Adami
1984–7	Carmelo Mifsud Bonnici	2004–	Lawrence Gonzi
1987–96	Edward Fenech-Adami		

Maltese Medal

In 1942 Malta was awarded the George Cross for its resistance to heavy air attacks in World War II.

MALVINAS *see* FALKLAND ISLANDS *under* UNITED KINGDOM

MAN, ISLE OF *see* UNITED KINGDOM

MARIANA ISLANDS, NORTHERN *see* UNITED STATES OF AMERICA

MARSHALL ISLANDS

Official name	Republic of the Marshall Islands (RMI)
Local name	Marshall Islands, Majol
Former name	formerly part of the Trust Territory of the Pacific Islands (1947–79)
Independence	1986
Area	approx 180 sq km/70 sq mi
Capital	Majuro
Population	62 000 (2007e)
Nationality	Marshallese
Languages	Marshallese, English
Ethnic groups	Micronesian 97%, others 3%
Religions	Christianity 93% (Prot 85%, RC 8%), Baha'i 1%, unaffiliated 2%, others 4%
Time zone	GMT +12
Currency	1 US Dollar ($, US$/USD) = 100 cents
Telephone	+692
Internet	.mh
Country code	MHL

Location
An archipelago republic in the central Pacific Ocean.

Physical description
Coral limestone and sand islands, atolls and reefs, with few natural resources; low-lying, rising to no more than 10m/33ft.

Climate
Hot and humid; wet season is from May to Nov; occasional typhoons.

National holidays
Jan 1, Mar 1 (Memorial), May 1 (Constitution), Nov 17 (President), Dec 25; GF; Culture (last Fri in Sep), Fishermen (1st Fri in Jul), Gospel (1st Fri in Dec), Labour (1st Fri in Sep).

Political leaders

President

1979–96	Amata Kabua	2000–8	Kessai Note
1996–7	Kunio Lemari *Acting*	2008–	Litokwa Tomeing
1997–2000	Imata Kabua		

The Real Bikini

The bikini swimsuit was named after Bikini Atoll in the Marshall Islands. The atoll was the scene of atom-bomb experiments in the late 1940s, and the bikini's effects on men were reputed to be similar. The real Bikini Atoll covers 6 sq km/2.3 sq mi of land and 594 sq km/229 sq mi of lagoon, and has 36 islets. The atoll's name is slightly different in Marshallese – had the word come into English in its original form, people might now be wearing a *pikinni* instead.

MARTINIQUE *see* FRANCE

MAURITANIA

Official name	Islamic Republic of Mauritania
Local name	Mauritanie; République Islamique de Mauritanie (French), Mūrītāniyā; Al-Jumhūriyya al-Islāmiyya al-Mawrītāniyya (Arabic)
Independence	1960
Area	1 029 920 sq km/397 549 sq mi
Capital	Nouakchott
Chief towns	Nouadhibou, Atar
Population	3 270 000 (2007e)
Nationality	Mauritanian
Languages	Arabic; French is also widely spoken
Ethnic groups	mixed Arab and black 40%, Arab 30%, black 30%
Religions	Islam 100%
Time zone	GMT
Currency	1 Ouguiya (U, UM/MRO) = 5 khoums
Telephone	+222
Internet	.mr
Country code	MRT

Location
A republic in north-west Africa, crossed by the Tropic of Cancer in the North; bounded to the north-west by Western Sahara; to the north-east by Algeria; to the south and east by Mali; to the south-west by Senegal; and to the west by the Atlantic Ocean.

Physical description
Saharan zone covers two-thirds of the country with sand dunes, mountainous plateaux and occasional oases; coastal area has minimal rainfall and little vegetation; Senegal River is the chief agricultural region; highest point is Kediet Idjill (915m/3002ft).

Climate
Dry and tropical with sparse rainfall; temperatures can rise to over 49°C in the Sahara.

National holidays
Jan 1, May 1, 25 (Africa), Nov 28 (Independence); Ad, ER, NY (Muslim), PB.

Political leaders

President

1961–78	Mokhtar Ould Daddah
1978–9	Mustapha Ould Mohammed Salek
1979–80	Mohammed Mahmoud Ould Ahmed Louly
1980–4	Mohammed Khouna Ould Haydallah
1984–2005	Maaouya Ould Sid'Ahmed Taya

Chairman of the Military Council for Justice and Democracy

2005–7	Ely Ould Mohammed Vall

President

2007–	Sidi Ould Cheikh Abdallahi

Prime Minister

1992–6	Sidi Mohammed Ould Boubaker
1996–7	Cheikh el Avia Ould Mohammed Khouna
1997–8	Mohammed Lemine Ould Guig
1998–2003	Cheikh el Avia Ould Mohammed Khouna
2003–5	Sghaïr Ould M'Bareck
2005–7	Sidi Mohammed Ould Boubaker
2007–	Zeine Ould Zeidane

Place of Winds

When Mauritania became independent in 1960 it lacked a capital, so a new city was built on the coast. It was named Nouakchott, supposedly meaning 'place of winds'.

MAURITIUS

Official name	Republic of Mauritius
Local name	Mauritius
Independence	1968
Area	1 865 sq km/720 sq mi
Capital	Port Louis
Population	1 251 000 (2007e)
Nationality	Mauritian
Languages	English; French is also spoken
Ethnic groups	Indo-Mauritian 68%, Creole 27%, others 5%
Religions	Hinduism 48%, Christianity 32% (RC 24%), Islam 17%, others 3%
Time zone	GMT +4
Currency	1 Mauritius Rupee (MR, MauRe/MUR) = 100 cents
Telephone	+230
Internet	.mu
Country code	MUS

Location

An island republic in the Indian Ocean, east of Madagascar.

Physical description

Volcanic, with a central plateau; highest peak is Piton de la Petite Rivière Noire (828m/2 717ft); dry, lowland coast, with wooded savanna, mangrove swamp and bamboo; surrounded by coral reefs enclosing lagoons and sandy beaches.

Climate

Tropical-maritime, with temperatures averaging 22–26°C; wide variation in rainfall with most rain falling in the central plateau.

National holidays

Jan 1, 2, Feb 1 (Abolition of Slavery), Mar 12 (National), May 1, Nov 1, 2 (First Labourers), Dec 25; D, ER, NY (Chinese) (Jan/Feb); Ganesh Chathurti (Aug/Sep), Maha Shivaratri (Feb/Mar), Ougadi (Mar/Apr), Thaipoosam Cavadee (Jan/Feb).

Political leaders

Head of State until 1992: British monarch, represented by Governor General.

President

1992	Veerasamy Ringadoo
1992–2002	Cassam Uteem
2002	Angidi Chettiar *Acting*
2002	Arianga Pillay *Acting*
2002–3	Karl Offmann
2003	Raouf Bundhun *Acting*
2003–	Anerood Jugnauth

Prime Minister

1968–82	Seewoosagur Ramgoolam
1982–95	Anerood Jugnauth
1995–2000	Navin Ramgoolam
2000–3	Anerood Jugnauth
2003–5	Paul Berengér
2005–	Navinchandra Ramgoolam

Dead as a Dodo

Perhaps the most famous native of Mauritius was the dodo, a clumsy flightless bird about the size of a turkey. The dodo amused early explorers, but when permanent settlements were set up its demise was swift; hunting and newly-introduced animal predators meant it became extinct about the end of the 17c. *Dodo* comes from the Portuguese word *doudo*, meaning silly.

MAYOTTE *see* FRANCE

MEXICO

Official name	United Mexican States
Local name	México; Estados Unidos Méxicanos
Independence	1821
Area	1 978 800 sq km/763 817 sq mi
Capital	Mexico City; Ciudad de México
Chief towns	Guadalajara, Léon, Monterrey, Ciudad Juárez
Population	108 701 000 (2007e)
Nationality	Mexican
Languages	Spanish; Native American languages are also spoken
Ethnic groups	mestizo 60%, Amerindian 30%, white 9%, others 1%
Religions	Christianity 95% (RC 89%, Prot 6%), others 5%
Time zone	GMT –6/8
Currency	1 Mexican Peso (Mex$/MXN) = 100 centavos
Telephone	+52
Internet	.mx
Country code	MEX

Location

A federal republic in southern North America, crossed by the Tropic of Cancer; bounded to the north by the United States of America; to the east by the Gulf of Mexico; to the south by Guatemala and Belize; to the west and south-west by the Pacific Ocean; and to the west by the Gulf of California.

Physical description

Narrow coastal plains rise steeply to a central plateau, reaching a height of approximately 2 400m/7 874ft around Mexico City; volcanic peaks to the south, notably Citlaltépetl (also called Volcan Pico de Orizaba; 5 699m/18 697ft); Yucatán peninsula lowlands in south-east; subject to very severe earthquakes.

Climate

Great climatic variation between the coastlands and mountains; desert or semi-desert conditions in the north-west; typically tropical climate on the east coast; generally wetter on the south coast; extreme temperature variations in the north.

National holidays

Jan 1, Feb 5 (Constitution), Mar 21 (Benito Juárez), May 1, 5 (Battle of Puebla), 10 (Mothers), Sep 16 (Independence), Nov 2, 20 (Revolution), Dec 12 (Our Lady of Guadalupe), 25; ES, GF, HT; *some holidays granted at discretion of employers*.

Political leaders

President

1876–1911	Porfirio Diaz
1911	Francisco León de la Barra
1911–13	Francisco I Madero
1913–14	Victoriano Huerta
1914	Francisco Carvajal
1914	Venustiano Carranza
1914–15	Eulalio Gutiérrez *Provisional*
1915	Roque González Garza *Provisional*
1915	Francisco Lagos Chazaro *Provisional*
1915–20	Venustiano Carranza
1920	Adolfo de la Huerta
1920–4	Alvaro Obregón
1924–8	Plutarco Elías Calles
1928–30	Emilio Portes Gil
1930–2	Pascual Ortíz Rubio
1932–4	Abelardo L Rodríguez
1934–40	Lazaro Cardenas
1940–6	Manuel Avila Camacho
1946–52	Miguel Alemán
1952–8	Adolfo Ruiz Cortines
1958–64	Adolfo López Mateos
1964–70	Gustavo Díaz Ordaz
1970–6	Luis Echeverría
1976–82	José López Portillo
1982–8	Miguel de la Madrid Hurtado

1988–94	Carlos Salinas de Gortari	2000–6	Vincente Fox Quesada
1994–2000	Ernesto Zedillo Ponce de León	2006–	Felipe Calderon

Aztec Capital

Mexico City is the oldest capital in continental America, and is built on the site of the Aztec capital, Tenochtitlán.

MICRONESIA

Official name	Federated States of Micronesia (FSM)
Local name	Micronesia
Former name	formerly part of the Trust Territory of the Pacific Islands (1947–79)
Independence	1986
Area	702 sq km/271 sq mi
Capital	Palikir (on Pohnpei)
Chief towns	Kolonia, Colonia, Weno, Lelu
Population	108 000 (2007e)
Nationality	Micronesian; also Chuukese, Kosraen, Pohnpeian, Yapese
Languages	English; eight major indigenous languages are also spoken
Ethnic groups	Chuukese 42%, Pohnpeian 27%, others 31%
Religions	Christianity 97% (RC 50%, Prot 47%), others 3%
Time zone	GMT +10/11
Currency	1 US Dollar (US$/USD) = 100 cents
Telephone	+691
Internet	.fm
Country code	FSM

Location

An archipelago republic of 607 islands divided into four states – Yap, Chuuk (formerly Truk), Pohnpei (formerly Ponape) and Kosrae (formerly Kosaie) – in the western Pacific Ocean.

Physical description

Islands vary geologically, from low, coral atolls to high mountainous islands; Pohnpei, Kosrae and Chuuk have volcanic outcroppings; highest point is Totolom (791m/2 595ft).

Climate

Tropical; heavy rainfall all year round, especially in the eastern islands; subject to typhoons.

National holidays

Jan 1, May 10 (Constitution), Oct 24 (United Nations), Nov 3 (Independence), 11 (Veterans), Dec 25; *additional days vary between states.*

Stone Money

The islanders of Yap still use traditional stone money as legal tender as well as the US dollar. The 'coins' are huge, doughnut-shaped stone discs, some taller than a person.

Political leaders

President

1979–87	Tosiwo Nakayama	1999–2003	Leo Falcam
1987–91	John Haglelgam	2003–7	Joseph Urusemal
1991–7	Bailey Olter	2007–	Emmanuel ('Manny') Mori
1997–9	Jacob Nena		

MOLDOVA

Official name	Republic of Moldova
Local name	Moldova; Republica Moldova
Former name	formerly part of Romania (1918–40), Moldavia or Moldavian Soviet Socialist Republic (until 1991), within the Union of Soviet Socialist Republics (USSR; 1922–91)
Independence	1991
Area	33 843 sq km/13 066 sq mi
Capital	Chisinau, Chişinău
Chief towns	Tiraspol, Bendery, Beltsy
Population	4 320 000 (2007e)
Nationality	Moldovan
Languages	Moldovan
Ethnic groups	Moldovan/Romanian 78%, Ukrainian 8%, Russian 6%, Gagauzi 4%, Bulgarian 2%, others 2%
Religions	Christianity 98% (Orthodox), Judaism 2%
Time zone	GMT +2
Currency	1 Leu (Mld/MDL) = 100 bani
Telephone	+373
Internet	.md
Country code	MDA

Location
A republic in eastern Europe, bounded to the west by Romania, and on all other sides by Ukraine.

Physical description
Terrain consists of a hilly plain, reaching a height of 429m/1 407ft at Mt Balanesti in the centre.

Climate
Moderate winters; warm summers.

National holidays
Jan 1, 7–8 (Orthodox Christmas), Mar 8 (Women), May 1, 9 (Victory), Aug 27 (Independence), 31 (Limba Noastra/Our Language); EM (Orthodox), ES (Orthodox); 1st Sun after Easter.

Political leaders

President

1991–6	Mircea Snegur
1996–2001	Petru Lucinschi
2001–	Vladimir Voronin

Prime Minister

1991–2	Valery Muravsky
1992–7	Andrei Sangheli
1997–9	Ion Ciubuc
1999	Ion Sturza
1999–2001	Dumitru Barghis
2001–	Vasile Tarlev

Spring City

The Moldovan capital, Chisinau, takes its name from a word meaning 'spring', 'pump' or 'pipe' in the Moldovan language.

MONACO

Official name	Principality of Monaco
Local name	Monaco; Principauté de Monaco
Area	1.9 sq km/0.75 sq mi
Capital	Monaco
Chief towns	Monte Carlo
Population	33 000 (2007e)
Nationality	Monégasque or Monacan
Languages	French
Ethnic groups	French 47%, Monégasque 16%, Italian 16%, others 21%
Religions	Christianity 95% (RC 90%, Prot 5%), others 5%
Time zone	GMT +1
Currency	1 Euro (€/EUR) = 100 cents
Telephone	+377
Internet	.mc
Country code	MCO

Location
A principality bounded to the south-east by the Mediterranean Sea and on all other sides by France, close to the Italian frontier.

Physical description
Hilly, rugged and rocky, rising to 63m/206ft; almost entirely urban.

Climate
Warm, dry summers and mild winters.

National holidays
Jan 1, 27 (St Devote), May 1, Aug 15, Nov 1, 19 (National), Dec 8, 25; A, CC, EM, WM.

Political leaders

Head of State (Monarch)

1889–1922 Albert
1922–49 Louis II
1949–2005 Rainier III
2005– Albert II

MONGOLIA

Official name	State of Mongolia
Local name	Mongol Uls
Former name	Outer Mongolia (until 1924); People's Republic of Mongolia (1924–92)
Independence	1911 (declared), 1924 (republic)
Area	1 564 619 sq km/604 099 sq mi
Capital	Ulan Bator; Ulaanbaatar
Chief towns	Darhan, Erdenet
Population	2 952 000 (2007e)
Nationality	Mongolian
Languages	Khalkha Mongolian
Ethnic groups	Mongol 94%, Kazakh 5%, Chinese, Russian and others 1%
Religions	Buddhist Lamaism 50%, Shamanism and Christianity 6%, Islam 4%, none 40%
Time zone	GMT +8
Currency	1 Tugrug (T/MNT) = 100 müngü
Telephone	+976
Internet	.mn
Country code	MNG

Location
A republic in eastern central Asia, bounded to the north by Russia and on all other sides by China.

Physical description
Mountainous, at an average height of 1580m/5184ft; highest point is Tavan Bogd (4374m/14350ft); high ground is mainly in the west, with mountains north-west to south-east, running into the Gobi Desert; lowland plains are mainly arid grasslands.

Climate
Continental, with hard and long-lasting frosts in winter; average temperature at Ulan Bator is 27°C in Jan and 9–24°C in Jul; rainfall is generally low; arid desert conditions prevail in the south.

National holidays
Jan 1, Mar 8 (Women), Jun 1 (Children), Jul 11–13 (National) , Nov 26 (Independence); NY (Lunar) (Jan/Feb) (3).

Political leaders

Prime Minister

1924–8	Tserendorji
1928–32	Amor
1932–6	Gendun
1936–8	Amor
1939–52	Korloghiin Choibalsan
1952–74	Yumsjhagiin Tsedenbal

Chairman of the Presidium

1948–53	Gonchighlin Bumatsende
1954–72	Jamsarangiin Sambu
1972–4	Sonomyn Luvsan
1974–84	Yumsjhagiin Tsedenbal
1984–90	Jambyn Batmunkh

President

1990–7	Punsalmaagiyn Ochirbat
1997–2005	Natsagiyn Bagabandi
2005–	Nambaryn Enkhbayar

Premier

1974–84	Jambyn Batmunkh
1984–90	Dumaagiyn Sodnom
1990–2	Dashiyn Byambasuren
1992–6	Puntsagiyn Jasray
1996–8	Mendsaihany Enkhsahan
1998	Tsahiagiyin Elbegdorj
1998–9	Janlaviyn Narantsatsralt
1999–2000	Rinchinnyamiyn Amarjagal
2000–4	Nambaryn Enkhbayar
2004	Chultern Ulaan *Acting*
2004–6	Tsakhia Elbegdorj
2006–7	Miyeegombo Enkhbold
2007–	Sanj Bayar

Outer Mongolia

Outer Mongolia is sometimes used light-heartedly to describe anywhere very far away and isolated. But it is actually the official former name of Mongolia. Mongolia was originally the homeland of nomadic tribes which united under Ghengis Khan in the 13c to become part of a great Mongol Empire. Mongolia was later assimilated into China, and divided into Inner and Outer Mongolia. Inner Mongolia remains an autonomous region of China, but Outer Mongolia declared itself independent in 1911.

MONTENEGRO

Official name	Republic of Montenegro
Local name	Crna Gora; Republika Crna Gora
Former name	part of Kingdom of Serbs, Croats and Slovenes (until 1929), Kingdom of Yugoslavia (1929–41), Federal People's Republic of Yugoslavia (1945–63), Socialist Federal Republic of Yugoslavia (1963–92), Federal Republic of Yugoslavia (1992–2003), Serbia and Montenegro (2003–6)
Area	13812 sq km/5333 sq mi
Capital	Podgorica (administrative centre); Cetinje (historic and cultural capital)
Chief towns	Nikšic, Bar
Population	685000 (2007e)
Nationality	Montenegrin
Languages	Montenegrin (Ijekavian dialect of Serbian), Serbian and Albanian
Ethnic groups	Montenegrin 43%, Serb 32%, Bosniac 8%, Albanian 5%, others 12%
Religions	Christianity 74% (Orthodox 70%, RC 4%), Islam 21%, others 5%
Time zone	GMT +1
Currency	1 Euro (€/EUR) = 100 cents
Telephone	+382
Internet	.me
Country code	MNE

Location

A republic in south-eastern Europe, bounded to the west and north-west by Bosnia and Herzegovina; to the north-east by Serbia; to the east by the Serbian province of Kosovo; to the south by Albania; and to the south-west by the Adriatic Sea and Croatia.

Physical description

Densely forested mountains in the interior are cut by river valleys and canyons; the highest point is Bobotov Kuk (2522m/8274ft); fertile lowlands lie alongside lakes and in river valleys; the low-lying, 293km-long Adriatic coastline is highly indented; the main river is the Tara.

Climate

Mediterranean climate, with hot, dry summers and autumns; colder upland climate inland, with heavy winter snow.

National holidays

Jan 1, 2, 7–8 (Orthodox Christmas), May 1–2, 21 (Independence), Jul 13 (Statehood); EM, ES, GF (all Orthodox).

Political leaders

See **Yugoslavia** for political leaders prior to 1991–2, and **Serbia** for political leaders 1992–2006.

President (within federation)

1991–8	Momir Bulatovic
1998–2002	Milo Djukanovic
2002–3	Filip Vujanović *Acting*
2003	Rifat Rastoder/Dragan Kujovic *Acting*
2003–6	Filip Vujanović

In 2006 Montenegro held a referendum on independence, which was widely supported, and the federation with Serbia was dissolved, with both countries becoming independent sovereign states.

President

2003–	Filip Vujanović

Prime Minister

2002–6	Milo Djukanovic
2006–8	Zeljko Sturanovic
2008–	*Position vacant*

MONTSERRAT *see* UNITED KINGDOM

MOROCCO

Official name	Kingdom of Morocco
Local name	Al Maghrib; Al-Mamlaka Al-Maghribiyya
Independence	1956
Area	446 550 sq km/172 412 sq mi
Capital	Rabat; Ar Ribāt, Er Ribât
Chief towns	Casablanca, Fez, Marrakesh, Tangier, Meknès, Kenitra, Tétouan, Oujda, Agadir
Population	33 757 000 (2007e)
Nationality	Moroccan
Languages	Arabic; Berber and French are also spoken
Ethnic groups	Arab-Berber 99%, others 1%
Religions	Islam 99% (mostly Sunni), Christianity 1%
Time zone	GMT
Currency	1 Dirham (DH/MAD) = 100 centimes
Telephone	+212
Internet	.ma
Country code	MAR

Location

A kingdom in North Africa, bounded to the north-east by the Mediterranean Sea; to the east and south-east by Algeria; to the south by Western Sahara, over which it claims sovereignty; and to the west by the Atlantic Ocean. The Tropic of Cancer crosses Western Sahara.

Physical description

Dominated by a series of mountain ranges, rising in the High Atlas in the south to 4 165m/13 665ft at Mt Toubkal; Atlas Mountains descend south-east to the north-west edge of the Sahara Desert; has a broad coastal plain.

Climate

Mediterranean climate on the north coast; settled and hot in May–Sep; Sahara is virtually rainless, with extreme heat in summer but chilly winter nights; average maximum temperatures of 17–28°C on Atlantic coast; heavy winter snowfall in the High Atlas.

National holidays

Jan 1, 11 (Independence Manifesto), May 1, Jul 30 (Feast of the Throne), Aug 14 (Oued-ed-Dahab Allegiance), Aug 20 (Revolution), 21 (Youth), Nov 6 (Green March), 18 (Independence); Ad (2), ER (2), NY (Muslim), PB.

Political leaders

Monarch

1927–61	Mohammed V
1961–99	Hassan II
1999–	Mohammed VI

Prime Minister

1955–8	Si Mohammed Bekkai
1958	Ahmad Balfrej
1958–60	Abdullah Ibrahim
1960–3	*As Monarch*
1963–5	Ahmad Bahnini
1965–7	*As Monarch*
1967–9	Moulay Ahmed Laraki
1969–71	Mohammed Ben Hima

1971–2	Mohammed Karim Lamrani	1992–4	Mohammed Karim Lamrani
1972–9	Ahmed Othman	1994–8	Abdellatif Filali
1979–83	Maati Bouabid	1998–2002	Abderrahmane el-Yousifi
1983–6	Mohammed Karim Lamrani	2002–7	Driss Jettou
1986–92	Izz Id-Dien Laraki	2007–	Abbas El Fassi

Western Sahara

Local name	Sahara Occidental; République Arabe Saharouie Démocratique
Former name	Spanish Sahara (until 1976)
Area	252 126 sq km/97 321 sq mi
Capital	El Aaiún; Laâyoune, La 'Youn
Chief towns	Smara, Bu Craa, Dakhla
Population	383 000 (2007e)
Nationality	Sahrawi, Sahraoui; Sahrawian, Sahraouian
Languages	Arabic; French, Berber and Spanish are also spoken
Ethnic groups	Arab, Berber
Religions	Islam (Sunni) 100%
Time zone	GMT
Currency	1 Moroccan Dirham (DH/MAD) = 100 centimes
Telephone	+212
Internet	.eh
Country code	ESH

Location
A disputed non-self-governing territory in north-west Africa, bounded to the north by Morocco; to the north-east by Algeria; to the east and south by Mauritania; and to the west by the Atlantic Ocean.

Physical description
Low, flat desert terrain, composed principally of plains and low plateaux; rises in the south to hills; rocky desert in the north-east, rising to steep hills; highest point reaches 463m/1 519ft; ergs and sand dunes inland, with sparse desert vegetation.

Climate
Hot, dry climate, with little rainfall; coastal fog, mists and dew; subject to the hot, dry *sirocco* wind in winter and spring.

Political leaders

Disputed; Morocco claims sovereignty and views Western Sahara as Moroccan provinces administered by the Moroccan government. The Western Saharan independence movement, the Polisario Front, proclaimed a government-in-exile in 1976 (see below).

Sahrawi Arab Democratic Republic

Chairman of Revolutionary Council

1976	El Wali Mustafa Sayed
1976	Mahfoud Ali Beiba *Acting*

Chairman of Revolutionary Command Council

1976–82	Mohamed Abdelaziz

President

1982–	Mohamed Abdelaziz

Prime Minister

1976–82	Mohamed Lamine Ould Ahmed	1985–8	Mohamed Lamine Ould Ahmed
1982–5	Mahfoud Ali Beiba	1988–93	Mahfoud Ali Beiba

1993–5	Bouchraya Hammoudi Bayoune	1999–2003	Bouchraya Hamoudi Bayoune
1995–9	Mahfoud Ali Beiba	2003–	Abdelkader Taleb Oumar

Coming of the Camel

It is thought that the camel first arrived in Western Sahara in the 1C AD.

MOZAMBIQUE

Official name	Republic of Mozambique
Local name	Moçambique; República de Moçambique
Former name	People's Republic of Mozambique (1975–90)
Independence	1975
Area	789 800 sq km/304 863 sq mi
Capital	Maputo
Chief towns	Nampula, Beira, Pemba
Population	20 905 000 (2007e)
Nationality	Mozambican
Languages	Portuguese; Swahili and other African languages are widely spoken
Ethnic groups	Makua 47%, Tsonga 23%, Malawi 12%, Shona 11%, Yao 4%, others 3%
Religions	Christianity 41% (RC 24%, others 17%), Islam 18%, others 18%, none 23%; *some aspects of traditional beliefs are widespread*
Time zone	GMT +2
Currency	1 Metical (Mt/MZM) = 100 centavos
Telephone	+258
Internet	.mz
Country code	MOZ

Location

A republic in south-eastern Africa, crossed by the Tropic of Capricorn in the south; bounded to the north-west by Zambia and Malawi; to the north by Tanzania; to the east by the Mozambique Channel and the Indian Ocean; to the south by Swaziland; to the south and south-west by South Africa; and to the west by Zimbabwe.

Physical description

South of the Zambezi River the low-lying coast has sandy beaches and mangroves; low hills of volcanic origin inland; coast north of the Zambezi is more rugged, with savanna plateau inland; highest peak is Mt Binga (2 436m/7 992ft).

Climate

Tropical, with relatively low rainfall in the coastal lowlands; maximum daily temperatures of 25–32°C in the central coast zone; rainfall decreases in the drier areas of the interior lowlands; one rainy season in Dec–Mar.

National holidays

Jan 1, Feb 3 (Heroes), Apr 7 (Women), May 1, Jun 25 (Independence), Sep 7 (Lusaka Accord), 25 (Armed Forces), Oct 4 (Peace and Reconciliation), Dec 25 (Christmas/Family).

Political leaders

President

1975–86	Samora Moïses Machel
1986–2005	Joaquim Alberto Chissano
2005–	Armando Guebuza

Prime Minister

1986–94	Mario de Graça Machungo
1994–2004	Pascoal Mocumbi
2004–	Luisa Diogo

First Lady of Africa

The first president of Mozambique, Samora Machel, was killed in an air crash in 1986. His widow, Graça Machel, is internationally respected for her work for women's and children's rights. She later married the former president of South Africa, Nelson Mandela.

MYANMAR (BURMA)

Official name	Union of Myanmar; still often referred to internationally as Burma
Local name	Myanmar; Pyidaungsu Myanmar Naingngandaw
Former name	Union of Burma (1948–74); Socialist Republic of the Union of Burma (1974–88), Union of Burma (1988–9)
Independence	1948
Area	678 576 sq km/261 930 sq mi
Capital	Rangoon; Yangon (historic capital), Naypyidaw (administrative capital since 2005)
Chief towns	Mandalay, Henzada, Pegu, Myingyan
Population	47 374 000 (2007e)
Nationality	Burmese or Myanmarese
Languages	Burmese; several minority languages are also spoken
Ethnic groups	Burman 68%, Shan 9%, Karen 7%, Rakhine 4%, Chinese 3%, Indian 2%, Mon 2%, others 5%
Religions	Buddhism 89%, Christianity 4%, Islam 4%, animist 1%, others 2%
Time zone	GMT +6.5
Currency	1 Kyat (K/MMK) = 100 pyas
Telephone	+95
Internet	.mm
Country code	MMR

Location
A republic in south-east Asia, crossed by the Tropic of Cancer; bounded to the north-west by India; to the north-east by China; to the east by Laos and Thailand; to the south and west by the Bay of Bengal and the Andaman Sea; and to the west by Bangladesh.

Physical description
Mountains in the north, east and west rise to Hkakabo Razi (5 881m/19 294ft) and descend in a series of ridges and valleys; Irrawaddy River delta extends over 240km/150mi.

Climate
Tropical monsoon climate, with a marked change between the cooler, dry season (Nov–Apr) and the hotter, wet season (May–Sep); lowlands are very hot all year; high coastal humidity.

National holidays
Jan 4 (Independence), Feb 12 (Union), Mar 2 (Peasants), 27 (Armed Forces), May 1, Jul 19 (Martyrs), Dec 25; NY (Burmese) (Apr); Kason Full Moon (Apr), Maha Thingyan/Water Festival (Apr) (4), National (Nov/Dec), Tabaung Full Moon (Mar), Tazaung Full Moon (Nov), Thadingyut Full Moon (Oct), Waso Full Moon (Jul); Ad, D *by some of population*.

Political leaders

President

1948–52 Sao Shwe Thaik
1952–7 Agga Maha Thiri Thudhamma Ba U
1957–62 U Wing Maung
1962 Sama Duwa Sinwa Nawng

Chairman of Revolutionary Council

1962–74 Ne Win

President

1974–81 Ne Win
1981–8 U San Yu
1988 U Sein Lwin
1988 Maung Maung

Chairman of State Law and Order Restoration Council

1988–92 Saw Maung
1992–7 Than Shwe

Chairman of State Peace and Development Council

1997–	Than Shwe

Prime Minister

1948–56	U Nu	1977–8	U Maung Maung Ka
1956–7	U Ba Swe	1988	U Tun Tin
1957–8	U Nu	1988–92	Saw Maung
1958–60	Ne Win	1992–2003	Than Shwe
1960–2	U Nu	2003–4	Khin Nyunt
1962–74	Ne Win	2004–7	Soe Win
1974–7	U Sein Win	2007–	Thein Sein

NAMIBIA

Official name	Republic of Namibia
Local name	Namibia
Former name	South West Africa (until 1968)
Independence	1990
Area	823 144 sq km/317 734 sq mi
Capital	Windhoek
Chief towns	Lüderitz, Keetmanshoop, Grootfontein
Population	2 055 000 (2007e)
Nationality	Namibian
Languages	English; Afrikaans, German and local languages are also widely spoken
Ethnic groups	Ovambo 50%, Kavango 9%, Damara 7%, Herero 7%, white 6%, mixed 6%, Nama 5%, others 10%
Religions	Christianity 90%, traditional beliefs 10%
Time zone	GMT +1
Currency	1 Namibian Dollar (N$/NAD) = 100 cents; the South African Rand is also used.
Telephone	+264
Internet	.na
Country code	NAM

Location
A republic in south-western Africa, crossed by the Tropic of Capricorn; bounded to the north by Angola; to the north-east by Zambia and Zimbabwe; to the east by Botswana; to the south by South Africa; and to the west by the Atlantic Ocean.

Physical description
Namib Desert runs along the Atlantic Ocean coast; inland plateau has a mean elevation of 1 500m/4 921ft; highest point is Konigstein peak on Brandberg (2 574m/8 445ft); Kalahari Desert lies to the east and south; Orange River forms the frontier with South Africa.

Climate
Low rainfall on the coast, higher in the interior; the average maximum daily temperature range at Windhoek, representative of the interior, is 20–30°C.

National holidays
Jan 1, Mar 21 (Independence), May 1, 4 (Cassinga), 25 (Africa), Aug 26 (Heroes), Dec 10 (Human Rights), Dec 25, 26 (Family); A, EM, GF.

Political leaders

President

1990–2005	Sam Daniel Nujoma
2005–	Hifikepunye Pohamba

Prime Minister

1990–2002	Hage Geingob
2002–5	Theo-Ben Gurirab
2005–	Nahas Angula

NAURU

Official name	Republic of Nauru
Local name	Naoero (Nauruan), Nauru (English)
Independence	1968
Area	21 sq km/8 sq mi
Capital	There is no capital as such; government offices are situated in Yaren District
Population	13000 (2007e)
Nationality	Nauruan
Languages	Nauruan; English is also widely understood
Ethnic groups	Nauruan 58%, other Pacific Islanders 26%, Chinese and Vietnamese 8%, European 8%
Religions	Christianity (predominantly Prot, with RC minority); also Buddhism
Time zone	GMT +12
Currency	1 Australian Dollar ($A/AUD) = 100 cents
Telephone	+674
Internet	.nr
Country code	NRU

Location

An independent republic in the west-central Pacific Ocean, 4000km/2500mi north-east of Sydney, Australia.

Physical description

A small, isolated island; ground rises from sandy beaches to form a fertile coastal belt, approximately 100–300m/330–980ft wide, the only cultivable soil; central plateau inland, which reaches 65m/213ft at its highest point, composed largely of phosphate-bearing rocks.

Climate

Tropical, with average daily temperatures of 24–34°C, and average humidity between 70% and 80%; rainfall mainly in the monsoon season from Nov to Feb, with marked yearly deviations.

National holidays

Jan 1, 31 (Independence), May 17 (Constitution), Sep 25 (Youth), Oct 26 (Angam), Dec 25, 26; EM, GF, Easter Tuesday.

Political leaders

President

1968–76	Hammer de Roburt
1976–8	Bernard Dowiyogo
1978	Lagumot Harris
1978–86	Hammer de Roburt
1986	Kennan Adeang
1986–9	Hammer de Roburt
1989	Kenas Aroi
1989–95	Bernard Dowiyogo
1995–6	Lagumot Harris
1996	Bernard Dowiyogo
1996	Kennan Adeang
1996–7	Rueben Kun
1997–8	Kinza Clodumar
1998–9	Bernard Dowiyogo
1999–2000	René Harris
2000–1	Bernard Dowiyogo
2001–3	René Harris
2003	Bernard Dowiyogo
2003	René Harris
2003	Bernard Dowiyogo
2003	Derog Gioura *Acting*
2003	Ludwig Scotty
2003–4	René Harris
2004–7	Ludwig Scotty
2007–	Marcus Stephens

NEPAL

Official name	Kingdom of Nepal
Local name	Nepāl Adhirājya
Area	145 391 sq km/56 121 sq mi
Capital	Kathmandu
Chief towns	Patan, Bhadgaon
Population	28 902 000 (2007e)
Nationality	Nepalese
Languages	Nepali; around 70 local dialects and languages are also spoken
Ethnic groups	Nepali 59%, Bihari 20%, Tamang 3%, Tharu 3%, Newar 3%, others 12%
Religions	Hinduism 81%, Buddhism 11%, Islam 4%, others 4%
Time zone	GMT +5.75
Currency	1 Nepalese Rupee (NRp, NRs/NPR) = 100 paise/pice
Telephone	+977
Internet	.np
Country code	NPL

Location

An independent kingdom in central Asia, bounded to the north by the Tibet region of China, and on all other sides by India.

Physical description

Rises steeply from the Ganges Basin; high fertile valleys in the hill country at 1 300m/4 265ft, such as the Vale of Kathmandu, are enclosed by mountain ranges; dominated by the glaciated peaks of the Himalayas; highest point is Mt Everest (8 850m/29 035ft).

Climate

Varies from subtropical lowland, with hot, humid summers and mild winters, to an alpine climate over 3 300m/10 827ft, with permanently snow-covered peaks; average temperatures at Kathmandu from 23°C (May–Aug) to 9°C (Jan); monsoon season during summer (Jun–Sep).

National holidays

Jan 30 (Martyrs), Feb 19 (Democracy), Mar 8 (Women), Apr 14 (NY), 24 (Restoration of Democracy), May 1; Buddha Jayanti (May), Dashain (Oct) (9), Ghatasthapana (Oct), Maha Shivaratri (Mar), Rakshya Bandhan (Aug), Ramnawami/Chaitay Dashain (Mar), Tihar (Nov) (3); *women only:* Mar 8 (Women); Hari Taika (Sep), Rhishi Panchami (Sep); *various regional and other religious festivals*.

Political leaders

Monarch

1881–1911	Prithvi Bir Bikram Shah
1911–50	Tribhuvan Bir Bikram Shah
1950–2	Bir Bikram
1952–5	Tribhuvan Bir Bikram Shah
1956–72	Mahendra Bir Bikram Shah
1972–2001	Birendra Bir Bikram Shah Dev
2001	Dipendra Bir Bikram Shah Dev
2001–	Gyanendra Bir Bikram Shah Dev

Prime Minister

1901–29	Chandra Sham Sher Jang Bahadur Rana
1929–31	Bhim Cham Sham Sher Jang Bahadur Rana
1931–45	Juddha Sham Sher Rana
1945–8	Padma Sham Sher Jang Bahadur Rana
1948–51	Mohan Sham Sher Jang Bahadur Rana
1951–2	Matrika Prasad Koirala
1952–3	*King also Prime Minister*
1953–5	Matrika Prasad Koirala
1955–6	Mahendra Bir Bikram Shah
1956–7	Tanka Prasad Acharya
1957–9	*King also Prime Minister*
1959–60	Sri Bishawa Prasad Koirala
1960–3	*No Prime Minister*
1963–5	Tulsi Giri
1965–9	Surya Bahadur Thapa
1969–70	Kirti Nidhi Bista
1970–1	*King also Prime Minister*

1971–3	Kirti Nidhi Bista
1973–5	Nagendra Prasad Rijal
1975–7	Tulsi Giri
1977–9	Kirti Nidhi Bista
1979–83	Surya Bahadur Thapa
1983–6	Lokendra Bahadur Chand
1986–91	Marich Man Singh Shrestha
1991–4	Girija Prasad Koirala
1994–5	Man Mohan Adhikari
1995–7	Sher Bahadur Deuba
1997	Lokendra Bahadur Chand
1997	Surya Bahadur Thapa
1998–9	Girija Prasad Koirala
1999–2000	Krishna Prasad Bhattari
2000–1	Girija Prasad Koirala
2001–2	Sher Bahadur Deuba
2002–3	Lokendra Bahadur Chand
2003–4	Surya Bahadur Thapa
2004–5	Sher Bahadur Deuba
2005–6	*King also Prime Minister*
2006–	Girija Prasad Koirala *Interim*

Nepalese Peoples

Nepal is home to a diverse range of peoples, with more than 60 ethnic groups. These include the Sherpas, famous for their mountaineering skill, the Dolpa people, who live in probably the world's highest human settlements at around 4,000m/13,123ft, and the Gurungs, whose traditions include a colourful dancing season.

THE NETHERLANDS

Official name	Kingdom of the Netherlands; often known as Holland
Local name	Nederlanden; Koninkrijk der Nederlanden
Area	33929 sq km/13097 sq mi
Capital	Amsterdam; The Hague (Den Haag) is the seat of government
Chief towns	Rotterdam, Utrecht, Haarlem, Eindhoven, Arnhem, Groningen
Population	16571000 (2007e)
Nationality	Dutch
Languages	Dutch; Frisian is spoken in Friesland, and English is widely spoken
Ethnic groups	Dutch 83%, Turks, Moroccans, Antilleans, Surinamese, Indonesians and others 17%
Religions	Christianity 51% (RC 31%, Prot 20%), Islam 6%, others 2%, none/unaffiliated 41%
Time zone	GMT +1
Currency	1 Euro (€/EUR) = 100 cents
Telephone	+31
Internet	.nl
Country code	NLD

Location
A kingdom in north-western Europe, bounded to the north and west by the North Sea; to the east by Germany; and to the south by Belgium.

Physical description
Generally low and flat, except in the south-east where hills rise to 321m/1053ft; 24% of the land is below sea level, including much of the coast, which is protected by dunes and artificial dykes; many canals, totalling 6340km/3940mi in length.

Climate
Cool, temperate, maritime; average temperatures 1.7°C (Jan) and 17°C (Jul); rainfall is distributed fairly evenly throughout the year.

National holidays
Jan 1, Apr 30 (Queen's Birthday), May 5 (Liberation), Dec 25, 26; A, EM, GF, WM.

Netherlands overseas territories

Aruba

Location	An island in the Caribbean Sea, about 30km/19mi north of Venezuela, and 70km/44mi west of Curaçao (the Netherlands).		
Area	193 sq km/75 sq mi	**Internet**	.aw
Capital	Oranjestad	**Country code**	ABW
Population	100 000 (2007e)		

Netherlands Antilles (Dutch Antilles)

Location	A group of islands in the Caribbean Sea, comprising the southern group of Curaçao and Bonaire north of the Venezuelan coast, and the northern group of St Maarten (southern half of the island of St Martin), St Eustatius and Saba, lying east of Puerto Rico (USA).		
Local name	Nederlandse Antillen	**Population**	224 000 (2007e)
Area	960 sq km/371 sq mi	**Internet**	.an
Capital	Willemstad	**Country code**	ANT

Political leaders

Monarch (House of Orange-Nassau)

1572–84 William the Silent
1584–1625 Maurice
1625–47 Frederick Henry
1647–50 William II
1672–1702 William III
1747–51 William IV
1751–95 William V
1806–10 Louis Bonaparte
1813–40 William I
1840–9 William II
1849–90 William III
1890–1948 Wilhelmina
1948–80 Juliana
1980– Beatrix

Prime Minister

1897–1901 Nicholas G Pierson
1901–5 Abraham Kuyper
1905–8 Theodoor H de Meester
1908–13 Theodorus Heemskerk
1913–18 Pieter W A Cort van der Linden
1918–25 Charles J M Ruys de Beerenbrouck
1925–6 Hendrikus Colijn
1926 Dirk J de Geer
1926–33 Charles J M Ruys de Beerenbrouck
1933–9 Hendrikus Colijn
1939–40 Dirk J de Geer
1940–5 Pieter S Gerbrandy (*in exile*)
1945–6 Willem Schemerhorn/Willem Drees
1946–8 Louis J M Beel
1948–51 Willem Drees/Josephus R H van Schaik
1951–8 Willem Drees
1958–9 Louis J M Beel
1959–63 Jan E de Quay
1963–5 Victor G M Marijnen
1965–6 Joseph M L T Cals
1966–7 Jelle Zijlstra
1967–71 Petrus J S de Jong
1971–3 Barend W Biesheuvel
1973–7 Joop M Den Uyl
1977–82 Andreas A M van Agt
1982–94 Ruud F M Lubbers
1994–2002 Wim Kok
2002– Jan Peter Balkenende

NEVIS *see* **ST KITTS AND NEVIS**

NEW CALEDONIA *see* **FRANCE**

NEW ZEALAND

Official name	New Zealand (NZ)
Local name	New Zealand (English), Aotearoa (Maori)
Independence	1907 (from Britain), 1947 (full)
Area	268812 sq km/103761 sq mi
Capital	Wellington; Te Whanganui-a-Tara
Chief towns	Auckland, Christchurch, Dunedin, Hamilton
Population	4116000 (2007e)
Nationality	Kiwi (*informal*), New Zealand
Languages	English, Maori
Ethnic groups	European 70%, Maori 8%, mixed 8%, Asian 6%, Pacific Islanders 4%, others 4%
Religions	Christianity 53% (Prot 32%, RC 12%, other 9%), others 3%, none/unaffiliated 44%
Time zone	GMT +12
Currency	1 New Zealand Dollar (NZ$/NZD) = 100 cents
Telephone	+64
Internet	.nz
Country code	NZL

Location

An independent state comprising a group of islands in the Pacific Ocean to the south-east of Australia, from which it is separated by the Tasman Sea; the two principal islands are North Island and South Island, separated by the Cook Strait.

Physical description

North Island is mountainous in the centre, with many hot springs; peaks rise to 2797m/9176ft at Mt Ruapehu; South Island is mountainous for its whole length, rising in the Southern Alps to 3753m/12312ft at Mt Cook, New Zealand's highest point; many glaciers and mountain lakes.

Climate

Highly changeable weather, with all months moderately wet; almost subtropical in the north and on the east coast, with mild winters and warm, humid summers; Auckland daily temperatures are 8–13°C (Jul), 16–23°C (Jan); generally cooler in South Island.

National holidays

Jan 1, 2, Feb 6 (Waitangi), Apr 25 (Anzac), Dec 25, 26; EM, GF, Queen's Birthday (Jun), Labour (Oct).

Self-governing territories

Cook Islands

Location	A widely scattered group of 15 volcanic and coral islands in the South Pacific Ocean, approximately 3200km/2000mi north-east of New Zealand.		
Area	238 sq km/92 sq mi	**Internet**	.ck
Chief town	Avarua	**Country code**	COK
Population	22000 (2007e)		

Niue

Location	A small island in the South Pacific Ocean, 2140km/1330mi north-east of New Zealand.		
Area	263 sq km/101 sq mi	**Internet**	.nu
Chief town	Alofi	**Country code**	NIU
Population	1000 (2007e)		

Non-self-governing territories

Tokelau

Location	Comprises three small atolls (Atafu, Nukunonu, Fakaofo) in the South Pacific Ocean, approximately 3500km/2200mi north-east of New Zealand.		
Area	10.1 sq km/3.9 sq mi	**Internet**	.tk
Population	1000 (2007e)	**Country code**	TKL

Ross Dependency

Location	A territory in Antarctica.
Area	413540 sq km/159626 sq mi (land); 336770 sq km/129993 sq mi (permanent shelf ice)
Population	Populated solely by scientists.

Political leaders

Head of State: British monarch, represented by Governor General (Anand Satyanand since 2006).

Prime Minister

1893–1906	Richard John Seddon *Lib*
1906	William Hall-Jones *Lib*
1906–12	Joseph George Ward *Lib/Nat*
1912	Thomas Mackenzie *Nat*
1912–25	William Ferguson Massey *Ref*
1925	Francis Henry Dillon Bell *Ref*
1925–8	Joseph Gordon Coates *Ref*
1928–30	Joseph George Ward *Lib/Nat*
1930–5	George William Forbes *Un*
1935–40	Michael Joseph Savage *Lab*
1940–9	Peter Fraser *Lab*
1949–57	Sidney George Holland *Nat*
1957	Keith Jacka Holyoake *Nat*
1957–60	Walter Nash *Lab*
1960–72	Keith Jacka Holyoake *Nat*
1972	John Ross Marshall *Nat*
1972–4	Norman Eric Kirk *Lab*
1974–5	Wallace Edward Rowling *Lab*
1975–84	Robert David Muldoon *Nat*
1984–89	David Russell Lange *Lab*
1989–90	Geoffrey Palmer *Lab*
1990	Mike Moore *Lab*
1990–7	James Bolger *Nat*
1997–9	Jenny Shipley *Nat*
1999–	Helen Clark *Lab*

Lab = Labor; Lib = Liberal; Nat = National; Ref = Reform; Un = United

Votes for Women

In 1893 New Zealand became the first country to give women the vote in national elections.

NICARAGUA

Official name	Republic of Nicaragua
Local name	Nicaragua; República de Nicaragua
Independence	1821
Area	130 668 sq km/50 451 sq mi
Capital	Managua
Chief towns	León, Granada, Masaya, Chinandega, Matagalpa, Corinto
Population	5 675 000 (2007e)
Nationality	Nicaraguan
Languages	Spanish; English and local languages in Caribbean coastal areas
Ethnic groups	mestizo 69%, white 17%, black 9%, Amerindian 5%
Religions	Christianity 90% (RC 73%, Prot 17%), others 2%, none 8%
Time zone	GMT –6
Currency	1 Córdoba (C$/NIO) = 100 centavos = 10 reales
Telephone	+505
Internet	.ni
Country code	NIC

Location
A republic in Central America, bounded to the north by Honduras; to the east by the Caribbean Sea; to the south by Costa Rica; and to the west by the Pacific Ocean.

Physical description
Mountainous west with volcanic ranges rising to over 2 000m/6 562ft in the north-west; highest point is the Dipilto-Jalapa ridge (2 107m/6 913ft); two large lakes behind the coastal mountains; rolling uplands and forested plains to the east; many short rivers.

Climate
Tropical, with average annual temperatures ranging from 15–35°C according to altitude; there is a rainy season from May to Nov when humidity is high; subject to devastating hurricanes.

National holidays
Jan 1, May 1, Jul 19 (Revolution), Sep 14 (Battle of San Jacinto), 15 (Independence), Nov 2, Dec 8, 25; ES, GF, HS, HT.

Political leaders

President

1893–1909	José Santos Zelaya
1909–10	José Madriz
1910–11	José Dolores Estrada
1911	Juan José Estrada
1911–17	Adolfo Díaz
1912	Luis Mena *rival President*
1917–21	Emiliano Chamorro Vargas
1921–3	Riego Manuel Chamorro
1923–4	Martínez Bartolo
1925–6	Carlos Solórzano
1926	Emiliano Chamorro Vargas
1926–8	Adolfo Díaz
1926	Juan Bautista Sacasa *rival President*
1928–32	José Marcia Moncada
1933–6	Juan Bautista Sacasa
1936	Carlos Brenes Jarquin
1937–47	Anastasio Somoza García
1947	Leonardo Argüello
1947	Benjamin Lascayo Sacasa
1947–50	Victor Manuel Román y Reyes
1950–6	Anastasio Somoza García
1956–63	Luis Somoza Debayle
1963–6	René Schick Gutiérrez
1966–7	Lorenzo Guerrero Gutiérrez
1967–72	Anastasio Somoza Debayle
1972–4	*Triumvirate*
1974–9	Anastasio Somoza Debayle
1979–84	*Government Junta of National Reconstruction*
1984–90	Daniel Ortega Saavedra
1990–7	Violeta Barrios de Chamorro
1997–2002	Arnoldo Alemán Lacayo
2002–7	Enrique Bolaños
2007–	Daniel Ortega Saavedra

NIUE *see* NEW ZEALAND

NIGER

Official name	Republic of Niger
Local name	Niger; République du Niger
Independence	1960
Area	1 267 000 sq km/489 189 sq mi
Capital	Niamey
Chief towns	Agadès, Diffa, Dosso, Maradi, Tahoua, Zinder
Population	12 895 000 (2007e)
Nationality	Nigerien
Languages	French; Hausa and Djerma are spoken widely
Ethnic groups	Hausa 56%, Djerma 22%, Fulani 9%, Tuareg 8%, others 5%
Religions	Islam 80%, Christianity and traditional beliefs 20%
Time zone	GMT +1
Currency	1 CFA Franc (CFAFr/XOF) = 100 centimes
Telephone	+227
Internet	.ne
Country code	NER

Location
A republic in West Africa, bounded to the north-west by Algeria; to the north-east by Libya; to the east by Chad; to the south by Nigeria and Benin; to the south-west by Burkina Faso; and to the west by Mali. The Tropic of Cancer passes the northern tip.

Physical description
Lies on the southern fringe of the Sahara Desert, on a high plateau; deserts in the east, centre and north; water in quantity is found only in the south-west around the River Niger and in the south-east around Lake Chad; highest point is Mt Greboun (2 310m/7 580ft).

Climate
One of the hottest countries in the world; marked rainy season in the south Jun–Oct; rainfall decreases in the north to almost negligible levels in desert areas; drought can occur.

National holidays
Jan 1, Apr 24 (Concord), May 1, Aug 3 (Independence), Dec 18 (Republic), 25; Ad, EM, ER, NY (Muslim), PB, Revelation of Koran.

Political leaders

President

1960–74	Hamani Diori
1974–87	Seyni Kountché
1987–93	Ali Saibou
1993–6	Mahamane Ousmane
1996–9	Ibrahim Baré Maïnassara
1999	Daouda Malam Wanke
1999–	Mamadou Tandja

Prime Minister

1957–8	Djibo Bakary
1958–60	Hamani Diori
1960–83	*No Prime Minister*
1983	Mamane Oumarou
1983–8	Ahmid Algabid
1988–9	Mamane Oumarou
1990–1	Aliou Mahamidou
1991–3	Amadou Cheiffou
1993–4	Mahamadou Issoufou
1994–5	Abdoulaye Souley
1995	Amadou Boubacar Cissé
1995–6	Hama Amadou
1996	Boukary Adji
1996–7	Amadou Boubacar Cissé

1997–2000	Ibrahim Assane Mayaki	2007–	Seyni Oumarou
2000–7	Hama Amadou		

Nomads of Niger

Northern Niger is home to several nomadic peoples, including the Bororo Fulani. In their traditional marriage rituals a young man must seduce his beloved, then 'kidnap' her, elope and travel widely. People gather at the annual Guérewol festival for – according to the Embassy of Niger – 'celebrations, engagements, kidnappings of wives and baptisms'.

NIGERIA

Official name	Federal Republic of Nigeria
Local name	Nigeria
Independence	1960
Area	923 768 sq km/356 574 sq mi
Capital	Abuja
Chief towns	Lagos, Ibadan, Ogbomosho, Kano, Oshogbo, Ilorin, Abeokuta, Port Harcourt
Population	135 031 000 (2007e)
Nationality	Nigerian
Languages	English; Hausa, Yoruba, Edo and Igbo are also spoken
Ethnic groups	Hausa/Fulani 29%, Yoruba 21%, Igbo 18%, Ijaw 10%, Kanuri 4%, Ibibio 3%, Tiv 2%, others 13%
Religions	Islam 50% (Sunni), Christianity 50%
Time zone	GMT +1
Currency	1 Naira (N, ₦/NGN) = 100 kobo
Telephone	+234
Internet	.ng
Country code	NGA

Location

A republic in West Africa, bounded to the north by Niger; to the north-east by Chad; to the east by Cameroon; to the south by the Gulf of Guinea and the Bight of Benin; and to the west by Benin.

Physical description

Coastal strip dominated by the River Niger delta; tropical rainforest and oil palm bush lie north; dry central plateau of open woodland and savanna; edge of the Sahara Desert in the far north; numerous rivers; highest point is Mt Vogel (2 024m/6 640ft).

Climate

Two rainy seasons in the coastal areas; wettest part is the Niger delta and mountainous south-eastern frontier; Ibadan has an average daily maximum temperature of 31°C; only one rainy season in the north; dry season extends from Oct to Apr.

National holidays

Jan 1, May 1, 29 (Democracy), Oct 1 (National), Dec 25, 26; Ad (2), EM, ER (2), GF, PB.

Political leaders

President

1960–6 Nnamdi Azikiwe

Prime Minister

1960–6 Abubakar Tafawa Balewa

Military Government

1966	J T U Aguiyi-Ironsi
1966–75	Yakubu Gowon
1975–6	Murtala R Mohamed
1976–9	Olusegun Obasanjo

President

1979–83	Alhaji Shehu Shagari

Military Government

1983–5	Mohammadu Buhari
1985–93	Ibrahim B Babangida
1993	Ernest Shonekan *Interim*

Chairman of Provisional Ruling Council

1993–8	Sani Abacha
1998–9	Abdulsalami Abubakar

President

1999–2007	Olusegun Obasanjo
2007–	Umaru Musa Yar'Adua

Agriculture, Peace and Unity

The Nigerian flag has two green stripes, representing agriculture, and a white centre that symbolizes peace and unity. The flag is accorded the utmost respect; the government states that 'next to Mother Earth, it is the only national symbol worth dying for'.

NORFOLK ISLAND *see* AUSTRALIA

NORTHERN IRELAND *see* UNITED KINGDOM

NORTHERN MARIANA ISLANDS *see* UNITED STATES OF AMERICA

NORTH KOREA *see* KOREA, NORTH

NORWAY

Official name	Kingdom of Norway
Local name	Norge; Kongeriket Norge
Independence	1905
Area	323 895 sq km/125 023 sq mi
Capital	Oslo
Chief towns	Bergen, Trondheim, Stavanger, Kristiansand
Population	4 628 000 (2007e)
Nationality	Norwegian
Languages	Norwegian, in the varieties of Bokmål and Nynorsk
Ethnic groups	Norwegian 96%, Sami (Lapp) 1%, others 3%
Religions	Christianity 90% (Prot 87%, RC 1%, other 2%), Islam 2%, others and none/unaffiliated 8%
Time zone	GMT +1
Currency	1 Norwegian Krone (NKr/NOK) = 100 øre
Telephone	+47
Internet	.no
Country code	NOR

NORWAY

Location

A kingdom in north-west Europe, bounded to the north by the Arctic Ocean; to the east by Russia, Finland and Sweden; to the south by the Skagerrak; and to the west by the North Sea and Norwegian Sea.

Physical description

Mountainous, with many ranges and extensive plateau regions, especially in the south-west and centre; much of the interior rises above 1500m/4921ft; highest point is Galdhøpiggen (2469m/8100ft); numerous lakes; irregular coastline with many small islands and long deep fjords.

Climate

Arctic winter climate in the interior highlands, with snow, strong winds and severe frosts; comparatively mild winter conditions on the coast; heavy rainfall on the west coast; colder winters and warmer, drier summers in southern lowlands.

National holidays

Jan 1, May 1, 17 (Constitution), Dec 25, 26; A, EM, GF, HT, WM.

Norwegian dependencies

Bouvet Island

Location	An inaccessible and uninhabited ice-covered island of volcanic origin in the South Atlantic ocean, lying approximately 1370km/850mi to the south-west of the Cape of Good Hope, South Africa.		
Local name	Bouvetøya	**Internet**	.bv
Area	59 sq km/23 sq mi	**Country code**	BVT

Svalbard and Jan Mayen islands

Location	Svalbard Islands lie to the north of Norway and to the east of Greenland (Denmark) at the eastern edges of the Barents Sea, south of the Arctic Ocean; Jan Mayen Island lies to the north-east of Iceland and east of Greenland between the Norwegian Sea and the Greenland Sea.		
Area	62049 sq km/23957 sq mi (Svalbard); 373 sq km/144 sq mi (Jan Mayen)	**Population**	2200 (Svalbard; 2007e); uninhabited (Jan Mayen)
		Internet	.sj
Capital	Longyearbyen	**Country code**	SJM

Political leaders

Monarch

1872–1905	Oscar II *union with Sweden*	1957–91	Olav V
1905–57	Haakon VII	1991–	Harald V

Prime Minister

1898–1902	Johannes Steen	1923–4	Abraham Berge
1902–3	Otto Albert Blehr	1924–6	Johan Ludwig Mowinckel
1903–5	George Francis Hagerup	1926–8	Ivar Lykke
1905–7	Christian Michelsen	1928	Christopher Hornsrud
1907–8	Jørgen Løvland	1928–31	Johan Ludwig Mowinckel
1908–10	Gunnar Knudsen	1931–2	Peder L Kolstad
1910–12	Wollert Konow	1932–3	Jens Hundseid
1912–13	Jens Bratlie	1933–5	Johan Ludwig Mowinckel
1913–20	Gunnar Knudsen	1935–45	Johan Nygaardsvold
1920–1	Otto Bahr Halvorsen	1945–51	Einar Gerhardsen
1921–3	Otto Albert Blehr	1951–5	Oscar Torp
1923	Otto Bahr Halvorsen	1955–63	Einar Gerhardsen

1963	John Lyng
1963–5	Einar Gerhardsen
1965–71	Per Borten
1971–2	Trygve Bratteli
1972–3	Lars Korvald
1973–6	Trygve Bratteli
1976–81	Odvar Nordli
1981	Gro Harlem Brundtland
1981–6	Kåre Willoch
1986–9	Gro Harlem Brundtland
1989–90	Jan P Syse
1990–6	Gro Harlem Brundtland
1996–7	Thorbjørn Jagland
1997–2000	Kjell Magne Bondevik
2000–1	Jens Stoltenberg
2001–5	Kjell Magne Bondevik
2005–	Jens Stoltenberg

Midnight Sun and Northern Lights

In the far north of Norway the sun never sets in summer, earning it the nickname 'the Land of the Midnight Sun', while in the winter the same area witnesses the Aurora Borealis or Northern Lights – luminous and shimmering colours and streamers of light in the dark night sky.

OMAN

Official name	Sultanate of Oman
Local name	'Umān; Saltanat 'Umān
Former name	Sultanate of Muscat and Oman (until 1970)
Area	300 000 sq km/115 800 sq mi
Capital	Muscat; Masqat
Chief towns	Matrah, Nazwa, Salalah
Population	3 205 000 (2007e)
Nationality	Omani
Languages	Arabic
Ethnic groups	Arab 74%, Pakistani 22%, others 4%
Religions	Islam 86% (Ibadhi 75%), Hinduism 13%, others 1%
Time zone	GMT +4
Currency	1 Omani Rial (RO/OMR) = 1 000 baisas
Telephone	+968
Internet	.om
Country code	OMN

Location

An independent state in the south-east of the Arabian Peninsula, crossed by the Tropic of Cancer in the north; bounded to the north-west by the United Arab Emirates; to the north-east by the Gulf of Oman; to the east by the Arabian Sea; to the south-west by Yemen; and to the west by Saudi Arabia; the tip of the Musandam peninsula in the Strait of Hormuz is separated from the rest of the country by an 80km/50mi strip of the United Arab Emirates.

Physical description

Hajar range runs north-west to south-east parallel to the coast; several peaks in the Jebal al Akhdar are over 3000m/9842ft; highest point is Jebel Shams (3075m/10088ft); alluvial plain of the Batinah lies east and north of the Hajar; a vast sand desert is to the north-east.

Climate

Desert climate with much regional variation; summer (Apr–Oct) is hot and humid on the coast (maximum temperature 47°C), hot and dry in the interior; relatively temperate in mountains; light monsoon rains in the south from Jun to Sep.

National holidays

Jan 1, Jul 23 (Renaissance), Nov 18 (National), 19 (Sultan's Birthday); Ad (3), ER (4), NY (Muslim), PA, PB.

Political leaders

Sultan

1888–1913	Faisal bin Turki
1913–32	Taimur bin Faisal
1932–70	Said bin Taimur
1970–	Qaboos bin Said

Prime Minister

1970–2	Tariq bin Taimur
1972–	*As Sultan*

Fragrant Oman

Incense-burning is an Omani tradition, and many villages will have a specialized craftsman who makes incense, known as *bokhur*, from local ingredients including ambergris, frankincense, myrrh, rosewater and sandalwood.

PAKISTAN

Official name	Islamic Republic of Pakistan
Local name	Pākistān; Islāmī Jamhūriya e Pākistān
Former name	formerly part of India (until 1947), Dominion of Pakistan (1947–56); known as West Pakistan (until 1971)
Independence	1947
Area	803 943 sq km/310 322 sq mi
Capital	Islamabad; Islāmābād
Chief towns	Karachi, Lahore, Faisalabad, Rawalpindi
Population	164 742 000 (2007e)
Nationality	Pakistani
Languages	Urdu; English and several local languages are also spoken
Ethnic groups	Punjabi 66%, Sindhi 13%, Pashtun 11%, Muhajir 8%, Balochi 2%
Religions	Islam 97% (Sunni 77%, Shia 20%), Hinduism, Christianity and others 3%
Time zone	GMT +5
Currency	1 Pakistan Rupee (PRs, Rp/PKR) = 100 paisa
Telephone	+92
Internet	.pk
Country code	PAK

Location

A republic in Asia, bounded to the north by China; to the north-east by the disputed area of Jammu and Kashmir; to the east by India; to the south by the Arabian Sea; and to the west by Afghanistan and Iran.

Physical description

Largely centred on the alluvial floodplain of the River Indus; bounded to the north and west by mountains rising to 8610m/28 251ft at K2 in the disputed Kashmir-Jammu region; mostly flat plateaux, low-lying plains, and arid desert to the south of the Karakoram range.

Climate

Dominated by the Asiatic monsoon; hottest season is Mar–Jun, with highest temperatures in south; rainy season is late Jun–early Oct; climate varies in the mountains and upland plateaux; Indus Valley is extremely hot in summer.

National holidays

Feb 5 (Kashmir), Mar 23 (Pakistan), May 1, Aug 14 (Independence), Nov 9 (Iqbal), Dec 25 (Quaid-e-Azam (Jinnah)/Christmas); Ad (2), As (2), ER (3), PB, R; *additional optional holidays observed by religious minorities*.

Political leaders

President

1956–8	Iskander Mirza	1988–93	Ghulam Ishaq Khan
1958–69	Mohammad Ayoub Khan	1993	Wasim Sajjad *Acting*
1969–71	Agha Mohammad Yahya Khan	1993–7	Farooq Ahmad Khan Leghari
1971–3	Zulfikar Ali Bhutto	1997–8	Wasim Sajjad *Acting*
1973–8	Fazal Elahi Chawdry	1998–2001	Muhammed Rafiq Tarar
1978–88	Mohammad Zia Ul-Haq	2001–	Pervez Musharraf

Prime Minister

1947–51	Liaqat Ali Khan	1988	Mohammad Aslam Khan Khattak
1951–3	Khawaja Nazimuddin	1988–90	Benazir Bhutto
1953–5	Mohammad Ali	1990	Ghulam Mustafa Jatoi
1955–6	Chawdry Mohammad Ali	1990–3	Mian Mohammad Nawaz Sharif
1956–7	Hussein Shahid Suhrawardi	1993–6	Benazir Bhutto
1957	Ismail Chundrigar	1996–7	Meraj Khalid *Acting*
1957–8	Malik Feroz Khan Noon	1997–9	Mian Mohammad Nawaz Sharif
1958	Mohammad Ayoub Khan	1999–2002	*No Prime Minister*
1958–73	*No Prime Minister*	2002–4	Mir Zafarullah Khan Jamali
1973–7	Zulfikar Ali Bhutto	2004	Chaudhry Shujaat Hussain
1977–85	*No Prime Minister*	2004–7	Shaukat Aziz
1985–8	Mohammad Khan Junejo	2007–	Mohammad Mian Soomro *Interim*

PALAU

Official name	Republic of Palau
Local name	Belau; Belu'u era Belau
Former name	formerly part of the Trust Territory of the Pacific Islands (1917–79)
Independence	1994
Area	494 sq km/191 sq mi
Capital	Melekeok
Population	21 000 (2007e)
Nationality	Palauan
Languages	Palauan, English
Ethnic groups	Palauan (Micronesian with Malaysian and Melanesian admixtures) 70%, Filipino 15%, Chinese 5%, other Asian 2%, white 2%, others 6%
Religions	Christianity 65% (RC 42%, Prot 23%), traditional beliefs (Modekngei) 9%, others 10%, none/unaffiliated 16%
Time zone	GMT +10
Currency	1 US Dollar ($, US$/USD) = 100 cents
Telephone	+680
Internet	.pw
Country code	PLW

Location

An island republic in the western Pacific Ocean, 960km/600mi east of the Philippines.

Physical description

A group of approximately 350 small islands and islets; varies from the mountainous main island of Babelthuap to low-lying coral islands often surrounded by coral reefs; highest point is Mt Ngerchelchauus (242m/794ft).

Climate

Warm all year, with high humidity; average annual temperature is 27°C; typhoons are rare.

National holidays
Jan 1, Mar 15 (Youth), May 5 (Senior Citizens), Jun 1 (President), Jul 9 (Constitution), Oct 1 (Independence), 24 (United Nations), Dec 25; Labour Day (1st Mon in Sep), Thanksgiving (4th Thurs in Nov).

Political leaders

President

1981–5	Haruo Remeliik	1988–9	Thomas Remengesau
1985	Thomas Remengesau *Acting*	1989–93	Ngiratkel Etpison
1985	Alfonso Oiterong	1993–2000	Kuniwo Nakamura
1985–8	Lazarus Salii	2001–	Thomas Remengesau

Get By in Palauan

The Palauan word for *hello* is *alii*, and *how are you?* is *ke ua ngerang?Goodbye* is *ak morolung*, while other useful phrases include *ngtecha ngklem?* for *what is your name?* and *bo momengur!* which means *have something to eat!*

PALESTINE, PALESTINIAN AUTONOMOUS AREAS *see* ISRAEL

PANAMA

Official name	Republic of Panama
Local name	Panamá; República de Panamá
Independence	1821 (from Spain), 1903 (from Gran Colombia union)
Area	77 082 sq km/29 753 sq mi
Capital	Panama City; La Ciudad de Panamá
Chief towns	David, Colón, Santiago
Population	3 242 000 (2007e)
Nationality	Panamanian
Languages	Spanish
Ethnic groups	mestizo (Amerindian and white) 70%, Amerindian and mixed (West Indian) 14%, white 10%, Amerindian 6%
Religions	Christianity 100% (RC 85%, Prot 15%)
Time zone	GMT –5
Currency	1 Balboa (B, Ba/PAB) = 100 centésimos; the US dollar is also used
Telephone	+507
Internet	.pa
Country code	PAN

Location
A republic in Central America, bounded to the north by the Caribbean Sea; to the east by Colombia; to the south by the Pacific Ocean; and to the west by Costa Rica.

Physical description
Mostly mountainous; Serranía de Tabasará in the west rises to over 2 000m/6 562ft; highest point is Barú volcano in Chiriqui (3 475m/11 400ft); Azuero peninsula lies to the south; lake-studded lowland cuts across the isthmus; dense tropical forests on the Caribbean coast; Panama Canal (approximately 80km/50mi long) links the Pacific and Caribbean coasts.

Climate
Tropical, with a mean annual temperature of 32°C.

National holidays
Jan 1, 9 (Martyrs), May 1, Nov 3 (Independence from Colombia), 5 (Colon), 10 (Los Santos Uprising), 28 (Independence), Dec 8 (Mothers), 25; C, ES, GF, HS; *some local variation*.

Political leaders

President

1904–8	Manuel Amador Guerrero
1908–10	José Domingo de Obaldia
1910	Federico Boyd
1910	Carlos Antonio Mendoza
1910–12	Pablo Arosemena
1912	Rodolfo Chiari
1912–16	Belisario Porras
1916–18	Ramón Maximiliano Valdés
1918	Pedro Antonio Diaz
1918	Cirilo Luis Urriola
1918–20	Belisario Porras
1920	Ernesto T Lefevre
1920–4	Belisario Porras
1924–8	Rodolfo Chiari
1928	Tomás Gabriel Duque
1928–31	Florencio Harmodio Arosemena
1931	Harmodio Arias
1931–2	Ricardo Joaquín Alfaro
1932–6	Harmodio Arias
1936–9	Juan Demóstenes Arosemena
1939	Ezequiel Fernández Jaén
1939–40	Augusto Samuel Boyd
1940–1	Arnulfo Arias Madrid
1941	Ernesto Jaén Guardia
1941	José Pezet
1941–5	Ricardo Adolfo de la Guardia
1945–8	Enrique Adolfo Jiménez Brin
1948–9	Domingo Diaz Arosemena
1949	Daniel Chanis
1949	Roberto Francisco Chiari
1949–51	Arnulfo Arias Madrid
1951–2	Alcibiades Arosemena
1952–5	José Antonio Remón
1955	José Ramón Guizado
1955–6	Ricardo Manuel Arias Espinosa
1956–60	Ernesto de la Guardia
1960–4	Roberto Francisco Chiari
1964–8	Marco A Robles
1968	Arnulfo Arias Madrid
1968	*Military Junta*
1968–9	Omar Torrijos Herrera
1969–78	Demetrio Basilio Lakas
1978–82	Aristides Royo
1982–4	Ricardo de la Esoriella
1984	Jorge Enrique Illueca Sibauste
1984–5	Nicolás Ardito Barletta
1985–8	Eric Arturo Delvalle
1988–9	Manuel Solís Palma
1989–94	Guillermo Endara Galimany
1994–9	Ernesto Pérez Balladares
1999–2004	Mireya Elisa Moscoso Rodriguez
2004–	Martin Torrijos

Fish and Butterflies

The name *Panama* is widely believed to mean 'an abundance of fish' or 'an abundance of butterflies' in the local Amerindian language.

PAPUA NEW GUINEA

Official name	Independent State of Papua New Guinea (PNG)
Local name	Papua New Guinea; Gau Hedinarai ai Papua-Matamata Guinea
Independence	1975
Area	462 840 sq km/178 656 sq mi
Capital	Port Moresby
Chief towns	Lae, Madang, Rabaul
Population	5 796 000 (2007e)
Nationality	Papua New Guinean
Languages	Pidgin English; approximately 800 other languages are spoken
Ethnic groups	Papuan 85%, Melanesian 1%, others 14%
Religions	Christianity 66% (Prot and others 44%, RC 22%), traditional beliefs 34%
Time zone	GMT +10
Currency	1 Kína (K/PGK) = 100 toea
Telephone	+675
Internet	.pg
Country code	PNG

Location
An independent state in the south-western Pacific Ocean, comprising the eastern half of the island of New Guinea, bounded by Indonesia to the west, and many smaller islands; separated from Australia to the south by the Torres Strait.

Physical description
Complex mountain system, with snow-covered peaks rising above 4000m/13123ft; highest point is Mt Wilhelm (4509m/14793ft); mainly covered with tropical rainforest; coastal mangrove swamps; other islands are also mountainous and mostly volcanic.

Climate
Typically monsoonal, with temperatures and humidity constantly high; the average temperature range is 22–33°C; high rainfall.

National holidays
Jan 1, Jul 23 (Remembrance), Sep 16 (Independence), Dec 25, 26; EM, ES, GF, HS; Queen's Birthday (Jun); *also various regional holidays*.

Political leaders

Head of State: British monarch, represented by Governor General (Sir Paulias Matane since 2004).

Prime Minister

1975–80	Michael T Somare
1980–2	Julius Chan
1982–5	Michael T Somare
1985–8	Paias Wingti
1988–92	Rabbie Namaliu
1992–4	Paias Wingti
1994–7	Julius Chan
1997	John Giheno *Acting*
1997	Julius Chan
1997–9	Bill Skate
1999–2002	Mekere Morauta
2002–	Sir Michael Somare

Birds of Paradise

The beautiful feathers of the bird of paradise are used for decoration and in cultural and religious ceremonies across Papua New Guinea. A yellow bird of paradise with trailing plumes is shown in flight on the national flag, while the national crest shows a striking crimson and gold bird with spread wings sitting on a ceremonial drum, with a traditional spear behind it.

PARAGUAY

Official name	Republic of Paraguay
Local name	Paraguay; República del Paraguay
Independence	1811
Area	406750 sq km/157000 sq mi
Capital	Asunción
Chief towns	Villarrica, Concepción
Population	6669000 (2007e)
Nationality	Paraguayan
Languages	Spanish, Guaraní
Ethnic groups	mestizo 95%, others 5%
Religions	Christianity 99% (RC 90%, Prot 9%, mostly Mennonite), others 1%
Time zone	GMT –4
Currency	1 Guaraní (Gs/PYG) = 100 céntimos
Telephone	+595
Internet	.py
Country code	PRY

Location

A republic in central South America, crossed by the Tropic of Capricorn in the south; bounded to the north-west by Bolivia; to the north and east by Brazil; and to the south and south-west by Argentina.

Physical description

Divided into two regions by the River Paraguay, lying mostly at altitudes below 450m/1 476ft; west is mostly cattle country or scrub forest; more fertile in the east; higher Paraná Plateau is mainly wet, treeless savanna; highest point is Cerro Pero (842m/2 762ft).

Climate

Tropical in the north-west, with hot summers and warm winters; temperate in the south-east; temperature at Asunción ranges from 12°C in winter to 35°C in summer.

National holidays

Jan 1, Mar 1 (Heroes), May 1, 15 (Independence), Jun 12 (Chaco Armistice), Aug 15 (Foundation of Asunción), Sep 29 (Battle of Boquerón), Dec 8 (Our Lady of Caacupé), 25; GF, HT.

Political leaders

President

1898–1902	Emilio Aceval
1902	Héctor Carvallo
1902–4	Juan Antonio Escurra
1904–5	Juan Gaona
1905–6	Cecilio Baez
1906–8	Benigno Ferreira
1908–10	Emiliano González Navero
1910–11	Manuel Gondra
1911	Albino Jara
1911	Liberato Marcial Rojas
1912	Pedro Peña
1912	Emiliano González Navero
1912–16	Eduardo Schaerer
1916–19	Manuel Franco
1919–20	José P Montero
1920–1	Manuel Gondra
1921	Félix Paiva
1921–3	Eusebio Ayala
1923–4	Eligio Ayala
1924	Luis Alberto Riart
1924–8	Eligio Ayala
1928–31	José Particio Guggiari
1931–2	Emiliano González Navero
1932	José Particio Guggiari
1932–6	Eusebio Ayala
1936–7	Rafael Franco
1937–9	Félix Paiva
1939–40	José Félix Estigarribia
1940–8	Higino Morínigo
1948	Juan Manuel Frutos
1948–9	Juan Natalicio González
1949	Raimundo Rolón
1949	Felipe Molas López
1949–54	Federico Chaves
1954	Tomás Romero Pareira
1954–89	Alfredo Stroessner
1989–93	Andrés Rodríguez
1993–8	Juan Carlos Wasmosy
1998–9	Raúl Cubas Grau
1999–2003	Luis González Mácchi
2003–	Nicanor Duarte Frutos

Pleistocene Peccary

The Chacoan peccary is a hairy, pig-like creature that lives in the Gran Chaco, a vast area of arid scrublands, cacti and thorny vegetation in north-west Paraguay. The Chacoan peccary was thought to be extinct but had been described from fossil records of the Pleistocene period; the creature was discovered alive, to great scientific astonishment, in the 1970s.

PERU

Official name	Republic of Peru
Local name	Perú; República del Perú
Independence	1821
Area	1 284 640 sq km/495 871 sq mi
Capital	Lima
Chief towns	Arequipa, Chiclayo, Cuzco, Trujillo
Population	28 675 000 (2007e)
Nationality	Peruvian
Languages	Spanish, Quechua; Aymara is also widely spoken
Ethnic groups	Amerindian 45% (principally Quechua), mestizo 37%, white 15%, black, Japanese, Chinese and others 3%
Religions	Christianity 83% (RC 81%, Prot 2%), others 1%, none/unaffiliated 16%
Time zone	GMT –5
Currency	1 Nuevo Sol (Pes/PEN) = 100 cénts
Telephone	+51
Internet	.pe
Country code	PER

Location

A republic on the west coast of South America, bounded to the north by Ecuador; to the north-east by Colombia; to the east by Brazil and Bolivia; to the south by Chile; and to the west by the Pacific Ocean.

Physical description

Arid plains and foothills on the coast, with desert areas and fertile river valleys; 50% of the population live on the central sierra, at an average altitude of 3000m/9842ft; highest point is Huascarán (6768m/22204ft); forested Amazon basin lies to the east; major rivers flow to the Amazon; Lake Titicaca lies on the Bolivian border.

Climate

Mild temperatures on the coast; dry, arid desert in the south; northern coastal region is affected by El Niño; Andean temperatures never rise above 23°C with a large daily range; the climate is typically wet and tropical in the Amazon basin.

National holidays

Jan 1, May 1, Jun 29 (SS Peter and Paul), Jul 28–29 (Independence), Aug 30 (St Rose of Lima), Oct 8 (Battle of Angamos), Nov 1, Dec 8, 25; ES, GF, HT.

Political leaders

President

1899–1903	Eduardo López de Romaña
1903–4	Manuel Candamo
1904	Serapio Calderón
1904–8	José Pardo y Barreda
1908–12	Augusto B Leguía
1912–14	Guillermo Billinghurst
1914–15	Oscar R Benavides
1915–19	José Pardo y Barreda
1919–30	Augusto B Leguía
1930	Manuel Ponce
1930–1	Luis M Sánchez Cerro
1931	Leoncio Elías
1931	Gustavo A Jiménez
1931	David Samanez Ocampo
1931–3	Luis M Sánchez Cerro
1933–9	Oscar R Benavides
1939–45	Manuel Prado
1945–8	José Luis Bustamante y Rivero
1948–56	Manuel A Odría
1956–62	Manuel Prado
1962–3	*Military Junta*
1963–8	Fernando Belaúnde Terry
1968–75	*Military Junta* (Juan Velasco Alvarado)
1975–80	*Military Junta* (Francisco Morales Bermúdez)
1980–5	Fernando Belaúnde Terry
1985–90	Alan García Pérez

1990–2000	Alberto Keinya Fujimori
2000–1	Valentín Paniagua *Interim*
2001–6	Alejandro Toledo Manrique
2006–	Alan García Pérez

Prime Minister

1900	Enrique Coronel Zegarra y Cortés
1900–1	Domingo M Almenara Butler
1901–2	Cesáreo Chacaltana Reyes
1902	Cesáreo Octavio Deustua Escarza
1902–3	Eugenio Larrabure y Unanue
1903–4	José Pardo y Barreda
1904	Alberto Elmore Fernández de Córdoba
1904–7	Augusto B Leguía y Salcedo
1907	Agustín Tovar
1907–8	Carlos A Washburn Salas
1908–9	Eulogio Romero Salcedo
1909–10	Rafael Fernández de Villanueva Cortez
1910	Javier Prado y Ugarteche
1910	Germán Schreiber Waddington
1910	José Salvador Cavero
1910–11	Enrique C Basadre Stevenson
1911–12	Agustín G Ganoza Cavero
1912	Elías Malpartida
1912–13	Enrique Varela
1913	Federico Luna y Peralta
1913	Aurelio Sousa Matute
1913–14	Enrique Varela
1914	Pedro E Muñiz
1914	Manuel Melitón Carvajal
1914	Aurelio Sousa Matute
1914–15	Germán Schreiber Waddington
1915	Carlos Isaac Abrill
1915–17	Enrique de la Riva-Agüero y Looz Corswaren
1917–18	Francisco Tudela y Varela
1918–19	Germán Arenas y Loayza
1919	Juan Manuel Zuloaga
1919–22	Germán Leguía y Martínez Jakeway
1922–4	Julio Enrique Ego Aguirre
1924–6	Alejandrino Maguiña
1926–9	Pedro José Rada y Gamio
1929–30	Benjamín Huamán de los Heros
1930–1	Fernando Sarmiento
1931–2	Germán Arenas y Loayza
1932	Francisco R Lanatta
1932	Luis A Flores
1932	Ricardo Rivadeneira
1932–3	José Matías Manzanilla Barrientos
1933	Jorge Prado y Ugarteche
1933–4	José de la Riva-Agüero y Osma
1934–5	Carlos Arenas y Loayza
1935–6	Manuel Esteban Rodríguez
1936–9	Ernesto Montagne Markholz
1939	Alberto Rey de Castro y Romaña
1939–44	Alfredo Solf y Muro
1944–5	Manuel Cisneros Sánchez
1945–6	Rafael Belaúnde y Diez Canseco
1946–7	Julio Ernesto Portugal Escobedo
1947	José Alcamora
1948	Roque Augusto Saldías Maninat
1948	Armando Revoredo Iglesias
1948–54	*No Prime Minister*
1954–6	Roque Augusto Saldías Maninat
1956–7	Manuel Cisneros Sánchez
1958–9	Luis Gallo Porras
1959–61	Pedro Gerardo Beltrán Espantos
1961–2	Carlos Moreyra y Paz Soldán
1962–3	Nicolás Lindley López
1963	Julio Óscar Trelles Montes
1963–5	Fernando Schwalb López Aldana
1965–7	Daniel Becerra de la Flor
1967	Edgardo Seoane Corrales
1967–8	Raúl Ferrero Rebagliati
1968	Oswaldo Hercelles García
1968	Miguel Mujica Gallo
1968–73	Ernesto Montagne Sánchez
1973–5	Edgardo Mercado Jarrín
1975	Francisco Morales Bermúdez
1975–6	Óscar Vargas Prieto
1976	Jorge Fernández Maldonado Solari
1976–8	Guillermo Arbulú Galliani
1978–9	Óscar Molina Pallochia
1979–80	Pedro Richter Prada
1980–3	Manuel Ulloa Elías
1983–4	Fernando Schwalb López Aldana
1984	Sandro Mariátegui Chiappe
1984–5	Luis Pércovich Roca
1985–7	Luis Alva Castro
1987–8	Guillermo Larco Cox
1988–9	Armando Villanueva del Campo
1989	Luis Alberto Sánchez
1989–90	Guillermo Larco Cox
1990–1	Juan Carlos Hurtado Miller
1991	Carlos Torres y Torres Lara
1991–2	Alfonso de los Heros
1992–3	Óscar de la Puente Raygada
1993–4	Alfonso Bustamante y Bustamante
1994–5	Efraín Goldenberg Schreiber
1995–6	Dante Córdova Blanco

1996–8	Alberto Pandolfi
1998	Javier Valle Riestra
1998–9	Alberto Pandolfi
1999	Víctor Joy Way
1999–2000	Alberto Bustamante Belaúnde
2000	Federico Salas Guevara
2001	Javier Perez de Cuellar
2001–2	Roberto Daniño Zapata
2002–3	Luis Solari de la Fuente
2003	Beatriz Merino
2003–5	Carlos Ferrero Costa
2005–6	Pedro Pablo Kuczynski
2006–	Jorge del Castillo

Peruvian Pisco

Peru's national drink is *pisco*, an alcoholic grape liqueur made nowhere else in the world which is named after the Quechua word for 'bird'. Grape vines were introduced to Peru during Spanish colonization of South America in the 16c, but the Peruvians proved so adept at winemaking that worried Spanish vineyards banned the trade. The Peruvian producers therefore switched from wines to liqueurs, using ancient Inca earthenware, and created pisco.

PHILIPPINES

Official name	Republic of the Philippines
Local name	Pilipinas; República Ñg Pilipinas
Independence	1946
Area	299679 sq km/115676 sq mi
Capital	Manila
Chief towns	Quezon City, Basilan, Cebu, Bacolod, Davao, Iloilo
Population	91077000 (2007e)
Nationality	Filipino (masculine), Filipina (feminine), Philippine
Languages	Pilipino; English and many local dialects are also spoken
Ethnic groups	Tagalog 28%, Cebuano 13%, Ilocano 9%, Ilongo 8%, Bisaya/Binisaya 8%, Bicol 6%, Waray 3%, others 25%
Religions	Christianity 92% (RC 81%, Prot 11%), Islam 5%, others 3%
Time zone	GMT +8
Currency	1 Philippine Peso (PHP) = 100 centavos
Telephone	+63
Internet	.ph
Country code	PHL

Location

An archipelago republic between the South China Sea to the west and the Pacific Ocean to the east, lying north of Indonesia, west of Vietnam and China; and to the south of Taiwan.

Physical description

More than 7100 islands and islets; largely mountainous, with north to south ridges rising to over 2500m/8200ft; highest point is Mt Apo (2954m/9691ft); narrow coastal margins and broad interior plateaux; forests cover half the land area; some islands are ringed by coral reefs.

Climate

Lowlands have a warm and humid tropical climate throughout the year, with an average temperature of 27°C; lying astride the typhoon belt, the Philippines are affected by approximately 15 cyclonic storms annually.

National holidays

Jan 1, Apr 9 (Araw ng Kagitingan/Valour), May 1, Jun 12 (Independence), Aug 20 (Aquino), 27 (Heroes), Nov 1, 30 (Bonifacio), Dec 25, 30 (Rizal), 31; GF, HS, HT; *Muslim festivals are official holidays in some provinces.*

Political leaders

President

1935–44	Manuel L Quezon (*in exile from 1942*)	1957–61	Carlos P Garcia
1943–4	José P Laurel (*Japanese occupation*)	1961–5	Diosdado Macapagal
1944–6	Sergio Osmeña	1965–86	Ferdinand E Marcos (*Martial law 1972–81*)
1946–8	Manuel A Roxas	1986–92	Corazon C Aquino
1948–53	Elpidio Quirino	1992–8	Fidel V Ramos
1953–7	Ramon Magsaysay	1998–2001	Joseph Estrada
		2001–	Gloria Macapagal-Arroyo

Seashells and Volcanoes

The Philippines Department of Tourism proudly reports that 488 of the world's 500 species of coral are found in its waters, along with seven of the eight known species of giant clam, five of the eight species of marine turtle and approximately 12,000 types of seashell. It adds that the province of Camiguin not only has more volcanoes per square kilometre than any other island in the world, but is 'the only place in the Philippines which has more volcanoes (seven) than towns (five)'.

PITCAIRN ISLANDS *see* UNITED KINGDOM

POLAND

Official name	Republic of Poland
Local name	Polska; Rzeczpospolita Polska
Former name	People's Republic of Poland (1952–89)
Independence	1918
Area	312 612 sq km/120 668 sq mi
Capital	Warsaw; Warszawa
Chief towns	Lódz, Kraków, Wroclaw, Poznań, Gdańsk, Katowice, Lublin
Population	38 518 000 (2007e)
Nationality	Pole, Polish
Languages	Polish
Ethnic groups	Polish 97%, German, Belarussian, Ukrainian and others 3%
Religions	Christianity 92% (RC 90%, Orthodox and Prot 2%), none/unaffiliated 8%
Time zone	GMT +1
Currency	1 Złoty (Zl/PLN) = 100 groszy
Telephone	+48
Internet	.pl
Country code	POL

Location

A republic in central Europe, bounded to the north by the Baltic Sea and the Russian region of Kaliningrad; to the north-east by Lithuania and Belarus; to the south-east by Ukraine; to the south by Slovakia; to the south-west by the Czech Republic; and to the west by Germany.

POLAND

Physical description
Mostly part of the great European plain; mountains in the south rise in the High Tatra to 2 499m/8 199ft at Mt Rysy; Europe's richest coal basin lies in the west (Silesia); lowlands with many lakes in the north.

Climate
Continental climate, with severe winters and hot summers; rain falls chiefly in summer.

National holidays
Jan 1, May 1, 3 (National), Aug 15, Nov 1, 11 (Independence), Dec 25, 26; CC, EM.

Political leaders

Republic of Poland

President

1945–52	Bolesław Bierut *Acting President until 1947*
1952–64	Aleksander Zawadzki
1964–8	Edward Ochab
1968–70	Marian Spychalski
1970–2	Józef Cyrankiewicz
1972–85	Henryk Jabłonski
1985–90	Wojciech Jaruzelski
1990–5	Lech Wałesa
1995–2005	Aleksander Kwasniewski
2005–	Lech Kaczynski

Prime Minister

1947–52	Józef Cyrankiewicz
1952–4	Bolesław Bierut
1954–70	Józef Cyrankiewicz
1970–80	Piotr Jecoszewicz
1980	Edward Babiuch
1980–1	Józef Pinkowski
1981–5	Wojciech Jaruzelski
1985–8	Zbigniew Messner
1988–9	Mieczyslaw Rakowski
1989	Czeslaw Kiszczak
1989–90	Tadeusz Mazowiecki
1991	Jan Krzysztof Bielecki
1991–2	Jan Olszewski
1992	Waldemar Pawlak
1992–3	Hanna Suchocka
1993–5	Waldemar Pawlak
1995–6	Józef Oleksy
1996–7	Wlodzimierz Cimoszewicz
1997–2001	Jerzy Buzek
2001–4	Leszek Miller
2004–5	Marek Belka
2005–6	Kazimierz Marcinkiewicz
2006–7	Jaroslaw Kaczynski
2007–	Donald Tusk

First Secretary

1945–8	Władysław Gomułka
1948–56	Bolesław Bierut
1956	Edward Ochab
1956–70	Władysław Gomułka
1970–80	Edward Gierek
1980–1	Stanisław Kania
1981–9	Wojciech Jaruzelski
1989	Mieczyslaw Rakowski

Polish Pines

Forests cover about 27% of Poland, with pine trees the most abundant species.

POLYNESIA, FRENCH *see* FRANCE

PORTUGAL

Official name	Portuguese Republic
Local name	Portugal; República Portuguesa
Former name	Kingdom of Portugal (until 1910)
Independence	1668
Area	91 982 sq km/35 142 sq mi
Capital	Lisbon; Lisboa
Chief towns	Oporto, Setúbal, Coimbra
Population	10 643 000 (2007e)
Nationality	Portuguese
Languages	Portuguese
Ethnic groups	Portuguese 95%, others 5%
Religions	Christianity 96% (RC 94%, Prot 2%), others 1%, none/unaffiliated 3%
Time zone	GMT
Currency	1 Euro (€/EUR) = 100 cents
Telephone	+351
Internet	.pt
Country code	PRT

Location
A republic in south-western Europe on the western side of the Iberian Peninsula, bounded to the north and east by Spain; and to the south and west by the Atlantic Ocean.

Physical description
Several mountain ranges formed by the west spurs of the Spanish mountain system; chief range is the Serra da Estrêla in the north, rising to 1 991m/6 532ft; highest point is Mt Pico on Ilha do Pico (Pico Island) in the Azores (2 351m/7 713ft).

Climate
Basically a maritime climate, with increased variation between summer and winter temperatures inland; west coast is relatively cool in summer; most rainfall in winter.

National holidays
Jan 1, Apr 25 (Liberty), May 1, Jun 10 (Camões-Portugal/National), Aug 15, Oct 5 (Republic), Nov 1, Dec 1 (Independence), 8, 25; C, CC, ES, GF.

Autonomous regions

Azores

Location	An island archipelago of volcanic origin in the North Atlantic ocean, lying 1 400–1 800km/870–1 100mi to the west of the Cabo da Roca on mainland Portugal.		
Area	2 300 sq km/900 sq mi	**Capital**	Ponta Delgada

Madeira

Location	The main island in a Portuguese archipelago off the coast of North Africa, 990km/615mi south-west of Lisbon.		
Area	796 sq km/307 sq mi	**Capital**	Funchal

Political leaders

Monarch

1095–1112	Henry of Burgundy	1211–23	Alfonso II
1112–85	Alfonso I	1223–45	Sancho II
1185–1211	Sancho I	1245–79	Alfonso III

1279–1325	Diniz
1325–57	Alfonso IV
1357–67	Peter I
1367–83	Ferdinand
1383–5	*disputed by John of Castile and John of Aviz*
1385–1433	John I of Aviz
1433–8	Edward
1438–81	Alfonso V
1481–95	John II
1495–1521	Manuel I
1521–57	John III
1557–78	Sebastian
1578–80	Henry
1580–98	Philip I (II of Spain)
1598–1621	Philip II (III of Spain)
1621–40	Philip III (IV of Spain)
1640–56	John IV of Braganza
1656–83	Alfonso VI
1683–1706	Peter II
1706–50	John V
1750–77	Joseph
1777–1816	Maria I
1777–86	Peter III (King Consort)
1816–26	John VI
1826	Peter IV (I of Brazil)
1826–8	Maria II
1828–34	Miguel
1834–53	Maria II
1853–61	Peter V
1861–89	Luis
1889–1908	Charles
1908–10	Manuel II

First Republic

President

1910–11	Teófilo Braga
1911–15	Manuel José de Arriaga
1915	Teófilo Braga
1915–17	Bernardino Machado
1917–18	Sidónio Pais
1918–19	Joâo do Canto e Castro
1919–23	António José de Almeida
1923–5	Manuel Teixeira Gomes
1925–6	Bernardino Machado

New State

President

1926	*Military Junta* (José Mendes Cabeçadas)
1926	*Military Junta* (Manuel de Oliveira Gomes da Costa)
1926–51	António Oscar Fragoso Carmona
1951–8	Francisco Craveiro Lopes
1958–74	Américo de Deus Tomás

Prime Minister

1932–68	António de Oliveira Salazar
1968–74	Marcelo Caetano

Second Republic

President

1974	*Military Junta* (António Spínola)
1974–6	*Military Junta* (Francisco da Costa Gomes)

Prime Minister

1974	Adelino da Palma Carlos
1974–5	Vasco Gonçalves
1975–6	José Pinheiro de Azevedo

Third Republic

President

1976–86	António dos Santos Ramalho Eanes	1996–2006	Jorge Sampaio
1986–96	Mário Soares	2006–	Anibal Cavaço Silva

Prime Minister

1976–8	Mário Soares	1983–5	Mário Soares
1978	Alfredo Nobre da Costa	1985–95	Aníbal Cavaço Silva
1978–9	Carlos Alberto de Mota Pinto	1995–2001	António Guterres
1979	Maria de Lurdes Pintasilgo	2002–4	José Manuel Durão Barroso
1980–1	Francisco de Sá Carneiro	2004–5	Pedro Santana Lopes
1981–3	Francisco Pinto Balsemão	2005–	José Sócrates

PRÍNCIPE *see* **SÃO TOMÉ AND PRÍNCIPE**

PUERTO RICO *see* **UNITED STATES OF AMERICA**

QATAR

Official name	State of Qatar
Local name	Qatar; Dawlat Qatar
Independence	1971
Area	11 437 sq km/4415 sq mi
Capital	Doha; Ad Dawhah
Chief towns	Dukhan, Al Khawr, Umm Sai'd, Al Wakrah
Population	907 000 (2007e)
Nationality	Qatari
Languages	Arabic
Ethnic groups	Arab 40%, Pakistani 18%, Indian 18%, Iranian 10%, others 14%
Religions	Islam 95%, others 5%
Time zone	GMT +3
Currency	1 Qatari Riyal (QR/QAR) = 100 dirhams
Telephone	+974
Internet	.qa
Country code	QAT

Location

A state on the east coast of the Arabian Peninsula, comprising the Qatar Peninsula and numerous small offshore islands, bounded to the south by Saudi Arabia, and on all other sides by the Arabian Gulf.

Physical description

The peninsula, 160km/100mi long and 55–80km/34–50mi wide, slopes gently from the Dukhān Heights (98m/322ft) to the east shore; highest point is Qurayn Abu al Bawl (103m/338ft); barren terrain, mainly sand and gravel; coral reefs offshore.

Climate

Desert climate with average temperatures of 23°C in the winter and 35°C in the summer; high humidity; sparse annual rainfall.

National holidays

Dec 18 (National); Ad (5), ER (4).

Political leaders

Emir

Family name: al-Thani

1971–2 Ahmad bin Ali
1972–95 Khalifa bin Hamad
1995– Hamad bin Khalifa

Prime Minister

1971–95 *As Emir*
1995–6 *As Emir*
1996–2007 Abdullah bin Khalifa al-Thani
2007– Hamad bin Jassem bin Jabr al-Thani

RAS AL-KHAIMAH *see* UNITED ARAB EMIRATES

REPUBLIC OF CHINA *see* TAIWAN

RÉUNION *see* FRANCE

ROMANIA

Official name	Romania
Local name	Romănia
Former name	Kingdom of Romania (until 1947), People's Republic of Romania (1947–65), Socialist Republic of Romania (1965–89); known as Rumania in English until 1966
Independence	1878
Area	237 500 sq km/91 675 sq mi
Capital	Bucharest; Bucureşti
Chief towns	Braşov, Constanşa, Iaşi, Timişoara, Cluj-Napoca
Population	22 276 000 (2007e)
Nationality	Romanian
Languages	Romanian
Ethnic groups	Romanian 89%, Magyar 7%, Romany 2%, others 2%
Religions	Christianity 99% (Orthodox 87%, Prot 7%, RC 5%), Islam and others 1%
Time zone	GMT +2
Currency	1 New Leu (L/RON) = 100 bani
Telephone	+40
Internet	.ro
Country code	ROU

Count Dracula's Castle

The classic vampire story *Dracula* (1897) by Bram Stoker is famed for its Transylvanian vampire. Transylvania is a real region of northern and central Romania, separated from the capital by the high Carpathian Mountains. The character of Dracula was inspired by one *Vlad Dracula*, a ruler of Romania in the mid-15c, whose nickname was Vlad the Impaler. Today the area thrives on the Dracula legend, with 'Dracula tours' taking in the real Dracula's birthplace in Sighisoara and his home at Castle Bran.

Location

A republic in south-eastern Europe, bounded to the north by Ukraine; to the east by Moldova, Ukraine and the Black Sea; to the south by Bulgaria; and to the west by Serbia and Hungary.

Physical description
Carpathian Mountains separate Old Romania from Transylvania, and form the heart of the country; highest peak is Mt Moldoveanu (2544m/8349ft); Romanian Plain in the south includes the richest arable area; over 25% of the land is forested.

Climate
Continental, with cold, snowy winters and warm summers; mildest area in winter is along the Black Sea coast; plains of the north and east can suffer from drought; average rainfall is higher in the mountains than in the Danube delta.

National holidays
Jan 1, 2, May 1, Dec 1 (National), 25, 26; EM (Orthodox); *other religious festivals are observed in many areas*.

Political leaders

Monarch

1881–1914 Carol I
1914–27 Ferdinand I
1927–30 Michael *Prince*
1930–40 Carol II
1940–7 Michael I

President

1947–8 Mihai Sadoveanu *Interim*
1948–52 Constantin I Parhon
1952–8 Petru Groza
1958–61 Ion Georghe Maurer
1961–5 Georghe Gheorghiu-Dej
1965–7 Chivu Stoica
1967–89 Nicolae Ceauşescu
1989–96 Ion Iliescu
1996–2000 Emil Constantinescu
2000–4 Ion Iliescu
2004– Traian Basescu

Prime Minister

1900–1 Petre P Carp
1901–6 Dimitrie A Sturdza
1906–7 Gheorge Grigore Cantacuzino
1907–9 Dimitrie A Sturdza
1909 Ionel Brătianu
1909–10 Mihai Pherekyde
1910–11 Ionel Brătianu
1911–12 Petre P Carp
1912–14 Titu Maiorescu
1914–18 Ionel Brătianu
1918 Alexandru Averescu
1918 Alexandru Marghiloman
1918 Constantin Coandă
1918 Ionel Brătianu
1919 Artur Văitoianu
1919–20 Alexandru Vaida-Voevod
1920–1 Alexandru Averescu
1921–2 Take Ionescu
1922–6 Ionel Brătianu
1926–7 Alexandru Averescu
1927 Ionel Brătianu
1927–8 Vintila I C Brătianu
1928–30 Juliu Maniu
1930 Gheorghe C Mironescu
1930 Juliu Maniu
1930–1 Gheorghe C Mironescu
1931–2 Nicolae Iorga
1932 Alexandru Vaida-Voevod
1932–3 Juliu Maniu
1933 Alexandru Vaida-Voevod
1933 Ion G Duca
1933–4 Constantin Angelescu
1934–7 Gheorghe Tătărescu
1937 Octavian Goga
1937–9 Miron Cristea
1939 Armand Călinescu
1939 Gheorghe Argeşanu
1939 Constantine Argetoianu
1939–40 Gheorghe Tătărescu
1940 Ion Gigurtu
1940–4 Ion Antonescu
1944 Constantin Savbnătescu
1944–5 Nicolae Rădescu
1945–52 Petru Groza
1952–5 Gheorghe Gheorghiu-Dej
1955–61 Chivu Stoica
1961–74 Ion Gheorghe Maurer
1974–80 Manea Mănescu
1980–3 Ilie Verdet
1983–9 Constantin Dăscălescu
1989–91 Petre Roman
1991–2 Theodor Stolojan

1992–6	Nicolae Vacaroiu
1996–8	Victor Ciorbea
1998	Gavril Dejeu *Interim*
1998–9	Radu Vasile
1999	Alexandru Athanesiu *Interim*
1999–2000	Mugur Isarescu
2000–4	Adrian Nastase
2004	Eugen Bejinariu *Interim*
2004–	Calin Popescu Tariceanu

General Secretary

1955–65	Georghe Gheorghiu-Dej
1965–89	Nicolae Ceauşescu

ROSS DEPENDENCY *see* NEW ZEALAND

RUSSIA

Official name	Russian Federation
Local name	Rossiya; Rossiiskaya Federatsiya
Former name	Russian Empire (until 1917), Russian Republic (1917), Russian Socialist Federal Soviet Republic (until 1991), within the Union of Soviet Socialist Republics (USSR; 1922–91)
Independence	1991
Area	17075400 sq km/6591104 sq mi
Capital	Moscow; Moskva
Chief towns	St Petersburg, Nizhniy Novgorod, Rostov-on-Don, Volgograd, Yekaterinburg, Novosibirsk, Chelyabinsk, Kazan, Samara, Omsk
Population	141378000 (2007e)
Nationality	Russian
Languages	Russian
Ethnic groups	Russian 80%, Tatar 4%, Ukrainian 2%, Chuvash 1%, Bashkir 1%, others 12%
Religions	Christianity 22% (Orthodox), Islam 15%, none/unaffiliated 63%
Time zone	GMT +2/12
Currency	1 Rouble (R/RUB) = 100 kopeks
Telephone	+7
Internet	.ru
Country code	RUS

Location

A republic occupying much of eastern Europe and northern Asia, bounded to the north by the Arctic Ocean; to the east by the Sea of Okhotsk and the Bering Sea; to the south-east by North Korea; to the south by Mongolia, China and Kazakhstan; to the south-west by the Caspian Sea, Azerbaijan, Georgia and the Black Sea; and to the west by Ukraine, Belarus, Latvia, Estonia, Finland and Norway.

Physical description

Vast plains dominate the western half; Ural Mountains separate the East European Plain in the west from the West Siberian Lowlands in the east; Central Siberian Plateau lies east of the River Yenisei; further east lies the North Siberian Plain; over 20000 lakes, the largest being the Caspian Sea, Lake Taymyr and Lake Baikal; highest point is Mt Elbrus (5642m/18510ft).

Climate

Several different climate regions; variable weather in the north and the centre; winter temperatures are increasingly severe in the east and north; Moscow average temperature is 9°C (Jan) and 18°C (Jul); Siberia has a continental climate, with very cold and prolonged winters and short, often warm summers.

National holidays

Jan 1–5, 7 (Orthodox Christmas), Feb 23 (Defenders of the Motherland), Mar 8 (Women), May 1 (Spring and Labour), 9 (Victory), Jun 12 (Russia), Nov 4 (National Unity).

Political leaders

Monarch (Tsar)

1283–1303	Daniel
1303–25	Yuri
1325–41	Ivan I
1341–53	Semeon
1353–9	Ivan II
1359–89	Dimitri Donskoy
1389–1425	Vasili I
1425–62	Vasili II
1462–1505	Ivan III (the Great)
1505–33	Vasili III
1533–84	Ivan IV (the Terrible)
1584–98	Feodor I
1598–1605	Boris Godunov
1605	Feodor II
1605–6	Dimitri II
1606–10	Vasili IV Shuisky
1610–13	*no Tsar*
1613–45	Michael Romanov
1645–76	Alexei
1676–82	Feodor III
1682–96	Ivan V *joint Tsar*
1682–1725	Peter I (the Great) *joint Tsar until 1696*
1725–7	Catherine I
1727–30	Peter II
1730–40	Anne
1740–1	Ivan VI
1741–62	Elizabeth
1762	Peter III
1762–96	Catherine II (the Great)
1796–1801	Paul
1801–25	Alexander I
1825–55	Nicholas I
1855–81	Alexander II
1881–94	Alexander III
1894–1917	Nicholas II

See separate entry for the **USSR** for the period 1917–91.

President

1991–9	Boris Yeltsin
2000–	Vladimir Putin

Prime Minister

1991–2	Boris Yeltsin
1992	Yegor Gaidar *Acting*
1992–8	Viktor Chernomyrdin
1998	Sergei Kiriyenko
1998	Viktor Chernomyrdin *Acting*
1998–9	Yevgeny Primakov
1999	Sergei Stepashin
1999–2000	Vladimir Putin
2000–4	Mikhail Kasyanov
2004	Viktor Khristenko
2004–7	Mikhail Fradkov
2007–	Viktor Zubkov

White, Blue and Red

Russia has had several flags – the Tsar's flag in the 19c, the Soviet flag and the current white, blue and red striped flag. The latter flag was first used in 1705 by Peter the Great, was used several times in the intervening centuries, and finally officially declared to be the modern Russian flag in 1993.

RWANDA

Official name	Republic of Rwanda
Local name	Rwanda; République Rwandaise, Republika y'u Rwanda
Former name	Ruanda, as part of Ruanda-Urundi (with Burundi, until 1962)
Independence	1962
Area	26 338 sq km/10 166 sq mi
Capital	Kigali
Chief towns	Butare, Ruhengeri
Population	9 907 000 (2007e)
Nationality	Rwandan
Languages	English, French, Kinyarwanda; Swahili is widely used in commerce
Ethnic groups	Hutu 84%, Tutsi 15%, Twa 1%
Religions	Christianity 82% (RC 56%, Prot 26%), Islam 5%, traditional beliefs and others 13%
Time zone	GMT +2
Currency	1 Rwanda Franc (RF, RWFr/RWF) = 100 centimes
Telephone	+250
Internet	.rw
Country code	RWA

Location
A republic in central Africa, bounded to the north by Uganda; to the east by Tanzania; to the south by Burundi; and to the west by Democratic Republic of the Congo and Lake Kivu.

Physical description
Situated at a relatively high altitude; highest point is Karisimbi volcano (4507m/14787ft) in the Virunga range; western third of the country drains into Lake Kivu and then the River Congo, remainder drains towards the River Nile; many lakes.

Climate
A highland tropical climate; the two wet seasons run from Oct to Dec and Mar to May, with the highest rainfall in the west, decreasing in the central uplands and to the north and east.

National holidays
Jan 1, Feb 1 (Heroes), Apr 7 (Genocide Memorial), May 1, Jul 1 (Independence), 4 (Liberation), Aug 15, Oct 1 (Patriotism), Dec 25, 26; EM, ER *by Muslims*, GF; *community-work half-day holidays each month*.

Political leaders

President

1962–73	Grégoire Kayibanda
1973–94	Juvénal Habyarimana
1994	Theodore Sindikubgabo *Interim*
1994–2000	Pasteur Bizimungu
2000–	Paul Kagame *Transitional President until 2003*

Prime Minister

1991–2	Sylvestre Nsanzimana
1992–4	Dismas Nsengiyaremye
1994	Jean Kambanda *Acting*
1994–5	Faustin Twagiramungu
1995–2000	Pierre-Célestin Rwigyema
2000–	Bernard Makuza

SAHARA, WESTERN *see* WESTERN SAHARA *under* MOROCCO

ST HELENA *see* UNITED KINGDOM

ST KITTS AND NEVIS

Official name	Federation of St Christopher and Nevis
Local name	St Kitts and Nevis
Independence	1983
Area	269 sq km/104 sq mi
Capital	Basseterre
Population	39 000 (2007e)
Nationality	Kittitian, Nevisian
Languages	English
Ethnic groups	black 93%, mulatto 4%, white 1%, others 2%
Religions	Christianity 75% (Prot 50%, RC 25%), others 25%
Time zone	GMT –4
Currency	1 East Caribbean Dollar (EC$/XCD) = 100 cents
Telephone	+1869
Internet	.kn
Country code	KNA

Location

An independent state comprising the islands of St Kitts and Nevis in the North Leeward Islands, in the eastern Caribbean Sea.

Physical description

St Kitts is 37km/23mi long and has an area of 168 sq km/65 sq mi; a mountain range rises to 1 156m/3 793ft at Mt Liamuiga; Nevis, 3km/2mi south-east, has an area of 93 sq km/36 sq mi and is dominated by a central peak rising to 985m/3 232ft.

Climate

Warm, with an average annual temperature of 26°C; low humidity; subject to hurricanes.

National holidays

Jan 1, 2, Aug 7 (Culturama), Sep 16 (Heroes), 19 (Independence), Dec 25, 26; EM, GF, WM, Labour (1st Mon in May).

Political leaders

Head of State: British monarch, represented by Governor General (Sir Cuthbert Sebastian since 1996).

Prime Minister

1983–95	Kennedy A Simmonds
1995–	Denzil Douglas

Nelson on Nevis

Lord Horatio Nelson (1758–1805), the British admiral, is popularly known for his exploits in naval battles in Europe. However, he spent much of his early career with the British navy in the Caribbean, and it was on Nevis that he met and married Frances Nisbet (1761–1831). Today there is a Nelson Museum on Nevis, which boasts 'the largest collection of Nelson memorabilia in the Americas'.

ST LUCIA

Official name	St Lucia
Local name	St Lucia
Area	616 sq km/238 sq mi
Independence	1979
Capital	Castries
Chief towns	Vieux Fort, Soufrière
Population	171 000 (2007e)
Nationality	St Lucian
Languages	English; French patois is also spoken
Ethnic groups	black 90%, mixed 6%, East Indian 3%, white 1%
Religions	Christianity 82% (RC 67%, Prot 10%, other 5%), Rastafarianism 2%, others 10%, none/unaffiliated 6%
Time zone	GMT –4
Currency	1 East Caribbean Dollar (EC$/XCD) = 100 cents
Telephone	+1758
Internet	.lc
Country code	LCA

Location
An independent country in the Windward Islands, in the eastern Caribbean Sea north of South America.

Physical description
The island is 43km/27mi long and 23km/14mi wide; mountainous centre, rising to 950m/3 117ft at Mt Gimie; twin volcanic peaks of Gros and Petit Piton rise steeply from the sea on the south-west coast of the island.

Climate
Tropical; annual temperatures range from 18°C to 34°C; wet season is Jun–Dec.

National holidays
Jan 1, 2, Feb 22 (Independence), May 1, Aug 6 (Emancipation), Oct 1 (Thanksgiving), Dec 13 (National), 25, 26; CC, EM, GF, WM.

Political leaders

Head of State: British monarch, represented by Governor General (Dame Pearlette Louisy since 1997).

Prime Minister

1979	John Compton
1979–81	Allan Louisy
1981–3	Winston Francis Cenac
1983–96	John Compton
1996–7	Vaughan Lewis
1997–2006	Kenny Anthony
2006–7	Sir John Compton
2007–	Stephenson King

Saints and Iguanas

The Arawak Indians and Caribs were the first inhabitants of St Lucia, and knew the island as *Ioüanalao* and *Hewanorra*, meaning 'place where the iguana is found'. The island was renamed St Lucia by explorers in the late 16c, probably because it was first sighted on St Lucia's day (13 Dec).

ST PIERRE AND MIQUELON *see* FRANCE

ST VINCENT AND THE GRENADINES

Official name	St Vincent and the Grenadines
Local name	St Vincent and the Grenadines
Independence	1979
Area	390 sq km/150 sq mi
Capital	Kingstown
Population	118 000 (2007e)
Nationality	St Vincentian or Vincentian
Languages	English; French patois is also spoken
Ethnic groups	black 66%, mixed 19%, East Indian 6%, Carib Amerindian 2%, others 7%
Religions	Christianity 88% (Prot 75%, RC 13%), others 12%
Time zone	GMT –4
Currency	1 East Caribbean Dollar (EC$/XCD) = 100 cents
Telephone	+1784
Internet	.vc
Country code	VCT

Location
An island country in the Windward Islands, situated in the eastern Caribbean Sea north of South America.

Physical description
Comprises the island of St Vincent (length 29km/18mi; width 16km/10mi) and the northern Grenadine Islands; St Vincent is volcanic in origin; highest peak is Soufrière, an active volcano rising to a height of 1 234m/4 049ft.

Climate
Tropical, with an average annual temperature of 25°C.

National holidays
Jan 1, Mar 14 (Heroes), Aug 6 (Emancipation), Oct 27 (Independence), Dec 25, 26; C (Jul) (2), EM, GF, WM; Labour (1st Mon in May).

Political leaders

Head of State: British monarch, represented by Governor General (Sir Frederick Ballantyne since 2002).

Prime Minister

1979–84	Milton Cato
1984–2000	James Fitz-Allen Mitchell
2000–1	Arnhim Eustace
2001–	Ralph Gonsalves

Land of the Blessed

Before European settlers arrived on St Vincent, the island was inhabited by an Amerindian people known as the Carib (after whom the Caribbean Sea was named). The Caribs named the island 'Hairoun', meaning 'Land of the Blessed'.

SAMOA

Official name	Independent State of Samoa
Local name	Samoa; 'O la Malo Tu To'atasi o Samoa
Former name	Western Samoa (until 1997)
Independence	1962
Area	2842 sq km/1097 sq mi
Capital	Apia
Population	214000 (2007e)
Nationality	Samoan
Languages	Samoan, English
Ethnic groups	Samoan 93%, mixed 6%, European 1%
Religions	Christianity 81% (Prot 57%, RC 20%, other 4%), others 19%
Time zone	GMT −11
Currency	1 Tala (ST$/WST) = 100 sene
Telephone	+685
Internet	.ws
Country code	WSM

Location
An island state in the south-west Pacific Ocean, 2600km/1600mi north-east of Auckland, New Zealand.

Physical description
Formed from ranges of mainly extinct volcanoes; many dormant volcanoes (last activity was between 1905 and 1911); highest point is Mt Silisili (1857m/6092ft); thick tropical vegetation; several coral reefs along the coast.

Climate
Tropical; rainy season is Dec–Apr; average annual temperatures are 22–30°C; hurricanes occur.

National holidays
Jan 1–2, 4 (King's Birthday), Apr 25 (Anzac), Jun 1–2 (Independence), Dec 25, 26; EM, GF; Arbor (Nov), Day after White Sunday (Oct), Fathers (Aug), Mothers (May).

Political leaders

Elective monarch

1962–3	Tupua Tamesehe Mea'ole *and* Malietoa Tanumafili II *Joint Monarchs*
1963–2007	Malietoa Tanumafili II
2007–	Tuiatua Tupua Tamasese Efi

Prime Minister

1962–1970	Fiame Mata'afa Faumuina Mulinu'u II
1970–6	Tupua Tamasese Leolofi IV
1976–82	Tupuola Taisi Efi
1982	Va'ai Kolone
1982	Tupuola Taisi Efi
1982–6	Tofilau Eti Alesana
1986–8	Va'ai Kolone
1988–98	Tofilau Eti Alesana
1998–	Tuilaepa Sailele Malielegaoi

SAMOA, AMERICAN *see* UNITED STATES OF AMERICA

SANDWICH ISLANDS, SOUTH *see* UNITED KINGDOM

SAN MARINO

Official name	Republic of San Marino
Local name	San Marino; Repubblica di San Marino
Area	61 sq km/24 sq mi
Capital	San Marino
Chief towns	Serravalle
Population	30 000 (2007e)
Nationality	Sammarinese
Languages	Italian
Ethnic groups	Sammarinese 88%, Italian 11%, others 1%
Religions	Christianity 95% (RC), others and none/unaffiliated 5%
Time zone	GMT +1
Currency	1 Euro (/EUR) = 100 cents
Telephone	+378
Internet	.sm
Country code	SMR

Location

A republic completely surrounded by eastern central Italy, lying 12mi/20km from the Adriatic Sea.

Physical description

Ruggedly mountainous, centred on the limestone ridges of Mt Titano (755m/2 477ft) and the valley of the River Ausa.

Climate

Temperate climate, with cool winters and warm summers (20–30°C); rainfall is moderate.

National holidays

Jan 1, 6, Feb 5 (Liberation/St Agatha), Mar 25 (Arengo), Apr 1 (New Captains Regent Investiture), May 1, Jul 28 (Fall of Fascism), Aug 15, Sep 3 (San Marino/Foundation of Republic), Oct 1 (New Captains Regent Investiture), Nov 1, 2, Dec 8, 24, 25, 26, 31; CC, EM, ES.

Political leaders

Regent

Heads of state are two *capitani reggenti* or 'Captains Regent' appointed every 6 months.

SÃO TOMÉ AND PRÍNCIPE

Official name	Democratic Republic of São Tomé and Príncipe
Local name	São Tomé e Príncipe; República Democrática de São Tomé e Príncipe
Independence	1975
Area	1 001 sq km/386 sq mi
Capital	São Tomé
Chief towns	Santo António
Population	199 000 (2007e)
Nationality	São Toméan, Santoméan
Languages	Portuguese
Ethnic groups	black 90%, Portuguese and Creole 10%
Religions	Christianity 75% (RC 70%, Prot 5%), others 5%, others 19%
Time zone	GMT
Currency	1 Dobra (Db/STD) = 100 céntimos
Telephone	+239
Internet	.st
Country code	STP

Location
An island republic in the Gulf of Guinea, off West Africa; São Tomé lies approximately 440km/275mi and Príncipe approximately 200km/125mi off the north coast of Gabon.

Physical description
Volcanic islands, heavily forested; São Tomé has an area of 860 sq km/332 sq mi and reaches a height of 2024m/6640ft at Pico de São Tomé; Príncipe, the smaller of the two islands, covers 140 sq km/54 sq mi and has similar terrain.

Climate
Tropical; average annual temperature is 27°C on the coast, 20°C in the mountains; rainy season from Oct to May.

National holidays
Jan 1, Feb 3 9Martyrs), May 1, Jul 12 (Independence), Sep 6 (Armed Forces), 30 (Agriculture), Dec 21 (St Thomas), 25; *also GF in some areas*.

Political leaders

President

1975–91	Manuel Pinto da Costa
1991–2001	Miguel Trovoada
2001–	Fradique de Menezes

Prime Minister

1974–5	Leonel Maria d'Alva
1975–8	Miguel Trovoada
1978–88	*No Prime Minister*
1988–91	Celestino Rocha da Costa
1991–2	Daniel Lima dos Santos Daio
1992–4	Norberto José d'Alva Costa Alegre
1994	Evaristo Carvalho
1994–5	Carlos da Graça
1995–6	Armindo Vaz d'Almeida
1996–9	Raul Bragança
1999–2002	Guilherme Posser da Costa
2002	Gabriel Costa
2002–4	Maria das Neves
2004–5	Damião Vaz d'Almeida
2005–6	Maria do Carmo Silveira
2006–	Tomé Vera Cruz

SAUDI ARABIA

Official name	Kingdom of Saudi Arabia
Local name	Al-Mamlaka al-'Arabiyya as-Sa'ūdiyya
Area	2 331 000 sq km/899 766 sq mi
Capital	Riyadh; Ar Riyād
Chief towns	Jeddah, Mecca, Medina, Ta'if, Ad Dammam, Abha
Population	27 601 000 (2007e)
Nationality	Saudi or Saudi Arabian
Languages	Arabic
Ethnic groups	Arab 90%, Afro-Asian 10%
Religions	Islam 100% (Sunni 90%, Shia 10%); *public practice of any religion other than Islam is forbidden*
Time zone	GMT +3
Currency	1 Saudi Riyal (SR, SRls/SAR) = 20 qursh = 100 halala
Telephone	+966
Internet	.sa
Country code	SAU

Location
A kingdom comprising about four-fifths of the Arabian Peninsula, crossed by the Tropic of Cancer; bounded to the north-west by Jordan; to the north by Iraq; to the north-east by Kuwait; to the east by the Arabian Gulf, Qatar and the United Arab Emirates, and Bahrain to which it is connected by a causeway; to the south-east by Oman; to the south by Yemen; and to the west by the Red Sea.

Physical description
Red Sea coastal plain is bounded to the east by mountains; south-west highlands include Jabal Sawda', the highest peak (3133m/10278ft); Arabian Peninsula slopes north and east to the oil-rich Al Hasa plain on the Arabian Gulf; large areas of sand desert in the interior; numerous salt flats in the eastern lowlands.

Climate
Hot and dry, with average temperatures from 21°C (north) to 26°C (south); day temperatures may rise to 50°C in the interior deserts; night frosts are common in the north and highlands; Red Sea coast is hot and humid; average rainfall is low.

National holidays
Sep 23 (National); Ad (5), ER (3); *government offices and some businesses close for 10 days for both festivals*.

Political leaders

Monarch

Family name: al-Saud

1932–53	Abdulaziz bin Abdur-Rahman
1953–64	Saud bin Abdulaziz
1964–75	Faisal bin Abdulaziz
1975–82	Khalid bin Abdulaziz
1982–2005	Fahd bin Abdulaziz
2005–	Abdullah bin Abdulaziz

SCOTLAND *see* UNITED KINGDOM

SENEGAL

Official name	Republic of Senegal
Local name	Sénégal; République du Sénégal
Former name	part of the Federation of Mali (1959–60); Senegambia (with the Gambia, 1982–9)
Independence	1960
Area	196840 sq km/75980 sq mi
Capital	Dakar
Chief towns	Thiès, Kaolack, St Louis, Ziguinchor
Population	12522000 (2007e)
Nationality	Senegalese
Languages	French, Wolof
Ethnic groups	Wolof 43%, Pular 24%, Serer 15%, Jola 4%, others 14%
Religions	Islam 94% (Sunni), Christianity 5% (mostly RC), traditional beliefs 1%
Time zone	GMT
Currency	1 CFA Franc (CFAFr/XOF) = 100 centimes
Telephone	+221
Internet	.sn
Country code	SEN

Location

A republic in West Africa, bounded to the north by Mauritania; to the east by Mali; to the south by Guinea and Guinea-Bissau; and to the west by the Atlantic Ocean; it surrounds the Gambia on three sides.

Physical description

Most westerly country in mainland Africa; coast is characterized by dunes, mangrove forests and mudbanks; extensive low-lying basin of savanna and semi-desert vegetation lies to the north; south rises to approximately 500m/1 640ft.

Climate

Tropical with a rainy season Jun–Sep; high humidity levels and high night-time temperatures, especially on the coast; rainfall decreases from the south to the north; average temperature at Dakar ranges from 22°C to 28°C.

National holidays

Jan 1, Apr 4 (Independence), May 1, Aug 15, Nov 1, Dec 25; A, Ad, As, EM, ER, PB, WM; *Magal de Touba (3) is unofficial but widely observed.*

Political leaders

President

1960–80	Léopold Sédar Senghor
1981–2000	Abdou Diouf
2000–	Abdoulaye Wade

Prime Minister

1958–62	Mamadou Dia
1962–70	*No Prime Minister*
1970–80	Abdou Diouf
1981–3	Habib Thiam
1983	Moustapha Niasse *Interim*
1983–91	*No Prime Minister*
1991–8	Habib Thiam
1998–2000	Mamadou Lamine Loum
2000–1	Moustapha Niasse
2001–2	Madior Boye
2002–4	Idrissa Seck
2004–7	Cherif Macky Sall
2007–	Cheikh Hadjibou Soumaré

SERBIA

Official name	Republic of Serbia
Local name	Srbija; Republika Srbija
Former name	part of Kingdom of Serbs, Croats and Slovenes (until 1929), Kingdom of Yugoslavia (1929–41), Federal People's Republic of Yugoslavia (1945–63), Socialist Federal Republic of Yugoslavia (1963–92), Federal Republic of Yugoslavia (1992–2003), Serbia and Montenegro (2003–6)
Area	88 361 sq km/34 116 sq mi
Capital	Belgrade; Beograd
Chief towns	Kragujevac, Niš, Novi Sad, Priština (Kosovo)[1], Subotica
Population	10 150 000 (2007e)
Nationality	Serbian
Languages	Serbian; Romanian, Hungarian, Slovak, Ukrainian and Croatian are also spoken in Vojvodina, and Albanian in Kosovo
Ethnic groups	Serb 66%, Albanian 17%, Magyar 3%, others 14%
Religions	Christianity 83% (Orthodox 79%, RC 4%), Islam 5%, others 12%
Time zone	GMT +1
Currency	1 Dinar (D, Din/RSD) = 100 paras
Telephone	+381
Internet	.rs
Country code	SRB

[1] Kosovo declared independence from Serbia in February 2008, with Priština as its capital; at the time of going to press this has not been universally recognized internationally.

Location
A republic in the Balkan peninsula of south-eastern Europe, bounded to the north by Hungary; to the north-east by Romania; to the east by Bulgaria; to the south by Macedonia and Albania; to the south-east by Montenegro; and to the west by Bosnia and Herzegovina and Croatia.

Physical description
Dominated in the north by the Danube, Tisza and Sava rivers; fertile plains in the north-east; drained in the centre by the River Morava; southern mountain ranges cut by deep river valleys; several great lakes in the south; highest point is Daravica (2656m/8714ft).

Climate
Continental climate; rain falls throughout the year; colder upland climate, with winter snow.

National holidays
Jan 1–2, 7 (Orthodox Christmas), Feb 15 (Constitution), May 1–2; ES (Orthodox), GF (Orthodox); *unofficial but widely observed are Jan 27 (St Sava), May 9 (Victory) and Jun 28 (St Vitus).*

Political leaders

After the secession of the other constituent states of Yugoslavia in 1991–2, Serbia and Montenegro formed the Federal Republic of Yugoslavia. To meet Montenegro's desire for greater autonomy, the Federal Republic was replaced by a looser federation of the two countries in 2003.

Federal Republic of Yugoslavia

President

1992–3 Dobrica Cosic
1993 Milos Radulovic *Acting President*
1993–7 Zoran Lilic
1997 Srdja Bozovic *Acting President*
1997–2000 Slobodan Milosevic
2000–3 Vojislav Kostunica

Prime Minister

1992–3 Milan Panic
1993–8 Radoje Kontic
1998–2000 Momir Bulatovic
2000–1 Zoran Zizic
2001–3 Dragisa Pesic

Serbia and Montenegro

President
2003–6 Svetozar Marović

Serbia

President (within federation)

1992–7 Slobodan Milosevic
1997 Dragan Tomic *Acting*
1997–2002 Milan Milutinovic
2002–4 Nataša Mićić *Acting*
2004 Dragan Maršićanin *Acting*
2004 Vojislav Mihailović *Acting*
2004 Predrag Marković *Acting*
2004– Boris Tadić

After Montenegrins voted in favour of independence in a referendum, the union was dissolved and the two countries became separate independent sovereign states in 2006.

President
2004– Boris Tadić

Prime Minister
2004– Vojislav Kostunica

See also **MONTENEGRO**

SEYCHELLES

Official name	Republic of Seychelles
Local name	Seychelles; République des Seychelles (French), Repiblik Sesel (Creole)
Independence	1976
Area	453 sq km/175 sq mi
Capital	Victoria
Population	82 000 (2007e)
Nationality	Seychellois
Languages	Creole; French and English are spoken
Ethnic groups	mulatto 94%, Malagasy 3%, Chinese 2%, English 1%
Religions	Christianity 92% (RC 82%, Prot and others 10%), Hinduism 2%, Islam 1%, others 5%
Time zone	GMT +4
Currency	1 Seychelles Rupee (SR/SCR) = 100 cents
Telephone	+248
Internet	.sc
Country code	SYC

Location

An island group in the south-west Indian Ocean, north of Madagascar.

Physical description

Comprises 115 islands in two main groups; first, a compact group of 41 steep granitic islands, are mountainous, rising to 905m/2 969ft at Morne Seychellois on Mahé; steep forest-clad slopes; coastal lowlands of grass and dense scrub; second group are low-lying coralline islands and atolls situated to the south-west.

Climate

Tropical with a rainfall that varies with altitude and is higher on the southern sides of the islands; wettest months are Nov to Mar; rarely affected by tropical storms.

National holidays

Jan 1, 2, May 1, Jun 5 (Liberation), 18 (National), 29 (Independence), Aug 15, Nov 1, Dec 8, 25; CC, GF, HS.

Political leaders

President

1976–7	James R Mancham
1977–2004	France-Albert René
2004–	James Michel

Sea Coconut

The Seychellois islands of Praslin and Curieuse are home to the palm tree *Lodoicea seychellarum*, commonly known as the 'sea coconut'. The coconuts from this species of tree are the largest seeds in the world; their diameter can be as large as 50cm (20in) and they weigh up to 25kg (50 lb). Their common name stems from the fact that sailors first saw these coconuts floating in the sea; it was many years before the parent plants were discovered.

SHARJAH *see* **UNITED ARAB EMIRATES**

SIERRA LEONE

Official name	Republic of Sierra Leone
Local name	Sierra Leone
Independence	1961
Area	72325 sq km/27917 sq mi
Capital	Freetown
Chief towns	Bo, Sefadu, Makeni, Kenema, Lunsar
Population	6144000 (2007e)
Nationality	Sierra Leonean
Languages	English, Mende, Temnel; Krio (a Creole language) is also widely spoken
Ethnic groups	African 90% (20 ethnic groups, including Mende 30%, Temne 30%), others 10%
Religions	Islam 60% (Sunni), traditional beliefs 30%, Christianity 10%
Time zone	GMT
Currency	1 Leone (Le/SLL) = 100 cents
Telephone	+232
Internet	.sl
Country code	SLE

Location

A republic in West Africa, bounded to the north by Guinea; to the south-east by Liberia; and to the south and south-west by the Atlantic Ocean.

Physical description

A low, narrow coastal plain; western half rises to an average height of 500m/1640ft in the Loma Mountains; highest point is Loma Mansa (also called Bintimani; 1948m/6391ft); Tingi Mountains in the south-east rise to 1853m/6079ft.

Climate

Equatorial, with a rainy season from May to Oct; highest rainfall is on the coast; temperatures are uniformly high throughout the year, approximately 27°C.

National holidays

Jan 1, Apr 27 (Independence), Dec 25, 26; Ad, EM, ER, GF, PB.

Political leaders

President

1971	Christopher Okero Cole
1971–85	Siaka Stevens
1985–92	Joseph Saidu Momoh
1992–6	Valentine Strasser
1996–7	Ahmad Tejan Kabbah
1997	*Military coup* (Johnny Koroma)
1998–2007	Ahmad Tejan Kabbah
2007–	Ernest Bai Koroma

Prime Minister

1961–4	Milton Margai
1964–7	Albert Michael Margai
1967	Siaka Stevens
1967	David Lansana
1967	Ambrose Genda
1967–8	*National Reformation Council* (Andrew Saxon-Smith)
1968	John Bangura
1968–71	Siaka Stevens
1971–5	Sorie Ibrahim Koroma
1975–8	Christian Alusine Kamara Taylor
1978–	*No Prime Minister*

SINGAPORE

Official name	Republic of Singapore
Local name	Singapore; Repablik Singapura (Malay), Singapur Kuţyara'su (Tamil), Xinjiapo Gongheguo (Chinese)
Former name	part of Straits Settlement (until 1942), State of Singapore (1959–63), part of the Federation of Malaysia (1963–65)
Independence	1965
Area	647 sq km/250 sq mi
Capital	Singapore; Singapura (Malay), Singapur (Tamil), Xinjiapo (Chinese)
Population	4553000 (2007e)
Nationality	Singaporean, Singapore
Languages	English, Chinese (Mandarin), Malay, Tamil; other Chinese dialects are also spoken
Ethnic groups	Chinese 77%, Malay 14%, Indian 8%, others 1%
Religions	Buddhism 42%, Islam 15%, Christianity 15%, (RC 5%, other 10%), Taoism 9%, Hinduism 4%, none/unaffiliated 15%
Time zone	GMT +8
Currency	1 Singapore Dollar (S$/SGD) = 1 Ringgit = 100 cents
Telephone	+65
Internet	.sg
Country code	SGP

Location
A republic at the southern tip of the Malay Peninsula, south-east Asia, comprising the island of Singapore (linked to Malaysia in the north by a causeway) and about 50 adjacent islets.

Physical description
Singapore Island measures approximately 42km/26mi by 22km/14mi at its widest; low-lying; highest point is Bukit Timah (177m/581ft); important deep-water harbour lies to the south-east.

Climate
Equatorial, with high humidity, and a daily temperature range from 21°C to 34°C.

National holidays
Jan 1, May 1, Aug 9 (National), Dec 25; Ad, D, ER, GF, NY (Chinese) (Jan/Feb) (2), Vesak.

Political leaders

President (Yang di-Pertuan Negara)

1959–70	Yusof bin Ishak
1970–81	Benjamin Henry Sheares
1981–5	Chengara Veetil Devan Nair
1985–93	Wee Kim Wee
1993–9	Ong Teng Cheong
1999–	Sellapan Rama Nathan

Prime Minister

1959–90	Lee Kuan Yew
1990–2004	Goh Chok Tong
2004–	Lee Hsien Loong

City of Lions

The name 'Singapore' comes from the Sanskrit-derived Malay name 'Singapura' meaning 'Lion City'. Malay mythology tells of a prince discovering the island and spotting a lion on the shore. However, lions have never lived there, and the beast in question was probably a tiger.

SLOVAKIA

Official name	Republic of Slovakia or the Slovak Republic
Local name	Slovensko; Slovenská Republika
Former name	formerly part of Czechoslovakia (until 1993)
Independence	1993
Area	49035 sq km/18927 sq mi
Capital	Bratislava
Chief towns	Košice, Banská Bystrica, Prešov
Population	5447000 (2007e)
Nationality	Slovak
Languages	Slovak
Ethnic groups	Slovak 86%, Magyar 10%, Roma 2%, others 2%
Religions	Christianity 84% (RC 69%, Prot 11%, Orthodox 4%), others/unaffiliated 3%, none 13%
Time zone	GMT +1
Currency	1 Slovak Koruna (Sk/SKK) = 100 halierov
Telephone	+421
Internet	.sk
Country code	SVK

Location

A republic in eastern Europe, bounded to the north by Poland; to the east by Ukraine; to the south by Hungary; to the south-west by Austria; and to the west by the Czech Republic.

Physical description

Lowlands in the south; Tatra Mountains in the north rise to 2655m/8710ft at Gerlachovsky Stit, Slovakia's highest point.

Climate

Continental; hot in summer, cold in winter.

National holidays

Jan 1 (New Year/Republic), 6, May 1, 8 (Victory), Jul 5 (SS Cyril and Methodius), Aug 29 (Slovak National Uprising), Sep 1 (Constitution), 15 (Our Lady of Sorrows), Nov 1, 17 (Freedom and Democracy), Dec 24, 25, 26; EM, GF.

Political leaders

See entry for **Czech Republic** for political leaders prior to 1993.

President

1993–8	Michal Kovác
1998–9	*No President*
1999–2004	Rudolf Schuster
2004–	Ivan Gašparović

Prime Minister

1993–4	Vladimír Mečiar
1994	Jozef Moravčik
1994–8	Vladimír Mečiar
1998–2006	Mikuláš Dzurinda
2006–	Robert Fico

Thunder and Lightning

Slovakia's mighty Tatra mountains are commemorated in its national anthem, *Nad Tatrou sa blýska*, meaning 'Lightning over the Tatras'. It speaks of the lightning over the mountains and the roar of thunder reawakening the spirit of the Slovak people.

SLOVENIA

Official name	Republic of Slovenia
Local name	Slovenija; Republika Slovenija
Former name	formerly part of Kingdom of Serbs, Croats and Slovenes (until 1929), Kingdom of Yugoslavia (1929–41), Federal People's Republic of Yugoslavia (1945–63), Socialist Federal People's Republic of Yugoslavia (1963–91)
Independence	1991
Area	20 251 sq km/7 817 sq mi
Capital	Ljubljana
Chief towns	Maribor, Kranj, Celje, Koper
Population	2 009 000 (2007e)
Nationality	Slovene, Slovenian
Languages	Slovene
Ethnic groups	Slovene 83%, Serb 2%, Croat 2%, Bosniak 1%, others 12%
Religions	Christianity 61% (RC 58%, Orthodox 2%, other 1%), Islam 2%, others 23%, none/unaffiliated 14%
Time zone	GMT +1
Currency	1 Euro (€/EUR) = 100 cents
Telephone	+386
Internet	.si
Country code	SVN

Location
A republic in central Europe, bounded to the north by Austria; to the east by Hungary; to the south by Croatia; and to the west by Italy.

Physical description
Forested and mountainous, linked to Austria by a number of pass roads; highest point is Mt Triglav (2 864m/9 396ft); drops down towards the Adriatic coast.

Climate
Hot summers and cold winters in the plateaux and valleys in the east; Mediterranean climate on the west coast.

National holidays
Jan 1, 2, Feb 8 (Culture), Apr 27 (National Resistance), May 1–2, Jun 25 (National), Aug 15, Oct 31 (Reformation), Nov 1, Dec 25, 26 (Independence); EM, ES, Whit Sunday.

Political leaders

See **Yugoslavia** for political leaders prior to 1991–2.

President

1991–2002	Milan Kučan
2002–7	Janez Drnovšek
2007–	Danilo Türk

Prime Minister

1990–2	Lojze Peterle
1992–2000	Janez Drnovšek
2000	Andrej Bajuk
2000–2	Janez Drnovšek
2002–4	Anton Rop
2004–	Janez Jansa

Slovenian Grammar

The Slovene language is unusual in that it has not only singular and plural forms but also an additional *dual* form. While most languages distinguish whether one person is doing something or many people are doing it, Slovene also has different words and grammar for two people.

SOLOMON ISLANDS

Official name	Solomon Islands
Local name	Solomon Islands
Former name	British Solomon Islands (until 1975)
Independence	1978
Area	27 556 sq km/10 637 sq mi
Capital	Honiara
Chief towns	Gizo, Auki, Kirakira
Population	567 000 (2007e)
Nationality	Solomon Islander (noun)
Languages	English; pidgin English and Melanesian dialects are also spoken
Ethnic groups	Melanesian 94%, Polynesian 3%, Micronesian 1%, others 2%
Religions	Christianity 97% (Prot 62%, RC 19%, others 16%), others 3%
Time zone	GMT +11
Currency	1 Solomon Islands Dollar (SI$/SBD) = 100 cents
Telephone	+677
Internet	.sb
Country code	SLB

Location

An independent country consisting of an archipelago of several hundred islands in the south-west Pacific Ocean east of Papua New Guinea.

Physical description

Six main islands are Choiseul, Guadalcanal, Malaita, New Georgia, Makira and Santa Isabel; larger islands have forested mountain ranges of mainly volcanic origin, deep, narrow valleys, and coastal belts lined with coconut palms; ringed by reefs; highest point is Mt Makarakomburu (2477m/8127ft) on Guadalcanal, the largest island.

Climate

Equatorial; average temperature is 27°C; high humidity.

National holidays

Jan 1, Jul 7 (Independence), Dec 25, 26 (Thanksgiving); EM, GF, HS, WM, Queen's Birthday (Jun); *each province has a Province Day*.

Political leaders

Head of State: British monarch, represented by Governor General (Sir Nathaniel Waena since 2004).

Prime Minister

1978–82	Peter Kenilorea
1982–4	Solomon Mamaloni
1984–6	Peter Kenilorea
1986–9	Ezekiel Alebua
1989–93	Solomon Mamaloni
1993–4	Francis Billy Hilly
1994–7	Solomon Mamaloni
1997–2000	Bartholomew Ulufa'alu
2000–1	Manasseh Sogavare
2001–6	Allan Kemakeza
2006	Snyder Rini
2006–7	Manasseh Sogavare
2007–	Derek Sikua

War in the Pacific

The idyllic tropical Solomon Islands were the site of some of the fiercest fighting of World War II. Following the attacks on Pearl Harbor and Singapore (7–8 Dec 1941), Japan advanced into the South Pacific, reaching Guadalcanal in May 1942. US forces reinvaded and after six months of bitter fighting, in one of the crucial actions of the war, they halted the Japanese advance. Wreckage from the fighting can still be seen in the islands and surrounding waters.

SOMALIA

Official name	Somalia
Local name	Soomaaliya; Jamhuuriyadda Dimoqraadiya Soomaaliya
Former name	British Somaliland (until 1960) and Italian Somalia (until 1936), Italian East Africa (1936–50), Somali Democratic Republic (1969–91)
Independence	1960
Area	637 657 sq km/246 199 sq mi
Capital	Mogadishu; Muqdisho (Somali), Muqdishu (Arabic)
Chief towns	Hargeysa, Berbera, Kismayu
Population	9 119 000 (2007e)
Nationality	Somali
Languages	Somali, Arabic; English and Italian are also spoken widely
Ethnic groups	Somali 85%, Bantu, Arab and others 15%
Religions	Islam 98% (Sunni), Christianity 2%
Time zone	GMT +3
Currency	1 Somali Shilling (SoSh/SOS) = 100 cents
Telephone	+252
Internet	.so
Country code	SOM

Location
A republic in north-east Africa, crossed by the Equator in the south; bounded to the north-west by Djibouti; to the north by the Gulf of Aden; to the east by the Indian Ocean; to the south-west by Kenya; and to the west by Ethiopia.

Physical description
Occupies the eastern Horn of Africa where a dry coastal plain broadens to the south and rises inland to a plateau at nearly 1 000m/3 280ft; forested mountains on the Gulf of Aden coast rise to 2 416m/7 926ft at Mt Shimbiris.

Climate
Considerable variation in climate; average maximum daily temperatures of 29–42°C (Berbera on the north coast) and 28–32°C (Mogadishu); higher rainfall on the east coast in Apr–Sep; serious and persistent threat of drought.

National holidays
Jan 1, May 1, Jun 26 (Independence), Jul 1 (Foundation of Republic); Ad, As, ER, NY (Muslim), PB.

Political leaders

President

1961–7	Aden Abdallah Osman
1967–9	Abdirashid Ali Shermarke
1969–80	Mohammed Siad Barre *Supreme Revolutionary Council*
1980–91	Mohammed Siad Barre
1991–2000	*Civil War*
2000	Abdullahi Derow Isaq *Acting*
2000–4	Abd-al-Qassim Salat Hasan
2004–	Abdullahi Yusuf Ahmed

Prime Minister

1960	Mohammed Haji Ibrahim Egal
1960–4	Abdirashid Ali Shermarke
1964–7	Abdirizak Haji Hussein
1967–9	Mohammed Haji Ibrahim Egal
1969–70	Mohammed Siad Barre
1970–87	*No Prime Minister*
1987–90	Mohammed Ali Samater
1990–1	Mohammed Hawadie Madar
1991	Umar Arteh Ghalib
1991–2000	*Civil War*
2000–1	Ali Khalif Galaid
2001–3	Hassan Abshir Farah
2003–4	Abdi Yusuf Mohammed
2004–7	Ali Mohamed Gedi
2007–	Nur Hassan Hussein

SOUTH AFRICA

Official name	Republic of South Africa (RSA)
Local name	South Africa; Republiek van Suid-Afrika
Independence	1931 (within Commonwealth), 1961 (republic)
Area	1228376 sq km/474275 sq mi
Capital	Pretoria (administrative), Bloemfontein (judicial) and Cape Town (Kaapstad) (legislative)
Chief towns	Durban, Johannesburg, Port Elizabeth
Population	43998000 (2007e)
Nationality	South African
Languages	Eleven official languages: Afrikaans, English, IsiNdebele, IsiXosa, IsiZulu, Sepedi, Sosetho, SiSwati, Setswana, Tshivenda, Xitsonga
Ethnic groups	black African 79%, white 10%, coloured 9%, Indian/Asian 2%
Religions	Christianity 80% (Prot 37%, RC 7%, others 36%), Islam 1%, others 2%, none/unaffiliated 17%
Time zone	GMT +2
Currency	1 Rand (R/ZAR) = 100 cents
Telephone	+27
Internet	.za
Country code	ZAF

Location

A republic in southern Africa, crossed by the Tropic of Capricorn in the north-east; bounded to the north-west by Namibia; to the north by Botswana; to the north-east by Zimbabwe, Mozambique and Swaziland; to the east and south-east by the Indian Ocean; and to the south-west and west by the southern Atlantic Ocean; it completely encloses Lesotho.

Physical description

Occupies the southern extremity of the African plateau, fringed by mountains and a lowland coastal margin; northern interior comprises the Kalahari Basin, scrub grassland and arid desert; highest point is Mafadi (3451m/11322ft).

Climate

Subtropical in the east, with lush vegetation; dry moistureless climate on the west coast; Cape Town has minimum daily temperatures of 7°C (Jul), to an average maximum of 26°C (Jan–Feb); desert region further north.

National holidays

Jan 1, Mar 21 (Human Rights), Apr 27 (Freedom Day), May 1, Jun 16 (Youth), Aug 9 (Women), Sep 24 (Heritage), Dec 16 (Reconciliation), 25, 26 (Goodwill); EM (Family), GF.

Political leaders

Head of State 1910–61: British monarch, represented by Governor General.

Governor General

1910–14	Herbert, Viscount Gladstone
1914–20	Sydney, Earl Buxton
1920–4	Arthur, Duke of Connaught
1924–31	Alexander, Earl of Athlone
1931–7	George Herbert Hyde Villiers
1937–43	Patrick Duncan
1943–5	Nicolaas Jacobus de Wet
1945–51	Gideon Brand Van Zyl
1951–9	Ernest George Jansen
1959	Lucas Cornelius Steyn
1959–61	Charles Robberts Swart

Republic

President

1961–7	Charles Robberts Swart
1967	Theophilus Ebenhaezer Dünges
1967–8	Jozua François Nandé
1968–75	Jacobus Johannes Fouché
1975–8	Nicolaas Diederichs
1978–9	Balthazar Johannes Vorster
1979–84	Marais Viljoen
1984–89	Pieter Willem Botha
1989–94	Frederick Willem de Klerk
1994–9	Nelson Rolihlahla Mandela
1999–	Thabo Mbeki

Prime Minister

1910–19	Louis Botha *SAf*
1919–24	Jan Christiaan Smuts *SAf*
1924–39	James Barry Munnick Hertzog *Nat*
1939–48	Jan Christiaan Smuts *Un*
1948–54	Daniel François Malan *Nat*
1954–8	Johannes Gerardus Strijdom *Nat*
1958–66	Hendrik Frensch Verwoerd *Nat*
1966–78	Balthazar Johannes Vorster *Nat*
1978–84	Pieter Willem Botha *Nat*
1984	*post abolished*

Nat = National; SAf = South African Party; Un = United

South Africa produces 20% of the world's gold, 62% of its vanadium and 48% of its chrome. It is the second-largest producer of platinum, titanium and zirconium and is also famous for diamonds.

SOUTHERN AND ANTARCTIC TERRITORIES, FRENCH *see* FRANCE

SOUTH GEORGIA *see* UNITED KINGDOM

SOUTH KOREA *see* KOREA, SOUTH

SOUTH SANDWICH ISLANDS *see* UNITED KINGDOM

SPAIN

Official name	Kingdom of Spain
Local name	España; Reino de España
Former name	Spanish Republic (1931–9), Spanish State (1936–78)
Area	492 431 sq km/190 078 sq mi
Capital	Madrid
Chief towns	Barcelona, Valencia, Seville, Zaragoza, Málaga
Population	40 448 000 (2007e)
Nationality	Spanish
Languages	Spanish (Castilian); Catalan, Galician (Gallego) and Basque (Euskera) are also spoken in certain regions
Ethnic groups	Castilian Spanish 72%, Catalan 17%, Galician 7%, Basque 2%, others 3%
Religions	Christianity 94% (RC), others 6%
Time zone	GMT +1
Currency	1 Euro (€/EUR) = 100 cents
Telephone	+34
Internet	.es
Country code	ESP

Location
A kingdom in south-western Europe, bounded to the north by France, Andorra and the Bay of Biscay; to the east by the Mediterranean Sea; to the south by Gibraltar (UK) and the Strait of Gibraltar; to the west by Portugal; and to the north-west by the Atlantic Ocean.

Physical description
Consists mainly of a furrowed central plateau (the Meseta, average height 700m/2 297ft) crossed by mountains; Andalusian or Baetic Mountains in the south-east rise to 3478m/11 410ft at Mulhacén; Pyrenees in the north rise to 3404m/11 168ft at Pico de Aneto; highest point is Pico de Teide (3718m/12 198ft) on the island of Tenerife in the Canary Islands.

Climate
Meseta has a continental climate, with hot summers, cold winters and low rainfall; high rainfall in the mountains, with deep winter snow; south Mediterranean coast has the warmest winter temperatures on the European mainland.

National holidays
Jan 1, 6 (*most areas*), May 1, Aug 15, Oct 12 (National), Nov 1, Dec 6 (Constitution), 8, 25; GF, HT (*most areas*); *much regional variation*.

Balearic Islands

Location	An archipelago of five major islands (Majorca, Minorca, Ibiza, Formentera and Cabrera) and eleven islets in the west Mediterranean Sea, situated near the east coast of Spain.		
Area	5014 sq km/1935 sq mi	**Capital**	Palma de Mallorca

Canary Islands

Location	An island archipelago of eight major islands (Tenerife, Gran Canaria, Fuerteventura, Lanzarote, La Palma, Hierro and Gomera) in the Atlantic Ocean, lying 100km/62mi off the north-west coast of Africa.		
Area	7273 sq km/2807 sq mi	**Capital**	Las Palmas

Political leaders

Monarch

1516–56	Charles I (Emperor Charles V)
1556–98	Philip II
1598–1621	Philip III
1621–65	Philip IV
1665–1700	Charles II
1700–24	Philip V
1724	Luis
1724–46	Philip V
1746–59	Ferdinand VI
1759–88	Charles III
1788–1808	Charles IV
1808	Ferdinand VII
1808–14	Joseph Bonaparte
1814–33	Ferdinand VII
1833–68	Isabella II
1868–70	*No monarchy*
1870–3	Amadeus of Savoy
1873–4	*Temporary republic*
1874–85	Alfonso XII
1886–1931	Alfonso XIII

President

1931	Niceto Alcalá Zamora y Torres
1931	Manuel Azaña y Díez
1931–6	Niceto Alcalá Zamora y Torres
1936	Diego Martínez Barrio *Acting*
1936–9	Manuel Azaña y Díez *Civil War*
1936–9	Miguel Cabanellas Ferrer *Civil War*

Head of State – Nationalist Government

1936–75	Francisco Franco Bahamonde

Monarch

1975–	Juan Carlos I

Prime Minister

1900–1	Marcelo de Azcárraga y Palmero
1901–2	Práxedes Mateo Sagasta
1902–3	Francisco Silvela y Le-Vielleuze
1903	Raimundo Fernández Villaverde
1903–4	Antonio Maura y Montaner
1904–5	Marcelo de Azcárraga y Palmero
1905	Raimundo Fernández Villaverde
1905	Eugenio Montero Ríos
1905–6	Segismundo Moret y Prendergast
1906	José López Domínguez
1906	Segismundo Moret y Prendergast
1906–7	Antonio Aguilar y Correa
1907–9	Antonio Maura y Montaner
1909–10	Segismundo Moret y Prendergast
1910–12	José Canalejas y Méndez
1912	Álvaro Figueroa y Torres
1912–13	Manuel García Prieto
1913–15	Eduardo Dato y Iradier
1915–17	Álvaro Figueroa y Torres
1917	Manuel García Prieto
1917	Eduardo Dato y Iradier
1917–18	Manuel García Prieto
1918	Antonio Maura y Montaner
1918	Manuel García Prieto
1918–19	Álvaro Figueroa y Torres
1919	Antonio Maura y Montaner
1919	Joaquín Sánchez de Toca
1919–20	Manuel Allendesalazar
1920–1	Eduardo Dato y Iradier
1921	Gabino Bugallal Araujo *Acting*
1921	Manuel Allendesalazar
1921–2	Antonio Maura y Montaner
1922	José Sánchez Guerra y Martínez
1922–3	Manuel García Prieto
1923–30	Miguel Primo de Rivera y Oraneja
1930–1	Dámaso Berenguer y Fusté
1931	Juan Bautista Aznar-Cabañas
1931	Niceto Alcalá Zamora y Torres
1931–3	Manuel Azaña y Díez
1933	Alejandro Lerroux y García
1933	Diego Martínez Barrio
1933–4	Alejandro Lerroux y García
1934	Ricardo Samper Ibáñez
1934–5	Alejandro Lerroux y García
1935	Joaquín Chapaprieta y Terragosa
1935–6	Manuel Portela Valladares
1936	Manuel Azaña y Díez
1936	Santiago Casares Quiroga
1936	Diego Martínez Barrio
1936	José Giral y Pereyra
1936–7	Francisco Largo Caballero
1937–9	Juan Negrín

Chairman of the Council of Ministers

1939–73	Francisco Franco Bahamonde

Prime Minister

1973	Torcuato Fernández Miranda y Hevía *Acting*
1973–6	Carlos Arias Navarro
1976–81	Adolfo Suárez
1981–2	Calvo Sotelo
1982–96	Felipe González
1996–2004	José María Aznar
2004–	José Zapatero

Talking Castles

The main language of Spain that most people consider to be 'Spanish' is actually Castilian Spanish – other regions also speak Galician, Basque, Catalan and Valencian. In Spain Castilian Spanish is often simply referred to as *castellano*, Castilian, rather than 'Spanish'. The word *castellano* comes from *Castilla*, the central area of Spain that started the 'reconquest' of the peninsula from eight centuries of dominance by the Moors. To defend themselves they built large numbers of castles, leading to the name.

SRI LANKA

Official name	Democratic Socialist Republic of Sri Lanka
Local name	Sri Lanka; Sri Lanka Prajatantrika Samajavadi Janarajaya
Former name	Ceylon (until 1972)
Independence	1948 (from Britain), 1972 (republic)
Area	65610 sq km/25325 sq mi
Capital	Colombo (commercial) and Sri Jayawardenepura Kotte (administrative)
Chief towns	Jaffna, Kandy, Galle, Trincomalee
Population	20926000 (2007e)
Nationality	Sri Lankan
Languages	Sinhala, Tamil
Ethnic groups	Sinhalese 74%, Sri Lankan Moor 7%, Indian Tamil 5%, Sri Lankan Tamil 4%, others 10%
Religions	Buddhism 69%, Islam 8%, Hinduism 7%, Christianity 6%, unspecified 10%
Time zone	GMT +5.5
Currency	1 Sri Lanka Rupee (SLR, SLRs/LKR) = 100 cents
Telephone	+94
Internet	.lk
Country code	LKA

Location

An island republic in the Indian Ocean off the south-east coast of India.

Physical description

Pear-shaped; low-lying areas in the north and south, surrounding the south-central uplands; highest peak is Pidurutalagala (2524m/8281ft); coastal plain is fringed by sandy beaches and lagoons; nearly half is tropical monsoon forest or open woodland.

Climate

High temperatures and humidity in the northern plains; average daily temperatures at Trincomalee are 24–33°C; temperatures in the interior are reduced by altitude; greatest rainfall on the south-west coast and in the mountains.

National holidays

Feb 4 (National), May 1, Dec 25; Ad, D, ER, GF, NY (Sinhala/Tamil) (Apr) (2), PB, Maha Sivarathri (Feb/Mar), Tamil Thai Pongal (Jan), Full Moon (*monthly*), day following Vesak Full Moon (May).

Political leaders

Head of State 1947–72: British monarch, represented by Governor General.

President

1972–8	William Gopallawa
1978–89	Junius Richard Jayawardene
1989–93	Ranasinghe Premadasa
1994–2005	Chandrika Bandaranaike Kumaratunga
2005–	Mahinda Rajapakse

Ceylon

Prime Minister

1947–52	Don Stephen Senanayake
1952–3	Dudley Shelton Senanayake
1953–6	John Lionel Kotelawala
1956–9	Solomon West Ridgeway Dias Bandaranaike
1959–60	Vijayananda Dahanayake
1960	Dudley Shelton Senanayake
1960–5	Sirimavo Ratwatte Dias Bandaranaike
1965–70	Dudley Shelton Senanayake
1970–7	Sirimavo Ratwatte Dias Bandaranaike

Sri Lanka

Prime Minister

1970–7	Sirimavo Ratwatte Dias Bandaranaike
1977–89	Ranasinghe Premadasa
1989–93	Dingiri Banda Wijetunge
1993–4	Ranil Wickremasinghe
1994	Chandrika Bandaranaike Kumaratunga
1994–2000	Sirimavo Ratwatte Dias Bandaranaike
2000–1	Ratnasiri Wickremanayake
2001–4	Ranil Wickremasinghe
2004–5	Mahinda Rajapakse
2005–	Ratnasiri Wickremanayake

Serendipity

Serendipity, meaning the state of frequently making lucky discoveries by accident, comes from an ancient name for Sri Lanka, *Serendip*. It arrived in English via a Persian fairytale, 'The Three Princes of Serendip', whose heroes made many lucky discoveries by chance; the writer Horace Walpole coined *serendipity* in reference to the tale.

SUDAN

Official name	Republic of Sudan
Local name	As-Sūdān; Al-Jumhūriyya as-Sūdān
Former name	Anglo-Egyptian Sudan (until 1956), Democratic Republic of The Sudan (1969–85)
Independence	1956
Area	2504530 sq km/966749 sq mi
Capital	Khartoum; Al Khartūm, Al Khurtūm
Chief towns	Port Sudan, Wad Medani, Omdurman
Population	39379000 (2007e)
Nationality	Sudanese
Languages	Arabic
Ethnic groups	African 52%, Arab 39%, Beja 6%, others 3%
Religions	Islam 70% (mostly Sunni), traditional beliefs 25%, Christianity 3%
Time zone	GMT +2
Currency	1 Sudanese Dinar (SD/SDG) = 10 pounds
Telephone	+249
Internet	.sd
Country code	SDN

Location

A republic in north-east Africa, bounded to the north-west by Libya; to the north by Egypt; to the north-east by the Red Sea; to the east by Ethiopia and Eritrea; to the south-east by Uganda and Kenya; to the south by Democratic Republic of the Congo; to the south-west by the Central African Republic; and to the west by Chad.

Physical description

Largest country on the African continent, astride the middle reaches of the River Nile; eastern edge formed by the Nubian Highlands and an escarpment rising to over 2000m/6562ft on the Red Sea; Imatong Mountains in the south rise to 3187m/10456ft at Kinyeti (the highest point); White Nile flows north to meet the Blue Nile at Khartoum.

Climate

Desert conditions in the north; in the hottest months (Jul–Aug), the temperature rarely falls below 24°C in the north.

National holidays

Jan 1 (Independence), 9 (Peace Agreement), Jun 30 (Revolution), Dec 25; Ad (4), ER (3), ES (Coptic) (2), NY (Muslim), PA, PB; *also* May 16, Jul 30 (Martyrs) *southern Sudan*.

Political leaders

Head of State

1956–8	*Council of State*
1958–64	Ibrahim Abboud
1964–5	*Council of Sovereignty*
1965–9	Ismail Al-Azhari
1969–85	Jaafar Mohammed Nimeiri *President from 1971*

Chairman of Transitional Military Council

1985–6 Abd Al-Rahman Siwar Al-Dahab

Chairman of Supreme Council

1986–9 Ahmad Al-Mirghani

Chairman of Revolutionary Command Council

1989–93 Omar Hassan Ahmed Al-Bashir

President

1993– Omar Hassan Ahmed Al-Bashir

Prime Minister

1955–6	Ismail Al-Azhari
1956–8	Abdullah Khalil
1958–64	*As President*
1964–5	Serr Al-Khatim Al-Khalifa
1965–6	Mohammed Ahmed Mahjoub
1966–7	Sadiq Al-Mahdi
1967–9	Mohammed Ahmed Mahjoub
1969	Babiker Awadalla
1969–76	*As President*
1976–7	Rashid Al-Tahir Bakr
1977–85	*As Head of State*
1985–6	*Transitional Military Council* (Al-Jazuli Dafallah)
1986–9	Sadiq Al-Mahdi *Military Council, Prime Minister*
1989–	*No Prime Minister*

SURINAME

Official name	Republic of Suriname
Local name	Suriname; Republiek Suriname
Former name	Netherlands Guiana, Dutch Guiana (until 1948)
Independence	1975
Area	163 265 sq km/63 020 sq mi
Capital	Paramaribo
Chief towns	Brokopondo, Nieuw Amsterdam
Population	471 000 (2007e)
Nationality	Surinamese
Languages	Dutch; English, Hindi, Javanese and Sranang Tongo are also spoken
Ethnic groups	Hindustani 37%, Creole 31%, Javanese 15%, black 10%, Amerindian 2%, Chinese 2%, others 3%
Religions	Christianity 48% (Prot 25%, RC 23%), Hinduism 27%, Islam 20%, traditional beliefs 5%
Time zone	GMT –3
Currency	1 Surinamese Dollar ($/SRD) = 100 cents
Telephone	+597
Internet	.sr
Country code	SUR

SURINAME

Location
A republic in north-eastern South America, bounded to the north by the Atlantic Ocean; to the east by French Guiana; to the south by Brazil; and to the west by Guyana.

Physical description
Diverse natural regions, ranging from coastal lowland through savanna to mountainous upland; coastal strip is mostly covered by swamp; highland interior in the south is overgrown with dense tropical forest; highest point is Julianatop (1 230m/4 035ft).

Climate
Tropically hot and humid, with two rainy seasons in May–Jul and Nov–Jan; Paramaribo temperatures range from 22–33°C.

National holidays
Jan 1, May 1, Jul 1 (Emancipation), Aug 9 (Indigenous Peoples), Nov 25 (Independence), Dec 25, 26; EM, ER, ES, GF, Holi (Mar).

Political leaders

President

1975–80	J H E Ferrier
1980–2	Henk Chin-a-Sen
1982–8	L F Ramdat-Musier *Acting*
1988–90	Ramsewak Shankar
1990–1	Johan Kraag
1991–6	Ronald Venetiaan
1996–2000	Jules Wijdenbosch
2000–	Ronald Venetiaan

Chairman of National Military Council

1980–7	Desi Bouterse
1987	Iwan Granoogst *Acting Prime Minister*

Prime Minister

1975–80	Henk Arron
1980	Henk Chin-a-Sen
1980–2	*No Prime Minister*
1982–3	Henry Weyhorst
1983–4	Errol Alibux
1984–6	Wim Udenhout
1986–7	Pretaapnarain Radhakishun
1987–8	Jules Wijdenbosch
1988–90	Henk Arron
1990–1	Jules Wijdenbosch
1991–6	Jules Ajodhia

Vice President/Chairman of the Council of Ministers

1996–2000	Pretaapnarain Radhakishun
2000–5	Jules Ajodhia
2005–	Ram Sardjoe

New Amsterdam, New York

Suriname was first settled by the British in 1651. However, in 1667 it was taken by a Dutch fleet. The British and the Dutch were also rivals in North America, and later in 1667 an agreement was reached by which the Dutch were allowed to keep Suriname in exchange for granting the British possession of Nieuw Amsterdam – later to become New York City.

SVALBARD ISLANDS *see* NORWAY

SWAZILAND

Official name	Kingdom of Swaziland
Local name	Umbuso we Swatini
Independence	1968
Area	17 363 sq km/6 702 sq mi
Capital	Mbabane (administrative) and Lobamba (legislative)
Population	1 133 000 (2007e)
Nationality	Swazi
Languages	English, Siswati
Ethnic groups	Swazi 97%, European 3%
Religions	Christianity 60% (Prot 35%, RC 25%), traditional beliefs (Zionism) 30%, Islam 1%, others 9%
Time zone	GMT +2
Currency	1 Lilangeni (plural Emalangeni) (Li, E/SZL) = 100 cents
Telephone	+268
Internet	.sz
Country code	SWZ

Location

A kingdom in south-east Africa, bounded to the north, west, south and south-east by South Africa, and to the north-east by Mozambique.

Physical description

Mountainous Highveld in the west; highest point is Emblembe (1 862m/6 109ft); more populated Middleveld in the centre descends to 600–700m/1 970–2 300ft; rolling, bush-covered Lowveld in the east is irrigated by river systems.

Climate

Humid, near-temperate climate in the west; subtropical and drier in the centre; tropical in the east, with relatively little rain (susceptible to drought); average annual temperature is 16°C in the west and 22°C in the east.

National holidays

Jan 1, Apr 19 (King's Birthday), 25 (National Flag), May 1, Jul 22 (late King Sobhuza's Birthday), Sep 6 (Somhlolo/Independence), Dec 25, 26; A, EM, GF, Incwala (Dec/Jan), Umhlanga/Reed Dance (Aug/Sep), Jul public holiday.

Political leaders

Monarch

1967–82	Sobhuza II *Chief since 1921*
1982–3	Dzeliwe *Queen Regent*
1983	Sozisa Dlamini *Regent*
1983–6	Ntombi *Queen Regent*
1986–	Mswati III

Prime Minister

1967–78	Prince Makhosini
1978–9	Prince Maphevu Dlamini
1979–83	Prince Mbandla Dlamini
1983–6	Prince Bhekimpi Dlamini
1986–9	Sotsha Dlamini
1989–93	Obed Dlamini *Acting*
1993–6	Jameson Mbilini Dlamini
1996–2003	Barnabas Sibusiso Dlamini
2003	Paul Shabangu
2003–	Absalom Themba Dlamini

Power Behind the Throne

Kings of Swaziland are permitted to have many wives, and King Sobhuza II is thought to have had more than 60. Upon the death of a king, the Royal Council chooses one of his favourite senior wives to be the new Queen Mother, an important position that makes her the most influential woman in the country. One of her unmarried sons is then chosen to be the new king.

SWEDEN

Official name	Kingdom of Sweden
Local name	Sverige; Konungariket Sverige
Area	411 479 sq km/158 830 sq mi
Capital	Stockholm
Chief towns	Gothenburg, Malmö, Uppsala, Norrköping, Västerås, Örebro, Linköping
Population	9 031 000 (2007e)
Nationality	Swedish
Languages	Swedish
Ethnic groups	Swedish 90%, Finnish and Lapp 3%, others 7%
Religions	Christianity 85% (Prot 83%, RC 2%), unaffiliated 14%, others 1%
Time zone	GMT +1
Currency	1 Swedish Krona (Skr/SEK) = 100 øre
Telephone	+46
Internet	.se
Country code	SWE

Location

A kingdom in northern Europe, occupying the eastern side of the Scandinavian Peninsula, bounded to the north-east by Finland; to the east by the Gulf of Bothnia and the Baltic Sea; to the south-west by the Skagerrak and Kattegat; and to the west and north-west by Norway.

Physical description

A large amount of inland water; many coastal islands; approximately 57% of the country is forested; Kjölen Mountains in the west form much of the boundary with Norway; highest peak is Kebnekaise (2 111m/6926ft); many waterfalls.

Climate

Typically continental, with a considerable temperature range between summer and winter, except in the south-west where winters are warmer; average number of days with a mean temperature below freezing increases from 71in Malmö to 184 near the Arctic Circle.

National holidays

Jan 1, 6, May 1, Jun 6 (National), Nov 1, Dec 25, 26; A, EM, ES, GF, Midsummer (Jun); *many public holidays preceded by an unofficial day or half-day holiday*.

Political leaders

Vasa

Monarch

1523–60	Gustav I	1599–1611	Karl IX
1560–8	Erik XIV	1611–32	Gustav II Adolf
1568–92	Johan III	1632–54	Kristina
1592–9	Sigismund		

Zweibrucken

Monarch

1654–60	Karl X Gustav	1697–1718	Karl XII
1660–97	Karl XI	1718–20	Ulrika Eleonora

Hesse

Monarch

1720–51 Fredrik

Oldenburg-Holstein-Gottorp

Monarch

1751–71	Adolf Fredrik
1771–92	Gustav III
1792–1809	Gustav IV Adolf
1809–18	Karl XIII

Bernadotte

Monarch

1818–44	Karl XIV Johan
1844–59	Oskar I
1859–72	Karl XV
1872–1907	Oskar II
1907–50	Gustav V
1950–73	Gustav VI Adolf
1973–	Karl XVI Gustav

Prime Minister

1900–2	Fredrik von Otter
1902–5	Erik Gustaf Boström
1905	Johan Ramstedt
1905	Christian Lundeberg
1905–6	Karl Staaf
1906–11	Arvid Lindman
1911–14	Karl Staaf
1914–17	Hjalmar Hammarskjöld
1917	Carl Swartz
1917–20	Nils Edén
1920	Hjalmar Branting
1920–1	Louis de Geer
1921	Oscar von Sydow
1921–3	Hjalmar Branting
1923–4	Ernst Trygger
1924–5	Hjalmar Branting
1925–6	Rickard Sandler
1926–8	Carl Gustaf Ekman
1928–30	Arvid Lindman
1930–2	Carl Gustaf Ekman
1932	Felix Hamrin
1932–6	Per Albin Hansson
1936	Axel Pehrsson-Branstorp
1936–46	Per Albin Hansson
1946–69	Tage Erlander
1969–76	Olof Palme
1976–8	Thorbjörn Fälldin
1978–9	Ola Ullsten
1979–82	Thorbjörn Fälldin
1982–6	Olof Palme
1986–91	Ingvar Carlsson
1991–4	Carl Bildt
1994–6	Ingvar Carlsson
1996–2006	Göran Persson
2006–	Fredrik Reinfeldt

Crayfish Parties

Every Aug, Swedes get together for big parties in celebration of crayfish. The crayfish party tradition began in the early 20c, when stocks of Swedish crayfish were threatened and fishing was restricted to Aug; the weeks when crayfish could be caught were celebrated with a big party at which crayfish were eaten. Today, silly hats, colourful decorations, songs in honour of the crayfish and copious quantities of schnapps to wash the crustaceans down are all part of the raucous festivities.

SWITZERLAND

Official name	Swiss Confederation
Local name	Schweiz; Schweizerische Eidgenossenschaft (German), Suisse; Confédération Suisse (French), Svizzera; Confederazione Svizzera (Italian), Svizra; Confederaziun Svizra (Romansch)
Area	41 228 sq km/15 914 sq mi
Capital	Berne; Bern, Berna
Chief towns	Zurich, Lucerne, St Gallen, Lausanne, Basle, Geneva
Population	7 555 000 (2007e)
Nationality	Swiss
Languages	German (65%), French (18%), Italian (12%) and Romansch (1%); many of the Swiss speak more than one of these
Ethnic groups	German 65%, French 18%, Italian 10%, Romansch 1%, others 6%
Religions	Christianity 79% (RC 42%, Prot 35%, other 2%), Islam 4%, others 1%, none/unaffiliated 16%
Time zone	GMT +1
Currency	1 Swiss Franc (SFr, SwF/CHF) = 100 centimes = 100 rappen
Telephone	+41
Internet	.ch
Country code	CHE

Location
A republic in central Europe, bounded to the north by Germany; to the east by Liechtenstein and Austria; to the south by Italy; and to the west by France.

Physical description
Mountainous; the Alps run roughly east to west in the south; highest peak is Dufourspitze (4634m/15203ft); average height of the Pre-Alps in the north-west is 2000m/6562ft; central plateau, at an average altitude of 580m/1903ft, is fringed by large lakes; approximately 3000 sq km/1160 sq mi of glaciers.

Climate
Temperate, varying greatly with relief and altitude; warm summers, with considerable rainfall; winter temperatures average 0°C; average annual temperature is 7–9°C; the *Föhn*, a warm wind, is noticeable in the Alps during late winter and spring.

National holidays
Jan 1, Aug 1 (National), Dec 25; A, EM, ES, GF, WM, Whit Sunday; *some regional variation; other canton and local holidays*.

Political leaders

President

1900	Walter Hauser
1901	Ernst Brenner
1902	Joseph Zemp
1903	Adolf Deucher
1904	Robert Comtesse
1905	Marc-Emile Ruchet
1906	Ludwig Forrer
1907	Eduard Müller
1908	Ernst Brenner
1909	Adolf Deucher
1910	Robert Comtesse
1911	Marc-Emile Ruchet
1912	Ludwig Forrer
1913	Eduard Müller
1914	Arthur Hoffmann
1915	Giuseppe Motta
1916	Camille Decoppet
1917	Edmund Schulthess
1918	Felix Calonder
1919	Gustave Ador
1920	Giuseppe Motta
1921	Edmund Schulthess
1922	Robert Haab
1923	Karl Scheurer
1924	Ernest Chuard
1925	Jean-Marie Musy

1926	Heinrich Häberlin
1927	Giuseppe Motta
1928	Edmund Schulthess
1929	Robert Haab
1930	Jean-Marie Musy
1931	Heinrich Häberlin
1932	Giuseppe Motta
1933	Edmund Schulthess
1934	Marcel Pilet-Golaz
1935	Rudolf Minger
1936	Albert Meyer
1937	Giuseppe Motta
1938	Johannes Baumann
1939	Philipp Etter
1940	Marcel Pilet-Golaz
1941	Ernst Wetter
1942	Philipp Etter
1943	Enrico Celio
1944	Walter Stampfli
1945	Eduard von Steiger
1946	Karl Kobelt
1947	Philipp Etter
1948	Enrico Celio
1949	Ernst Nobs
1950	Max Petitpierre
1951	Eduard von Steiger
1952	Karl Kobelt
1953	Philipp Etter
1954	Rodolphe Rubattel
1955	Max Petitpierre
1956	Markus Feldmann
1957	Hans Streuli
1958	Thomas Holenstein
1959	Paul Chaudet
1960	Max Petitpierre
1961	Friedrich Wahlen
1962	Paul Chaudet
1963	Willy Spühler
1964	Ludwig von Moos
1965	Hans Peter Tschudi
1966	Hans Schaffner
1967	Roger Bonvin
1968	Willy Spühler
1969	Ludwig von Moos
1970	Hans Peter Tschudi
1971	Rudolf Gnägi
1972	Nello Celio
1973	Roger Bonvin
1974	Ernst Brugger
1975	Pierre Graber
1976	Rudolf Gnägi
1977	Kurt Furgler
1978	Willi Ritschard
1979	Hans Hürlimann
1980	Georges-André Chevallaz
1981	Kurt Furgler
1982	Fritz Honegger
1983	Pierre Aubert
1984	Leon Schlumpf
1985	Kurt Furgler
1986	Alphons Egli
1987	Pierre Aubert
1988	Otto Stich
1989	Jean-Pascal Delamuraz
1990	Arnold Koller
1991	Flavio Cotti
1992	René Felber
1993	Adolf Ogi
1994	Otto Stich
1995	Kaspar Villiger
1996	Jean-Pascal Delamuraz
1997	Arnold Koller
1998	Flavio Cotti
1999	Ruth Dreifuss
2000	Adolf Ogi
2001	Moritz Leuenberger
2002	Kaspar Villinger
2003	Pascal Couchepin
2004	Joseph Deiss
2005	Samuel Schmid
2006	Moritz Leuenberger
2007	Micheline Calmy-Rey
2008	Pascal Couchepin

Orson Welles on Switzerland

'In Italy for thirty years under the Borgias they had warfare, terror, murder, bloodshed – they produced Michelangelo, Leonardo da Vinci and the Renaissance. In Switzerland they had brotherly love, five hundred years of democracy and peace, and what did they produce? The cuckoo clock.'

1949 Orson Welles (1915–85) US director and actor (from the film *The Third Man*).

SYRIA

Official name	Syrian Arab Republic
Local name	As-Sūriyya; Al-Jumhūriyya Al-'Arabiyya as-Sūriyya
Former name	formerly part of the United Arab Republic, with Egypt (1958–61)
Independence	1946
Area	185 180 sq km/71 479 sq mi
Capital	Damascus; Dimashq
Chief towns	Halab (Aleppo), Homs, Hama, Latakia
Population	19 315 000 (2007e)
Nationality	Syrian
Languages	Arabic
Ethnic groups	Arab 90%, Kurds, Armenian and others 10%
Religions	Islam 90% (Sunni 74%, others 16%), Christianity 10%
Time zone	GMT +2
Currency	1 Syrian Pound (LS, S$/SYP) = 100 piastres
Telephone	+963
Internet	.sy
Country code	SYR

Location

A republic in the Middle East, bounded to the north by Turkey; to the east by Iraq; to the south-west by Israel and Jordan; and to the west by the Mediterranean Sea and Lebanon.

Physical description

Behind a narrow coastal plain, the Jabal al Nusayriyah Mountains rise to approximately 1 500m/4 921ft; steep drop in the east to the Orontes River valley; Anti-Lebanon range in the south-west rises to 2 814m/9 232ft at Mt Hermon; open steppe and desert to the east.

Climate

Coastal Mediterranean climate, with hot, dry summers and mild, wet winters; 60% has a desert or semi-desert climate; the *khamsin* wind causes temperatures to rise to 43–49°C; in Damascus average temperatures from 7°C (Jan) to 27°C (Jul).

National holidays

Jan 1, Mar 8 (Revolution), 21 (Mothers), Apr 17 (Independence), May 1, 6 (Martyrs), Oct 6 (Liberation War), Dec 25; Ad (4), ER (3), ES, ES (Orthodox), NY (Muslim), PB.

Political leaders

President

1943–9	Shukri Al-Quwwatli
1949	Husni Az-Zaim
1949–51	Hashim Al-Atassi
1951–4	Adib Shishaqli
1954–5	Hashim Al-Atassi
1955–8	Shukri Al-Quwwatli
1958–61	*Part of United Arab Republic*
1961–3	Nazim Al-Qudsi
1963	Luai Al-Atassi
1963–6	Amin Al-Hafiz
1966–70	Nureddin Al-Atassi
1970–1	Ahmad Al-Khatib
1971–2000	Hafez Al-Assad
2000–	Bashar Al-Assad

Prime Minister

1946–8	Jamil Mardam Bey
1948–9	Khalid Al-Azm
1949	Husni Az-Zaim
1949	Muhsi Al-Barazi
1949	Hashim Al-Atassi
1949	Nazim Al-Qudsi
1949–50	Khalid Al-Azm
1950–1	Nazim Al-Qudsi
1951	Khalid Al-Azm
1951	Hassan Al-Hakim
1951	Maruf Ad-Dawalibi
1951–3	Fauzi As-Salu

1953–4	Adib Shishaqli
1954	Shewqet Shuqair
1954	Sabri Al-Asali
1954	Said Al-Ghazzi
1954–5	Faris Al-Khuri
1955	Sabri Al-Asali
1955–6	Said Al-Ghazzi
1956–8	Sabri Al-Asali
1958–61	*Part of United Arab Republic*
1961	Abd Al-Hamid As-Sarraj
1961	Mamun Kuzbari
1961	Izzat An-Nuss
1961–2	Maruf Ad-Dawalibi
1962	Bashir Azmah
1962–3	Khalid Al-Azm
1963	Salah Ad-Din Al-Bitaar
1963	Sami Al-Jundi
1963	Salah Ad-Din Al-Bitaar
1963–4	Amin Al-Hafez
1964	Salah Ad-Din Al-Bitaar
1964–5	Amin Al-Hafez
1965	Yousif Zeayen
1966	Salah Ad-Din Al-Bitaar
1966–8	Yousif Zeayen
1968–70	Nureddin Al-Atassi *Acting*
1970–1	Hafez Al-Assad
1971–2	Abdel Rahman Khleifawi
1972–6	Mahmoud Bin Saleh Al-Ayoubi
1976–8	Abdul Rahman Khleifawi
1978–80	Mohammed Ali Al-Halabi
1980–7	Abdel Rauof Al-Kasm
1987–2000	Mahmoud Al-Zubi
2000–3	Muhammad Mustafa Mero
2003–	Muhammad Naji al-Otari

Ancient City

Damascus claims to be the world's oldest continuously inhabited city. It dates back to at least the third millennium BC, or perhaps even to the seventh. Documented history shows that Damascus was an important regional centre by the second millennium BC. It has been suggested that the name Damascus may come from old Arabic *Dar Meshq*, meaning 'well-watered place'. In ancient times it was a great trade and commercial centre.

TAIWAN

Official name	Republic of China; also sometimes known as Chinese Taipei
Local name	T'ai-wan; Chung-hua Min-kuo
Former name	Formosa (until 1949)
Independence	1949 (creation of republic)
Area	36000 sq km/13896 sq mi
Capital	T'aipei
Chief towns	Chilung, Kaohsiung, Taichung
Population	22859000 (2007e)
Nationality	Taiwanese, Chinese
Languages	Mandarin Chinese
Ethnic groups	Taiwanese Chinese (including Hakka) 84%, mainland Chinese 14%, Ainu 2%
Religions	Buddhism and Taoism 93%, Christianity 4%, Islam and others 3%
Time zone	GMT +8
Currency	1 New Taiwan Dollar (NT$/TWD) = 100 cents
Telephone	+886
Internet	.tw
Country code	TWN

TAIWAN

Location

An island republic, lying approximately 80mi/130km off the south-east coast of China between the East China Sea and the South China Sea; crossed by the Tropic of Cancer.

Physical description

Mountain range runs north to south, covering two thirds of Taiwan Island; highest peak is Yu Shan (3997m/13113ft); low-lying land is mainly on the west; crossed by the Tropic of Cancer.

Climate

Tropical monsoon-type climate; wettest period is May–Sep, when it is hot and humid; typhoons bring heavy rains in Jul–Sep; short mild winters; average daily temperature at T'aipei is 12–19°C (Jan), 24–33°C (Jul–Aug).

National holidays

Jan 1 (Foundation of the Republic), Feb 28 (Peace Memorial), Apr 5 (Tomb Sweeping), May 1, Oct 10 (National); NY (Chinese) (Jan/Feb) (3), Dragon Boat Festival (Jun), Mid-Autumn Moon Festival (Sep/Oct).

Political leaders

President

1950–75	Chiang Kai-shek	1987–2000	Lee Teng-hui
1975–8	Yen Chia-kan	2000–	Chen Shui-bian
1978–87	Chiang Ching-kuo		

President of Executive Council

1950–4	Ch'eng Ch'eng	1978–84	Sun Yun-suan
1954–8	O K Yui	1984–9	Yu Kuo-hwa
1958–63	Ch'eng Ch'eng	1989–90	Lee Huan
1963–72	Yen Chia-ken	1990–3	Hau Pei-tsun
1972–8	Chiang Ching-kuo	1993–6	Lien Chan

Prime Minister

1996–7	Lien Chan	2002–5	Yu Shyi-kun
1997–2000	Vincent Siew	2005–6	Frank Hsieh
2000	Tang Fei	2006–7	Su Tseng-chang
2000–2	Chang Chun-hsiung	2007–	Chang Chun-hsiung

What's in a Name?

'Taiwan' is perhaps the most controversial country name in the world, for complex historical reasons. When the Communists took control of China in 1949, renaming it the People's Republic of China, the defeated Nationalist government fled to the island of Formosa and set up a 'Chinese government-in-exile'. They kept China's old name and so renamed the island Republic of China, which is still Taiwan's official name. Today there is a movement to rename the country simply as Taiwan and move on as an independent country. But China claims that Taiwan is a Chinese province that should be under mainland Chinese control, and many people fear that renaming the country would be viewed by the Chinese authorities as an act of wilful independence that would provoke violent retaliation.

TAJIKISTAN

Official name	Republic of Tajikistan
Local name	Cumhurii Tocikiston
Former name	Tajik Soviet Socialist Republic (until 1991), within the Union of Soviet Socialist Republics (USSR; 1929–91)
Independence	1991
Area	143 100 sq km/55 200 sq mi
Capital	Dushanbe; Dušanbe
Chief towns	Khudzand, Kulyab, Kurgan-Tyube
Population	7 076 000 (2007e)
Nationality	Tajik or Tadzhik, Tajikistani
Languages	Tajik, Uzbek, Russian
Ethnic groups	Tajik 80%, Uzbek 15%, Russian 1%, Kyrgyz 1%, others 3%
Religions	Islam 90% (Sunni 85%, Shia 5%), others 10%
Time zone	GMT +5
Currency	1 Somoni (S/TJS) = 100 dirams
Telephone	+992
Internet	.tj
Country code	TJK

Location
A republic in central Asia, bounded to the north by Kyrgyzstan; to the east by China; to the south by Afghanistan; and to the west and north by Uzbekistan.

Physical description
Tien Shan, Gissar-Alai and Pamir mountain ranges cover over 90% of the area; highest peak is Peak Ismoili Somoni (formerly Communism Peak; 7 495m/24 590ft); River Amudarya flows east to west along the southern border; largest lake is Lake Kara-Kul.

Climate
Predominantly continental; hot summers and mild winters.

National holidays
Jan 1, Mar 8 (Women), 21–22 (Navrus), May 1, 9 (Victory), Jun 27 (National Unity), Sep 9 (Independence), Nov 6 (Constitution); Ad, ER.

Political leaders

President

1991–2	Rakhman Nabiev
1992	Akbarsho Iskandrov *Acting*
1992–	Emomali Sharipovich Rakhmonov

Prime Minister

1991–2	Akbar Mirzoyev
1992–3	Abdumalik Abdullojanov
1993–4	Abduljalil Samadov *Acting*
1994–6	Jamshed Karimov
1996–9	Yahya Azimov
1999–	Akil Akilov

Ice White

The flag of Tajikistan has three horizontal stripes of green, white and red, with a gold crown and seven stars above it. The green is said to represent the country's valleys and the white to symbolize not only the snow and ice of Tajikistan's many mountains but also cotton, a major export. The red stripe suggests the unified republic and sympathy with other countries.

TANZANIA

Official name	United Republic of Tanzania
Local name	Tanzania
Former name	Republic of Tanganyika (1962–4), United Republic of Tanganyika and Zanzibar (1964)
Independence	1961
Area	939652 sq km/362706 sq mi
Capital	Dodoma (political) and Dar es Salaam (commercial)
Chief towns	Dar es Salaam, Zanzibar, Mwanza, Tanga, Arusha
Population	39384000 (2007e)
Nationality	Tanzanian
Languages	Kiswahili, English; local languages are also spoken
Ethnic groups	Tanganyika: Bantu 95% (includes over 120 tribes, none more than 10% of population), other African 4%, Asian, European, Arab and others 1%; Zanzibar: Arab, African, mixed
Religions	Tanganyika: Islam 35%, traditional beliefs 35%, Christianity 30%; Zanzibar: Islam 99%, others 1%
Time zone	GMT +3
Currency	1 Tanzanian Shilling (Tsh/TZS) = 100 cents
Telephone	+255
Internet	.tz
Country code	TZA

Location

A republic in eastern Africa, bounded to the north-west by Burundi and Rwanda; to the north by Uganda (Lake Victoria) and Kenya; to the east by the Indian Ocean; to the south by Mozambique, Lake Nyasa and Malawi; to the south-west by Zambia; and to the west by Democratic Republic of the Congo (Lake Tanganyika).

Physical description

Largest East African country, just south of the Equator; central plateau at average elevation of 1000m/3281ft; high grasslands and mountain ranges to the centre and south; Rift Valley branches around Lake Victoria in the north; several high volcanic peaks, notably Mt Kilimanjaro, the highest point (5895m/19340ft); extensive Serengeti plain to the west; island of Zanzibar lies off the coast.

Climate

Hot, humid and tropical on the coast and offshore islands; average temperature is approximately 23°C (Jun–Sept) and 27°C (Dec–Mar); hot and dry on the central plateau; semi-temperate at altitudes above 1500m/4921ft; permanent snow on high peaks.

National holidays

Jan 1, 12 (Zanzibar Revolution), Apr 26 (Union), May 1, Jul 7 (Industry), Aug 8 (Farmers), Oct 14 (Nyerere), Dec 9 (Independence/Republic), 25, 26; Ad, EM, ER (2), GF, PB.

That Sinking Feeling

The name 'Dodoma' comes from a local word meaning 'it has sunk', supposedly referring to an elephant that became stuck in a swamp in the area.

Political leaders

President

1964–85	Julius Kambarage Nyerere	1995–2005	Benjamin William Mkapa
1985–95	Ali Hassan Mwinyi	2005–	Jakaya Mrisho Kikwete

Prime Minister

1964–72	Rashid M Kawawa *Vice President*	1977–80	Edward M Sokoine
1972–7	Rashid M Kawawa	1980–3	Cleopa D Msuya

1983–4	Edward M Sokoine	1994–5	Cleopa Msuya
1984–5	Salim A Salim	1995–2005	Frederick Sumaye
1985–90	Joseph S Warioba	2005–	Edward Lowassa
1990–4	John Malecela		

THAILAND

Official name	Kingdom of Thailand
Local name	Prathet Thai
Former name	Siam (until 1939 and 1945–49)
Area	513 115 sq km/198 062 sq mi
Capital	Bangkok; Krung Thep
Chief towns	Chiang Mai, Nakhon Ratchasima
Population	65 068 000 (2007e)
Nationality	Thai
Languages	Thai
Ethnic groups	Thai 75%, Chinese 14%, others 11%
Religions	Buddhism 95%, Islam 4%, others 1%
Time zone	GMT +7
Currency	1 Baht (B/THB) = 100 satang
Telephone	+66
Internet	.th
Country code	THA

Location
A kingdom in south-east Asia, bounded to the north-east and east by Laos; to the south-east by Cambodia; to the south by Malaysia and the Gulf of Thailand; to the west by the Andaman Sea; and to the west and north-west by Myanmar.

Physical description
Central agricultural region dominated by the Chao Phraya River floodplain; large north-eastern plateau; mountainous north rises to 2 595m/8 514ft at Doi Inthanon; low-lying south covered in tropical rainforest; mangrove-forested coastal islands.

Climate
Equatorial climate in the south; tropical monsoon climate in the north and centre.

National holidays
Jan 1, Apr 6 (Chakri), 13–15 (Songkran/Thai NY), May 5 (Coronation), Jul 1, Aug 12 (Queen's Birthday), Oct 23 (Chulalongkorn Memorial), Dec 5 (King's Birthday), 10 (Constitution), 31; Buddhist Lent (Jul), Makha Bucha (Feb/Mar), Visakha (May/Jun).

Political leaders

Monarch

1868–1910	Chulalongkorn, Rama V	1939–46	Nai Pridi Phanomyong *Regent*
1910–25	Rama VI	1946–	Bhumibol Adulyadej, Rama IX (*regency 1946–50*)
1925–35	Rama VII	1946–50	Rangsit of Chainat *Regent*
1935–9	Ananda Mahidol, Rama VIII		

Prime Minister

1932–3	Phraya Manopakom	1945–6	Mom Rachawongse Seni Pramoj
1933–8	Phraya Phahon Phonphahuyasena	1946	Nai Khuang Aphaiwong
1938–44	Luang Phibun Songgram	1946	Nai Pridi Phanomyong
1944–5	Nai Khuang Aphaiwong	1946–7	Luang Thamrong Nawasawat
1945	Thawi Bunyaket	1947–8	Nai Khuang Aphaiwong

1948–57	Luang Phibun Songgram	1987–91	Chatichai Choonhaven
1957	Sarit Thanarat	1991–2	Anand Panyarachun
1957	Nai Pote Sarasin	1992	Suchinda Kraprayoon
1957–8	Thanom Kittikatchom	1992	Anand Panyarachun
1958–63	Sarit Thanarat	1992–5	Chuan Leekpai
1963–73	Thanom Kittikatchom	1995–6	Banharn Silpa-Archa
1973–5	Sanya Dharmasaki	1996–7	Chavalit Yongchaiyudh
1975–6	Mom Rachawongse Kukrit Pramoj	1997–2001	Chuan Leekpai
1976	Seni Pramoj	2001–6	Thaksin Shinawatra
1976–7	Thanin Kraivichien	2006–8	Surayd Chulanont *Interim*
1977–80	Kriangsak Chammanard	2008–	Samak Sundaravej
1980–7	Prem Tinsulanonda		

TOBAGO *see* TRINIDAD AND TOBAGO

TOGO

Official name	Republic of Togo (also Togolese Republic)
Local name	Togo; République Togolaise
Former name	French Togoland (until 1956)
Independence	1960
Area	56 600 sq km/21 848 sq mi
Capital	Lomé
Chief towns	Sokodé, Kpalimé, Atakpamé
Population	5 701 000 (2007e)
Nationality	Togolese
Languages	French; many local languages are also spoken
Ethnic groups	African 99% (mainly Ewe, Dagomba, Mina and Kabye), others 1%
Religions	traditional beliefs 51%, Christianity 29%, Islam 20%
Time zone	GMT
Currency	1 CFA Franc (CFAFr/XOF) = 100 centimes
Telephone	+228
Internet	.tg
Country code	TGO

Location

A republic in West Africa, bounded to the north by Burkina Faso; to the east by Benin; to the south by the Bight of Benin in the Gulf of Guinea; and to the west by Ghana.

Physical description

Rises from the lagoon coast of the Gulf of Guinea, past low-lying plains to the Atakora Mountains, which run north-east to south-west across the north of the country; highest peak is Pic Baumann (Mt Agou; 986m/3 235ft); flat plains lie to the north-west.

Climate

Tropical; rain throughout the year in the south; one rainy season in the north Jul–Sep.

National holidays

Jan 1, 13 (National Liberation), Apr 27 (Independence), May 1, Jun 21 (Pya Martyrs), Aug 15, Nov 1, Dec 25; A, Ad, EM, ER, WM.

Political leaders

President

1960–3	Sylvanus Olympio	2005	Faure Gnassingbé *Acting*
1963–7	Nicolas Grunitzky	2005	Abass Bonfoh *Acting*
1967–2005	Gnassingbé Eyadéma	2005–	Faure Gnassingbé

Prime Minister

1991–4	Joseph Koukou Koffigoh	2002–5	Koffi Sama
1994–6	Edem Kodjo	2005–6	Edem Kodjo
1996–9	Kwassi Klutse	2006–7	Yawovi Madji Agboyibo
1999–2000	Eugene Koffi Adoboli	2007–	Komlan Mally
2000–2	Messan Agbeyome Kodjo		

TOKELAU *see* NEW ZEALAND

TONGA

Official name	Kingdom of Tonga; also sometimes known as the Friendly Islands
Local name	Tonga; Pule'anga Fakatu'I 'O Tonga
Independence	1970
Area	748 sq km/289 sq mi
Capital	Nuku'alofa
Population	117 000 (2007e)
Nationality	Tongan
Languages	English, Tongan
Ethnic groups	Tongan 98%, others 2%
Religions	Christianity 79% (Prot 63%, RC 16%), others 21%
Time zone	GMT +13
Currency	1 Pa'anga/Tongan Dollar (T$/TOP) = 100 seniti
Telephone	+676
Internet	.to
Country code	TON

Location

An independent island kingdom in the south-west Pacific Ocean, north-east of New Zealand.

Physical description

Comprises 171 islands, 45 of which are inhabited, divided into three main groups (coral formations of Ha'apai and Tongatapu-Eua, mountainous Vava'u); largest island is Tongatapu; western islands are mainly volcanic (some still active); highest point is the extinct volcano Kao (1 046m/3 432ft).

Climate

Semi-tropical; average annual temperature on Tongatapu is 23°C; occasional hurricanes in the summer months.

National holidays

Jan 1, Apr 25 (Anzac), Jun 4 (Emancipation), Jul 12 (Crown Prince's Birthday), Aug 1 (King's Birthday), Nov 4 (National), Dec 4 (King Tupou I), 25, 26; EM, GF.

Political leaders

Monarch

1893–1918	George Tupou II	1965–2006	Taufa'ahau Tupou IV
1918–65	Salote Tupou III	2006–	George Tupou V

Prime Minister

1970–91	Fatafehi Tu'ipelehake	2000–6	Prince 'Ulukalala Lavaka Ata
1991–2000	Baron Vaea	2006–	Feleti Sevele

TRINIDAD AND TOBAGO

Official name	Republic of Trinidad and Tobago
Local name	Trinidad and Tobago
Independence	1962
Area	5 128 sq km/1 979 sq mi
Capital	Port of Spain
Chief towns	San Fernando, Arima, Scarborough
Population	1 057 000 (2007e)
Nationality	Trinidadian, Tobagonian
Languages	English
Ethnic groups	East Indian 40%, black 37%, mixed 20%, others 3%
Religions	Christianity 54% (RC 26%, Prot 22%, other 6%), Hinduism 22%, Islam 6%, others 15%, none/unaffiliated 3%
Time zone	GMT –4
Currency	1 Trinidad and Tobago Dollar (TT$/TTD) = 100 cents
Telephone	+1868
Internet	.tt
Country code	TTO

Location

A republic in the Lesser Antilles in the south-east Caribbean Sea, just north of South America; Trinidad is separated from Venezuela in the south by the 11km/7mi wide Gulf of Paria; Tobago lies 30km/19mi north-east of Trinidad.

Physical description

Trinidad is roughly rectangular; crossed by three mountain ranges; highest point is El Cerro del Aripo (940m/3 084ft); rest is low-lying, with large coastal mangrove swamps; Pitch Lake is the world's largest reservoir of natural asphalt; Tobago's Main Ridge extends along most of the island, rising to 576m/1 890ft.

Climate

Tropical, with an annual average temperature of 29°C.

National holidays

Jan 1, Mar 30 (Spiritual Shouter Baptist Liberation), May 30 (Indian Arrival), Jun 19 (Labour), Aug 1 (Emancipation), 31 (Independence), Sep 24 (Republic), Dec 25, 26; CC, D, EM, ER, GF.

Political leaders

President

1976–87 Ellis Emmanuel Clarke
1987–97 Noor Mohammed Hassanali
1997–2003 Arthur Ray Robinson
2003– George Maxwell Richards

Premier

1956–62 Eric Williams

Prime Minister

1962–81 Eric Williams
1981–6 George Chambers
1986–91 Raymond Robinson
1991–5 Patrick Manning
1995–2001 Basdeo Panday
2001– Patrick Manning

Steel Band Music

The music of steel bands plays a central part in the culture of Trinidad and Tobago, and the government lists the steel pan as one of the national symbols alongside the national bird, the national flower, the state flag and the coat of arms.

TUNISIA

Official name	Republic of Tunisia
Local name	Tūnisiya; Al-Jumhūriyya at-Tūnisiyya
Independence	1956
Area	164 150 sq km/63 362 sq mi
Capital	Tunis; Toûnis, Tunus
Chief towns	Bizerta, Sousse, Sfax, Gabes
Population	10 276 000 (2007e)
Nationality	Tunisian
Languages	Arabic; French is also spoken
Ethnic groups	Arab and Berber 98%, European 1%, Jewish and others 1%
Religions	Islam 98%, Christianity 1%, Judaism and others 1%
Time zone	GMT +1
Currency	1 Tunisian Dinar (TD, D/TND) = 1 000 millimes
Telephone	+216
Internet	.tn
Country code	TUN

Location

A republic in North Africa, bounded to the north-east and north by the Mediterranean Sea; to the south-east by Libya; and to the west by Algeria.

Physical description

Atlas Mountains in the north-west rise to 1 544m/5 066ft at Djebel Chambi; central depression runs west to east, containing several salty lakes; dry, sandy upland lies to the south.

Climate

Mediterranean climate on the coast, with hot, dry summers and wet winters; daily maximum temperature is 14–33°C; higher rainfall in the Atlas Mountains; further south, rainfall decreases and temperatures can be extreme.

National holidays

Jan 1, Mar 20 (Independence), 21 (Youth), Apr 9 (Martyrs), May 1, Jul 25 (Republic), Aug 13 (Women), Nov 7 (New Era); Ad (2), ER (2), NY (Muslim), PB.

Political leaders

Bey

1943–57	Muhammad VIII

President

1957–87	Habib Bourguiba
1987–	Zine al-Abidine Ben Ali

Prime Minister

1956–7	Habib Bourguiba
1957–69	*No Prime Minister*
1969–70	Bahi Ladgham
1970–80	Hadi Nouira
1980–6	Mohammed Mezali
1986–7	Rashid Sfar
1987	Zine Al-Abidine Bin Ali
1987–9	Hadi Baccouche
1989–99	Hamed Karoui
1999–	Mohammed Ghannouchi

TURKEY

Official name	Republic of Turkey
Local name	Türkiye; Türkiye Çumhuriyeti
Area	779 452 sq km/300 868 sq mi
Capital	Ankara; Angora
Chief towns	Istanbul, Izmir, Adana, Bursa, Gaziantep
Population	71 159 000 (2007e)
Nationality	Turkish
Languages	Turkish
Ethnic groups	Turkish 80%, Kurdish 16%, others 4%
Religions	Islam 99% (mostly Sunni), others 1%
Time zone	GMT +2
Currency	1 New Turkish Lira (TL/TRY) = 100 new kurus
Telephone	+90
Internet	.tr
Country code	TUR

Location
A republic lying between Europe and Asia, bounded to the north by Bulgaria and the Black Sea; to the north-east by Georgia, Armenia, Azerbaijan and Iran; and to the south by Iraq, Syria and the Mediterranean Sea.

Physical description
Mountainous (average height 1 100m/3 609ft); average altitude of the central plateau is 1 000–2 000m/3 281–6 562ft; Taurus Mountains cover the entire southern part of Anatolia; highest peak is Mt Ararat (5 165m/16 945ft); alluvial coastal plains; the Turkish Straits (the Dardanelles, Sea of Marmara and Bosporus) connect the Black Sea in the north-east and the Mediterranean Sea in the south-west.

Climate
Typically Mediterranean climate on the Aegean and Mediterranean coasts, with hot, dry summers and warm, wet winters; further east along the Black Sea coast, rainfall becomes heavy in summer and autumn; low rainfall on the interior plateau, with cold winters and warm or hot summers.

National holidays
Jan 1, Apr 23 (National Sovereignty and Children), May 19 (Atatürk Commemoration/Youth and Sports), Aug 30 (Victory), Oct 29 (Republic); Ad (4), ER (3).

Political leaders

Sultan of the Ottoman Empire

1876–1909 Abdülhamit
1909–18 Mehmet Reşat
1918–22 Mehmet Vahideddin

President

1923–38 Mustafa Kemal Atatürk
1938–50 İsmet İnönü
1950–60 Celal Bayar
1960–6 Cemal Gürsel
1966–73 Cevdet Sunay
1973–80 Fahri S Korutürk
1980 Ihsan Çaglayangil *Acting*
1980–9 Kenan Evren *Chairman of National Security Council until 1982*
1989–93 Turgut Özal
1993–2000 Süleyman Demirel
2000–7 Ahmet Necdet Sezer
2007– Abdullah Gül

Prime Minister

1923–4 İsmet İnönü
1924–5 Ali Fethi Okyar
1925–37 İsmet İnönü
1937–9 Celal Bayar
1939–42 Dr Refik Saydam
1942–6 Şükrü Saracoğlu
1946–7 Recep Peker
1947–9 Hasan Saka

1949–50	Şemşettin Günaltay	1978–9	Bülent Ecevit
1950–60	Adnan Menderes	1979–80	Süleyman Demirel
1960–1	Cemal Gürsel	1980–3	Bülent Ülüsü
1961–5	İsmet İnönü	1983–9	Turgut Özal
1965	S Hayri Ürgüplü	1989–91	Yildrim Akbulut
1965–71	Süleyman Demirel	1991	Mesut Yilmaz
1971–2	Nihat Erim	1991–3	Süleyman Demirel
1972–3	Ferit Melen	1993–6	Tansu Çiller
1973–4	Naim Talu	1996	Mesut Yilmaz
1974	Bülent Ecevit	1996–7	Necmettin Erbakan
1974–5	Sadi Irmak	1997–8	Mesut Yilmaz
1975–7	Süleyman Demirel	1999–2002	Bülent Ecevit
1977	Bülent Ecevit	2002–3	Abdullah Gül
1977–8	Süleyman Demirel	2003–	Recep Tayyip Erdoğan

TURKMENISTAN

Official name	Republic of Turkmenistan
Local name	Turkmenostan; Turkmenostan Respublikasy
Former name	Turkmen Soviet Socialist Republic (1924–91), within the Union of Soviet Socialist Republics (USSR; 1925–91)
Independence	1991
Area	488 100 sq km/188 400 sq mi
Capital	Ashgabat; Ašgabat, Ašhabad
Chief towns	Chardzhou, Mary, Türkmenbashi, Nebit-Dag
Population	5 097 000 (2007e)
Nationality	Turkmen
Languages	Turkmen, Russian, Uzbek
Ethnic groups	Turkmen 85%, Uzbek 5%, Russian 4%, others 6%
Religions	Islam 89% (mostly Sunni), Christianity 9% (Orthodox), others 2%
Time zone	GMT +5
Currency	1 Manat (TMM) = 100 tenesi
Telephone	+993
Internet	.tm
Country code	TKM

Location

A republic in central Asia, bounded to the north by Kazakhstan and Uzbekistan; to the south by Afghanistan and Iran; and to the west by the Caspian Sea.

Physical description

Low-lying with hills in the south; mainly desert; highest point is Ayrybaba (3 139m/10 298ft).

Climate

Continental, hot and arid in the large desert areas.

National holidays

Jan 1, 12 (Memorial), Feb 19 (National Flag), 20–22 (Novrus), May 8 (Heroes), 9 (Victory), 18 (Revival and Unity), Oct 6 (Earthquake Remembrance), 27–28 (Independence), Dec 12 (Neutrality); Ad (3), ER.

Beard Ban

President Niyazov of Turkmenistan renamed January after himself, April after his late mother and built a 12m/39ft gold statue of himself which revolves to face the sun. He also banned opera, ballet, beards and gold teeth.

Political leaders

President

1991–2006	Saparmurad Niyazov
2006–	Gurbanguly Berdymukhamedov *Acting President until 2007*

Prime Minister

1991–2	Khan Akhmedov
1992–	*As President*

TURKS AND CAICOS ISLANDS *see* UNITED KINGDOM

TUVALU

Official name	Tuvalu
Local name	Tuvalu; Fakavae Aliki-Malo I Tuvalu
Former name	Ellice Islands, as part of the Gilbert and Ellice Islands (until 1975)
Independence	1978
Area	26 sq km/10 sq mi
Capital	Fongafale (on Funafuti)
Population	12 000 (2007e)
Nationality	Tuvaluan
Languages	Tuvaluan, English
Ethnic groups	Polynesian 96%, others 4%
Religions	Christianity 97%, Baha'i 1%, others 2%
Time zone	GMT +12
Currency	1 Australian Dollar (A$/AUD) = 100 cents
Telephone	+688
Internet	.tv
Country code	TUV

Location
An island state in the south-west Pacific, 1 050km/650mi north of Fiji.

Physical description
Comprises nine low-lying coral atolls, rising no higher than 5m/16ft, running north-west to south-east in a chain 580km/360mi long.

Climate
Hot and humid; average annual temperature is 30°C.

National holidays
Jan 1, Dec 25, 26; EM, ES, GF, HS; Children (Aug), Commonwealth Day (Mar), Gospel Day (May), Independence (Oct) (2), Queen's Birthday (Jun).

Political leaders

Head of State: British monarch, represented by Governor General (Filoimea Telito since 2005).

Prime Minister

1978–81	Toalipi Lauti
1981–9	Tomasi Puapua
1989–93	Bikenibeu Paeniu
1993–6	Kamuta Lataasi
1996–9	Bikenibeu Paeniu
1999–2000	Ionatana Ionatana
2000–1	Lagitupu Tuilimu *Acting*
2001	Faimalaga Luka
2001–2	Koloa Talake
2002–4	Saufatu Sopoanga
2004–6	Maatia Toafa
2006–	Apisai Ielemia

UGANDA

Official name	Republic of Uganda
Local name	Uganda
Independence	1962
Area	238 461 sq km/92 029 sq mi
Capital	Kampala
Chief towns	Jinja, Mbale, Tororo, Soroti, Entebbe
Population	30 263 000 (2007e)
Nationality	Ugandan
Languages	English; Swahili and other languages are also spoken
Ethnic groups	Baganda 17%, Banyankole 8%, Basogo 8%, Iteso 8%, Bakiga 7%, Langi 6%, Rwanda 6%, Bagisu 5%, Acholi 4%, Lugbara 4%, non-African (European, Asian, Arab) 1%, others 26%
Religions	Christianity 66% (RC 33%, Prot 33%), traditional beliefs 18%, Islam 16%
Time zone	GMT +3
Currency	1 Uganda Shilling (USh/UGX) = 100 cents
Telephone	+256
Internet	.ug
Country code	UGA

Location

A republic in East Africa, crossed by the Equator in the south; bounded to the north by Sudan; to the east by Kenya; to the south by Tanzania (Lake Victoria) and Rwanda; and to the west by Democratic Republic of the Congo.

Physical description

Mainly on a plateau with an elevation of 900–1 000m/2 950ft–3 280ft; population is concentrated in the fertile Lake Victoria basin; highest point is Margherita Peak (5 110m/16 765ft) in the Mt Stanley massif; main rivers are the upper reaches of the River Nile.

Climate

Highest rainfall is in the mountains to the west and south-west and along the shores of Lake Victoria; daily temperatures at Entebbe on the north shore of the lake are 24–28°C; central and north-eastern areas receive less rain.

National holidays

Jan 1, 26 (Liberation), Mar 8 (Women), May 1, Jun 3 (Martyrs), 9 (Heroes), Oct 9 (Independence), Dec 25, 26; Ad, EM, ER, GF.

Political leaders

Governor-General

1962–3 Walter Fleming Coutts

Antelope Hill

The name of Uganda's capital city, Kampala, comes from *Kasozi Kampala*, meaning 'the hill of antelopes'.

President

1963–6	Edward Muteesa II
1966–71	Apollo Milton Obote
1971–9	Idi Amin
1979	Yusuf Kironde Lule
1979–80	Godfrey Lukongwa Binaisa
1981–5	Apollo Milton Obote
1985–6	*Military Council* (Tito Okello Lutwa)
1986–	Yoweri Museveni

Prime Minister

1962–71	Apollo Milton Obote
1971–81	*No Prime Minister*
1981–5	Eric Otema Alimadi
1985	Paulo Muwanga
1985–6	Abraham N Waliggo
1986–91	Samson B Kisekka
1991–4	George Cosmas Adyebo
1994–9	Kintu Musoke
1999–	Apolo Nsibambi

UKRAINE

Official name	Ukraine
Local name	Ukraïna
Former name	Ukrainian Soviet Socialist Republic (1919–91), within the Union of Soviet Socialist Republics (USSR; 1922–91)
Independence	1991
Area	603 700 sq km/233 028 sq mi
Capital	Kiev; Kyïv
Chief towns	Kharkov, Donetsk, Odessa, Dnepropetrovsk, Lvov, Zaporozhye, Krivoy Rog
Population	46 300 000 (2007e)
Nationality	Ukrainian
Languages	Ukrainian, Russian
Ethnic groups	Ukrainian 78%, Russian 17%, others (including Tartar) 5%
Religions	Christianity 75% (Orthodox), unaffiliated 22%, others 1%
Time zone	GMT +2
Currency	1 Hryvnia (UAH) = 100 kopiykas
Telephone	+380
Internet	.ua
Country code	UKR

Location
A republic in eastern Europe, bounded to the north by Belarus; to the east by Russia; to the south by the Black Sea; to the south-west by Moldova and Romania; and to the west by Hungary, Slovakia and Poland.

Physical description
Generally a plain with high elevations in the west, south and south-east; Ukrainian Carpathian Mountains in the west rise to 2 061 m/6 762 ft at Hora Hoverla; Crimean Peninsula separates the Black Sea from the Sea of Azov; Crimean Mountains lie along the south coast of the peninsula; many reservoirs and lakes.

Climate
Temperate, continental; cold winters and warm summers.

National holidays
Jan 1, 7 (Orthodox Christmas), Mar 8 (Women), May 1–2, 9 (Victory), Jun 28 (Constitution), Aug 24 (Independence); EM (Orthodox), ES (Orthodox), Orthodox Pentecost (May/Jun) (2).

Political leaders

President

1991–4	Leonid Kravchuk
1994–2005	Leonid Kuchma
2005–	Viktor Yushchenko

Prime Minister

1990–2	Vitold Fokin
1992	Valentin Symonenko
1992–3	Leonid Kuchma
1993–4	Yukhim Zvyahilski *Acting*
1994–5	Vitalii Masol
1995–6	Yevhenii Maruk
1996–7	Pavlo Lazarenko
1997	Vasyl Durdynets *Acting*
1997–9	Valery Pustovoytenko
1999–2001	Viktor Yushchenko
2001–2	Anatoli Kinakh
2002–5	Viktor Yanukovich
2005	Mykola Azarov *Acting*
2005–5	Yuliya Tymoshenko
2005–6	Yuri Yekhanurov
2006–7	Viktor Yanukovych
2007–	Yulia Tymoshenko

UMM AL-QAIWAIN *see* UNITED ARAB EMIRATES

UNITED ARAB EMIRATES

Official name	United Arab Emirates (UAE)
Local name	Ittihād al-imārāt al-'Arabīyah
Former name	Trucial States (until 1971)
Independence	1971
Area	83 600 sq km/32 300 sq mi
Capital	Abu Dhabi; Abū Zhaby
Chief towns	Dubai, Sharjah, Ras al-Khaimah
Population	4 444 000 (2007e)
Nationality	Emirati
Languages	Arabic, English
Ethnic groups	Arab 55% (UAE citizens approximately 20%), South Asian 28%, Iranian 8%, others 9%
Religions	Islam 96% (Sunni 80%, Shia 16%), others 4%
Time zone	GMT +4
Currency	1 Dirham (DH/AED) = 100 fils
Telephone	+971
Internet	.ae
Country code	ARE

Location
A federation in the eastern central Arabian Peninsula comprising seven internally self-governing emirates (Abu Dhabi, Ajman, Dubai, Fujairah, Ras al-Khaimah, Sharjah and Umm al-Qaiwain), crossed by the Tropic of Cancer; bounded to the north by the Arabian Gulf; to the east by Oman; and to the south and west by Saudi Arabia.

Physical description
Located along the southern shore of the Arabian Gulf; Fujairah has a coastline along the Gulf of Oman; salt marshes predominate on the coast; barren desert and gravel plain inland; Hajar Mountains in Fujairah rise to over 1 000m/3 280ft; highest point is Jabal Yibir (1 527m/5 010ft).

Climate
Hot with limited rainfall; winter temperatures average 21°C, with high humidity (in excess of 70%); less humid in summer, with maximum temperatures rising to 45°C; sandstorms are common.

National holidays
Jan 1, Dec 2–3 (National); Ad (4), ER (3), NY (Muslim), PA, PB.

Political leaders

President

1971–2004 Zayed bin Sultan al-Nahayan
2004– Khalifa bin Zayed al-Nahayan

Prime Minister

1971–9 Maktoum bin Rashid al-Maktoum
1979–91 Rashid bin Said al-Maktoum
1991–2006 Maktoum bin Rashid al-Maktoum
2006– Mohammed bin Rashid al-Maktoum

Abu Dhabi

Tribe: al Bu Falah or al Nahyan (Bani Yas)

Family name: al-Nahyan

Sheikh

1855–1909 Zayed
1909–12 Tahnoun
1912–22 Hamdan
1922–6 Sultan
1926–8 Saqr
1928–66 Shakhbout
1966–2004 Zayed
2004– Khalifa

Ajman

Tribe: al Bu Kharayban (Naim)
Family name: al-Nuaimi

Sheikh

1900–10	Abdel-Aziz
1910–28	Humaid
1928–81	Rashid
1981–	Humaid

Dubai

Tribe: al Bu Flasah (Bani Yas)
Family name: al-Maktoum

Sheikh

1894–1906	Maktoum
1906–12	Butti
1912–58	Said
1958–90	Rashid
1990–2006	Maktoum
2006–	Mohammed

Fujairah

Tribe: Sharqiyyin
Family name: al-Sharqi

Sheikh

1952–75	Mohammed
1975–	Hamad

Ras al-Khaimah

Tribe: Huwalah
Family name: al-Qasimi

Sheikh

1921–48	Sultan
1948–	Saqr

Sharjah

Tribe: Huwalah
Family name: al-Qasimi

Sheikh

1883–1914	Saqr
1914–24	Khaled
1924–51	Sultan
1951–65	Saqr
1965–72	Khaled
1972–87	Sultan
1987	Abdel-Aziz
1987–	Sultan

Umm al-Qaiwain

Tribe: al-Ali
Family name: al-Mualla

Sheikh

1873–1904	Ahmad
1904–22	Rashid
1922–3	Abdullah
1923–9	Hamad
1929–81	Ahmad
1981–	Rashid

UNITED KINGDOM

Official name	United Kingdom of Great Britain and Northern Ireland (UK)
Local name	United Kingdom
Area[1]	242 495 sq km/93 627 sq mi
Capital	London
Chief towns	Birmingham, Leeds, Glasgow, Sheffield, Bradford, Edinburgh, Liverpool, Manchester, Cardiff, Belfast, Newcastle upon Tyne
Population	60 776 000 (2007e)
Nationality	British
Languages	English; Welsh and Gaelic are also spoken
Ethnic groups	white 92%, Asian or Asian British[2] 4%, Black or Black British[3] 2%, mixed 1.2%, Chinese 0.4%, others 0.4%
Religions	Christianity[4] 71.6%, Islam 2.7%, Hinduism 1%, Sikhism 0.6%, Judaism 0.5%, Buddhism 0.3%, others 0.3%, unknown 7.3%, none/unaffiliated 15.5%
Time zone	GMT
Currency	1 Pound Sterling (£/GBP) = 100 pence
Telephone	+44
Internet	.uk
Country code	GBR

Location

An island kingdom in western Europe, comprising England, Scotland, Wales and Northern Ireland; separated from France to the south by the English Channel, and from Ireland to the west by the Irish Sea; Northern Ireland borders Ireland to the south.

Climate

Temperate maritime climate, moderated by prevailing south-west winds; generally wetter and warmer in the west.

[1] *Data source: Office for National Statistics*
[2] *Includes Indian, Pakistani, Bangladeshi and other*
[3] *Includes Black African, Black Caribbean and other*
[4] *2001 Census data; did not distinguish different Christian denominations*

Political leaders

House of Stuart

Monarch

1603–25 James I (VI of Scotland)
1625–49 Charles I

Commonwealth and Protectorate

Monarch

1649–53 *Council of State*
1653–8 Oliver Cromwell *Lord Protector*
1658–9 Richard Cromwell *Lord Protector*

House of Stuart (restored)

Monarch

1660–85 Charles II
1685–8 James II
1689–94 Mary II and William III (*jointly*)
1694–1702 William III (*alone*)
1702–14 Anne

House of Hanover

Monarch

1714–27 George I
1727–60 George II
1760–1820 George III
1820–30 George IV
1830–7 William IV
1837–1901 Victoria

House of Saxe-Coburg

Monarch

1901–10	Edward VII

House of Windsor

Monarch

1910–36	George V
1936	Edward VIII
1936–52	George VI
1952–	Elizabeth II

Prime Minister

1721–42	Robert Walpole *Whig*
1742–3	Earl of Wilmington (Spencer Compton) *Whig*
1743–54	Henry Pelham *Whig*
1754–6	Duke of Newcastle (Thomas Pelham-Holles) *Whig*
1756–7	Duke of Devonshire (William Cavendish) *Whig*
1757–62	Duke of Newcastle *Whig*
1762–3	Earl of Bute (John Stuart) *Tory*
1763–5	George Grenville *Whig*
1765–6	Marquess of Rockingham (Charles Watson Wentworth) *Whig*
1766–70	Duke of Grafton (Augustus Henry Fitzroy) *Whig*
1770–82	Lord North (Frederick North) *Tory*
1782	Marquess of Rockingham *Whig*
1782–3	Earl of Shelburne (William Petty-Fitzmaurice) *Whig*
1783	Duke of Portland (William Henry Cavendish Bentinck) *Coal*
1783–1801	William Pitt *Tory*
1801–4	Henry Addington *Tory*
1804–6	William Pitt *Tory*
1806–7	Lord Grenville (William Wyndham) *Whig*
1807–9	Duke of Portland (William Henry Cavendish Bentinck) *Tory*
1809–12	Spencer Perceval *Tory*
1812–27	Earl of Liverpool (Robert Banks Jenkinson) *Tory*
1827	George Canning *Tory*
1827–8	Viscount Goderich (Frederick John Robinson) *Tory*
1828–30	Duke of Wellington (Arthur Wellesley) *Tory*
1830–4	Earl Grey (Charles Grey) *Whig*
1834	Viscount Melbourne (William Lamb) *Whig*
1834–5	Robert Peel *Con*
1835–41	Viscount Melbourne *Whig*
1841–6	Robert Peel *Con*
1846–52	Lord John Russell *Lib*
1852	Earl of Derby (Edward George Smith Stanley) *Con*
1852–5	Lord Aberdeen (George Hamilton-Gordon) *Peelite*
1855–8	Viscount Palmerston (Henry John Temple) *Lib*
1858–9	Earl of Derby *Con*
1859–65	Viscount Palmerston *Lib*
1865–6	Lord John Russell *Lib*
1866–8	Earl of Derby *Con*
1868	Benjamin Disraeli *Con*
1868–74	William Ewart Gladstone *Lib*
1874–80	Benjamin Disraeli *Con*
1880–5	William Ewart Gladstone *Lib*
1885–6	Marquess of Salisbury (Robert Gascoyne-Cecil) *Con*
1886	William Ewart Gladstone *Lib*
1886–92	Marquess of Salisbury *Con*
1892–4	William Ewart Gladstone *Lib*
1894–5	Earl of Rosebery (Archibald Philip Primrose) *Lib*
1895–1902	Marquess of Salisbury *Con*
1902–5	Arthur James Balfour *Con*
1905–8	Henry Campbell-Bannerman *Lib*
1908–15	Herbert Henry Asquith *Lib*
1915–16	Herbert Henry Asquith *Coal*
1916–22	David Lloyd George *Coal*
1922–3	Andrew Bonar Law *Con*
1923–4	Stanley Baldwin *Con*
1924	James Ramsay MacDonald *Lab*
1924–9	Stanley Baldwin *Con*
1929–31	James Ramsay MacDonald *Lab*
1931–5	James Ramsay MacDonald *Nat*
1935–7	Stanley Baldwin *Nat*
1937–40	Arthur Neville Chamberlain *Nat*
1940–5	Winston Churchill *Coal*
1945–51	Clement Attlee *Lab*
1951–5	Winston Churchill *Con*
1955–7	Anthony Eden *Con*
1957–63	Harold Macmillan *Con*
1963–4	Alec Douglas-Home *Con*
1964–70	Harold Wilson *Lab*

1970–4	Edward Heath *Con*
1974–6	Harold Wilson *Lab*
1976–9	James Callaghan *Lab*
1979–90	Margaret Thatcher *Con*
1990–7	John Major *Con*
1997–2007	Tony Blair *Lab*
2007–	Gordon Brown *Lab*

Coal = Coalition   Lib = Liberal   Lab = Labour   Con = Conservative   Nat = Nationalist

England

Area[1]	130 279 sq km/50 301 sq mi
Capital	London
Chief towns	Birmingham, Bradford, Liverpool, Leeds, Manchester, Newcastle, Sheffield
Population	50 432 000 (2005e)
Nationality	English
Physical description	Largely undulating lowland, rising in the south to the Mendips, Cotswolds, Chilterns and North Downs, in the north to the north–south ridge of the Pennines and in the north-west to the Cumbria Mountains; drained in the east by the Tyne, Tees, Humber, Ouse and Thames rivers, and in the west by the Eden, Ribble, Mersey and Severn rivers; Lake District in the north-west includes Derwent Water, Ullswater, Windermere and Bassenthwaite; highest point is Scafell Pike at 978m/3 209ft.
National holidays	Jan 1, Dec 25, 26; EM, GF, May Day (1st Mon), Spring (last Mon in May) and Summer (last Mon in Aug) Bank Holidays.

[1] *Data source: Office for National Statistics*

West Saxon Kings

Monarch	
802–39	Egbert
839–58	Æthelwulf
858–60	Æthelbald
860–5	Æthelbert
866–71	Æthelred
871–99	Alfred
899–924	Edward (the Elder)
924–39	Athelstan
939–46	Edmund
946–55	Edred
955–9	Edwy
959–75	Edgar
975–8	Edward (the Martyr)
978–1016	Æthelred (the Unready)
1016	Edmund (Ironside)

Danish Kings

Monarch	
1016–35	Knut (Canute)
1035–7	Harold Regent
1037–40	Harold I (Harefoot)
1040–2	Hardaknut
1042–66	Edward (the Confessor)
1066	Harold II

House of Normandy

Monarch	
1066–87	William I (the Conqueror)
1087–1100	William II (Rufus)
1100–35	Henry I

House of Blois

Monarch	
1135–54	Stephen

House of Plantagenet

Monarch	
1154–89	Henry II
1189–99	Richard I (the Lionheart)
1199–1216	John
1216–72	Henry III
1272–1307	Edward I
1307–27	Edward II
1327–77	Edward III
1377–99	Richard II

House of Lancaster

Monarch	
1399–1413	Henry IV
1413–22	Henry V
1422–61	Henry VI

House of York

Monarch	
1461–70	Edward IV

House of Lancaster

Monarch	
1470–1	Henry VI

House of York

Monarch	
1471–83	Edward IV
1483	Edward V
1483–5	Richard III

House of Tudor

Monarch	
1485–1509	Henry VII
1509–47	Henry VIII
1547–53	Edward VI
1553–8	Mary I
1558–1603	Elizabeth I

Divorced, Beheaded, Died

King Henry VIII (1491–1547) is famous for his six wives who, as the schoolchildren's rhyme goes, were sequentially divorced, beheaded, died, divorced, beheaded and survived:

Catherine of Aragon (1485–1536) First married to Henry's brother Arthur, she was betrothed following his early death to her brother-in-law, Henry, who was then aged just 11. She married him in 1509. In 1527 Henry began a procedure for divorce, which he obtained in 1533. Catherine retired to lead an austere religious life until her death.

Anne Boleyn (c.1504–36) Secretly married to Henry in 1533, she was soon declared his legal wife but within months his passion for her had cooled. It was not revived by the birth of a daughter (later Elizabeth I), still less by that of a stillborn son. She was arrested and brought to the Tower, convicted of treason on flimsy evidence and beheaded in 1536.

Jane Seymour (c.1509–37) A lady-in-waiting to Henry's first two wives, she married him 11 days after the execution of Anne Boleyn. She died soon after the birth of her son, the future Edward VI.

Anne of Cleves (1515–57) A Lutheran princess who became Henry's fourth queen in 1540, as part of a strategy to develop an alliance with German Protestant rulers. The marriage was declared null and void on grounds of non-consummation six months afterwards. On agreeing to the divorce, Anne was given a large income and she remained in England until her death.

Catherine Howard (c.1520–42) Became Queen in the same month as Anne of Cleves was divorced (Jul 1540). A year later she was charged with having had an affair before her marriage with a musician and a relation, and she was beheaded for treason.

Catherine Parr (1512–48) Married Henry in 1543. A learned and tactful woman, she persuaded Henry to restore the succession to his daughters, and showed them much kindness. Soon after Henry's death in 1547 she married a former suitor and died in childbirth the following year.

Northern Ireland

Area[1]	13576 sq km/5242 sq mi
Capital	Belfast
Chief towns	Armagh, Londonderry
Population	1724000 (2005e)
Nationality	Northern Irish
Physical description	Northern Ireland occupies the north-eastern part of Ireland, and is centred on Lough Neagh; to the north and east are the Antrim Mountains; Mourne Mountains are in the south-east; highest point is Slieve Donard at 852m/2795ft.
National holidays	Jan 1, Mar 17 (St Patrick), Jul 12 (Battle of the Boyne/Orangemen), Dec 25, 26; EM, GF; May Day (1st Mon), Spring (last Mon in May), and Summer (last Mon in Aug) Bank Holidays.

[1] *Data source: Office for National Statistics*

Political leaders

Devolved power was transferred to the Northern Ireland Assembly in Dec 1999. Devolution was suspended Feb–May 2000, Aug 2001, Sep 2001 and from Oct 2002–May 2007.

First Minister

1999–2001	David Trimble *(First Minister designate from 1998)*
2001	Reg Empey *Acting*
2001–2	David Trimble
2002–7	*Direct rule by UK government*
2007–	Ian Paisley

Scotland

Area[1]	77907 sq km/30080 sq mi
Capital	Edinburgh
Chief towns	Aberdeen, Dundee, Glasgow, Inverness, Perth
Population	5095000 (2005e)
Nationality	Scottish
Physical description	Divided into the Southern Uplands (rising to 843m/2766ft at Merrick), the Central Lowlands (the most densely populated area) and the Northern Highlands (divided by the fault line following the Great Glen); highest point is Ben Nevis (1343m/4406ft); 787 islands, most of which lie off the heavily-indented west coast and only approximately 60 exceed 8 sq km/3 sq mi; several wide estuaries on the east coast, primarily the firths of Forth, Tay and Moray; interior has many freshwater lochs, the largest being Loch Lomond (70 sq km/27 sq mi) and the deepest Loch Morar (310m/1017ft); longest river is the River Tay (192km/119mi).
National holidays	Jan 1, 2, Nov 30 (St Andrew), Dec 25, 26; GF, May Day (1st Mon), Spring (last Mon in May) and Summer (1st Mon in Aug) Bank Holidays; *local holidays may also be observed, in addition to or instead of the statutory days, and there is no automatic entitlement to time off on these days.*

[1] *Data source: Office for National Statistics*

Monarch

1005–34	Malcolm II
1034–40	Duncan I
1040–57	Macbeth
1057–8	Lulach
1058–93	Malcolm III
1093–4	Donald Bane
1094	Duncan II
1094–7	Donald Bane
1097–1107	Edgar

1107–24	Alexander I	1329–71	David II
1124–53	David I	1371–90	Robert II
1153–65	Malcolm IV	1390–1406	Robert III
1165–1214	William I	1406–37	James I
1214–49	Alexander II	1437–60	James II
1249–86	Alexander III	1460–88	James III
1286–90	Margaret	1488–1513	James IV
1290–2	*Interregnum*	1513–42	James V
1292–96	John Balliol	1542–67	Mary Queen of Scots
1296–1306	*Interregnum*	1567–1625	James VI[1]
1306–29	Robert I (the Bruce)		

[1] *In 1603, James VI succeeded Elizabeth I to the English throne and united the thrones of Scotland and England (Union of the Crowns).*

Political leaders

The Scottish parliament was officially opened on 1 Jul 1999.

First Minister

1999–2000	Donald Dewar	2001	Jim Wallace *Acting*
2000	Jim Wallace *Acting*	2001–7	Jack McConnell
2000–1	Henry McLeish	2007–	Alex Salmond

Wales

Area[1]	20733 sq km/8005 sq mi
Capital	Cardiff
Chief towns	Swansea, Wrexham
Population	2959000 (2005e)
Nationality	Welsh
Physical description	Rises in the north-west to 1085m/3560ft at Snowdon in the Snowdonia range (the highest point); the Cambrian Mountains rise in the centre, and the Brecon Beacons in the south; drained by the Severn, Clwyd, Conwy, Dee, Dovey, Taff, Tawe, Teifi, Towy, Usk and Wye rivers.
National holidays	Jan 1, Dec 25, 26; EM, GF, May Day (1st Mon), Spring (last Mon in May) and Summer (last Mon in Aug) Bank Holidays.

[1] *Data source: Office for National Statistics*

Political leaders

The opening session of the Welsh Assembly was held in June 1999. The post of First Minister was called First Secretary until Oct 2000.

First Minister

1999–2000	Alun Michael
2000–	Rhodri Morgan

British islands[1]

Channel Islands

Location	An island group of the British Isles in the English Channel, west of the Cotentin Peninsula of Normandy. A dependent territory of the British Crown, it has individual legislative assemblies and legal system and is divided into the Bailiwicks of Jersey and of Guernsey. Main islands: Guernsey, Jersey, Alderney, Sark; other islands include Herm, Jethou, Brechou, the Caskets, the Minquiers and the Chauseys.		
Area	194 sq km/75 sq mi	**Language**	Both English and Norman-French are spoken
Capital	St Helier (Jersey); St Peter Port (Guernsey)	**Internet**	.gg (Guernsey), .je (Jersey)
Population	159 000 (2006e)	**Country code**	GGY (Guernsey), JEY (Jersey)

Isle of Man

Location	A British Crown Dependency in the Irish Sea, west of England and east of Northern Ireland.		
Area	572 sq km/221 sq mi	**Languages**	English; Manx is also spoken
Capital	Douglas		
Population	76 000 (2007e)	**Internet**	.im
Nationality	Manx	**Country code**	IMN

[1]*Part of the British Isles but not included in the United Kingdom.*

UK dependent territories

Anguilla

Location	The most northerly of the Leeward Islands, in the east Caribbean Sea.		
Area	90 sq km/35 sq mi	**Nationality**	Anguillan
Capital	The Valley	**Internet**	.ai
Population	14 000 (2007e)	**Country code**	AIA

Bermuda

Location	A group of approximately 150 low-lying, coral islands and islets situated in the west Atlantic Ocean approximately 900km/560mi east of Cape Hatteras, North Carolina (USA).		
Area	53 sq km/20 sq mi	**Nationality**	Bermudian
Capital	Hamilton	**Internet**	.bm
Population	66 000 (2007e)	**Country code**	BMU

Bermuda Triangle

The *Bermuda Triangle* is an area in the Atlantic Ocean off the south-eastern USA where ships and aeroplanes have mysteriously disappeared. The points of the triangle are thought to be the city of Miami in Florida, the island of Bermuda and the city of San Juan, Puerto Rico. The US Coast Guard reports rather sniffily that it 'is not impressed with supernatural explanations of disasters at sea'. It suggests that unpredictable weather, dangerous currents and seabed hazards are the more likely culprits. However, it does point out that the Bermuda Triangle area is one of only two places on Earth where a compass needle points to true north, rather than magnetic north. Inexperienced navigators who forget this may end up lost and miles off course.

British Antarctic Territory

Location	Includes the South Orkney Islands, the South Shetland Islands, the Antarctic Graham Land Peninsula, and the land mass extending to the South Pole.
Area	1709400 sq km/666000 sq mi
Population	Populated solely by scientists of the British Antarctic Survey.

British Indian Ocean Territory

Location	Consists of 2300 islands in the Chagos Archipelago in the Indian Ocean, 1900km/1180mi north-east of Mauritius; the largest island is Diego Garcia.		
Area	60 sq km/23 sq mi	**Internet**	.io
Population	Indigenous population relocated; military personnel and civilian support staff only.	**Country code**	IOT

British Virgin Islands

Location	An island group at the north-western end of the Lesser Antilles chain in the east Caribbean Sea.		
Area	153 sq km/59 sq mi	**Nationality**	British Virgin Islander
Capital	Road Town	**Internet**	.vg
Population	23000 (2007e)	**Country code**	VGB

Cayman Islands

Location	An island group in the west Caribbean Sea, comprising the islands of Grand Cayman, Cayman Brac and Little Cayman, approximately 240km/150mi south of Cuba.		
Area	260 sq km/100 sq mi	**Nationality**	Caymanian
Capital	George Town	**Internet**	.ky
Population	47000 (2007e)	**Country code**	CYM

Falkland Islands

Location	Situated in the South Atlantic Ocean, approximately 650km/400mi north-east of the Magellan Strait. Also known as the Malvinas.		
Area	12200 sq km/4700 sq mi	**Nationality**	Falkland Islander
Capital	Stanley	**Internet**	.fk
Population	3000 (2006e)	**Country code**	FLK

Gibraltar

Location	The narrow peninsula rising steeply from the low-lying coast of south-west Spain at the eastern end of the Strait of Gibraltar, which is an important strategic point of control for the western Mediterranean.		
Area	6.5 sq km/2.5 sq mi	**Nationality**	Gibraltarian
Capital	Gibraltar	**Internet**	.gi
Population	29000 (2006e)	**Country code**	GIB

Montserrat

Location	A volcanic island in the Leeward Islands, Lesser Antilles, in the east Caribbean Sea.		
Area	102 sq km/39 sq mi	**Population**	9000 (2007e) *Note: The population dropped from 10639 in 1991 to approximately 4000 as a result of an exodus after volcanic activity resumed in 1995, but some refugees have now returned.*
Capital	Brades *Note: The original capital, Plymouth, lies within the Exclusion Zone – an area into which entry is prohibited after a devastating volcanic eruption from the Soufrière Hills volcano in 1997 made it uninhabitable.*	**Nationality**	Montserratian
		Internet	.ms
		Country code	MSR

Pitcairn Islands

Location	An island group in the south-east Pacific Ocean, east of French Polynesia, comprising Pitcairn Island and the uninhabited islands of Ducie, Henderson and Oeno.		
Area	4.5 sq km/2 sq mi	**Nationality**	Pitcairn Islander
Capital	Adamstown	**Internet**	.pn
Population	48 (2007e)	**Country code**	PCN

St Helena and Dependencies[1]

Location	A volcanic island in the South Atlantic Ocean, lying 1920km/1200mi from the south-west coast of Africa.		
Area	310 sq km/120 sq mi	**Population**	7000 (2007e)
Capital	Jamestown (St Helena); Georgetown (Ascension); Edinburgh of the Seven Seas (Tristan da Cunha)	**Nationality**	St Helenian
		Internet	.sh
		Country code	SHN

[1] *The territories of Ascension (area: 90 sq km/35 sq mi) and Tristan da Cunha (area: 98 sq km/38 sq mi).*

South Georgia and the South Sandwich Islands

Location	South Georgia is a barren, mountainous snow-covered uninhabited island in the South Atlantic Ocean, about 500km/300mi east of the Falkland Islands. The South Sandwich Islands are a group of small, uninhabited islands in the South Atlantic Ocean, lying approximately 720km/450mi south-east of South Georgia.
Area	approximately 3750 sq km/1450 sq mi (S Georgia); 1152 sq km/445 sq mi (S Sandwich Is)
Internet	.gs

Turks and Caicos Islands

Location	A pair of island groups which form the south-eastern part of the Bahamas archipelago; they lie 920km/570mi south-east of Miami (USA).		
Area	430 sq km/166 sq mi	**Population**	22000 (2007e)
Capital	Grand Turk (Cockburn Town)	**Internet**	.tc
		Country code	TCA

UNITED STATES OF AMERICA

Official name	United States of America (USA)
Local name	United States of America; United States; US
Independence	1776
Area	9160454 sq km/3535935 sq mi
Capital	Washington, DC (District of Columbia)
Chief towns	New York City, Los Angeles, Chicago, Houston, Philadelphia, Phoenix, San Diego, Dallas, San Antonio, Detroit
Population	301140000 (2007e)
Nationality	American
Languages	English; there is a sizeable Spanish-speaking minority
Ethnic groups	white (including Hispanic) 82%, black 13%, Asian 4%, Amerindian, Alaskan native, native Hawaiian or Pacific islander 1%
Religions	Christianity 76%, Mormon 2%, Islam 1%, Judaism 1%, others 10%, none 10%
Time zone	GMT –5/10
Currency	1 US Dollar ($, US$/USD) = 100 cents
Telephone	+1
Internet	.us
Country code	USA

Location

A republic in North America, bounded to the north by Canada; to the east by the northern Atlantic Ocean; to the south by Mexico and the Gulf of Mexico; and to the west by the Pacific Ocean.

Physical description

Fourth-largest country in the world; East Atlantic coastal plain is backed by the Appalachian Mountains from the Great Lakes in the north to Alabama in the south; this series of parallel ranges includes the Allegheny, Blue Ridge and Catskill mountains; to the south the plain broadens out towards the Gulf of Mexico and into the Florida Peninsula; to the west, the Gulf Plains stretch north to meet the higher Great Plains from which they are separated by the Ozark Mountains; further west, the Rocky Mountains rise to over 4500m/14760ft; highest point is Mt McKinley, Alaska, at 6194m/20322ft; lowest point is in Death Valley (–86m/–282ft); major rivers include the Hudson, Delaware, Potomac, Columbia, Colorado and the great Red River–Missouri–Mississippi River System.

Climate

Varies from conditions in hot tropical deserts (in the south-west) to those typical of Arctic continental regions; most regions are affected by westerly depressions that can bring changeable weather; rainfall is heaviest in the Pacific north-west, lightest in the south-west; in the Great Plains, wide temperature variation is the result of cold air from the Arctic as well as warm tropical air from the Gulf of Mexico; on the west coast the influence of the Pacific Ocean results in a smaller range of temperatures between summer and winter; on the east coast there is a gradual increase in winter temperatures southwards; the states bordering the Gulf of Mexico are subject to hurricanes and tornadoes moving north-east from the Caribbean Sea.

National holidays

Jan 1, Jul 4 (Independence), Nov 11 (Veterans), Dec 25; Martin Luther King's Birthday (3rd Mon in Jan), Presidents' Day (3rd Mon in Feb), Memorial (last Mon in May), Labor (1st Mon in Sep), Columbus (2nd Mon in Oct), Thanksgiving (4th Thurs in Nov); *federal organizations; each state determines its own holidays, although federal holidays are widely observed*.

States of the USA

State (abbrev.; ZIP)	**Entry to Union**	**Population** (2006e)	**Area**	**Capital**	**Inhabitant**	**Nickname**
Alabama (Ala; AL)	1819 (22nd)	4599030	131443 sq km/50750 sq mi	Montgomery	Alabamian	Camellia State, Heart of Dixie
Alaska (Alaska; AK)	1959 (49th)	670053	1477268 sq km/570373 sq mi	Juneau	Alaskan	Mainland State, The Last Frontier
Arizona (Ariz; AZ)	1912 (48th)	6166318	295276 sq km/114006 sq mi	Phoenix	Arizonan	Apache State, Grand Canyon State
Arkansas (Ark; AR)	1836 (25th)	2810872	137754 sq km/53187 sq mi	Little Rock	Arkansan	Bear State, Land of Opportunity
California (Calif; CA)	1850 (31st)	36457549	403971 sq km/155973 sq mi	Sacramento	Californian	Golden State
Colorado (Colo; CO)	1876 (38th)	4753377	268658 sq km/103729 sq mi	Denver	Coloradan	Centennial State
Connecticut (Conn; CT)	1788 (5th)	3504809	12547 sq km/4844 sq mi	Hartford	Nutmegger	Nutmeg State, Constitution State
Delaware (Del; DE)	1787 (1st)	853476	5133 sq km/1985 sq mi	Dover	Delawarean	Diamond State, First State
District of Columbia (DC; DC)	*Established* 1791	581530	159 sq km/61 sq mi	Washington	Washingtonian	—
Florida (Fla; FL)	1845 (27th)	18089888	139697 sq km/53937 sq mi	Tallahassee	Floridian	Everglade State, Sunshine State
Georgia (Ga; GA)	1788 (4th)	9363941	152571 sq km/58908 sq mi	Atlanta	Georgian	Empire State of the South, Peach State
Hawaii (Hawaii; HI)	1959 (50th)	1285498	16636 sq km/6423 sq mi	Honolulu	Hawaiian	Aloha State
Idaho (Idaho; ID)	1890 (43rd)	1466465	214325 sq km/82751 sq mi	Boise	Idahoan	Gem State
Illinois (Ill; IL)	1818 (21st)	12831970	144123 sq km/55646 sq mi	Springfield	Illinoisan	Prairie State, Land of Lincoln
Indiana (Ind; IN)	1816 (19th)	6313520	92903 sq km/35870 sq mi	Indianapolis	Hoosier	Hoosier State
Iowa (Iowa; IA)	1846 (29th)	2982085	144716 sq km/55875 sq mi	Des Moines	Iowan	Hawkeye State, Corn State
Kansas (Kans; KS)	1861 (34th)	2764075	211922 sq km/81823 sq mi	Topeka	Kansan	Sunflower State, Jayhawker State
Kentucky (Ky; KY)	1792 (15th)	4206074	102907 sq km/39732 sq mi	Frankfort	Kentuckian	Bluegrass State
Louisiana (La; LA)	1812 (18th)	4287768	112836 sq km/43566 sq mi	Baton Rouge	Louisianian	Pelican State, Sugar State, Creole State

State (abbrev.; ZIP)	Entry to Union	Population (2006e)	Area	Capital	Inhabitant	Nickname
Maine (Maine; ME)	1820 (23rd)	1321574	79931 sq km/30861 sq mi	Augusta	Downeaster	Pine Tree State
Maryland (Md; MD)	1788 (7th)	5615727	25316 sq km/9775 sq mi	Annapolis	Marylander	Old Line State, Free State
Massachusetts (Mass; MA)	1788 (6th)	6437193	20300 sq km/7838 sq mi	Boston	Bay Stater	Bay State, Old Colony
Michigan (Mich; MI)	1837 (26th)	10095643	150544 sq km/58125 sq mi	Lansing	Michigander	Wolverine State, Great Lake State
Minnesota (Minn; MN)	1858 (32nd)	5167101	206207 sq km/79617 sq mi	St Paul	Minnesotan	Gopher State, North Star State
Mississippi (Miss; MS)	1817 (20th)	2910540	123510 sq km/47687 sq mi	Jackson	Mississippian	Magnolia State
Missouri (Mo; MO)	1821 (24th)	5842713	178446 sq km/68898 sq mi	Jefferson City	Missourian	Bullion State, Show Me State
Montana (Mont; MT)	1889 (41st)	944632	376991 sq km/145556 sq mi	Helena	Montanan	Treasure State, Big Sky Country
Nebraska (Nebr; NE)	1867 (37th)	1768331	199113 sq km/76878 sq mi	Lincoln	Nebraskan	Cornhusker State, Beef State
Nevada (Nev; NV)	1864 (36th)	2495529	273349 sq km/105540 sq mi	Carson City	Nevadan	Silver State, Sagebrush State
New Hampshire (NH; NH)	1788 (9th)	1314895	23292 sq km/8993 sq mi	Concord	New Hampshirite	Granite State
New Jersey (NJ; NJ)	1787 (3rd)	8724560	19210 sq km/7417 sq mi	Trenton	New Jerseyite	Garden State
New Mexico (N Mex; NM)	1912 (47th)	1954599	314334 sq km/121364 sq mi	Santa Fe	New Mexican	Sunshine State, Land of Enchantment
New York (NY; NY)	1788 (11th)	19306183	122310 sq km/47224 sq mi	Albany	New Yorker	Empire State
North Carolina (NC; NC)	1789 (12th)	8856505	126180 sq km/48718 sq mi	Raleigh	North Carolinian	Old North State, Tar Heel State
North Dakota (N Dak; ND)	1889 (39th)	635867	178695 sq km/68994 sq mi	Bismarck	North Dakotan	Flickertail State, Sioux State, Peace Garden State
Ohio (Ohio; OH)	1803 (17th)	11478006	106067 sq km/40952 sq mi	Columbus	Ohioan	Buckeye State
Oklahoma (Okla; OK)	1907 (46th)	3579212	177877 sq km/68678 sq mi	Oklahoma City	Oklahoman	Sooner State
Oregon (Oreg; OR)	1859 (33rd)	3700758	251385 sq km/97060 sq mi	Salem	Oregonian	Sunset State, Beaver State
Pennsylvania (Pa; PA)	1787 (2nd)	12440621	116083 sq km/44820 sq mi	Harrisburg	Pennsylvanian	Keystone State

State (abbrev.; ZIP)	**Entry to Union**	**Population (2006e)**	**Area**	**Capital**	**Inhabitant**	**Nickname**
Rhode Island (RI; RI)	1790 (13th)	1 067 610	2 707 sq km/1 045 sq mi	Providence	Rhode Islander	Little Rhody, Plantation State
South Carolina (SC; SC)	1788 (8th)	4 321 249	77 988 sq km/30 111 sq mi	Columbia	South Carolinian	Palmetto State
South Dakota (S Dak; SD)	1889 (40th)	781 919	196 576 sq km/75 898 sq mi	Pierre	South Dakotan	Sunshine State, Coyote State
Tennessee (Tenn; TN)	1796 (16th)	6 038 803	106 759 sq km/41 220 sq mi	Nashville	Tennessean	Volunteer State
Texas (Tex; TX)	1845 (28th)	23 507 783	678 358 sq km/261 914 sq mi	Austin	Texan	Lone Star State
Utah (Utah; UT)	1896 (45th)	2 550 063	212 816 sq km/82 168 sq mi	Salt Lake City	Utahn	Mormon State, Beehive State
Vermont (Vt; VT)	1791 (14th)	623 908	23 955 sq km/9 249 sq mi	Montpelier	Vermonter	Green Mountain State
Virginia (Va; VA)	1788 (10th)	7 642 884	102 558 sq km/39 598 sq mi	Richmond	Virginian	Old Dominion State, Mother of Presidents
Washington (Wash; WA)	1889 (42nd)	6 395 798	172 447 sq km/66 582 sq mi	Olympia	Washingtonian	Evergreen State, Chinook State
West Virginia (W Va; WV)	1863 (35th)	1 818 470	62 758 sq km/24 231 sq mi	Charleston	West Virginian	Panhandle State, Mountain State
Wisconsin (Wis; WI)	1848 (30th)	5 556 506	145 431 sq km/56 151 sq mi	Madison	Wisconsinite	Badger State, America's Dairyland
Wyoming (Wyo; WY)	1890 (44th)	515 004	251 501 sq km/97 105 sq mi	Cheyenne	Wyomingite	Equality State

US non-self-governing territories

American Samoa (AS)

Location	A group of islands in the South Pacific Ocean, some 3500km/2175mi north-east of New Zealand.		
Area	199 sq km/77 sq mi	**Nationality**	American Samoan
Capital	Pago Pago	**Internet**	.as
Population	58000 (2007e)	**Country code**	ASM

Guam

Location	The largest and southernmost island of the Mariana Islands, west Pacific Ocean.		
Area	541 sq km/209 sq mi	**Nationality**	Guamanian
Capital	Hagatna (Agaña)	**Internet**	.gu
Population	173000 (2007e)	**Country code**	GUM

Northern Mariana Islands

Location	A group of 14 islands in the north-west Pacific Ocean, approximately 2400km/1500mi to the east of the Philippines.		
Area	477 sq km/184 sq mi	**Internet**	.mp
Capital	Saipan	**Country code**	MNP
Population	84000 (2007e)		

US Virgin Islands

Location	A group of more than 50 islands in the south and west of the Virgin Islands group, Lesser Antilles, Caribbean Sea, 64km/40mi east of Puerto Rico (USA). There are three main islands: St Croix, St Thomas and St John.		
Area	342 sq km/132 sq mi	**Nationality**	Virgin Islander
Capital	Charlotte Amalie	**Internet**	.vi
Population	108000 (2007e)	**Country code**	VIR

US associated commonwealth

Puerto Rico

Location	The easternmost island of the Greater Antilles, situated between the Dominican Republic in the west and the US Virgin Islands in the east, approximately 1600km/1000mi south-east of Miami (USA).		
Area	8870 sq km/3424 sq mi	**Nationality**	Puerto Rican, American
Capital	San Juan	**Internet**	.pr
Population	3944000 (2007e)	**Country code**	PRI

Note: The USA also possesses Baker Island, Howland Island, Johnston Atoll, Kingman Reef, Midway Island, Palmyra Atoll and Wake Island in the North Pacific Ocean, Jarvis Island in the South Pacific Ocean and Navassa Island in the Caribbean Sea, all largely uninhabited.

Political leaders

President *(Vice President in parentheses)*

1789–97	George Washington (1st) (John Adams)
1797–1801	John Adams (2nd) *Fed* (Thomas Jefferson)
1801–9	Thomas Jefferson (3rd) *Dem-Rep* (Aaron Burr, 1801–5) (George Clinton, 1805–9)
1809–17	James Madison (4th) *Dem-Rep* (George Clinton, 1809–12) *no Vice President* 1812–13 (Elbridge Gerry, 1813–14) *no Vice President* 1814–17
1817–25	James Monroe (5th) *Dem-Rep* (Daniel D Tompkins)
1825–9	John Quincy Adams (6th) *Dem-Rep* (John C Calhoun)
1829–37	Andrew Jackson (7th) *Dem* (John C Calhoun, 1829–32) *no Vice President* 1832–3 (Martin van Buren, 1833–7)
1837–41	Martin van Buren (8th) *Dem* (Richard M Johnson)
1841	William Henry Harrison (9th) *Whig* (John Tyler)
1841–5	John Tyler (10th) *Whig no Vice President*
1845–9	James Knox Polk (11th) *Dem* (George M Dallas)
1849–50	Zachary Taylor (12th) *Whig* (Millard Fillmore)
1850–3	Millard Fillmore (13th) *Whig no Vice President*
1853–7	Franklin Pierce (14th) *Dem* (William R King, 1853) *no Vice President* 1853–7
1857–61	James Buchanan (15th) *Dem* (John C Breckinridge)
1861–5	Abraham Lincoln (16th) *Rep* (Hannibal Hamlin, 1861–5) (Andrew Johnson, 1865)
1865–9	Andrew Johnson (17th) *Dem-Nat no Vice President*
1869–77	Ulysses Simpson Grant (18th) *Rep* (Schuyler Colfax, 1869–73) (Henry Wilson, 1873–5) *no Vice President* 1875–7
1877–81	Rutherford Birchard Hayes (19th) *Rep* (William A Wheeler)
1881	James Abram Garfield (20th) *Rep* (Chester A Arthur)
1881–5	Chester Alan Arthur (21st) *Rep no Vice President*
1885–9	Grover Cleveland (22nd) *Dem* (Thomas A Hendricks, 1885) *no Vice President* 1885–9
1889–93	Benjamin Harrison (23rd) *Rep* (Levi P Morton)
1893–7	Grover Cleveland (24th) *Dem* (Adlai E Stevenson)
1897–1901	William McKinley (25th) *Rep* (Garrat A Hobart, 1897–9) *no Vice President* 1899–1901 (Theodore Roosevelt, 1901)
1901–9	Theodore Roosevelt (26th) *Rep no Vice President* 1901–5 (Charles W Fairbanks, 1905–9)
1909–13	William Howard Taft (27th) *Rep* (James S Sherman, 1909–12) *no Vice President* 1912–13
1913–21	Woodrow Wilson (28th) *Dem* (Thomas R Marshall)
1921–3	Warren Gamaliel Harding (29th) *Rep* (Calvin Coolidge)
1923–9	Calvin Coolidge (30th) *Rep no Vice President* 1923–5 (Charles G Dawes,1925–9)
1929–33	Herbert Clark Hoover (31st) *Rep* (Charles Curtis)
1933–45	Franklin Delano Roosevelt (32nd) *Dem* (John N Garner, 1933–41) (Henry A Wallace, 1941–5) (Harry S Truman, 1945)
1945–53	Harry S Truman (33rd) *Dem no Vice President* 1945-9 (Alben W Barkley, 1949–53)
1953–61	Dwight David Eisenhower (34th) *Rep* (Richard M Nixon)
1961–3	John Fitzgerald Kennedy (35th) *Dem* (Lyndon B Johnson)
1963–9	Lyndon Baines Johnson (36th) *Dem no Vice President* 1963–5 (Hubert H Humphrey, 1965–9)
1969–74	Richard Milhous Nixon (37th) *Rep* (Spiro T Agnew, 1969–73) *no Vice President* 1973,Oct–Dec (Gerald R Ford,1973–4)
1974–7	Gerald Rudolph Ford (38th) *Rep no Vice President* 1974, Aug–Dec (Nelson A Rockefeller, 1974–7)
1977–81	Jimmy Carter (39th) *Dem* (Walter F Mondale)
1981–9	Ronald Wilson Reagan (40th) *Rep* (George H W Bush)

1989–93	George Herbert Walker Bush (41st) *Rep* (J Danforth Quayle)	2001–	George Walker Bush (43rd) *Rep* (Richard B Cheney)
1993–2001	William Jefferson Blythe IV Clinton (42nd) *Dem* (Albert Gore)		

Dem = Democrat; Nat = National Union; Fed = Federalist; Rep = Republican

Keeping It in the Family

John Quincy Adams, the 6th President, was the son of John Adams, the 2nd President; Benjamin Harrison, the 23rd President, was the grandson of William Henry Harrison, the 9th President; Theodore Roosevelt, the 26th President, and Franklin D Roosevelt, the 32nd, were distant cousins; and George Bush, the 41st President, saw his son George W Bush become the 43rd President.

URUGUAY

Official name	Eastern Republic of Uruguay
Local name	Uruguay; República Oriental del Uruguay
Independence	1828
Area	176215 sq km/68018 sq mi
Capital	Montevideo
Chief towns	Salto, Paysandú, Mercedes, Las Piedras
Population	3461000 (2007e)
Nationality	Uruguayan
Languages	Spanish; Portunol or Brazilero, a mix of Portuguese and Spanish, is also spoken on the Brazilian border
Ethnic groups	white 88%, mestizo 8%, black 4%
Religions	Christianity 68% (RC 66%, Prot 2%), Judaism 1%, others/unaffiliated 31%
Time zone	GMT –3
Currency	1 Uruguayan Peso (Ur$, Urug$/UYU) = 100 centésimos
Telephone	+598
Internet	.uy
Country code	URY

Location
A republic in eastern South America, bounded to the north by Brazil; to the east and south by the Atlantic Ocean; and to the west by Argentina.

Physical description
Grass-covered plains of the south rise north to a high sandy plateau; River Negro flows south to west to meet the River Uruguay on the Argentine frontier; highest point is Cerro Catedral (514m/1686ft).

Climate
Temperate with warm summers and mild winters; the average temperature at Montevideo is 16°C.

National holidays
Jan 1, 6, Apr 19 (Landing of the 33 Patriots), May 1, 18 (Battle of Las Piedras), Jun 19 (José Artigas/Nunca Más), Jul 18 (Constitution), Aug 25 (Independence), Oct 12 (Battle of Sarandí), Nov 2, Dec 25; C (2), ES, GF, HT.

Political leaders

President

1899–1903	Juan Lindolfo Cuestas	1907–11	Claudio Williman
1903–7	José Batlle y Ordóñez	1911–15	José Batlle y Ordóñez

1915–19	Feliciano Viera	1938–43	Alfredo Baldomir
1919–23	Baltasar Brum	1943–7	Juan José de Amézaga
1923–7	José Serrato	1947	Tomás Berreta
1927–31	Juan Capisteguy	1947–51	Luis Batlle Berres
1931–8	Gabriel Terra	1951–5	Andrés Martínez Trueba

President of the National Government Council

1955–6	Luis Batlle Berres	1961–2	Eduardo Victor Haedo
1956–7	Alberto F Zubiría	1962–3	Faustino Harrison
1957–8	Alberto Lezama	1963–4	Daniel Fernández Crespo
1958–9	Carlos L Fischer	1964–5	Luis Giannattasio
1959–60	Martín R Etchegoyen	1965–6	Washington Beltrán
1960–1	Benito Nardone	1966–7	Alberto Heber Usher

President

1967	Oscar Daniel Gestido	1985	Rafael Addiego Bruno *Acting*
1967–72	Jorge Pacheco Areco	1985–90	Julio María Sanguinetti Cairolo
1972–6	Juan María Bordaberry Arocena	1990–5	Luis Alberto Lacalle Herrera
1976–81	Aparicio Méndez	1995–2000	Julio María Sanguinetti
1981–5	Gregorio Conrado Álvarez Armelino	2000–5	Jorge Batlle Ibáñez
		2005–	Tabaré Vázquez

USSR (UNION OF SOVIET SOCIALIST REPUBLICS)

Political leaders

No longer in existence, but included for reference. See separate entries for former constituent states of the USSR since 1990–91 (Armenia, Azerbaijan, Belarus, Estonia, Georgia, Kazakhstan, Kyrgyzstan, Latvia, Lithuania, Moldova, Russia, Tajikistan, Turkmenistan, Ukraine, Uzbekistan).

President

1917	Leo Kamenev	1977–82	Leonid Brezhnev
1917–19	Yakov Sverlov	1982–3	Vasily Kuznetsov *Acting*
1919–46	Mikhail Kalinin	1983–4	Yuri Andropov
1946–53	Nikolai Shvernik	1984	Vasily Kuznetsov *Acting*
1953–60	Klimentiy Voroshilov	1984–5	Konstantin Chernenko
1960–4	Leonid Brezhnev	1985	Vasily Kuznetsov *Acting*
1964–5	Anastas Mikoyan	1985–8	Andrei Gromyko
1965–77	Nikolai Podgorny	1988–90	Mikhail Gorbachev

Executive President

1990–91	Mikhail Gorbachev
1991	Gennady Yanayev *Acting*
1991	Mikhail Gorbachev

Chairman of the Council of Ministers

1917	Georgy Lvov
1917	Aleksandr Kerensky

Chairman of the Council of People's Commissars

1917–24	Vladimir Ilyich Lenin	1930–41	Vyacheslav Molotov
1924–30	Aleksei Rykov	1941–53	Josef Stalin

Chairman of the Council of Ministers

1953–5	Georgiy Malenkov
1955–8	Nikolai Bulganin
1958–64	Nikita Khrushchev
1964–80	Alexei Kosygin
1980–5	Nikolai Tikhonov
1985–90	Nikolai Ryzhkov
1990–1	Yuri Maslyukov *Acting*
1991	Valentin Pavlov
1991	Ivan Silayev *Acting*

General Secretary of the Communist Party

1922–53	Josef Stalin
1953	Georgiy Malenkov
1953–64	Nikita Khrushchev
1964–82	Leonid Brezhnev
1982–4	Yuri Andropov
1984–5	Konstantin Chernenko
1985–91	Mikhail Gorbachev

US VIRGIN ISLANDS *see* UNITED STATES OF AMERICA

UZBEKISTAN

Official name	Republic of Uzbekistan
Local name	Özbekiston; Özbekiston Respublikasia
Former name	Uzbek Soviet Socialist Republic (1924–91), within the Union of Soviet Socialist Republics (USSR; 1924–91)
Independence	1991
Area	447 400 sq km/172 696 sq mi
Capital	Tashkent; Toškent, Taškent
Chief towns	Samarkand, Andizhan, Namangan
Population	27 780 000 (2007e)
Nationality	Uzbek
Languages	Uzbek; Russian, Tajik and Kazakh are also spoken
Ethnic groups	Uzbek 71%, Russian 8%, Tajik 5%, Kazakh 4%, Tartars 3%, others 9%
Religions	Islam 88% (mostly Sunni), Christianity 9% (Orthodox), others/unaffiliated 3%
Time zone	GMT +5
Currency	1 Sum (UZS) = 100 tiyin
Telephone	+998
Internet	.uz
Country code	UZB

Location

A republic in central Asia, bounded to the north and west by Kazakhstan; to the east by Kyrgyzstan and Tajikistan; to the south by Afghanistan; and to the south-west by Turkmenistan.

Physical description

Large area occupied by the Kyzyl-Kum desert; highest point is Beshtor Peak (4 299m/14 104ft); the Aral Sea lies to the north on the border with Kazakhstan.

Climate

Long, hot summers, mild winters.

National holidays

Jan 1, Mar 8 (Women), 21, May 9 (Memory and Respect), Sep 1 (Independence), Oct 1 (Teachers), Dec 8 (Constitution); Ad, ER.

Political leaders

President

1991–	Islam Karimov

Prime Minister

1991–5	Abdulhashim Mutalov
1995–2003	Otkir Sultonov
2003–	Shavkat Mirziyayev

VANUATU

Official name	Republic of Vanuatu
Local name	Vanuatu; Ripablik Blong Vanuatu, République de Vanuatu
Former name	New Hebrides (until 1980)
Independence	1980
Area	12 336 sq km/4 763 sq mi
Capital	Port-Vila
Population	212 000 (2007e)
Nationality	Ni-Vanuatu
Languages	Bislama, English, French
Ethnic groups	Melanesian 95%, others 5%
Religions	Christianity 83% (Prot 70%, RC 13%), traditional beliefs 5%, unaffiliated 7%, others 5%
Time zone	GMT +11
Currency	1 Vatu (V, VT/VUV) = 100 centimes
Telephone	+678
Internet	.vu
Country code	VUT

Location

An independent island republic in the south-west Pacific Ocean, 400km/250mi north-east of the French islands of New Caledonia.

Physical description

Comprises an irregular Y-shaped island chain; actively volcanic and rugged, with raised coral beaches fringed by reefs; highest peak, Tabwemasana, rises to 1 888m/6 194ft; densely forested, narrow strips of cultivated coastal land.

Climate

Tropical, with a hot and rainy season in Nov–Apr when cyclones may occur; annual temperatures at Port-Vila are 16–33°C.

National holidays

Jan 1, Feb 21 (Walter Lini), Mar 5 (Custom Chiefs), May 1, Jul 24 (Children), 30 (Independence), Aug 15, Oct 5 (Constitution), Nov 29 (Unity), Dec 25, 26 (Family); A, EM, ES, GF.

Political leaders

President

1980–4	George Sokomanu (*formerly* Kalkoa)
1984	Fred Timakata *Acting*
1984–9	George Sokomanu
1989	Onneyn Tahi *Acting*
1989–94	Fred Timakata
1994	Alfred Maseng *Acting*
1994–9	Jean-Marie Léyé
1999	Edward Natapei *Acting*
1999–2004	John Bani
2004	Roger Abiut *Interim*
2004	Alfred Maseng
2004	Roger Abiut *Interim*
2004	Josias Moli *Interim*
2004–	Kalkot Mataskelekele

Prime Minister

1980–91	Walter Lini
1991	Donald Kalpokas
1991–5	Maxime Carlot Korman
1995–6	Serge Vohor

1996	Maxime Carlot Korman	2001–4	Edward Natapei
1996–8	Serge Vohor	2004	Serge Vohor
1998–9	Donald Kalpokas	2004–	Ham Lini
1999–2001	Barak Sopé		

VATICAN

Official name	Vatican City State; the Holy See
Local name	Città del Vaticano; Stato della Città del Vaticano; Santa Sede
Independence	1929 (formally)
Area	0.4 sq km/0.2 sq mi
Capital	Vatican City
Population	1 000 (2007e)
Languages	Latin; Italian is widely spoken
Ethnic groups	predominantly European, especially Italian
Religions	Christianity 100% (RC)
Time zone	GMT +1
Currency	1 Euro (€/EUR) = 100 cents
Telephone	+39
Internet	.va
Country code	VAT

Location
A papal sovereign state, the smallest independent state in the world, surrounded by Rome, Italy.

Physical description
Landlocked, urban and entirely enclosed within the Italian city of Rome; reaches 75m/246ft at its highest point.

Climate
Mediterranean; hot summers and mild winters.

National holidays
Jan 1, 6, Feb 11 (Lateran Treaty), Mar 19 (St Joseph), May 1, Jun 29 (SS Peter and Paul), Aug 15, 16, Nov 1, Dec 8, 25, 26; A, CC, EM, ES, WM; *the Pope's birthday and the anniversary of his election are sometimes declared public holidays*.

Political leaders

The head of state is the Supreme Pontiff of the Roman Catholic Church, the pope, who is elected for life by the Sacred College of Cardinals and has full legislative, judicial and executive powers (see **Religions, Beliefs and Folklore** for lists of **popes**). The head of government is a Secretary of State appointed by the pope (since 2006, Cardinal Tarcisio Bertone).

Swiss Guards

The Vatican and the pope himself are protected by the distinctive Swiss Guards, with their blue- and yellow-striped dress uniform and red-tufted helmets. The Swiss Guards were instituted as the papal police corps by Pope Julius II, pope from 1503 to 1513. Their distinctive uniform was designed by Michelangelo. To be admitted to the Swiss Guards, one must be Roman Catholic, of good moral and ethical background, have attended military school in Switzerland, be 19–30 years old, at least 1.74m/5.7ft tall, unmarried, hold a professional diploma or high school degree, and, of course, be Swiss.

VENEZUELA

Official name	Bolivarian Republic of Venezuela
Local name	Venezuela; República Bolivariana de Venezuela
Independence	1830
Area	912050 sq km/352051 sq mi
Capital	Caracas
Chief towns	Maracaibo, Ciudad Guayana, Valencia, Barquisimeto
Population	26023000 (2007e)
Nationality	Venezuelan
Languages	Spanish; indigenous languages are also spoken
Ethnic groups	mestizo 67%, white 21%, black 10%, Amerindian 2%
Religions	Christianity 98% (RC 96%, Prot 2%), others/unaffiliated 2%
Time zone	GMT –4
Currency	1 Bolívar (Bs/VEF) = 100 céntimos
Telephone	+58
Internet	.ve
Country code	VEN

Location
A republic in northern South America, bounded to the north by the Caribbean Sea; to the east by Guyana; to the south by Brazil; and to the south-west and west by Colombia.

Physical description
Guiana Highlands in the south-east cover over half the country; Venezuelan Highlands in the west and along the coast reach heights of around 5000m/16400ft; highest point is Pico Bolívar (5007m/16427ft); lowlands around Lake Maracaibo and in the Orinoco River valley, which runs south to north-east.

Climate
Generally hot and humid; one rainy season from Apr to Oct; annual temperatures at Caracas are 13–27°C; very little rainfall on the coast around Lake Maracaibo, increasing in the east.

National holidays
Jan 1, Apr 19 (Declaration of Independence), May 1, Jun 24 (Battle of Carabobo), Jul 5 (Independence), 24 (Bolívar's Birthday), Oct 12 (Indigenous Resistance), Dec 25; C (2), GF, HT; *also additional religious holidays observed by banks and in regions*.

Political leaders

President

1899–1908	Cipriano Castro
1908–36	Juan Vicente Gomez
1936–41	Eleazar Lopez Contreras
1941–5	Isaias Medina Angarita
1945–7	*Military Junta* (Rómulo Betancourt)
1947–8	Romulo Gallegos
1948–50	*Military Junta* (Carlos Delgado Chalbaud)
1950–9	*Military Junta* (Marcos Pérez Jiménez)
1959–64	Rómulo Betancourt
1964–9	Raul Leoni
1969–74	Rafael Caldera Rodriguez
1974–9	Carlos Andres Pérez
1979–84	Luis Herrera Campins
1984–9	Jaime Lusinchi
1989–93	Carlos Andres Pérez
1994–8	Rafael Caldera Rodríguez
1998–2002	Hugo Chávez Frías
2002	Pedro Carmona *Head of Transitional Government*
2002–	Hugo Chávez Frías

VIETNAM

Official name	Socialist Republic of Vietnam (SRV)
Local name	Viêt Nam; Công-Hòa Xã-Hôi Chu-Ngh Viêt Nam
Former name	formerly part of Indochina (until 1945), *post-1945 as listed below under Political leaders*
Independence	1945 (declared), 1976 (republic)
Area	329 566 sq km/127 213 sq mi
Capital	Hanoi; Hà Nội
Chief towns	Ho Chi Minh City (formerly Saigon), Haiphong, Da Nang, Nha Trang
Population	85 262 000 (2007e)
Nationality	Vietnamese
Languages	Vietnamese
Ethnic groups	Kinh Vietnamese 86%, others (53 ethnic groups) 14%
Religions	Buddhism 12%, Christianity 8%, Cao Dai 3%, Hao Hao 1%, others, unaffiliated or none 76%
Time zone	GMT +7
Currency	1 Dông (D/VND) = 10 hào = 100 xu
Telephone	+84
Internet	.vn
Country code	VNM

Location

An independent republic in south-east Asia, bounded to the north by China; to the east by the South China Sea and the Gulf of Tongking; to the south-west by the Gulf of Thailand; and to the west by Laos and Cambodia.

Physical description

Occupies a narrow strip along the coast of the Gulf of Tongking and the South China Sea; broader at the Mekong River Delta, in the south, and along the Red River Valley to the north; highest peak is Fan si Pan (3 143m/10 312ft).

Climate

Tropical monsoon-type, dominated by south to south-east winds during May–Sep and north to north-east winds during Oct–Apr; high humidity in the rainy season; temperatures are high in the south during Oct–Apr.

National holidays

Jan 1, Apr 30 (Liberation), May 1, Sep 2 (National); NY (Vietnamese) (Jan/Feb) (4), Hung Kings (Mar/Apr).

Political leaders

Democratic Republic of Vietnam (North Vietnam)

President

1945–69	Ho Chi Minh
1969–76	Ton Duc Thang

Prime Minister

1945–55	*As President*
1955–76	Pham Van Dong

State of Vietnam (South Vietnam)

Head of State

1949–55	Bao Dai

Prime Minister

1949–50	Nguyen Van Xuan
1950	Nguyen Phan Long
1950–2	Tran Van Huu
1952	Tran Van Huong
1952–3	Nguyen Van Tam
1953–4	Buu Loc
1954–5	Ngo Dinh Diem

Republic of Vietnam (South Vietnam)

President

1955–63	Ngo Dinh Diem
1963–4	Duong Van Minh
1964	Nguyen Khanh
1964	Duong Van Minh
1964	Nguyen Khanh
1964	Duong Van Minh
1964–5	Phan Khac Suu
1965–75	Nguyen Van Thieu
1975	Tran Van Huong
1975	Duong Van Minh
1975–6	*Provisional Revolutionary Government* (Huynh Tan Phat)

Prime Minister

1955–63	Ngo Dinh Diem
1963–4	Nguyen Ngoc Tho
1964	Nguyen Khanh
1964–5	Tran Van Huong
1965	Phan Huy Quat
1965–7	Nguyen Cao Ky
1967–8	Nguyen Van Loc
1968–9	Tran Van Huong
1969–75	Tran Thien Khiem
1975	Nguyen Ba Can
1975–6	Vu Van Mau

Socialist Republic of Vietnam

President

1976–80	Ton Duc Thang
1980–1	Nguyen Hun Tho *Acting*
1981–7	Truong Chinh
1987–92	Vo Chi Cong
1992–7	Le Duc Anh
1997–2006	Tran Duc Luong
2006–	Nguyen Minh Triet

Premier

1976–87	Pham Van Dong
1987–8	Pham Hung
1988	Vo Van Kiet *Acting*
1988–91	Do Muoi
1991–7	Vo Van Kiet
1997–2006	Phan Van Khai
2006–	Nguyen Tan Dung

General Secretary

1976–86	Le Duan
1986	Truong Chinh
1986–91	Nguyen Van Linh
1991–7	Do Muoi
1997–2001	Le Kha Phieu
2001–	Nong Duc Manh

Vietnamese Customs

Chewing betel and areca is an old Vietnamese custom. Betel and areca nuts are shared for enjoyment at weddings, are a source of comfort at funerals, are used during ancestor worship, and as a symbol of friendship during festivals. Betel is a relaxant and intoxicant; the chewed quid often comprises a mixture of betel bark, areca leaf, chay root and hydrated lime, giving a mixture of hot, sweet, bitter and pungent tastes.

VIRGIN ISLANDS, BRITISH *see* **UNITED KINGDOM**

VIRGIN ISLANDS, US *see* **UNITED STATES OF AMERICA**

WALES *see* **UNITED KINGDOM**

WALLIS AND FUTUNA ISLANDS *see* **FRANCE**

WEST BANK *see* **PALESTINIAN AUTONOMOUS AREAS** *under* **ISRAEL**

WESTERN SAHARA *see* MOROCCO

see MOROCCO

WESTERN SAMOA *see* SAMOA

YEMEN

Official name	Republic of Yemen
Local name	Al-Yamaniyya; Al-Jumhūriyya Al-Yamaniyya
Former name	*as listed below under Political leaders*
Independence	1990 (united republic)
Area	531 570 sq km/205 186 sq mi
Capital	Sana'a; San'ā, Sanaa
Chief towns	Ta'iz
Population	22 230 000 (2007e)
Nationality	Yemeni
Languages	Arabic
Ethnic groups	Arab 96%, others 4%
Religions	Islam 100% (Sunni 70%, Shia 30%)
Time zone	GMT +3
Currency	1 Yemeni Rial (YR, YRI/YER) = 100 fils
Telephone	+967
Internet	.ye
Country code	YEM

Location
A republic in the south of the Arabian Peninsula, bounded to the north by Saudi Arabia; to the east by Oman; to the south by the Gulf of Aden; and to the west by the Red Sea.

Physical description
Narrow desert plain bordering the Red Sea rises abruptly to mountains at 3 000–3 700m/9 840–12 140ft; highest point is Jabal an Nabi Shu'ayb (3 760m/12 336ft); to the north, a plateau merges with the gravel plains and sand of the Rub al Khali Basin.

Climate
Hot and humid on the western coastal strip, with an annual temperature of 29°C; milder in the highlands; rainfall is highest in the north and west; hot all year round in the south, with maximum temperatures over 40°C (Jul–Aug) and very high humidity.

National holidays
May 1, 22 (Unification), Sep 26 (Revolution), Oct 14 (Liberation), Nov 30 (Independence); Ad (5), ER (4), NY (Muslim).

Political leaders

Yemen Arab Republic (North Yemen)

Monarch (Imam)

1918–48	Yahya Mohammed bin Mohammed
1948–62	Ahmed bin Yahya
1962–70	Mohammed bin Ahmed
1962	*Civil War*

President

1962–7	Abdullah al-Sallal
1967–74	Abdur Rahman al-Iriani
1974–7	*Military Command Council* (Ibrahim al-Hamadi)
1977–8	Ahmed bin Hussein al-Ghashmi
1978–90	Ali Abdullah Saleh

Prime Minister

1964	Hamud al-Jaifi
1965	Hassan al-Amri
1965	Ahmed Mohammed Numan
1965	*As President*
1965–6	Hassan al-Amri
1966–7	*As President*
1967	Muhsin al-Aini
1967–9	Hassan al-Amri
1969–70	Abd Allah Kurshumi
1970–1	Muhsin al-Aini
1971	Abdel Salam Sabra *Acting*
1971	Ahmed Mohammed Numan
1971	Hassan al-Amri
1971–2	Muhsin al-Aini
1972–4	Qadi Abdullah al-Hijri
1974	Hassan Makki
1974–5	Muhsin al-Aini
1975	Abdel Latif Deifallah *Acting*
1975–90	Abdel-Aziz Abdel-Ghani

People's Democratic Republic of Yemen (South Yemen)

President

1967–9	Qahtan Mohammed al-Shaabi
1969–78	Salim Ali Rubai
1978	Ali Nasir Mohammed Husani
1978–80	Abdel Fattah Ismail
1980–6	Ali Nasir Mohammed Husani
1986–90	Haidar Abu Bakr al-Attas

Prime Minister

1969	Faisal Abd al-Latif al-Shaabi
1969–71	Mohammed Ali Haithem
1971–85	Ali Nasir Mohammed Husani
1985–6	Haidar Abu Bakr al-Attas
1986–90	Yasin Said Numan

Republic of Yemen

President

1990–	Ali Abdullah Saleh

Prime Minister

1990–3	Haidar Abu Bakr al-Attas
1993–7	Abdel-Aziz Abdel-Ghani
1997	Farag Said Ben Ghanem
1998–2001	Abdul Ali al-Karim al-Iryani
2001–7	Abd al-Qadir Abd al-Rahman Bajammal
2007–	Ali Mohammad Mujawar

YUGOSLAVIA

No longer in existence, but included for reference. See separate entries for former constituent states of Yugoslavia since 1991–92 (Bosnia and Herzegovina, Croatia, the Former Yugoslav Republic of Macedonia, Montenegro, Serbia and Slovenia).

Political leaders

Kingdom of Yugoslavia[1]

Monarch

1921–34	Aleksandar II
1934–45	Petar II (*in exile from* 1941)

Prime Minister

1929–32	Pear Živkovic
1932	Vojislav Marinković
1932–4	Milan Sršić
1934	Nikola Uzunović
1934–5	Bogoljub Jevtić
1935–9	Milan Stojadinović
1939–41	Dragiša Cvetković
1941–2	Dušan Simović

Prime Minister of government-in-exile

1942–3	Slobodan Jovanović	1944–5	Ivan Šubašić
1943	Miloš Trifunović	1945	Drago Marušić
1943–4	Božidar Purić		

[1]*Name from 1929; previously called Kingdom of Serbs, Croats and Slovenes.*

Socialist Federal Republic of Yugoslavia[2]

Chairman

1945–53	Ivan Ribar

President

1953–80	Josip Broz Tito

Collective Presidency

1980	Lazar Koliševski	1987–8	Lazar Mojsov
1980–1	Cvijetin Mijatović	1988–9	Raif Dizdarević
1981–2	Serghei Kraigher	1989–90	Janez Drnovšek
1982–3	Petar Stambolić	1990–1	Borisav Jovic
1983–4	Mika Spiljak	1991	*vacant*
1984–5	Veselin Ðuranović	1991	Stjepan Mesić
1985–6	Radovan Vlajković	1991–2	Branko Kostic *Acting*
1986–7	Sinan Hasani		

Prime Minister/Premier

1941–4	Milan Nedić	1977–82	Veselin Ðuranović
1943–63	Josip Broz Tito	1982–6	Milka Planinc
1963–7	Petar Stambolić	1986–9	Branko Mikulić
1967–9	Mika Špiljak	1989–91	Ante Marković
1969–71	Mitja Ribičič	1992	Aleksandar Mitrovic *Acting*
1971–7	Džemal Bijedić		

[2]*Name from 1963; was Federal People's Republic of Yugoslavia 1945–63.*

Communist Party

Secretary-General

1937–52	Josip Broz Tito

League of Communists

Secretary-General

1952–63	Josip Broz Tito

President of the Central Committee

1963–80	Josip Broz Tito	1984–5	Ali Sukrija
1979–80	Stevan Doronjski *Acting*	1985–6	Vidoje Žarkovic
1980–1	Lazar Mojsov	1986–7	Milanko Renovica
1981–2	Dušan Dragosavac	1987–8	Boško Krunić
1982–3	Mitja Ribicic	1988–9	Stipe Suvar
1983–4	Dragoslav Marković	1989–90	Milan Pancevski

ZAÏRE *see* CONGO, DEMOCRATIC REPUBLIC OF THE

ZAMBIA

Official name	Republic of Zambia
Local name	Zambia
Former name	Northern Rhodesia (until 1964), part of the Federation of Rhodesia and Nyasaland (1953–63)
Independence	1964
Area	752 613 sq km/290 509 sq mi
Capital	Lusaka
Chief towns	Ndola, Kitwe, Kabwe, Livingstone
Population	11 477 000 (2007e)
Nationality	Zambian
Languages	English; local languages are also spoken
Ethnic groups	African 99% (over 70 ethnic groups, including Bemba, Maravi, Tonga and Lozi), European and others 1%
Religions	Christianity 50%–75%, Islam and Hinduism 24%–49%, others 1%
Time zone	GMT +2
Currency	1 Kwacha (K/ZMK) = 100 ngwee
Telephone	+260
Internet	.zm
Country code	ZMB

Location

A republic in southern Africa, bounded to the north by Democratic Republic of the Congo; to the north-east by Tanzania; to the east by Malawi; to the south-east by Zimbabwe and Mozambique; to the south by Botswana and Namibia; and to the west by Angola.

Physical description

Occupies a high plateau at an altitude of 1 000–1 400m/3 280–4 590ft; highest point is 2 067m/6 781ft south-east of Mbala; Zambezi River rises in the north extremity of North-West Province.

Climate

Temperate climate on upland plateau; rainy season is Oct–Mar; at Lusaka the maximum average daily temperatures range between 23°C and 35°C; tropical climate in the lower river valleys.

National holidays

Jan 1, May 1, 25 (Africa Freedom), Oct 24 (Independence), Dec 25; EM, GF, HS, Youth (2nd Mon in Mar), Heroes (1st Mon in Jul), Unity (1st Tues in Jul), Farmers (1st Mon in Aug).

Smoke that Thunders

Zambia is renowned for the Victoria Falls, the waterfalls on the Zambezi River which lie on the border with Zimbabwe. The falls are 61–108m/200–350ft high and 1,688m/5,538ft wide. In 1855 the explorer David Livingstone became the first European to see the falls, which he named after Queen Victoria. However, the indigenous Kololo people knew the falls as *Mosi oa Tunya*, 'the smoke that thunders', while the Leya people called the falls *Shongwe*, meaning 'rainbow'.

Political leaders

President

1964–91	Kenneth Kaunda
1991–2002	Frederick Chiluba
2002–	Levy Mwanawasa

Prime Minister

1964–73	Kenneth Kaunda
1973–5	Mainza Chona
1975–7	Elijah Mudenda
1977–8	Mainza Chona
1978–81	Daniel Lisulu
1981–5	Nalumino Mundia
1985–9	Kebby Musokotwane
1989–91	Malimba Masheke
1991–	*No Prime Minister*

ZIMBABWE

Official name	Republic of Zimbabwe
Local name	Zimbabwe
Former name	Southern Rhodesia (until 1965), part of the Federation of Rhodesia and Nyasaland (1953–63), Rhodesia (1965–80)
Independence	1980
Area	391 090 sq km/150 961 sq mi
Capital	Harare
Chief towns	Bulawayo, Gweru, Mutare
Population	12 311 000 (2007e)
Nationality	Zimbabwean
Languages	English; Shona, Sindebele and other local languages are also spoken
Ethnic groups	African 98% (Shona 82%, Ndebele 14%, other 2%), mixed and Asian 1%, white less than 1%
Religions	mixture of Christian and traditional beliefs 50%, Christianity 25%, traditional beliefs 24%, Islam and others 1%
Time zone	GMT +2
Currency	1 Zimbabwe Dollar (Z$/ZWD) = 100 cents
Telephone	+263
Internet	.zw
Country code	ZWE

Location

A republic in southern Africa, bounded to the north-west by Zambia; to the north-east, east and south-east by Mozambique; to the south by South Africa; and to the south-west by Botswana.

Physical description

High plateau country, with the Middleveld at 900–1 200m/2 950–3 940ft and the Highveld at 1 200–1 500m/3 940–4 920ft; lower towards the Zambezi River in the north and the Limpopo River in the south; mountains in the east rise to 2 592m/8 504ft at Mt Inyangani.

Climate

Generally subtropical, strongly influenced by altitude; warm and dry in the lowlands; average maximum daily temperatures at Harare, in the Highveld, range between 21°C and 29°C.

National holidays

Jan 1, Apr 18 (Independence), May 1, 25 (Africa), Dec 22 (Unity), 25, 26; EM, GF, HS, Heroes (Aug), Defence Forces (Aug).

Political leaders

President

1980–7	Canaan Sodindo Banana
1987–	Robert Gabriel Mugabe

Prime Minister

1980–7	Robert Gabriel Mugabe

Politicians and Chiefs

Zimbabwe's capital was founded in 1890 and was named Salisbury after the British prime minister of the time, Lord Salisbury. After Zimbabwe gained its independence the capital was renamed Harare in 1982, this time after Chief Neharawa, a former indigenous ruler of the area.

HISTORICAL EMPIRES

For the Roman Empire see **Ancient Greece and Rome**, for ancient Chinese dynasties see **China** in **Countries A–Z**, for ancient Egyptian dynasties see **Egypt** in **Countries A–Z** and for ancient Japanese emperors see **Japan** in **Countries A–Z**.

Holy Roman Empire

The establishment of the Holy Roman Empire (HRE) is usually dated to the coronation of Charlemagne in 800 as emperor over most of Christian Western Europe. It was known as the Roman Empire and the Holy Empire before its full title was adopted in 1254. It was always based principally in the territory of modern-day Germany, though its full extent fluctuated considerably. It was at its zenith in the early Middle Ages, but remained officially in existence until 1806. It was abolished by Francis II, who restyled himself Emperor of Austria to evade the threat of Napoleon I trying to appropriate the Holy Roman title and establish a European hegemony.

800–814	Charlemagne (Charles I)
814–840	Louis I (the Pious)
840–843	*Civil War*
843–855	Lothair I
855–875	Louis II
875–877	Charles II (the Bald)
877–881	*Interregnum*
881–887	Charles III (the Fat)
887–891	*Interregnum*
891–894	Guido of Spoleto
892–898	Lambert of Spoleto[1]
896–899	Arnulf[2]
901–905	Louis III
905–924	Berengar
911–918	Conrad I[2,4]
919–936	Henry I, the Fowler[4]
936–973	Otto I (the Great)
973–983	Otto II
983–1002	Otto III
1002–24	Henry II (the Saint)
1024–39	Conrad II
1039–56	Henry III (the Black)
1056–1106	Henry IV
1077–80	Rudolf of Rheinfelden[2,4]
1081–93	Hermann[2,4]
1093–1101	Conrad[2,4]
1106–25	Henry V
1125–37	Lothair II
1138–52	Conrad III[4]
1152–90	Frederick I (Barbarossa)
1190–7	Henry VI
1198–1214	Otto IV
1198–1208	Philip[2,4]
1215–50	Frederick II
1246–7	Henry Raspe[2,4]
1247–56	William of Holland[2,4]
1250–4	Conrad IV[4]
1254–73	*Great Interregnum*
1257–72	Richard[2,4]
1257–75	Alfonso (Alfonso X of Castile)[2,4]
1273–91	Rudolf I[4]
1292–8	Adolf[4]
1298–1308	Albert[4]
1308–13	Henry VII
1314–26	Frederick (III)[3,4]
1314–46	Louis IV
1346–78	Charles IV
1378–1400	Wenceslas[4]
1400–10	Rupert[4]
1410–37	Sigismund
1438–9	Albert II[4]
1440–93	Frederick III
1493–1519	Maximilian I[4]
1519–56	Charles V[4]
1556–64	Ferdinand I[4]
1564–76	Maximilian II[4]
1576–1612	Rudolf II[4]
1612–19	Matthias[4]
1619–37	Ferdinand II[4]
1637–57	Ferdinand III[4]
1658–1705	Leopold I[4]
1705–11	Joseph I[4]
1711–40	Charles VI[4]
1740–42	*Interregnum*
1742–5	Charles VII[4]
1745–65	Francis I[4]
1765–90	Joseph II[4]
1790–2	Leopold II[4]
1792–1806	Francis II[4]

[1] *Co-emperor.*
[2] *Rival.*
[3] *Co-regent.*
[4] *Ruler not crowned at Rome; therefore, strictly speaking, only King of Germany.*

Inca Empire

The Incas were originally a small group of Quechua-speaking Indians living in the Cuzco Basin of the central Andean highlands. In the 11c the Inca established their capital at Cuzco, the Sacred City of the Sun, where they built huge stone temples and fortresses, and occasionally covered important buildings in sheets of gold. During the 15c they brought together much of the Andean area, stretching along the entire western length of South America, from near the present Ecuador–Columbia border to south central Chile, and occupied much of the Andean region of Bolivia as well. They ruled more than 12 million people. The Inca emperor was a despotic ruler of a highly stratified society, and a quasi-religious figure thought to be a direct descendant of the sun god, Inti. In 1532 Spanish invaders under Pizarro encountered the Incas. They captured the emperor, Atahualpa, whom they later murdered, and seized control of the empire. By the 1570s Inca power was totally destroyed.

Note: The earliest Inca emperors are considered to be mythical, rather than historical figures. Dates are not known for the early emperors. The Spanish names, rather than the Inca names, of the emperors are given.

dates unknown	Manco Capac
dates unknown	Sinchi Roca
dates unknown	Lloque Yupanqui
dates unknown	Mayta Capac
dates unknown	Capac Yupanqui
dates unknown	Inca Roca
dates unknown	Yahuar Huacac
dates unknown	Viracocha Inca
dates unknown	Inca Urcon
1438–71	Pachacuti Inca Yupanqui
1471–93	Topa Inca Yupanqui
1493–1525	Huayna Capac
1525–32	Huascar
1532–3	Atahualpa
1533	Topa Huallpa
1533–45	Manco Inca Yupanqui
1545–60	Sayri Tupac
1560–71	Titu Cusi Yupanqui
1571–2	Tupac Amaru

Mughal Empire

The Mughal Empire was an important Indian Muslim state, founded in 1526 by Babur. The empire was extended during the 16c and 17c, but its last great emperor was Aurangzeb and by the mid-18c it ruled only a small area around Delhi, although its administrative forms and culture continued to have great influence.

1526–30	Babur
1530–56	Humayun[1]
1556–1605	Akbar
1605–27	Jahangir
1627–58	Shah Jahan
1658–1707	Aurangzeb (Alamgir)
1707–12	Bahadur Shah I (or Shah Alam I)
1712–13	Jahandar Shah
1713–19	Farruksiyar
1719	Rafid-ud-Darajat
1719	Rafi-ud-Daulat
1719	Nekusiyar
1719	Ibrahim
1719–48	Muhammad Shah
1748–54	Ahmad Shah
1754–9	Alamgir II
1759–1806	Shah Alam II
1806–37	Akbar II
1837–57	Bahadur Shah II[2]

[1] *Humayun lost his throne to the Afghan chieftain Sher Shah in 1540, became a fugitive, and did not regain his title until 1555.*
[2] *Bahadur Shah II was exiled by the British to Rangoon after the Indian Uprising of 1857–8.*

WORLD POLITICAL MAPS

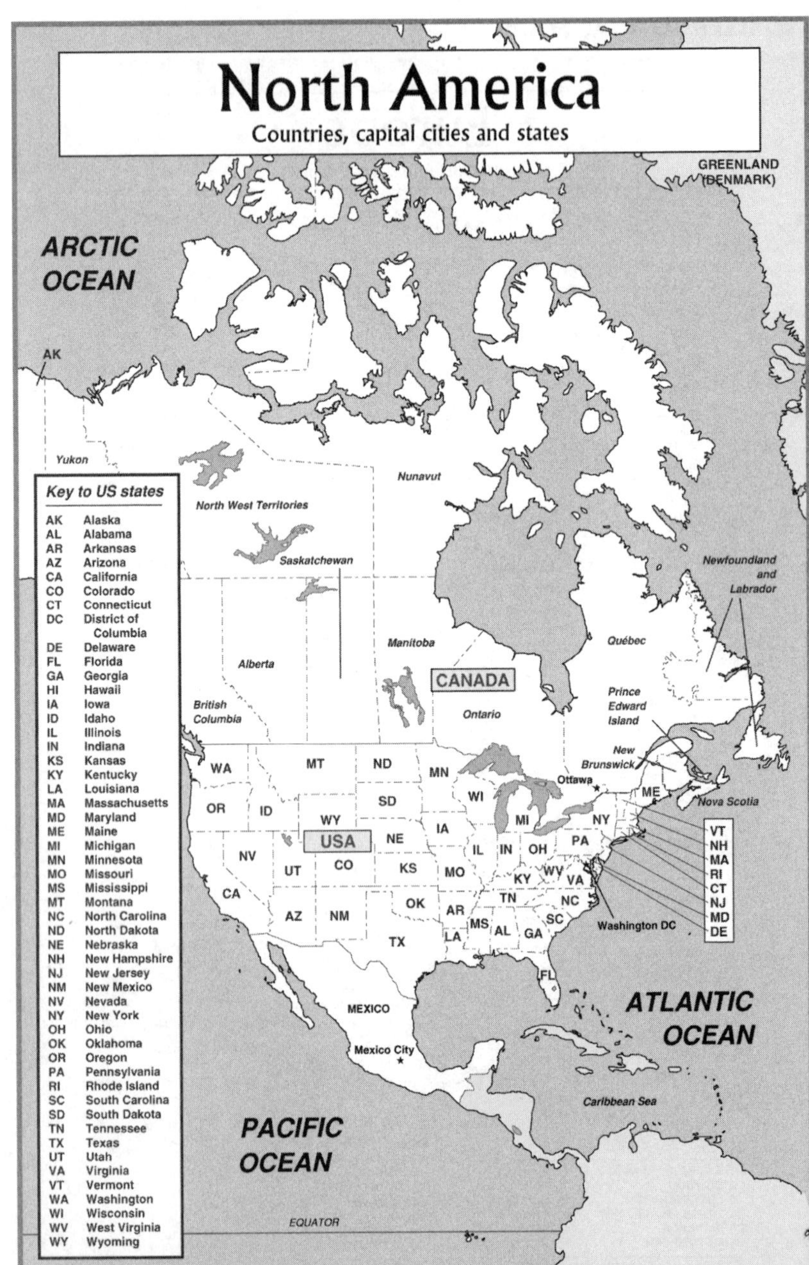
North America
Countries, capital cities and states
GREENLAND (DENMARK)
ARCTIC OCEAN
AK
Yukon
Nunavut
North West Territories
Saskatchewan
Newfoundland and Labrador
Manitoba
Québec
Alberta
CANADA
British Columbia
Ontario
Prince Edward Island
New Brunswick
Ottawa
Nova Scotia
WA
MT
ND
MN
OR
ID
SD
WI
ME
WY
MI
NY
USA
NE
IA
PA
NV
UT
CO
KS
IL
IN
OH
MO
KY
WV
VA
CA
TN
NC
OK
AZ
NM
AR
SC
MS
AL
GA
LA
TX
FL
Washington DC
VT
NH
MA
RI
CT
NJ
MD
DE
MEXICO
Mexico City
ATLANTIC OCEAN
Caribbean Sea
PACIFIC OCEAN
EQUATOR
Key to US states
AK Alaska
AL Alabama
AR Arkansas
AZ Arizona
CA California
CO Colorado
CT Connecticut
DC District of Columbia
DE Delaware
FL Florida
GA Georgia
HI Hawaii
IA Iowa
ID Idaho
IL Illinois
IN Indiana
KS Kansas
KY Kentucky
LA Louisiana
MA Massachusetts
MD Maryland
ME Maine
MI Michigan
MN Minnesota
MO Missouri
MS Mississippi
MT Montana
NC North Carolina
ND North Dakota
NE Nebraska
NH New Hampshire
NJ New Jersey
NM New Mexico
NV Nevada
NY New York
OH Ohio
OK Oklahoma
OR Oregon
PA Pennsylvania
RI Rhode Island
SC South Carolina
SD South Dakota
TN Tennessee
TX Texas
UT Utah
VA Virginia
VT Vermont
WA Washington
WI Wisconsin
WV West Virginia
WY Wyoming

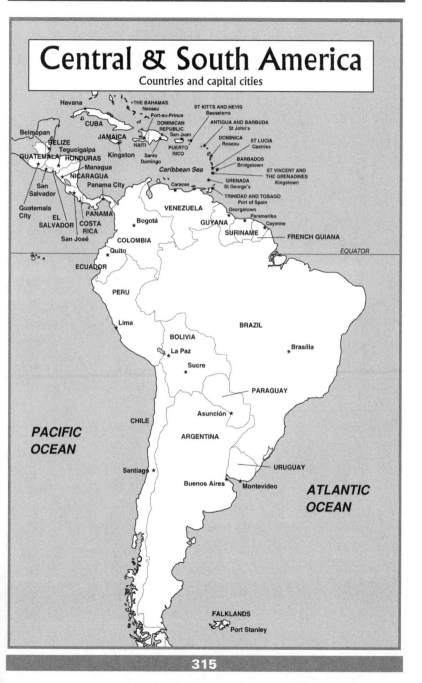

Central & South America

Countries and capital cities

Havana
THE BAHAMAS
Nassau
Port-au-Prince
ST KITTS AND NEVIS
Basseterre
CUBA
DOMINICAN REPUBLIC
ANTIGUA AND BARBUDA
St John's
Belmopan
BELIZE
JAMAICA
San Juan
DOMINICA
Roseau
ST LUCIA
Castries
HAITI
PUERTO RICO
Tegucigalpa
GUATEMALA
HONDURAS
Kingston
Santo Domingo
BARBADOS
Bridgetown
Managua
Caribbean Sea
ST VINCENT AND THE GRENADINES
Kingstown
NICARAGUA
GRENADA
St George's
San Salvador
Panama City
Caracas
TRINIDAD AND TOBAGO
Port of Spain
Guatemala City
PANAMA
VENEZUELA
Georgetown
EL SALVADOR
COSTA RICA
Bogotá
GUYANA
Paramaribo
Cayenne
San José
SURINAME
FRENCH GUIANA
COLOMBIA
Quito
EQUATOR
ECUADOR
PERU
Lima
BRAZIL
BOLIVIA
La Paz
Brasília
Sucre
PARAGUAY
Asunción
CHILE
PACIFIC OCEAN
ARGENTINA
URUGUAY
Santiago
Buenos Aires
Montevideo
ATLANTIC OCEAN
FALKLANDS
Port Stanley

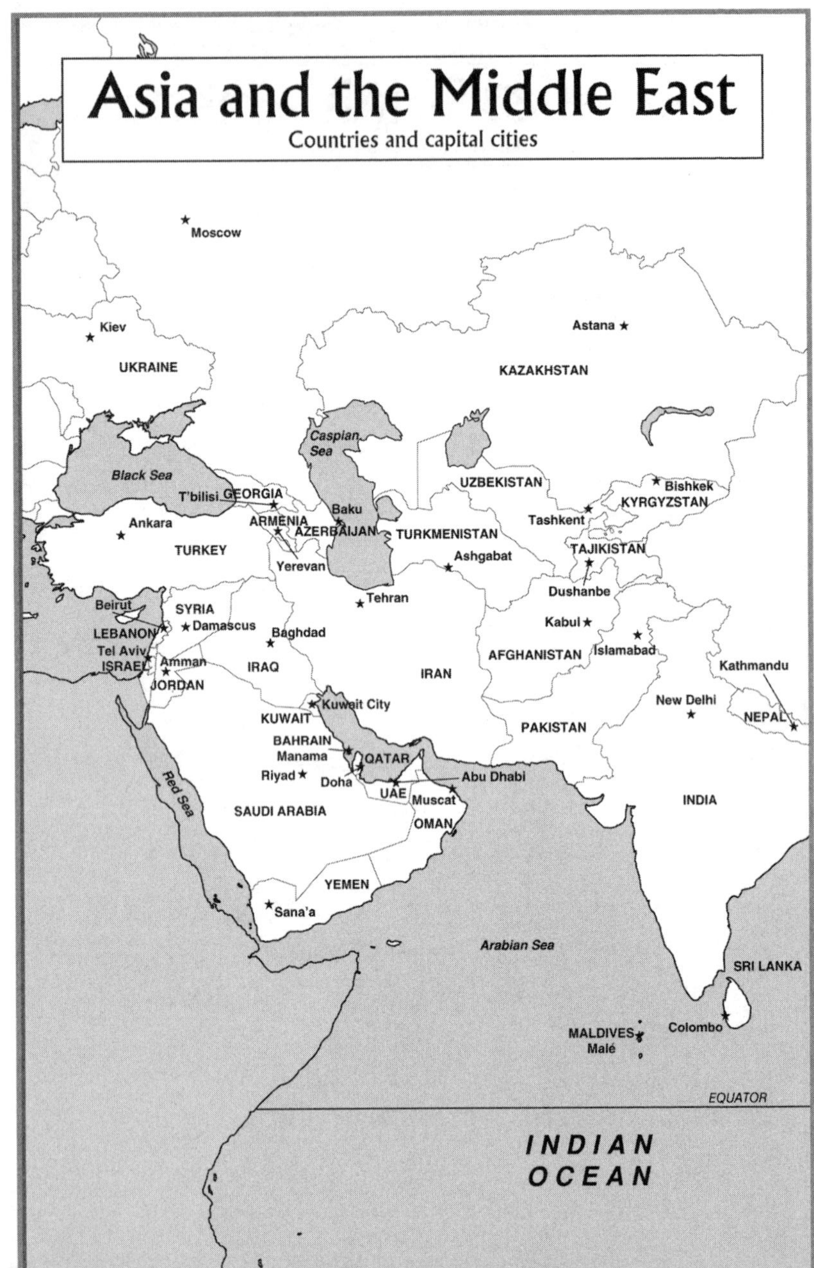
Asia and the Middle East
Countries and capital cities
Moscow
Kiev
UKRAINE
Astana
KAZAKHSTAN
Caspian Sea
Black Sea
T'bilisi
GEORGIA
UZBEKISTAN
Bishkek
KYRGYZSTAN
Tashkent
Baku
ARMENIA
AZERBAIJAN
TURKMENISTAN
Ankara
TURKEY
Yerevan
Ashgabat
TAJIKISTAN
Dushanbe
Tehran
Beirut
SYRIA
Damascus
Kabul
LEBANON
Baghdad
Islamabad
Tel Aviv
ISRAEL
Amman
JORDAN
IRAQ
IRAN
AFGHANISTAN
Kathmandu
Kuwait City
KUWAIT
New Delhi
NEPAL
PAKISTAN
BAHRAIN
Manama
QATAR
Riyad
Doha
Abu Dhabi
UAE
Muscat
Red Sea
SAUDI ARABIA
OMAN
INDIA
YEMEN
Sana'a
Arabian Sea
SRI LANKA
MALDIVES
Malé
Colombo
EQUATOR
INDIAN OCEAN

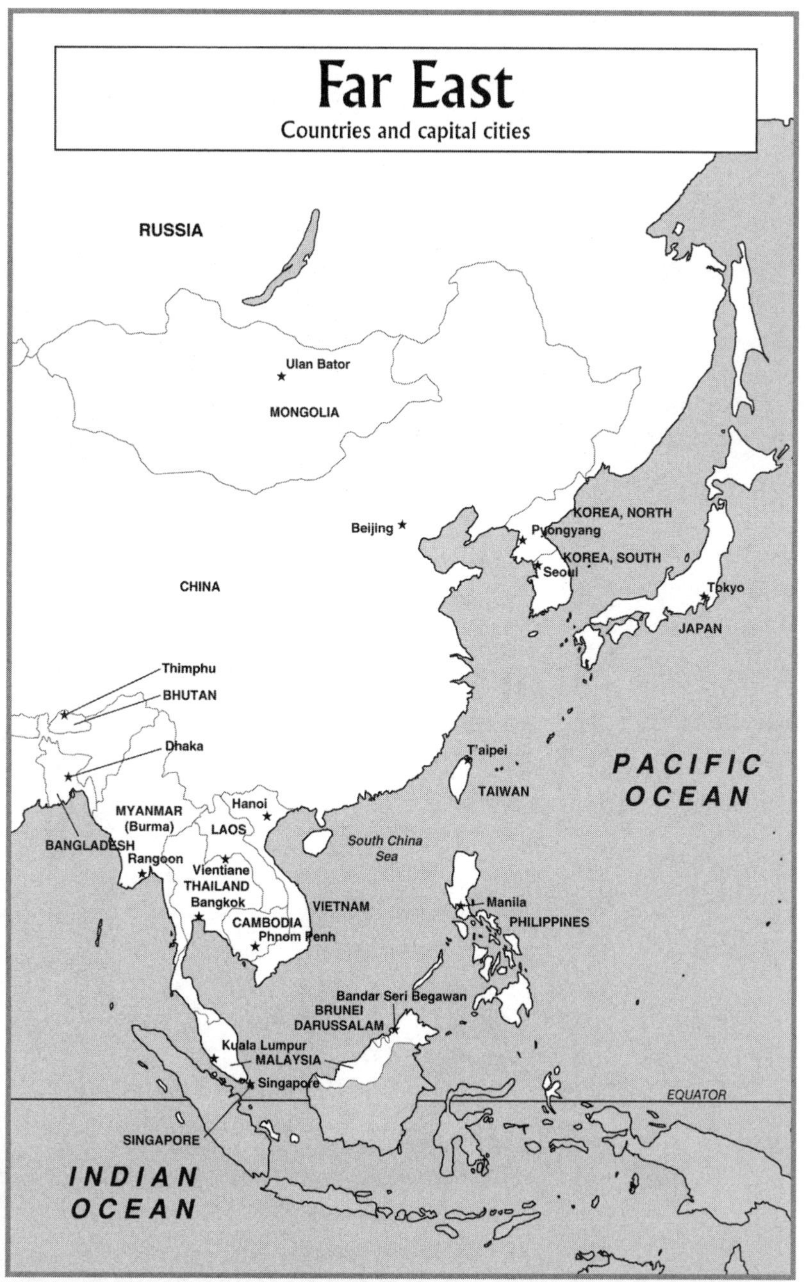
Far East
Countries and capital cities
RUSSIA
Ulan Bator
MONGOLIA
Beijing
CHINA
KOREA, NORTH
Pyongyang
KOREA, SOUTH
Seoul
Tokyo
JAPAN
Thimphu
BHUTAN
Dhaka
T'aipei
TAIWAN
PACIFIC
OCEAN
MYANMAR
(Burma)
Hanoi
LAOS
BANGLADESH
Rangoon
South China
Sea
Vientiane
THAILAND
Bangkok
VIETNAM
Manila
CAMBODIA
PHILIPPINES
Phnom Penh
Bandar Seri Begawan
BRUNEI
DARUSSALAM
Kuala Lumpur
MALAYSIA
Singapore
EQUATOR
SINGAPORE
INDIAN
OCEAN

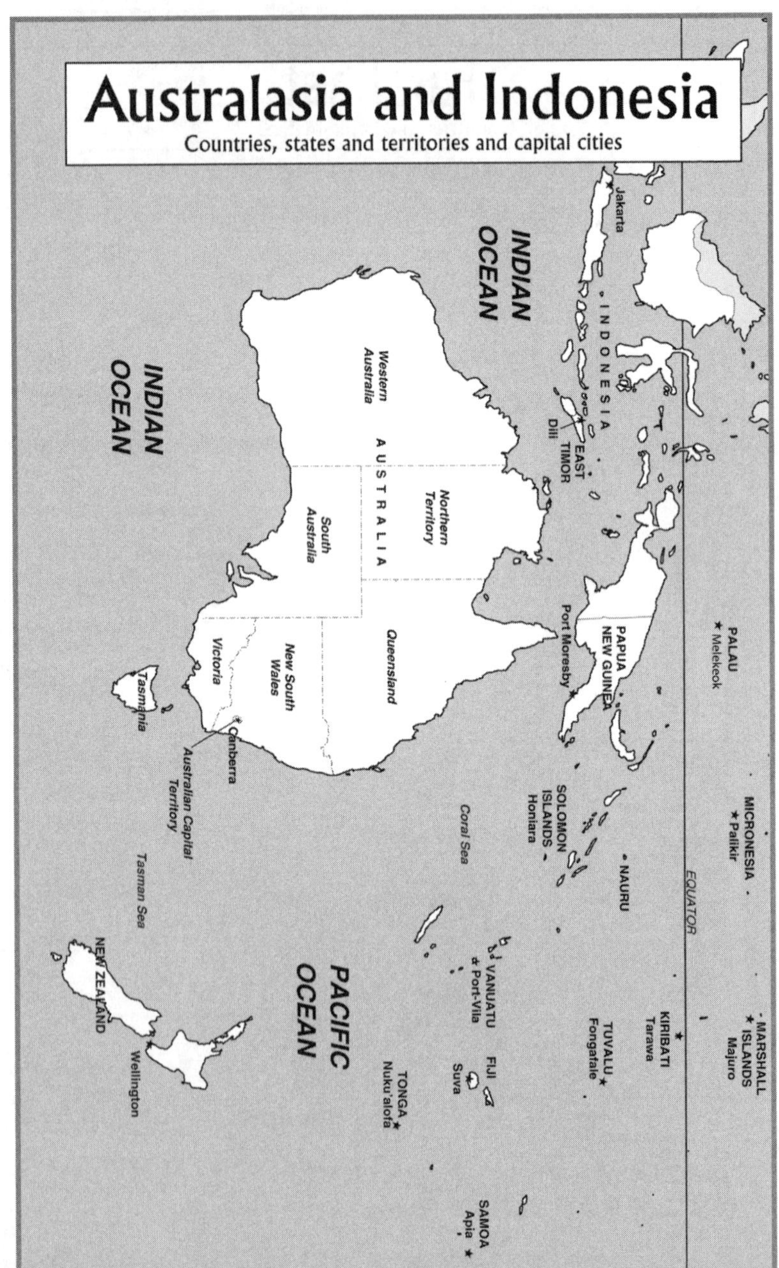
Australasia and Indonesia
Countries, states and territories and capital cities
Jakarta
INDIAN OCEAN
INDIAN OCEAN
INDONESIA
EAST TIMOR
Dili
Western Australia
AUSTRALIA
Northern Territory
South Australia
Queensland
New South Wales
Victoria
Tasmania
Canberra
Australian Capital Territory
PALAU
Melekeok
PAPUA NEW GUINEA
Port Moresby
MICRONESIA
Palikir
SOLOMON ISLANDS
Honiara
NAURU
EQUATOR
Coral Sea
Tasman Sea
PACIFIC OCEAN
VANUATU
Port-Vila
MARSHALL ISLANDS
Majuro
KIRIBATI
Tarawa
TUVALU
Fongafale
FIJI
Suva
TONGA
Nuku'alofa
NEW ZEALAND
Wellington
SAMOA
Apia

Africa

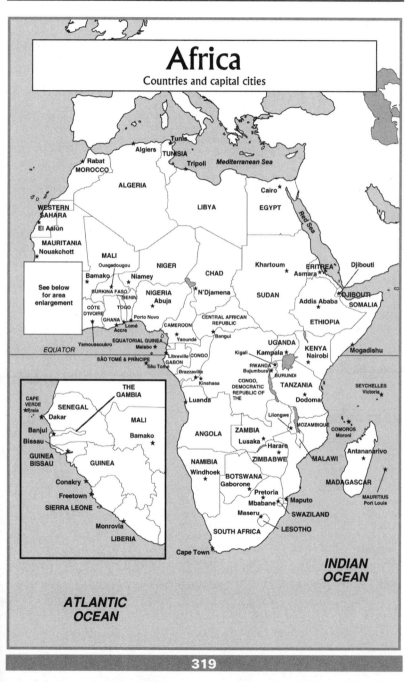

Countries and capital cities

Tunis
TUNISIA
Algiers
Tripoli
Mediterranean Sea
Rabat
MOROCCO
ALGERIA
Cairo
LIBYA
EGYPT
Red Sea
WESTERN SAHARA
El Aaiún
MAURITANIA
Nouakchott
MALI
Ouagadougou
NIGER
CHAD
Khartoum
ERITREA
Asmara
Djibouti
Bamako
Niamey
BURKINA FASO
BENIN
NIGERIA
Abuja
N'Djamena
SUDAN
DJIBOUTI
Addis Ababa
SOMALIA
See below for area enlargement
CÔTE D'IVOIRE
TOGO
GHANA
Lomé
Accra
Porto Novo
Yamoussoukro
CAMEROON
Yaoundé
CENTRAL AFRICAN REPUBLIC
Bangui
ETHIOPIA
EQUATORIAL GUINEA
Malabo
EQUATOR
SÃO TOMÉ & PRÍNCIPE
São Tomé
Libreville
GABON
CONGO
Brazzaville
Kinshasa
UGANDA
Kigali
Kampala
KENYA
Nairobi
Mogadishu
RWANDA
Bujumbura
BURUNDI
CONGO, DEMOCRATIC REPUBLIC OF THE
TANZANIA
Dodoma
SEYCHELLES
Victoria
Luanda
ANGOLA
ZAMBIA
Lusaka
Lilongwe
MOZAMBIQUE
COMOROS
Moroni
Harare
ZIMBABWE
MALAWI
Antananarivo
MADAGASCAR
MAURITIUS
Port Louis
NAMIBIA
Windhoek
BOTSWANA
Gaborone
Pretoria
Mbabane
Maputo
SWAZILAND
Maseru
LESOTHO
SOUTH AFRICA
Cape Town
INDIAN OCEAN
ATLANTIC OCEAN

THE GAMBIA
CAPE VERDE
Praia
SENEGAL
Dakar
MALI
Banjul
Bamako
Bissau
GUINEA BISSAU
GUINEA
Conakry
Freetown
SIERRA LEONE
Monrovia
LIBERIA

LARGEST COUNTRIES

The ten largest countries in the world by area.

Country	Area
Russia	17 075 400 sq km/6 591 104 sq mi
Canada	9 970 610 sq km/3 848 655 sq mi
China	9 597 000 sq km/3 704 000 sq mi
United States of America	9 160 454 sq km/3 535 935 sq mi
Brazil	8 511 965 sq km/3 285 618 sq mi
Australia	7 692 300 sq km/2 969 228 sq mi
Argentina	3 761 274 sq km/1 451 852 sq mi
India	3 166 829 sq km/1 222 396 sq mi
Kazakhstan	2 717 300 sq km/1 048 878 sq mi
Sudan	2 504 530 sq km/966 749 sq mi

SMALLEST COUNTRIES

The ten smallest countries in the world by area.

Country	Area
Vatican	0.4 sq km/0.2 sq mi
Monaco	1.9 sq km/0.75 sq mi
Nauru	21 sq km/8 sq mi
Tuvalu	26 sq km/10 sq mi
San Marino	61 sq km/24 sq mi
Liechtenstein	160 sq km/62 sq mi
Marshall Islands	180 sq km/70 sq mi
St Kitts and Nevis	269 sq km/104 sq mi
Maldives	300 sq km/120 sq mi
Malta	316 sq km/122 sq mi

MOST POPULOUS COUNTRIES

The ten most populous countries in the world.

Country	Population estimate[1]
China	1 321 852 000
India	1 129 866 000
United States of America	301 140 000
Indonesia	234 694 000
Brazil	190 010 000
Pakistan	164 742 000
Bangladesh	150 448 000
Russia	141 378 000
Nigeria	135 031 000
Japan	127 433 000

[1] *Population figures are 2007 estimates rounded to the nearest 1 000. Data source: CIA World Factbook.*

LEAST POPULOUS COUNTRIES

The ten least populous countries in the world.

Country	Population estimate[1]
Vatican	1 000
Tuvalu	12 000
Nauru	13 000
Palau	21 000
San Marino	30 000
Monaco	33 000
Liechtenstein	34 000
St Christopher and Nevis	39 000
Marshall Islands	62 000
Antigua and Barbuda	69 000

[1] *Population figures are 2007 estimates rounded to the nearest 1 000. Data source: CIA World Factbook.*

COUNTRY POPULATION ESTIMATES

The six most populous countries in the world.

	1950		*2000*		*2050*	
	Country	**Population estimate[1]**	**Country**	**Population estimate[1]**	**Country**	**Population estimate[1]**
1	China	554 760 000	China	1 275 133 000	India	1 592 704 000
2	India	357 561 000	India	1 008 937 000	China	1 392 307 000
3	USA	157 813 000	USA	283 230 000	USA	394 976 000
4	Russia	102 702 000	Indonesia	212 092 000	Pakistan	304 700 000
5	Japan	83 625 000	Brazil	170 406 000	Indonesia	284 640 000
6	Indonesia	79 538 000	Russia	145 491 000	Nigeria	258 108 000

[1] *Population figures are rounded to the nearest 1 000. Data source: United Nations Population Division, 'World Population Prospects: The 2004 Revision'.*

WORLD POPULATION

World population estimates (medium variant predictions) published by the UN in 2002. In 2005 the estimated world population in 2050 was revised to 9076 million.

Date (AD)	Millions[1]	Date (AD)	Millions[1]	Date (AD)	Millions[1]
1	300	1900	1 650	2010	6 830
1000	310	1950	2 519	2020	7 540
1250	400	1960	3 021	2030	8 130
1500	500	1970	3 692	2040	8 594
1750	790	1980	4 435	2050	8 919
1800	980	1990	5 264		
1850	1 260	2000	6 071		

[1] *Population figures are rounded to the nearest 1 000 000. Data source: United Nations Population Division.*

LIFE EXPECTANCY

Highest life expectancy at birth		Lowest life expectancy at birth	
Country	**Years**[1]	**Country**	**Years**[1]
Japan	81.9	Swaziland	32.9
Hong Kong, China	81.5	Botswana	36.6
Iceland	80.6	Lesotho	36.7
Switzerland	80.4	Zimbabwe	37.2
Australia	80.2	Zambia	37.4
Sweden	80.1	Central African Republic	39.4
Italy	80.0	Malawi	39.6
Macao, China	80.0	Sierra Leone	40.6
Canada	79.9	Angola	40.7
Israel	79.6	Mozambique	41.9

[1] *Figures are 2005 estimates. Data source: United Nations Population Division, 'World Population Prospects: The 2004 Revision'.*

Oldest and Youngest

Japan has the oldest overall population in the world, with a median average age in 2005 estimated to be 42.9 years. The youngest population is that of Uganda, where the median average age in 2005 was estimated to be 14.8 years.

CAPITAL CITIES

The principal English names of capital cities are listed. For local names, names in other languages and alternative spellings, see the entry for the country in **Countries A–Z**. Capitals of states, provinces, dependencies, overseas possessions and other territories are not listed.

Capital city	Country
Abidjan	Côte d'Ivoire *(administrative and economic capital)*
Abu Dhabi	United Arab Emirates
Abuja	Nigeria
Accra	Ghana
Addis Ababa	Ethiopia
Algiers	Algeria
Amman	Jordan
Amsterdam	The Netherlands (*official capital*)
Andorra la Vella	Andorra
Ankara	Turkey
Antananarivo	Madagascar
Apia	Samoa
Ashgabat	Turkmenistan
Asmara	Eritrea
Astana	Kazakhstan
Asunción	Paraguay
Athens	Greece
Baghdad	Iraq
Baku	Azerbaijan
Bamako	Mali
Bandar Seri Begawan	Brunei Darussalam
Bangkok	Thailand
Bangui	Central African Republic
Banjul	The Gambia
Basseterre	St Christopher and Nevis
Beijing	China
Beirut	Lebanon
Belgrade	Serbia
Belmopan	Belize
Berlin	Germany
Berne	Switzerland
Bishkek	Kyrgyzstan
Bissau	Guinea-Bissau
Bloemfontein	South Africa *(judicial capital)*
Bogotá	Colombia
Brasília	Brazil
Bratislava	Slovakia
Brazzaville	Congo

Capital city	Country
Bridgetown	Barbados
Brussels	Belgium
Bucharest	Romania
Budapest	Hungary
Buenos Aires	Argentina
Bujumbura	Burundi
Cairo	Egypt
Canberra	Australia
Cape Town	South Africa *(legislative capital)*
Caracas	Venezuela
Castries	St Lucia
Cetinje	Montenegro (*historic and cultural capital*)
Chisinau	Moldova
Colombo	Sri Lanka *(commercial capital)*
Conakry	Guinea
Copenhagen	Denmark
Cotonou	Benin *(seat of government and economic capital)*
Dakar	Senegal
Damascus	Syria
Dar es Salaam	Tanzania (*commercial capital*)
Dhaka	Bangladesh
Dili	East Timor
Djibouti	Djibouti
Dodoma	Tanzania (*political capital*)
Doha	Qatar
Dublin	Ireland
Dushanbe	Tajikistan
Freetown	Sierra Leone
Funafuti	Tuvalu
Gaborone	Botswana
Georgetown	Guyana
Guatemala City	Guatemala
Hanoi	Vietnam
Harare	Zimbabwe
Havana	Cuba
Helsinki	Finland
Honiara	Solomon Islands
Islamabad	Pakistan
Jakarta	Indonesia
Kabul	Afghanistan
Kampala	Uganda
Kathmandu	Nepal
Khartoum	Sudan
Kiev	Ukraine
Kigali	Rwanda
Kingston	Jamaica

Capital city	Country
Kingstown	St Vincent and the Grenadines
Kinshasa	Democratic Republic of the Congo
Kuala Lumpur	Malaysia (*official capital*)
Kuwait City	Kuwait
La Paz	Bolivia *(administrative capital)*
Libreville	Gabon
Lilongwe	Malawi
Lima	Peru
Lisbon	Portugal
Ljubljana	Slovenia
Lobamba	Swaziland *(legislative capital)*
Lomé	Togo
London	United Kingdom
Luanda	Angola
Lusaka	Zambia
Luxembourg	Luxembourg
Madrid	Spain
Majuro	Marshall Islands
Malabo	Equatorial Guinea
Malé	Maldives
Managua	Nicaragua
Manama	Bahrain
Manila	Philippines
Maputo	Mozambique
Maseru	Lesotho
Mbabane	Swaziland *(administrative capital)*
Melekeok	Palau
Mexico City	Mexico
Minsk	Belarus
Mogadishu	Somalia
Monaco	Monaco
Monrovia	Liberia
Montevideo	Uruguay
Moroni	Comoros
Moscow	Russia
Muscat	Oman
Nairobi	Kenya
Nassau	The Bahamas
Naypyidaw	Myanmar (Burma) (*administrative capital*)
N'Djamena	Chad
New Delhi	India
Niamey	Niger
Nicosia	Cyprus
Nouakchott	Mauritania
Nuku'alofa	Tonga

CAPITAL CITIES

Capital city	Country
Oslo	Norway
Ottawa	Canada
Ouagadougou	Burkina Faso
Palikir	Federated States of Micronesia
Panama City	Panama
Paramaribo	Suriname
Paris	France
Phnom Penh	Cambodia
Podgorica	Montenegro (*administrative centre*)
Port-au-Prince	Haiti
Port Louis	Mauritius
Port Moresby	Papua New Guinea
Port of Spain	Trinidad and Tobago
Porto Novo	Benin *(administrative and constitutional capital)*
Port-Vila	Vanuatu
Prague	Czech Republic
Praia	Cape Verde
Pretoria	South Africa *(administrative capital)*
Putrajaya	Malaysia (*seat of government and administrative capital*)
Pyongyang	North Korea
Quito	Ecuador
Rabat	Morocco
Rangoon	Myanmar (Burma) (*historic capital*)
Reykjavík	Iceland
Riga	Latvia
Riyadh	Saudi Arabia
Rome	Italy
Roseau	Dominica
St George's	Grenada
St John's	Antigua and Barbuda
San José	Costa Rica
San Marino	San Marino
San Salvador	El Salvador
Sana'a	Yemen
Santiago	Chile
Santo Domingo	Dominican Republic
São Tomé	São Tomé and Príncipe
Sarajevo	Bosnia and Herzegovina
Seoul	South Korea
Singapore	Singapore
Skopje	Macedonia
Sofia	Bulgaria
Sri Jayawardenepura Kotte	Sri Lanka *(administrative capital)*
Stockholm	Sweden
Sucre	Bolivia *(official and legislative capital)*
Suva	Fiji
T'aipei	Taiwan
Tallinn	Estonia
Tarawa	Kiribati
Tashkent	Uzbekistan
T'bilisi	Georgia
Tegucigalpa	Honduras
Tehran	Iran
Tel Aviv-Jaffa[1]	Israel
The Hague	The Netherlands (*seat of government*)
Thimphu	Bhutan
Tirana	Albania
Tokyo	Japan
Tripoli	Libya
Tunis	Tunisia
Ulan Bator	Mongolia
Vaduz	Liechtenstein
Valletta	Malta
Vatican City	Vatican
Victoria	Seychelles
Vienna	Austria
Vientiane	Laos
Vilnius	Lithuania
Warsaw	Poland
Washington, DC	United States of America
Wellington	New Zealand
Windhoek	Namibia
Yamoussoukro	Côte d'Ivoire *(official capital)*
Yaoundé	Cameroon
Yaren District[2]	Nauru
Yerevan	Armenia
Zagreb	Croatia

[1] *Israel claims Jerusalem as its capital, but this is not recognized internationally.*
[2] *There is no capital as such, but government offices are situated in this area.*

City of the North

The Icelandic city of Reykjavík, founded in 874, is the most northerly capital city in the world.

CAPITAL CITIES ON RIVERS

Information for selected major capital cities is given. Capital cities that are sea ports or that lie on bays, estuaries, lakes or other water expanses are not included.

Capital city	Country	River
Amman	Jordan	Zarqa
Amsterdam	The Netherlands	Amstel (and the IJsselmeer)
Ankara	Turkey	a tributary of the Ova
Baghdad	Iraq	Tigris
Bangkok	Thailand	Chao Phraya
Belgrade	Serbia	Danube, Sava
Berlin	Germany	Spree, Havel (and others)
Bratislava	Slovakia	Danube
Brussels	Belgium	Senne
Bucharest	Romania	Dambovit
Budapest	Hungary	Danube
Buenos Aires	Argentina	Plate
Cairo	Egypt	Nile
Canberra	Australia	Molonglo
Damascus	Syria	Barada
Dhaka	Bangladesh	Meghna
Dublin	Ireland	Liffey
Hanoi	Vietnam	Red
Islamabad	Pakistan	Jhelum
Jakarta	Indonesia	Liwung
Kiev	Ukraine	Dnieper
Lima	Peru	Rímac
Lisbon	Portugal	Tagus
Ljubljana	Slovenia	Sava, Ljubljanica
London	United Kingdom	Thames
Luxembourg	Luxembourg	Alzette, Petrusse
Madrid	Spain	Manzanares
Manila	Philippines	Pasig
Minsk	Belarus	Svisloch
Moscow	Russia	Moskva
New Delhi	India	Yamuna (Old Delhi)
Ottawa	Canada	Ottawa, Rideau
Paris	France	Seine
Phnom Penh	Cambodia	Mekong (at confluence with the Tonlé Sap lake)
Podgorica	Montenegro	Morača
Prague	Czech Republic	Vltava
Pyongyang	North Korea	Taedong
Rabat	Morocco	Bou Regreg
Riga	Latvia	Daugava
Rome	Italy	Tiber
Santiago	Chile	Mapocho
Sarajevo	Bosnia and Herzegovina	Miljacka
Seoul	South Korea	Han
Skopje	Macedonia	Vardar
Tokyo	Japan	Sumida

CAPITAL CITY POPULATION

Capital city	Country	River
Vienna	Austria	Danube
Vilnius	Lithuania	Vilnya
Warsaw	Poland	Vistula
Washington, DC	United States of America	Potomac, Anacostia
Zagreb	Croatia	Sava

Skinny-Dipping Presidents

Rivers in capital cities are liable to receive unexpected visitors. John Quincy Adams (1767–1848), the sixth president of the United States of America, reportedly swam naked in the Potomac every day.

CAPITAL CITY POPULATION

Capital city	Population[1]	Capital city	Population[1]
Abidjan	3577000 (2005e)	Bratislava	422000 (2006e)
Abu Dhabi	1850000 (2006e)	Brazzaville	1327000 (2006e)
Abuja	1405000 (2006)	Bridgetown	99000 (2007e)
Accra	2981000 (2005e)	Brussels	1012000 (2005e)
Addis Ababa	2893000 (2005e)	Bucharest	1934000 (2005e)
Algiers	3221000 (2006e)	Budapest	1693000 (2005e)
Amman	1292000 (2005e)	Buenos Aires	11612000 (2006e)
Amsterdam	1147000 (2005e)	Bujumbura	342000 (2007e)
Andorra la Vella	20000 (2007e)	Cairo	7438000 (2005e)
Ankara	3573000 (2005e)	Canberra	325000 (2005e)
Antananarivo	1585000 (2005e)	Cape Town	3083000 (2005e)
Apia	41000 (2007e)	Caracas	2913000 (2005e)
Ashgabat	848000 (2007e)	Castries	13000 (2007e)
Asmara	594000 (2007e)	Cetinje	15000 (2003)
Astana	357000 (2007e)	Chisinau	611000 (2007e)
Asunción	1858000 (2005e)	Colombo	649000 (2006e)
Athens	3131000 (2005e)	Conakry	1425000 (2005e)
Baghdad	5904000 (2005e)	Copenhagen	1088000 (2005e)
Baku	1856000 (2005e)	Cotonou	761000 (2006e)
Bamako	1368000 (2005e)	Dakar	2159000 (2005e)
Bandar Seri Begawan	70000 (2007e)	Damascus	2272000 (2005e)
Bangkok	6593000 (2005e)	Dar es Salaam	2676000 (2005e)
Bangui	735000 (2006e)	Dhaka	6725000 (2005e)
Banjul	34000 (2006e)	Dili	167000 (2007e)
Basseterre	13000 (2007e)	Djibouti	643000 (2007e)
Beijing	7725000 (2007e)	Dodoma	196000 (2007e)
Beirut	1777000 (2005e)	Doha	351000 (2006e)
Belgrade	1106000 (2005e)	Dublin	1037000 (2005e)
Belmopan	16000 (2007e)	Dushanbe	538000 (2006e)
Berlin	3400000 (2006e)	Freetown	799000 (2005e)
Berne	957000 (2006e)	Funafuti	4000 (2002)
Bishkek	934000 (2007e)	Gaborone	221000 (2007e)
Bissau	404000 (2006e)	Georgetown	237000 (2006e)
Bloemfontein	498000 (2007e)	Guatemala City	1024000 (2006e)
Bogotá	7235000 (2006e)	Hanoi	4164000 (2005e)
Brasília	2384000 (2006e)	Harare	1515000 (2005e)

Capital city	Population[1]
Havana	2 189 000 (2005e)
Helsinki	1 091 000 (2005e)
Honiara	58 000 (2007e)
Islamabad	834 000 (2007e)
Jakarta	8 569 000 (2006e)
Kabul	2 994 000 (2005e)
Kampala	1 319 000 (2005e)
Kathmandu	815 000 (2005e)
Khartoum	4 518 000 (2005e)
Kiev	2 470 000 (2007e)
Kigali	779 000 (2005e)
Kingston	585 000 (2006e)
Kingstown	18 000 (2007e)
Kinshasa	8 419 000 (2007e)
Kuala Lumpur[2]	1 405 000 (2005e)
Kuwait City	32 000 (2005)
La Paz	1 527 000 (2005e)
Libreville	591 000 (2006e)
Lilongwe	722 000 (2007e)
Lima	7 186 000 (2005e)
Lisbon	499 000 (2007e)
Ljubljana	254 000 (2006e)
Lobamba	5 000 (2007e)
Lomé	1 337 000 (2005e)
London	7 518 000 (2005e)
Luanda	2 766 000 (2005e)
Lusaka	1 260 000 (2005e)
Luxembourg	76 000 (2006e)
Madrid	3 155 000 (2005e)
Majuro	28 000 (2006e)
Malabo	167 000 (2007e)
Malé	89 000 (2007e)
Managua	1 165 000 (2005e)
Manama	149 000 (2007e)
Manila	1 581 000 (2000e)
Maputo	1 320 000 (2005e)
Maseru	116 000 (2007e)
Mbabane	81 000 (2007e)
Melekeok	400 (2007e)
Mexico City	8 659 000 (2006e)
Minsk	1 778 000 (2005e)
Mogadishu	1 320 000 (2005e)
Monaco	1 000 (2007e)
Monrovia	936 000 (2005e)
Montevideo	1 264 000 (2005e)
Moroni	45 000 (2007e)
Moscow	10 568 000 (2007e)
Muscat	24 000 (2007e)
Nairobi	2 773 000 (2005e)
Nassau	232 000 (2006e)
N'Djamena	888 000 (2005e)

Capital city	Population[1]
New Delhi	322 000 (2006e)
Niamey	850 000 (2005e)
Nicosia	202 000 (2006e)
Nouakchott	753 000 (2007e)
Nuku'alofa	24 000 (2007e)
Oslo	802 000 (2005e)
Ottawa	1 149 000 (2005e)
Ouagadougou	1 152 000 (2007e)
Palikir	4 000 (2007e)
Panama City	404 000 (2007e)
Paramaribo	226 000 (2007e)
Paris	2 154 000 (2006e)
Phnom Penh	1 364 000 (2005e)
Podgorica	163 000 (2007e)
Port-au-Prince	2 129 000 (2005e)
Port Louis	134 000 (2006e)
Port Moresby	290 000 (2006e)
Port of Spain	50 000 (2006e)
Porto Novo	242 000 (2007e)
Port-Vila	38 000 (2007e)
Prague	1 171 000 (2005e)
Praia	121 000 (2007e)
Pretoria	1 271 000 (2005e)
Pyongyang	3 351 000 (2005e)
Quito	1 514 000 (2005e)
Rabat	1 647 000 (2005e)
Rangoon[3]	4 574 000 (2006e)
Reykjavík	195 000 (2006e)
Riga	738 000 (2006e)
Riyadh	4 193 000 (2005e)
Rome	2 817 000 (2005e)
Roseau	17 000 (2007e)
St George's	37 000 (2001c)
St John's	25 000 (2007e)
San José	912 000 (2005e)
San Marino	4 000 (2007e)
San Salvador	1 517 000 (2005e)
Sana'a	1 801 000 (2005e)
Santiago	5 683 000 (2005e)
Santo Domingo	2 022 000 (2005e)
São Tomé	65 000 (2007e)
Sarajevo	737 000 (2006e)
Seoul	10 297 000 (2005e)
Singapore	4 326 000 (2005e)
Skopje	582 000 (2006e)
Sofia	1 093 000 (2005e)
Sri Jayewardenepura Kotte	119 000 (2007e)
Stockholm	1 708 000 (2005e)
Sucre	241 000 (2007e)
Suva	203 000 (2006e)

LARGEST CITIES

Capital city	Population[1]	Capital city	Population[1]
T'aipei	2492000 (2006e)	Valletta	7000 (2007e)
Tallinn	392000 (2006e)	Vatican City	1000 (2007e)
Tarawa	47000 (2007e)	Victoria	23000 (2006e)
Tashkent	2181000 (2005e)	Vienna	1651000 (2005e)
T'bilisi	1047000 (2005e)	Vientiane	698000 (2006e)
Tegucigalpa	927000 (2005e)	Vilnius	542000 (2006e)
Tehran	7314000 (2005e)	Warsaw	1680000 (2005e)
Tel Aviv-Jaffa[4]	388000 (2006e)	Washington, DC	544000 (2007e)
Thimphu	79000 (2007e)	Wellington	179000 (2006)
Tirana	380000 (2006e)	Windhoek	277000 (2006e)
Tokyo	8404000 (2006e)	Yamoussoukro	206000 (2007e)
Tripoli	2098000 (2005e)	Yaoundé	1391000 (2007e)
Tunis	941000 (2006e)	Yaren[5]	5000 (207e)
Ulan Bator	863000 (2005e)	Yerevan	1103000 (2005e)
Vaduz	5000 (2007e)	Zagreb	701000 (2006e)

[1] *Population figures are rounded to the nearest 1000; c = census; e = estimate.*
[2] *No accurate figure available for Putrajaya, Malaysia's administrative capital.*
[3] *No figure available for Naypyidaw, Myanmar's administrative capital.*
[4] *Israel claims Jerusalem as its capital, but this is not recognized internationally.*
[5] *Nauru has no capital, but government offices are located in Yaren District.*

LARGEST CITIES

World

UN estimates for the world's ten largest urban agglomerations ranked by population size. The agglomeration includes not only the city itself but also the greater metropolitan area. This means that the figures vary from estimates for the city alone. Population estimates also vary according to the criteria used in their calculation.

City	Country	Population
Tokyo	Japan	35200000
Mexico City	Mexico	19400000
New York-Newark	United States of America	18700000
São Paulo	Brazil	18300000
Mumbai	India	18200000
Delhi	India	15000000
Shanghai	China	14500000
Kolkata	India	14300000
Jakarta	Indonesia	13200000
Buenos Aires	Argentina	12600000

[1] *Population figures are 2005 estimates. Data source: United Nations Population Division, 'World Urbanization Prospects: The 2005 Revision'.*

UK

The ten largest cities in the United Kingdom ranked by population size.

City	Population[1]
London	7517700
Birmingham	994900
Leeds	719600
Glasgow	577700
Sheffield	516100
Bradford	481100
Edinburgh	453700
Liverpool	444500
Manchester	437000
Bristol	393900

[1] *Population figures are 2004 estimates. Data source: Office for National Statistics and General Register Office for Scotland.*

Cities of the Future

People are increasingly living in cities in the modern world. The United Nations predicts that more than half of the world's population will live in urban areas by 2008 – compared with just 2% of people in 1800, 30% in 1950 and 47% in 2000.

USA

The ten largest cities in the United States of America ranked by population size.

City	State	Population (2006e)
New York	New York	8214400
Los Angeles	California	3849400
Chicago	Illinois	2833300
Houston	Texas	2144500
Phoenix	Arizona	1513000
Philadelphia	Pennsylvania	1448400
San Antonio	Texas	1296700
San Diego	California	1257000
Dallas	Texas	1233000
San José	California	930000

Data source: Population Division, US Census Bureau.

World's Best City

According to a study by the Economist Intelligence Unit in 2005, Vancouver is the best city in the world in which to live. Based on five criteria – stability, healthcare, culture and environment, education and infrastructure – the study put the Canadian west coast city ahead of runners-up Melbourne, Vienna, Geneva, Perth, Adelaide, Sydney, Zurich, Toronto and Calgary.

UNITED NATIONS (UN)

An organization formed to maintain world peace and foster international co-operation, formally established on 24 Oct 1945 with 51 member states. It has six 'principal organs': the General Assembly, the Security Council, the Secretariat, the International Court of Justice, the Economic and Social Council and the Trusteeship Council.

United Nations membership

The United Nations has 192 member states. Countries are grouped according to year of entry; only the country's current name is given, although its name may have changed during its membership (for example Belarus joined the UN in 1945 as Byelorussia). For information on former names see each country's entry in **Countries A–Z** under **Human Geography**.

1945	Argentina, Australia, Belarus, Belgium, Bolivia, Brazil, Canada, Chile, China[1], Colombia, Costa Rica, Cuba, Czechoslovakia (until 1992), Denmark, Dominican Republic, Ecuador, Egypt, El Salvador, Ethiopia, France, Greece, Guatemala, Haiti, Honduras, India, Iran, Iraq, Lebanon, Liberia, Luxembourg, Mexico, The Netherlands, New Zealand, Nicaragua, Norway, Panama, Paraguay, Peru, Philippines, Poland, Russia, Saudi Arabia, South Africa, Syria, Turkey, Ukraine, United Kingdom, United States of America, Uruguay, Venezuela, Yugoslavia (until 1992)
1946	Afghanistan, Iceland, Sweden, Thailand
1947	Pakistan, Yemen[2]
1948	Myanmar (Burma)
1949	Israel
1950	Indonesia
1955	Albania, Austria, Bulgaria, Cambodia, Finland, Hungary, Ireland, Italy, Jordan, Laos, Libya, Nepal, Portugal, Romania, Spain, Sri Lanka
1956	Japan, Morocco, Sudan, Tunisia
1957	Ghana, Malaysia
1958	Guinea
1960	Benin, Burkina Faso, Cameroon, Central African Republic, Chad, Congo, Congo (Democratic Republic of the), Côte d'Ivoire, Cyprus, Gabon, Madagascar, Mali, Niger, Nigeria, Senegal, Somalia, Togo
1961	Mauritania, Mongolia, Sierra Leone, Tanzania[3]
1962	Algeria, Burundi, Jamaica, Rwanda, Trinidad and Tobago, Uganda
1963	Kenya, Kuwait
1964	Malawi, Malta, Zambia
1965	The Gambia, Maldives, Singapore
1966	Barbados, Botswana, Guyana, Lesotho
1968	Equatorial Guinea, Mauritius, Swaziland
1970	Fiji
1971	Bahrain, Bhutan, Oman, Qatar, United Arab Emirates
1973	The Bahamas, East Germany (until 1990), Germany
1974	Bangladesh, Grenada, Guinea-Bissau
1975	Cape Verde, Comoros, Mozambique, Papua New Guinea, São Tomé and Príncipe, Suriname
1976	Angola, Samoa, Seychelles
1977	Djibouti, Vietnam
1978	Dominica, Solomon Islands
1979	St Lucia
1980	St Vincent and the Grenadines, Zimbabwe
1981	Antigua and Barbuda, Belize, Vanuatu

1983	St Kitts and Nevis
1984	Brunei Darussalam
1990	Liechtenstein, Namibia
1991	Estonia, Korea (North), Korea (South), Latvia, Lithuania, Marshall Islands, Micronesia
1992	Armenia, Azerbaijan, Bosnia and Herzegovina, Croatia, Georgia, Kazakhstan, Kyrgyzstan, Moldova, San Marino, Slovenia, Tajikistan, Turkmenistan, Uzbekistan
1993	Andorra, Czech Republic, Eritrea, Macedonia, Monaco, Slovakia
1994	Palau
1999	Kiribati, Nauru, Tonga
2000	Tuvalu, Serbia[4]
2002	East Timor, Switzerland
2006	Montenegro

[1] *Taiwan, as the Republic of China, represented China at the UN until 25 Oct 1971, when the People's Republic of China was recognized instead; Taiwan has not since been a member of the UN.*

[2] *North Yemen joined the UN in 1947 and South Yemen joined in 1967; since unification in 1990 as Yemen the UN has considered 1947 to be the state's date of joining.*

[3] *Tanganyika joined the UN in 1961 and Zanzibar joined in 1963; since unification in 1964 as Tanzania the UN has considered 1961 to be the state's date of joining.*

[4] *The Federal Republic of Yugoslavia joined the UN in 2000 and was renamed Serbia and Montenegro in 2003. Since Montenegro's declaration of independence in 2006 and a subsequent declaration by Serbia of its intention to retain UN membership, the UN has considered 2000 to be Serbia's date of joining.*

Blue Berets for Peace

Between 1948 and Jun 2007, UN peacekeepers took part in 61 operations. They are currently deployed in 15 ongoing missions. The UN calculates that peacekeeping since 1948 has cost $47.2 billion.

United Nations Secretaries-General

The United Nations Secretariat, under the Secretary-General, employs around 8,900 people worldwide. The Secretary-General is often a significant figure in international diplomacy.

Secretary-General

1946–53	Trygve Lie *Norway*
1953–61	Dag Hammarskjöld *Sweden*
1962–71	U Thant *Burma*
1972–81	Kurt Waldheim *Austria*
1982–91	Javier Pérez de Cuéllar *Peru*
1992–6	Boutros Boutros-Ghali *Egypt*
1997–2006	Kofi Annan *Ghana*
2006–	Ban Ki-moon *South Korea*

UNITED NATIONS (UN)

United Nations Security Council

The United Nations Security Council has 15 members: five permanent members, which each have the power of veto over any resolutions, and ten that are elected for two-year periods. The primary role of the Council is to maintain international peace and security; its decisions are binding on all other members. Only the permanent members are listed.

China
France
Russia
United Kingdom
United States of America

United Nations organizations

In addition to the bodies established under the UN Charter there is a range of subsidiary agencies, many with their own constitutions and membership. There are also a number of functional and regional commissions and research and training institutes.

UN specialized agencies

Food and Agriculture Organization of the United Nations (FAO)
International Civil Aviation Organization (ICAO)
International Fund for Agricultural Development (IFAD)
International Labour Organization (ILO)
International Maritime Organization (IMO)
International Monetary Fund (IMF)
International Telecommunication Union (ITU)
United Nations Educational, Scientific and Cultural Organization (UNESCO)
United Nations Industrial Development Organization (UNIDO)
Universal Postal Union (UPU)
World Bank Group[1]
World Health Organization (WHO)
World Intellectual Property Organization (WIPO)
World Meteorological Organization (WMO)
World Tourism Organization (WTO)

[1] *Includes the International Bank for Reconstruction and Development (IBRD), the International Development Association (IDA), the International Finance Corporation (IFC), the Multilateral Investment Guarantee Agency (MIGA) and the International Centre for Settlement of Investment Disputes (ICSID).*

UN programmes and funds

International Trade Centre (ITC)
Office of the United Nations High Commissioner for Refugees (UNHCR)
United Nations Capital Development Fund (UNCDF)
United Nations Children's Fund (UNICEF)
United Nations Conference on Trade and Development (UNCTAD)
United Nations Development Fund for Women (UNIFEM)
United Nations Development Programme (UNDP)
United Nations Drug Control Programme (UNDCP)
United Nations Environment Programme (UNEP)
United Nations Human Settlements Programme (UNHSP/UN-Habitat)
United Nations Population Fund (UNFPA)
United Nations Relief and Works Agency for Palestine Refugees in the Near East (UNRWA)
United Nations Volunteers (UNV)
World Food Programme (WFP)

Other UN entities

Joint United Nations Programme on HIV/AIDS (UNAIDS)
Office of the United Nations High Commissioner for Human Rights (OHCHR)
United Nations Office for Project Services (UNOPS)
United Nations System Staff College (UNSSC)
United Nations University (UNU)

UN related organizations

International Atomic Energy Agency (IAEA)
Organization for the Prohibition of Chemical Weapons (OPCW)
PrepCom for the Nuclear-Test-Ban-Treaty Organization (CTBTO Prep.com)
World Trade Organization (WTO)

International HQ

Deep in the heart of New York City in the United States of America lie 7.3 hectares/18 acres of foreign land. The United Nations headquarters on Manhattan Island is an 'international territory', owned by the UN and beyond US jurisdiction.

COMMONWEALTH

The Commonwealth is a voluntary organization of autonomous states, most of which have in the past been imperial possessions of Britain. It was formally established by the Statute of Westminster (1931) and meets frequently to discuss matters of mutual interest and concern. Its head is Queen Elizabeth II. There are 53 member states, encompassing 1.8 billion people, or 30% of the world's population.

Commonwealth membership

Member countries are listed by year of entry.

1931	Australia, Canada, Irish Free State (left 1949), Newfoundland (joined Canada 1949), New Zealand, United Kingdom, South Africa (left 1961, rejoined 1994)
1947	India, Pakistan (left 1972, rejoined 1989; suspended 1999, readmitted 2004)
1948	Sri Lanka
1957	Ghana, Malaysia
1960	Nigeria (suspended 1995, readmitted 1999)
1961	Cyprus, Sierra Leone, Tanzania
1962	Jamaica, Trinidad and Tobago, Uganda
1963	Kenya
1964	Malawi, Malta, Zambia
1965	The Gambia, Singapore
1966	Barbados, Botswana, Guyana, Lesotho
1968	Mauritius, Nauru, Swaziland
1970	Tonga, Samoa, Fiji (left 1987, rejoined 1997; suspended 2000, readmitted 2001, suspended 2006)
1972	Bangladesh
1973	The Bahamas
1974	Grenada
1975	Papua New Guinea
1976	Seychelles
1978	Dominica, Solomon Islands, Tuvalu
1979	Kiribati, St Lucia, St Vincent and the Grenadines
1980	Vanuatu, Zimbabwe (suspended 2002; left 2003)

1981	Antigua and Barbuda, Belize
1982	Maldives
1983	St Kitts and Nevis
1984	Brunei Darussalam
1990	Namibia
1995	Cameroon, Mozambique[1]

[1] *Although Mozambique is a former Portuguese colony it was allowed to join the Commonwealth because of its close relationship with the Commonwealth since its independence.*

Commonwealth Secretaries-General

Secretary-General	
1965–75	Arnold Smith *Canada*
1975–90	Shridath Ramphal *Guyana*
1990–2000	Emeka Anyaoku *Nigeria*
2000–	Donald C McKinnon *New Zealand*

EUROPEAN UNION (EU)

European Union membership

Member countries are listed by year of entry.

1958	Belgium, France, Germany, Italy, Luxembourg, The Netherlands
1973	Denmark, Republic of Ireland, United Kingdom
1981	Greece
1986	Portugal, Spain
1995	Austria, Finland, Sweden
2004	Cyprus, Czech Republic, Estonia, Hungary, Latvia, Lithuania, Malta, Poland, Slovakia, Slovenia
2007	Bulgaria, Romania

Candidate countries: Croatia, Former Yugoslav Republic of Macedonia, Turkey.

European Union Commission presidents

The European Commission is an executive body composed of 25 Commissioners from EU member countries led by a president.

President	
1958–67	Walter Hallstein *West Germany*
1967–70	Jean Rey *Belgium*
1970–2	Franco Maria Malfatti *Italy*
1972–3	Sicco L Mansholt *The Netherlands*
1973–7	François-Xavier Ortoli *France*
1977–81	Roy Jenkins *United Kingdom*
1981–5	Gaston Thorn *Luxembourg*
1985–95	Jacques Delors *France*
1995–9	Jacques Santer *Luxembourg*
1999–2004	Romano Prodi *Italy*
2004–	José Manuel Barroso *Portugal*

Note: The current Commission's term of office will end in 2009.

United in Diversity

'United in Diversity' is the official motto of the EU. There is also an official European anthem, Beethoven's Ninth Symphony, but this is always played without words. The EU celebrates its birthday on 9 May, 'Europe Day', as this was the day on which the idea of a European Union was first proposed in 1950.

AFRICAN UNION (AU)

The Organization of African Unity (OAU) was established in 1963 and changed its name to the African Union (AU) in 2002. Its stated aim is to promote accelerated socioeconomic integration of the continent, leading to greater unity and solidarity between African countries and peoples. It has 53 member states.

Algeria
Angola
Benin
Botswana
Burkina Faso
Burundi
Cameroon
Cape Verde
Central African Republic
Chad
Comoros
Congo
Congo, Democratic Republic of the
Côte d'Ivoire
Djibouti
Egypt
Equatorial Guinea
Eritrea
Ethiopia
Gabon
The Gambia
Ghana
Guinea
Guinea-Bissau
Kenya
Lesotho
Liberia
Libya
Madagascar
Malawi
Mali
Mauritania
Mauritius
Mozambique
Namibia
Niger
Nigeria
Rwanda
São Tomé and Príncipe
Senegal
Seychelles
Sierra Leone
Somalia
South Africa
Sudan
Swaziland
Tanzania
Togo
Tunisia
Uganda
Western Sahara
Zambia
Zimbabwe

ARAB LEAGUE

The League of Arab States, known as the Arab League, was established in 1945 and has 22 members from the Middle East and Africa. It exists primarily to promote political and economic co-operation, and its charter forbids its members from resorting to force against each other. Seven countries originally signed the treaty. Member countries are listed by year of entry.

1945	Egypt (suspended 1979–89), Iraq, Jordan (as Transjordan), Lebanon, Saudi Arabia, Syria, Yemen
1953	Libya
1956	Sudan
1958	Morocco, Tunisia
1961	Kuwait
1962	Algeria
1971	Bahrain, Oman, Qatar, United Arab Emirates
1973	Mauritania
1974	Somalia
1976	Palestine (as Palestine Liberation Organization)
1977	Djibouti
1993	Comoros

Atlantic Ocean, Arabian Sea

The Arab League estimates that the Arabic world covers approximately 14.2 million sq km/ 5.5 million sq mi, stretching across two continents from northern Africa's Atlantic coast to the Middle East and Asia, and encompassing a population of approximately 334 million people.

ASSOCIATION OF SOUTH EAST ASIAN NATIONS (ASEAN)

The Association of South East Asian Nations (ASEAN) was established in 1967 and has ten member states. Its aims are 'to accelerate economic growth, social progress and cultural development in the region' and 'to promote regional peace and stability'. Member countries are listed by year of entry.

1967	Indonesia, Malaysia, Philippines, Singapore, Thailand
1984	Brunei Darussalam
1995	Vietnam
1997	Laos, Myanmar (Burma)
1999	Cambodia

COMMONWEALTH OF INDEPENDENT STATES (CIS)

The Commonwealth of Independent States (CIS) is a grouping of twelve independent states formed in 1991 from the 15 republics which previously made up the USSR. Each member state has sovereign equality, and in 1993 all states signed an agreement to co-ordinate policies on taxation, customs, labour movement and other aspects of economic activity. Eleven countries originally joined the CIS in 1991; Georgia joined in 1993, but suspended membership of the defence council in 2006 and is reviewing its membership. Turkmenistan discontinued permanent membership in 2005 and became an associate member.

Armenia
Azerbaijan
Belarus
Georgia
Kazakhstan
Kyrgyzstan
Moldova
Russia
Tajikistan
Turkmenistan*
Ukraine
Uzbekistan

* Associate member.

GROUP OF EIGHT (G8)

The Group of Eight (G8) comprises the world's leading industrialized democracies. The first G8 summit was held in 1975; the annual summit meetings have a wide remit, dealing with economic, political and social issues on a global level. At other times these and other economically powerful countries have met to discuss matters of mutual interest as the Group of Five (G5), Seven (G7), Ten (G10), etc. Current member countries are listed by year of entry.

1975	France, Germany, Italy, Japan, United Kingdom, United States of America
1976	Canada
1998	Russia

G8 presidency and summits

The presidency of the G8 is held by each country in rotation for one year; that country hosts the annual summit meeting, at which the European Union is also represented.

2000	Japan (Okinawa)
2001	Italy (Genoa)
2002	Canada (Kananaskis)
2003	France (Evian)
2004	United States of America (Sea Island)
2005	United Kingdom (Gleneagles)
2006	Russia (St Petersburg)
2007	Germany (Heiligendamm)
2008	Japan (Hokkaido)
2009	Italy
2010	Canada

NORTH ATLANTIC TREATY ORGANIZATION (NATO)

The North Atlantic Treaty Organization (NATO) comprises 26 countries from Europe and North America. It was created from the signatories to the North Atlantic Treaty in 1949. Its stated aim is to 'safeguard the freedom and security of its member countries by political and military means'. Member countries are listed by year of entry.

1949	Belgium, Canada, Denmark, France, Iceland, Italy, Luxembourg, The Netherlands, Norway, Portugal, United Kingdom, United States of America
1952	Greece, Turkey
1955	Germany
1982	Spain
1999	Czech Republic, Hungary, Poland
2004	Bulgaria, Estonia, Latvia, Lithuania, Romania, Slovakia, Slovenia

ORGANIZATION OF AMERICAN STATES (OAS)

The Organization of American States (OAS) comprises 35 countries from North and South America and the Caribbean. It seeks to promote unity and co-operation on economic, social and political issues. Member countries are listed by year of entry.

1948	Argentina, Bolivia, Brazil, Chile, Colombia, Costa Rica, Cuba[1], Dominican Republic, Ecuador, El Salvador, Guatemala, Haiti, Honduras, Mexico, Nicaragua, Panama, Paraguay, Peru, United States of America, Uruguay, Venezuela
1967	Barbados, Trinidad and Tobago
1969	Jamaica
1975	Grenada
1977	Suriname
1979	Dominica, St Lucia
1981	Antigua and Barbuda, St Vincent and the Grenadines
1982	The Bahamas
1984	St Kitts and Nevis
1990	Canada
1991	Belize, Guyana

[1] *Since 1962 the current government of Cuba, while remaining a member, has been excluded from participation in the OAS.*

ORGANIZATION OF PETROLEUM EXPORTING COUNTRIES (OPEC)

The Organization of Petroleum Exporting Countries (OPEC) comprises twelve countries from Africa, Asia, the Middle East and Latin America whose economies rely on oil export revenues. Member countries are listed by year of entry.

1960	Iran, Iraq, Kuwait, Saudi Arabia, Venezuela
1961	Qatar
1962	Indonesia, Libya
1967	United Arab Emirates
1969	Algeria
1971	Nigeria
1973	Ecuador (left 1992)
1975	Gabon (left 1994)
2007	Angola

Black Gold

OPEC estimates that the total world consumption of oil (refined products) in 2006 was 78 million barrels per day; demand is expected to rise to 90 million barrels per day by 2010. Saudi Arabia is the world's biggest crude oil producer, pumping out over 92 million barrels every day.

WARSAW PACT

The Warsaw Pact was a military alliance, formed in 1955, comprising the USSR and the Communist states of Eastern Europe (excluding Yugoslavia). It was intended as a counterbalance to NATO. The Warsaw Pact was dissolved in 1991 after the break-up of the USSR.

Albania (seceded 1968)
Bulgaria
Czechoslovakia
East Germany (from 1990 part of united Germany)
Hungary
Poland
Romania
USSR

GENEVA CONVENTIONS

The four Geneva Conventions and two additional Protocols are a series of international agreements regulating the treatment of victims of war. They deal with such matters as torture, deportation, treatment of women and children, hostage-taking and the use of chemical and biological weapons, and are signed by most states and some non-governmental bodies.

Convention/Protocol	Date	Application
Convention I	12 Aug 1949	For the amelioration of the condition of the wounded and sick in armed forces in the field.
Convention II	12 Aug 1949	For the amelioration of the condition of wounded, sick and shipwrecked members of armed forces at sea.
Convention III	12 Aug 1949	Relative to the treatment of prisoners of war.
Convention IV	12 Aug 1949	Relative to the protection of civilian persons in time of war.
Protocol I	8 Jun 1977	Relative to the protection of victims of international armed conflicts.
Protocol II	8 Jun 1977	Relative to the protection of victims of non-international armed conflicts.

NOBEL PEACE PRIZE

Nobel Prizes were established by a bequest in the will of Alfred Nobel (1833–96) to honour 'those who, during the preceding year, shall have conferred the greatest benefit on mankind'. The Nobel Peace Prize is awarded annually to a person or organization judged to have 'done the most or the best work for fraternity between nations, for the abolition or reduction of standing armies and for the holding and promotion of peace congresses'; first awarded in 1901.

1901	Henri Dunant, Frédéric Passy
1902	Élie Ducommun, Albert Gobat
1903	Randal Cremer
1904	Institute of International Law
1905	Bertha von Suttner
1906	Theodore Roosevelt
1907	Ernesto Teodoro Moneta, Louis Renault
1908	Klas Pontus Arnoldson, Fredrik Bajer
1909	Auguste Beernaert, Paul Henri d'Estournelles de Constant
1910	Permanent International Peace Bureau
1911	Tobias Asser, Alfred Fried
1912	Elihu Root
1913	Henri La Fontaine
1914	*no award*
1915	*no award*
1916	*no award*

1917	International Committee of the Red Cross
1918	*no award*
1919	Woodrow Wilson
1920	Léon Bourgeois
1921	Hjalmar Branting, Christian Lange
1922	Fridtjof Nansen
1923	*no award*
1924	*no award*
1925	Sir Austen Chamberlain, Charles G Dawes
1926	Aristide Briand, Gustav Stresemann
1927	Ferdinand Buisson, Ludwig Quidde
1928	*no award*
1929	Frank B Kellogg
1930	Nathan Söderblom
1931	Jane Addams, Nicholas Murray Butler
1932	*no award*
1933	Sir Norman Angell
1934	Arthur Henderson
1935	Carl von Ossietzky
1936	Carlos Saavedra Lamas
1937	Robert Cecil
1938	Nansen International Office for Refugees
1939	*no award*
1940	*no award*
1941	*no award*
1942	*no award*
1943	*no award*
1944	International Committee of the Red Cross
1945	Cordell Hull
1946	Emily Greene Balch, John R Mott
1947	Friends Service Council, American Friends Service Committee
1948	*no award*
1949	Lord Boyd Orr
1950	Ralph Bunche
1951	Léon Jouhaux
1952	Albert Schweitzer
1953	George C Marshall
1954	Office of the United Nations High Commissioner for Refugees
1955	*no award*
1956	*no award*
1957	Lester Bowles Pearson
1958	Georges Pire
1959	Philip Noel-Baker
1960	Albert Lutuli
1961	Dag Hammarskjöld
1962	Linus Pauling
1963	International Committee of the Red Cross, League of Red Cross Societies
1964	Martin Luther King
1965	United Nations Children's Fund
1966	*no award*
1967	*no award*
1968	René Cassin
1969	International Labour Organization
1970	Norman Borlaug
1971	Willy Brandt
1972	*no award*
1973	Henry Kissinger, Le Duc Tho
1974	Seán MacBride, Eisaku Sato
1975	Andrei Sakharov
1976	Betty Williams, Mairead Corrigan
1977	Amnesty International
1978	Anwar al-Sadat, Menachem Begin
1979	Mother Teresa
1980	Adolfo Pérez Esquivel
1981	Office of the United Nations High Commissioner for Refugees
1982	Alva Myrdal, Alfonso García Robles
1983	Lech Walesa
1984	Desmond Tutu
1985	International Physicians for the Prevention of Nuclear War
1986	Elie Wiesel
1987	Oscar Arias Sánchez
1988	United Nations Peacekeeping Forces
1989	The 14th Dalai Lama
1990	Mikhail Gorbachev
1991	Aung San Suu Kyi
1992	Rigoberta Menchú Tum
1993	Nelson Mandela, F W de Klerk
1994	Yasser Arafat, Shimon Peres, Yitzhak Rabin
1995	Joseph Rotblat, Pugwash Conferences on Science and World Affairs
1996	Carlos Filipe Ximenes Belo, José Ramos-Horta
1997	International Campaign to Ban Landmines, Jody Williams
1998	John Hume, David Trimble
1999	Médecins Sans Frontières

2000	Kim Dae-jung
2001	United Nations, Kofi Annan
2002	Jimmy Carter
2003	Shirin Ebadi
2004	Wangari Maathai
2005	International Atomic Energy Agency, Mohamed ElBaradei
2006	Muhammad Yunus, Grameen Bank
2007	Intergovernmental Panel on Climate Change (IPCC), Al Gore

RANKS OF THE POLICE

UK-wide police service

Chief Constable
Deputy Chief Constable
Assistant Chief Constable
Chief Superintendent
Superintendent
Chief Inspector
Inspector
Sergeant
Constable

Metropolitan Police

Commissioner
Deputy Commissioner
Assistant Commissioner
Deputy Assistant Commissioner
Commander
Chief Superintendent
Superintendent
Chief Inspector
Inspector
Sergeant
Constable

ASSASSINS

The list includes convicted, alleged and attempted assassins. Assassins working together, such as the three men who killed Malcolm X, have not been included.

Assassin	Victim	Date
Mehmet Ali Agca	Pope John Paul II	13 May 1981 (attempt)
Yigal Amir	Yitzhak Rabin	4 Nov 1995
John Wilkes Booth	Abraham Lincoln	14 Apr 1865
Marcus Junius Brutus and Cassius	Julius Caesar	15 May 44 BC
Mark Chapman	John Lennon	8 Dec 1980
Charlotte Corday	Jean Paul Marat	13 Jul 1793
Leon Czolgosz	William McKinley	6 Sep 1901
Nathuram Godse	Mahatma Gandhi	30 Jan 1948
Charles J Guiteau	James Garfield	2 Jul 1881
John Hinckley	Ronald Reagan	30 Mar 1981 (attempt)
Ramón Mercader	Leon Trotsky	20 Aug 1940
Lee Harvey Oswald	John F Kennedy	23 Nov 1963
Gavrilo Princip	Archduke Franz Ferdinand	28 Jun 1914
James Earl Ray	Martin Luther King, Jnr	4 Apr 1968
Sirhan Sirhan	Robert Kennedy	5 Jun 1968
Valerie Solanas	Andy Warhol	3 Jun 1968 (attempt)

Ra, Ra, Rasputin

One of history's most infamous assassinations was that of Russian mystic Rasputin in Dec 1916. The assassins, a clique of Russian aristocrats, first tried to poison him; when that failed they reportedly beat him and shot him three times. His body was then thrown into an icy river, and the post-mortem was reported to show that he had drowned.

PRECEDENCE OF LAW COURTS

Courts are listed from highest to lowest. The European Court of Justice is the recourse for cases concerning European Union law in the UK.

Criminal law

England and Wales
House of Lords
Court of Appeal
Crown Court
Magistrates' Court

Scotland
High Court of Justiciary
Sheriff's Court
District Court

Northern Ireland
House of Lords
Northern Ireland Court of Appeal
Crown Court
Magistrates' Court

Civil law

England and Wales
House of Lords
Court of Appeal
High Court of Justice
County Court
Magistrates' Court

Scotland
House of Lords
Court of Session
Sheriff's Principal Court
Sheriff's Court

Northern Ireland
House of Lords
Northern Ireland Court of Appeal
High Court Of Justice
County Court
Magistrates' Court

MILITARY RANKS

UK officer ranks

Army	Air Force	Navy
Field Marshal	Marshal of the Royal Air Force	Admiral of the Fleet
General	Air Chief Marshal	Admiral
Lieutenant-General	Air Marshal	Vice-Admiral
Major-General	Air Vice-Marshal	Rear-Admiral
Brigadier	Air Commodore	Commodore Admiral
Colonel	Group Captain	Captain RN
Lieutenant-Colonel	Wing Commander	Commander
Major	Squadron Leader	Lieutenant Commander
Captain	Flight Lieutenant	Lieutenant
Lieutenant	Flying Officer	Sub-Lieutenant
Second-Lieutenant	Pilot Officer	Midshipman

USA officer ranks

Army	Air Force	Navy
General of the Army	General of the Air Force	Fleet Admiral
General	General	Admiral
Lieutenant General	Lieutenant General	Vice Admiral
Major General	Major General	Rear Admiral (Upper Half)
Brigadier General	Brigadier General	Rear Admiral (Lower Half)
Colonel	Colonel	Captain
Lieutenant Colonel	Lieutenant Colonel	Commander
Major	Major	Lieutenant Commander

Army	Air Force	Navy
Captain	Captain	Lieutenant
First Lieutenant	First Lieutenant	Lieutenant Junior Grade
Second Lieutenant	Second Lieutenant	Ensign

PARLIAMENT (UK)

All information is for the year 2007–8 unless otherwise stated. For British prime ministers, monarchs and first ministers of devolved regional governments see **United Kingdom** in **Countries A–Z** under **Human Geography**.

Number of MPs (House of Commons)	646
Number of peers (House of Lords)	738, plus 12 on leave of absence (7 Jan 2008)
MP's annual parliamentary salary	£60,675 (1 Apr 2007)
Prime minister's annual salary	£188,849 (inclusive of MP's salary) (1 Apr 2007)
Days that the House of Commons sits	162 (annual average, 1979–2007); 146 (2006–7)
Days that the House of Lords sits	130 (annual average, 1979–2007); 142 (2006–7)
Father of the House	A traditional title given to the MP who has the 'longest unbroken service in the Commons'. Alan Williams MP became the Father of the House in May 2005; he entered Parliament in 1964.
Speaker	The person who presides over the debates in the House of Commons. Michael Martin MP became the 156th Speaker in Oct 2000.
Women MPs	126 (2007)
Maximum length of a Parliament	5 years, as decreed by the Parliament Act (1911); this term has only been extended twice, during World War I and World War II.
Palace of Westminster	The current Palace of Westminster dates to the mid-19c; it was built 1840–70 after the previous Palace was destroyed by a fire in 1834.
Big Ben	Big Ben weighs 13.8 tonnes/13.6 tons. It is believed that the bell was named after one Sir Benjamin Hall, the Commissioner of Works at the Houses of Parliament (1855–8), whose name is engraved on the bell. The famous clock tower that houses Big Ben is 96.3m/316ft tall.
Voting	Women aged 30 years and over were given the vote in 1918. In 1928 women aged 21 and over were allowed to vote, giving them equality with men. The voting age was reduced to 18 in 1969.

Parliamentary Pay

The tradition of paying parliamentary representatives dates back to the 13th century, when local shires and boroughs typically gave them a daily allowance of a few shillings. Local variations were common, however – the most unusual payment surely being that made to the representatives of Weymouth in 1463, who received a wage of 500 mackerel for their troubles. Regular salaries from public funds were not paid to MPs until 1911, when they received £400 per year.

US CONSTITUTIONAL AMENDMENTS

The US Constitution was framed in 1787 and came into effect in 1789. Amendments to the Constitution were later proposed, and the following is a list of those that have been ratified. The first ten Amendments collectively are known as the Bill of Rights.

Amendment	Date	Main areas of application
I	1791	Freedom of religion, speech, the press, assembly and petition
II	1791	Right to bear arms
III	1791	Restrictions on the quartering of troops
IV	1791	Restrictions on search and seizure
V	1791	Grand jury trial, double jeopardy, self-incrimination, due process
VI	1791	Criminal prosecutions, jury trial, right to confront and to counsel
VII	1791	Common law suits, jury trial
VIII	1791	Excess bail or fines, cruel and unusual punishment
IX	1791	Non-enumerated rights
X	1791	Rights reserved to states
XI	1795	Suits against a state
XII	1804	Election of the president and vice-president
XIII	1865	Abolition of slavery
XIV	1868	Privileges and immunities, due process, equal protection, apportionment of representatives, Civil War disqualification and debt
XV	1870	Rights not to be denied on account of race
XVI	1913	Income tax
XVII	1913	Election of senators
XVIII	1919	Prohibition
XIX	1920	Women's right to vote
XX	1933	Presidential term and succession
XXI	1933	Repeal of Prohibition
XXII	1951	Two term limit on president
XXIII	1961	Presidential voting powers
XXIV	1964	Poll tax
XXV	1967	Presidential succession
XXVI	1971	Right to vote at age 18
XXVII	1992	Compensation of members of Congress

Constitutional Prohibition

The only constitutional amendment ever to have been repealed is the 18th, relating to Prohibition, which was ratified in Jan 1919. It stated that 'after one year ... the manufacture, sale, or transportation of intoxicating liquors within, the importation thereof into, or the exportation thereof from the United States ... for beverage purposes is hereby prohibited'. It was repealed by the 21st amendment, ratified in Dec 1933, but both remain in the Constitution.

Ancient Greece and Rome

GREEK GODS

Adonis	God of vegetation and rebirth
Aeolus	God of the winds
Alphito	Barley goddess of Argos
Aphrodite	Goddess of love and beauty
Apollo	God of prophecy, music, youth, archery and healing
Ares	God of war
Arethusa	Goddess of springs and fountains
Artemis	Goddess of fertility, chastity and hunting
Asclepius	God of healing
Athene	Goddess of prudence and wise counsel; protectress of Athens
Atlas	Titan who bears up the Earth
Attis	God of vegetation
Boreas	God of the north wind
Cronus	Father of Zeus
Cybele	Goddess of the earth
Demeter	Goddess of the harvest
Dionysus	God of wine, vegetation and ecstasy
Eos	Goddess of the dawn
Eros	God of love
Gaia	Goddess of the earth
Ganymede	God of rain
Hades/Pluto	God of the Underworld
Hebe	Goddess of youth
Hecate	Goddess of the Moon
Helios	God of the Sun
Hephaestus	God of fire
Hera	Goddess of marriage and childbirth; queen of heaven
Hermes	Messenger of the gods
Hestia	Goddess of the hearth
Hypnos	God of sleep
Iris	Goddess of the rainbow
Morpheus	God of dreams
Nemesis	God of destiny
Nereus	God of the sea
Nike	Goddess of victory
Oceanus	God of the river Oceanus
Pan	God of male sexuality and of herds
Persephone	Goddess of the Underworld and of corn
Poseidon	God of the sea
Rhea	Original mother goddess; wife of Cronus
Selene	Goddess of the Moon
Thanatos	God of death
Zeus	Overlord of the Olympian gods and goddesses; god of the sky and all its properties

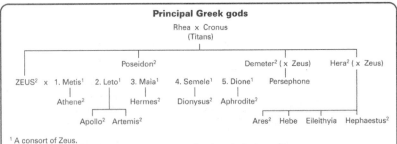

Principal Greek gods

Rhea x Cronus
(Titans)

ZEUS[2] x 1. Metis[1] — Athene[2]
ZEUS[2] x 2. Leto[1] — Apollo[2], Artemis[2]
ZEUS[2] x 3. Maia[1] — Hermes[2]
ZEUS[2] x 4. Semele[1] — Dionysus[2]
ZEUS[2] x 5. Dione[1] — Aphrodite[2]
Poseidon[2]
Demeter[2] (x Zeus) — Persephone
Hera[2] (x Zeus) — Ares[2], Hebe, Eileithyia, Hephaestus[2]

[1] A consort of Zeus.
[2] One of the twelve Olympians in the 'central group' of gods on the Parthenon frieze.

ROMAN GODS

Apollo	God of the Sun
Bacchus	God of wine and ecstasy
Bellona	Goddess of war
Ceres	Goddess of corn
Consus	God of seed sowing
Cupid	God of love
Diana	Goddess of fertility and hunting
Egreria	Goddess of fountains and childbirth
Epona	Goddess of horses

Fauna	Goddess of fertility
Faunus	God of crops and herbs
Feronia	Goddess of spring flowers
Fides	God of honesty
Flora	Goddess of fruitfulness and flowers
Fortuna	Goddess of chance and fate
Genius	Protective god of individuals, groups and the state
Janus	God of entrances, travel and the dawn
Juno	Goddess of marriage, childbirth and light
Jupiter	God of the sky and its attributes (Sun, Moon, thunder, rain, etc)
Lares	Gods of the house
Liber Pater	God of agricultural and human fertility
Libitina	Goddess of funeral rites
Luna	Goddess of the Moon
Maia	Goddess of fertility
Mars	God of war
Mercury	Messenger of the gods; also god of merchants
Minerva	Goddess of war, craftsmen, education and the arts
Mithras	Sun god; also god of regeneration
Neptune	God of the sea
Ops	Goddess of the harvest
Orcus	God of death
Pales	Goddess of flocks
Penates	Gods of food and drink
Picus	God of woods
Pluto/Dis	God of the Underworld
Pomona	Goddess of fruit trees
Portunus	God of husbands
Proserpina	Goddess of the Underworld
Rumina	Goddess of nursing mothers
Saturn	God of fertility and agriculture
Silvanus	God of trees and forests
Venus	Goddess of spring, gardens and love
Vertumnus	God of fertility
Vesta	Goddess of the hearth
Victoria	Goddess of victory
Vulcan	God of fire

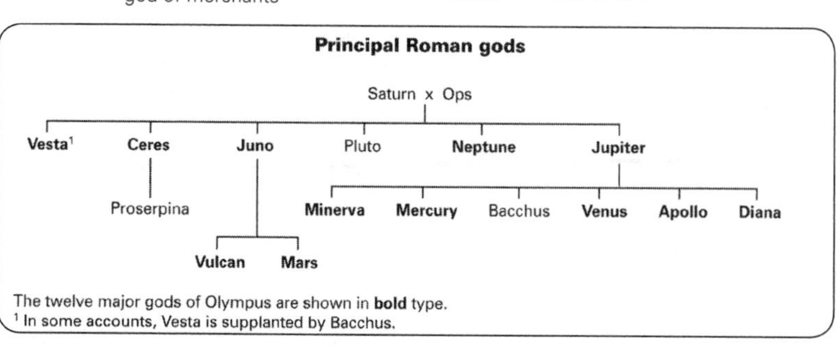

The twelve major gods of Olympus are shown in **bold** type.
[1] In some accounts, Vesta is supplanted by Bacchus.

ROMAN EMPERORS

Dates overlap where there are periods of joint rule (eg Marcus Aurelius and Lucius Verus) and where the government of the empire divides between east and west. All dates are AD unless otherwise indicated.

Regnal dates	Name
27 BC–AD 14	Augustus (Caesar Augustus)
14–37	Tiberius
37–41	Caligula (Gaius Caesar)
41–54	Claudius
54–68	Nero
68–69	Galba
69	Otho
69	Vitellius
69–79	Vespasian
79–81	Titus
81–96	Domitian
96–98	Nerva
98–117	Trajan
117–138	Hadrian

ROMAN EMPERORS

Regnal dates	Name
138–161	Antoninus Pius
161–180	Marcus Aurelius
161–169	Lucius Verus
176–192	Commodus
193	Pertinax
193	Didius Julianus
193–211	Septimius Severus
198–217	Caracalla
209–212	Geta
217–218	Macrinus
218–222	Elagabalus
222–235	Alexander Severus
235–238	Maximin
238	Gordian I
238	Gordian II
238	Maximus
238	Balbinus
238–244	Gordian III
244–249	Philip
249–251	Decius
251	Hostilian
251–253	Gallus
253	Aemilian
253–260	Valerian
253–268	Gallienus
268–269	Claudius II (the Goth)
269–270	Quintillus
270–275	Aurelian
275–276	Tacitus
276	Florian
276–282	Probus
282–283	Carus
283–285	Carinus
283–284	Numerian
284–305	Diocletian (East)

Regnal dates	Name
286–305	Maximian (West)
305–311	Galerius (East)
305–306	Constantius I
306–307	Severus (West)
306–312	Maxentius (West)
306–337	Constantine I
308–324	Licinius (East)
337–340	Constantine II
337–350	Constans I
337–361	Constantius II
350–351	Magnentius
360–363	Julian
364–375	Valentinian I (West)
364–378	Valens (East)
365–366	Procopius (East)
375–383	Gratian (West)
375–392	Valentinian II (West)
379–395	Theodosius I
395–408	Arcadius (East)
395–423	Honorius (West)
408–450	Theodosius II (East)
421–423	Constantius III (West)
423–455	Valentinian III (West)
450–457	Marcian (East)
455	Petronius Maximus (West)
455–456	Avitus (West)
457–474	Leo I (East)
457–461	Majorian (West)
461–467	Libius Severus (West)
467–472	Anthemius (West)
472–473	Olybrius (West)
474–480	Julius Nepos (West)
474	Leo II (East)
474–491	Zeno (East)
475–476	Romulus Augustus (West)

Fiddling While Rome Burned

Nero, the Roman emperor from AD 54–68, lived a wild and violent life. His reign was infamous for its debauchery, extravagance and tyranny. He caused his stepbrother to be poisoned, murdered his mother and his first wife and subsequently murdered his second wife in a fit of passion. He then proposed marriage to his murdered stepbrother's daughter, had her executed when she refused, and finally married a third wife after murdering her husband. Nero was also said to have been responsible for the fire which destroyed two-thirds of Rome in Jul AD 64, but this is doubtful, as is the story that he admired the spectacle from a distance while reciting his poetry and playing his lyre. He finally met his end in AD 68, when the army and guards rose against him; he fled Rome and committed suicide.

ROMAN KINGS

According to Roman literary tradition, Rome was founded by Romulus.

753–715 BC	Romulus	616–578 BC	Tarquinius Priscus
715–673 BC	Numa Pompilius	578–534 BC	Servius Tullius
673–642 BC	Tullus Hostilius	534–509 BC	Tarquinius Superbus
642–616 BC	Ancus Marcius		

SEVEN WONDERS OF THE WORLD

Originally compiled by Antipater of Sidon, a Greek poet, c.100 BC. Modern locations are shown in italics.

Pyramids of Egypt *Egypt*	Oldest and only surviving 'wonder'. Built c.2000 BC as royal tombs, about 80 are still standing. The largest, the Great Pyramid of Cheops, at el-Gizeh, is approximately 146m/482ft high, covering 5.3 hectares/13 acres at the base.
Hanging Gardens of Babylon *Iraq*	Terraced gardens adjoining Nebuchadnezzar's palace, said to rise 23–91m/75–300ft. Supposedly built by the king c.600 BC to please his wife, a princess from the mountains, they are also associated with the Assyrian Queen Semiramis.
Statue of Zeus at Olympia *Greece*	Carved by Phidias, the 12m/40ft statue marked the site of the original Olympic Games c.400 BC. It was constructed of ivory and gold, and showed Zeus (Jupiter) on his throne.
Temple of Artemis (Diana) at Ephesus *Turkey*	Constructed of Parian marble and more than 122m/400ft long with over 100 columns 18m/60ft high, it was begun c.350 BC and took some 120 years to build. Destroyed by the Goths in AD 262.
Mausoleum at Halicarnassus *Turkey*	Erected by Queen Artemisia in memory of her husband King Mausolus of Caria (in Asia Minor), who died 353 BC. It stood 43m/140ft high. All that remains are a few pieces in the British Museum.
Colossus of Rhodes *Greece*	Gigantic bronze statue of sun god Helios (or Apollo); stood about 36m/117ft high, dominating the harbour entrance at Rhodes. The sculptor Chares supposedly laboured for twelve years before he completed it in 280 BC. It was destroyed by an earthquake in 224 BC.
Pharos of Alexandria *Egypt*	Marble lighthouse and watchtower built c.270 BC on the island of Pharos in Alexandria's harbour. Possibly standing 122m/400ft high, it was destroyed by an earthquake in 1375.

SEVEN HILLS OF ROME

The ancient city of Rome was built around seven hills.

Aventine
Esquiline
Palatine
Cælian
Quirinal
Viminal
Capitoline

Language Legacy

The monument to King Mausolus at Halicarnassus was destroyed centuries ago, but his name still lives on in the English word *mausoleum*, a magnificent tomb or monument.

FURIES

Three Greek goddesses, inhabitants of hell who were responsible for punishing bloody crimes; represented as winged spirits with long hair entwined with snakes, carrying whips and torches; they tortured their victims and made them mad. Also known as *Erinyes*.

Alecto
Megara
Tisiphone

TWELVE LABOURS OF HERCULES

Hercules, also known as Heracles, was a Greek hero famous for his great strength. The son of Zeus and Alcmene, he demonstrated his strength from birth, choking the serpents sent by the jealous Hera, Zeus's wife. He undertook the twelve famous labours for Eurystheus of Tiryns.

To kill and flay the Nemean lion
To kill the monster Hydra
To capture the Arcadian stag
To destroy the Erymanthian boar
To clean the stables of Augeas, King of Elis, in a day
To destroy the man-eating birds of the Stymphalian marshes
To capture the Cretan bull
To catch the savage horses of the Thracian king Diomedes
To obtain the golden girdle of the Amazonian queen Hippolyta
To steal the oxen of the giant Geryon
To fetch the golden apples of the Hesperides
To capture Cerberus, the three-headed dog of Hades, the underworld

FATES

Three Greek goddesses, daughters of Zeus; the first spun a thread which signified birth, the second unravelled the thread, symbolizing the unravelling of life, and the third cut the thread, signifying death. Also known as *Moerae*.

Atropos
Clotho
Lachesis

THREE GRACES

Three daughters of Zeus and Hera; embodied beauty and social accomplishments.

Aglaia
Euphrosyne
Thalia

MUSES

Nine Greek goddesses, daughters of Zeus, each with the vocation to promote an area of the arts.

Calliope
epic poetry
Erato
lyric poetry and hymns
Melpomene
tragedy
Terpsichore
dance and lyric poetry
Clio
history and lyre-playing
Euterpe
flute-playing
Polyhymnia
dance, mime and acting
Thalia
comedy and idyllic poetry
Urania
astronomy

SEVEN AGAINST THEBES

Seven Greek champions; defeated by another seven champions at the seven gates of Thebes; all were killed in battle, except for Amphiarus, whom the earth swallowed alive, and Adrastus, who escaped.

Adrastus *or* Eteoklos
Hippomedon
Polynices
Amphiarus
Capaneus
Parthenopaeus
Tydeus

RELIGIONS, BELIEFS AND FOLKLORE

For Greek and Roman gods see **Ancient Greece and Rome**.

NORSE GODS

Aegir	God of the sea
Aesir	Race of warlike gods
Alcis	Twin gods of the sky
Balder	Odin's son; favourite of the gods
Bor	Father of Odin
Bragi	God of poetry
Fafnir	Dragon god
Fjorgynn	Mother of Thor
Frey	God of fertility
Freyja	Goddess of libido
Frigg	Goddess of fertility; wife of Odin
Gefion	Goddess who received virgins after death
Heimdall	Guardian of the bridge Bifrost
Hel	Goddess of death; Queen of Niflheim, the land of mists
Hermod	Son of Odin
Hoder	Blind god who killed Balder
Hoenir	Companion to Odin and Loki
Idunn	Guardian goddess of the golden apples of youth
Kvasir	God of wise utterances
Logi	Fire god
Loki	God of mischief
Mimir	God of wisdom
Nanna	Goddess wife of Balder
Nehallenia	Goddess of plenty
Nerthus	Goddess of earth
Njord	God of ships and the sea
Norns	Goddesses of destiny
Odin, Woden, Wotan	Chief of the Aesir family of gods, the 'father' god; the god of battle, death, inspiration
Otr	Otter god
Ran	Goddess of the sea
Sif	Goddess wife of Thor
Sigyn	Goddess wife of Loki
Thor, Donar	God of thunder and sky; good crops
Tyr	God of battle
Ull	Stepson of Thor, an enchanter
Valkyries	Female helpers of the gods of war
Vanir	Race of benevolent gods
Vidar	Slayer of the wolf, Fenrir
Weland, Volundr	Craftsman god

World Tree

In Norse mythology the World Tree, a giant ash known as *Yggdrasil*, supported the sky, held the different realms of gods and men in its branches and had its roots in the Underworld. Odin created *Asgard*, the home of the gods, in the upper branches of the World Tree. Asgard was reached from earth by the rainbow bridge *Bifrost*, guarded by Heimdall, the watchman of the gods.

EGYPTIAN GODS

Amun-Re	Universal god
Anubis	God of funerals
Apis	God of fertility
Aten	Unique god
Geb	God of the earth
Hathor	Goddess of love
Horus	God of light
Isis	Goddess of magic
Khnum	Goddess of creation
Khonsou	Son of Amun-Re
Maat	Goddess of order
Nephthys	Goddess of funerals
Nut	God of the sky
Osiris	God of vegetation
Ptah	God of creation
Re, Ra	Sun god (later Amun-Re)
Sekhmet	Goddess of might
Seth	God of evil
Thoth	Supreme scribe

Gods and Beasts

The gods of Ancient Egypt were often portrayed with human bodies but the heads of animals, for example Anubis (the head of a jackal), Hathor (cow), Horus (falcon), Sekhmet (lioness) and Thoth (ibis or baboon). Re was depicted as a falcon with the Sun's disc on his head during the day, while at night he appeared as a ram-headed god who sailed through the Underworld.

CELTIC GODS

Many Celtic gods and goddesses were known by different names by different Celtic peoples; where names differ, the British spelling is given.

Anna	Mother goddess of fecundity and plenty
Arianrhod	Earth goddess
Badhbh	Goddess of war
Boann	River goddess
Bel, Beli, Belinus	God of the Sun, light and fire
Blodeuwedd	Goddess of love and generosity
Brigantia, Brighid	Goddess of livestock, agriculture, midwifery, poetry and crafts
Cernunnos	Ruler of all the animals and lord of the Underworld
Cerridwen	Goddess of the Underworld
Cliodna	Goddess of peace and beauty
Dea Arduinna	Goddess of wild animals
Don	Chief of the Irish gods; the lord of the Otherworld
Dylan	God of the sea
Édain, Étain	Goddess of the Otherworld
Epona	Goddess of horses
Flidhais	Goddess of wild animals
Gofannon	God of smiths and of strength
Grannos	God of healing
Llyr, Lir	God of the sea
Lleu	Hero god, deity of crafts, commerce and (in some traditions) youth and games
Mabon	God of youth, healing, music and hunting
Macha	Goddess of horses
Manawydan, Manawyddan	God of wisdom and patience
Matres, Matronae	Trio of goddesses associated with earth, fecundity and motherhood
Medhbh	Warrior-goddess representing sexuality
Merlin	Guardian god of the land
Modron	Mother goddess
Morrighan	Goddess of war
Nemhain	Goddess of war
Ogmia	God of strength and eloquence
Rhiannon	Goddess of horses, birds and the Moon, known as the Great Queen
Silvanus, Sucellus	God of the Underworld
Taran	God of thunder and war

Talking Heads

In Celtic mythology Bran was a gigantic god who featured in the Welsh tales *The Mabinogion* (14c) as King of Britain. He died in Ireland, and his severed head provided his followers with advice and entertainment for 80 years. It was finally buried at the site of the Tower of London, from where it protected Britain from invaders until it was eventually dug up.

BAHA'I

Founded	1863
Founder	Mirza Husayn Ali (1817–92)
Sacred texts	Most Holy Book, The Seven Valleys, The Hidden Words, The Bayan.
Place of worship	Shrine, temple
Beliefs	The oneness of God, the unity of all faiths, the inevitable unification of humankind, universal education and obedience to government.
Organization	There is a network of elected local and national level bodies, and an elected international governing body. There is little formal ritual.
Divisions	No major divisions.

BUDDHISM

Founded	c.500 BC
Founder	Prince Siddhartha Gautama (c.563–c.483 BC)
Sacred texts	The Pali Canon or Tripitaka. Other texts include the Mahayana Sutras, the Milindapanha (Questions of Milinda) and the Bardo Thodol (Tibetan Book of the Dead).
Place of worship	Temple
Beliefs	The Four Noble Truths concerning suffering and freedom from it; the Eightfold Path leading to Nirvana; the law of Karma.
Organization	Monastic system; numerous festivals and ceremonies for the laity.
Divisions	Two main historical divisions: Theravada and Mahayana. Other schools include Zen, Lamaism, Tendai, Nichiren and Soka Gakkai.

The Enlightened One

Buddha was born in c.563 BC as Prince Siddhartha Gautama, the son of the rajah in a ruling tribe in Nepal. When he was about 30 he left the luxuries of the court, his beautiful wife and all earthly ambitions in exchange for the life of an ascetic; after six years of extreme self-mortification he saw in the contemplative life the perfect way to self-enlightenment. According to tradition, he achieved enlightenment when sitting beneath a banyan tree near Buddh Gaya in Bihar. For the next 40 years he taught, gaining many disciples and followers. He died aged about 80 in c.483 BC.

DALAI LAMAS

Dalai Lama is the title given to the spiritual and political leader of Tibetan Buddhists. Each successive Dalai Lama is held to be a reincarnation of the previous one, and is also regarded as a manifestation of the Bodhisattva Avalokiteshavara, the Buddha of Compassion.

1391–1475	Gedun Truppa
1475–1542	Gedun Gyatso
1543–88	Sonam Gyatso
1589–17	Yonten Gyatso
1617–82	Ngawang Lobzang Gyatso
1683–1706	Tsang-yang Gyatso
1708–57	Kezang Gyatso
1758–1804	Jampel Gyatso
1806–15	Luntok Gyatso
1816–37	Tshultrim Gyatso
1838–56	Khedrup Gyatso
1856–75	Trinle Gyatso
1876–1933	Thupten Gyatso
1935–	Tenzin Gyatso

Ocean-like Guru

The name *Dalai Lama* comes from the Mongolian word *dalai*, meaning ocean, and the Tibetan word *lama*, high priest, and is sometimes translated as 'ocean-like guru' or 'ocean of wisdom'. The Panchen Lama, the Tibetan religious leader second in importance to the Dalai Lama, is named from the Tibetan *pandita chen-po*, meaning 'great scholar'.

FOUR NOBLE TRUTHS

The Four Noble Truths are a summary of the central teachings of Buddha.

Suffering is always present in life.
The origin of suffering is desire.
By ceasing to desire one ceases to suffer.
The Eightfold Path is the way of achieving release from desire and suffering.

EIGHTFOLD PATH

The fourth of Buddha's Four Noble Truths, prescribing the way to enlightenment.

Right views
Right thoughts
Right speech
Right action
Right livelihood
Right effort
Right mindfulness
Right concentration

CHRISTIANITY

Founded	1C AD
Founder	Jesus Christ, 'the Son of God' (c.4 BC–c.30 AD)
Sacred texts	The Bible consisting of the Old and New Testaments.
Old Testament:	Genesis, Exodus, Leviticus, Numbers, Deuteronomy, Joshua, Judges, Ruth, 1 Samuel, 2 Samuel, 1 Kings, 2 Kings, 1 Chronicles, 2 Chronicles, Ezra, Nehemiah, Esther, Job, Psalms, Proverbs, Ecclesiastes, Song of Solomon, Isaiah, Jeremiah, Lamentations, Ezekiel, Daniel, Hosea, Joel, Amos, Obadiah, Jonah, Micah, Nahum, Habakkuk, Zephaniah, Haggai, Zechariah, Malachi.
New Testament:	Matthew, Mark, Luke, John, Acts of the Apostles, Romans, 1 Corinthians, 2 Corinthians, Galatians, Ephesians, Philippians, Colossians, 1 Thessalonians, 2 Thessalonians, 1 Timothy, 2 Timothy, Titus, Philemon, Hebrews, James, 1 Peter, 2 Peter, 1 John, 2 John, 3 John, Jude, Revelation. *Apocrypha (Revised standard version 1957)*: 1 Esdras, 2 Esdras, Tobit, Judith, Additions to Esther, Wisdom of Solomon, Ecclesiasticus, Epistle of Jeremiah, Baruch, Prayer of Azariah and the Song of the Three Young Men, (History of) Susanna, Bel and the Dragon, Prayer of Manasseh, 1 Maccabees, 2 Maccabees. (The Authorized version incorporates Jeremiah into Baruch; The prayer of Azariah is simply called the Song of the Three Holy Children. The Roman Catholic Church includes Tobit, Judith, all of Esther, Maccabees 1 and 2, Wisdom of Solomon, Ecclesiasticus and Baruch in its canon.)
Place of worship	Cathedral, chapel, church
Beliefs	Monotheistic: centred on the life and works of Jesus of Nazareth. Christians believe that Jesus was crucified and resurrected from the dead.
Organization	Various priestly hierarchies, often involving bishops and lesser clergy, ultimately deriving from the traditions of the Apostles and their successors.
Divisions	Major divisions are the Orthodox or Eastern church, the Roman Catholic church and the Protestant churches.

POPES

Antipopes (who claimed to be pope in opposition to those canonically chosen) are given in square brackets. All dates listed are AD.

until c.64	Peter
c.64–c.76	Linus
c.76–c.90	Anacletus
c.90–c.99	Clement I
c.99–c.105	Evaristus
c.105–c.117	Alexander I
c.117–c.127	Sixtus I
c.127–c.137	Telesphorus
c.137–c.140	Hyginus
c.140–c.154	Pius I
c.154–c.166	Anicetus
c.166–c.175	Soter
175–89	Eleutherius
189–98	Victor I
198–217	Zephyrinus
217–22	Callistus I
[217–c.235	Hippolytus]
222–30	Urban I
230–5	Pontian
235–6	Anterus
236–50	Fabian
251–3	Cornelius
[251–c.258	Novatian]
253–4	Lucius I
254–7	Stephen I
257–8	Sixtus II
259–68	Dionysius
269–74	Felix I
275–83	Eutychianus
283–96	Caius
296–304	Marcellinus
304–8	*interregnum*
308–9	Marcellus I
310	Eusebius
311–14	Miltiades
314–35	Sylvester I
336	Mark
337–52	Julius I
352–66	Liberius
[355–65	Felix II]
366–84	Damasus I
[366–7	Ursinus]
384–99	Siricius
399–401	Anastasius I
402–17	Innocent I
417–18	Zosimus
418–22	Boniface I
[418–19	Eulalius]
422–32	Celestine I
432–40	Sixtus III
440–61	Leo I
461–8	Hilarus
468–83	Simplicius
483–92	Felix III (II)
492–6	Gelasius I
496–8	Anastasius II
498–514	Symmachus
[498, 501–5	Laurentius]
514–23	Hormisdas
523–6	John I
526–30	Felix IV (III)
530–2	Boniface II
[530	Dioscorus]
533–5	John II
535–6	Agapetus I
536–7	Silverius
537–55	Vigilius
556–61	Pelagius I
561–74	John III
575–9	Benedict I
579–90	Pelagius II
590–604	Gregory I
604–6	Sabinianus
607	Boniface III
608–15	Boniface IV
615–18	Deusdedit *or* Adeodatus I
619–25	Boniface V
625–38	Honorius I
640	Severinus
640–2	John IV
642–9	Theodore I
649–55	Martin I
654–7	Eugenius I[1]
657–72	Vitalian
672–6	Adeodatus II
676–8	Donus
678–81	Agatho
682–3	Leo II
684–5	Benedict II
685–6	John V
686–7	Cono
[687	Theodore]
[687–92	Paschal]
687–701	Sergius I
701–5	John VI
705–7	John VII
708	Sisinnius
708–15	Constantine
715–31	Gregory II
731–41	Gregory III
741–52	Zacharias
752	Stephen II (*not consecrated*)
752–7	Stephen II (III)
757–67	Paul I
[767–9	Constantine II]
[768	Philip]
768–72	Stephen III (IV)
772–95	Hadrian I
795–816	Leo III
816–17	Stephen IV (V)
817–24	Paschal I
824–7	Eugenius II
827	Valentine
827–44	Gregory IV
[844	John]
844–7	Sergius II
847–55	Leo IV
855–8	Benedict III
[855	Anastasius Bibliothecarius]
858–67	Nicholas I
867–72	Hadrian II
872–82	John VIII
882–4	Marinus I
884–5	Hadrian III
885–91	Stephen V (VI)
891–6	Formosus
896	Boniface VI
896–7	Stephen VI (VII)
897	Romanus
897	Theodore II
898–900	John IX
900–3	Benedict IV
903	Leo V
[903–4	Christopher]
904–11	Sergius III
911–13	Anastasius III
913–14	Lando

Dates	Pope
914–28	John X
928	Leo VI
928–31	Stephen VII (VIII)
931–5	John XI
936–9	Leo VII
939–42	Stephen IX
942–6	Marinus II
946–55	Agapetus II
955–64	John XII
[963–5	Leo VIII]
964	Benedict V
965–72	John XIII
973–4	Benedict VI
[974, 984–5	Boniface VII]
974–83	Benedict VII
983–4	John XIV
985–96	John XV
996–9	Gregory V
[997–8	John XVI]
999–1003	Sylvester II
1003	John XVII
1004–9	John XVIII
1009–12	Sergius IV
1012–24	Benedict VIII
[1012	Gregory]
1024–32	John XIX
1032–44	Benedict IX
1045	Sylvester III
1045	Benedict IX (*second reign*)
1045–6	Gregory VI
1046–7	Clement II
1047–8	Benedict IX (*third reign*)
1048	Damasus II
1048–54	Leo IX
1055–7	Victor II
1057–8	Stephen IX (X)
[1058–9	Benedict X]
1059–61	Nicholas II
1061–73	Alexander II
[1061–72	Honorius II]
1073–85	Gregory VII
[1080, 1084–1100	Clement VII]
1086–7	Victor III
1088–99	Urban II
1099–1118	Paschal II
[1100–2	Theodoric]
[1102	Albert]
[1105–11	Sylvester IV]
1118–19	Gelasius II
[1118–21	Gregory VIII]
1119–24	Callistus II
1124–30	Honorius II
[1124	Celestine II]
1130–43	Innocent II
[1130–8	Anacletus II]
[1138	Victor IV][2]
1143–4	Celestine II
1144–5	Lucius II
1145–53	Eugenius III
1153–4	Anastasius IV
1154–9	Hadrian IV
1159–81	Alexander III
[1159–64	Victor IV][2]
[1164–8	Paschal III]
[1168–78	Callistus III]
[1179–80	Innocent III]
1181–5	Lucius III
1185–7	Urban III
1187	Gregory VIII
1187–91	Clement III
1191–8	Celestine III
1198–1216	Innocent III
1216–27	Honorius III
1227–41	Gregory IX
1241	Celestine IV
1241–3	*interregnum*
1243–54	Innocent IV
1254–61	Alexander IV
1261–4	Urban IV
1265–8	Clement IV
1268–71	*interregnum*
1271–6	Gregory X
1276	Innocent V
1276	Hadrian V
1276–7	John XXI[3]
1277–80	Nicholas III
1281–5	Martin IV
1285–7	Honorius IV
1288–92	Nicholas IV
1292–4	*interregnum*
1294	Celestine V
1294–1303	Boniface VIII
1303–4	Benedict XI
1304–5	*interregnum*
1305–14	Clement V
1314–16	*interregnum*
1316–34	John XXII
[1328–30	Nicholas V]
1334–42	Benedict XII
1342–52	Clement VI
1352–62	Innocent VI
1362–70	Urban V
1370–8	Gregory XI
1378–89	Urban VI
[1378–94	Clement VII]
1389–1404	Boniface IX
[1394–1423	Benedict XIII]
1404–6	Innocent VII
1406–15	Gregory XII
[1409–10	Alexander V]
[1410–15	John XXIII]
1416	*interregnum*
1417–31	Martin V
[1423–9	Clement VIII]
[1425–30	Benedict XIV]
1431–47	Eugenius IV
[1439–49	Felix V]
1447–55	Nicholas V
1455–8	Callistus III
1458–64	Pius II
1464–71	Paul II
1471–84	Sixtus IV
1484–92	Innocent VIII
1492–1503	Alexander VI
1503	Pius III
1503–13	Julius II
1513–21	Leo X
1522–3	Hadrian VI
1523–34	Clement VII
1534–49	Paul III
1550–5	Julius III
1555	Marcellus II
1555–9	Paul IV
1559–65	Pius IV
1566–72	Pius V
1572–85	Gregory XIII
1585–90	Sixtus V
1590	Urban VII
1590–1	Gregory XIV
1591	Innocent IX
1592–1605	Clement VIII
1605	Leo XI
1605–21	Paul V
1621–3	Gregory XV
1623–44	Urban VIII
1644–55	Innocent X
1655–67	Alexander VII
1667–9	Clement IX
1670–6	Clement X
1676–89	Innocent XI

1689–91	Alexander VIII	1775–99	Pius VI	1922–39	Pius XI
1691–1700	Innocent XII	1800–23	Pius VII	1939–58	Pius XII
1700–21	Clement XI	1823–9	Leo XII	1958–63	John XXIII
1721–4	Innocent XIII	1829–30	Pius VIII	1963–78	Paul VI
1724–30	Benedict XIII	1831–46	Gregory XVI	1978	John Paul I
1730–40	Clement XII	1846–78	Pius IX	1978–2005	John Paul II
1740–58	Benedict XIV	1878–1903	Leo XIII	2005–	Benedict XVI
1758–69	Clement XIII	1903–14	Pius X		
1769–74	Clement XIV	1914–22	Benedict XV		

[1] *Elected during the banishment of Martin I*
[2] *Different individuals.*
[3] *There was no John XX.*

Choosing the Pope

Upon the death of the pope a set of ancient ceremonies are held to choose a successor. Firstly, the *camerlengo* (papal treasurer) strikes the dead pope's forehead three times with a silver hammer and calls him by his real name to ensure he is truly dead. All the cardinals of the Roman Catholic church who are younger than 80 years then assemble in a *conclave*. The cardinals are locked into a specially prepared area of the Vatican palace, guarded and unable to leave or communicate with the outside world; the door will not be reopened until a successor has been elected, which may take days. The election itself is by secret ballot in the Sistine Chapel; the ballot papers are burned with chemicals after each inconclusive round of voting, sending black smoke into the air above the Vatican, while burning of the ballots alone after a successful vote sends up white smoke and signals to the waiting crowds outside that a new pope has been chosen.

ARCHBISHOPS OF YORK

The date of succession is given.

627	Paulinus[1]	1023	Aelfric Puttoc
644	Chad (Ceadda)[1]	1051	Cynesige
669	Wilfrid I (St Wilfrid)[1]	1061	Ealdred
678	Bosa[1]	1070	Thomas I
705	John (St John of Beverley)[1]	1101	Gerard
718	Wilfrid II[1]	1109	Thomas II
735	Egbert	1119	Thurstan
767	Ethelbert	1143	William Fitzherbert
780	Eanbald I	1147	Henry Fitzherbert/William Fitzherbert
796	Eanbald II		
808	Wulfsige	1154	William Fitzherbert
837	Wigmund	1154	Roger of Pont-L'Eveque
854	Wulfhere	1181	Geoffrey Plantagenet
900	Ethelbald	1215	Walter de Grey
904	Hrotheweard (or Lodeward)	1256	Sewal de Bovill
931	Wulfstan I	1258	Godfrey of Ludham (or Kineton)
958	Oskytel	1265	Walter Giffard
971	Edwald (or Ethelwold)	1279	William Wickwane
972	Oswald	1286	John le Romeyn (Romanus)
992	Ealdulf (Abbot of Peterborough)	1298	Henry of Newark
1003	Wulfstan II	1300	Thomas of Corbridge

ARCHBISHOPS OF CANTERBURY

1306	William Greenfield
1317	William of Melton
1342	William le Zouche
1352	John of Thoresby
1374	Alexander Neville
1388	Thomas Arundel
1396	Robert Waldby
1398	Richard le Scrope
1407	Henry Bowet
1425	John Kempe
1452	William Booth
1465	George Neville
1476	Lawrence Booth
1480	Thomas Rotheram (or Scott)
1501	Thomas Savage
1508	Christopher Bainbridge
1514	Thomas Wolsey
1531	Edward Lee
1545	Robert Holgate
1555	Nicholas Heath
1561	Thomas Young
1570	Edmund Grindal
1577	Edwin Sandys
1589	John Piers
1595	Matthew Hutton
1606	Tobias Matthew
1628	George Monteigne
1628	Samuel Harsnett
1632	Richard Neile
1641	John Williams
1660	Accepted Frewen
1664	Richard Sterne
1683	John Dolben
1688	Thomas Lamplugh
1691	John Sharp
1714	Sir William Dawes
1724	Lancelot Blackburne
1743	Thomas Herring
1747	Matthew Hutton
1757	John Gilbert
1761	Robert Hay Drummond
1777	William Markham
1807	Edward Venables Vernon (afterwards Harcourt)
1847	Thomas Musgrave
1860	Charles Thomas Longley
1862	William Thomson
1890	William Connor Magee
1891	William Dalrymple
1908	Cosmo Gordon Lang
1929	William Temple
1942	Cyril Forster Garbett
1956	Arthur Michael Ramsey
1961	Frederic Donald Coggan
1975	Stuart Yarworth Blanch
1983	John Stapylton Habgood
1995	David Hope
2005	John Sentamu

[1] *Bishop of York; the first Archbishop was Egbert in 735.*
Note: Gaps in the chronology indicate that the see was vacant or subject to conflict.

ARCHBISHOPS OF CANTERBURY

The date of succession is given.

597	Augustine
604	Laurentius
619	Mellitus
624	Justus
627	Honorius
655	Deusdedit
668	Theodore
693	Berhtwald
731	Tatwine
735	Nothelm
740	Cuthbert
761	Bregowine
765	Jaenbert
793	Ethelhard
805	Wulfred
832	Feologeld
833	Ceolnoth
870	Ethelred
890	Plegmund
914	Athelm
923	Wulfhelm
942	Oda
959	Aelfsige
959	Brithelm
960	Dunstan
990	Sigeric
995	Aelfric
c.988	Ethelgar

ARCHBISHOPS OF CANTERBURY

1005 Alphege
1013 Lyfing
1020 Ethelnoth
1038 Eadsige
1051 Robert of Jumieges
1052 Stigand
1070 Lanfranc
1093 Anselm
1114 Ralph d'Escures
1123 William de Corbeil
1139 Theobald
1162 Thomas à Becket
1174 Richard (of Dover)
1184 Baldwin
1193 Hubert Walter
1207 Stephen Langton
1229 Richard le Grant
1234 Edmund of Abingdon
1245 Boniface of Savoy
1273 Robert Kilwardby
1279 John Peckham
1294 Robert Winchelsey
1313 Walter Reynolds
1328 Simon Meopham
1333 John de Stratford
1349 Simon Islip
1349 Thomas Bradwardine
1366 Simon Langham
1368 William Whittlesey
1375 Simon Sudbury
1381 William Courtenay
1396 Thomas Arundel
1398 Roger Walden
1399 Thomas Arundel (*restored*)
1414 Henry Chichele
1443 John Stafford
1452 John Kempe
1454 Thomas Bourchier
1486 John Morton
1501 Henry Deane
1503 William Warham
1533 Thomas Cranmer
1556 Reginald Pole
1559 Matthew Parker
1576 Edmund Grindal
1583 John Whitgift
1604 Richard Bancroft
1611 George Abbot
1633 William Laud
1660 William Juxon
1663 Gilbert Sheldon
1678 William Sancroft
1691 John Tillotson
1695 Thomas Tenison
1716 William Wake
1737 John Potter
1747 Thomas Herring
1757 Matthew Hutton
1758 Thomas Secker
1768 Frederick Cornwallis
1783 John Moore
1805 Charles Manners-Sutton
1828 William Howley
1848 John Sumner
1862 Charles Longley
1868 Archibald Tait
1883 Edward Benson
1896 Frederick Temple
1903 Randall Davidson
1928 William Lang
1942 William Temple
1945 Geoffrey Fisher
1961 Arthur Ramsey
1974 Frederick Coggan
1980 Robert Runcie
1991 George Carey
2002 Rowan Williams

Chair of St Augustine

The post of Archbishop of Canterbury is known as the 'Chair of St Augustine', after the first Archbishop. St Augustine was probably born in Rome, where he became the prior of a Benedictine monastery. In 596 he was sent by Pope Gregory I to convert the Anglo-Saxons to Christianity, and it is recorded that he baptized 1,000 people in the River Swale in a single day. Augustine became Bishop of the English in 597 and established his church at Canterbury, where he died in 604.

APOSTLES

In Christianity, the Apostles were Christ's twelve chosen followers. The Apostles are generally taken to include the twelve original followers of Christ (excluding Judas Iscariot in some versions), who witnessed the resurrected Jesus and were charged with proclaiming his gospel.

Peter (brother of Andrew)
Andrew (brother of Peter)
James, son of Zebedee (brother of John)
John (brother of James)
Philip
Bartholomew
Thomas
Matthew
James of Alphaeus
Simon the Canaanite (*in Matthew and Mark*) or **Simon the Zealot** (*in Luke and Acts*)
Judas Iscariot

The twelfth Apostle is Thaddeus in the biblical gospels of Matthew and Mark; in Luke and Acts it is Judas or James. Matthias succeeded to Judas's place.

FATHERS OF THE CHURCH

'Father of the Church' is a title usually applied to the leaders of the early Christian church. Recognized as eminent teachers of the faith, they were characterized by orthodoxy of doctrine and personal holiness, and were usually beatified.

Note: The title has also been subsequently awarded by the Roman Catholic church to later Christian writers.

Sent Away

The word 'apostle' comes from the Greek word *apostolos* meaning 'someone who is sent away'. The Bible describes the Twelve Apostles as being sent forth by Jesus to establish the Church throughout the nations.

Apostolic Fathers

The Apostolic Fathers were the immediate disciples and fellow labourers of the Apostles, more especially those who have left writings. Only the three major Fathers are listed.

St Clement of Rome
St Ignatius of Antioch
St Polycarp of Smyrna

Doctors of the Church

A small number of especially revered early ecclesiastical writers are known as Doctors of the Church. There were eight from medieval times, originally four from the Greek Church and four from the Latin Church.

St Basil the Great
St Gregory Nazianzen
St John Chrysostom
St Gregory the Great
St Ambrose
St Jerome
St Augustine
St Athanasius

TEN COMMANDMENTS

In the Bible, the Ten Commandments given by God to Moses on Mount Sinai, as described in the Old Testament Book of Exodus.

I	I am the Lord your God, who brought you out of the land of Egypt, out of the house of bondage. You shall have no other gods before me.
II	You shall not make for yourself a graven image. You shall not bow down to them or serve them.
III	You shall not take the name of the Lord your God in vain.
IV	Remember the sabbath day, to keep it holy.
V	Honour your father and your mother.
VI	You shall not kill.
VII	You shall not commit adultery.
VIII	You shall not steal.
IX	You shall not bear false witness against your neighbour.
X	You shall not covet.

The Ten Commandments appear in two different places in the Bible – Exodus 20.17 and Deuteronomy 5.6–21. Most Protestant, Anglican and Orthodox Christians enumerate the Commandments differently from Roman Catholics and Lutherans.

A Most Unfortunate Error

The 1631 edition of the King James version of the Bible is known as 'The Wicked Bible' or 'The Adulterous Bible'. The word 'not' was accidentally left out of the seventh commandment, meaning that it read 'Thou shalt commit adultery'.

CHAMPIONS OF CHRISTENDOM

In medieval times the patron saints of seven nations were known as the Champions of Christendom. Their supposed exploits were celebrated in *The Famous History of the Seven Champions of Christendom*, published c.1597 by Richard Johnson (1573–c.1659).

St George of England
St Andrew of Scotland
St Patrick of Ireland
St David of Wales
St Denys of France
St James of Spain
St Anthony of Italy

PATRON SAINTS

A patron saint is a saint regarded as the protector of a particular group.

Accountants	Matthew
Actors	Genesius, Vitus
Advertisers	Bernardino of Siena
Architects	Thomas (Apostle)
Artists	Luke, Angelico
Astronauts	Joseph (Cupertino)
Astronomers	Dominic
Athletes	Sebastian
Authors	Francis de Sales
Aviators	Our Lady of Loreto
Bakers	Honoratus
Bankers	Bernardino (Feltre)
Barbers	Cosmas and Damian
Blacksmiths	Eligius
Bookkeepers	Matthew
Book trade	John of God
Brewers	Amand, Wenceslaus
Builders	Barbara, Thomas (Apostle)
Butchers	Luke
Carpenters	Joseph

PATRON SAINTS

Chemists	Cosmas and Damian
Comedians	Vitus
Cooks	Lawrence, Martha
Dancers	Vitus
Dentists	Apollonia
Doctors	Cosmas and Damian, Luke
Editors	Francis de Sales
Farmers	Isidore
Firemen	Florian
Fishermen	Andrew, Peter
Florists	Dorothy, Thérèse of Lisieux
Gardeners	Adam, Fiacre
Glassworkers	Luke, Lucy
Gravediggers	Joseph of Arimathea
Grocers	Michael
Hotelkeepers	Amand, Julian the Hospitaler
Housewives	Martha
Jewellers	Eligius
Journalists	Francis de Sales
Labourers	James, John Bosco
Lawyers	Ivo, Thomas More
Librarians	Jerome, Catherine of Alexandria
Merchants	Francis of Assisi
Messengers	Gabriel
Metalworkers	Eligius
Midwives	Raymond Nonnatus
Miners	Anne, Barbara
Motorists	Christopher
Musicians	Cecilia, Gregory the Great
Nurses	Camillus de Lellis, John of God
Philosophers	Thomas Aquinas, Catherine of Alexandria
Poets	Cecilia, David
Police	Michael
Politicians	Thomas More
Postal Workers	Gabriel
Priests	Jean-Baptiste Vianney
Printers	John of God
Prisoners	Leonard
Radio Workers	Gabriel
Sailors	Christopher, Erasmus, Francis of Paola
Scholars	Thomas Aquinas
Scientists	Albert the Great
Sculptors	Luke, Louis
Secretaries	Genesius
Servants	Martha, Zita
Shoemakers	Crispin, Crispinian
Singers	Cecilia, Gregory
Soldiers	George, Joan of Arc, Martin of Tours, Sebastian
Students	Thomas Aquinas
Surgeons	Luke, Cosmas and Damian
Tailors	Homobonus
Tax Collectors	Matthew
Taxi Drivers	Fiacre
Teachers	Gregory the Great, John Baptiste de la Salle
Television Workers	Gabriel
Theologians	Augustine, Alphonsus Liguori, Thomas Aquinas
Undertakers	Dismas, Joseph of Arimathea
Waiters	Martha
Writers	Lucy

Politicians' Patron

In 2000 Pope John Paul II declared the martyr Sir Thomas More (1478–1535) to be the patron saint of politicians and statesmen. More was Speaker of the House of Commons and Lord Chancellor under King Henry VIII; he was beheaded in 1535.

SAINTS

Information on selected well-known saints is given below. The official recognition of saints, and the choice of a saint's day, varies greatly between different branches of Christianity, calendars and localities. Where there are major variations, the dates given refer to the dates in the Western church calendar.

Saint	Lived	Saint's Day
Alban	3c AD	22 Jun

The first Christian martyr in Britain, he was a pagan living in the town of Verulamium who was scourged and beheaded around AD300 for helping a fugitive Christian priest who had converted him. A monastery was founded on the site in 793, and the place was renamed St Albans.

Andrew	1c AD	30 Nov

One of the twelve Apostles of Jesus Christ, he was a fisherman who preached the Gospel in Asia Minor, and was crucified in Greece. The belief that his cross was X-shaped dates only from the 14c. He is a patron saint not only of Scotland but of Greece and Russia.

Bernard	923–1008	28 May or 15 Jun

Also known as the Apostle of the Alps, he founded hospices in Alpine passes which were named after him, as were St Bernard dogs, trained by the monks to go to the aid of travellers.

Catherine	died AD307	25 Nov

Born in Alexandria, she is said to have publicly confessed the Gospel at a sacrificial feast appointed by Emperor Maximinus, and was consequently beheaded, after being tortured on a spiked wheel (later known as a 'catherine wheel').

Christopher	3c AD	25 Jul

He was, according to tradition, a man some 3.5m/11.5ft tall. His name in Greek (*Christophoros*) means 'Christ-bearing', which gave rise to the legend that he had carried the Christ-child (and all the weight of the world's sin) across a river. He is the patron saint of travellers.

David	c.520–601	1 Mar

He presided over two Welsh synods and is believed to have died in 601 as Bishop of Moni Judeorum, or Menevia, afterwards St David's. He is the patron saint of Wales.

George	early 4c AD	23 Apr

Little is known about him, the date of his death is uncertain, and he has been confused with others; his name was soon obscured by fables and myth. The famous story of his fight with the dragon cannot be traced much earlier than the 13c. He is the patron saint of England and Portugal.

Nicholas	4c AD	6 Dec

In legend he gave gifts of gold to three poor girls for their dowries, which gave rise to the custom of giving gifts on his feast day. His identification with Father Christmas began in Europe and spread to the USA. He is a patron saint of Greece and Russia, and also of children, scholars, merchants, sailors, travellers and thieves.

Pancras	died AD304	12 May

He was killed in persecutions while still a child, and is one of the patron saints of children.

Patrick	5c	17 Mar

In AD432 it is thought he was sent by the Pope as a missionary to Ireland. He converted his old master Milchu and other chiefs, and after 20 years spent in missionary work fixed his see at Armagh (AD454). He is the patron saint of Ireland.

Stephen	1c AD	26 Dec

All that is known is from the Bible, Acts 6–7. He was appointed by the Apostles to manage the finances and alms of the early Church, was tried for blasphemy and stoned to death.

Saint	Lived	Saint's Day
Swithin	died 862	15 Jul

An English ecclesiastic, he was made Bishop of Winchester in 852. When the monks exhumed his body in 971 to bury it in the rebuilt cathedral, the removal, which was to have taken place on 15 Jul, is said to have been delayed by violent rain. This led to the belief that if it rains on his feast day it will rain for a further 40 days.

Saint	Lived	Saint's Day
Valentine	died AD 269	14 Feb

He is said to have been executed during Roman persecutions, but claims have been made for another St Valentine who was martyred in Rome. Neither is associated with romance, hardly surprisingly; the custom of sending love letters on his feast day originated in the Middle Ages, when it was thought the birds' mating season started then.

Death of Saints

Many early saints met a premature end through martyrdom. Their gruesome fates include being rolled over burning coals (St Agatha, died AD 251), tortured on a spiked wheel and beheaded (St Catherine, died AD 307), pressed to death (St Margaret Clitherow, c.1556–86), tied to a tree and shot to death with arrows by the Danes (St Edmund, c.841–70), murdered by a heathen daughter-in-law (St Ludmilla, died 921), impaled or crucified head downward (St Peter, 1c AD), beaten to death with rods (St Sebastian, died AD 288) and being killed, along with 11,000 virgin companions, by a horde of Huns (St Ursula, 4c AD).

DAYS OF CHRISTMAS

According to the old song, 'my true love' gave a present on each of the twelve days of Christmas.

Day	Gift
1st	Partridge in a pear tree
2nd	Turtle doves
3rd	French hens
4th	Calling birds
5th	Gold rings
6th	Geese a-laying
7th	Swans a-swimming
8th	Maids a-milking
9th	Ladies dancing
10th	Lords a-leaping
11th	Pipers piping
12th	Drummers drumming

Christmas Birds

It is thought that 'calling birds' is a corruption of the older 'colly birds' – a dialect word for blackbirds. 'Gold rings' may be ring-necked birds, rather than jewellery, meaning that the first seven gifts are all birds.

TRIBES OF ISRAEL

In the Bible (Genesis 49), a confederacy of twelve tribes generally traced to Jacob's twelve sons – six by Leah (Reuben, Simeon, Levi, Judah, Issachar, Zebulun), two by Rachel (Joseph, Benjamin), two by Rachel's maid Bilhah (Dan, Naphtali), and two by Leah's maid Zilpah (Gad, Asher). Joseph's sons Ephraim and Manasseh gave rise to two tribes; the Tribe of Levi is not conventionally listed as they served in the Holy Temple rather than owning land. Jacob had received the name Israel (Genesis 32.28) when he wrestled with a divine being.

Reuben	Simeon	Gad
Judah	Issachar	Zebulun
Ephraim	Manasseh	Benjamin
Dan	Asher	Naphtali

PLAGUES OF EGYPT

Ten biblical plagues, described in the book of Exodus, that afflicted the Egyptians as a result of the Pharaoh's refusal to release the Israelites from captivity.

Water turns to blood	Boils
Frogs	Hail
Lice	Locusts
Flies	Darkness
Cattle disease	Death of first-born

SEVEN DEADLY SINS

Pride *or* vanity	Envy	Gluttony
Lust	Anger *or* wrath	Sloth
Avarice, greed *or* covetousness		

VIRTUES

Cardinal virtues

Also known as the natural virtues.

Justice	Prudence	Temperance
Fortitude		

Theological virtues

Also known as the supernatural or Christian virtues.

Faith	Hope	Charity

SEVEN SLEEPERS

The Seven Sleepers of Ephesus in medieval legend were seven persecuted Christians who fled into a cave at the time of the emperor Decius (AD 250). They slept for 200 years, emerging in AD 447 at the time of Theodosius II. The story was thought to confirm the resurrection of Christ.

Achillides	Diomedes	Diogenus
Probatus	Stephanus	Sambatus
Quiriacus		

HORSEMEN OF THE APOCALYPSE

The symbolic biblical characters described in Revelation 6 and Zechariah 6.1–7, who signal the beginning of the messianic age. Each comes on a steed of different colour, symbolizing devastations associated with the end of the world, except for the white horse's rider, who is given a crown and sent to conquer (Revelation 6.2).

Black horse	Famine
Red	Bloodshed and War
Pale	Pestilence and Death
White	various interpretations

GIFTS OF THE WISE MEN

In the Bible, a group who came from 'the East' guided by a star (Matthew 2.1–12) to visit the infant Jesus in Bethlehem, bringing three gifts.

gold	frankincense	myrrh

We Three Kings

The three wise men are a Christian tradition. But the Bible doesn't specify how many wise men there were: the belief that there were three developed in later centuries. Tradition also suggests the three were called Balthasar, Gaspar and Melchior. The wise men are also sometimes known as the *Magi*. The word is the plural of *magus*, which comes from the Old Persian word for magician.

CONFUCIANISM

Founded	6c BC
Founder	K'ung-fu-tzu (Confucius) (c.551–479 BC), a Chinese philosopher
Sacred texts	Shih Ching, Li Ching, Shu Ching, Chu'un Ch'iu, I Ching.
Place of worship	Temple
Beliefs	Confucius was concerned with the best way to live and behave in this world and was not concerned with the afterlife. He laid particular emphasis on the family.
Organization	Confucianism is not an institution and has no church or clergy. Weddings and funerals follow a tradition handed down by Confucian scholars.
Divisions	Two major divisions: the first is associated with Confucius and Hsun Tzu (c.298–238 BC), and the second with Mencius (c.371–289 BC) and medieval neo-Confucians.

Act Wisely

'Man has three ways of acting wisely. First, on meditation; that is the noblest. Secondly, on imitation; that is the easiest. Thirdly, on experience; that is the bitterest.'

From *The Analects* (c.479 BC), a collection of the sayings and doings of Confucius.

HINDUISM

Founded	c.1500 BC
Founder	No single founder
Sacred texts	The Vedas ('knowledge') including the Upanishads, the Ramayana and the Mahabharata, the Bhagavad Gita, the Agamas.
Place of worship	Temple
Beliefs	Many diverse religious beliefs and practices, including dharma (right living), the law of karma and reincarnation; numerous gods.
Organization	A Brahmanic priesthood officiates at prayer and festivals.
Divisions	The three major living traditions are those devoted to Vishnu, Shiva and the goddess Shakti. Many folk traditions exist.

HINDU GODS

Agni	God of fire
Brahma	God of creation
Durga	Shiva's wife
Ganesh	Elephant-headed son of Shiva
Garuda	Bird that carries Shiva
Hanuman	Monkey god
Indra	God of storms and war
Iswara	God of nature and the soul
Kali	Goddess of destruction and wife of Shiva
Kama	God of lust and desire
Kartikeya	Six-headed war god mounted on a peacock
Krishna	Incarnation of Vishnu
Kurma	Incarnation of Vishnu in the form of a tortoise
Lakshmana	Half-brother of Rama
Lakshmi	Goddess of wealth and good luck
Narada	Incarnation of Vishnu
Narasimha	Incarnation of Vishnu as a lion-man
Nataraja	Aspect of Shiva as the Lord of Dance
Parvati	Shiva's wife
Pushan	God of enlightenment
Radha	Goddess of love and consort of Krishna
Rama	Incarnation of Vishnu

Rudra	Destructive aspect of Shiva	**Sita**	Rama's wife
Sarasvati	Mother goddess representing art, learning and music	**Soma**	God of speech and deity of the soma creeper
Shakti	Female principle of power and energy	**Surya**	God of the Sun
		Varuna	God of the sea
Shani	Bringer of bad luck	**Vishnu**	God of creation
Shiva	God of creation and destruction	**Yama**	God of death

HINDU CALENDAR

The Indian classical calendar was based on the Sun for purposes of astrology, but the lunar one was necessary for the sacred calendar. In the 6c AD the practice of dating years relative to the revolutions of the orbit of Jupiter was introduced, creating a 60-year cycle. In recent times the National Calendar of India was introduced in 1957, using Gregorian dates alongside the Saka era calendar (calculated from AD 78, each year beginning on 22 Mar, or 21 Mar in a leap year). Other calendars in use include the Vikrama era calendar (calculated from 58 BC) and the Kalacuri era calendar (calculated from AD 248). Other important Hindu eras include the Gupta era (AD 320) and Harsa era (AD 606).

Months (solar days)
Basis: Moon
Chaitra (29 or 30)
Vaisakha (29 or 30)
Jyaistha (29 or 30)
Asadha (29 or 30)
Dvitiya Asadha (*certain leap years*)
Sravana (29 or 30)
Dvitiya Sravana (*certain leap years*)
Bhadrapada (29 or 30)
Asvina (29 or 30)
Karttika (29 or 30)
Margasirsa (29 or 30)
Pausa (29 or 30)
Magha (29 or 30)
Phalguna (29 or 30)

Saka era

Year	Gregorian equivalents (AD)
1917	(22 Mar 1995–20 Mar 1996)
1918	(21 Mar 1996–21 Mar 1997)
1919	(22 Mar 1997–21 Mar 1998)
1920	(22 Mar 1998–21 Mar 1999)
1921	(22 Mar 1999–20 Mar 2000)
1922	(21 Mar 2000–21 Mar 2001)
1923	(22 Mar 2001–21 Mar 2002)
1924	(22 Mar 2002–21 Mar 2003)
1925	(22 Mar 2003–20 Mar 2004)
1926	(21 Mar 2004–21 Mar 2005)
1927	(22 Mar 2005–21 Mar 2006)
1928	(22 Mar 2006–21 Mar 2007)
1929	(22 Mar 2007–20 Mar 2008)

Saka era

Year	Gregorian equivalents (AD)
1930	(21 Mar 2008–21 Mar 2009)
1931	(22 Mar 2009–21 Mar 2010)
1932	(22 Mar 2010–21 Mar 2011)
1933	(22 Mar 2011–20 Mar 2012)
1934	(21 Mar 2012–21 Mar 2013)
1935	(22 Mar 2013–21 Mar 2014)
1936	(22 Mar 2014–21 Mar 2015)
1937	(22 Mar 2015–20 Mar 2016)
1938	(21 Mar 2016–21 Mar 2017)
1939	(22 Mar 2017–21 Mar 2018)
1940	(22 Mar 2018–21 Mar 2019)
1941	(22 Mar 2019–20 Mar 2020)

Vikrama era

Year	Gregorian equivalents (AD)
2052	(14 Mar 1995–13 Mar 1996)
2053	(14 Mar 1996–13 Mar 1997)
2054	(14 Mar 1997–13 Mar 1998)
2055	(14 Mar 1998–13 Mar 1999)
2056	(14 Mar 1999–13 Mar 2000)
2057	(14 Mar 2000–13 Mar 2001)
2058	(14 Mar 2001–13 Mar 2002)
2059	(14 Mar 2002–13 Mar 2003)
2060	(14 Mar 2003–13 Mar 2004)
2061	(14 Mar 2004–13 Mar 2005)
2062	(14 Mar 2005–13 Mar 2006)
2063	(14 Mar 2006–13 Mar 2007)
2064	(14 Mar 2007–13 Mar 2008)

Vikrama era

Year	Gregorian equivalents (AD)
2065	(14 Mar 2008–13 Mar 2009)
2066	(14 Mar 2009–13 Mar 2010)
2067	(14 Mar 2010–13 Mar 2011)
2068	(14 Mar 2011–13 Mar 2012)
2069	(14 Mar 2012–13 Mar 2013)
2070	(14 Mar 2013–13 Mar 2014)
2071	(14 Mar 2014–13 Mar 2015)
2072	(14 Mar 2015–13 Mar 2016)
2073	(14 Mar 2016–13 Mar 2017)
2074	(14 Mar 2017–13 Mar 2018)
2075	(14 Mar 2018–13 Mar 2019)
2076	(14 Mar 2019–13 Mar 2020)

ISLAM

Founded	7C AD
Founder	Muhammad (c.570–c.632)
Sacred texts	The Koran (the word of God as revealed to Muhammad) and the Hadith (a collection of the Prophet's sayings).
Place of worship	Mosque
Beliefs	Monotheistic: God is the creator of all things and holds absolute power over man; the perfect word of God was revealed to the Prophet Muhammad.
Organization	No organized priesthood, but great respect is accorded to descendants of Muhammad and holy men, scholars and teachers such as mullahs and ayatollahs.
Divisions	Two main groups: the Sunni (the majority and the more orthodox) and the Shiites. Other subsects include the Sufis, the Ismailis and the Wahhabis.

PILLARS OF ISLAM

Islam has five essential religious duties.

Shahada	Profession of faith, the sincere recitation of the two-fold creed, 'There is no god but God' and 'Muhammad is the Messenger of God'.
Salat	Formal prayer, to be performed at fixed hours five times a day while facing towards the holy city of Mecca.
Zakat	Almsgiving, through the payment of zakat, is the duty of sharing one's wealth out of gratitude for God's favour, according to the uses laid down in the Koran.
Saum	Fasting, during the hours of daylight of the month of Ramadan.
Hajj	Pilgrimage to Mecca, to be performed if at all possible at least once during one's lifetime.

ISLAMIC CALENDAR

The Islamic calendar is calculated from the Hegira (the year Muhammad migrated from Mecca to Medina, and the beginning of the Muslim era) in AD 622. Still used by Muslims for religious purposes, it has twelve lunar months, with no intercalations.

Months (solar days)

Basis: Moon
Muharram (30)
Safar (29)
Rabi I (30)
Rabi II (29)
Jumada I (30)
Jumada II (29)

Months (solar days)

Rajab (30)
Shaban (29)
Ramadan (30)
Shawwal (29)
Dhu al-Qadah (30)
Dhu al-Hijjah (29 or 30)

Year	Gregorian equivalents (AD)
1416	(31 May 1995–18 May 1996)
1417	(19 May 1996–8 May 1997)
1418	(9 May 1997–27 Apr 1998)
1419	(28 Apr 1998–16 Apr 1999)
1420	(17 Apr 1999–5 Apr 2000)
1421	(6 Apr 2000–25 Mar 2001)
1422	(26 Mar 2001–14 Mar 2002)
1423	(15 Mar 2002–3 Mar 2003)
1424	(4 Mar 2003–21 Feb 2004)
1425	(22 Feb 2004–9 Feb 2005)
1426	(10 Feb 2005–30 Jan 2006)
1427	(31 Jan 2006–20 Jan 2007)
1428	(21 Jan 2007–9 Jan 2008)

Year	Gregorian equivalents (AD)
1429	(10 Jan 2008–28 Dec 2008)
1430	(29 Dec 2008–17 Dec 2009)
1431	(18 Dec 2009–6 Dec 2010)
1432	(7 Dec 2010–26 Nov 2011)
1433	(27 Nov 2011–14 Nov 2012)
1434	(15 Nov 2012–4 Nov 2013)
1435	(5 Nov 2013–24 Oct 2014)
1436	(25 Oct 2014–13 Oct 2015)
1437	(14 Oct 2015–1 Oct 2016)
1438	(2 Oct 2016–21 Sep 2017)
1439	(22 Sep 2017–10 Sep 2018)
1440	(11 Sep 2018–31 Aug 2019)
1441	(1 Sep 2019–19 Aug 2020)

One God

Allah is simply the Arabic name for 'God'. Muslims, Christians and Jews all worship this same God.

JAINISM

Founded	6c BC
Founder	Vardhamana Mahavira (c.540–468 BC)
Sacred texts	The Svetambara canon of scripture and Digambara texts.
Place of worship	Temple
Beliefs	Salvation and freedom from the working of karma can be acquired by ascetic practices. All living things are sacred and must not be harmed.
Organization	Jain monks and nuns have a strong relationship with lay people and officiate at temple rituals.
Divisions	Svetambara and Digambara.

JUDAISM

Founded	c.2000 BC
Founder	Abraham (c.2000–1650 BC) and Moses (c.1500–1300 BC)
Sacred texts	The Hebrew Bible: Torah (Pentateuch): Genesis, Exodus, Leviticus, Numbers, Deuteronomy. Also the books of the Prophets, Psalms, Chronicles and Proverbs, as well as the Talmud (made up of the Mishna, the oral law, and the Gemara, an extensive commentary). The Zohar (Book of Splendour) is a famous cabbalistic book.
Place of worship	Synagogue
Beliefs	Monotheistic: God created the world, delivered the Israelites out of bondage in Egypt, and chose them to be a light to all humankind.
Organization	Hierarchy of chief rabbis, rabbis and congregations.
Divisions	Today most Jews are descendants of either the Ashkenazim or the Sephardim.

CHIEF RABBIS

The spiritual leader of the Jewish community in the UK is given the title of Chief Rabbi of the United Hebrew Congregations of the Commonwealth. The Chief Rabbinate consists of the Chief Rabbi and his Cabinet.

1704–56	Aaron Hart
1756–8	*post vacant*
1758–64	Hart Lyon
1765–91	David Tevele Schiff
1791–1802	*post vacant*
1802–42	Solomon Hirschell
1842–5	*post vacant*
1845–91	Nathan Marcus Adler
1891–1911	Hermann Marcus Adler
1911–13	*post vacant*
1913–46	Joseph Herman Hertz
1946–8	*post vacant*
1948–65	Israel Brodie
1966–91	Lord Immanuel Jakobovits
1991–	Sir Jonathan Sacks

JEWISH CALENDAR

The Jewish religious calendar dates in its modern form from the Babylonian Exile in the 6c BC, when the Jews adopted the Babylonian calendar. This was lunar-solar, with a lunar year of 354 days and a solar year (important to agriculture) of 365 days. By the 4c BC an accurate system of intercalation had been devised. Each month starts with the new moon, but each day begins at sunset. These features were retained in the Jewish calendar. The year count of the Jewish era is calculated from 3761 BC, said to be the year of the creation of the world.

Months (solar days)
Basis: Moon
Tishri (30)
Heshvan (29 or 30)
Kislev (29 or 30)
Tevet (29)
Shevat (30)
Adar (29 or 30)

Months (solar days)
Adar Sheni (*leap years only*)
Nisan (30)
Iyar (29)
Sivan (30)
Tammuz (29)
Av (30)
Elul (29)

Year	Gregorian equivalents (AD)	Year	Gregorian equivalents (AD)
5756	(25 Sep 1995–13 Sep 1996)	5769	(30 Sep 2008–18 Sep 2009)
5757	(14 Sep 1996–1 Oct 1997)	5770	(19 Sep 2009–8 Sep 2010)
5758	(2 Oct 1997–20 Sep 1998)	5771	(9 Sep 2010–28 Sep 2011)
5759	(21 Sep 1998–10 Sep 1999)	5772	(29 Sep 2011–16 Sep 2012)
5760	(11 Sep 1999–29 Sep 2000)	5773	(17 Sep 2012–4 Sep 2013)
5761	(30 Sep 2000–17 Sep 2001)	5774	(5 Sep 2013–24 Sep 2014)
5762	(18 Sep 2001–6 Sep 2002)	5775	(25 Sep 2014–13 Sep 2015)
5763	(7 Sep 2002–26 Sep 2003)	5776	(14 Sep 2015–2 Oct 2016)
5764	(27 Sep 2003–15 Sep 2004)	5777	(3 Oct 2016–20 Sep 2017)
5765	(16 Sep 2004–3 Oct 2005)	5778	(21 Sep 2017–9 Sep 2018)
5766	(4 Oct 2005–22 Sep 2006)	5779	(10 Sep 2018–29 Sep 2019)
5767	(23 Sep 2006–12 Sep 2007)	5780	(30 Sep 2019–18 Sep 2020)
5768	(13 Sep 2007–29 Sep 2008)		

SHINTOISM

Founded	8c
Founder	No single founder
Sacred texts	Kojiki and Nihon Shoki
Place of worship	Shrine
Beliefs	Founded on Japanese folk religions, Shinto is made up of many elements, including animism, veneration of nature and ancestor worship.
Organization	Shamans originally performed the ceremonies; in the 8c the imperial family were ascribed divine origins and state Shintoism was established.
Divisions	In the 19c Shinto was divided into Shrine (jinga) Shinto and Sectarian (kyoko) Shinto. Jinga was a state cult until 1945.

SIKHISM

Founded	15c
Founder	Guru Nanak (1469–1539)
Sacred texts	Adi Granth
Place of worship	Temple
Beliefs	Monotheistic; a fusion of Brahmanism and Islam, preaching tolerance and equality in the sight of God; initiates wear the Five Ks.
Organization	No priestly caste. All Sikhs are empowered to perform rituals connected with births, marriages and deaths.
Divisions	There are several religious orders of Sikhs based either on disputes over the succession of gurus or points of ritual and tradition.

FIVE KS OF SIKHISM

The Five Ks are the symbols of a Sikh's spiritual and cultural allegiance to Sikhism, worn by baptized Sikhs.

Kesh (uncut hair)
Kanga (comb)
Kara (steel bangle symbolizing the one God)
Kirpan (ceremonial dagger to fight injustice)
Kaccha (short trousers signifying willingness to ride into battle)

TAOISM

Founded	c.600 BC
Founder	Lao-tzu (6c BC)
Sacred texts	Chuang-tzu, Lao-tzu (Tao-te-ching)
Place of worship	Temple
Beliefs	Tao ('the way') stresses harmony with nature, meditation, worship of a pantheon of gods and spirits and the theory of Yin-Yang.
Organization	Monastic orders and priests practise temple worship and divination, including the I Ching.
Divisions	Taoism emerged from many sects, each emphasizing different aspects such as worship of the Immortals, exorcism, faith healing, alchemy or meditative practice.

TEMPLETON PRIZE

Awarded annually for progress towards research or discoveries about spiritual realities; first awarded in 1973.

1973	Mother Teresa
1974	Brother Roger
1975	Sir Sarvepalli Radhakrishnan
1976	Leon Joseph Suenens
1977	Chiara Lubich
1978	Thomas F Torrance
1979	Nikkyo Niwano
1980	Ralph Wendell Burhoe
1981	Dame Cicely Saunders
1982	Billy Graham
1983	Aleksandr Solzhenitsyn
1984	Michael Bourdeaux
1985	Alister Hardy
1986	James McCord
1987	Stanley L Jaki
1988	Inamullah Khan
1989	Lord MacLeod; Carl Friedrich von Weizsäcker
1990	Baba Amte; L Charles Birch
1991	Lord Jakobovits
1992	Kyung-Chik Han
1993	Charles W Colson
1994	Michael Novak
1995	Paul Davies
1996	William R Bright
1997	Pandurang Shastri Athavale
1998	Sir Sigmund Sternberg
1999	Ian Graeme Barbour
2000	Freeman J Dyson
2001	Arthur Peacocke
2002	John C Polkinghorne
2003	Holmes Rolston III
2004	George F R Ellis
2005	Charles H Townes
2006	John D Barrow
2007	Charles Taylor

A Prodigious Prize

The Templeton Prize was founded by the US financial analyst and philanthropist Sir John Templeton (1912–). The monetary value of the prize is always set to be higher than the Nobel prizes; in fact, the Templeton Prize is the world's largest monetary prize awarded to an individual.

SIGNS OF THE ZODIAC

The zodiac is the band of sky, about 18° wide, through the centre of which the Sun appears to move. It forms the background for the motions of the Sun, Moon and major planets, and is divided into twelve equal parts of 30°, each of which once contained one of the zodiacal constellations. The passing of time means that the Sun no longer passes through each constellation on the accepted dates.

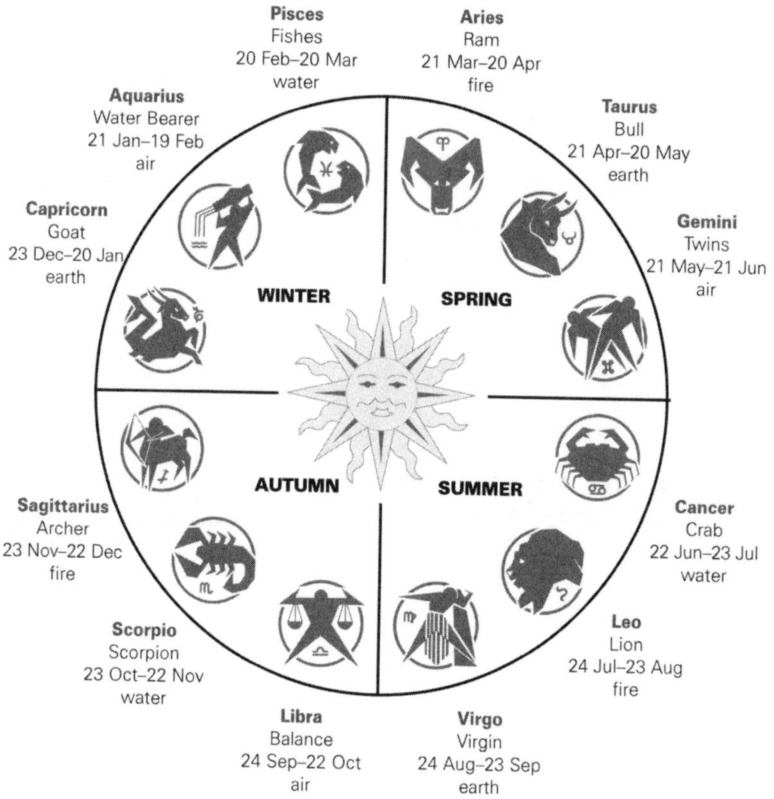

Sky Figures

The word *zodiac* comes from the French word *zodiaque* but is originally from the Greek word *zōidion*, a small carved or painted figure, which itself comes from the word *zōion*, an animal.

BIRTHSTONES

In many Western countries, the months are traditionally associated with gemstones. There is considerable variation between countries; the following combinations are widely recognized in North America and the UK.

Month	Gemstone	Month	Gemstone
Jan	garnet	Jul	ruby
Feb	amethyst	Aug	peridot, sardonyx
Mar	aquamarine, bloodstone	Sep	sapphire
Apr	diamond	Oct	opal, tourmaline
May	emerald	Nov	topaz
Jun	alexandrite, moonstone, pearl	Dec	turquoise, zircon

BIRTH FLOWERS

In many Western countries, the months are traditionally associated with flowers. There is considerable variation between countries; the following combinations are widely recognized in North America and the UK.

Month	Flower	Month	Flower
Jan	carnation, snowdrop	Jul	larkspur, water lily
Feb	primrose, violet	Aug	gladiolus, poppy
Mar	jonquil, violet	Sep	aster, morning glory
Apr	daisy, sweet pea	Oct	calendula, cosmos
May	hawthorn, lily of the valley	Nov	chrysanthemum
Jun	honeysuckle, rose	Dec	holly, narcissus, poinsettia

KNIGHTS OF THE ROUND TABLE

Tradition has it that King Arthur and his knights sat at the Round Table, a table shaped so that no individual knight should have precedence. Lists of the knights vary considerably; below are those recorded on the Winchester Round Table.

Sir Alymere
King Arthur
Sir Bedivere
Sir Bleoberis
Sir Bors de Ganis
Sir Brunor le Noir
La Cote Male Taile
Sir Dagonet
Sir Degore
Sir Ector de Maris
Sir Galahad
Sir Gareth
Sir Gawaine
Sir Kay
Sir Lamorak
Sir Lancelot (Launcelot) Du Lac
Sir Le Bel Desconneu
Sir Lionell
Sir Lucan
Sir Mordred
Sir Palomedes
Sir Pelleas
Sir Percivale
Sir Safer
Sir Tristan (Tristram)

SANTA'S REINDEER

Clement Clarke Moore (1779–1863) christened Santa's reindeer in his poem 'A Visit from St Nicholas' (1823), popularly known as ''Twas the Night Before Christmas'.

Blitzen
Comet
Cupid
Dasher
Dancer
Donder[1]
Prancer
Vixen

[1] *Donder is also known as Donner.*

Rudolph the Red-Nosed Reindeer

Shopping chains and promotional gimmicks might not seem to have anything to do with the spirit of Christmas. However, Rudolph, the famous reindeer with the 'very shiny nose', was originally devised as a character in a storybook to be given away as a Christmas freebie in 1939 to customers of Montgomery Ward department stores in Chicago, USA. His creator, Robert L May, supposedly went through a number of names before settling on Rudolph: Santa's red-nosed pal was nearly called Rollo, or even Reginald.

SEASONS

Northern hemisphere

Season	Duration
Spring	From vernal equinox (c.21 Mar) to summer solstice (c.21 Jun)
Summer	From summer solstice (c.21 Jun) to autumnal equinox (c.23 Sep)
Autumn	From autumnal equinox (c.23 Sep) to winter solstice (c.21 Dec)
Winter	From winter solstice (c.21 Dec) to vernal equinox (c.21 Mar)

Southern hemisphere

Season	Duration
Spring	From vernal equinox (c.23 Sep) to summer solstice (c.21 Dec)
Summer	From summer solstice (c.21 Dec) to autumnal equinox (c.21 Mar)
Autumn	From autumnal equinox (c.21 Mar) to winter solstice (c.21 Jun)
Winter	From winter solstice (c.21 Jun) to vernal equinox (c.23 Sep)

MONTHS

Month	Days	Name origin
January	31	From the Latin *Jānuārius* (*mēnsis*), the month dedicated to Janus, the god of gates, doorways, and beginnings, usually depicted with a two-faced head.
February	28 or 29	From the Latin *Februārius* (*mēnsis*) the month of expiation, and *februa* the feast of expiation.
March	31	From the Latin *Martius* (*mēnsis*) the month dedicated to Mars, the Roman god of war.
April	30	From the Latin *Aprīlis*, probably from Latin *aperire*, to open.
May	31	From the Old French *Mai*, from Latin *Māius* (*mēnsis*), probably meaning the month sacred to Māia, the Roman goddess of fertility.
June	30	From the Latin *Jūnius* (*mēnsis*) the month of Juno, the Roman goddess of marriage, childbirth and light.
July	31	From the Latin *Jūlius*, from the Roman emperor Julius Caesar, who was born in it.
August	31	From the first Roman emperor, Augustus, who amended the Roman calendar in 8 BC.
September	30	From the Latin *September*, from *septem* seven; in the original Roman calendar, September was the seventh month of a ten-month year.
October	31	From the Latin *Octōber*, from *octō* eight; in the original Roman calendar, October was the eighth month of a ten-month year.
November	30	From the Latin *November*, from *novem* nine; in the original Roman calendar, November was the ninth month of a ten-month year.
December	31	From the Latin *December*, from *decem* ten; in the original Roman calendar, December was the tenth month of a ten-month year.

For the Hindu, Islamic and Jewish calendars and months see **Religions, Beliefs and Folklore**.

Gregorian Calendar

The calendar in general use throughout the world is the Gregorian New Style calendar. The calendar was reformed by Pope Gregory XIII in 1582.

The Julian calendar that was previously in use had a shortcoming in that the value of 365¼ days placed on the solar year was too long by 11 minutes and 14 seconds. By 1545 the vernal equinox, used by the Church to determine the date of Easter, had moved ten days. It took time for astronomers to work out a satisfactory method of correction, but finally the Pope instructed that ten days should be omitted from Oct 1582.

Britain didn't adopt the new calendar until 1752. At that time the difference between the two calendars was eleven days. The changeover meant that 2 Sep was immediately followed by 14 Sep. This led to popular protests; people who felt swindled out of the missing days chanted 'Give us back our eleven days!'

DAYS

Day	Name origin
Sunday	From the Old English *sunnan dæg*, a translation of the Latin *diēs sōlis*, meaning day of the Sun.
Monday	From the Old English *mōnandæg*, from *mōnan*, *tōna* meaning Moon, and *dæg* meaning day, a translation of the Latin *diēs lūnae*, Moon's day.
Tuesday	From the Old English *Tiwes dæg*, the day of Tiw, the god of war, corresponding to the Latin *diēs Martis*, the day of Mars.
Wednesday	From the Old English *Wōdnes dæg*, the day of Woden, or Odin, the chief god.
Thursday	From the Old English *Thunres dæg*, the day of Thunor, the thunder god, and the Old Norse *Thōrsdagr*, Thor's day.
Friday	From the Old English *Frīgedæg*, the day of *Frīg*, the goddess of married love, corresponding to the Latin *diēs Veneris*, the day of Venus.
Saturday	From the Old English *Sæterdæg* or *Sætern(es)dæg*, a translation of the Latin *diēs Saturni*, the day of Saturn.

Hot Dogs

The hottest days of the year are known as the *dog days*, and are associated with the rising of the Dog Star (Sirius). The definition of this period varies, but it is generally reckoned to last from 3 Jul to 11 Aug. According to ancient superstition, disease and disaster were rife at this time and dogs were at their most susceptible to rabies: in some towns and cities all dogs had to wear muzzles in public places for the duration.

QUARTER DAYS

Traditionally, the quarter days were those days in each of the year's quarters on which rent or interest was due to be paid.

England, Wales and Ireland

Lady Day	25 Mar
Midsummer Day	24 Jun
Michaelmas Day	29 Sep
Christmas Day	25 Dec

Scotland[1]

Candlemas	28 Feb
Whitsunday	28 May
Lammas	28 Aug
Martinmas	28 Nov

[1] *As defined in the Term and Quarter Days (Scotland) Act 1990.*

FRENCH REVOLUTIONARY CALENDAR

The French Revolutionary Calendar, also known as the French Republican Calendar, was introduced in 1793 and attempted to move the organization of the calendar away from all religious connections. Instead, Year 1 dated from the declaration of the First Republic on 22 Sep 1792. Twelve 30-day months were introduced, named to be appropriate to the season, and were divided into three ten-day weeks called *decadi*. Five supplementary days (or six in leap years) were known as *sans-culottides*. The calendar worked well enough in France but caused problems for international communications, and Napoleon I replaced it with the Gregorian calendar in 1805.

Month	Derivation of name	Month	Derivation of name
Vendémiaire	vintage	Germinal	seed
Brumaire	mist	Floréal	blossom
Frimaire	frost	Prairial	meadow
Nivôse	snow	Messidor	harvest
Pluviôse	rain	Thermidor	heat
Ventôse	wind	Fructidor	fruits

CHINESE ANIMAL YEARS AND TIMES

	Years								
Rat	1924	1936	1948	1960	1972	1984	1996	2008	2020
Ox	1925	1937	1949	1961	1973	1985	1997	2009	2021
Tiger	1926	1938	1950	1962	1974	1986	1998	2010	2022
Hare	1927	1939	1951	1963	1975	1987	1999	2011	2023
Dragon	1928	1940	1952	1964	1976	1988	2000	2012	2024
Serpent	1929	1941	1953	1965	1977	1989	2001	2013	2025
Horse	1930	1942	1954	1966	1978	1990	2002	2014	2026
Sheep	1931	1943	1955	1967	1979	1991	2003	2015	2027
Monkey	1932	1944	1956	1968	1980	1992	2004	2016	2028
Cock	1933	1945	1957	1969	1981	1993	2005	2017	2029
Dog	1934	1946	1958	1970	1982	1994	2006	2018	2030
Boar	1935	1947	1959	1971	1983	1995	2007	2019	2031

	Time of day (hours)
Rat	2300–0100
Ox	0100–0300
Tiger	0300–0500
Hare	0500–0700
Dragon	0700–0900
Serpent	0900–1100
Horse	1100–1300
Sheep	1300–1500
Monkey	1500–1700
Cock	1700–1900
Dog	1900–2100
Boar	2100–2300

WEDDING ANNIVERSARIES

In many Western countries, wedding anniversaries have become associated with gifts of different materials. There is some variation between countries.

Anniversary	Traditional gift	Modern gift
1st	paper	clocks
2nd	cotton	china
3rd	leather	crystal, glass
4th	fruit, flowers	appliances
5th	wood	silverware
6th	sugar, iron	wood
7th	copper, wool	desk sets
8th	bronze, pottery	linen, lace
9th	pottery, willow	leather
10th	tin, aluminium	diamond jewellery
11th	steel	fashion jewellery
12th	silk, linen	pearl
13th	lace	textiles, fur
14th	ivory	gold jewellery
15th	crystal	watches
20th	china	platinum
25th	silver	silver
30th	pearl	diamond
35th	coral	jade
40th	ruby	ruby
45th	sapphire	sapphire
50th	gold	gold
55th	emerald	emerald
60th	diamond	diamond
70th	platinum	platinum

A Call from the Queen

It is well known that the monarch will send congratulations to centenarians upon their 100th birthday, a tradition that dates back to 1917. But the sovereign will also send royal best wishes to couples reaching their diamond wedding anniversary, and also to husbands and wives celebrating 65 years of marriage, 70 years and every subsequent anniversary.

CHEMICAL ELEMENTS

Chemical elements with atomic numbers between 1 and 112 are listed.

Symbol	Element	Derived from	Atomic no
Ac	actinium	Greek *aktis* = ray	89
Ag	silver	Old English *silfer, seolfor*	47
Al	aluminium	Latin *alumen* = alum	13
Am	americium	America	95
Ar	argon	Greek *argon* = inactive	18
As	arsenic	Greek *arsenikon* = orpiment, a yellow mineral (arsenic trisulphide)	33
At	astatine	Greek *astatos* = unstable	85
Au	gold	Old English *gold*	79
B	boron	Arabic *buraq* = borax	5
Ba	barium	Greek *barys* = heavy	56
Be	beryllium	Greek *beryllos* = beryl	4
Bh	bohrium	Niels Bohr, Danish physicist	107
Bi	bismuth	German (origin unknown)	83
Bk	berkelium	Berkeley, California	97
Br	bromine	Greek *bromos* = stink	35
C	carbon	Latin *carbo* = coal, charcoal	6
Ca	calcium	Latin *calx* = lime	20
Cd	cadmium	Greek *kadmeia* = calamine	48
Ce	cerium	asteroid Ceres	58
Cf	californium	California	98
Cl	chlorine	Greek *chloros* = pale green	17
Cm	curium	Marie and Pierre Curie, French physicists	96
Co	cobalt	German *Kobold* = demon	27
Cr	chromium	Greek *chroma* = colour	24
Cs	caesium	Latin *caesius* = bluish-grey	55
Cu	copper	Cyprus	29
Db	dubnium	Dubna, Russia	105
Ds	darmstadtium	Darmstadt, Germany	110
Dy	dysprosium	Greek *dysprositos* = difficult to reach	66
Er	erbium	Ytterby, Sweden	68
Es	einsteinium	Albert Einstein, US physicist	99
Eu	europium	Europe	63
F	fluorine	Latin *fluor* = flow	9
Fe	iron	Old English *iren*	26
Fm	fermium	Enrico Fermi, Italian physicist	100
Fr	francium	France	87
Ga	gallium	Latin *Gallia* = France, or *gallus* = cock	31
Gd	gadolinium	Johan Gadolin, Finnish chemist	64
Ge	germanium	Germany	32
H	hydrogen	Greek *hydor* = water + *gennaein* = to produce	1
He	helium	Greek *helios* = sun	2
Hf	hafnium	Latin *Hafnia* = Copenhagen	72
Hg	mercury	Latin *Mercurius*	80
Ho	holmium	Latin *Holmia* = Stockholm	67

Symbol	Element	Derived from	Atomic no
Hs	hassium	Latin *Hassias* = Hesse	108
I	iodine	Greek *ioeides* = violet-coloured	53
In	indium	indigo lines in the spectrum	49
Ir	iridium	Latin *iris* = rainbow goddess	77
K	potassium	potash	19
Kr	krypton	Greek *kryptein* = to hide	36
La	lanthanum	Greek *lanthanein* = to escape notice	57
Li	lithium	Greek *lithos* = stone	3
Lr	lawrencium	Ernest O Lawrence, US physicist	103
Lu	lutetium	Latin *Lutetia* = Paris	71
Md	mendelevium	Dmitri Mendeleev, Russian scientist	101
Mg	magnesium	Magnesia, Thessaly, Greece	12
Mn	manganese	Latin *magnesia*	25
Mo	molybdenum	Greek *molybdos* = lead	42
Mt	meitnerium	Lise Meitner, Austrian physicist	109
N	nitrogen	Greek *nitron* = sodium carbonate + *gennaein* = to produce	7
Na	sodium	soda	11
Nb	niobium	Niobe (Greek myth)	41
Nd	neodymium	Greek *neos* = new + *didymos* = twin	60
Ne	neon	Greek *neos* = new	10
Ni	nickel	German *Kupfernickel* = niccolite	28
No	nobelium	Nobel Institute	102
Np	neptunium	planet Neptune	93
O	oxygen	Greek *oxys* = acid + *gennaein* = to produce	8
Os	osmium	Greek *osme* = smell	76
P	phosphorus	Greek *phosphoros* = light-bearer	15
Pa	protactinium	Greek *protos* = first + *actinium* (see above)	91
Pb	lead	Old English *lead*	82
Pd	palladium	minor planet Pallas	46
Pm	promethium	Prometheus (Greek myth)	61
Po	polonium	Poland	84
Pr	praseodymium	Greek *prasios* = leek green + *didymos* = twin	59
Pt	platinum	Spanish *plata* = silver	78
Pu	plutonium	planet Pluto	94
Ra	radium	Latin *radius* = ray	88
Rb	rubidium	Latin *rubidus* = red	37
Re	rhenium	Latin *Rhenus* = the Rhine	75
Rf	rutherfordium	Ernest Rutherford, British physicist	104
Rg	roentgenium	Wilhelm Roentgen, German physicist	111
Rh	rhodium	Greek *rhodon* = rose	45
Rn	radon	radium	86
Ru	ruthenium	Latin *Ruthenia* = Russia	44
S	sulphur	Latin *sulphur*	16
Sb	antimony	Latin *antimonium*	51
Sc	scandium	Scandinavian	21
Se	selenium	Greek *selene* = moon	34
Sg	seaborgium	Glenn Seaborg, US physicist	106
Si	silicon	Latin *silex* = flint	14

CHEMICAL ELEMENTS

Symbol	Element	Derived from	Atomic no
Sm	samarium	Colonel M S Samarski, Russian engineer	62
Sn	tin	Old English *tin*	50
Sr	strontium	Strontian, Scotland	38
Ta	tantalum	Tantalus (Greek myth)	73
Tb	terbium	Ytterby, Sweden	65
Tc	technetium	Greek *technetos* = artificial	43
Te	tellurium	Latin *tellus* = earth	52
Th	thorium	Scandinavian god Thor	90
Ti	titanium	Greek *Titan* = Titan	22
Tl	thallium	Greek *thallos* = a young shoot	81
Tm	thulium	Latin *Thule* = an island in the far north	69
U	uranium	planet Uranus	92
Uub	ununbium	systematic name, 'one hundred and twelve'	112
V	vanadium	Old Norse *Vanadis* = goddess Freya	23
W	tungsten	Swedish *tungsten* = heavy stone	74
Xe	xenon	Greek *xenos* = stranger	54
Y	yttrium	Ytterby, Sweden	39
Yb	ytterbium	Ytterby, Sweden	70
Zn	zinc	German *zink*	30
Zr	zirconium	Persian *zargun* = gold-coloured	40

Radioactive Family

Curium is named after the French physicists Pierre (1859–1906) and Marie Curie (1867–1934). They were jointly awarded the Nobel Prize for Physics in 1903; Marie later received the Nobel Prize for Chemistry (1911). Their daughter, Irène Joliot-Curie (1897–1956), and her husband, Frédéric (1900–58), also won the Nobel Prize for Chemistry in 1935.

PERIODIC TABLE

element symbol atomic number
element name

Transition metals

1	2	3	4	5	6	7	8	9	10	11	12	13	14	15	16	17	18
H 1 hydrogen																	He 2 helium
Li 3 lithium	Be 4 beryllium											B 5 boron	C 6 carbon	N 7 nitrogen	O 8 oxygen	F 9 fluorine	Ne 10 neon
Na 11 sodium	Mg 12 magnesium											Al 13 aluminium	Si 14 silicon	P 15 phos-phorus	S 16 sulphur	Cl 17 chlorine	Ar 18 argon
K 19 potassium	Ca 20 calcium	Sc 21 scandium	Ti 22 titanium	V 23 vanadium	Cr 24 chromium	Mn 25 manganese	Fe 26 iron	Co 27 cobalt	Ni 28 nickel	Cu 29 copper	Zn 30 zinc	Ga 31 gallium	Ge 32 germanium	As 33 arsenic	Se 34 selenium	Br 35 bromine	Kr 36 krypton
Rb 37 rubidium	Sr 38 strontium	Y 39 yttrium	Zr 40 zirconium	Nb 41 niobium	Mo 42 moly-bdenum	Tc 43 technetium	Ru 44 ruthenium	Rh 45 rhodium	Pd 46 palladium	Ag 47 silver	Cd 48 cadmium	In 49 indium	Sn 50 tin	Sb 51 antimony	Te 52 tellurium	I 53 iodine	Xe 54 xenon
Cs 55 caesium	Ba 56 barium	57–71 *	Hf 72 hafnium	Ta 73 tantalum	W 74 tungsten	Re 75 rhenium	Os 76 osmium	Ir 77 iridium	Pt 78 platinum	Au 79 gold	Hg 80 mercury	Tl 81 thallium	Pb 82 lead	Bi 83 bismuth	Po 84 polonium	At 85 astatine	Rn 86 radon
Fr 87 francium	Ra 88 radium	89–103 **	Rf 104 ruther-fordium	Db 105 dubnium	Sg 106 sea-borgium	Bh 107 bohrium	Hs 108 hassium	Mt 109 meitnerium	Ds 110 darmstadtium	Rg 111 röntgenium	Uub 112 ununbium						

*Lanthanide series	La 57 lanthanum	Ce 58 cerium	Pr 59 praseo-dymium	Nd 60 neo-dymium	Pm 61 pro-methium	Sm 62 samarium	Eu 63 europium	Gd 64 gadolinium	Tb 65 terbium	Dy 66 dysprosium	Ho 67 holmium	Er 68 erbium	Tm 69 thulium	Yb 70 ytterbium	Lu 71 lutetium
**Actinide series	Ac 89 actinium	Th 90 thorium	Pa 91 pro-tactinium	U 92 uranium	Np 93 neptunium	Pu 94 plutonium	Am 95 americium	Cm 96 curium	Bk 97 berkelium	Cf 98 californium	Es 99 einsteinium	Fm 100 fermium	Md 101 men-delevium	No 102 nobelium	Lr 103 law-rencium

SUBATOMIC PARTICLES

Subatomic particles are those that constitute the atom.

hadrons	quarks	leptons	gauge bosons
baryons	up quark	electron	photon
proton	down quark	positron	W
neutron	charmed quark	muon	Z
	strange quark	tau lepton	gluon
mesons	bottom quark	neutrino (electron)	graviton
pion	top quark	neutrino (muon)	
kaon		neutrino (tau)	
J/psi			
upsilon			

Flavours of Quark

The language of *quarks* is one of the quirkier areas of particle physics. The six types of quark – *up*, *down*, *top*, *bottom*, *strange* and *charmed* – are known as *flavours*. *Bottom* is sometimes also known as *beauty*, and *top* as *truth*. Each flavour of quark is also believed to have an antiparticle known as an *antiquark*. Flavours of quark come in three *colours*: red, blue and green; and for antiquarks, three *anticolours*. The term *quark* was chosen by the US physicist Murray Gell-Mann (1929–); some people believe he was inspired by the line 'three quarks for Muster Mark' in *Finnegans Wake* by James Joyce (1882–1941) since at that time there were thought to be only three flavours of quark.

DECIBEL SCALE

A decibel is a term used to express a level of sound. It is the tenth part of a bel, a measure for comparing the intensity of noises, which was named after Alexander Graham Bell (1847–1922), the inventor of the telephone.

Source	Decibel level (dB)	Source	Decibel level (dB)
Breathing	10	Traffic	60–90
Whisper	20	Pneumatic drill	110
Conversation	50–60	Jet aircraft	120
Vacuum cleaner	80	Space vehicle launch	140–170

WENTWORTH SCALE

The Wentworth scale is one of the main scales used in geology to describe the general dimensions of grains in a rock, especially sediment. It was devised by Chester K Wentworth (1891–1969), a US geologist.

Name	Dimension[1]	Name	Dimension[1]
boulder	greater than 256mm	sand	$\frac{1}{16}$–2mm
cobble	64–256mm	silt	$\frac{1}{256}$–$\frac{1}{16}$mm
pebble	4–64mm	clay	less than $\frac{1}{256}$mm
gravel	2–4mm		

[1] *To convert millimetres to inches, multiply by 0.0394.*

SCOVILLE SCALE *see* **Food and Drink**

MOHS HARDNESS SCALE

The relative hardness of solids can be expressed using a scale of numbers from 1 to 10, each relating to a mineral. The method was devised by Friedrich Mohs (1773–1839), a German mineralogist. Sets of hardness pencils are used to test specimens to see what will scratch them. Other useful instruments for testing include: fingernail (will scratch a specimen with a hardness of 2.5 or lower), old (non-magnetic) copper coin (3.5 or lower), steel knife (5.5 or lower) and glass (6.0 or lower).

Talc	1	Fluorite	4	Quartz	7	Diamond	10
Gypsum	2	Apatite	5	Topaz	8		
Calcite	3	Orthoclase	6	Corundum	9		

PH SCALE

pH or pH value is a number used to express degrees of acidity or alkalinity in solutions. The term comes from the German word *Potenz* meaning power, and *H* the symbol for hydrogen. The scale ranges from 0 to 14; a pH below 7 indicates acidity, and one above 7 alkalinity. A solution with a pH of 7 is neutral.

ELECTROMAGNETIC SPECTRUM

The electromagnetic spectrum ranges from long to short wavelengths, with a length of between approximately 10^4m and 10^{-12}m. *To convert metres to feet multiply by 3.2808.*

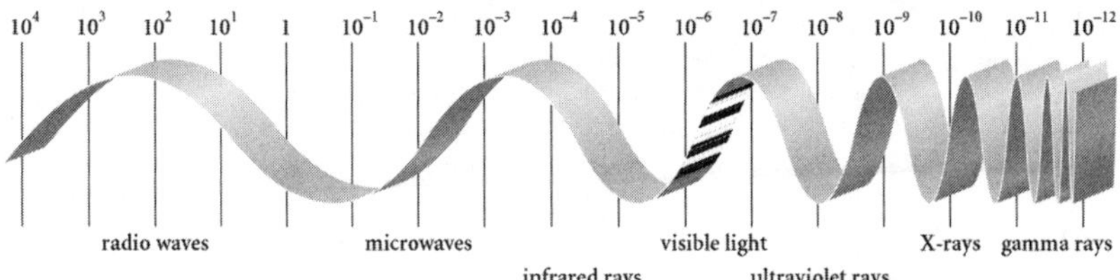

Light Speed

The speed of light in a vacuum is 2.99792458×10^8m/sec, equivalent to 300,000km, or 186,000mi, per second. It is very slightly slower in air, by around 0.3%. The speed of sound in air is a tardy 331.4m/sec, or 1,193kph/741mph.

SI PREFIXES

Factor	Prefix	Symbol	Factor	Prefix	Symbol
10^{24}	yotta	Y	10^{-1}	deci	d
10^{21}	zetta	Z	10^{-2}	centi	c
10^{18}	exa	E	10^{-3}	milli	m
10^{15}	peta	P	10^{-6}	micro	μ
10^{12}	tera	T	10^{-9}	nano	n
10^9	giga	G	10^{-12}	pico	p
10^6	mega	M	10^{-15}	femto	f
10^3	kilo	k	10^{-18}	atto	a
10^2	hecto	h	10^{-21}	zepto	z
10^1	deca	da	10^{-24}	yocto	y

GEMSTONES

Nearly all gemstones are minerals; the four non-mineral gems are amber, coral, jet and pearl. Their hardness is expressed on the Mohs scale.

Gem	Colour	Mohs of hardness
agate	brown, red, blue, green, yellow	7.0
alexandrite	green, red	8.5
amber	yellow, brown and other colours	2–2.5
amethyst	violet	7.0
aquamarine	sky blue, greenish blue	7.5
beryl	green, blue, pink	7.5
bloodstone	green with red spots	7.0
chalcedony	all colours	7.0
chrysoprase	apple green	7.0
citrine	yellow	7.0
coral	white, pink, red, orange, blue, violet and other colours	3.5–4
diamond	colourless, tints of various colours	10.0
emerald	green	7.5
garnet	red and other colours	6.5–7.25
jade	green, whitish, mauve, brown	7.0
jasper	dark red, multi-coloured	7.0
jet	black	2.5–4
lapis lazuli	deep blue	5.5
malachite	dark green banded	3.5
moonstone	whitish with blue shimmer	6.0
onyx	various colours with straight coloured bands	7.0
opal	black, white, orange-red, rainbow coloured	6.0
pearl	cream, white, pink and other colours	2.5–4.5
peridot	green	6.5
ruby	red	9.0
sapphire	blue and other colours	9.0
serpentine	red and green	3.0
soapstone	white, may be stained with impurities	2.0
sunstone	whitish red-brown flecked with golden particles	6.0
topaz	blue, green, pink, yellow, colourless	8.0
tourmaline	brown-black, blue, pink, red, violet-red, yellow, green	7.5
turquoise	greenish grey, sky blue	6.0
zircon	all colours	7.5

Diamonds are Forever

Until the 18c, all the world's diamonds came from India, where they were mined from c.2000 BC. The largest diamond ever found is the Cullinan, a huge 3,106 carat crystal mined in South Africa in 1903.

DRUGS DERIVED FROM PLANTS AND FUNGI

Some commonly prescribed drugs of plant and fungal origin are listed.

Drug	Origin	Effect
aspirin	white willow	pain relief
cocaine	coca	local anaesthetic/central nervous system stimulant
codeine	opium poppy	pain relief
curare	various tropical American plants	muscle relaxant
digitalis	foxglove	heart stimulant
morphine	opium poppy	pain relief/narcotic
penicillin	*Penicillium notatum* fungus	antibiotic
quinine	yellow cinchona	antimalarial
strychnine	nux vomica	central nervous system stimulant

MEASURING DEVICES

Device	Measures
accelerometer	acceleration
altimeter	height
ammeter	electric current
anemometer	wind speed
barometer	atmospheric pressure
calorimeter	heat capacities, etc
chronometer	time
cryometer	low temperatures
decelerometer	deceleration
dosimeter	cumulative exposure to radiation
dynamometer	force
evaporimeter, evaporometer	rate of evaporation
flowmeter	rate of flow of a fluid in a pipe
focimeter	focal length of a lens
galvanometer	electric currents
Geiger counter	radioactivity
geothermometer	subterranean temperatures
gravimeter	variations in the Earth's surface gravity
hyetometer, ombrometer, pluviometer	rain
hygrometer	humidity of the air or of other gases
inclinometer, clinometer	slopes
interferometer	wavelengths, wave speeds, angles, etc
luxmeter	illumination
magnetometer	strength/direction of a magnetic field
mileometer, milometer	miles that a vehicle, etc has travelled
odometer, hodometer	distance travelled by a wheeled vehicle
ohmmeter	electrical resistance
optometer	vision
pedometer	paces (approximate distance walked)
photometer	luminous intensity
pulsimeter	strength or quickness of the pulse
pyrometer	high temperatures
respirometer	breathing

Device	Measures
seismometer	intensity, frequency and duration of earthquakes
spectrometer	wavelengths
speedometer	speed at which a vehicle is travelling
sphygmomanometer, sphygmometer	arterial blood pressure
tachometer	velocity
theodolite	horizontal and vertical angles
thermometer	temperature
vaporimeter	vapour pressure or vapour
velocimeter	velocity
vibrograph, vibrometer	vibrations
viscometer, viscosimeter	viscosity
voltmeter	electromotive force
volumeter	volumes of gases and liquids
wattmeter	circuit power
wavemeter	wavelengths

Unusual Measuring Devices

In the realm of science there are instruments to measure almost everything. Some of the less common are the *cyanometer* (measures the blueness of the sky or ocean), *diaphanometer* (the transparency of the air), *drosometer* (dew), *konimeter* (dust in the air), *oenometer* (the alcoholic strength of wines), *Nilometer* (the height of the River Nile), *weatherometer* (the weather-resisting properties of paints or other surfaces) and *xylometer* (the specific gravity of wood). The specific gravity, relative density and purity or richness of milk are measured by the *galactometer*, *lactometer* and *lactoscope* respectively, while the *plethysmograph* measures variations in the size of body parts, for example when varying amounts of blood flow through them.

NOBEL PRIZE IN PHYSICS

Nobel Prizes were established by a bequest in the will of Alfred Nobel (1833–96) to honour 'those who, during the preceding year, shall have conferred the greatest benefit on mankind'. The Nobel Prize in Physics is awarded annually to a person who has 'made the most important discovery or invention within the field of physics'; first awarded in 1901.

1901 Wilhelm Conrad Röntgen
1902 Hendrik A Lorentz, Pieter Zeeman
1903 Henri Becquerel, Pierre Curie, Marie Curie
1904 Lord Rayleigh
1905 Philipp Lenard
1906 J J Thomson
1907 Albert A Michelson
1908 Gabriel Lippmann
1909 Guglielmo Marconi, Ferdinand Braun
1910 Johannes Diderik van der Waals
1911 Wilhelm Wien
1912 Gustaf Dalén
1913 Heike Kamerlingh Onnes
1914 Max von Laue
1915 William Bragg, Lawrence Bragg
1916 *no award*
1917 Charles Glover Barkla
1918 Max Planck
1919 Johannes Stark
1920 Charles Edouard Guillaume
1921 Albert Einstein
1922 Niels Bohr
1923 Robert A Millikan
1924 Manne Siegbahn
1925 James Franck, Gustav Hertz
1926 Jean Baptiste Perrin
1927 Arthur H Compton, C T R Wilson
1928 Owen Willans Richardson
1929 Louis de Broglie

NOBEL PRIZE IN PHYSICS

1930 Venkata Raman
1931 *no award*
1932 Werner Heisenberg
1933 Erwin Schrödinger, Paul A M Dirac
1934 *no award*
1935 James Chadwick
1936 Victor F Hess, Carl D Anderson
1937 Clinton Davisson, George Paget Thomson
1938 Enrico Fermi
1939 Ernest Lawrence
1940 *no award*
1941 *no award*
1942 *no award*
1943 Otto Stern
1944 Isidor Isaac Rabi
1945 Wolfgang Pauli
1946 Percy W Bridgman
1947 Edward V Appleton
1948 Patrick M S Blackett
1949 Hideki Yukawa
1950 Cecil Powell
1951 John Cockcroft, Ernest T S Walton
1952 Felix Bloch, E M Purcell
1953 Frits Zernike
1954 Max Born, Walther Bothe
1955 Willis E Lamb, Polykarp Kusch
1956 William B Shockley, John Bardeen, Walter H Brattain
1957 Chen Ning Yang, Tsung-Dao Lee
1958 Pavel A Cherenkov, Iĺja M Frank, Igor Y Tamm
1959 Emilio Segrè, Owen Chamberlain
1960 Donald A Glaser
1961 Robert Hofstadter, Rudolf Mössbauer
1962 Lev Landau
1963 Eugene Wigner, Maria Goeppert-Mayer, J Hans D Jensen
1964 Charles H Townes, Nicolay G Basov, Aleksandr M Prokhorov
1965 Sin-Itiro Tomonaga, Julian Schwinger, Richard P Feynman
1966 Alfred Kastler
1967 Hans Bethe
1968 Luis Alvarez
1969 Murray Gell-Mann
1970 Hannes Alfvén, Louis Néel
1971 Dennis Gabor
1972 John Bardeen, Leon N Cooper, Robert Schrieffer
1973 Leo Esaki, Ivar Giaever, Brian D Josephson
1974 Martin Ryle, Antony Hewish
1975 Aage N Bohr, Ben R Mottelson, James Rainwater
1976 Burton Richter, Samuel C C Ting
1977 Philip W Anderson, Sir Nevill F Mott, John H van Vleck
1978 Pyotr Kapitsa, Arno Penzias, Robert Woodrow Wilson
1979 Sheldon Glashow, Abdus Salam, Steven Weinberg
1980 James Cronin, Val Fitch
1981 Nicolaas Bloembergen, Arthur L Schawlow, Kai M Siegbahn
1982 Kenneth G Wilson
1983 Subramanyan Chandrasekhar, William A Fowler
1984 Carlo Rubbia, Simon van der Meer
1985 Klaus von Klitzing
1986 Ernst Ruska, Gerd Binnig, Heinrich Rohrer
1987 J Georg Bednorz, K Alex Müller
1988 Leon M Lederman, Melvin Schwartz, Jack Steinberger
1989 Norman F Ramsey, Hans G Dehmelt, Wolfgang Paul
1990 Jerome I Friedman, Henry W Kendall, Richard E Taylor
1991 Pierre-Gilles de Gennes
1992 Georges Charpak
1993 Russell A Hulse, Joseph H Taylor Jr
1994 Bertram N Brockhouse, Clifford G Shull
1995 Martin L Perl, Frederick Reines
1996 David M Lee, Douglas D Osheroff, Robert C Richardson
1997 Steven Chu, Claude Cohen-Tannoudji, William D Phillips
1998 Robert B Laughlin, Horst L Stürmer, Daniel C Tsui
1999 Gerardus 't Hooft, Martinus JG Veltman
2000 Zhores I Alferov, Herbert Kroemer, Jack S Kilby
2001 Eric A Cornell, Wolfgang Ketterle, Carl E Wieman
2002 Raymond Davis Jr, Masatoshi Koshiba, Riccardo Giacconi
2003 Alexei A Abrikosov, Vitaly L Ginzburg, Anthony J Leggett
2004 David J Gross, H David Politzer, Frank Wilczek
2005 Roy J Glauber, John L Hall, Theodor W Hänsch
2006 John C Mather, George F Smoot
2007 Albert Fert, Peter Grünberg

Bragging About Physics

Lawrence Bragg (1890–1971) was just 25 years old when he won the Nobel Prize in Physics, making him the youngest ever winner of a Nobel award.

NOBEL PRIZE IN CHEMISTRY

Nobel Prizes were established by a bequest in the will of Alfred Nobel (1833–96) to honour 'those who, during the preceding year, shall have conferred the greatest benefit on mankind'. The Nobel Prize in Chemistry is awarded annually to a person who has 'made the most important chemical discovery or improvement'; first awarded in 1901.

1901 Jacobus H van't Hoff
1902 Emil Fischer
1903 Svante Arrhenius
1904 Sir William Ramsay
1905 Adolf von Baeyer
1906 Henri Moissan
1907 Eduard Buchner
1908 Ernest Rutherford
1909 Wilhelm Ostwald
1910 Otto Wallach
1911 Marie Curie
1912 Victor Grignard, Paul Sabatier
1913 Alfred Werner
1914 Theodore W Richards
1915 Richard Willstätter
1916 *no award*
1917 *no award*
1918 Fritz Haber
1919 *no award*
1920 Walther Nernst
1921 Frederick Soddy
1922 Francis W Aston
1923 Fritz Pregl
1924 *no award*
1925 Richard Zsigmondy
1926 The Svedberg
1927 Heinrich Wieland
1928 Adolf Windaus
1929 Arthur Harden, Hans von Euler-Chelpin
1930 Hans Fischer
1931 Carl Bosch, Friedrich Bergius
1932 Irving Langmuir
1933 *no award*
1934 Harold C Urey
1935 Frédéric Joliot, Irène Joliot-Curie
1936 Peter Debye
1937 Norman Haworth, Paul Karrer
1938 Richard Kuhn
1939 Adolf Butenandt, Leopold Ruzicka
1940 *no award*
1941 *no award*
1942 *no award*
1943 George de Hevesy
1944 Otto Hahn
1945 Artturi Virtanen
1946 James B Sumner, John H Northrop, Wendell M Stanley
1947 Sir Robert Robinson
1948 Arne Tiselius
1949 William F Giauque
1950 Otto Diels, Kurt Alder
1951 Edwin M McMillan, Glenn T Seaborg
1952 Archer J P Martin, Richard L M Synge
1953 Hermann Staudinger
1954 Linus Pauling
1955 Vincent du Vigneaud
1956 Sir Cyril Hinshelwood, Nikolay Semenov
1957 Lord Todd
1958 Frederick Sanger
1959 Jaroslav Heyrovsky
1960 Willard F Libby
1961 Melvin Calvin
1962 Max F Perutz, John C Kendrew
1963 Karl Ziegler, Giulio Natta
1964 Dorothy Crowfoot Hodgkin
1965 Robert B Woodward
1966 Robert S Mulliken
1967 Manfred Eigen, Ronald G W Norrish, George Porter
1968 Lars Onsager
1969 Derek Barton, Odd Hassel
1970 Luis Leloir
1971 Gerhard Herzberg
1972 Christian Anfinsen, Stanford Moore, William H Stein
1973 Ernst Otto Fischer, Geoffrey Wilkinson
1974 Paul J Flory

1975 John Cornforth, Vladimir Prelog
1976 William Lipscomb
1977 Ilya Prigogine
1978 Peter Mitchell
1979 Herbert C Brown, Georg Wittig
1980 Paul Berg, Walter Gilbert, Frederick Sanger
1981 Kenichi Fukui, Roald Hoffmann
1982 Aaron Klug
1983 Henry Taube
1984 Bruce Merrifield
1985 Herbert A Hauptman, Jerome Karle
1986 Dudley R Herschbach, Yuan T Lee, John C Polanyi
1987 Donald J Cram, Jean-Marie Lehn, Charles J Pedersen
1988 Johann Deisenhofer, Robert Huber, Hartmut Michel
1989 Sidney Altman, Thomas R Cech
1990 Elias James Corey
1991 Richard R Ernst
1992 Rudolph A Marcus
1993 Kary B Mullis, Michael Smith
1994 George A Olah
1995 Paul J Crutzen, Mario J Molina, F Sherwood Rowland
1996 Robert F Curl Jr, Sir Harold Kroto, Richard E Smalley
1997 Paul D Boyer, John E Walker, Jens C Skou
1998 Walter Kohn, John Pople
1999 Ahmed Zewail
2000 Alan Heeger, Alan G MacDiarmid, Hideki Shirakawa
2001 William S Knowles, Ryoji Noyori, K Barry Sharpless
2002 John B Fenn, Koichi Tanaka, Kurt Wüthrich
2003 Peter Agre, Roderick MacKinnon
2004 Aaron Ciechanover, Avram Hershko, Irwin Rose
2005 Yves Chauvin, Robert H Grubbs, Richard R Schrock
2006 Roger D Kornberg
2007 Gerhard Ertl

When Professor Dorothy Hodgkin won the Nobel Prize in Chemistry in 1964, the *Daily Mail*'s headline ran 'Nobel Prize for British Wife'.

NOBEL PRIZE IN PHYSIOLOGY OR MEDICINE

Nobel Prizes were established by a bequest in the will of Alfred Nobel (1833–96) to honour 'those who, during the preceding year, shall have conferred the greatest benefit on mankind'. The Nobel Prize in Physiology or Medicine is awarded annually to a person who has 'made the most important discovery within the domain of physiology or medicine'; first awarded in 1901.

1901 Emil von Behring
1902 Ronald Ross
1903 Niels Ryberg Finsen
1904 Ivan Pavlov
1905 Robert Koch
1906 Camillo Golgi, Santiago Ramón y Cajal
1907 Alphonse Laveran
1908 Ilya Mechnikov, Paul Ehrlich
1909 Theodor Kocher
1910 Albrecht Kossel
1911 Allvar Gullstrand
1912 Alexis Carrel
1913 Charles Richet
1914 Robert Bárány
1915 *no award*
1916 *no award*
1917 *no award*
1918 *no award*
1919 Jules Bordet
1920 August Krogh
1921 *no award*
1922 Archibald V Hill, Otto Meyerhof
1923 Frederick G Banting, John Macleod
1924 Willem Einthoven
1925 *no award*
1926 Johannes Fibiger
1927 Julius Wagner-Jauregg
1928 Charles Nicolle
1929 Christiaan Eijkman, Sir Frederick Hopkins
1930 Karl Landsteiner
1931 Otto Warburg
1932 Sir Charles Sherrington, Edgar Adrian
1933 Thomas H Morgan

1934 George H Whipple, George R Minot, William P Murphy
1935 Hans Spemann
1936 Sir Henry Dale, Otto Loewi
1937 Albert Szent-Györgyi
1938 Corneille Heymans
1939 Gerhard Domagk
1940 *no award*
1941 *no award*
1942 *no award*
1943 Henrik Dam, Edward A Doisy
1944 Joseph Erlanger, Herbert S Gasser
1945 Sir Alexander Fleming, Ernst B Chain, Sir Howard Florey
1946 Hermann J Muller
1947 Carl Cori, Gerty Cori, Bernardo Houssay
1948 Paul Müller
1949 Walter Hess, Egas Moniz
1950 Edward C Kendall, Tadeus Reichstein, Philip S Hench
1951 Max Theiler
1952 Selman A Waksman
1953 Hans Krebs, Fritz Lipmann
1954 John F Enders, Thomas H Weller, Frederick C Robbins
1955 Hugo Theorell
1956 André F Cournand, Werner Forssmann, Dickinson W Richards
1957 Daniel Bovet
1958 George Beadle, Edward Tatum, Joshua Lederberg
1959 Severo Ochoa, Arthur Kornberg
1960 Sir Frank Macfarlane Burnet, Peter Medawar
1961 Georg von Békésy
1962 Francis Crick, James Watson, Maurice Wilkins
1963 Sir John Eccles, Alan L Hodgkin, Andrew F Huxley
1964 Konrad Bloch, Feodor Lynen
1965 François Jacob, André Lwoff, Jacques Monod
1966 Peyton Rous, Charles B Huggins
1967 Ragnar Granit, Haldan K Hartline, George Wald
1968 Robert W Holley, H Gobind Khorana, Marshall W Nirenberg
1969 Max Delbrück, Alfred D Hershey, Salvador E Luria
1970 Sir Bernard Katz, Ulf von Euler, Julius Axelrod
1971 Earl W Sutherland, Jr
1972 Gerald M Edelman, Rodney R Porter
1973 Karl von Frisch, Konrad Lorenz, Nikolaas Tinbergen
1974 Albert Claude, Christian de Duve, George E Palade
1975 David Baltimore, Renato Dulbecco, Howard M Temin
1976 Baruch S Blumberg, D Carleton Gajdusek
1977 Roger Guillemin, Andrew V Schally, Rosalyn Yalow
1978 Werner Arber, Daniel Nathans, Hamilton O Smith
1979 Allan M Cormack, Godfrey N Hounsfield
1980 Baruj Benacerraf, Jean Dausset, George D Snell
1981 Roger W Sperry, David H Hubel, Torsten N Wiesel
1982 Sune K Bergström, Bengt I Samuelsson, John R Vane
1983 Barbara McClintock
1984 Niels K Jerne, Georges JF Köhler, César Milstein
1985 Michael S Brown, Joseph L Goldstein
1986 Stanley Cohen, Rita Levi-Montalcini
1987 Susumu Tonegawa
1988 Sir James W Black, Gertrude B Elion, George H Hitchings
1989 J Michael Bishop, Harold E Varmus
1990 Joseph E Murray, E Donnall Thomas
1991 Erwin Neher, Bert Sakmann
1992 Edmond H Fischer, Edwin G Krebs
1993 Richard J Roberts, Phillip A Sharp
1994 Alfred G Gilman, Martin Rodbell
1995 Edward B Lewis, Christiane Nüsslein-Volhard, Eric F Wieschaus
1996 Peter C Doherty, Rolf M Zinkernagel
1997 Stanley B Prusiner
1998 Robert F Furchgott, Louis J Ignarro, Ferid Murad
1999 Günter Blobel
2000 Arvid Carlsson, Paul Greengard, Eric R Kandel
2001 Leland H Hartwell, Tim Hunt, Sir Paul Nurse
2002 Sydney Brenner, H Robert Horvitz, John E Sulston
2003 Paul C Lauterbur, Sir Peter Mansfield
2004 Richard Axel, Linda B Buck
2005 Barry J Marshall, J Robin Warren
2006 Andrew Z Fire, Craig C Mello
2007 Mario R Capecchi, Sir Martin J Evans, Oliver Smithies

SKELETON

Humans have an internal skeleton or endoskeleton made of bone or cartilage. It supports the tissues and organs of the body, and protects soft internal organs such as the lungs. The muscles are attached to the bones of the skeleton by means of tendons; these pull against the bones when the muscles contract, causing them to move. Bones are connected to one another by ligaments. The point of articulation or contact between two or more bones of the skeleton is known as a joint, different types of joint allowing varying degrees of movement. In total, the adult human skeleton has 206 bones; some are illustrated below.

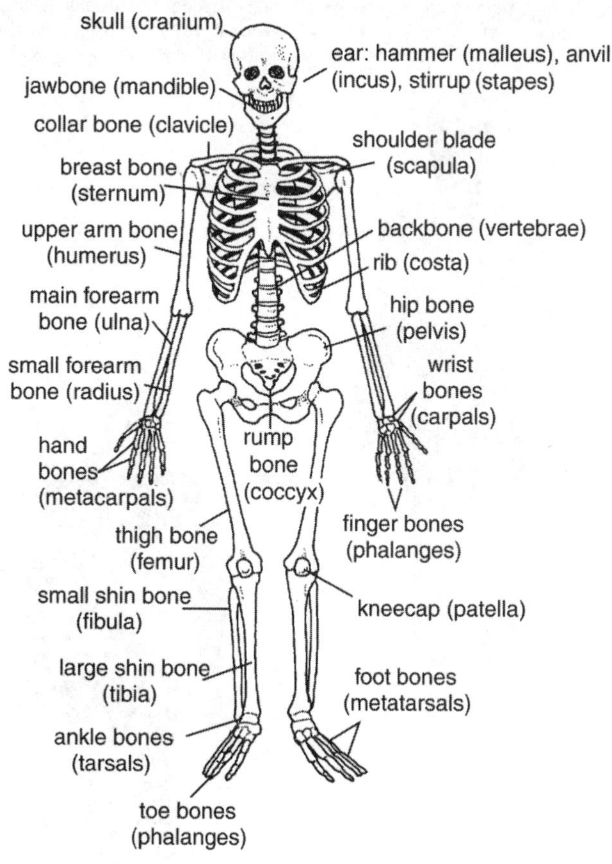

MUSCLES

Muscles consist of bundles of small fibres, each of which is in turn composed of many protein myofibrils, which lengthen or shorten as their filaments slide past each other. This movement, which occurs in response to a stimulus from the nervous system, or a hormonal signal, causes contraction of the whole muscle. *Voluntary muscle*, which is under conscious control, produces voluntary movements by pulling against the bones of the skeleton, to which it is attached by means of tendons, so that contractions of such muscles cause the bones to move. *Involuntary muscle* (also called *smooth muscle*) maintains the movements of the internal body systems, and forms part of many internal organs, such as the intestines, bladder and uterus. *Cardiac muscle*, found only in the heart, does not become fatigued, and continues to contract rhythmically even when it is disconnected from the nervous system. Some of the body's major superficial muscles are illustrated below.

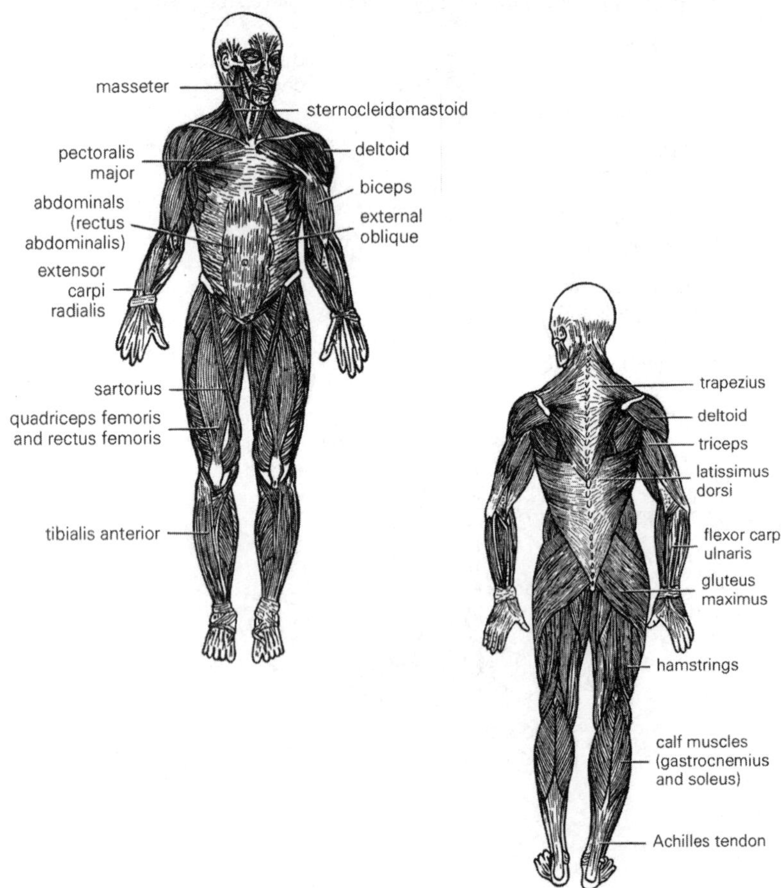

TEETH

In humans, the first set of teeth, consisting of 20 deciduous or milk teeth, is gradually replaced from about six years of age by 32 permanent teeth. These consist of chisel-shaped incisors for cutting, situated at the front of each jaw, and behind them the pointed canine teeth, for tearing food. Behind the canines are the molars and premolars, which have uneven surfaces for grinding and chewing food.

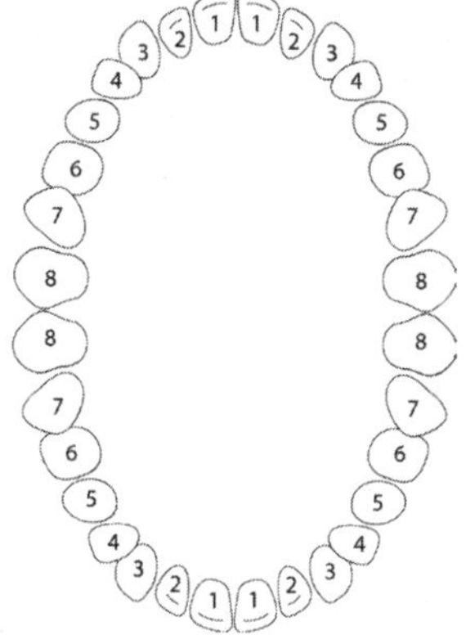

1 central incisors
2 lateral incisors
3 canines (cuspids)
4 first premolars (bicuspids)
5 second premolars (bicuspids)
6 first molars
7 second molars
8 third molars (wisdom teeth)

BLOOD

Blood performs many important functions as it circulates through the tissues of the body. It transports oxygen, nutrients and hormones, and carries waste products to the organs of excretion. It also helps to maintain a uniform temperature in humans and other warm-blooded organisms.

Blood composition

Component	Functions
Red blood cells	Carry oxygen, by means of haemoglobin
White blood cells	Defend the body against infection
Platelets	Needed for blood clotting
Plasma	Distribution of nutrients, salts, hormones, clotting factors and proteins needed for defence

ABO blood group system

Every person has a particular blood group, determined by genes inherited from their parents. The red blood cells of the A, B, AB and O groups carry, respectively, the A antigen, B antigen, both antigens and neither. The blood contains natural antibodies against the blood group antigens that are absent from the red blood cells. Before a transfusion, the blood of the recipient and donor is cross-matched to ensure that red blood cells from the donor are not given to a person possessing antibodies against them, as this could have fatal consequences.

Blood group	Can receive blood type	Blood group	Can receive blood type
A	A and O	AB	A, B, AB, O
B	B and O	O	O

SKIN

The skin consists of two main layers. The epidermis is a thin outer layer, which is continually being renewed as dead cells are shed from its surface. The thicker underlying layer is called the dermis and is composed of a network of collagen and elastic fibres. The dermis contains blood and lymph vessels, sensory nerve endings, hair follicles, sweat and sebaceous glands, and smooth muscle. In humans, as well as other warm-blooded animals, the skin has an important role in temperature regulation. Heat loss is achieved by sweating and by dilation of the skin capillaries. In order to conserve heat, the skin capillaries contract and the hairs on the surface are raised, trapping a layer of warm air next to the skin. The skin is an important sense organ, sensitive to touch, pressure, changes in temperature, and painful stimuli. It prevents fluid loss and dehydration, and protects the body from invasion by micro-organisms and parasites.

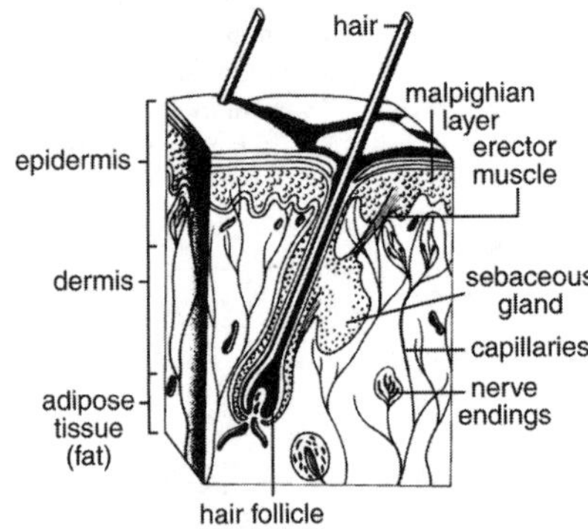

HUMAN BODY DATA

Number of bones	206
Number of muscles	approx 650
Number of chromosomes	22 pairs and two sex chromosomes
Average body temperature	37°C/98.6°F
Average pulse rate	72 beats per minute (men), 80 beats per minute (women)
Average weight of brain	1.4kg/3 lb
Number of nerve cells in the brain	more than 10 billion
Total surface area of the skin of an adult	approx 1.86 sq m/20 sq ft
Total dead skin cells shed per person per lifetime	approx 18kg/40 lb
Total surface area of the alveoli in the lungs	70 sq m/753 sq ft
Average total blood volume	5 l/8pt

FIELDS MEDAL

The Fields Medal is the world's highest award for achievement in mathematics. Named after a Canadian mathematician, Professor J C Fields (1863–1932), the medals are awarded at the International Congress of Mathematicians (ICM) every four years to 'recognize outstanding mathematical achievement' in a mathematician of no older than 40 years. Up to four medals may be awarded on each occasion.

1936	Lars Valerian Ahlfors, Jesse Douglas
1950	Laurent Schwartz, Atle Selberg
1954	Kunihiko Kodaira, Jean-Pierre Serre
1958	Klaus Friedrich Roth, René Thom
1962	Lars Hörmander, John Willard Milnor
1966	Michael Francis Atiyah, Paul Joseph Cohen, Alexander Grothendieck, Stephen Smale
1970	Alan Baker, Heisuke Hironaka, Serge Novikov, John Griggs Thompson
1974	Enrico Bombieri, David Bryant Mumford
1978	Pierre René Deligne, Charles Louis Fefferman, Gregori Alexandrovitch Margulis, Daniel G Quillen
1982	Alain Connes, William P Thurston, Shing-Tung Yau
1986	Simon K Donaldson, Gerd Faltings, Michael H Freedman
1990	Vladimir Drinfeld, Vaughan F R Jones, Shigefumi Mori, Edward Witten
1994	Jean Bourgain, Pierre-Louis Lions, Jean-Christophe Yoccoz, Efim Zelmanov
1998	Richard E Borcherds, W Timothy Gowers, Maxim Kontsevich, Curtis T McMullen
2002	Laurent Lafforgue, Vladimir Voevodsky
2006	Andrei Okounkov, Grigori Perelman (Russia)[1], Terence Tao, Wendelin Werner

[1] Declined the award.

Fermat's Last Theorem

The most famous problem in mathematics was scrawled by the French mathematician Pierre de Fermat (1601–65) in the margin of a page of a book.

Fermat had studied law at Toulouse University, where he became a councillor of parliament, but his passion was mathematics. Most of his work was communicated in letters to friends, containing results without proof.

In what became known as his 'Last Theorem', Fermat stated that it is impossible to find a solution to the equation

$$x^n + y^n = z^n$$

if n is greater than 2. He added tantalizingly that 'I have a truly marvellous demonstration of this proposition which this margin is too narrow to contain'.

The puzzle to find Fermat's proof went on to baffle and outwit mathematicians for almost 350 years. The proof was finally announced in 1993 by the British mathematician Andrew Wiles, and revised by him in 1994. Wiles was just too old to qualify for the Fields Medal, so the International Mathematical Union instead honoured him with a silver plaque as a special tribute.

NUMERALS

Arabic	Roman	Greek	Binary numbers
1	I	α′	1
2	II	β′	10
3	III	γ′	11
4	IV	δ′	100
5	V	ε′	101
6	VI	ϛ′	110
7	VII	ζ′	111
8	VIII	η′	1000
9	IX	θ′	1001
10	X	ι′	1010
11	XI	ια′	1011
12	XII	ιβ′	1100
13	XIII	ιγ′	1101
14	XIV	ιδ′	1110
15	XV	ιε′	1111
16	XVI	ιϛ′	10000
17	XVII	ιζ′	10001
18	XVIII	ιη′	10010
19	XIX	ιθ′	10011
20	XX	κ′	10100
30	XXX	λ′	11110
40	XL	μ′	101000
50	L	ν′	110010
60	LX	ξ′	111100
70	LXX	ο′	1000110
80	LXXX	π′	1010000
90	XC	,ο′	1011010
100	C	ρ′	1100100
200	CC	σ′	11001000
300	CCC	τ′	100101100
400	CD	υ′	110010000
500	D	φ′	111110100
1000	M	,α	1111101000
5000	V	,ε	1001110001000
10000	X	,ι	10011100010000
100000	C	,ρ	11000011010100000

FRACTIONS AND DECIMALS

%	Decimal	Fraction	%	Decimal	Fraction
1	0.01	1/100	10	0.10	1/10
2	0.02	1/50	11	0.11	11/100
3	0.03	3/100	12	0.12	3/25
4	0.04	1/25	12½	0.125	1/8
5	0.05	1/20	13	0.13	13/100
6	0.06	3/50	14	0.14	7/50
7	0.07	7/100	15	0.15	3/20
8	0.08	2/25	16	0.16	4/25
8⅓	0.083	1/12	16⅔	0.167	1/6
9	0.09	9/100	17	0.17	17/100

%	Decimal	Fraction	%	Decimal	Fraction
18	0.18	9/50	39	0.39	39/100
19	0.19	19/100	40	0.40	2/5
20	0.20	1/5	41	0.41	41/100
21	0.21	21/100	42	0.42	21/50
22	0.22	11/50	43	0.43	43/100
23	0.23	23/100	44	0.44	11/25
24	0.24	6/25	45	0.45	9/20
25	0.25	1/4	46	0.46	23/50
26	0.26	13/50	47	0.47	47/100
27	0.27	27/100	48	0.48	12/25
28	0.28	7/25	49	0.49	49/100
29	0.29	29/100	50	0.50	1/2
30	0.30	3/10	55	0.55	11/20
31	0.31	31/100	60	0.60	3/5
32	0.32	8/25	65	0.65	13/20
33	0.33	33/100	70	0.70	7/10
33⅓	0.333	1/3	75	0.75	3/4
34	0.34	17/50	80	0.80	4/5
35	0.35	7/20	85	0.85	17/20
36	0.36	9/25	90	0.90	9/10
37	0.37	37/100	95	0.95	19/20
38	0.38	19/50	100	1.00	1

Fraction	Decimal	Fraction	Decimal	Fraction	Decimal
1/2	0.5000	8/9	0.8889	15/16	0.9375
1/3	0.3333	1/10	0.1000	1/20	0.0500
2/3	0.6667	3/10	0.3000	3/20	0.1500
1/4	0.2500	7/10	0.7000	7/20	0.3500
3/4	0.7500	9/10	0.9000	9/20	0.4500
1/5	0.2000	1/11	0.0909	11/20	0.5500
2/5	0.4000	2/11	0.1818	13/20	0.6500
3/5	0.6000	3/11	0.2727	17/20	0.8500
4/5	0.8000	4/11	0.3636	19/20	0.9500
1/6	0.1667	5/11	0.4545	1/32	0.0313
5/6	0.8333	6/11	0.5454	3/32	0.0938
1/7	0.1429	7/11	0.6363	5/32	0.1563
2/7	0.2857	8/11	0.7272	7/32	0.2188
3/7	0.4286	9/11	0.8181	9/32	0.2813
4/7	0.5714	10/11	0.9090	11/32	0.3438
5/7	0.7143	1/12	0.0833	13/32	0.4063
6/7	0.8571	5/12	0.4167	15/32	0.4688
1/8	0.1250	7/12	0.5833	17/32	0.5313
3/8	0.3750	11/12	0.9167	19/32	0.5938
5/8	0.6250	1/16	0.0625	21/32	0.6563
7/8	0.8750	3/16	0.1875	23/32	0.7188
1/9	0.1111	5/16	0.3125	25/32	0.7813
2/9	0.2222	7/16	0.4375	27/32	0.8438
4/9	0.4444	9/16	0.5625	29/32	0.9063
5/9	0.5556	11/16	0.6875	31/32	0.9688
7/9	0.7778	13/16	0.8125		

MULTIPLICATION TABLE

	2	**3**	**4**	**5**	**6**	**7**	**8**	**9**	**10**	**11**	**12**	**13**	**14**	**15**	**16**	**17**	**18**	**19**	**20**	**21**	**22**	**23**	**24**	**25**
2	4	6	8	10	12	14	16	18	20	22	24	26	28	30	32	34	36	38	40	42	44	46	48	50
3	6	9	12	15	18	21	24	27	30	33	36	39	42	45	48	51	54	57	60	63	66	69	72	75
4	8	12	16	20	24	28	32	36	40	44	48	52	56	60	64	68	72	76	80	84	88	92	96	100
5	10	15	20	25	30	35	40	45	50	55	60	65	70	75	80	85	90	95	100	105	110	115	120	125
6	12	18	24	30	36	42	48	54	60	66	72	78	84	90	96	102	108	114	120	126	132	138	144	150
7	14	21	28	35	42	49	56	63	70	77	84	91	98	105	112	119	126	133	140	147	154	161	168	175
8	16	24	32	40	48	56	64	72	80	88	96	104	112	120	128	136	144	152	160	168	176	184	192	200
9	18	27	36	45	54	63	72	81	90	99	108	117	126	135	144	153	162	171	180	189	198	207	216	225
10	20	30	40	50	60	70	80	90	100	110	120	130	140	150	160	170	180	190	200	210	220	230	240	250
11	22	33	44	55	66	77	88	99	110	121	132	143	154	165	176	187	198	209	220	231	242	253	264	275
12	24	36	48	60	72	84	96	108	120	132	144	156	168	180	192	204	216	228	240	252	264	276	288	300
13	26	39	52	65	78	91	104	117	130	143	156	169	182	195	208	221	234	247	260	273	286	299	312	325
14	28	42	56	70	84	98	112	126	140	154	168	182	196	210	224	238	252	266	280	294	308	322	336	350
15	30	45	60	75	90	105	120	135	150	165	180	195	210	225	240	255	270	285	300	315	330	345	360	375
16	32	48	64	80	96	112	128	144	160	176	192	208	224	240	256	272	288	304	320	336	352	368	384	400
17	34	51	68	85	102	119	136	153	170	187	204	221	238	255	272	289	306	323	340	357	374	391	408	425
18	36	54	72	90	108	126	144	162	180	198	216	234	252	270	288	306	324	342	360	378	396	414	432	450
19	38	57	76	95	114	133	152	171	190	209	228	247	266	285	304	323	342	361	380	399	418	437	456	475
20	40	60	80	100	120	140	160	180	200	220	240	260	280	300	320	340	360	380	400	420	440	460	480	500
21	42	63	84	105	126	147	168	189	210	231	252	273	294	315	336	357	378	399	420	441	462	483	504	525
22	44	66	88	110	132	154	176	198	220	242	264	286	308	330	352	374	396	418	440	462	484	506	528	550
23	46	69	92	115	138	161	184	207	230	253	276	299	322	345	368	391	414	437	460	483	506	529	552	575
24	48	72	96	120	144	168	192	216	240	264	288	312	336	360	384	408	432	456	480	501	528	552	576	600
25	50	75	100	125	150	175	200	225	250	275	300	325	350	375	400	425	450	475	500	525	550	575	600	625

SQUARES, CUBES AND ROOTS

Number	Square	Cube	Square root	Cube root
1	1	1	1.000	1.000
2	4	8	1.414	1.260
3	9	27	1.732	1.442
4	16	64	2.000	1.587
5	25	125	2.236	1.710
6	36	216	2.449	1.817
7	49	343	2.646	1.913
8	64	512	2.828	2.000
9	81	729	3.000	2.080
10	100	1000	3.162	2.154
11	121	1331	3.317	2.224
12	144	1728	3.464	2.289
13	169	2197	3.606	2.351
14	196	2744	3.742	2.410
15	225	3375	3.873	2.466
16	256	4096	4.000	2.520
17	289	4913	4.123	2.571
18	324	5832	4.243	2.621
19	361	6859	4.359	2.668
20	400	8000	4.472	2.714
25	625	15625	5.000	2.924
30	900	27000	5.477	3.107
40	1600	64000	6.325	3.420
50	2500	125000	7.071	3.684

POLYGONS

A polygon is a many-sided plane figure.

Sides	Polygon	Sides	Polygon
n	*n*-gon	12	dodecagon
3	trigon, triangle	13	tridecagon, triskaidecagon
4	tetragon, quadrilateral	14	tetradecagon, tetrakaidecagon
5	pentagon	15	pentadecagon, pentakaidecagon
6	hexagon	16	hexadecagon, hexakaidecagon
7	heptagon	17	heptadecagon, heptakaidecagon
8	octagon	18	octadecagon, octakaidecagon
9	enneagon, nonagon	19	enneadecagon, enneakaidecagon
10	decagon	1 000	chiliagon
11	hendecagon, undecagon		

Other names have been proposed for larger polygons using a system of prefixes but the form n-gon, eg 76-gon for a figure with 76 sides, is more common. The name myriagon has been proposed for a polygon with 10,000 sides.

LARGE NUMBERS

The names of large numbers formerly differed between the UK and the USA. In the UK, a billion was one million millions, rather than one thousand millions, as below. International economics has led to the US system becoming increasingly used worldwide. The US system is given below; to find the former British equivalents, increase the power by 6 each time (hence one billion becomes 10^{12}, one trillion becomes 10^{18} and one centillion 10^{600}).

thousand	10^{3}	1 000
million	10^{6}	1 000 000
billion	10^{9}	1 000 000 000
trillion	10^{12}	1 000 000 000 000
quadrillion	10^{15}	1 000 000 000 000 000
quintillion	10^{18}	1 000 000 000 000 000 000
sextillion	10^{21}	1 000 000 000 000 000 000 000
septillion	10^{24}	1 000 000 000 000 000 000 000 000
octillion	10^{27}	1 000 000 000 000 000 000 000 000 000
nonillion	10^{30}	1 000 000 000 000 000 000 000 000 000 000
decillion	10^{33}	1 000 000 000 000 000 000 000 000 000 000 000
googol	10^{100}	1 followed by 100 zeros
centillion	10^{303}	1 followed by 303 zeros
googolplex	10 to the power of a googol	1 followed by a googol of zeros

Googol, Google

The popular internet search engine Google® is named after the *googol*, one followed by 100 zeros. The company's world headquarters in Mountain View, California, USA, is affectionately known as 'the Googleplex'.

ECONOMICS

NOBEL PRIZE FOR ECONOMICS

Nobel Prizes were established by a bequest in the will of Alfred Nobel (1833–96) to honour 'those who, during the preceding year, shall have conferred the greatest benefit on mankind'. However, the prize for economics was not among the original awards set up in this way. Instead, it was instituted by the Bank of Sweden and is officially called the 'Bank of Sweden Prize in Economic Sciences in Memory of Alfred Nobel'; first awarded in 1969.

1969	Ragnar Frisch, Jan Tinbergen
1970	Paul A Samuelson
1971	Simon Kuznets
1972	John R Hicks, Kenneth J Arrow
1973	Wassily Leontief
1974	Gunnar Myrdal, Friedrich August von Hayek
1975	Leonid Vitaliyevich Kantorovich, Tjalling C Koopmans
1976	Milton Friedman
1977	Bertil Ohlin, James E Meade
1978	Herbert A Simon
1979	Theodore W Schultz, Sir Arthur Lewis
1980	Lawrence R Klein
1981	James Tobin
1982	George J Stigler
1983	Gerard Debreu
1984	Richard Stone
1985	Franco Modigliani
1986	James M Buchanan Jr
1987	Robert M Solow
1988	Maurice Allais
1989	Trygve Haavelmo
1990	Harry M Markowitz, Merton H Miller, William F Sharpe
1991	Ronald H Coase
1992	Gary S Becker
1993	Robert W Fogel, Douglass C North
1994	John C Harsanyi, John F Nash Jr, Reinhard Selten
1995	Robert E Lucas Jr
1996	James A Mirrlees, William Vickrey
1997	Robert C Merton, Myron S Scholes
1998	Amartya Sen
1999	Robert A Mundell
2000	James J Heckman, Daniel L McFadden
2001	George A Akerlof, A Michael Spence, Joseph E Stiglitz
2002	Daniel Kahneman, Vernon L Smith
2003	Robert F Engle, Clive W J Granger
2004	Finn E Kydland, Edward C Prescott
2005	Robert J Aumann, Thomas C Schelling
2006	Edmund S Phelps
2007	Leonid Hurwicz, Eric S Maskin, Roger B Myerson

STOCK EXCHANGE INDICES

Some of the world's major stock exchange indices are listed.

Index	Country
FTSE 100	United Kingdom
Dow Jones Industrial Average	United States of America
Nasdaq	United States of America
Nikkei 225	Japan
Hang Seng	Hong Kong
Dax	Germany
CAC 40	France

BANKNOTE DESIGNS

Bank of England

Banknotes featuring people were first issued by the Bank in 1970.

£50	Sir John Houblon (1632–1711, first Governor of the Bank of England)
£20	Sir Edward Elgar (1857–1934); Adam Smith (1723–90) (issued from 13 March 2007)
£10	Charles Darwin (1809–82)
£5	Elizabeth Fry (1780–1845)

Financial Faces

Famous people to have featured on now-withdrawn banknotes include Sir Christopher Wren (£50), William Shakespeare (£20), Michael Faraday (£20), Charles Dickens (£10), Florence Nightingale (£10), George Stephenson (£5), the Duke of Wellington (£5) and Sir Isaac Newton (£1).

Bank of Scotland

All banknotes feature Sir Walter Scott (1771–1832) on the front. On the back of banknotes issued before autumn 2007 are illustrations of various aspects of Scottish industry, commerce and culture. A new set of banknotes was issued from autumn 2007 featuring illustrations of Scottish bridges, representing the pioneering enterprise and heritage of Scotland.

	Issued before autumn 2007	**Issued from autumn 2007**
£100	Leisure and tourism	Kessock Bridge
£50	Arts and culture	The Falkirk Wheel
£20	Education and research	Forth Bridge
£10	Distilling and brewing	Glenfinnan Viaduct
£5	Oil and energy	Brig o'Doon

Royal Bank of Scotland

All banknotes feature Lord Ilay (1682–1761), first Governor of the Bank. On the back are illustrations of some of Scotland's famous castles.

£100	Balmoral Castle
£50	Inverness Castle
£20	Brodick Castle
£10	Glamis Castle
£5	Culzean Castle
£1	Edinburgh Castle

Clydesdale Bank

Banknotes feature a notable figure on the front. On the back are relevant scenes from the person's life.

£100	Lord Kelvin (1824–1907)
£50	Adam Smith (1723–90)
£20	King Robert the Bruce (1274–1329)
£10	Mary Slessor (1848–1915)
£5	Robert Burns (1759–96)

Million Pound Notes

The Bank of England is obliged to back notes issued by the Scottish and Northern Irish banks on a 'pound for pound' basis. The Bank calculates that over a billion pounds is needed to do so – far too much money to be stored in normal Bank of England notes. To get round the problem, they issue special £1,000,000 notes for the purpose. But it is unlikely that most people will ever see one: the Bank sternly declares that the notes 'are for internal use only and are never seen outside the Bank'.

First Trust Bank

All banknotes feature generic people of Northern Ireland on the front. On the back are coastal scenes or designs featuring the Spanish Armada.

£100	The Armada
£50	A commemorative medal
£20	The chimney at Lagada Point
£10	The ship *Girona*
£5	Dunluce Castle

Northern Bank

All banknotes except the £5 feature a notable figure on the front and a representation of Belfast City Hall on the back. New £100, £50, £20 and £10 banknotes were issued from March 2005 in response to a £26.5m robbery at the Northern Bank's cash centre in December 2004; the new banknotes feature the same illustrations as the old, but the colours, bank logo and serial number prefix were changed.

£100	Sir James Martin (1893–1981)
£50	Sir Samuel Davidson (1846–1921)
£20	Harry Ferguson (1884–1960)
£10	John Boyd Dunlop (1840–1921)
£5	US space shuttle

Ulster Bank

Banknotes are in £50, £20, £10 and £5 denominations. All notes feature a view of Belfast City Harbour, flanked by landscape views. On the back of each is the Bank's coat of arms.

Bank of Ireland

Banknotes are in £100, £50, £20, £10 and £5 denominations. All notes feature a seated woman representing Hibernia on the front. On the back of each is a view of Queen's University Belfast.

Surfing and Spending

Consumers in the UK are increasingly spending their hard-earned cash online. According to the Office for National Statistics, the value of Internet sales to UK households quadrupled between 2002 and 2005, reaching £21.4 billion. The e-retail organization IMRG estimates that this figure will approach £60 billion by 2010, and that online shopping will account for almost 20% of all retail.

POUND COIN INSCRIPTIONS

Scotland
nemo me impune lacessit
no one provokes me with impunity
(from the Motto of the Order of the Thistle)

Wales
pleidiol wyf i'm gwlad
true am I to my Country
(from the Welsh National Anthem)

England, Northern Ireland, United Kingdom
decus et tutamen
an ornament and a safeguard
(from Virgil's *Aeneid*)

BRITISH PRE-DECIMAL CURRENCY

Coins	Nickname	Value
Farthing	Jenny	¼ penny
Half penny	Ha'penny	½ penny
Penny	Copper	1/240 pound, 1/12 shilling
Three pence	Thruppence, throppence, threppence, thruppenny bit, joey	3 pence, ¼ shilling, 1/80 pound
Six pence	Tanner	6 pence, ½ shilling, 1/40 pound
Shilling	Bob	12 pence, 1/20 pound
Florin	Two bob	24 pence, 2 shillings, 1/10 pound
Half crown	Half a crown, two and six	30 pence, 2 shillings and 6 pence, ⅛ pound
Crown	Five bob	60 pence, 5 shillings, ¼ pound

Notes	Nickname	Value
Ten shilling note	Half a quid	120 pence, 10 shillings, ½ pound
Pound note	Quid	240 pence, 20 shillings

CURRENCY ABBREVIATIONS

International currency codes are regulated by the International Organization for Standardization's ISO 4217 standard. Countries which use the currency of another (for example Liechtenstein uses the Swiss Franc) do not have a separate currency code. For currency by country see **Human Geography**.

Abbrev	Country	Currency
AED	United Arab Emirates	UAE Dirham
AFN	Afghanistan	Afghani
ALL	Albania	Lek
AMD	Armenia	Armenian Dram
AOA	Angola	Kwanza
ARS	Argentina	Argentine Peso
AUD	Australia	Australian Dollar
AZM	Azerbaijan	Azerbaijani Manat

CURRENCY ABBREVIATIONS

Abbrev	Country	Currency
BAM	Bosnia and Herzegovina	Convertible Mark
BBD	Barbados	Barbados Dollar
BDT	Bangladesh	Taka
BGN	Bulgaria	Bulgarian Lev
BHD	Bahrain	Bahraini Dinar
BIF	Burundi	Burundi Franc
BND	Brunei Darussalam	Brunei Dollar
BOB	Bolivia	Boliviano
BRL	Brazil	Brazilian Real
BSD	The Bahamas	Bahamian Dollar
BTN	Bhutan	Ngultrum
BWP	Botswana	Pula
BYR	Belarus	Belarussian Rouble
BZD	Belize	Belize Dollar
CAD	Canada	Canadian Dollar
CDF	Congo, Democratic Republic of the	Congolese Franc
CHF	Switzerland	Swiss Franc
CLP	Chile	Chilean Peso
CNY	China	Yuan[1]
COP	Colombia	Colombian Peso
CRC	Costa Rica	Costa Rican Colón
CUP	Cuba	Cuban Peso
CVE	Cape Verde	Cape Verde Escudo
CZK	Czech Republic	Koruna
DJF	Djibouti	Djibouti Franc
DKK	Denmark	Danish Krone
DOP	Dominican Republic	Dominican Peso
DZD	Algeria	Algerian Dinar
EEK	Estonia	Kroon
EGP	Egypt	Egyptian Pound
ERN	Eritrea	Nakfa
ETB	Ethiopia	Ethiopian Birr
EUR	Euro member countries	Euro
FJD	Fiji	Fiji Dollar
GBP	United Kingdom	Pound Sterling
GEL	Georgia	Lari
GHS	Ghana	Cedi
GMD	The Gambia	Dalasi
GNF	Guinea	Guinea Franc
GTQ	Guatemala	Quetzal
GYD	Guyana	Guyana Dollar
HNL	Honduras	Lempira
HRK	Croatia	Kuna
HTG	Haiti	Gourde
HUF	Hungary	Forint
IDR	Indonesia	Rupiah
ILS	Israel	New Israeli Shekel
INR	India	Indian Rupee
IQD	Iraq	Iraqi Dinar
IRR	Iran	Iranian Rial

Abbrev	Country	Currency
ISK	Iceland	Iceland Króna
JMD	Jamaica	Jamaican Dollar
JOD	Jordan	Jordanian Dinar
JPY	Japan	Yen
KES	Kenya	Kenyan Shilling
KGS	Kyrgyzstan	Som
KHR	Cambodia	Riel
KMF	Comoros	Comoran Franc
KPW	Korea (North)	North Korean Won
KRW	Korea (South)	Won
KWD	Kuwait	Kuwaiti Dinar
KZT	Kazakhstan	Tenge
LAK	Laos	Kip
LBP	Lebanon	Lebanese Pound
LKR	Sri Lanka	Sir Lanka Rupee
LRD	Liberia	Liberian Dollar
LSL	Lesotho	Loti
LTL	Lithuania	Litas
LVL	Latvia	Lat
LYD	Libya	Libyan Dinar
MAD	Morocco	Moroccan Dirham
MDL	Moldova	Moldovan Leu
MGA	Madagascar	Ariary
MKD	Macedonia	Denar
MMK	Myanmar (Burma)	Kyat
MNT	Mongolia	Tugrik
MRO	Mauritania	Ouguiya
MUR	Mauritius	Mauritius Rupee
MVR	Maldives	Rufiyaa
MWK	Malawi	Kwacha
MXN	Mexico	Mexican Peso
MYR	Malaysia	Malaysian Ringgit
MZM	Mozambique	Metical
NAD	Namibia	Namibian Dollar
NGN	Nigeria	Naira
NIO	Nicaragua	Córdoba
NOK	Norway	Norwegian Krone
NPR	Nepal	Nepalese Rupee
NZD	New Zealand	New Zealand Dollar
OMR	Oman	Omani Rial
PAB	Panama	Balboa
PEN	Peru	Nuevo Sol
PGK	Papua New Guinea	Kina
PHP	Philippines	Philippine Peso
PKR	Pakistan	Pakistan Rupee
PLN	Poland	Zloty
PYG	Paraguay	Guaraní
QAR	Qatar	Qatari Riyal
RMB	China	Renminbi[1]
RON	Romania	Leu

CURRENCY ABBREVIATIONS

Abbrev	Country	Currency
RSD	Serbia	Serbian Dinar
RUB	Russia	Russian Rouble
RWF	Rwanda	Rwanda Franc
SAR	Saudi Arabia	Saudi Riyal
SBD	Solomon Islands	Solomon Islands Dollar
SCR	Seychelles	Seychelles Rupee
SDG	Sudan	Sudanese Dinar
SEK	Sweden	Swedish Krona
SGD	Singapore	Singapore Dollar
SIT	Slovenia	Tolar
SKK	Slovakia	Slovak Koruna
SLL	Sierra Leone	Leone
SOS	Somalia	Somali Shilling
SRD	Suriname	Surinam Dollar
STD	São Tomé and Príncipe	Dobra
SVC	El Salvador	El Salvador Colón
SYP	Syria	Syrian Pound
SZL	Swaziland	Lilangeni
THB	Thailand	Baht
TJS	Tajikistan	Somoni
TMM	Turkmenistan	Manat
TND	Tunisia	Tunisian Dinar
TOP	Tonga	Pa'anga
TRY	Turkey	New Turkish Lira
TTD	Trinidad and Tobago	Trinidad and Tobago Dollar
TWD	Taiwan	New Taiwan Dollar
TZS	Tanzania	Tanzanian Shilling
UAH	Ukraine	Hryvnia
UGX	Uganda	Uganda Shilling
USD	United States of America	United States Dollar
UYU	Uruguay	Uruguayan Peso
UZS	Uzbekistan	Uzbekistan Sum
VEF	Venezuela	Bolívar
VND	Vietnam	Dông
VUV	Vanuatu	Vatu
WST	Samoa	Tala
XAF	African Financial Community, *Communautè Financière Africaine* (CFA); Bank of Central African States, *Banque des États de l'Afrique Centrale* (BEAC)	CFA Franc
XCD	East Caribbean states	East Caribbean Dollar
XOF	African Financial Community, *Communauté Financière Africaine* (CFA); Central Bank of West African States, *Banque Centrale des États de l'Afrique de l'Ouest* (BCEAO)	CFA Franc
XPF	Pacific Financial Community, *Comptoirs Français du Pacifique* (CFP)	CFP Franc
YER	Yemen	Yemeni Rial
ZAR	South Africa	Rand
ZMK	Zambia	Kwacha
ZWD	Zimbabwe	Zimbabwe Dollar

[1] *The Yuan is also known as the Renminbi; although the ISO code CNY covers both terms, RMB is also used.*

MEASUREMENT, CONVERSION AND SIZE

Figures in tables are rounded to two decimal places.

LENGTH

All miles are statute miles. See **Nautical Measurements** for nautical miles.

Metric units

1 millimetre (mm)
10 millimetres (mm) = 1 centimetre (cm)
10 centimetres (cm) = 1 decimetre (dm)
100 centimetres (cm) = 1 metre (m)
1 000 metres (m) = 1 kilometre (km)

Imperial units

1 inch (in)
12 inches (in) = 1 foot (ft)
3 feet (ft) = 1 yard (yd)
1 760 yards (yd) = 1 mile (mi)

Exact conversions

1mm = 0.03937in
1cm = 0.3937in
1cm = 0.0328ft
1cm = 0.0109yd
1dm = 3.937in
1m = 39.37in
1m = 3.2808ft
1m = 1.0936yd
1m = 0.00062mi
1km = 3 280.8ft
1km = 1 093.6yd
1km = 0.6214mi

1in = 25.4mm
1in = 2.54cm
1in = 0.254dm
1in = 0.0254m
1ft = 30.48cm
1ft = 0.3048m
1ft = 0.0003km
1yd = 91.44cm
1yd = 0.9144m
1yd = 0.0009km
1mi = 1 609.3m
1mi = 1.6093km

Inches to centimetres		Centimetres to inches		Inches to millimetres		Millimetres to inches	
in	*cm*	*cm*	*in*	*in*	*mm*	*mm*	*in*
⅛	0.32	1	0.39	⅛	3.18	1	0.04
¼	0.64	2	0.79	¼	6.35	2	0.08
⅜	0.95	3	1.18	⅜	9.53	3	0.12
½	1.27	4	1.57	½	12.70	4	0.16
⅝	1.59	5	1.97	⅝	15.88	5	0.20
¾	1.91	6	2.36	¾	19.05	6	0.24
⅞	2.22	7	2.76	⅞	22.23	7	0.28
1	2.54	8	3.15	1	25.40	8	0.31
2	5.08	9	3.54	2	50.80	9	0.35
3	7.62	10	3.94	3	76.20	10	0.39
4	10.16	20	7.87	4	101.60	20	0.79
5	12.70	30	11.81	5	127.00	30	1.18
6	15.24	40	15.75	6	152.40	40	1.58
7	17.78	50	19.69	7	177.80	50	1.97
8	20.32	60	23.62	8	203.20	60	2.36
9	22.86	70	27.56	9	228.60	70	2.76
10	25.40	80	31.50	10	254.00	80	3.15
11	27.94	90	35.43	11	279.40	90	3.54
12	30.48	100	39.37	12	304.80	100	3.94

Feet to metres

ft	*m*
1	0.30
2	0.61
3	0.91
4	1.22
5	1.52
6	1.83
7	2.13
8	2.44
9	2.74
10	3.05
20	6.10
30	9.14
40	12.19
50	15.24
75	22.86
100	30.48
200	60.96
300	91.44
400	121.92
500	152.40
1000	304.80
2000	609.60
3000	914.40
4000	1219.20
5000	1524.00

Metres to feet

m	*ft*
1	3.28
2	6.56
3	9.84
4	13.12
5	16.40
6	19.68
7	22.97
8	26.25
9	29.53
10	32.81
20	65.62
30	98.42
40	131.23
50	164.04
75	246.06
100	328.08
200	656.16
300	984.24
400	1312.32
500	1640.40
1000	3280.80
2000	6561.60
3000	9842.40
4000	13123.20
5000	16404.00

Yards to metres

yd	*m*
1	0.91
2	1.83
3	2.74
4	3.66
5	4.57
6	5.49
7	6.40
8	7.32
9	8.23
10	9.14
20	18.29
30	27.43
40	36.58
50	45.72
75	68.58
100	91.44
200	182.88
300	274.32
400	365.76
500	457.20
1000	914.40
2000	1828.80
3000	2743.20
4000	3657.60
5000	4572.00

Metres to yards

m	*yd*
1	1.09
2	2.19
3	3.28
4	4.37
5	5.47
6	6.56
7	7.66
8	8.75
9	9.84
10	10.94
20	21.87
30	32.81
40	43.74
50	54.68
75	82.02
100	109.36
200	218.72
300	328.08
400	437.44
500	546.80
1000	1093.60
2000	2187.20
3000	3280.80
4000	4374.40
5000	5468.00

Miles to kilometres

mi	*km*
1	1.61
2	3.22
3	4.83
4	6.44
5	8.05
6	9.66
7	11.27
8	12.87
9	14.48
10	16.09
20	32.19
30	48.28
40	64.37

Miles to kilometres

mi	*km*
50	80.47
75	120.70
100	160.93
200	321.86
300	482.79
400	643.72
500	804.65
1000	1609.30
2000	3218.60
3000	4827.90
4000	6437.20
5000	8046.50

Kilometres to miles

km	*mi*
1	0.62
2	1.24
3	1.86
4	2.49
5	3.11
6	3.73
7	4.35
8	4.97
9	5.59
10	6.21
20	12.43
30	18.64
40	24.86

Kilometres to miles

km	*mi*
50	31.07
75	46.61
100	62.14
200	124.28
300	186.42
400	248.56
500	310.70
1000	621.40
2000	1242.80
3000	1864.20
4000	2485.60
5000	3107.00

AREA

Metric units

1 square millimetre (sq mm)
100 square millimetres (sq mm) = 1 square centimetre (sq cm)
100 square centimetres (sq cm) = 1 square decimetre (sq dm)
100 square decimetres (sq dm) = 1 square metre (sq m)

10 000 square centimetres (sq cm) = 1 square metre (sq m)
10 000 square metres (sq m) = 1 hectare (ha)
100 hectares (ha) = 1 square kilometre (sq km)
1 000 000 square metres (sq m) = 1 square kilometre (sq km)

Imperial units

1 square inch (sq in)
144 square inches (sq in) = 1 square foot (sq ft)
9 square feet (sq ft) = 1 square yard (sq yd)
4 840 square yards (sq yd) = 1 acre (a)
640 acres (a) = 1 square mile (sq mi)

Exact conversions

1 sq mm = 0.0016 sq in
1 sq cm = 0.155 sq in
1 sq cm = 0.0011 sq ft
1 sq dm = 15.5 sq in
1 sq m = 1 550 sq in
1 sq m = 10.7639 sq ft
1 sq m = 1.196 sq yd
1 sq m = 0.0002a
1 ha = 2.471a
1 ha = 11 959.9 sq yd
1 ha = 0.0039 sq mi
1 sq km = 0.3861 sq mi
1 sq km = 247.1a
1 sq in = 645.16 sq mm
1 sq in = 6.4516 sq cm
1 sq in = 0.0645 sq dm
1 sq in = 0.0006 sq m
1 sq ft = 929.03 sq cm
1 sq ft = 0.0929 sq m
1 sq yd = 0.8361 sq m
1 sq yd = 0.00008ha
1 a = 4 046.85 sq m
1 a = 0.4047ha
1 a = 0.0016 sq km
1 sq mi = 258.9988 ha
1 sq mi = 2.5899 sq km

Square inches to square centimetres

sq in	*sq cm*
1	6.45
2	12.90
3	19.35
4	25.81
5	32.26
6	38.71
7	45.16
8	51.61
9	58.06
10	64.52
11	70.97
12	77.42
13	83.87
14	90.32
15	96.77
16	103.23
17	109.68
18	116.13
19	122.58
20	129.03
25	161.29
50	322.58
75	483.87
100	645.16

Square centimetres to square inches

sq cm	*sq in*
1	0.16
2	0.31
3	0.47
4	0.62
5	0.78
6	0.93
7	1.09
8	1.24
9	1.40
10	1.55
11	1.71
12	1.86
13	2.02
14	2.17
15	2.33
16	2.48
17	2.64
18	2.79
19	2.95
20	3.10
25	3.88
50	7.75
75	11.63
100	15.50

Square feet to square metres

sq ft	*sq m*
1	0.09
2	0.19
3	0.28
4	0.37
5	0.46
6	0.56
7	0.65
8	0.74
9	0.84
10	0.93
11	1.02
12	1.11
13	1.21
14	1.30
15	1.39
16	1.49
17	1.58
18	1.67
19	1.77
20	1.86
50	4.65
100	9.29
250	23.23
500	46.45
1 000	92.90

Square metres to square feet

sq m	*sq ft*
1	10.76
2	21.53
3	32.29
4	43.06
5	53.82
6	64.58
7	75.35
8	86.11
9	96.88
10	107.64
11	118.40
12	129.17
13	139.93
14	150.69
15	161.46
16	172.22
17	182.99
18	193.75
19	204.51
20	215.28
50	538.20
100	1 076.39
250	2 690.98
500	5 381.95
1 000	10 763.90

Acres to hectares	
a	*ha*
1	0.40
2	0.81
3	1.21
4	1.62
5	2.02
6	2.43
7	2.83
8	3.24
9	3.64
10	4.05
11	4.45
12	4.86
13	5.26
14	5.67
15	6.07
16	6.48
17	6.88
18	7.28
19	7.69
20	8.09
25	10.12
50	20.23
75	30.35
100	40.47
250	101.17
500	202.35
750	303.52
1 000	404.69

Hectares to acres	
ha	*a*
1	2.47
2	4.94
3	7.41
4	9.88
5	12.36
6	14.83
7	17.30
8	19.77
9	22.24
10	24.71
11	27.18
12	29.65
13	32.12
14	34.59
15	37.07
16	39.54
17	42.01
18	44.48
19	46.95
20	49.42
25	61.78
50	123.55
75	185.33
100	247.10
250	617.75
500	1 235.50
750	1 853.25
1 000	2 471.00

Square miles to square kilometres	
sq mi	*sq km*
1	2.59
2	5.18
3	7.77
4	10.36
5	12.95
6	15.54
7	18.13
8	20.72
9	23.31
10	25.90
20	51.80
30	77.70
40	103.60
50	129.50
100	258.99
200	517.98
300	776.97
400	1 035.96
500	1 294.95
1 000	2 589.90
1 500	3 884.85
2 000	5 179.80

Square kilometres to square miles	
sq km	*sq mi*
1	0.39
2	0.77
3	1.16
4	1.54
5	1.93
6	2.32
7	2.70
8	3.09
9	3.47
10	3.86
20	7.72
30	11.58
40	15.44
50	19.31
100	38.61
200	77.22
300	115.83
400	154.44
500	193.05
1 000	386.10
1 500	579.15
2 000	772.20

VOLUME

Metric units

1 cubic centimetre (cu cm[1])
1 000 cubic centimetres (cu cm) = 1 cubic decimetre (cu dm)
1 000 cubic decimetres (cu dm) = 1 cubic metre (cu m)

[1] *Cubic centimetres sometimes abbreviated as cc.*

Imperial units

1 cubic inch (cu in)
1 728 cubic inches (cu in) = 1 cubic foot (cu ft)
27 cubic feet (cu ft) = 1 cubic yard (cu yd)

Exact conversions

1 cu cm = 0.0610 cu in
1 cu dm = 61.024 cu in
1 cu m = 61 023.74 cu in
1 cu m = 35.3147 cu ft
1 cu m = 1.308 cu yd

1 cu in = 16.3871 cu cm
1 cu in = 0.0164 cu dm
1 cu in = 0.000016 cu m
1 cu ft = 0.0283 cu m
1 cu yd = 0.7646 cu m

Cubic inches to cubic centimetres

cu in	cu cm
1	16.39
2	32.77
3	49.16
4	65.55
5	81.93
6	98.32
7	114.71
8	131.10
9	147.48
10	163.87
15	245.81
20	327.74
50	819.36
100	1638.71

Cubic centimetres to cubic inches

cu cm	cu in
1	0.06
2	0.12
3	0.18
4	0.24
5	0.31
6	0.37
7	0.43
8	0.49
9	0.55
10	0.61
15	0.92
20	1.22
50	3.05
100	6.10

Cubic feet to cubic metres

cu ft	cu m
1	0.03
2	0.06
3	0.08
4	0.11
5	0.14
6	0.17
7	0.20
8	0.23
9	0.25
10	0.28
15	0.42
20	0.57
50	1.41
100	2.83

Cubic metres to cubic feet

cu m	cu ft
1	35.31
2	70.63
3	105.94
4	141.26
5	176.57
6	211.89
7	247.20
8	282.52
9	317.83
10	353.15
15	529.72
20	706.29
50	1765.74
100	3531.47

Cubic yards to cubic metres

cu yd	cu m
1	0.76
2	1.53
3	2.29
4	3.06
5	3.82
6	4.59
7	5.35

Cubic yards to cubic metres

cu yd	cu m
8	6.12
9	6.88
10	7.65
15	11.47
20	15.29
50	38.23
100	76.46

Cubic metres to cubic yards

cu m	cu yd
1	1.31
2	2.62
3	3.92
4	5.23
5	6.54
6	7.85
7	9.16

Cubic metres to cubic yards

cu m	cu yd
8	10.46
9	11.77
10	13.08
15	19.62
20	26.16
50	65.40
100	130.80

CAPACITY

Liquid capacity measures

Metric units

1 millilitre (ml)
10 millilitres (ml) = 1 centilitre (cl)
100 centilitres (cl) = 1 litre (l)
100 litres (l) = 1 hectolitre (hl)

Imperial units

1 fluid ounce (fl oz)
20 fluid ounces (fl oz) = 1 pint (pt)
2 pints (pt) = 1 quart (qt)
8 pints (pt) = 1 gallon (gal)
4 quarts (qt) = 1 gallon (gal)

Exact conversions

1 ml = 0.035fl oz
1 cl = 0.352fl oz
1 l = 35.196fl oz
1 l = 1.7598pt
1 l = 0.220gal
1 hl = 22gal

1 fl oz = 28.41ml
1 fl oz = 2.84cl
1 fl oz = 0.0284l
1 pt = 0.5682l
1 qt = 1.14l
1 gal = 4.546l

CAPACITY

US measures

8 fl oz = 1 cup

1 pt (UK) = 1.20pt (US)
1 pt (US) = 0.83pt (UK)

1 fl oz = 0.0296 l
1 pt = 0.4732 l
1 gal = 3.7854 l

1 l = 33.8140fl oz
1 l = 2.1134pt
1 l = 0.2642gal

1 gal (UK) = 1.200929gal (US)
1 gal (US) = 0.832688gal (UK)

UK fluid ounces to litres

UK fl oz	*l*
1	0.03
2	0.06
3	0.09
4	0.11
5	0.14
6	0.17
7	0.20
8	0.23
9	0.26
10	0.28
11	0.31
12	0.34
13	0.37
14	0.40
15	0.43
20	0.57
50	1.42
100	2.84

US fluid ounces to litres

US fl oz	*l*
1	0.03
2	0.06
3	0.09
4	0.12
5	0.15
6	0.18
7	0.21
8	0.24
9	0.27
10	0.30
11	0.33
12	0.36
13	0.39
14	0.41
15	0.44
20	0.59
50	1.48
100	2.96

Litres to fluid ounces

l	*UK fl oz*	*US fl oz*
1	35.20	33.81
2	70.39	67.63
3	105.59	101.44
4	140.78	135.26
5	175.98	169.07
6	211.18	202.88
7	246.37	236.70
8	281.57	270.51
9	316.76	304.33
10	351.96	338.14
11	387.16	371.95
12	422.35	405.77
13	457.55	439.58
14	492.75	473.40
15	527.94	507.21
20	703.92	676.28
50	1759.81	1690.70
100	3519.61	3381.40

UK pints to litres

UK pt	*l*
1	0.57
2	1.14
3	1.70
4	2.27
5	2.84
6	3.41
7	3.98
8	4.55
9	5.11
10	5.68
15	8.52
20	11.36
50	28.41
100	56.82

US pints to litres

US pt	*l*
1	0.47
2	0.95
3	1.42
4	1.89
5	2.37
6	2.84
7	3.31
8	3.78
9	4.26
10	4.73
15	7.10
20	9.46
50	23.66
100	47.32

Litres to pints

l	*UK pt*	*US pt*
1	1.76	2.11
2	3.52	4.23
3	5.28	6.34
4	7.04	8.45
5	8.80	10.57
6	10.56	12.68
7	12.32	14.79
8	14.08	16.91
9	15.84	19.02
10	17.60	21.13
15	26.40	31.70
20	35.20	42.27
50	87.99	105.67
100	175.98	211.34

UK gallons to litres

UK gal	l
1	4.55
2	9.09
3	13.64
4	18.18
5	22.73
6	27.28
7	31.82
8	36.37
9	40.91
10	45.46
11	50.01
12	54.55
13	59.10
14	63.64
15	68.19
16	72.74
17	77.28
18	81.83
19	86.37
20	90.92
50	227.30
100	454.61

US gallons to litres

US gal	l
1	3.78
2	7.57
3	11.36
4	15.14
5	18.93
6	22.71
7	26.50
8	30.28
9	34.07
10	37.85
11	41.64
12	45.42
13	49.21
14	52.99
15	56.78
16	60.57
17	64.35
18	68.14
19	71.92
20	75.71
50	189.27
100	378.54

Litres to gallons

l	UK gal	US gal
1	0.22	0.26
2	0.44	0.53
3	0.66	0.79
4	0.88	1.06
5	1.10	1.32
6	1.32	1.58
7	1.54	1.85
8	1.76	2.11
9	1.98	2.38
10	2.20	2.64
11	2.42	2.91
12	2.64	3.17
13	2.86	3.43
14	3.08	3.70
15	3.30	3.96
16	3.52	4.23
17	3.74	4.49
18	3.96	4.76
19	4.18	5.02
20	4.40	5.28
50	11.00	13.20
100	22.00	26.42

UK gallons to US gallons

UK gal	US gal
1	1.20
2	2.40
3	3.60
4	4.80
5	6
6	7.21
7	8.41
8	9.61
9	10.81
10	12.01
11	13.21
12	14.41
13	15.61
14	16.81
15	18.01
20	24.02
25	30.02
50	60.05

US gallons to UK gallons

US gal	UK gal
1	0.83
2	1.67
3	2.50
4	3.33
5	4.16
6	5.00
7	5.83
8	6.66
9	7.49
10	8.33
11	9.16
12	9.99
13	10.82
14	11.66
15	12.49
20	16.65
25	20.82
50	41.63

Pottles and Kilderkins

The world of liquid capacity measures used not to be so regimented. Measures in use in past centuries included the *anker*, the *bath*, the *kilderkin*, the *pipe*, the *pottle*, the *puncheon* and the *rundlet*.

Dry capacity measures

Metric units

Cubic metres (cu m) see **Volume** above.
Litres (l) see **Liquid capacity measures** above.

Imperial units

1 gallon (gal)
2 gallons (gal) = 1 peck (pk)
4 pecks (pk) = 1 bushel (bu)
8 gallons (gal) = 1 bushel (bu)

Exact conversions

1 cu m = 219.97gal
1 cu m = 109.98pk
1 cu m = 27.4962bu
1 l = 0.2200gal
1 l = 0.1100pk
1 l = 0.0275bu
1 gal = 0.0045 cu m
1 gal = 4.546 l
1 pk = 0.0091 cu m
1 pk = 9.0919 l
1 bu = 0.0369 cu m
1 bu = 36.3677 l

US measures

1 cu m = 227.02gal
1 cu m = 113.51pk
1 cu m = 28.3776bu
1 l = 0.227gal
1 l = 0.1135pk
1 l = 0.0284bu
1 gal = 0.0044 cu m
1 gal = 4.4049 l
1 pk = 0.0088 cu m
1 pk = 8.8095 l
1 bu = 0.0353 cu m
1 bu = 35.2381 l
1 qt = 1 101.22 cu cm
1 qt = 0.0011012 cu m
1 qt = 1.1012 l
1 pt = 550.61 cu cm
1 pt = 0.0006 cu m
1 pt = 0.5506 l
1 cu cm = 0.0009qt
1 cu m = 908.08qt
1 l = 0.908qt
1 cu cm = 0.0018pt
1 cu m = 1816.17pt
1 l = 1.816pt

UK bushels to cubic metres and litres

UK bu	*cu m*	*l*
1	0.04	36.37
2	0.07	72.74
3	0.11	109.10
4	0.15	145.47
5	0.18	181.84
10	0.37	363.68

US bushels to cubic metres and litres

US bu	*cu m*	*l*
1	0.04	35.24
2	0.07	70.48
3	0.11	105.71
4	0.14	140.95
5	0.18	176.19
10	0.35	352.38

Cubic metres to bushels

cu m	*UK bu*	*US bu*
1	27.50	28.38
2	54.99	56.76
3	82.49	85.13
4	109.98	113.51
5	137.48	141.89
10	274.96	283.78

Litres to bushels

l	*UK bu*	*US bu*
1	0.03	0.03
2	0.06	0.06
3	0.08	0.09
4	0.11	0.11
5	0.14	0.14
10	0.28	0.28

UK pecks to litres

UK pk	*l*
1	9.09
2	18.18
3	27.28
4	36.37
5	45.46
10	90.92

US pecks to litres

US pk	*l*
1	8.81
2	17.62
3	26.43
4	35.24
5	44.05
10	88.10

Litres to pecks

l	*UK pk*	*US pk*
1	0.11	0.11
2	0.22	0.23
3	0.33	0.34
4	0.44	0.45
5	0.55	0.57
10	1.10	1.14

US dry quarts to cubic centimetres and litres

US qt	cu cm	l
1	1101	1.1
2	2202	2.2
3	3304	3.3
4	4405	4.4
5	5506	5.5
10	11012	11.0

US dry pints to cubic centimetres and litres

US pt	cu cm	l
1	551	0.55
2	1101	1.10
3	1652	1.65
4	2202	2.20
5	2753	2.75
10	5506	5.51

WEIGHT

All ounces are avoirdupois.

Metric units

1 gram (g)
1000 grams (g) = 1 kilogram (kg)
1000 kilograms (kg) = 1 tonne[1]

[1] *The tonne is sometimes known as the metric ton.*

Imperial units

1 ounce (oz)
16 ounces (oz) = 1 pound (lb)
14 pounds (lb) = 1 stone (st)
8 stones (st) = 1 hundredweight[1] (cwt)
20 hundredweights (cwt) = 1 ton[2]
1 pound (lb) = 0.0714 stones (st)
1 hundredweight (cwt) = 112 pounds (lb)
1 ton = 2240 pounds (lb)
1 ton = 160 stone (st)

[1] *The UK hundredweight of 112lb is sometimes known as the long hundredweight.*
[2] *The UK ton of 2,240lb is sometimes known as the long ton.*

Exact conversions

1 g = 0.0353oz
1 kg = 35.274oz
1 kg = 2.2046lb
1 kg = 0.1575st
1 kg = 0.0197cwt
1 tonne = 157.5st
1 tonne = 19.684cwt
1 tonne = 0.9842 tons
1 oz = 28.3495g
1 lb = 0.4536kg
1 st = 6.350kg
1 cwt = 50.8023kg
1 cwt = 0.0508 tonnes
1 ton = 1016.06kg
1 ton = 1.0160 tonnes

US measures

100 pounds (lb) = 1 hundredweight[1] (cwt)
2000 pounds (lb) = 1 ton[2]
20 hundredweights (cwt) = 1 ton

1 kg = 0.0220cwt
1 tonne = 1.1023 tons

1 cwt = 45.3592kg
1 ton = 0.9072 tonnes

1 cwt (UK) = 1.1199cwt (US)
1 cwt (US) = 0.8929cwt (UK)
1 ton (UK) = 1.1199 tons (US)
1 ton (US) = 0.8929 ton (UK)

[1] *The US hundredweight of 100lb is sometimes known as the short hundredweight.*
[2] *The US ton of 2,000lb is sometimes known as the short ton.*

WEIGHT

Ounces to grams

oz	g
1	28.35
2	56.70
3	85.05
4	113.40
5	141.75
6	170.10
7	198.45
8	226.80
9	255.15
10	283.50
11	311.84
12	340.19
13	368.54
14	396.89
15	425.24
16	453.59

Grams to ounces

g	oz
1	0.04
2	0.07
3	0.11
4	0.14
5	0.18
6	0.21
7	0.25
8	0.28
9	0.32
10	0.35
20	0.71
30	1.06
40	1.41
50	1.76
60	2.12
70	2.47
80	2.82
90	3.18
100	3.53

Pounds to kilograms

lb	kg
1	0.45
2	0.91
3	1.36
4	1.81
5	2.27
6	2.72
7	3.18
8	3.63
9	4.08
10	4.54
11	4.99
12	5.44
13	5.90
14	6.35
15	6.80
16	7.26
17	7.71
18	8.16
19	8.62
20	9.07
50	22.68
100	45.36
200	90.72
500	226.80
1 000	453.59

Kilograms to pounds

kg	lb
1	2.21
2	4.41
3	6.62
4	8.82
5	11.03
6	13.23
7	15.44
8	17.64
9	19.85
10	22.05
11	24.26
12	26.46
13	28.67
14	30.87
15	33.08
16	35.28
17	37.49
18	39.69
19	41.90
20	44.10
50	110.25
100	220.50
200	441.00
500	1 102.50
1 000	2 205.00

Stones to kilograms

st	kg
1	6.35
2	12.70
3	19.05
4	25.40
5	31.75
6	38.10
7	44.45
8	50.80
9	57.15
10	63.50

Kilograms to stones

kg	st
1	0.16
2	0.32
3	0.47
4	0.63
5	0.79
6	0.95
7	1.10
8	1.26
9	1.42
10	1.58

Stones to pounds

st	lb
1	14
2	28
3	42
4	56
5	70
6	84
7	98
8	112
9	126
10	140
11	154
12	168
13	182
14	196
15	210
16	224
17	238
18	252
19	266
20	280

Pounds to stones

lb	st
1	0.07
2	0.14
3	0.21
4	0.29
5	0.36
6	0.43
7	0.50
8	0.57
9	0.64
10	0.71
11	0.79
12	0.86
13	0.93
14	1.00

UK hundredweights to kilograms

UK cwt	kg
1	50.80
2	101.60
3	152.41
4	203.21
5	254.01
10	508.02
20	1016.05
50	2540.12
75	3810.17
100	5080.23

US hundredweights to kilograms

US cwt	kg
1	45.36
2	90.72
3	136.08
4	181.44
5	226.80
10	453.59
20	907.18
50	2267.96
75	3401.94
100	4535.92

Kilograms to hundredweights

kg	UK cwt	US cwt
1	0.02	0.02
2	0.04	0.04
3	0.06	0.07
4	0.08	0.09
5	0.10	0.11
10	0.20	0.22
20	0.40	0.44
50	0.99	1.10
75	1.48	1.65
100	1.97	2.20

UK hundredweights to US hundredweights

UK cwt	US cwt
1	1.12
2	2.24
3	3.36
4	4.48
5	5.60
10	11.20
20	22.40
50	56.00
75	83.99
100	111.99

US hundredweights to UK hundredweights

US cwt	UK cwt
1	0.89
2	1.79
3	2.68
4	3.57
5	4.46
10	8.93
20	17.86
50	44.64
75	66.96
100	89.29

UK tons to tonnes

UK tons	tonnes
1	1.02
2	2.03
3	3.05
4	4.06
5	5.08
10	10.16
20	20.32
50	50.80
75	76.20
100	101.60

US tons to tonnes

US tons	tonnes
1	0.91
2	1.81
3	2.72
4	3.63
5	4.54
10	9.07
20	18.14
50	45.36
75	68.04
100	90.72

Tonnes to tons

tonnes	UK tons	US tons
1	0.98	1.10
2	1.97	2.20
3	2.95	3.30
4	3.94	4.40
5	4.92	5.50
10	9.84	11.02
20	19.68	22.05
50	49.21	55.11
75	73.82	82.67
100	98.42	110.23

UK tons to US tons

UK tons	US tons
1	1.12
2	2.24
3	3.36
4	4.48
5	5.60
10	11.20
20	22.40
50	56.00
75	83.99
100	111.99

US tons to UK tons

US tons	UK tons
1	0.89
2	1.79
3	2.68
4	3.57
5	4.46
10	8.93
20	17.86
50	44.64
75	66.96
100	89.29

TYRE PRESSURE

1 pound per square inch = 0.070307 kilogram per square centimetre.

lb per sq in	kg per sq cm	lb per sq in	kg per sq cm
10	0.70	28	1.97
15	1.05	30	2.11
20	1.41	40	2.81
24	1.69		
26	1.83		

TEMPERATURE

Temperature conversion

Carry out operations in sequence.

To convert	To	Equation
°Fahrenheit	°Celsius[1]	−32, ×5, ÷9
°Fahrenheit	°Rankine	+459.67
°Fahrenheit	°Réaumur	−32, ×4, ÷9
°Celsius[1]	°Fahrenheit	×9, ÷5, +32
°Celsius[1]	Kelvin	+273.15
°Celsius[1]	°Réaumur	×4, ÷5
Kelvin	°Celsius[1]	−273.15
°Rankine	°Fahrenheit	−459.67
°Réaumur	°Fahrenheit	×9, ÷4, +32
°Réaumur	°Celsius[1]	×5, ÷4

[1] *Celsius is also known as Centigrade.*

Fahrenheit to Celsius (Centigrade)

°F	°C	°F	°C	°F	°C	°F	°C
1	−17.2	32	0.0	63	17.2	94	34.4
2	−16.7	33	0.6	64	17.8	95	35.0
3	−16.1	34	1.1	65	18.3	96	35.6
4	−15.6	35	1.7	66	18.9	97	36.1
5	−15.0	36	2.2	67	19.4	98	36.7
6	−14.4	37	2.8	68	20.0	99	37.2
7	−13.9	38	3.3	69	20.6	100	37.8
8	−13.3	39	3.9	70	21.1	102	38.9
9	−12.8	40	4.4	71	21.7	104	40.0
10	−12.2	41	5.0	72	22.2	106	41.1
11	−11.6	42	5.6	73	22.8	108	42.2
12	−11.1	43	6.1	74	23.3	110	43.3
13	−10.6	44	6.7	75	23.9	112	44.4
14	−10.0	45	7.2	76	24.4	114	45.6
15	−9.4	46	7.8	77	25.0	116	46.7
16	−8.9	47	8.3	78	25.6	118	47.8
17	−8.3	48	8.9	79	26.1	120	48.9
18	−7.8	49	9.4	80	26.7	122	50.0
19	−7.2	50	10.0	81	27.2	124	51.1
20	−6.7	51	10.6	82	27.8	126	52.2
21	−6.1	52	11.1	83	28.3	128	53.3
22	−5.6	53	11.7	84	28.9	130	54.4
23	−5.0	54	12.2	85	29.4	132	55.6
24	−4.4	55	12.8	86	30.0	134	56.7
25	−3.9	56	13.3	87	30.6	136	57.8
26	−3.3	57	13.9	88	31.1	138	58.9
27	−2.8	58	14.4	89	31.7	140	60.0
28	−2.2	59	15.0	90	32.2	142	61.1
29	−1.7	60	15.6	91	32.8	144	62.2
30	−1.1	61	16.1	92	33.3	146	63.3
31	−0.5	62	16.7	93	33.9	148	64.4

°F	°C	°F	°C	°F	°C	°F	°C
150	65.6	182	83.3	235	112.8	330	165.6
152	66.7	184	84.4	240	115.6	340	171.1
154	67.8	186	85.6	245	118.3	350	176.7
156	68.9	188	86.7	250	121.1	360	182.2
158	70.0	190	87.8	255	123.9	370	187.8
160	71.1	192	88.8	260	126.7	380	193.3
162	72.2	194	90.0	265	129.4	390	198.9
164	73.3	196	91.1	270	132.2	400	204.4
166	74.4	198	92.2	275	135.0	410	210.0
168	75.6	200	93.3	280	137.8	420	215.6
170	76.7	205	96.1	285	140.6	430	221.1
172	77.8	210	98.9	290	143.3	440	226.7
174	78.9	215	101.7	295	146.1	450	232.2
176	80.0	220	104.4	300	148.9		
178	81.1	225	107.2	310	154.4		
180	82.2	230	110.0	320	160.0		

Celsius (Centigrade) to Fahrenheit

°C	°F	°C	°F	°C	°F	°C	°F
1	33.8	26	78.8	52	125.6	105	221
2	35.6	27	80.6	54	129.2	110	230
3	37.4	28	82.4	56	132.8	115	239
4	39.2	29	84.2	58	136.4	120	248
5	41.0	30	86.0	60	140.0	125	257
6	42.8	31	87.8	62	143.6	130	266
7	44.6	32	89.6	64	147.2	135	275
8	46.4	33	91.4	66	150.8	140	284
9	48.2	34	93.2	68	154.4	145	293
10	50.0	35	95.0	70	158.0	150	302
11	51.8	36	96.8	72	161.6	155	311
12	53.6	37	98.6	74	165.2	160	320
13	55.4	38	100.4	76	168.8	165	329
14	57.2	39	102.2	78	172.4	170	338
15	59.0	40	104.0	80	176.0	175	347
16	60.8	41	105.8	82	179.6	180	356
17	62.6	42	107.6	84	183.2	185	365
18	64.4	43	109.4	86	186.8	190	374
19	66.2	44	111.2	88	190.4	195	383
20	68.0	45	113.0	90	194.0	200	392
21	69.8	46	114.8	92	197.6	210	410
22	71.6	47	116.6	94	201.2	220	428
23	73.4	48	118.4	96	204.8	230	446
24	75.2	49	120.2	98	208.4	240	464
25	77.0	50	122.0	100	212	250	482

ASTRONOMICAL MEASUREMENTS

1 astronomical unit (AU) = 149 598 073 kilometres = 92 955 933 miles[1]
1 light year = 9 460 753 090 819 kilometres = 5 878 639 427 505 miles
1 parsec = 30 856 780 000 000 kilometres = 19 173 514 177 205 miles

[1] *The astronomical unit is equivalent to the mean distance between the Sun and the Earth.*

BREWING MEASUREMENTS

4.5 gallons = 1 pin
2 pins = 9 gallons = 1 firkin
4 firkins = 1 barrel = 36 gallons
6 firkins = 1 hogshead = 54 gallons
4 hogsheads = 1 tun

CLOTH MEASUREMENTS

1 ell = 45 inches
1 bolt = 120 feet = 32 ells

CRUDE OIL MEASUREMENTS (PETROLEUM)

1 barrel = 35 UK gallons = 42 US gallons

HORSE MEASUREMENTS

The height of horses is measured in hands.

1 hand = 4 inches = 10 centimetres

NAUTICAL MEASUREMENTS

1 span = 9 inches = 23 centimetres
8 spans = 1 fathom = 6 feet
1 cable's length = ⅒ nautical mile
1 nautical mile (old) = 6 080 feet
1 nautical mile (international) = 6 076.1 feet = 1.151 statute mile = 1 852 metres[1]
60 nautical mile = 1 degree
3 nautical mile = 1 league (nautical)
1 knot = 1 nautical mile per hour
1 ton (shipping) = 42 cubic feet
1 ton (displacement) = 35 cubic feet
1 ton (register) = 100 cubic feet

[1] 1 kilometre = 0.54 nautical miles.

PRINTING MEASUREMENTS

1 point = 0.3515 millimetres
1 pica = 4.2175 millimetres
1 pica = 12 points

TIMBER MEASUREMENTS

1 000 millisteres = 1 stere = 1 cubic metre
1 board foot = 144 cubic inches (12 × 12 × 1 inches)
1 cord foot = 16 cubic feet
1 cord = 8 cord feet
1 hoppus foot = 4/π cubic feet (round timber)
1 Petrograd standard = 165 cubic feet

COMPUTER MEMORY SIZES

1 byte = 8 bits
1 kilobyte (KB) = 1 024 bytes[1]
1 megabyte (MB) = 1 024 kilobytes = 1 048 576 bytes[1]
1 gigabyte (GB) = 1 024 megabytes = 1 048 576 kilobytes = 1 073 741 824 bytes[1]

[1] These measures have officially been renamed the kibibit, mebibit and gibibit respectively, with 1 kilobyte being equal to 1,000 bytes etc. However, the usage given above is still by far the most widespread.

CLOTHING SIZES

Size equivalents are approximate, and may display some variation between manufacturers.

Women's suits/dresses

UK	USA	UK/Continent
8	6	36
10	8	38
12	10	40
14	12	42
16	14	44
18	16	46
20	18	48
22	20	50
24	22	52

Adults' shoes – women

UK	USA	UK/Continent
3	4½	36
3½	5	37
4	5½	37
4½	6	38
5	6½	38
5½	7	39
6	7½	39
6½	8	40
7	8½	41
7½	9	42

Adults' shoes – men

UK	USA	UK/Continent
6½	7	40
7	7½	41
7½	8	41
8	8½	42
8½	9	43
9	9½	43
9½	10	44
10	10½	44
10½	11	45
11	11½	45

Children's shoes

UK/USA	UK/Continent
0	15
½	16
1	17
2	18
3	19
4	20
4½	21
5	22
6	23
7	24
8	25
8½	26
9	27
10	28
11	29
12	30
12½	31
13	32

Women's hosiery

UK/USA	Continent
8	0
8½	1
9	2
9½	3
10	4
10½	5

Men's suits and overcoats

UK/USA	Continent
36	46
38	48
40	50
42	52
44	54
46	56

Men's socks

UK/USA	Continent
9½	38–39
10	39–40
10½	40–41
11	41–42
11½	42–43

Men's shirts

UK/USA	UK/Continent
12	30–31
12½	32
13	33
13½	34–35
14	36
14½	37
15	38
15½	39–40
16	41
16½	42
17	43
17½	44–45

EGG SIZES

There are four weight grades for Class A eggs ('fresh eggs') as follows:

XL	Very large (73g and above)	M	Medium (53g–63g)
L	Large (63g–73g)	S	Small (under 53g)

Egg Science

Dr Charles Williams of the School of Physics at the University of Exeter has worked out a scientific formula to calculate the exact cooking time needed to produce a perfect soft-boiled egg. His investigation concluded that the equation is:

$$t = aM^{2/3}\log_e\left[2x\ \frac{(T_{egg} - T_{water})}{(T_{yolk} - T_{water})}\right]$$

where: *t* is the total cooking time in minutes;
a is a constant which depends on the egg's specific heat capacity and thermal conductivity (use $a = 16\ s\ g^{-2/3}$ for eggs that are a week or two old – very fresh eggs will need a higher value, old eggs may need a lower value);
M is the mass of the egg in grams;
*T*egg is the temperature in °C of the egg at the beginning;
*T*yolk is the temperature in °C at which the egg is ready to be eaten (for soft-boiled eggs use 45°C);
*T*water is the temperature in °C of the boiling water.

PAPER SIZES

All sizes in these series have sides in the proportion of 1: 2.

A series Used for writing paper, books and magazines.

	mm	*in*		*mm*	*in*
A0	841 × 1 189	33.11 × 46.81	A6	105 × 148	4.13 × 5.83
A1	594 × 841	23.39 × 33.11	A7	74 × 105	2.91 × 4.13
A2	420 × 594	16.54 × 23.39	A8	52 × 74	2.05 × 2.91
A3	297 × 420	11.69 × 16.54	A9	37 × 52	1.46 × 2.05
A4	210 × 297	8.27 × 11.69	A10	26 × 37	1.02 × 1.46
A5	148 × 210	5.83 × 8.27			

B series Used for posters.

	mm	*in*		*mm*	*in*
B0	1 000 × 1 414	39.37 × 55.67	B6	125 × 176	4.92 × 6.93
B1	707 × 1 000	27.83 × 39.37	B7	88 × 125	3.46 × 4.92
B2	500 × 707	19.68 × 27.83	B8	62 × 88	2.44 × 3.46
B3	353 × 500	13.90 × 19.68	B9	44 × 62	1.73 × 2.44
B4	250 × 353	9.84 × 13.90	B10	31 × 44	1.22 × 1.73
B5	176 × 250	6.93 × 9.84			

C series Used for envelopes.

	mm	*in*		*mm*	*in*
C0	917 × 1 297	36.00 × 51.20	C7	81 × 114	3.19 × 4.50
C1	648 × 917	25.60 × 36.00	C8	57 × 81	2.24 × 3.19
C2	458 × 648	18.00 × 25.60	C9	40 × 57	1.57 × 2.24
C3	324 × 458	12.80 × 18.00	C10	28 × 40	1.10 × 1.57
C4	229 × 324	9.00 × 12.80			
C5	162 × 229	6.40 × 9.00	DL	110 × 220	4.33 × 8.66
C6	114 × 162	4.50 × 6.40			

Writing paper sizes

25 sheets = 1 quire
20 quires = 1 ream
500 sheets = 1 ream

PENCIL HARDNESS

Pencil lead classification uses *black*, abbreviated to B, to indicate softness in quality and darkness in use, and *hard*, abbreviated to H, to indicate durability in quality and faintness in use.

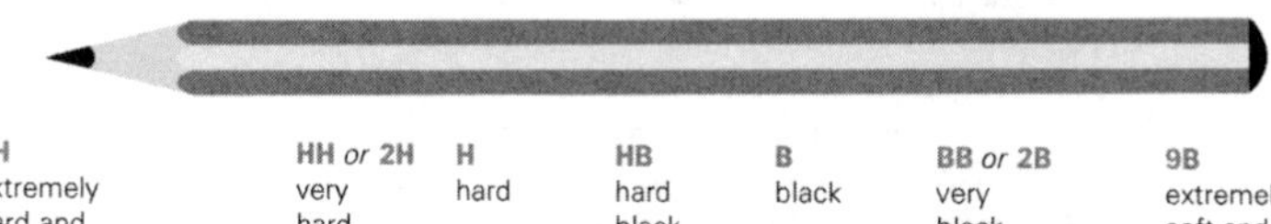

9H extremely hard and faint

HH *or* **2H** very hard

H hard

HB hard black

B black

BB *or* **2B** very black

9B extremely soft and dark

INVENTIONS, DISCOVERIES AND FIRSTS

Date	Invention, discovery or first
c.4000 BC	**Lock** is invented in Mesopotamia.
c.3500 BC	**Wheel** is invented in Mesopotamia.
c.3000 BC	**Writing** (pictography) is invented in Egypt.
c.2500 BC	**Soap** is invented in Sumer, Babylonia.
c.2250 BC	**Maps** are invented in Mesopotamia.
245 BC	**Gun** is invented by Ctesibius (fl.3c BC).
3c BC	**Cannon** is invented by Archimedes (c.287–212 BC).
c.2c BC	**Parachute** is invented in China.
59 BC	**Newspaper** is invented by Julius Caesar (100 or 102–44 BC).
25 BC	**Suspension bridge** is invented in China.
1c	Discovery of **magnetite** leads to the invention of the **compass** in China.
1c	**Concrete** is invented in Rome.
AD 105	**Paper** is invented in China. **Parchment** had been invented by Eumenes II of Pergamon (died 159 BC) in the 2c BC.
c.600	**Windmill** is invented in Syria.
725	**Mechanical clock** is invented in China.
c.10c	**Vaccination** is invented in Turkey and China.
c.980–1020	Coast of **America** is explored by first European, Leif Erikson (fl.1000).
1232	**Rocket** is invented by the Mongols in China.
c.1450	**Wooden printing press** is invented by Johannes Gutenberg (1400–68).
1513	**Pacific Ocean** is sighted by Vasco Nuñez de Balboa (1475–1519).
1519–22	First **circumnavigation of the world** by crew members of Ferdinand Magellan's (c.1480–1521) expedition.
1590	**Microscope** is invented by Zacharias Janssen (1580–1638).
1608	**Refractor telescope** is invented by Hans Lippershey (c.1570–c.1619).
1620	**Submarine** is invented by Cornelis Drebbel (c.1772–1633).
1628	**Blood circulation** is discovered by William Harvey (1578–1677).
1643	**Barometer** is invented by Evangelista Torricelli (1608–47).
1657	**Pendulum clock** is invented by Christiaan Huygens (1629–93).
1675	**Protozoa** are observed by Anton van Leeuwenhoek (1632–1723).
1675 or 1684	**Red corpuscles** are observed by Anton van Leeuwenhoek (1632–1723).
1677	**Spermatozoa** are observed by Anton van Leeuwenhoek (1632–1723).
1680	**Match** is invented by Robert Boyle (1627–91).
1698	**Steam engine** is invented by Thomas Savery (c.1650–1715); it is later refined by Thomas Newcomen (1663–1729) and James Watt (1736–1819).
1714	**Mercury thermometer** is invented by Daniel Fahrenheit (1686–1736). The **thermometer** itself had been invented by Ctesibius (fl.3c BC) in the 3c BC.
1718	**Machine gun** is invented by James Puckle (dates unknown).
1720	**Pianoforte** is invented by Bartolomeo Cristofori (1655–1731).
1735	**Chronometer** is invented by John Harrison (1693–1776).
1751	**Nickel** is discovered by Baron Axel Fredrik Cronstedt (1722–65).
1766	Existence of **carbon dioxide** and **hydrogen** in atmospheric air is demonstrated by Henry Cavendish (1731–1810).
1771	**Fluorine** is discovered by Carl Wilhelm Scheele (1742–86).
1772	**Nitrogen** is discovered by Daniel Rutherford (1749–1819).
1774	**Oxygen** is discovered by Joseph Priestley (1733–1804).
1774	**Chlorine** is discovered by Carl Wilhelm Scheele (1742–86).

Date	Invention, discovery or first
1776	**Nitrous oxide** (laughing gas) is discovered by Joseph Priestley (1733–1804). Its analgesic and laughter-provoking effects are later discovered by Humphry Davy (1778–1829).
1783	**Balloon** able to carry human passengers is invented by Jacques (1745–99) and Joseph (1740–1810) Montgolfier.
1789	**Uranium** is discovered by Martin Heinrich Klaproth (1743–1817).
1789	**Titanium** is discovered by William Gregor (1761–1817).
1795	**Pencil** is invented by Nicholas Jacques Conté (1755–1805).
1796	**Smallpox vaccination** is discovered by Edward Jenner (1749–1823).
1800	**Electric battery** is invented by Alessandro Volta (1745–1827).
1804	**Railed locomotive** is invented by Richard Trevithick (1771–1833).
1807	**Potassium** and **sodium** are discovered by Humphry Davy (1778–1829).
1808	**Barium** and **calcium** are discovered by Humphry Davy (1778–1829).
1811	**Iodine** is discovered by Bernard Courtois (1777–1838).
1816	**Photography** (on metal) is invented by Nicéphore Niepce (1765–1833). In 1838 William Henry Fox Talbot (1800–77) invents photography on paper. Colour photography is invented by James Clerk Maxwell (1831–79) in 1861.
1817	**Lithium** is discovered by Johan August Arfvedson (1792–1841).
1823	**Silicon** is discovered by Jöns Jacob Berzelius (1779–1848).
1828	**Aluminium** is discovered by Friedrich Wöhler (1800–82).
1829	**Magnesium** is discovered by Antoine Alexandre Brutus Bussy (1794–1882).
1829	A basic **typewriter**, called a typographer, is invented by William Burt (1792–1858). The first practical working typewriter was patented in 1868 by Christopher Sholes (1819–90). The electric typewriter was invented by Thomas Alva Edison (1847–1931) in 1872.
1835	'**Difference engine**', considered to be the first computer, is invented by Charles Babbage (1791–1871).
1835	**Revolver** is invented by Samuel Colt (1814–62).
1837	**Telegraph code** is invented by Samuel Morse (1791–1872).
1839–40	**Bicycle** is invented by Kirkpatrick Macmillan (1813–78).
c.1840	**General anaesthetic** is invented; priority is claimed by Crawford Long (1815–78), Gardner Cotton (1814–98), Horace Wells (1815–48) and Charles Jackson (1805–80). **Local anaesthetic** had been described centuries before in *Natural History* by Pliny the Elder (AD 23–79).
1844	**Ship with a metal hull and propeller** is built by Isambard Kingdom Brunel (1806–59).
1846	**Ether** is discovered by William Thomas Morton (1819–68).
1847	**Anaesthetic properties of chloroform** are discovered by James Young Simpson (1811–70).
1851	**Mechanical lift** is invented by Elisha G Otis (1811–61).
1855	**Cellular division** is discovered by Rudolph Virchow (1821–1902).
1858	**Theory of evolution** is presented by Charles Darwin (1809–82).
1859	Synthesis of **aspirin** by Hermann Kolbe (1818–84). Aspirin is introduced into medicine by Felix Hoffmann (1868–1946) in 1899.
1863	**Pasteurization** is invented by Louis Pasteur (1822–95).
1865	**Heredity** is discovered by Gregor Johann Mendel (1822–84).
1865	**Antisepsis** is developed by Joseph Lister (1827–1912).
1866	**Dynamite** is invented by Alfred Nobel (1833–96).
1868	**Plastics** are invented by John Wesley Hyatt (1837–1920).
1870	**DC electric motor** is invented by Zenobe Gramme (1826–1901).
1875	**Fertilization** is discovered by Oskar Hertwig (1849–1922).

Date	Invention, discovery or first
1876	**Telephone** is invented by Alexander Graham Bell (1847–1922).
1877	**Phonograph** and the **gramophone** are invented by Thomas Alva Edison (1847–1931).
1879	**Electric light bulb** is invented by Thomas Alva Edison (1847–1931).
1884	First practical working **fountain pen** is patented by Lewis Waterman (1837–1901). It is not until 1938 that Laszlo Biró (1899–1985) invents the **ballpoint pen**.
1885	**Car** is built using a high-speed internal combustion engine by Gottlieb Daimler (1834–1900).
1885	**Rabies vaccination** is pioneered by Louis Pasteur (1822–95).
1885	**Motorcycle** is invented by Gottlieb Daimler (1834–1900).
1886	**Petrol engine** is pioneered by Karl Benz (1844–1929).
1887	**Contact lenses** are invented by Adolph E Fick (1829–1901).
1888	**Chromosomes** are discovered by Thomas Hunt Morgan (1866–1945).
1888	**Radio telegraphy** is invented by Heinrich Hertz (1857–94).
1888	**AC electric motor** is invented by Nikola Tesla (1856–1943).
1889	**Photographic film** is invented by George Eastman (1854–1932).
1892	**Diesel engine** is invented by Rudolf Diesel (1858–1913).
1892	**X-rays** are discovered by Heinrich Hertz (1857–94). Their properties are discovered by Wilhelm Konrad von Röntgen (1845–1923) in 1895.
1895	**Helium** is discovered by William Ramsay (1852–1916).
1895	**Cinema** is pioneered by Auguste (1862–1954) and Louis (1865–1948) Lumière.
1895	**Safety razor** is invented by King Camp Gillette (1855–1932). The **electric razor** was invented by Jacob Schick (1878–1937) in 1928.
1898	**Radium** is discovered by Marie (1867–1934) and Pierre (1859–1906) Curie.
1898	**Neon** is discovered by William Ramsay (1852–1916) and Morris William Travers (1872–1961).
1900	**Rigid airship** is invented by Graf Ferdinand von Zeppelin (1838–1917).
1901	**Adrenaline** is discovered by Jokichi Takamine (1854–1922) based on work by Edward Sharpey-Schafer (1850–1935) and George Oliver (1841–1915).
1901	**Blood groups** A, O, B and AB are discovered by Karl Landsteiner (1868–1943).
1901	**Radio** (transatlantic) is invented by Guglielmo Marconi (1874–1937).
1903	**Aeroplane** is invented by Orville (1871–1948) and Wilbur (1867–1912) Wright.
1906	**Necessity of vitamins** in diet is demonstrated by Sir Frederick Gowland Hopkins (1861–1947).
1907	Electric **washing machine** is invented by Hurley Machine Co.
1909	**North Pole** is reached by Robert Edwin Peary (1856–1920).
1909	First **cross-Channel flight** is made by Louis Blériot (1872–1936).
1911	**South Pole** is reached by Roald Amundsen (1872–1928).
1919	First **nonstop transatlantic flight** is made by John Alcock (1892–1919) and Arthur Whitten Brown (1886–1948).
1921	**Insulin** is isolated by Frederick Grant Banting (1891–1941), Charles Herbert Best (1899–1978) and John James McLeod (1876–1935).
1926	**Television** is invented by John Logie Baird (1888–1946). Peter Goldmark (1906–77) went on to invent **colour television** in 1940.
1927	First **solo transatlantic flight** is made by Charles Lindbergh (1902–74). The first solo transatlantic flight by a woman was made by Amelia Earhart (1897–1937) in 1932.
1928	**Turbojet** is invented by Frank Whittle (1907–96).
1928	**Penicillin** is discovered by Alexander Fleming (1881–1955).
1933	First **solo circumnavigation of the globe by aeroplane** is made by Wiley Post (1900–35).
1935	**Sulphonamides** (the first **antibiotics**) are discovered by Gerhard (Johannes Paul) Domagk (1895–1964).

Date	Invention, discovery or first
1937	**Nylon** is invented by Wallace H Carothers (1896–1937).
1938	**Xerography** is invented by Chester Carlson (1906–68).
1939–45	**Atomic bomb** is invented by Otto Frisch (1904–79).
1940	**Plutonium** is discovered by Glenn Theodore Seaborg (1912–99), Edwin Mattison McMillan (1907–91) and others.
1945	**Microwave oven** is invented by Percy L Spencer (1894–1970).
1947	**Polaroid camera** is invented by Edwin Land (1909–91).
1947	First **piloted supersonic flight** is made by Charles E Yeager (1923–).
1948	**Transistor** is invented by John Bardeen (1908–91).
1949	First **nonstop circumnavigation of the globe by aeroplane** is made by a US B-50 Superfortress and crew of 15 in 94 hours.
1950	**Contraceptive pill** is invented by Gregor Pincus (1903–67) and others.
1952	**Chemical regulation by genes** is discovered by Jacques Monod (1910–76) and Edwin Joseph Cohn (1892–1953).
1953	**Structure of DNA** is unravelled by Francis Crick (1916–2004) and James D Watson (1928–).
1953	First people to reach the **summit of Mt Everest** are Edmund Hillary (1919–2008) and Tenzing Norgay (1914–86).
1955	**Hovercraft** is invented by Christopher Cockerell (1910–99).
1956	**Video recorder** is invented by Ampex Co.
1957	First **satellite** to orbit the Earth, Sputnik 1, is launched by the USSR.
1958	**Microchip** is invented by Jack Kilby (1923–2005).
1960	The first working **laser** is invented by Theodore Maiman (1927–2007); the laser was patented by Arthur L Schawlow (1921–99) and Charles H Townes (1915–).
1961	First **human being in space** as Yuri Gagarin (1934–68) makes one orbit of the Earth.
1961	**Silicon chip** is invented by Texas Instruments.
1969	First **human beings to walk on the moon** are Neil Armstrong (1930–) and Buzz Aldrin (1930–) of the Apollo 11 mission.
1971	**Microprocessor** is invented by Marcian E Hoff (1937–).
1979	**Compact disc** is invented by the Philips and Sony companies.
1981	**AIDS** (Acquired Immune Deficiency Syndrome) is identified by scientists in Los Angeles.
1981	**Space shuttle flights** are commenced by the USA.
1983	**HIV** (the Human Immuno-Deficiency Virus) is isolated by Luc Montagnier (1932–) and others.
1989	**World Wide Web** is invented by Tim Berners-Lee (1955–).
1990	**Hubble Space Telescope** (the first optical space-based telescope) is launched by NASA.
1999	First **nonstop circumnavigation of the globe by balloon** is made by Bertrand Piccard (1958–) and Brian Jones (1947–).
2001	First **space tourist** visits the International Space Station.
2003	Scientists **sequencing the human genome** announce its completion.
2004	Scientists in Korea announce the first successful, independently verified **cloning of human embryos**.
2005	First **solo circumnavigation of the globe by aeroplane without refuelling** is made by Steve Fossett (1944–2008[1]) in the *Virgin Global Flyer*.
2006	Gardasil®, a **vaccine against human papilloma viruses that cause cervical cancer**, is approved for use.

[1] Went missing Sep 2007; declared legally dead Feb 2008.

See also Space Firsts in **Astronomy and Space Exploration**.

ARCHITECTURE AND ENGINEERING

TALLEST BUILDINGS

The list includes only completed structures and buildings; proposed projects or those under construction have been excluded. Heights of tallest inhabited buildings include integral architectural features such as spires, but exclude antennas, aerials and flagpoles.

Tallest structures

Name	Location	Height	Date completed
KVLY-TV Mast	Blanchard, North Dakota, USA	629m/2 063ft	1963
CN Tower	Toronto, Canada	553m/1 815ft	1975

Tallest inhabited buildings

Name	Location	Height	Date completed
Taipei 101	Taipei, Taiwan	508m/1 667ft	2003
Petronas Twin Towers	Kuala Lumpur, Malaysia	452m/1 483ft	1998
Sears Tower	Chicago, USA	442m/1 451ft	1974
Jin Mao Building	Shanghai, China	421m/1 381ft	1998
Two International Finance Centre	Hong Kong, China	415m/1 362ft	2003
CITIC Plaza	Guangzhou, China	391m/1 283ft	1997
Shun Hing Square	Shenzhen, China	384m/1 260ft	1996
Empire State Building	New York City, USA	381m/1 250ft	1931
Central Plaza	Hong Kong, China	374m/1 227ft	1992
Bank of China	Hong Kong, China	367m/1 205ft	1990

Towering Craziness

The CN Tower has had its fair share of wild and wacky climbers. Records have been set for carrying a piano, lugging a 91kg/200lb pumpkin, driving a motorbike and bouncing on a pogo stick up the Tower's many stairs. World records have also been set for the descent, notably in 1984 when a stuntman tumbled his way to the bottom, falling down the 1,760-odd steps in just under two hours.

LONGEST BRIDGES

Figures refer to main unsupported spans. All bridges are of the suspension type. The list includes only completed bridges; proposed projects or those under construction have been excluded.

Name	Location	Length	Date completed
Akashi-Kaikyo (Pearl Bridge)	Honshu–Shikoku, Japan	1 990m/6 527ft	1998
Great Belt East (Storebaelt)	Halsskov–Kudshoved, Denmark	1 624m/5 327ft	1998
Runyang South	Jiangsu Province, China	1 490m/4 888ft	2005
Humber Estuary	Hull–Grimsby, UK	1 410m/4 625ft	1981
Jiangyin	Jiangsu Province, China	1 385m/4 543ft	1999
Tsing Ma	Hong Kong, China	1 377m/4 516ft	1997
Verrazano Narrows	Brooklyn–Staten Island, New York Harbour, USA	1 298m/4 257ft	1964
Golden Gate	San Francisco, California, USA	1 280m/4 198ft	1937

Name	Location	Length	Date completed
Höga Kusten	Kramfors, Sweden	1 210m/3 969ft	1997
Mackinac	Mackinaw City–St Ignace, Michigan, USA	1 158m/3 799ft	1957
Minami Bisan-Seto	Honshu–Shikoku, Japan	1 100m/3 608ft	1988
Fatih Sultan (Bosporus II)	Istanbul, Turkey	1 090m/3 575ft	1988
Bosporus	Istanbul, Turkey	1 074m/3 523ft	1973
George Washington	Hudson River, New York City, USA	1 067m/3 500ft	1931
Kurushima-3	Onomichi–Imabari, Japan	1 030m/3 378ft	1999
Kurushima-2	Onomichi–Imabari, Japan	1 020m/3 346ft	1999
Ponte 25 de Abril	Lisbon, Portugal	1 013m/3 323ft	1966
Forth Road	Edinburgh, UK	1 006m/3 300ft	1964
Kita Bisan-seto	Kojima–Sakaide, Japan	990m/3 247ft	1988
Severn	Bristol, UK	988m/3 240ft	1966

Sky Bridge

In Dec 2004 the Millau Viaduct, the world's highest road bridge, was opened to traffic. Designed by British architect Lord Foster, the bridge spans the River Tarn in southern France. It is 2,460m/8,070ft long and the tallest pylon is 343m/1,125ft high; the road deck itself is at 270m/885ft.

LONGEST TUNNELS

The list includes only completed tunnels; proposed projects or those under construction have been excluded.

Name	Location	Length	Type	Date completed
Seikan	Honshu–Hokkaido, Japan	53.9km/33.4mi	rail	1985
Channel	Cheriton, England–Coquelles, France	50.4km/31.3mi	rail	1994
Moscow subway	Moscow, Russia	37.9km/23.5mi	rail	1990
Loetschberg Base Tunnel	Berne–Visp, Switzerland	34.6km/21.5mi	rail	2007
Northern tube line	London, UK	27.8km/17.2mi	rail	1926
Iwate Ichinohe	Tanigawa Mountains, Japan	25.8km/16.0mi	rail	2002
Laerdal	Laerdal–Aurland, Norway	24.5km/15.2mi	road	2000
Dai-shimizu	Honshu, Japan	22.2km/13.8mi	rail	1979
Wushaoling	Gansu, China	21.1km/13.1mi	rail	2006
Simplon I & II	Brigue, Switzerland–Iselle, Italy	19.8km/12.3mi	rail	1906, 1922
Vereina	Klosters–Sagliains, Switzerland	19.1km/11.8mi	rail	1999
Kanmon	Kanmon Strait, Japan	18.7km/11.6mi	rail	1975
Apennine	Vernio, Italy	18.5km/11.5mi	rail	1934
Qinling I-II	Qinling Mountains, China	18.5km/11.5mi	rail	2002
Qinling Zhongnanshan	Shanxi, China	18.0km/11.2mi	road	2007
St Gotthard (road)	Göschenen, Switzerland–Airolo, Italy	16.3km/10.1mi	road	1980
Rokko	Osaka–Kōbe, Japan	16.1km/10.0mi	rail	1972
Furka Base	Andermatt–Brig, Switzerland	15.4km/9.5mi	rail	1982
Haruna	Gunma Prefecture, Japan	15.4km/9.5mi	rail	1982
Severomuyskiy	Baikal–Amur, Russia	15.3km/9.4mi	rail	2001
Gorigamine	Takasaki–Nagano, Japan	15.2km/9.4mi	rail	1997
Monte Santomarco	Paola–Cosenza, Italy	15.0km/9.3mi	rail	1987

Name	Location	Length	Type	Date completed
St Gotthard (rail)	Göschenen, Switzerland–Airolo, Italy	14.9km/9.2mi	rail	1882
Nakayama	Nakayama Pass, Hokkaido, Japan	14.9km/9.2mi	rail	1982
Mount MacDonald	British Columbia, Canada	14.7km/9.1mi	rail	1989
Lötschberg	Thun–Brig, Switzerland	14.6km/9.0mi	rail	1913
Romeriksporten	Oslo–Gardermoen airport, Norway	14.6km/9.1mi	rail	1999
Dayaoshan	Nanling Mountains, China	14.3km/8.9mi	rail	1987
Arlberg	Austrian Alps	14.0km/8.7mi	road	1979
Hokuriku	Sea of Japan coast, Japan	13.8km/8.6mi	rail	1962

HIGHEST DAMS

The list includes only completed dams; proposed projects or those under construction have been excluded.

Name	River, country	Structural height	Date completed
Nurek	Vakhsh, Tajikistan	300m/984ft	1980
Xiaowan	Mekong, China	292m/958ft	2007
Grande Dixence	Dixence, Switzerland	285m/935ft	1962
Inguri	Inguri, Georgia	272m/892ft	1984
Vaiont	Vaiont, Italy	262m/859ft	1961
Manuel M Torres	Grijalva, Mexico	261m/856ft	1981
Alvaro Obregon	Tenasco, Mexico	260m/853ft	1946
Mauvoisin	Drance de Bagnes, Switzerland	250m/820ft	1957
Alberto Lleras	Guavio, Colombia	243m/797ft	1989
Mica	Columbia, Canada	243m/797ft	1972
Sayano-Shushensk	Yenisei, Russia	242m/794ft	1980
Ertan	Yangtze/Yalong, China	240m/787ft	1999

STIRLING PRIZE

The Stirling Prize of the Royal Institute of British Architects (RIBA) is awarded annually to the architects of the building which is judged to have made the greatest contribution to British architecture in the foregoing year. The building must be sited within the European Union and the architects must be RIBA members. The prize is named after the architect Sir James Stirling (1926–92).

Date	Building	Architects
1996	University of Salford Centenary Building, Salford, UK	Hodder Associates
1997	Stuttgart Music School, Stuttgart, Germany	James Stirling, Michael Wilford and Partners
1998	American Air Museum, Duxford, UK	Foster and Partners
1999	Natwest Media Centre, Lord's Cricket Ground, London, UK	Future Systems
2000	Peckham Library, London, UK	Alsop Architects
2001	Magna Centre, Rotherham, UK	Wilkinson Eyre Architects
2002	Millennium Bridge, Gateshead, UK	Wilkinson Eyre Architects
2003	Laban Centre, London, UK	Herzog and de Meuron
2004	30 St Mary Axe ('the Gherkin'), London, UK	Foster and Partners
2005	Scottish Parliament Building, Edinburgh, UK	EMBT/RMJM Ltd
2006	Barajas Airport, Madrid, Spain	Richard Rogers Partnership
2007	Museum of Modern Literature, Marbach am Necker, Germany	David Chipperfield Architects

LIBERAL ARTS

In the Middle Ages, the *trivium* and *quadrivium* were studied.

Trivium	Quadrivium
grammar	arithmetic
rhetoric	geometry
logic	astronomy
	music

OXFORD UNIVERSITY COLLEGES

Oxford University has 39 official colleges and seven permanent private halls.

College	Date founded	College	Date founded
All Souls College	1438	Oriel College	1326
Balliol College	1263	Pembroke College	1624
Blackfriars Hall[3]	1994	Queen's College, The	1341
Brasenose College	1509	Regent's Park College	1810
Campion Hall	1896	St Anne's College	1952
Christ Church	1546	St Antony's College[1]	1950
Corpus Christi College	1517	St Benet's Hall	1897
Exeter College	1314	St Catherine's College	1962
Green College[1]	1979	St Cross College[1]	1965
Greyfriars Hall[3]	1957	St Edmund Hall	c.1278
Harris Manchester College[3]	1889	St Hilda's College[2]	1893
Hertford College	1282	St Hugh's College	1886
Jesus College	1571	St John's College	1555
Keble College	1870	St Peter's College	1929
Kellogg College[3]	1994	St Stephen's House	1876
Lady Margaret Hall	1878	Somerville College	1879
Linacre College[1]	1962	Templeton College[1]	1965
Lincoln College	1427	Trinity College	1555
Magdalen College	1448	University College	1249
Mansfield College	1886	Wadham College	1609
Merton College	1264	Wolfson College[1]	1965
New College	1379	Worcester College	1714
Nuffield College[1]	1937	Wycliffe Hall	1877

[1] *Graduates only.*
[2] *Women only.*
[3] *Date that Private Hall status was granted, or that the College or Hall joined the University; may have been established previously.*

Old Oxford

Oxford University is the oldest university in Britain, having its origins in informal groups of masters and students that gathered in Oxford in the 12c. The closure of the University of Paris to the English in 1167 accelerated Oxford's development. Cambridge is the second oldest university; its first college, Peterhouse, was founded in 1284.

CAMBRIDGE UNIVERSITY COLLEGES

Cambridge University has 31 official colleges and halls.

College	Date founded	College	Date founded
Christ's College	1505	Magdalene College	1428
Churchill College	1960	New Hall[2]	1954
Clare College	1326	Newnham College[2]	1871
Clare Hall[1]	1965	Pembroke College	1347
Corpus Christi College	1352	Peterhouse	1284
Darwin College[1]	1964	Queens' College	1448
Downing College	1800	Robinson College	1979
Emmanuel College	1584	St Catharine's College	1473
Fitzwilliam College	1966	St Edmund's College	1896
Girton College	1869	St John's College	1511
Gonville & Caius College	1348	Selwyn College	1882
Homerton College	1976	Sidney Sussex College	1596
Hughes Hall	1885	Trinity College	1546
Jesus College	1497	Trinity Hall	1350
King's College	1441	Wolfson College	1965
Lucy Cavendish College[2]	1965		

[1] *Graduates only.*
[2] *Women only.*

IVY LEAGUE

The Ivy League is a group of eight long-established universities, of particular academic and social prestige, in the north-eastern USA. The league was formally established in 1956.

Brown University
Columbia University
Cornell University
Dartmouth College
Harvard University
Princeton University
University of Pennsylvania
Yale University

SEVEN SISTERS COLLEGES

The Seven Sisters Colleges are a group of long-established, prestigious women's colleges (some now co-educational) in the north-eastern USA. The group was formally established in 1927.

Barnard College
Bryn Mawr College
Mt Holyoke College
Radcliffe College
Smith College
Vassar College
Wellesley College

PRESIDENTS OF THE ROYAL SOCIETY

The Royal Society was founded in 1660 and is the UK's foremost body for the encouragement of research and development in science, engineering and technology. Since the late 19c the president has been appointed for a five-year term. Names are listed in their original form, regardless of later knighthoods, peerages, etc.

Dates	Names
1662–77	William, Viscount Brouncker
1677–80	Sir Joseph Williamson
1680–2	Sir Christopher Wren
1682–3	Sir John Hoskins
1683–4	Sir Cyril Wyche
1684–6	Samuel Pepys
1686–9	John, Earl of Carbery
1689–90	Thomas, Earl of Pembroke
1690–5	Sir Robert Southwell
1695–8	Charles Montagu
1698–1703	John, Lord Somers
1703–27	Sir Isaac Newton
1727–41	Sir Hans Sloane
1741–52	Martin Folkes
1752–64	George, Earl of Macclesfield
1764–8	James, Earl of Morton
1768	James Burrow
1768–72	James West
1772–8	Sir John Pringle
1778–1820	Sir Joseph Banks
1820	William Hyde Wollaston
1820–7	Sir Humphry Davy
1827–30	Davies Gilbert
1830–8	HRH The Duke of Sussex
1838–48	Joshua Alwyne Compton, Marquess of Northampton
1848–54	William Parsons, Earl of Rosse
1854–8	John, Lord Wrottesley
1858–61	Sir Benjamin Collins Brodie
1861–71	Sir Edward Sabine
1871–3	Sir George Biddell Airy
1873–8	Sir Joseph Dalton Hooker
1878–83	William Spottiswoode
1883–5	Thomas Henry Huxley
1885–90	Sir George Gabriel Stokes
1890–5	Lord Kelvin
1895–1900	Lord Lister
1900–5	Sir William Huggins
1905–8	John William Strutt, Lord Rayleigh
1908–13	Sir Archibald Geikie
1913–15	Sir William Crookes
1915–20	Sir Joseph John Thomson
1920–5	Sir Charles Scott Sherrington
1925–30	Ernest, Lord Rutherford of Nelson
1930–5	Sir Frederick Gowland Hopkins
1935–40	Sir William Henry Bragg
1940–5	Sir Henry Dale
1945–50	Sir Robert Robinson
1950–5	Edgar Douglas Adrian
1955–60	Sir Cyril Hinshelwood
1960–5	Sir Howard Florey
1965–70	Patrick Maynard Stuart Blackett
1970–5	Sir Alan Hodgkin
1975–80	Alexander Robertus Todd
1980–5	Sir Andrew Huxley
1985–90	George Porter, Lord Porter of Luddenham
1990–5	Sir Michael Atiyah
1995–2000	Sir Aaron Klug
2000–2005	Lord May of Oxford
2005–	Sir Martin Rees

RANKS OF THE ARISTOCRACY (UK)

king
prince
duke
marquess
earl
viscount
baron

ROYAL SUCCESSION (UK)

The Prince of Wales
Prince William of Wales
Prince Henry of Wales
Prince Andrew, The Duke of York
Princess Beatrice of York
Princess Eugenie of York
Prince Edward, The Earl of Wessex
James, Viscount Severn
The Lady Louise Windsor
Princess Anne, The Princess Royal

LITERATURE

POETS LAUREATE

The Poet Laureate is a poet appointed to a lifetime post in the royal household. He or she is required to compose poems for state occasions, etc. The date of appointment is given.

1617	Ben Jonson
1638	Sir William D'Avenant
1668	John Dryden
1689	Thomas Shadwell
1692	Nahum Tate
1715	Nicholas Rowe
1718	Laurence Eusden
1730	Colley Cibber
1757	William Whitehead
1785	Thomas Warton
1790	Henry Pye
1813	Robert Southey
1843	William Wordsworth
1850	Alfred, Lord Tennyson
1896	Alfred Austin
1913	Robert Bridges
1930	John Masefield
1968	Cecil Day-Lewis
1972	Sir John Betjeman
1984	Ted Hughes
1999	Andrew Motion

CHILDREN'S LAUREATE

The title of Children's Laureate is awarded once every two years to an eminent writer or illustrator of children's books.

1999	Quentin Blake
2001	Anne Fine
2003	Michael Morpurgo
2005	Jacqueline Wilson
2007	Michael Rosen

PLAYS OF SHAKESPEARE

William Shakespeare (1564–1616) was an English playwright and poet, born in Stratford-upon-Avon. He is considered to be the greatest English dramatist.

Title	Date	Category
The Two Gentlemen of Verona	1590–1	comedy
Henry VI Part One	1592	history
Henry VI Part Two	1592	history
Henry VI Part Three	1592	history
Titus Andronicus	1592	tragedy
Richard III	1592–3	history
The Taming of the Shrew	1593	comedy
The Comedy of Errors	1594	comedy
Love's Labour's Lost	1594–5	comedy
Richard II	1595	history
Romeo and Juliet	1595	tragedy
A Midsummer Night's Dream	1595	comedy
King John	1596	history
The Merchant of Venice	1596–7	comedy
Henry IV Part One	1596–7	history
The Merry Wives of Windsor	1597–8	comedy
Henry IV Part Two	1597–8	history
Much Ado About Nothing	1598	dark comedy
Henry V	1598–9	history

Title	Date	Category
Julius Caesar	1599	tragedy
As You Like It	1599–1600	comedy
Hamlet, Prince of Denmark	1600–1	tragedy
Twelfth Night	1601	comedy
Troilus and Cressida	1602	tragedy
Measure for Measure	1603	dark comedy
Othello	1603–4	tragedy
All's Well That Ends Well	1604–5	dark comedy
Timon of Athens	1605	romantic drama
The Tragedy of King Lear	1605–6	tragedy
Macbeth	1606	tragedy
Antony and Cleopatra	1606	tragedy
Pericles	1607	romance
Coriolanus	1608	tragedy
The Winter's Tale	1609	romance
Cymbeline	1610	romance
The Tempest	1611	romance
Henry VIII	1613	history

Writers on Shakespeare

'The remarkable thing about Shakespeare is that he is really very good – in spite of all the people who say he is very good.'

Robert Graves, 1964 attributed.

'I have tried lately to read Shakespeare, and found it so intolerably dull that it nauseated me.'

Charles Darwin, 1860 autobiography.

'Shakespeare one gets acquainted with without knowing how. It is part of an Englishman's constitution. His thoughts and beauties are so spread abroad that one touches them everywhere, one is intimate with him by instinct.'

Jane Austen, 1814 *Mansfield Park*, chapter 34.

NOBEL PRIZE IN LITERATURE

Nobel Prizes were established by a bequest in the will of Alfred Nobel (1833–96) to honour 'those who, during the preceding year, shall have conferred the greatest benefit on mankind'. The Nobel Prize for Literature is awarded annually to a person who has 'produced in the field of literature the most outstanding work in an ideal direction'; first awarded in 1901.

1901	Sully Prudhomme
1902	Theodor Mommsen
1903	Bjørnstjerne Bjørnson
1904	Frédéric Mistral, José Echegaray
1905	Henryk Sienkiewicz
1906	Giosuè Carducci
1907	Rudyard Kipling
1908	Rudolf Eucken
1909	Selma Lagerlöf
1910	Paul Heyse
1911	Maurice Maeterlinck
1912	Gerhart Hauptmann
1913	Rabindranath Tagore
1914	*no award*
1915	Romain Rolland
1916	Verner von Heidenstam

NOBEL PRIZE IN LITERATURE

1917	Karl Gjellerup, Henrik Pontoppidan
1918	*no award*
1919	Carl Spitteler
1920	Knut Hamsun
1921	Anatole France
1922	Jacinto Benavente
1923	William Butler Yeats
1924	Wladyslaw Reymont
1925	George Bernard Shaw
1926	Grazia Deledda
1927	Henri Bergson
1928	Sigrid Undset
1929	Thomas Mann
1930	Sinclair Lewis
1931	Erik Axel Karlfeldt
1932	John Galsworthy
1933	Ivan Bunin
1934	Luigi Pirandello
1935	*no award*
1936	Eugene O'Neill
1937	Roger Martin du Gard
1938	Pearl S Buck
1939	Frans Eemil Sillanpää
1940	*no award*
1941	*no award*
1942	*no award*
1943	*no award*
1944	Johannes V Jensen
1945	Gabriela Mistral
1946	Hermann Hesse
1947	André Gide
1948	Thomas Stearns Eliot
1949	William Faulkner
1950	Bertrand Russell
1951	Pär Lagerkvist
1952	François Mauriac
1953	Winston Churchill
1954	Ernest Hemingway
1955	Halldór Kiljan Laxness
1956	Juan Ramón Jiménez
1957	Albert Camus
1958	Boris Pasternak
1959	Salvatore Quasimodo
1960	Saint-John Perse
1961	Ivo Andric
1962	John Steinbeck
1963	Giorgos Seferis
1964	Jean-Paul Sartre *declined*
1965	Michail Sholokhov
1966	Samuel Agnon, Nelly Sachs
1967	Miguel Angel Asturias
1968	Yasunari Kawabata
1969	Samuel Beckett
1970	Alexander Solzhenitsyn
1971	Pablo Neruda
1972	Heinrich Böll
1973	Patrick White
1974	Eyvind Johnson, Harry Martinson
1975	Eugenio Montale
1976	Saul Bellow
1977	Vicente Aleixandre
1978	Isaac Bashevis Singer
1979	Odysseus Elytis
1980	Czeslaw Milosz
1981	Elias Canetti
1982	Gabriel García Márquez
1983	William Golding
1984	Jaroslav Seifert
1985	Claude Simon
1986	Wole Soyinka
1987	Joseph Brodsky
1988	Naguib Mahfouz
1989	Camilo José Cela
1990	Octavio Paz
1991	Nadine Gordimer
1992	Derek Walcott
1993	Toni Morrison
1994	Kenzaburo Oe
1995	Seamus Heaney
1996	Wislawa Szymborska
1997	Dario Fo
1998	José Saramago
1999	Günter Grass
2000	Gao Xingjian
2001	V S Naipaul
2002	Imre Kertész
2003	J M Coetzee
2004	Elfriede Jelinek
2005	Harold Pinter
2006	Orhan Pamuk
2007	Doris Lessing

No Thanks!

The French existentialist philosopher, dramatist and novelist Jean-Paul Sartre declined the Nobel Prize for Literature in 1964 on the grounds that he had 'always declined official honours'; he said that 'a writer should not allow himself to be turned into an institution'.

BOOKER PRIZE

Awarded for the year's best novel, and open to all citizens of Commonwealth countries or the Republic of Ireland. It was established in 1968 in the UK.

1969 P H Newby *Something to Answer For*
1970 Bernice Rubens *The Elected Member*
1971 V S Naipaul *In a Free State*
1972 John Berger *G*
1973 J G Farrell *The Siege of Krishnapur*
1974 Nadine Gordimer *The Conservationist* and Stanley Middleton *Holiday*
1975 Ruth Prawer Jhabvala *Heat and Dust*
1976 David Storey *Saville*
1977 Paul Scott *Staying On*
1978 Iris Murdoch *The Sea, the Sea*
1979 Penelope Fitzgerald *Offshore*
1980 William Golding *Rites of Passage*
1981 Salman Rushdie *Midnight's Children*
1982 Thomas Keneally *Schindler's Ark*
1983 J M Coetzee *Life and Times of Michael K*
1984 Anita Brookner *Hotel du Lac*
1985 Keri Hulme *The Bone People*
1986 Kingsley Amis *The Old Devils*
1987 Penelope Lively *Moon Tiger*
1988 Peter Carey *Oscar and Lucinda*
1989 Kazuo Ishiguro *The Remains of the Day*
1990 A S Byatt *Possession*
1991 Ben Okri *The Famished Road*
1992 Michael Ondaatje *The English Patient* and Barry Unsworth *Sacred Hunger*
1993 Roddy Doyle *Paddy Clarke, Ha Ha Ha*
1994 James Kelman *How Late It Was, How Late*
1995 Pat Barker *The Ghost Road*
1996 Graham Swift *Last Orders*
1997 Arundhati Roy *The God of Small Things*
1998 Ian McEwan *Amsterdam*
1999 J M Coetzee *Disgrace*
2000 Margaret Atwood *The Blind Assassin*
2001 Peter Carey *True History of the Kelly Gang*
2002 Yann Martel *Life of Pi*
2003 D B C Pierre *Vernon God Little*
2004 Alan Hollinghurst *The Line of Beauty*
2005 John Banville *The Sea*
2006 Kiran Desai *The Inheritance of Loss*
2007 Anne Enright *The Gathering*

Booze and Curtains

When Kingsley Amis was asked what he intended to spend his prize money on, his answer was 'Booze, of course, and then curtains'.

BOOKER INTERNATIONAL PRIZE

Awarded to a living author of any nationality whose work is available in English. Established in 2005; awarded every two years.

2005 Ismail Kadaré (Albania)
2007 Chinua Achebe (Nigeria)

ORANGE PRIZE FOR FICTION

Awarded for the year's best English-language novel by a female author. It was established in 1996 in reaction to the perceived male domination of other literary awards.

1996 Helen Dunmore *A Spell of Winter*
1997 Anne Michaels *Fugitive Pieces*
1998 Carol Shields *Larry's Party*
1999 Suzanne Berne *A Crime in the Neighborhood*
2000 Linda Grant *When I Lived in Modern Times*
2001 Kate Grenville *The Idea of Perfection*
2002 Ann Patchett *Bel Canto*
2003 Valerie Martin *Property*

2004 Andrea Levy *Small Island*
2005 Lionel Shriver *We Need To Talk About Kevin*
2006 Zadie Smith *On Beauty*
2007 Chimamanda Ngozi Adichie *Half of a Yellow Sun*

COSTA BOOK AWARDS

Since their establishment in 1971 in the UK as the Whitbread Book Awards, prizes have been awarded in several varying categories. Today there are five: Novel, First Novel, Biography, Poetry and Children's Book. Since 1985, one book has been chosen from these winners to be Costa Book of the Year.

1985 Douglas Dunn *Elegies* (Poetry)
1986 Kazuo Ishiguro *An Artist of the Floating World* (Novel)
1987 Christopher Nolan *Under the Eye of the Clock* (Biography)
1988 Paul Sayer *The Comforts of Madness* (First Novel)
1989 Richard Holmes *Coleridge: Early Visions* (Biography)
1990 Nicholas Mosley *Hopeful Monsters* (Novel)
1991 John Richardson *A Life of Picasso* (Biography)
1992 Jeff Torrington *Swing Hammer Swing!* (First Novel)
1993 Joan Brady *Theory of War* (Novel)
1994 William Trevor *Felicia's Journey* (Novel)
1995 Kate Atkinson *Behind the Scenes at the Museum* (First Novel)
1996 Seamus Heaney *The Spirit Level* (Poetry)
1997 Ted Hughes *Tales from Ovid* (Poetry)
1998 Ted Hughes *Birthday Letters* (Poetry)
1999 Seamus Heaney *Beowulf* (Poetry)
2000 Matthew Kneale *English Passengers* (Novel)
2001 Philip Pullman *The Amber Spyglass* (Children's Book)
2002 Claire Tomalin *Samuel Pepys: The Unequalled Self* (Biography)
2003 Mark Haddon *The Curious Incident of the Dog in the Night-time* (Novel)
2004 Andrea Levy *Small Island* (Novel)
2005 Hilary Spurling *Matisse the Master* (Biography)
2006 Stef Penney *The Tenderness of Wolves* (First Novel)
2007 A L Kennedy *Day* (Novel)

Lengthy Literature

The French novelist Marcel Proust wrote what is widely considered to be the world's longest novel, *À la recherche du temps perdu* ('Remembrance of Things Past'; published between 1913 and 1927). Guinness World Records® estimate that the novel, originally published in 13 volumes, contains a whopping 9,609,000 letters.

PRIX GONCOURT

The Académie Goncourt was founded in the will of Edmond de Goncourt (1822–96), to further the aims of the 'Brothers Goncourt' – Goncourt and his brother Jules (1830–70). Its purpose is to foster fiction with the annual Prix Goncourt for 'the best imaginary prose work of the year'; first awarded in France in 1903.

1903 John-Antoine Nau *Force ennemie*
1904 Léon Frapié *La maternelle*
1905 Claude Farrère *Les civilisés*
1906 Jérôme et Jean Tharaud *Dingley, l'illustre écrivain*
1907 Émile Moselly *Terres lorraines*
1908 Francis de Miomandre *Écrit sur de l'eau*
1909 Marius et Ary Leblond *En France*
1910 Louis Pergaud *De Goupil à Margot*
1911 Alphonse de Châteaubriant *Monsieur des Lourdines*

1912 André Savignon *Filles de la pluie*
1913 Marc Elder *Le peuple de la mer*
1914 Adrien Bertrand *L'appel du sol*[1]
1915 René Benjamin *Gaspard*
1916 Henri Barbusse *Le feu*
1917 Henri Malherbe *La flamme au poing*
1918 Georges Duhamel *Civilisation*
1919 Marcel Proust *A l'ombre des jeunes filles en fleurs*
1920 Ernest Pérochon *Nêne*
1921 René Maran *Batouala*
1922 Henri Béraud *Le vitriol de lune*
1923 Lucien Fabre *Rabevel ou le mal des ardents*
1924 Thierry Sandre *Le chèvrefeuille*
1925 Maurice Genevoix *Raboliot*
1926 Henry Deberly *Le supplice de Phèdre*
1927 Maurice Bedel *Jérôme, 60° latitude Nord*
1928 Maurice Constantin-Weyer *Un homme se penche sur son passé*
1929 Marcel Arland *L'ordre*
1930 Henri Fauconnier *Malaisie*
1931 Jean Fayard *Mal d'amour*
1932 Guy Mazeline *Les loups*
1933 André Malraux *La condition humaine*
1934 Roger Vercel *Capitaine Conan*
1935 Joseph Peyré *Sang et lumières*
1936 Maxence Van der Meersch *L'empreinte du Dieu*
1937 Charles Plisnier *Faux passeports*
1938 Henri Troyat *L'araigne*
1939 Philippe Hériat *Les enfants gâtés*
1940 Francis Ambrière *Les grandes vacances*
1941 Henri Pourrat *Vent de mars*
1942 Marc Bernard *Pareils à des enfants*
1943 Marius Grout *Passage de l'homme*
1944 Elsa Triolet *Le premier accroc coûte deux cents francs*
1945 Jean-Louis Bory *Mon village à l'heure allemande*
1946 Jean-Jacques Gautier *Histoire d'un fait divers*
1947 Jean-Louis Curtis *Les forêts de la nuit*
1948 Maurice Druon *Les grandes familles*
1949 Robert Merle *Week-end à Zuydcoote*
1950 Paul Colin *Les jeux sauvages*
1951 Julien Gracq *Le rivage des Syrtes*
1952 Béatrice Beck *Léon Morin, prêtre*
1953 Pierre Gascar *Les bêtes, Le temps des morts*
1954 Simone de Beauvoir *Les Mandarins*
1955 Roger Ikor *Les eaux mêlées* (volume two of *Les fils d'Avrom*)
1956 Romain Gary *Les racines du ciel*
1957 Roger Vailland *La loi*
1958 Francis Walder *Saint-Germain ou la négociation*
1959 André Schwartz-Bart *Le dernier des justes*
1960 Vintila Horia *Dieu est né en exil*[2]
1961 Jean Cau *La pitié de Dieu*
1962 André Langfus *Les bagages de sable*
1963 Armand Lanoux *Quand la mer se retire*
1964 Georges Conchon *L'état sauvage*
1965 Jacques Borel *L'adoration*
1966 Edmonde Charles-Roux *Oublier Palerme*
1967 André Pieyre de Mandiargues *La marge*
1968 Bernard Clavel *Les fruits de l'hiver*
1969 Félicien Marceau *Creezy*
1970 Michel Tournier *Le roi des aulnes*
1971 Jacques Laurent *Les bêtises*
1972 Jean Carrière *L'épervier de Maheux*
1973 Jacques Chessex *L'ogre*
1974 Pascal Laîné *La dentellière*
1975 Émile Ajar *La vie devant soi*
1976 Patrick Grainville *Les flamboyants*
1977 Didier Decoin *John l'Enfer*
1978 Patrick Modiano *Rue des boutiques obscures*
1979 Antonine Maillet *Pélagie-la-Charrette*
1980 Yves Navarre *Le jardin d'acclimatation*
1981 Lucien Bodard *Anne-Marie*
1982 Dominique Fernandez *Dans la main de l'ange*
1983 Frédérick Tristan *Les égarés*
1984 Marguerite Duras *L'amant*
1985 Yann Queffélec *Les noces barbares*
1986 Michel Host *Valet de nuit*
1987 Tahar Ben Jelloun *La nuit sacrée*
1988 Erik Orsenna *L'exposition coloniale*
1989 Jean Vautrin *Un grand pas vers le Bon Dieu*
1990 Jean Rouaud *Les champs d'honneur*
1991 Pierre Combescot *Les filles du calvaire*
1992 Patrick Chamoiseau *Texaco*
1993 Amin Maalouf *Le rocher de Tanios*
1994 Didier Van Cauwelaert *Un aller simple*
1995 Andreï Makine *Le testament français*
1996 Pascale Roze *Le chasseur Zéro*

1997 Patrick Rambaud *La bataille*
1998 Paule Constant *Confidence pour confidence*
1999 Jean Echenoz *Je m'en vais*
2000 Jean-Jacques Schuhl *Ingrid Caven*
2001 Jean-Christophe Rufin *Rouge Brésil*
2002 Pascal Quignard *Les ombres errantes*
2003 Jacques-Pierre Amette *La maîtresse de Brecht*
2004 Laurent Gaudé *Le soleil des Scorta*
2005 François Weyergans *Trois jours chez ma mère*
2006 Jonathan Littell *Les Bienveillantes*
2007 Gilles Leroy *Alabama Song*

[1] *Prize awarded retrospectively in 1916 as a result of disruption caused by World War I.*
[2] *Horia refused the prize as a result of political pressure.*

PULITZER PRIZE IN LETTERS: FICTION

Pulitzer Prizes, first awarded in the United States of America in 1917, are given annually for literature, drama, music and journalism. Established in the will of Joseph Pulitzer (1847–1911); prize for fiction was first awarded in 1918; the prize was known as the prize for a novel, rather than fiction, until 1948.

1917 *no award*
1918 Ernest Poole *His Family*
1919 Booth Tarkington *The Magnificent Ambersons*
1920 *no award*
1921 Edith Wharton *The Age of Innocence*
1922 Booth Tarkington *Alice Adams*
1923 Willa Cather *One of Ours*
1924 Margaret Wilson *The Able McLaughlins*
1925 Edna Ferber *So Big*
1926 Sinclair Lewis *Arrowsmith*
1927 Louis Bromfield *Early Autumn*
1928 Thornton Wilder *The Bridge of San Luis Rey*
1929 Julia Peterkin *Scarlet Sister Mary*
1930 Oliver Lafarge *Laughing Boy*
1931 Margaret Ayer Barnes *Years of Grace*
1932 Pearl S Buck *The Good Earth*
1933 T S Stribling *The Store*
1934 Caroline Miller *Lamb in His Bosom*
1935 Josephine Winslow Johnson *Now in November*
1936 Harold L Davis *Honey in the Horn*
1937 Margaret Mitchell *Gone With the Wind*
1938 John Phillips Marquand *The Late George Apley*
1939 Marjorie Kinnan Rawlings *The Yearling*
1940 John Steinbeck *The Grapes of Wrath*
1941 *no award*
1942 Ellen Glasgow *In This Our Life*
1943 Upton Sinclair *Dragon's Teeth*
1944 Martin Flavin *Journey in the Dark*
1945 John Hersey *A Bell for Adano*
1946 *no award*
1947 Robert Penn Warren *All the King's Men*
1948 James A Michener *Tales of the South Pacific*
1949 James Gould Cozzens *Guard of Honor*
1950 A B Guthrie, Jnr *The Way West*
1951 Conrad Richter *The Town*
1952 Herman Wouk *The Caine Mutiny*
1953 Ernest Hemingway *The Old Man and the Sea*
1954 *no award*
1955 William Faulkner *A Fable*
1956 MacKinlay Kantor *Andersonville*
1957 *no award*
1958 James Agee *A Death in the Family*
1959 Robert Lewis Taylor *The Travels of Jaimie McPheeters*
1960 Allen Drury *Advise and Consent*
1961 Harper Lee *To Kill a Mockingbird*
1962 Edwin O'Connor *The Edge of Sadness*
1963 William Faulkner *The Reivers*
1964 *no award*
1965 Shirley Ann Grau *The Keepers of the House*
1966 Katherine Anne Porter *Collected Stories*
1967 Bernard Malamud *The Fixer*
1968 William Styron *The Confessions of Nat Turner*
1969 N Scott Momaday *House Made of Dawn*
1970 Jean Stafford *Collected Stories*
1971 *no award*
1972 Wallace Stegner *Angle of Repose*
1973 Eudora Welty *The Optimist's Daughter*
1974 *no award*

1975 Michael Shaara *The Killer Angels*
1976 Saul Bellow *Humboldt's Gift*
1977 *no award*
1978 James Alan McPherson *Elbow Room*
1979 John Cheever *The Stories of John Cheever*
1980 Norman Mailer *The Executioner's Song*
1981 John Kennedy Toole *A Confederacy of Dunces*
1982 John Updike *Rabbit is Rich*
1983 Alice Walker *The Color Purple*
1984 William Kennedy *Ironweed*
1985 Alison Lurie *Foreign Affairs*
1986 Larry McMurtry *Lonesome Dove*
1987 Peter Taylor *A Summons to Memphis*
1988 Toni Morrison *Beloved*
1989 Anne Tyler *Breathing Lessons*
1990 Oscar Hijuelos *The Mambo Kings Play Songs of Love*
1991 John Updike *Rabbit at Rest*
1992 Jane Smiley *A Thousand Acres*
1993 Robert Olen Butler *A Good Scent From a Strange Mountain*
1994 E Annie Proulx *The Shipping News*
1995 Carol Shields *The Stone Diaries*
1996 Richard Ford *Independence Day*
1997 Steven Millhauser *Martin Dressler: The Tale of an American Dreamer*
1998 Philip Roth *American Pastoral*
1999 Michael Cunningham *The Hours*
2000 Jhumpa Lahiri *Interpreter of Maladies*
2001 Michael Chabon *The Amazing Adventures of Kavalier & Clay*
2002 Richard Russo *Empire Falls*
2003 Jeffrey Eugenides *Middlesex*
2004 Edward P Jones *The Known World*
2005 Marilynne Robinson *Gilead*
2006 Geraldine Brooks *March*
2007 Cormac McCarthy *The Road*

LIBRARY BOOKS

Most borrowed authors in the UK

Most Borrowed Adult Fiction Author: James Patterson
Most Borrowed Children's Author: Jacqueline Wilson
Most Borrowed Classic Author: Roald Dahl

Top ten most borrowed authors in the UK

1 James Patterson
2 Jacqueline Wilson
3 Daisy Meadows
4 Josephine Cox
5 Nora Roberts
6 Danielle Steel
7 Ian Rankin
8 Mick Inkpen
9 Janet and Allan Ahlberg
10 Francesca Simon

Most borrowed books in the UK

Most Borrowed Adult Fiction Title: Patricia Cornwell *At Risk*
Most Borrowed Children's Fiction Title: J K Rowling *Harry Potter and the Half Blood Prince*
Most Borrowed Non-Fiction Title: James Martin *The Meaning of the 21st Century*

Top ten most borrowed fiction titles in the UK

1 *At Risk* Patricia Cornwell
2 *The Island* Victoria Hislop
3 *Judge and Jury* James Patterson and Andrew Gross
4 *The Da Vinci Code* Dan Brown
5 *Mary, Mary* James Patterson
6 *Journey's End* Josephine Cox
7 *My Best Friend's Girl* Dorothy Koomson
8 *The 5th Horseman* James Patterson and Maxine Paetro
9 *The Hard Way* Lee Child
10 *The Historian* Elizabeth Kostova

Data compiled and supplied by Public Lending Right, Stockton-on-Tees. Information is for Jul 2006–Jun 2007.

FICTIONAL LITERARY PLACES

Place	Author	Book
Airstrip One	George Orwell (1903–50)	*Nineteen Eighty-Four* (1949)
Ankh-Morpork	Terry Pratchett (1948–)	Discworld® books (since 1983)
Barchester	Anthony Trollope (1815–82)	Barsetshire Novels (1855–67)
Barset	Anthony Trollope (1815–82)	Barsetshire Novels (1855–67)
Barsetshire	Anthony Trollope (1815–82)	Barsetshire Novels (1855–67)
Brobdingnag	Jonathan Swift (1667–1745)	*Gulliver's Travels* (1726)
Celestial City	John Bunyan (1628–88)	*The Pilgrim's Progress* (1678–84)
Christminster	Thomas Hardy (1840–1928)	various novels (1871–95[1]), especially *Jude the Obscure* (1895)
Discworld®	Terry Pratchett (1948–)	Discworld® books (since 1983)
Earthsea	Ursula Le Guin (1929–)	Earthsea Tetralogy (1968–91)
Emerald City	L Frank Baum (1856–1919)	*The Wonderful Wizard of Oz* (1900)
Erehwon	Samuel Butler (1835–1902)	*Erehwon* (1872)
Eurasia	George Orwell (1903–50)	*Nineteen Eighty-Four* (1949)
Gormenghast	Mervyn Peake (1911–68)	Gormenghast Trilogy (1946–59)
Hogwarts	J K Rowling (1965–)	Harry Potter books (since 1997)
Lake Wobegon	Garrison Keillor (1942–)	various (since 1985)
Laputa	Jonathan Swift (1667–1745)	*Gulliver's Travels* (1726)
Lilliput	Jonathan Swift (1667–1745)	*Gulliver's Travels* (1726)
Llaregyb	Dylan Thomas (1914–53)	*Under Milk Wood* (1954)
Looking-Glass Land	Lewis Carroll (1832–98)	*Through the Looking-Glass* (1872)
Maple White Land	Arthur Conan Doyle (1859–1930)	*The Lost World* (1912)
Maycomb	Harper Lee (1926–)	*To Kill a Mockingbird* (1960)
Middle-Earth	J R R Tolkien (1892–1973)	*The Hobbit, The Lord of the Rings* (1937, 1954–5)
Narnia	C S Lewis (1898–1963)	*Chronicles of Narnia* (1950–6)
Never-Never Land	J M Barrie (1860–1937)	*Peter Pan* (1904 play; 1911 book)
Oceania	George Orwell (1903–50)	*Nineteen Eighty-Four* (1949)
Oz	L Frank Baum (1856–1919)	*The Wonderful Wizard of Oz* (1900)
Rivendell	J R R Tolkien (1892–1973)	*The Hobbit, The Lord of the Rings* (1937, 1954–5)
Shangri-la	James Hilton (1900–54)	*Lost Horizon* (1933)
The Shire	J R R Tolkien (1892–1973)	*The Hobbit, The Lord of the Rings* (1937, 1954–5)
Toyland	Enid Blyton (1897–1968)	*Noddy Goes to Toyland* (1949)
Treasure Island	Robert Louis Stevenson (1850–94)	*Treasure Island* (1883)
Utopia	Thomas More (1478–1535)	*Utopia* (1516)
Vanity Fair	John Bunyan (1628–88)	*The Pilgrim's Progress* (1678–84)
Wessex	Thomas Hardy (1840–1928)	various (1871–95[1])
Wonderland	Lewis Carroll (1832–98)	*Alice's Adventures in Wonderland* (1865)
Xanadu	Samuel Taylor Coleridge (1772–1834)	'Kubla Khan: A Vision in a Dream' (1816)
Yoknapatawpha County	William Faulkner (1897–1962)	various (1929–62[2])
Zenda	Anthony Hope (1863–1933)	*The Prisoner of Zenda* (1894)

[1] *Years between which he published novels, not those specifically set in Christminster or Wessex.*
[2] *Specifically covers period of works set in Yoknapatawpha County.*

AUTHORS' REAL NAMES

Pseudonym	Real name
Bachman, Richard	Stephen King
Bell, Acton	Anne Brontë
Bell, Currer	Charlotte Brontë
Bell, Ellis	Emily Brontë
Burgess, Anthony	John Anthony Burgess Wilson
Carroll, Lewis	Charles Lutwidge Dodgson
Charteris, Leslie	Leslie Charles Bowyer Yin
Conrad, Joseph	Józef Teodor Konrad Nalecz Korzeniowski
Coolidge, Susan	Sarah Chauncy Woolsey
Dinesen, Isak	Karen Blixen
Eliot, George	Mary Ann *or* Marian Evans
Farrell, M J	Molly Keane, *originally* Mary Nesta Skrine
Ford, Ford Madox	Ford Hermann Hueffer
France, Anatole	Anatole François Thibault
Gibbon, Lewis Grassic	James Leslie Mitchell
Gorky, Maxim	Aleksei Maksimovich Peshkov
Henry, O	William Sydney Porter
Higgins, Jack	Harry Patterson
Hite, Shere	Shirley Diana Gregory
Kincaid, Jamaica	Elaine Potter Richardson
Le Carré, John	David John Moore Cornwell
London, Jack	John Griffith Chaney
McBain, Ed	Salvatore A Lambino
Molière	Jean Baptiste Poquelin
Morrison, Toni	Chloe Anthony Morrison, *née* Wofford
Orwell, George	Eric Arthur Blair
Peters, Ellis	Edith Mary Pargeter
Queen, Ellery	Frederick Dannay *and* Manfred B Lee
Rhys, Jean	Gwen Williams
Robbins, Harold	Francis Kane
Saki	Hector Hugh Munro
Salten, Felix	Siegmund Salzmann
Sand, George	Amandine Aurore Lucie Dupin, Baronne Dudevant
Sapper	Herman Cyril McNeile
Seuss, Dr	Theodor Seuss Geisel
Shute, Nevil	Nevil Shute Norway
Smith, Stevie	Florence Margaret Smith
Stern, Daniel	Marie de Flavigny, Comtesse d'Agoult
Stoppard, Tom	Thomas Straussler
Tey, Josephine	Elizabeth Mackintosh
Twain, Mark	Samuel Langhorne Clemens
Voltaire	François Marie Arouet
Weldon, Fay	Franklin Birkinshaw
Wesley, Mary	Mary Aline Siepmann, *née* Farmar
West, Dame Rebecca	Cecily Isabel Andrews, *née* Fairfield
West, Nathanael	Nathan Wallenstein Weinstein
Westmacott, Mary	Dame Agatha Christie, *née* Miller
Williams, Tennessee	Thomas Lanier
Wyndham, John	John Wyndham Parkes Lucas Beynon Harris

THREE MUSKETEERS

The Three Musketeers appear in the novel *The Three Musketeers* (1844) by Alexandre Dumas (1802–70). As the novel progresses, the three are joined by d'Artagnan.

Aramis
Athos
Porthos

SNOW WHITE'S DWARFS

In the fairy tale by the Brothers Grimm the seven dwarfs are not mentioned by name, but these names were used in the Walt Disney animated film of 1937.

Bashful
Doc
Dopey
Grumpy
Happy
Sleepy
Sneezy

Hi Ho, Hi Ho

When *Snow White and the Seven Dwarfs* (1937) won an honorary Oscar® at the 11th Academy Awards®, the award comprised one normal-sized statuette – and seven miniature Oscars, one for each of the dwarfs.

SUPERHEROES' REAL NAMES

Superhero	Real name
Batman	Bruce Wayne
Captain America	Steve Rogers
Captain Marvel	Billy Batson
Daredevil	Matt Murdock
The Incredible Hulk	Dr Robert Bruce Banner
Spiderman	Peter Parker
Superman	Kal-El (on Krypton); Clark Kent (on Earth)
Wonder Woman	Diana Prince

Speeding Bullets

'Faster than a speeding bullet! More powerful than a locomotive! Able to leap tall buildings in a single bound!'

Jerome Siegel; introduction for the Superman radio serial. Quoted in *Time*, 14 Mar 1988.

TURNER PRIZE

The Turner Prize was founded in 1984 by the Patrons of New Art. It is awarded to a contemporary British artist under the age of 50 for an 'outstanding exhibition of work in the past twelve months'.

1984	Malcolm Morley, painter
1985	Sir Howard Hodgkin, painter
1986	Gilbert and George (Gilbert Proesch and George Passmore), performance and photopiece artists
1987	Richard Deacon, sculptor
1988	Tony Cragg, sculptor
1989	Richard Long, land artist
1990	*no award*
1991	Anish Kapoor, sculptor
1992	Grenville Davey, sculptor
1993	Rachel Whiteread, sculptor
1994	Antony Gormley, sculptor
1995	Damien Hirst, painter and conceptual and installation artist
1996	Douglas Gordon, video artist
1997	Gillian Wearing, photographer and video artist
1998	Chris Ofili, painter
1999	Steve McQueen, video artist
2000	Wolfgang Tillmans, photographer
2001	Martin Creed, conceptual and installation artist
2002	Keith Tyson, conceptual and installation artist
2003	Grayson Perry, potter
2004	Jeremy Deller, mixed media and video artist
2005	Simon Starling, conceptual and installation artist
2006	Tomma Abts, painter
2007	Mark Wallinger, conceptual and installation artist

Angel of the North

Antony Gormley, the Turner Prize winner in 1994, created the largest sculpture in the UK with his *Angel of the North* (1998) in Gateshead. Weighing 200 tonnes/197 tons, the *Angel* stands 20m/65ft high and has a wingspan of 54m/175ft. As a result of its prominent location by the A1 and the east coast railway line, it is estimated that the *Angel* is seen by 33 million people each year, or at least one person every second.

FAMOUS WORKS OF ART

Works are listed by the name by which they are popularly known.

Art work	Artist or sculptor	Location	Date
The Age of Bronze	Auguste Rodin	several castings in various collections worldwide	1877
The Ambassadors	Hans Holbein the Younger	National Gallery, London, UK	1533
Angel of the North	Antony Gormley	Gateshead, UK	1998
The Arnolfini Portrait	Jan Van Eyck	National Gallery, London, UK	1434
The Artist's Mother (also known as *Arrangement in Grey and Black: the Artist's Mother*)	James Abbott McNeill Whistler	Musée d'Orsay, Paris, France	1871–2
At the Moulin Rouge	Henri de Toulouse-Lautrec	Art Institute of Chicago, USA	1895
The Baptism of Christ	Piero della Francesca	National Gallery, London, UK	c.1450
A Bar at the Folies-Bergère	Édouard Manet	Courtauld Institute of Art, London, UK	1882

FAMOUS WORKS OF ART

Art work	Artist or sculptor	Location	Date
The Birth of Venus	Sandro Botticelli	Uffizi Gallery, Florence, Italy	c.1485
Campbell's Soup Cans	Andy Warhol	Museum of Modern Art, New York City, USA	1962
Christ of St John of the Cross	Salvador Dalí	Kelvingrove Art Gallery and Museum, Glasgow, UK	1951
David	Michelangelo	Accademia Gallery, Florence, Italy	1504
Le Déjeuner sur l'herbe	Édouard Manet	Musée d'Orsay, Paris, France	1863
Les Demoiselles d'Avignon	Pablo Picasso	Museum of Modern Art, New York City, USA	1907
The Fighting Téméraire	J M W Turner	National Gallery, London, UK	1839
Girl with a Pearl Earring	Jan Vermeer	Mauritshuis, The Hague, The Netherlands	c.1665
Guernica	Pablo Picasso	Museo Reina Sofia, Madrid, Spain	1937
Haystacks	Claude Monet	various collections worldwide	1890–1
The Hay Wain	John Constable	National Gallery, London, UK	1821
Impression: Rising Sun	Claude Monet	Marmottan Monet Museum, Paris, France	1872
The Kiss	Auguste Rodin	Rodin Museum, Paris, France	1888–9
The Kiss	Gustav Klimt	Österreichische Galerie Belvedere, Vienna, Austria	1907–08
The Last of England	Ford Madox Brown	Birmingham Museum and Art Gallery	1852–5
The Last Supper	Leonardo da Vinci	Santa Maria delle Grazie, Milan, Italy	completed c.1498
Mona Lisa	Leonardo da Vinci	Louvre, Paris, France	1503–6
Mother and Child Divided	Damien Hirst	Astrup Fearnley Museum, Oslo, Norway	1993
Mr and Mrs Clark and Percy	David Hockney	Tate Britain, London, UK	1970–1
Night Café	Vincent Van Gogh	Yale University Art Gallery, New Haven, USA	1888
The Night Watch	Rembrandt	Rijksmuseum, Amsterdam, The Netherlands	1642
The Persistence of Memory (Limp Watches)	Salvador Dalí	Museum of Modern Art, New York City, USA	1931
The Physical Impossibility of Death in the Mind of Someone Living	Damien Hirst	Metropolitan Museum of Art, New York City, USA	1991
The Potato Eaters	Vincent Van Gogh	Van Gogh Museum, Amsterdam, The Netherlands	1885
Rain, Steam and Speed	J M W Turner	National Gallery, London, UK	before 1844
A Rake's Progress	William Hogarth	Sir John Soane's Museum, London, UK	1733–5
Reverend Dr Robert Walker Skating on Duddingston Loch	Henry Raeburn	National Gallery of Scotland, Edinburgh, UK	1795
Rouen Cathedral	Claude Monet	various collections worldwide	1892–4
St George and the Dragon	Paolo Uccello	National Gallery, London, UK	c.1470

Art work	Artist or sculptor	Location	Date
The Scream	Edvard Munch	National Gallery, Oslo, Norway	1893
The Starry Night	Vincent Van Gogh	Museum of Modern Art, New York City, USA	1889
Sunflowers	Vincent Van Gogh	National Gallery, London, UK (and other versions elsewhere)	1888
The Thinker	Auguste Rodin	Rodin Museum, Paris, France (and other versions elsewhere)	1881
36 Views of Mount Fuji	Hokusai	various collections worldwide	c.1826–33
The Three Graces	Antonio Canova	shared between the Victoria and Albert Museum, London, UK, and the National Gallery of Scotland, Edinburgh, UK	1814
The Toilet of Venus (also known as '*The Rokeby Venus*')	Diego Velázquez	National Gallery, London, UK	1647–51
Venus de Milo (also known as *Aphrodite of Melos*)	unknown	Louvre, Paris, France	c.100 BC
Venus Rising from the Sea	Titian	National Gallery of Scotland, Edinburgh, UK	1520
Water Lilies	Claude Monet	various collections worldwide	1899–1906

Scissors, Paper, Stone

In April 2005 the auction houses Christie's and Sotheby's were rivals for the chance to sell a collection of paintings by Picasso, Cezanne and Van Gogh. Unable to decide between the two, the seller asked them to play the children's game of 'scissors, paper, stone'; Sotheby's chose paper but Christie's chose scissors, thus winning the right to sell the £11 million collection.

MUSEUMS AND ART GALLERIES

Museum/Gallery	City	Country
Acropolis Museum	Athens	Greece
Ashmolean Museum of Art and Archaeology	Oxford	United Kingdom
Guggenheim Museum	New York	United States of America
Louvre	Paris	France
Metropolitan Museum of Art	New York	United States of America
Musée d'Orsay	Paris	France
Museum of Modern Art (MoMA)	New York	United States of America
Museum of Modern Art at the Pompidou Centre	Paris	France
National Gallery	London	United Kingdom
Prado Museum	Madrid	Spain
Reina Sofia	Madrid	Spain
Rijksmuseum	Amsterdam	The Netherlands
Stedelijk Museum of Modern Art	Amsterdam	The Netherlands
Tate Gallery	London	United Kingdom
Tate Modern	London	United Kingdom
Uffizi Gallery	Florence	Italy
Van Gogh Museum	Amsterdam	The Netherlands
Victoria and Albert Museum	London	United Kingdom

ACADEMY AWARDS®

Awarded annually by the Academy of Motion Picture Arts and Sciences. Popularly known as Oscars®. Best Actor and Best Actress awards are for performance in a leading role.

Year	**Best Picture** (director)	**Best Actor**	**Best Actress**	**Best Director**
1927/8	*Wings* (William A Wellman)	Emil Jannings *The Last Command*, *The Way of All Flesh*	Janet Gaynor *7th Heaven*, *Street Angel*, *Sunrise*	Lewis Milestone *Two Arabian Knights*; Frank Borzage *7th Heaven*
1928/9	*The Broadway Melody* (Harry Beaumont)	Warner Baxter *In Old Arizona*	Mary Pickford *Coquette*	Frank Lloyd *The Divine Lady*
1929/30	*All Quiet on the Western Front* (Lewis Milestone)	George Arliss *Disraeli*	Norma Shearer *The Divorcee*	Lewis Milestone *All Quiet on the Western Front*
1930/1	*Cimarron* (Wesley Ruggles)	Lionel Barrymore *A Free Soul*	Marie Dressler *Min and Bill*	Norman Taurog *Skippy*
1931/2	*Grand Hotel* (Edmund Goulding)	Wallace Beery *The Champ*; Fredric March *Dr Jekyll and Mr Hyde*	Helen Hayes *The Sin of Madame Claudet*	Frank Borzage *Bad Girl*
1932/3	*Cavalcade* (Frank Lloyd)	Charles Laughton *The Private Life of Henry VIII*	Katharine Hepburn *Morning Glory*	Frank Lloyd *Cavalcade*
1934	*It Happened One Night* (Frank Capra)	Clark Gable *It Happened One Night*	Claudette Colbert *It Happened One Night*	Frank Capra *It Happened One Night*
1935	*Mutiny on the Bounty* (Frank Lloyd)	Victor Laglen *The Informer*	Bette Davis *Dangerous*	John Ford *The Informer*
1936	*The Great Ziegfeld* (Robert Z Leonard)	Paul Muni *The Story of Louis Pasteur*	Luise Rainer *The Great Ziegfeld*	Frank Capra *Mr Deeds Goes to Town*
1937	*The Life of Emile Zola* (William Dieterle)	Spencer Tracy *Captains Courageous*	Luise Rainer *The Good Earth*	Leo McCarey *The Awful Truth*
1938	*You Can't Take It with You* (Frank Capra)	Spencer Tracy *Boys Town*	Bette Davis *Jezebel*	Frank Capra *You Can't Take It with You*
1939	*Gone with the Wind* (Victor Fleming)	Robert Donat *Goodbye, Mr Chips*	Vivien Leigh *Gone with the Wind*	Victor Fleming *Gone with the Wind*
1940	*Rebecca* (Alfred Hitchcock)	James Stewart *The Philadelphia Story*	Ginger Rogers *Kitty Foyle*	John Ford *The Grapes of Wrath*
1941	*How Green Was My Valley* (John Ford)	Gary Cooper *Sergeant York*	Joan Fontaine *Suspicion*	John Ford *How Green Was My Valley*
1942	*Mrs Miniver* (William Wyler)	James Cagney *Yankee Doodle Dandy*	Greer Garson *Mrs Miniver*	William Wyler *Mrs Miniver*

Year	**Best Picture** (director)	**Best Actor**	**Best Actress**	**Best Director**
1943	*Casablanca* (Michael Curtiz)	Paul Lukas *Watch on the Rhine*	Jennifer Jones *The Song of Bernadette*	Michael Curtiz *Casablanca*
1944	*Going My Way* (Leo McCarey)	Bing Crosby *Going My Way*	Ingrid Bergman *Gaslight*	Leo McCarey *Going My Way*
1945	*The Lost Weekend* (Billy Wilder)	Ray Milland *The Lost Weekend*	Joan Crawford *Mildred Pierce*	Billy Wilder *The Lost Weekend*
1946	*The Best Years of Our Lives* (William Wyler)	Fredric March *The Best Years of Our Lives*	Olivia de Havilland *To Each His Own*	William Wyler *The Best Years of Our Lives*
1947	*Gentleman's Agreement* (Elia Kazan)	Ronald Colman *A Double Life*	Loretta Young *The Farmer's Daughter*	Elia Kazan *Gentleman's Agreement*
1948	*Hamlet* (Laurence Olivier)	Laurence Olivier *Hamlet*	Jane Wyman *Johnny Belinda*	John Huston *The Treasure of the Sierra Madre*
1949	*All the King's Men* (Robert Rossen)	Broderick Crawford *All the King's Men*	Olivia de Havilland *The Heiress*	Joseph L Mankiewicz *A Letter to Three Wives*
1950	*All About Eve* (Joseph L Mankiewicz)	José Ferrer *Cyrano de Bergerac*	Judy Holliday *Born Yesterday*	Joseph L Mankiewicz *All About Eve*
1951	*An American in Paris* (Vincente Minnelli)	Humphrey Bogart *The African Queen*	Vivien Leigh *A Streetcar Named Desire*	George Stevens *A Place in the Sun*
1952	*The Greatest Show on Earth* (Cecil B De Mille)	Gary Cooper *High Noon*	Shirley Booth *Come Back, Little Sheba*	John Ford *The Quiet Man*
1953	*From Here to Eternity* (Fred Zinnemann)	William Holden *Stalag 17*	Audrey Hepburn *Roman Holiday*	Fred Zinnemann *From Here to Eternity*
1954	*On the Waterfront* (Elia Kazan)	Marlon Brando *On the Waterfront*	Grace Kelly *The Country Girl*	Elia Kazan *On the Waterfront*
1955	*Marty* (Delbert Mann)	Ernest Borgnine *Marty*	Anna Magnani *The Rose Tattoo*	Delbert Mann *Marty*
1956	*Around the World in 80 Days* (Michael Anderson)	Yul Brynner *The King and I*	Ingrid Bergman *Anastasia*	George Stevens *Giant*
1957	*The Bridge on the River Kwai* (David Lean)	Alec Guinness *The Bridge on the River Kwai*	Joanne Woodward *The Three Faces of Eve*	David Lean *The Bridge on the River Kwai*
1958	*Gigi* (Vincente Minnelli)	David Niven *Separate Tables*	Susan Hayward *I Want To Live!*	Vincente Minnelli *Gigi*
1959	*Ben-Hur* (William Wyler)	Charlton Heston *Ben-Hur*	Simone Signoret *Room at the Top*	William Wyler *Ben-Hur*
1960	*The Apartment* (Billy Wilder)	Burt Lancaster *Elmer Gantry*	Elizabeth Taylor *Butterfield 8*	Billy Wilder *The Apartment*
1961	*West Side Story* (Robert Wise, Jerome Robbins)	Maximilian Schell *Judgment at Nuremberg*	Sophia Loren *Two Women*	Robert Wise, Jerome Robbins *West Side Story*

ACADEMY AWARDS®

Year	**Best Picture** (director)	**Best Actor**	**Best Actress**	**Best Director**
1962	*Lawrence of Arabia* (David Lean)	Gregory Peck *To Kill a Mockingbird*	Anne Bancroft *The Miracle Worker*	David Lean *Lawrence of Arabia*
1963	*Tom Jones* (Tony Richardson)	Sidney Poitier *Lilies of the Field*	Patricia Neal *Hud*	Tony Richardson *Tom Jones*
1964	*My Fair Lady* (George Cukor)	Rex Harrison *My Fair Lady*	Julie Andrews *Mary Poppins*	George Cukor *My Fair Lady*
1965	*The Sound of Music* (Robert Wise)	Lee Marvin *Cat Ballou*	Julie Christie *Darling*	Robert Wise *The Sound of Music*
1966	*A Man for All Seasons* (Fred Zinnemann)	Paul Scofield *A Man for All Seasons*	Elizabeth Taylor *Who's Afraid of Virginia Woolf?*	Fred Zinnemann *A Man for All Seasons*
1967	*In the Heat of the Night* (Norman Jewison)	Rod Steiger *In the Heat of the Night*	Katharine Hepburn *Guess Who's Coming to Dinner*	Mike Nichols *The Graduate*
1968	*Oliver!* (Carol Reed)	Cliff Robertson *Charly*	Katharine Hepburn *The Lion in Winter*; Barbra Streisand *Funny Girl*	Carol Reed *Oliver!*
1969	*Midnight Cowboy* (John Schlesinger)	John Wayne *True Grit*	Maggie Smith *The Prime of Miss Jean Brodie*	John Schlesinger *Midnight Cowboy*
1970	*Patton* (Franklin J Schaffner)	George C Scott *Patton*	Glenda Jackson *Women in Love*	Franklin J Schaffner *Patton*
1971	*The French Connection* (William Friedkin)	Gene Hackman *The French Connection*	Jane Fonda *Klute*	William Friedkin *The French Connection*
1972	*The Godfather* (Francis Ford Coppola)	Marlon Brando *The Godfather*	Liza Minnelli *Cabaret*	Bob Fosse *Cabaret*
1973	*The Sting* (George Roy Hill)	Jack Lemmon *Save the Tiger*	Glenda Jackson *A Touch of Class*	George Roy Hill *The Sting*
1974	*The Godfather Part II* (Francis Ford Coppola)	Art Carney *Harry and Tonto*	Ellen Burstyn *Alice Doesn't Live Here Anymore*	Francis Ford Coppola *The Godfather Part II*
1975	*One Flew Over the Cuckoo's Nest* (Milos Forman)	Jack Nicholson *One Flew Over the Cuckoo's Nest*	Louise Fletcher *One Flew Over the Cuckoo's Nest*	Milos Forman *One Flew Over the Cuckoo's Nest*
1976	*Rocky* (John G Avildsen)	Peter Finch *Network*	Faye Dunaway *Network*	John G Avildsen *Rocky*
1977	*Annie Hall* (Woody Allen)	Richard Dreyfuss *The Goodbye Girl*	Diane Keaton *Annie Hall*	Woody Allen *Annie Hall*
1978	*The Deer Hunter* (Michael Cimino)	Jon Voight *Coming Home*	Jane Fonda *Coming Home*	Michael Cimino *The Deer Hunter*
1979	*Kramer vs Kramer* (Robert Benton)	Dustin Hoffman *Kramer vs Kramer*	Sally Field *Norma Rae*	Robert Benton *Kramer vs Kramer*
1980	*Ordinary People* (Robert Redford)	Robert De Niro *Raging Bull*	Sissy Spacek *Coal Miner's Daughter*	Robert Redford *Ordinary People*

Year	**Best Picture** (director)	**Best Actor**	**Best Actress**	**Best Director**
1981	*Chariots of Fire* (Hugh Hudson)	Henry Fonda *On Golden Pond*	Katharine Hepburn *On Golden Pond*	Warren Beatty *Reds*
1982	*Gandhi* (Richard Attenborough)	Ben Kingsley *Gandhi*	Meryl Streep *Sophie's Choice*	Richard Attenborough *Gandhi*
1983	*Terms of Endearment* (James L Brooks)	Robert Duvall *Tender Mercies*	Shirley MacLaine *Terms of Endearment*	James L Brooks *Terms of Endearment*
1984	*Amadeus* (Milos Forman)	F Murray Abraham *Amadeus*	Sally Field *Places in the Heart*	Milos Forman *Amadeus*
1985	*Out of Africa* (Sydney Pollack)	William Hurt *Kiss of the Spider Woman*	Geraldine Page *The Trip to Bountiful*	Sydney Pollack *Out of Africa*
1986	*Platoon* (Oliver Stone)	Paul Newman *The Color of Money*	Marlee Matlin *Children of a Lesser God*	Oliver Stone *Platoon*
1987	*The Last Emperor* (Bernardo Bertolucci)	Michael Douglas *Wall Street*	Cher *Moonstruck*	Bernardo Bertolucci *The Last Emperor*
1988	*Rain Man* (Barry Levinson)	Dustin Hoffman *Rain Man*	Jodie Foster *The Accused*	Barry Levinson *Rain Man*
1989	*Driving Miss Daisy* (Bruce Beresford)	Daniel Day-Lewis *My Left Foot*	Jessica Tandy *Driving Miss Daisy*	Oliver Stone *Born on the Fourth of July*
1990	*Dances With Wolves* (Kevin Costner)	Jeremy Irons *Reversal of Fortune*	Kathy Bates *Misery*	Kevin Costner *Dances With Wolves*
1991	*The Silence of the Lambs* (Jonathan Demme)	Anthony Hopkins *The Silence of the Lambs*	Jodie Foster *The Silence of the Lambs*	Jonathan Demme *The Silence of the Lambs*
1992	*Unforgiven* (Clint Eastwood)	Al Pacino *Scent of a Woman*	Emma Thompson *Howards End*	Clint Eastwood *Unforgiven*
1993	*Schindler's List* (Steven Spielberg)	Tom Hanks *Philadelphia*	Holly Hunter *The Piano*	Steven Spielberg *Schindler's List*
1994	*Forrest Gump* (Robert Zemeckis)	Tom Hanks *Forrest Gump*	Jessica Lange *Blue Sky*	Robert Zemeckis *Forrest Gump*
1995	*Braveheart* (Mel Gibson)	Nicolas Cage *Leaving Las Vegas*	Susan Sarandon *Dead Man Walking*	Mel Gibson *Braveheart*
1996	*The English Patient* (Anthony Minghella)	Geoffrey Rush *Shine*	Frances McDormand *Fargo*	Anthony Minghella *The English Patient*
1997	*Titanic* (James Cameron)	Jack Nicholson *As Good As It Gets*	Helen Hunt *As Good As It Gets*	James Cameron *Titanic*
1998	*Shakespeare in Love* (Guy Madden)	Roberto Benigni *Life Is Beautiful*	Gwyneth Paltrow *Shakespeare in Love*	Steven Spielberg *Saving Private Ryan*

Year	**Best Picture** (director)	**Best Actor**	**Best Actress**	**Best Director**
1999	*American Beauty* (Sam Mendes)	Kevin Spacey *American Beauty*	Hilary Swank *Boys Don't Cry*	Sam Mendes *American Beauty*
2000	*Gladiator* (Ridley Scott)	Russell Crowe *Gladiator*	Julia Roberts *Erin Brockovich*	Steven Soderbergh *Traffic*
2001	*A Beautiful Mind* (Ron Howard)	Denzel Washington *Training Day*	Halle Berry *Monster's Ball*	Ron Howard *A Beautiful Mind*
2002	*Chicago* (Rob Marshall)	Adrien Brody *The Pianist*	Nicole Kidman *The Hours*	Roman Polanski *The Pianist*
2003	*The Lord of the Rings: The Return of the King* (Peter Jackson)	Sean Penn *Mystic River*	Charlize Theron *Monster*	Peter Jackson *The Lord of the Rings: The Return of the King*
2004	*Million Dollar Baby* (Clint Eastwood)	Jamie Foxx *Ray*	Hilary Swank *Million Dollar Baby*	Clint Eastwood *Million Dollar Baby*
2005	*Crash* (Paul Haggis)	Philip Seymour Hoffman *Capote*	Reese Witherspoon *Walk the Line*	Ang Lee *Brokeback Mountain*
2006	*The Departed* (Martin Scorsese)	Forest Whitaker *The Last King of Scotland*	Helen Mirren *The Queen*	Martin Scorsese *The Departed*
2007	*No Country For Old Men* (Joel and Ethan Coen)	Daniel Day-Lewis *There Will Be Blood*	Marion Cotillard *La Vie en Rose*	Joel and Ethan Coen *No Country for Old Men*

Most Successful

It Happened One Night (1934), *One Flew Over the Cuckoo's Nest* (1975) and *The Silence of the Lambs* (1991) are members of a very exclusive club: the only three films to have won all of the five most prestigious Oscars® (for Best Film, Actor, Actress, Director and Writing).

ORANGE BRITISH ACADEMY FILM AWARDS

The British Film Academy was founded in 1947, and in 1975 changed its name to the British Academy of Film and Television Arts (BAFTA). Best Actor and Best Actress awards are for performance in a leading role.

Year	**Best Film** (director)	**Best Actor**	**Best Actress**	**Best Direction**
1947	*The Best Years of our Lives* (William Wyler)			
1948	Hamlet (Laurence Olivier)			
1949	*The Bicycle Thief* (Vittorio De Sica)			
1950	*All About Eve* (Joseph L Mankiewicz)			
1951	*La Ronde* (Max Ophuls)			
1952	*The Sound Barrier* (David Lean)	Ralph Richardson *The Sound Barrier*	Vivien Leigh *A Streetcar Named Desire*	
1953	*Forbidden Games* (René Clément)	John Gielgud *Julius Caesar*	Audrey Hepburn *Roman Holiday*	
1954	*The Wages of Fear* (Henri-Georges Clouzot)	Kenneth More *Doctor in the House*	Yvonne Mitchell *The Divided Heart*	
1955	*Richard III* (Laurence Olivier)	Laurence Olivier *Richard III*	Katie Johnson *The Ladykillers*	
1956	*Gervaise* (René Clément)	Peter Finch *A Town Like Alice*	Virginia McKenna *A Town Like Alice*	
1957	*The Bridge on the River Kwai* (David Lean)	Alec Guinness *The Bridge on the River Kwai*	Heather Sears *The Story of Esther Costello*	
1958	*Room at the Top* (Jack Clayton)	Trevor Howard *The Key*	Irene Worth *Orders to Kill*	
1959	*Ben-Hur* (William Wyler)	Peter Sellers *I'm All Right Jack*	Audrey Hepburn *The Nun's Story*	
1960	*The Apartment* (Billy Wilder)	Peter Finch *The Trials of Oscar Wilde*	Rachel Roberts *Saturday Night and Sunday Morning*	
1961	*Ballad of a Soldier* (Grigori Chukhraj); *The Hustler* (Robert Rossen)	Peter Finch *No Love for Johnnie*	Dora Bryan *A Taste of Honey*	
1962	*Lawrence of Arabia* (David Lean)	Peter O'Toole *Lawrence of Arabia*	Leslie Caron *The L-shaped Room*	
1963	*Tom Jones* (Tony Richardson)	Dirk Bogarde *The Servant*	Rachel Roberts *This Sporting Life*	
1964	*Dr Strangelove* (Stanley Kubrick)	Richard Attenborough *Séance on a Wet Afternoon, Guns at Batasi*	Audrey Hepburn *Charade*	
1965	*My Fair Lady* (George Cukor)	Dirk Bogarde *Darling*	Julie Christie *Darling*	

ORANGE BRITISH ACADEMY FILM AWARDS

Year	**Best Film** (director)	**Best Actor**	**Best Actress**	**Best Direction**
1966	*Who's Afraid of Virginia Woolf?* (Mike Nichols)	Richard Burton *The Spy Who Came in from the Cold*	Elizabeth Taylor *Who's Afraid of Virginia Woolf?*	
1967	*A Man for All Seasons* (Fred Zinnemann)	Paul Scofield *A Man for All Seasons*	Edith Evans *The Whisperers*	
1968	*The Graduate* (Mike Nichols)	Spencer Tracy *Guess Who's Coming to Dinner?*	Katharine Hepburn *Guess Who's Coming to Dinner? The Lion in Winter*	Mike Nichols *The Graduate*
1969	*Midnight Cowboy* (John Schlesinger)	Dustin Hoffman *Midnight Cowboy, John and Mary*	Maggie Smith *The Prime of Miss Jean Brodie*	John Schlesinger *Midnight Cowboy*
1970	*Butch Cassidy and the Sundance Kid* (George Roy Hill)	Robert Redford *Butch Cassidy and the Sundance Kid, Tell Them Willie Boy is Here, Downhill Racer*	Katharine Ross *Butch Cassidy and the Sundance Kid, Tell Them Willie Boy is Here*	George Roy Hill *Butch Cassidy and the Sundance Kid*
1971	*Sunday, Bloody Sunday* (John Schlesinger)	Peter Finch *Sunday, Bloody Sunday*	Glenda Jackson *Sunday, Bloody Sunday*	John Schlesinger *Sunday, Bloody Sunday*
1972	*Cabaret* (Bob Fosse)	Gene Hackman *The French Connection, The Poseidon Adventure*	Liza Minnelli *Cabaret*	Bob Fosse *Cabaret*
1973	*Day for Night* (François Truffaut)	Walter Matthau *Pete 'n' Tillie, Charley Varrick*	Stéphane Audran *The Discreet Charm of the Bourgeoisie, Just Before Nightfall*	François Truffaut *Day for Night*
1974	*Lacombe Lucien* (Louis Malle)	Jack Nicholson *Chinatown, The Last Detail*	Joanne Woodward *Summer Wishes, Winter Dreams*	Roman Polanski *Chinatown*
1975	*Alice Doesn't Live Here Anymore* (Martin Scorsese)	Al Pacino *Dog Day Afternoon, The Godfather II*	Ellen Burstyn *Alice Doesn't Live Here Anymore*	Stanley Kubrick *Barry Lyndon*
1976	*One Flew Over the Cuckoo's Nest* (Milos Forman)	Jack Nicholson *One Flew Over the Cuckoo's Nest*	Louise Fletcher *One Flew Over the Cuckoo's Nest*	Milos Forman *One Flew Over the Cuckoo's Nest*
1977	*Annie Hall* (Woody Allen)	Peter Finch *Network*	Diane Keaton *Annie Hall*	Woody Allen *Annie Hall*
1978	*Julia* (Fred Zinnemann)	Richard Dreyfuss *The Goodbye Girl*	Jane Fonda *Julia*	Alan Parker *Midnight Express*
1979	*Manhattan* (Woody Allen)	Jack Lemmon *The China Syndrome*	Jane Fonda *The China Syndrome*	Francis Ford Coppola *Apocalypse Now*
1980	*The Elephant Man* (Jonathan Sanger)	John Hurt *The Elephant Man*	Judy Davis *My Brilliant Career*	Akira Kurosawa *Kagemusha*
1981	*Chariots of Fire* (Hugh Hudson)	Burt Lancaster *Atlantic City*	Meryl Streep *The French Lieutenant's Woman*	Louis Malle *Atlantic City*
1982	*Gandhi* (Richard Attenborough)	Ben Kingsley *Gandhi*	Katharine Hepburn *On Golden Pond*	Richard Attenborough *Gandhi*

ORANGE BRITISH ACADEMY FILM AWARDS

Year	**Best Film** (director)	**Best Actor**	**Best Actress**	**Best Direction**
1983	*Educating Rita* (Lewis Gilbert)	Michael Caine *Educating Rita*; Dustin Hoffman *Tootsie*	Julie Walters *Educating Rita*	Bill Forsyth *Local Hero*
1984	*The Killing Fields* (Roland Joffe)	Haing S Ngor *The Killing Fields*	Maggie Smith *A Private Function*	Wim Wenders *Paris, Texas*
1985	*The Purple Rose of Cairo* (Woody Allen)	William Hurt *Kiss of the Spider Woman*	Peggy Ashcroft *A Passage to India*	*no award*
1986	*A Room With a View* (James Ivory)	Bob Hoskins *Mona Lisa*	Maggie Smith *A Room With a View*	Woody Allen *Hannah and Her Sisters*
1987	*Jean de Florette* (Claude Berri)	Sean Connery *The Name of the Rose*	Anne Bancroft *84 Charing Cross Road*	Oliver Stone *Platoon*
1988	*The Last Emperor* (Bernardo Bertolucci)	John Cleese *A Fish Called Wanda*	Maggie Smith *The Lonely Passion of Judith Hearne*	Louis Malle *Au Revoir Les Enfants*
1989	*Dead Poets Society* (Peter Weir)	Daniel Day-Lewis *My Left Foot*	Pauline Collins *Shirley Valentine*	Kenneth Branagh *Henry V*
1990	*Goodfellas* (Martin Scorsese)	Philippe Noiret *Cinema Paradiso*	Jessica Tandy *Driving Miss Daisy*	Martin Scorsese *Goodfellas*
1991	*The Commitments* (Alan Parker)	Anthony Hopkins *The Silence of the Lambs*	Jodie Foster *The Silence of the Lambs*	Alan Parker *The Commitments*
1992	*Howards End* (James Ivory)	Robert Downey Jnr *Chaplin*	Emma Thompson *Howards End*	Robert Altman *The Player*
1993	*Schindler's List* (Steven Spielberg)	Anthony Hopkins *The Remains of the Day*	Holly Hunter *The Piano*	Steven Spielberg *Schindler's List*
1994	*Four Weddings and a Funeral* (Mike Newell)	Hugh Grant *Four Weddings and a Funeral*	Susan Sarandon *The Client*	Mike Newell *Four Weddings and a Funeral*
1995	*Sense and Sensibility* (Ang Lee)	Nigel Hawthorne *The Madness of King George*	Emma Thompson *Sense and Sensibility*	Michael Radford *Il Postino*
1996	*The English Patient* (Anthony Minghella)	Geoffrey Rush *Shine*	Brenda Blethyn *Secrets and Lies*	Joel Coen *Fargo*
1997	*The Full Monty* (Peter Cattaneo)	Tom Wilkinson *The Full Monty*	Judi Dench *Mrs Brown*	Baz Luhrmann *Romeo and Juliet*
1998	*Shakespeare in Love* (John Madden)	Roberto Benigni *Life is Beautiful*	Cate Blanchett *Elizabeth*	Peter Weir *The Truman Show*
1999	*American Beauty* (Sam Mendes)	Kevin Spacey *American Beauty*	Annette Bening *American Beauty*	Pedro Almodovar *All About My Mother*
2000	*Gladiator* (Ridley Scott)	Jamie Bell *Billy Elliot*	Julia Roberts *Erin Brockovich*	Ang Lee *Crouching Tiger, Hidden Dragon*
2001	*The Lord of the Rings: The Fellowship of the Ring* (Peter Jackson)	Russell Crowe *A Beautiful Mind*	Judi Dench *Iris*	Peter Jackson *The Lord of the Rings: The Fellowship of the Ring*
2002	*The Pianist* (Roman Polanski)	Daniel Day-Lewis *Gangs of New York*	Nicole Kidman *The Hours*	Roman Polanski *The Pianist*

Year	**Best Film** (director)	**Best Actor**	**Best Actress**	**Best Direction**
2003	*The Lord of the Rings: The Return of the King* (Peter Jackson)	Bill Murray *Lost in Translation*	Scarlett Johansson *Lost in Translation*	Peter Weir *Master and Commander: The Far Side of the World*
2004	*The Aviator* (Martin Scorsese)	Jamie Foxx *Ray*	Imelda Staunton *Vera Drake*	Mike Leigh *Vera Drake*
2005	*Brokeback Mountain* (Ang Lee)	Philip Seymour Hoffman *Capote*	Reese Witherspoon *Walk the Line*	Ang Lee *Brokeback Mountain*
2006	*The Queen* (Steven Frears)	Forest Whitaker *The Last King of Scotland*	Helen Mirren *The Queen*	Paul Greengrass *United 93*
2007	*Atonement* (Joe Wright)	Daniel Day-Lewis *There Will Be Blood*	Marion Cotillard *La Vie en Rose*	Joel and Ethan Coen *No Country for Old Men*

Continuity Chaos

Sharp-eyed movie buffs are constantly on the lookout for continuity errors, anachronisms and other mistakes in films. From camera crews reflected in plate-glass windows to Roman centurions wearing watches, some of the worst howlers have passed into film legend. These include the Von Trapp family fleeing over the mountains straight into enemy Germany at the end of *The Sound of Music* (1965), Dorothy's hair varying in length in *The Wizard of Oz* (1939) and a passenger in a lifeboat wearing a digital watch in *Titanic* (1997). Other classic gaffes include a distant aeroplane flying past in one scene in *Ben-Hur* (1959), a storm trooper banging his head in *StarWars* (1977) and a building marked 'Est. 1953' in World War II film *Pearl Harbor* (2001). Scenes involving food, drink and cigars or cigarettes are also a continuity nightmare for filmmakers: watch the fluctuating levels of alcohol in the wine glasses in *The Godfather* (1972) and the half-eaten hamburgers in *Pulp Fiction* (1994).

PALME D'OR

The Cannes Film Festival began in 1946 and is the world's leading festival of its kind. The *Palme d'Or* (Golden Palm) for best film has been awarded every year since 1955. The director is given in brackets.

1955	*Marty* (Delbert Mann)
1956	*The Silent World* (*Le monde du silence*) (Jacques-Yves Cousteau)
1957	*Friendly Persuasion* (William Wyler)
1958	*The Cranes are Flying* (*Letiat zhuravli*) (Mikhail Kalatozov)
1959	*Black Orpheus* (*Orfeu negro*) (Marcel Camus)
1960	*La Dolce Vita* (Federico Fellini)
1961	*Viridiana* (Luis Buñuel); *Une aussi longue absence* (Henri Colpi)
1962	*The Given Word* (*O Pagador de promessas*) (Anselmo Duarte)
1963	*The Leopard* (*Il gattopardi*) (Luchino Visconti)
1964	*The Umbrellas of Cherbourg* (*Les parapluies de Cherbourg*) (Jacques Demy)
1965	*The Knack … And How to Get It* (Richard Lester)
1966	*A Man and a Woman* (*Un homme et une femme*) (Claude Lelouch)
1967	*Blow-Up* (Michelangelo Antonioni)
1968	*festival cancelled*
1969	*If …* (Lindsay Anderson)
1970	*M*A*S*H* (Robert Altman)
1971	*The Go-Between* (Joseph Losey)

1972 *The Mattei Affair* (*Il caso Mattei*) (Francesco Rossi); *The Working Class Go to Heaven* (*La classe operaia va in paradiso*) (Elio Petri)
1973 *Scarecrow* (Jerry Schatzberg); *The Hireling* (Alan Bridges)
1974 *The Conversation* (Francis Ford Coppola)
1975 *Chronicle of the Years of Embers* (*Ahdat danawouach eldjamr*) (Mohammed Lakhdar Hamina)
1976 *Taxi Driver* (Martin Scorsese)
1977 *Padro Padrone* (Paolo and Vittorio Taviani)
1978 *The Tree of Wooden Clogs* (*L'albero degli zoccoli*) (Ermanno Olmi)
1979 *Apocalypse Now* (Francis Ford Coppola); *The Tin Drum* (*Die Blechtrommel*) (Volker Schlöndorff)
1980 *Kagemusha* (Akira Kurosawa); *All That Jazz* (Bob Fosse)
1981 *Man of Iron* (*Człowieck z żelaza*) (Andrzej Wajda)
1982 *Missing* (Costa-Gavras); *Yol* (Yilmaz Güney)
1983 *The Ballad of Narayama* (*Narayama bushi ko*) (Shohei Imamura)
1984 *Paris, Texas* (Wim Wenders)
1985 *When Father was Away on Business* (*Otak na sluažbenom putu*) (Emir Kusturica)
1986 *The Mission* (Roland Joffe)
1987 *Under Satan's Sun* (*Sous le soleil de satan*) (Maurice Pialat)
1988 *Pelle the Conquerer* (*Pell erobreren*) (Bille August)
1989 *sex, lies and videotape* (Steven Soderbergh)
1990 *Wild at Heart* (David Lynch)
1991 *Barton Fink* (Joel and Ethan Coen)
1992 *The Best Intentions* (*Den goda vilijan*) (Bille August)
1993 *The Piano* (Jane Campion); *Farewell my Concubine* (Chen Kaige)
1994 *Pulp Fiction* (Quentin Tarantino)
1995 *Underground* (Emir Kusturica)
1996 *Secrets and Lies* (Mike Leigh)
1997 *The Eel* (*Unagi*) (Shohei Imamura); *A Taste of Cherry* (*Ta'me guilass*) (Abbas Kiarostami)
1998 *Eternity and a Day* (*Mia eoniotita ke mia mera*) (Theo Angelopoulos)
1999 *Rosetta* (Luc and Jean-Pierre Dardenne)
2000 *Dancer in the Dark* (Lars von Trier)
2001 *The Son's Room* (*La stanza del figlio*) (Nanni Moretti)
2002 *The Pianist* (Roman Polanski)
2003 *Elephant* (Gus Van Sant)
2004 *Fahrenheit 9/11* (Michael Moore)
2005 *L'enfant* (Jean-Pierre and Luc Dardenne)
2006 *The Wind that Shakes the Barley* (Ken Loach)
2007 *4 Months, 3 Weeks and 2 Days* (*4 luni, 3 săptămâni şi 2 zile*) (Cristian Mungiu)

Fear Factor

In 2004, researchers from King's College in London announced that they had calculated the formula for the perfect horror film:

(es + u + cs + t) squared + s + (tl + f)/2 + (a + dr + fs)/n + sin x − 1

In the equation es = escalating music, u = the unknown, cs = chase scenes, t = being trapped, s = shock, tl = true life, f = fantasy, a = being alone, dr = in the dark, fs = film setting, n = number of people, sin x = blood and guts and 1 = stereotypes. Using the equation, the researchers announced that *The Shining* was the best horror film of all time.

MAJOR FILM FESTIVALS

Festival	Location	Major Prize
Bangkok	Bangkok, Thailand	Golden Kinnaree
Berlin	Berlin, Germany	Golden Bear
Cairo	Cairo, Egypt	Golden Pyramid
Cannes	Cannes, France	Palme d'Or
Cartagena	Cartagena, Colombia	Golden India Catalina
Chicago	Chicago, Illinois, USA	Gold Hugo
Cleveland	Cleveland, Ohio, USA	Best Film
Copenhagen	Copenhagen, Denmark	Golden Swan
Edinburgh	Edinburgh, Scotland, UK	Audience Award
Havana	Havana, Cuba	Grand Coral
Istanbul	Istanbul, Turkey	Golden Tulip
Locarno	Locarno, Switzerland	Golden Leopard
London	London, England, UK	Sutherland Trophy
Melbourne	Melbourne, Australia	Best Film
Montreal	Montreal, Canada	Grand Prix des Amériques
Moscow	Moscow, Russia	Golden St George
Paris	Paris, France	Grand Prix
Rotterdam	Rotterdam, The Netherlands	Tiger Award
San Francisco	San Francisco, California, USA	Golden Gate
San Sebastian	San Sebastian, Spain	Golden Seashell
Seattle	Seattle, Washington, USA	Golden Space Needle
Stockholm	Stockholm, Sweden	Bronze Horse
Sundance	Park City, Utah, USA	Grand Jury Prize
Tokyo	Tokyo, Japan	Grand Prix
Toronto	Toronto, Canada	People's Choice Award
Venice	Venice, Italy	Golden Lion
Vevey	Vevey, Switzerland	Golden Cane

ACTORS' REAL NAMES

Pseudonym	Real name
Alda, Alan	Alphonso Joseph d'Abruzzo
Allen, Woody	Allen Stewart Konigsberg
Andrews, Dame Julie	Julia Elizabeth Wells
Astaire, Fred	Frederick Austerlitz
Bacall, Lauren	Betty Perske
Bancroft, Anne	Anna Maria Louisa Italiano
Bardot, Brigitte	Camille Javal
Bernhardt, Sarah	Sarah-Marie-Henriette Rosine Bernard
Bogarde, Sir Dirk	Derek Jules Ulric Niven van den Bogaerde
Bronson, Charles	Charles Buchinsky
Brooks, Mel	Melvin Kaminsky
Burton, Richard	Richard Walter Jenkins
Cage, Nicolas	Nicholas Coppola
Caine, Sir Michael	Maurice Micklewhite
Cher	Cheryl Sarkisian La Pier
Coltrane, Robbie	Robin McMillan
Crawford, Joan	Lucille Le Sueur
Crosby, Bing	Harry Lillis Crosby
Cruise, Tom	Tom Cruise Mapother IV
Curtis, Tony	Bernard Schwartz
Day, Doris	Doris Kappelhoff
Deneuve, Catherine	Catherine Dorléac
Dietrich, Marlene	Maria Magdalena von Losch
Dors, Diana	Diana Fluck
Douglas, Kirk	Issur Danielovich
Fairbanks, Douglas	Douglas Elton Ullman
Fields, W C	William Claude Dukenfield
Flynn, Errol	Leslie Thomson Flynn
Foster, Jodie	Alicia Christian Foster
Garbo, Greta	Greta Lovisa Gustafsson

Pseudonym	Real name
Gardner, Ava	Lucy Johnson
Garland, Judy	Frances Ethel Gumm
Gish, Lillian Diana	Lillian de Guiche
Goldberg, Whoopi	Caryn Johnson
Grant, Cary	Archibald Leach
Grant, Richard E	Richard Grant Esterhuysen
Hardy, Oliver	Norvell Hardy Junior
Harlow, Jean	Harlean Carpentier
Hayworth, Rita	Margarita Carmen Cansino
Hepburn, Audrey	Edda Van Heemstra Hepburn-Ruston
Heston, Charlton	Charles Carter
Hill, Benny	Alfred Hawthorne Hill
Holm, Sir Ian	Ian Holm Cuthbert
Irving, Sir Henry	John Henry Brodribb
Jacques, Hattie	Josephine Edwina Jacques
Jason, David	David John White
Jolson, Al	Asa Yoelson
Karloff, Boris	William Henry Pratt
Keaton, Diane	Diane Hall
Keith, Penelope	Penelope Hatfield
Kingsley, Ben	Krishna Bhanji
Lancaster, Burt	Stephen Burton Lancaster
Laurel, Stan	Arthur Stanley Jefferson
Leigh, Vivien	Vivian Mary Hartley
Lindsay, Robert	Robert Lindsay Stevenson
Lombard, Carole	Jane Alice Peters
Loren, Sophia	Sofia Scicolone
Lugosi, Bela	Bela Ferenc Denzso Blasko
MacLaine, Shirley	Shirley MacLean Beaty
Matthau, Walter	Walter Matuschanskavasky
Mirren, Helen	Helen Lydia Mironoff
Monroe, Marilyn	Norma Jean Mortenson
Montand, Yves	Ivo Livi
Moore, Demi	Demi Guynes
Moore, Julianne	Julie Anne Smith
Neeson, Liam	William John Neeson
Niven, David	James David Graham Nevins
Pickford, Mary	Gladys Mary Smith
Robinson, Edward G	Emanuel Goldenberg
Rogers, Ginger	Virginia Katherine McMath
Russell, Lillian	Helen Louise Leonard
Ryder, Winona	Winona Horowitz
Scales, Prunella	Prunella Margaret Rumney Illingworth
Shepard, Sam	Samuel Shepard Rogers
Spacey, Kevin	Kevin Fowler
Stanwyck, Barbara	Ruby Stevens
Streisand, Barbra	Barbara Joan Rosen
Swanson, Gloria	Gloria May Josephine Svensson
Turner, Lana	Julia Jean Mildred Frances Turner
Valentino, Rudolph	Rodolpho Alphonso Guglielmi di Valentina d'Antonguolla
Wayne, John	Marion Michael Morrison
Welch, Raquel	Raquel Tejada
Wood, Natalie	Natasha Gurdin
York, Susannah	Susannah Yolande-Fletcher

Cameo Leach

Cary Grant used to enjoy sneaking his real name into his films. In *His Girl Friday* (1940) Grant refers in conversation to a man named Archie Leach, while the same name appears on a tombstone behind Grant in a graveyard scene in *Arsenic and Old Lace* (1944).

FILM RECORDS

First film	Thomas Edison and William Dickson pioneered the Kinetoscope in the early 1890s, showing short films such as 'The Sneeze' (1894); in 1895 Auguste and Louis Lumière patented the Cinematograph which they demonstrated in public with such short films as 'Arrival of Train at Station'.
First feature film with sound	*The Jazz Singer* (1927) featured short spoken clips and music, though other experiments with sound had been made with shorter films.

Oldest star	Jeanne Louise Calment appeared as herself in the film *Vincent and Me* (1990) at the age of 114. She lived to the age of 122.
Youngest star	Leroy Overacker appeared in the film *A Bedtime Story* (1933) at the age of 6 months, and received star billing.
Longest shot in a feature film	*Russian Ark* (2001) consists entirely of one long shot lasting 96 minutes.
Highest box office gross	*Titanic* (1997) is the most successful film of all time, and was the first to gross more than $1 billion internationally.
Film with most Academy Awards®	*Ben-Hur* (1959), *Titanic* (1997) and *The Lord of the Rings: The Return of the King* (2003) have won 11 Academy Awards®.
Most Academy Awards® for Best Actress	Katharine Hepburn won four Academy Awards, all for Best Actress, in 1932, 1967, 1968 and 1981.
Most Academy Awards® for Best Actor	Seven actors have won two Academy Awards® for Best Actor: Fredric March, Spencer Tracy, Gary Cooper, Marlon Brando, Jack Nicholson, Dustin Hoffman and Tom Hanks.
Most Academy Awards® in total	Walt Disney won 26 Academy Awards®.
Most Academy Award® nominations	Composer John Williams is the most nominated living person with 45 nominations (including 5 wins); another composer, Alfred Newman, also received 45 nominations (including 9 wins). Metro-Goldwyn-Mayer holds the overall record with 62 nominations.

Play It Again, Sam

Perhaps the most famous line associated with *Casablanca* (1942), 'Play it again, Sam', was never actually spoken by either star. Rick, played by Humphrey Bogart, declares 'Play it!' while Ingrid Bergman's character Ilsa requests 'Play it, Sam. Play *As Time Goes By*' – but neither ever utters the famous line.

BRITISH ACADEMY TELEVISION AWARDS

The British Academy of Film and Television Arts (BAFTA) has awarded prizes for outstanding work in television entertainment since 1954. Programmes associated with the awards are given from 1968.

Year	Best Actress	Best Actor
1954	Googie Withers	Paul Rogers
1955	Virginia McKenna	Peter Cushing
1956	Rosalie Crutchley	Michael Gough
1957	*no award*	Michael Hordern
1958	Gwen Watford	Donald Pleasence
1959	Catherine Lacey	Patrick McGoohan
1960	Billie Whitelaw	Lee Montague
1961	Ruth Dunning	Rupert Davies
1962	Brenda Bruce	Harry H Corbett
1963	Vivien Merchant	Alan Badel
1964	Katherine Blake	Patrick Wymark
1965	Gwen Watford	Alan Badel
1966	Vanessa Redgrave	Warren Mitchell
1967	Judi Dench	Eric Porter
1968	Wendy Craig *Not in Front of the Children*	Roy Dotrice *Brief Lives*

Year	Best Actress	Best Actor
1969	Margaret Tyzack *The First Churchills*	Edward Woodward *Callan, A Dream Divided* (Omnibus), *A Bit of a Holiday*
1970	Annette Crosbie *The Six Wives of Henry VIII*	Keith Michell *The Six Wives of Henry VIII, An Ideal Husband*
1971	Patricia Hayes *Edna, the Inebriate Woman*	John Le Mesurier *Traitor*
1972	Billie Whitelaw *The Sextet* (eight plays)	Anthony Hopkins *War and Peace*
1973	Celia Johnson *Mrs Palfrey at the Claremont*	Frank Finlay *The Adventures of Don Quixote, Candide, The Death of Adolf Hitler*
1974	Lee Remick *Jennie*	Peter Barkworth *Crown Matrimonial*
1975	Annette Crosbie *Edward the Seventh*	John Hurt *The Naked Civil Servant, Nijinsky, God of the Dance*
1976	Siân Phillips *I, Claudius*	Derek Jacobi *I, Claudius*
1977	Penelope Keith *The Norman Conquests Saving It for Albie*	Peter Barkworth *Professional Foul, The Country Party*
1978	Francesca Annis *Lillie, The Comedy of Errors*	Edward Fox *Edward and Mrs Simpson*
1979	Cheryl Campbell *Testament of Youth, The Duke of Wellington, Malice Aforethought*	Alec Guinness *Tinker Tailor Soldier Spy*
1980	Peggy Ashcroft *Caught on a Train, Cream in My Coffee*	Denholm Elliott *Gentle Folk/In Hiding/Blade on the Feather/The Stinker*
1981	Judi Dench *Going Gently, A Fine Romance, The Cherry Orchard*	Anthony Andrews *Brideshead Revisited*
1982	Beryl Reid *Smiley's People*	Alec Guinness *Smiley's People*
1983	Coral Browne *An Englishman Abroad*	Alan Bates *An Englishman Abroad*
1984	Peggy Ashcroft *The Jewel in the Crown*	Tim Pigott-Smith *The Jewel in the Crown*
1985	Claire Bloom *Shadowlands*	Bob Peck *Edge of Darkness*
1986	Anna Massey *Hotel Du Lac*	Michael Gambon *The Singing Detective*
1987	Emma Thompson *Fortunes of War, Tutti Frutti*	David Jason *Porterhouse Blue*
1988	Thora Hird *A Cream Cracker under the Settee*	Ray McAnally *A Very British Coup*
1989	Diana Rigg *Mother Love*	John Thaw *Inspector Morse*
1990	Geraldine McEwan *Oranges are not the Only Fruit*	Ian Richardson *House of Cards*
1991	Helen Mirren *Prime Suspect*	Robert Lindsay *G.B.H.*
1992	Helen Mirren *Prime Suspect 2*	John Thaw *Inspector Morse*
1993	Helen Mirren *Prime Suspect 3*	Robbie Coltrane *Cracker*
1994	Juliet Aubrey *Middlemarch*	Robbie Coltrane *Cracker*
1995	Jennifer Ehle *Pride and Prejudice*	Robbie Coltrane *Cracker*
1996	Gina McKee *Our Friends in the North*	Nigel Hawthorne *The Fragile Heart*
1997	Daniela Nardini *This Life*	Simon Russell Beale *A Dance to the Music of Time*
1998	Thora Hird *Waiting for the Telegram*	Tom Courtenay *A Rather English Marriage*
1999	Thora Hird *Lost for Words*	Michael Gambon *Wives and Daughters*
2000	Judi Dench *Last of the Blonde Bombshells*	Michael Gambon *Longitude*
2001	Julie Walters *My Beautiful Son*	Michael Gambon *Perfect Strangers*
2002	Julie Walters *Murder*	Albert Finney *The Gathering Storm*
2003	Julie Walters *The Wife of Bath – Canterbury Tales*	Bill Nighy *State of Play*
2004	Anamarcia Marinca *Sex Traffic*	Rhys Ifans *Not Only But Always*

Year	Best Actress	Best Actor
2005	Anna Maxwell Martin *Bleak House*	Mark Rylance *The Government Inspector*
2006	Victoria Wood *Housewife, 49*	Jim Broadbent *Longford*

SOAP OPERA PLACES

Soap opera	Setting
The Archers	Ambridge, South Borsetshire, UK
The Bill	Sun Hill, Canley, London, UK
Brookside	Brookside Close, Liverpool, UK
Casualty	Holby City Hospital, Holby, UK
Coronation Street	Weatherfield, Manchester, UK
EastEnders	Albert Square, Walford, London, UK
Emmerdale	Emmerdale, Yorkshire, UK
Holby City	Holby City Hospital, Holby, UK
Hollyoaks	Hollyoaks, Chester, UK
Home and Away	Summer Bay, Australia
Neighbours	Ramsay Street, Erinsborough, Australia
River City	Montego Street, Shieldinch, Glasgow, UK

Soap and Beer

The pubs in television soaps are some of the best known in the country. From The Bull (*The Archers*) to The Rover's Return (*Coronation Street*) and The Woolpack (*Emmerdale*), the characters in soap operas are often found having a pint and mulling over their problems at their local. Perhaps the most famous imaginary pub is *EastEnders*' Queen Vic. The BBC says that the booze served in the Vic is real, albeit low-alcohol, beer.

ORCHESTRAS

Orchestra layout

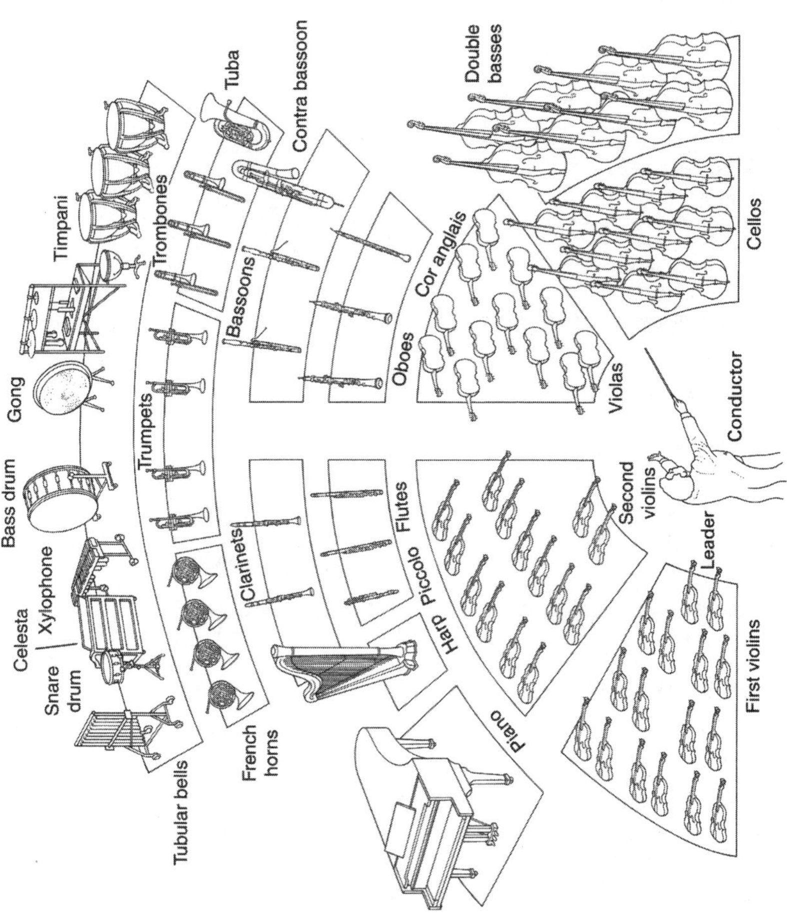

Empty Orchestra

The Japanese word *karaoke* literally means 'empty orchestra'.

Major orchestras

Name	Date founded	Location
Academy of Ancient Music	1973	UK (London)
Academy of St Martin-in-the-Fields	1959	UK (London)
Australian Chamber	1975	Sydney
BBC Philharmonic	1934	UK (Manchester)
BBC Scottish Symphony	1935	UK (Glasgow)
BBC Symphony	1930	UK (London)
BBC Welsh Symphony	1935	UK (Cardiff)
Berliner Philharmonic	1882	Germany
Boston Symphony	1881	USA
Bournemouth Symphony	1893	UK
Chicago Symphony	1891	USA
City of Birmingham Symphony	1920	UK
City of Glasgow Philharmonic	1990	UK
Cleveland Symphony	1918	USA
Concertgebouw	1888	The Netherlands (Amsterdam)
Detroit Symphony	1914	USA
English Chamber	1948	UK (London)
Hallé	1858	UK (Manchester)
Israel Philharmonic	1936	Israel (Tel Aviv)
London Philharmonic	1904	UK
London Symphony	1904	UK
Los Angeles Philharmonic	1904	USA
Melbourne Symphony	1906	Australia
Milan La Scala	1778	Italy
National Symphony	1931	USA (Washington DC)
NBC Symphony	1937–54	USA (New York)
New Orleans Philharmonic Symphony	1936	USA
New York Philharmonic	1842	USA
New York Symphony	1878	USA
Northern Sinfonia	1958	UK (Newcastle upon Tyne)
Orchestre Symphonique de Montréal	1842	Canada
Oslo Philharmonic	1919	Norway
Philadelphia	1900	USA
The Philharmonia	1945	UK (London)
Pittsburgh Symphony	1926	USA
Royal Liverpool Philharmonic	1840	UK
Royal Philharmonic	1946	UK (London)
Royal Scottish National	1891	UK (Glasgow)
St Petersburg Philharmonic	1921	Russia
San Francisco	1911	USA
Santa Cecelia Academy	1895	Italy (Rome)
Scottish Chamber	1974	UK (Edinburgh)
Seattle Symphony	1903	USA
Staatskapelle	1923	Germany (Dresden)
Sydney Symphony	1934	Australia
Toronto Symphony	1922	Canada
Ulster	1966	UK (Belfast)
Vienna Philharmonic	1842	Austria
Vienna Symphony	1900	Austria

OPERAS AND OPERETTAS

Name	Composer	Date
Aïda	Verdi	1871
Andrea Chénier	Umberto Giordano	1896
Ariadne auf Naxos	Richard Strauss	1916
Un Ballo in Maschera	Verdi	1859
The Barber of Seville	Rossini	1816
The Bartered Bride	Smetana	1866
La Bohème	Puccini	1896
Boris Godunov	Mussorgsky	1874
Carmen	Bizet	1875
Cavalleria Rusticana	Mascagni	1890
Così Fan Tutte	Mozart	1790
The Cunning Little Vixen	Janácek	1924
Dido and Aeneas	Purcell	1689
Don Carlos	Verdi	1867
Don Giovanni	Mozart	1787
Don Pasquale	Donizetti	1843
Duke Bluebeard's Castle	Bartók	1918
Einstein on the Beach	Philip Glass	1976
Elektra	Richard Strauss	1909
Eugene Onegin	Tchaikovsky	1879
Falstaff	Verdi	1893
Faust	Gounod	1859
Fidelio	Beethoven	1814
La Fille du Régiment	Donizetti	1840
Die Fledermaus	Johann Strauss	1874
The Flying Dutchman	Wagner	1843
Hansel and Gretel	Humperdinck	1893
HMS Pinafore	Gilbert and Sullivan	1878
Jenufa	Janácek	1904
King Priam	Tippett	1962
Lady Macbeth of Mtsensk	Shostakovich	1934
Lohengrin	Wagner	1850
The Love for Three Oranges	Prokofiev	1920
Lucia di Lammermoor	Donizetti	1835
Lulu	Berg	1937
Macbeth	Verdi	1847
Madame Butterfly	Puccini	1904
The Magic Flute	Mozart	1791
Manon	Massenet	1884
Manon Lescaut	Puccini	1893
The Marriage of Figaro	Mozart	1786
The Merry Wives of Windsor	Otto Nicolai	1849
The Midsummer Marriage	Tippett	1955
The Mikado	Gilbert and Sullivan	1885
Moses und Aron	Schönberg	1954
Nabucco	Verdi	1842
Nixon in China	Peter Adams	1990
Norma	Bellini	1831
Orfeo ed Euridice	Gluck	1762
Orpheus in the Underworld	Offenbach	1858
Otello	Verdi	1887
Pagliacci	Leoncavallo	1892
Parsifal	Wagner	1882
Pelléas et Mélisande	Debussy	1902
Peter Grimes	Britten	1945
Porgy and Bess	Gershwin	1935
The Rake's Progress	Stravinsky	1951
Rigoletto	Verdi	1851
The Ring	Wagner	1876
Salome	Richard Strauss	1911
Samson et Dalila	Saint-Saëns	1877
Simon Boccanegra	Verdi	1857
La Sonnambula	Bellini	1831
The Tales of Hoffman	Offenbach	1881
Tannhäuser	Wagner	1845
The Threepenny Opera	Weill	1928
Tosca	Puccini	1900
La Traviata	Verdi	1853
Tristan und Isolde	Wagner	1865
Il Trovatore	Verdi	1853
Turandot	Puccini	1926
The Turn of the Screw	Britten	1954
Werther	Massenet	1892
William Tell	Rossini	1829
Wozzeck	Berg	1925

BALLETS

Ballet	Composer	Choreographer	First performance
Bolero	Ravel	Bejart	1961
Cinderella	Prokofiev	Ashton	1948
Coppélia	Delibes	St Léon	1870
La Fille mal gardée	Various (French popular songs and airs)	Dauberval	1789
The Firebird	Stravinsky	Fokine	1910
Giselle	Adam	Coralli and Perro (later revised by Petipa)	1841
Manon	Massenet	MacMillan	1974
The Nutcracker	Tchaikovsky	Ivanov	1892
Romeo and Juliet	Prokofiev	Lavrovsky	1940
Le Sacré du printemps (The Rite of Spring)	Stravinsky, Roerich	Nijinsky	1913
Sheherazade	Rimsky-Korsakov	Fokine	1910
The Sleeping Beauty	Tchaikovsky	Petipa	1890
'Still Life' at the Penguin Café	Jeffes	Bintley	1988
Swan Lake	Tchaikovsky	Petipa and Ivanov	1895
La Sylphide	Løvenskjold	Bournonville	1836

Manuscript Millions

Original manuscripts of works by renowned composers are highly sought after by collectors and can fetch millions at auction. In May 2003 the working manuscript of Beethoven's 'Ninth Symphony' was sold for £2,133,600, setting a new record price both for a work by Beethoven and for a single musical manuscript. Described by Sotheby's as 'perhaps the single most important musical work ever to appear at auction', the pages, dating from 1826, have Beethoven's handwritten revisions scrawled throughout, including frustrated comments to his copyist such as *du verfluchter Kerl!* – 'you damned fool!' The record for the highest price ever paid for a manuscript was set in May 1987, when nine complete Mozart symphonies reached almost £2.6 million.

GRAMMY® AWARDS

Grammy® Awards are awarded annually, in a number of categories, by the US National Academy of Recording Arts and Sciences 'to honor excellence in the recording arts and sciences'; first awarded in 1958.

Year	Best record	Best album
1958	Domenico Modugno 'Nel Blu Dipinto Di Blu (Volare)'	Henry Mancini *Peter Gunn*
1959	Bobby Darin 'Mack the Knife'	Frank Sinatra *Come Dance with Me*
1960	Percy Faith 'Theme from *A Summer Place*'	Bob Newhart *Button Down Mind*
1961	Henry Mancini 'Moon River'	Judy Garland *Judy at Carnegie Hall*
1962	Tony Bennett 'I Left My Heart in San Francisco'	Vaughn Meader *The First Family*
1963	Henry Mancini 'The Days of Wine and Roses'	Barbra Streisand *The Barbra Streisand Album*
1964	Stan Getz, Astrud Gilberto 'The Girl from Ipanema'	Stan Getz, João Gilberto *Getz/Gilberto*
1965	Herb Alpert 'A Taste of Honey'	Frank Sinatra *September of My Years*

Year	Best record	Best album
1966	Frank Sinatra 'Strangers in the Night'	Frank Sinatra *A Man and His Music*
1967	5th Dimension 'Up, Up and Away'	The Beatles *Sgt Pepper's Lonely Hearts Club Band*
1968	Simon and Garfunkel 'Mrs Robinson'	Glen Campbell *By the Time I Get to Phoenix*
1969	5th Dimension 'Aquarius/Let the Sunshine In'	Blood, Sweat and Tears *Blood, Sweat and Tears*
1970	Simon and Garfunkel 'Bridge Over Troubled Water'	Simon and Garfunkel *Bridge Over Troubled Water*
1971	Carole King 'It's Too Late'	Carole King *Tapestry*
1972	Roberta Flack 'The First Time Ever I Saw Your Face'	Various artists *The Concert for Bangladesh*
1973	Roberta Flack 'Killing Me Softly with His Song'	Stevie Wonder *Innervisions*
1974	Olivia Newton-John 'I Honestly Love You'	Stevie Wonder *Fulfillingness' First Finale*
1975	Captain and Tennille 'Love Will Keep Us Together'	Paul Simon *Still Crazy After All These Years*
1976	George Benson 'This Masquerade'	Stevie Wonder *Songs in the Key of Life*
1977	Eagles 'Hotel California'	Fleetwood Mac *Rumours*
1978	Billy Joel 'Just the Way You Are'	Bee Gees *Saturday Night Fever*
1979	The Doobie Brothers 'What a Fool Believes'	Billy Joel *52nd Street*
1980	Christopher Cross 'Sailing'	Christopher Cross *Christopher Cross*
1981	Kim Carnes 'Bette Davis Eyes'	John Lennon, Yoko Ono *Double Fantasy*
1982	Toto 'Rosanna'	Toto *Toto IV*
1983	Michael Jackson 'Beat It'	Michael Jackson *Thriller*
1984	Tina Turner 'What's Love Got to Do with It'	Lionel Richie *Can't Slow Down*
1985	USA for Africa 'We Are the World'	Phil Collins *No Jacket Required*
1986	Steve Winwood 'Higher Love'	Paul Simon *Graceland*
1987	Paul Simon 'Graceland'	U2 *The Joshua Tree*
1988	Bobby McFerrin 'Don't Worry, Be Happy'	George Michael *Faith*
1989	Bette Midler 'Wind Beneath My Wings'	Bonnie Raitt *Nick of Time*
1990	Phil Collins 'Another Day in Paradise'	Quincy Jones *Back on the Block*
1991	Natalie Cole with Nat 'King' Cole 'Unforgettable'	Natalie Cole with Nat 'King' Cole *Unforgettable*
1992	Eric Clapton 'Tears in Heaven'	Eric Clapton *Unplugged*
1993	Whitney Houston 'I Will Always Love You'	Whitney Houston *The Bodyguard*
1994	Sheryl Crow 'All I Wanna Do'	Tony Bennett *MTV Unplugged*
1995	Seal 'Kiss From a Rose'	Alanis Morissette *Jagged Little Pill*
1996	Eric Clapton 'Change the World'	Celine Dion *Falling into You*
1997	Shawn Colvin 'Sunny Came Home'	Bob Dylan *Time Out of Mind*
1998	Celine Dion 'My Heart Will Go On'	Lauryn Hill *The Miseducation of Lauryn Hill*
1999	Santana, featuring Rob Thomas 'Smooth'	Santana *Supernatural*
2000	U2 'Beautiful Day'	Steely Dan *Two Against Nature*
2001	U2 'Walk On'	Various artists *O Brother, Where Art Thou?*
2002	Norah Jones 'Don't Know Why'	Norah Jones *Come Away With Me*
2003	Coldplay 'Clocks'	Outkast *Speakerboxxx/The Love Below*
2004	Ray Charles and Norah Jones 'Here We Go Again'	Ray Charles and various artists *Genius Loves Company*
2005	Green Day 'Boulevard Of Broken Dreams'	U2 *How To Dismantle An Atomic Bomb*
2006	Dixie Chicks 'Not Ready To Make Nice'	Dixie Chicks *Taking The Long Way*

EUROVISION SONG CONTEST

The Eurovision Song Contest is held annually to choose a winning pop song from among those entered by the participating countries. Open to member countries of the European Broadcasting Union; first held in 1956.

1956	Switzerland
1957	The Netherlands
1958	France
1959	The Netherlands
1960	France
1961	Luxembourg
1962	France
1963	Denmark
1964	Italy
1965	Luxembourg
1966	Austria
1967	UK
1968	Spain
1969	France, The Netherlands, Spain and UK[1]
1970	Ireland
1971	Monaco
1972	Luxembourg
1973	Luxembourg
1974	Sweden
1975	The Netherlands
1976	UK
1977	France
1978	Israel
1979	Israel
1980	Ireland
1981	UK
1982	Germany
1983	Luxembourg
1984	Sweden
1985	Norway
1986	Belgium
1987	Ireland
1988	Switzerland
1989	Yugoslavia
1990	Italy
1991	Sweden
1992	Ireland
1993	Ireland
1994	Ireland
1995	Norway
1996	Ireland
1997	UK
1998	Israel
1999	Sweden
2000	Denmark
2001	Estonia
2002	Latvia
2003	Turkey
2004	Ukraine
2005	Greece
2006	Finland
2007	Serbia

[1] Four-way tie.

La La Land

Eurovision entries are not usually noted for their lyrical brilliance. Silly Eurovision song titles have included 'Bana Bana' (Turkey, 1989), 'Boom Bang-a-Bang' (UK, 1969), 'Diggi-Loo-Diggi-Ley' (Sweden, 1984), 'A-Ba-Ni-Bi' (Israel, 1978) and 'Ding Dinge Dong' (The Netherlands, 1975), while Spain's 1968 entry 'La La La …' contained almost 140 instances of the word 'la'.

JAMES BOND FILM THEME SONGS

Year	Film	Song	Artist
1962	*Dr No*	'The James Bond Theme'	John Barry and orchestra
1963	*From Russia with Love*	'From Russia With Love'	Matt Munro
1964	*Goldfinger*	'Goldfinger'	Shirley Bassey
1965	*Thunderball*	'Thunderball'	Tom Jones
1967	*You Only Live Twice*	'You Only Live Twice'	Nancy Sinatra

Year	Film	Song	Artist
1969	*On Her Majesty's Secret Service*	'We Have All the Time in the World'	Louis Armstrong
1971	*Diamonds Are Forever*	'Diamonds Are Forever'	Shirley Bassey
1973	*Live and Let Die*	'Live and Let Die'	Paul McCartney and Wings
1974	*The Man With the Golden Gun*	'The Man with the Golden Gun'	Lulu
1977	*The Spy Who Loved Me*	'Nobody Does It Better'	Carly Simon
1979	*Moonraker*	'Moonraker'	Shirley Bassey
1981	*For Your Eyes Only*	'For Your Eyes Only'	Sheena Easton
1983	*Octopussy*	'All Time High'	Rita Coolidge
1985	*A View to a Kill*	'A View to a Kill'	Duran Duran
1987	*The Living Daylights*	'The Living Daylights'	A-Ha
1989	*Licence to Kill*	'Licence to Kill'	Gladys Knight
1995	*GoldenEye*	'GoldenEye'	Tina Turner
1997	*Tomorrow Never Dies*	'Tomorrow Never Dies'	Sheryl Crow
1999	*The World Is Not Enough*	'The World Is Not Enough'	Garbage
2002	*Die Another Day*	'Die Another Day'	Madonna
2006	*Casino Royale*	'You Know My Name (Look Up the Number)'	Chris Cornell

The Name's Norman

The famous signature tune of the James Bond movies, 'The James Bond Theme', was composed by Londoner Monty Norman. Norman, who insists that it was only the all-expenses paid trip to the *Dr No* set in Jamaica that convinced him to take on the project, based the theme on a song that he had written for a long-since abandoned musical. He reworked the song's simple melody into the now instantly recognizable riff that he describes as 'Dum de-de-dum-dum, dum dum dum, dum de-de dum dum, dum dum dum …'. The theme was then orchestrated by John Barry, who went on to have a lasting involvement in later Bond film scores. More than 25 million copies of the theme tune have since been sold worldwide.

MUSICAL REAL NAMES

Pseudonym	Real name
Bennett, Tony	Anthony Dominick Benedetto
Berlin, Irving	Israel Baline
Bizet, Georges	Alexandre Césare Léopold
Black, Cilla	Priscilla Maria Veronica White
Bo Diddley	Elias Bates, later McDaniel
Bon Jovi, Jon	John Francis Bongiovi, Jnr
Bono	Paul Hewson
Bowie, David	David Robert Jones
Boy George	George O'Dowd
Bygraves, Max	Walter William Bygraves
Charles, Ray	Ray Charles Robinson
Cher	Cheryl Sarkisian La Pier
Clark, Petula	Sally Owen
Cline, Patsy	Virginia Petterson Hensley
Cole, Nat 'King'	Nathaniel Adams Coles
Cooper, Alice	Vincent Damon Furnier
Costello, Elvis	Declan Patrick McManus
Crosby, Bing	Harry Lillis Crosby
Dylan, Bob	Robert Allen Zimmerman
The Edge	David Evans
Eminem	Marshall Mathers III
Fields, Dame Gracie	Grace Stansfield
Gershwin, George	Jacob Gershvin
Gershwin, Ira	Israel Gershvin
Holiday, Billie	Eleanora Fagan
Holly, Buddy	Charles Hardin
Howlin' Wolf	Chester Arthur Burnett

MUSICAL REAL NAMES

Pseudonym	Real name
John, Sir Elton Hercules	Reginald Kenneth Dwight
Jones, Tom	Thomas Jones Woodward
King, B B	Riley B King
Laine, Dame Cleo	Clementina Dinah Campbell
Lanza, Mario	Alfredo Arnold Coccozza
Leadbelly	Huddie William Ledbetter
Little Richard	Richard Wayne Penniman
Lulu	Marie McDonald McLaughlin Lawrie
Lynn, Dame Vera	Vera Margaret Welch
Madonna	Madonna Louise Veronica Ciccone
Manilow, Barry	Barry Allen Pincus
Manson, Marilyn	Brian Warner
Meat Loaf	Marvin Lee Aday
Mercury, Freddie	Farookh Bulsara
Michael, George	Georgios Kyriacos Panayiotou
Miranda, Carmen	Maria do Carmo Miranda Da Cunha
Morton, Jelly Roll	Ferdinand Joseph La Menthe or Lamothe
Novello, Ivor	David Ivor Davies
Offenbach, Jacques	Jakob Eberst
Osbourne, Ozzy	John Osbourne
Piaf, Edith	Edith Giovanna Gassion
Pop, Iggy	James Newell Osterberg
Prince	Prince Rogers Nelson
Rainey, Ma	Gertrude Pridgett Rainey *née* Pridgett
Reed, Lou	Louis Firbank
Richard, Sir Cliff	Harry Rodger Webb
Ross, Diana	Diane Earle
Rotten, Johnny	John Lydon
Scott, Ronnie	Ronald Schatt
Simone, Nina	Eunice Kathleen Waymon
Sly Stone	Sylvester Stewart
Solti, Sir Georg	Gyürgy Stern
Springfield, Dusty	Mary O'Brien
Starr, Ringo	Richard Starkey
Steele, Tommy	Thomas Hicks
Stevens, Cat	Stephen Demetre Georgiou
Sting	Gordon Matthew Sumner
Streisand, Barbra	Barbara Joan Rosen
Twain, Shania	Eileen Regina Edwards
Turner, Tina	Annie Mae Bullock
Vicious, Sid	John Simon Ritchie
Washington, Dinah	Ruth Jones
Waters, Muddy	McKinley Morganfield
Wonder, Stevie	Steveland Judkins
Wyman, Bill	William Perks
Wynette, Tammy	Virginia Wynette Pugh

Musical Monikers

Musicians, not content with renaming themselves, are also renowned for the intriguing and often unusual names with which they christen their offspring. In the 1960s, Keith Richards of the Rolling Stones named his daughter *Dandelion*, Sonny Bono and Cher christened their daughter *Chastity* and Frank Zappa famously called his daughter *Moon Unit*. From the 1970s came the euphonious *Zowie Bowie* (son of David) and *Rolan Bolan* (son of Marc). More recent additions to the pop world's second generation include children named after places (Victoria Beckham's son *Brooklyn*, Madonna's daughter *Lourdes* and Michael Jackson's daughter *Paris*), musical heroes (Liam Gallagher's son *Lennon*) and fruits (Chris Martin's daughter *Apple*). Other famous names include *Blue Angel* (U2's The Edge), *Fifi Trixibelle*, *Peaches Honeyblossom* and *Pixie* (Bob Geldof), *Heavenly Hiraani Tiger Lily* (Michael Hutchence), *Elijah Bob Patricius Guggi Q* (U2's Bono) and *Phoenix Chi* (the Spice Girls' Mel B).

VITAMINS

Vitamins are any of numerous organic substances present in minute quantities in nutritive foods, and are essential for the health of animals.

Fat-soluble vitamins

Vitamin	Chemical name	Source
A	retinol (carotene)	dairy products, egg yolk, fortified margarine, liver, oily fish
D	calciferols (eg cholecalciferol)	egg yolk, liver, oily fish; made on skin in sunlight
E	tocopherols	vegetable oils, nuts, seeds, wheatgerm
K	phytomenadione	green leafy vegetables, vegetable oils, cereals, beef, liver

Water-soluble vitamins

Vitamin	Chemical name	Source
B1	thiamin	pork, fruit, vegetables, dairy products, eggs, whole grains, some fortified breakfast cereals
B2	riboflavin	dairy products, eggs, fortified breakfast cereals, rice, mushrooms; destroyed by light
B3	niacin	milk, eggs, poultry, meats, wheat flour, maize flour
B5	pantothenic acid	found in virtually all meat and vegetable foods; destroyed in heavily-processed food
B6	pyridoxine	liver, meats, fruits, cereals, leafy vegetables
B7	biotin	liver, kidney, egg yolk, dried fruit, yeast extract; made by micro-organisms in large intestine
B9	folic acid	liver, green leafy vegetables, some fruits, brown rice, yeast extract; cooking and processing can cause serious losses in food
B12	cyanocobalamin	liver, kidney, other meats, fish, eggs, dairy products, some fortified breakfast cereals; none in plants
C	ascorbic acid	soft and citrus fruits, green leafy vegetables, potatoes, liver, kidney; losses occur during storage and cooking

MINERALS

Mineral	Source
calcium	dairy products, green leafy vegetables, soya beans, nuts, fortified cereals and flours
chromium	processed meats, whole grains, pulses, spices
copper	nuts, shellfish, offal
fluoride	fluoridated drinking water, seafood, tea
iodine	shellfish, saltwater fish, seaweed, iodized table salt
iron	liver, other meats, dark green leafy vegetables, beans, nuts, dried fruit, whole grains, fortified cereals and flours
magnesium	green leafy vegetables (eaten raw), nuts, whole grains
manganese	green vegetables, cereals, bread, tea
molybdenum	legumes, leafy vegetables, cauliflower, cereals, nuts
phosphorus	meat, poultry, fish, dairy products, cereals, bread
potassium	milk, fruits, vegetables, fish, shellfish, meats, liver
selenium	eggs, fish, offal, brazil nuts, cereals
sodium	table salt, cereals, bread, meat products, processed foods
zinc	meat, shellfish, dairy products, whole grains

WINE BOTTLE SIZES

Name	Capacity[1]	Equivalent (standard bottles)
wine bottle	75cl	1
magnum	1.5l	2
jeroboam	3l	4
rehoboam	4.5l	6
methuselah	6l	8
salmanazar	9l	12
balthazar	12l	16
nebuchadnezzar	15l	20

[1] *To convert litres to pints, multiply by 0.56821.*
Note: A flagon of wine contains 1.13l/2pt.

Biblical Bottles

Many bottle sizes are named after biblical figures from the Old Testament. The *balthazar* and the *nebuchadnezzar* were both named after kings of Babylon, the *methuselah* after a patriarch said to have lived 969 years, the *salmanazar* by allusion to Shalmaneser, king of Assyria, and the *jeroboam* and *rehoboam* after figures in the Book of Kings. In contrast, the *magnum* simply comes from the Latin word for 'big'.

EUROPEAN CHEESES

Belgium
Limburger

Cyprus
halloumi

Denmark
Danish blue

England
Cheddar
Cheshire
Derby
double Gloucester
Ilchester
Lancashire
Red Leicester
Stilton®
Wensleydale

France
Boursin
Brie
Camembert
Cantal
Chaumes
Coulommiers
crottin
Munster
Pont l'Évêque
Port Salut
reblochon
Roquefort
St Paulin
vacherin

Germany
Cambozola®
Münster
Tilsit

Greece
feta

Italy
bel paese
dolcelatte
Fontina
Gorgonzola
mascarpone
mozzarella
Parmesan
pecorino
provolone
ricotta
Romano
stracchino
Taleggio

The Netherlands
Edam
Gouda
Leerdammer

Norway
Jarlsberg®

Scotland
crowdie
Dunlop

Spain
Manchego

Switzerland
Emmental
Gruyère
sapsago

Wales
Caerphilly

Red Hot Chilli Peppers

The heat of chilli peppers is measured by the Scoville scale, which was developed by pharmacologist Wilbur Scoville in 1912. Although originally a taste test, today it scientifically measures the amount of capsaicin – the substance that makes chillis taste hot – in each pepper. The higher the number of Scoville units, the hotter the pepper; pure capsaicin measures a sizzling 16 million Scoville units. A bell pepper measures 0 Scoville units, a jalapeño pepper measures 2,500–5,000 units and cayenne pepper measures 30,000–50,000 units. Guinness World Records® states that the world's hottest chilli pepper is the Red Savina habañero, which can contain up to an eye-watering 570,000 Scoville units; most habañero peppers peak at around 325,000 to 350,000 units.

COCKTAILS

There are many variations in cocktail ingredients; only the most common are listed.

Cocktail	Alcohol	Other common ingredients
Bellini	chilled champagne	peach nectar or peach schnapps
Between the Sheets	rum, brandy, Cointreau®	lemon juice
Black Russian	vodka, Kahlúa®	none
Bloody Mary	vodka	tomato juice and seasoning
Brandy Alexander	brandy, crème de cacao	cream
Bullshot	vodka	beef consommé
Caipirinha	cachaça	crushed lime and sugar
Champagne Cocktail	champagne, brandy	sugar and Angostura bitters
Collins	a spirit, for example vodka or whisky	lemon or lime juice, sugar and soda water
Cosmopolitan	vodka, orange liqueur	lime juice and cranberry juice
Daiquiri	rum	lime juice
Gimlet	gin or vodka	lime juice
Harvey Wallbanger	Galliano, vodka	orange juice
Horse's Neck	brandy	ginger ale and a twist of lemon
Mai tai	rum, triple sec, grenadine	lime juice
Manhattan	vermouth, whisky and sometimes curaçao or maraschino	Angostura bitters
Margarita	tequila, orange liqueur	lime or lemon juice
Martini	vermouth, gin, sometimes vodka	bitters etc and a twist of lemon
Moscow Mule	vodka	ginger ale and lemon juice
Old Fashioned	whisky	bitters, water and sugar
Pink Lady	gin, grenadine	cream, egg white and lemon juice
Planter's Punch	rum	lime or lemon juice and sugar
Rickey	gin or vodka	lime juice and soda water with ice
Rusty Nail	whisky and Drambuie®	
Sazerac®	Pernod and whisky	
Screwdriver	vodka	orange juice
Sea Breeze	vodka	cranberry juice and grapefruit juice
Sidecar	brandy, orange liqueur	lemon juice
Singapore Sling	brandy, gin, Cointreau®, Benedictine and grenadine	orange juice, lime juice
Slammer	tequila	
Sour	gin or whisky	lemon or lime juice
Stinger	brandy and white crème de menthe	
Tequila Sunrise	tequila, grenadine	orange juice
Tom Collins	gin	lime juice, soda and sugar or syrup
White Lady	gin, orange liqueur	lemon juice
White Russian	vodka, Kahlúa®	milk

Cocktail Salvation

'The greatest of all the contributions of the American way of life to the salvation of humanity.'

H L Mencken on the cocktail. Quoted by William Grimes in 'The American Cocktail', ***Americana*****, Dec 1992.**

LIQUEURS

A liqueur is a potent alcoholic preparation that is flavoured or perfumed and sweetened.

Liqueur	Description
absinthe	bitter, green, aniseed-flavoured; containing (originally) extract of wormwood
advocaat	containing raw eggs and flavourings
amaretto	Italian; flavoured with almonds
anisette	prepared from anise seed (aromatic seeds, of a flavour similar to liquorice)
Benedictine	resembles Chartreuse; distilled at Fécamp in Normandy, formerly by Benedictine monks
Chartreuse	green or yellow; manufactured at La Grande Chartreuse monastery near Grenoble, France, by the monks; made from aromatic herbs, flowers and brandy
cherry brandy	made by steeping Morello cherries in brandy
Cointreau®	orange-flavoured
crème de cacao	chocolate-flavoured
crème de menthe	green, peppermint-flavoured
curaçao	flavoured with bitter orange peel
Drambuie®	Scotch whisky liqueur
eau des creoles	from Martinique; made by distilling the flowers of the mammee-apple with alcohol
Frangelico	Italian; flavoured with hazelnuts
Galliano	Italian; flavoured with anise
Grand Marnier®	orange-flavoured, with a cognac base
Kahlúa®	Mexican; made from coffee beans, cocoa beans and vanilla
kirsch	made from the wild cherry
kümmel	flavoured with cumin and caraway seeds
maraschino	distilled from a cherry grown in the Croatian region of Dalmatia
mirabelle	colourless; distilled from mirabelle plums
noyau	made from brandy flavoured with bitter almonds or peach kernels
ouzo	aniseed
ratafia	flavoured with fruit kernels
rum shrub	made from rum, sugar, lime or lemon juice, etc
sambuca	Italian; made from aniseed
Southern Comfort®	whisky liqueur originally produced in the southern US
Strega®	Italian; sweet, orange-flavoured
Tia Maria®	coffee-flavoured
Triple sec	clear, orange-flavoured
Van der Hum	South African; flavoured with tangerines

Monks and Sour Cherries

Liqueur names come from a variety of sources. Some reflect the liqueur's origin, for example *curaçao*, named after the island in the Caribbean where it was first made, or *Benedictine* after the Benedictine monks who first created it. Other names are derived from the taste of the liqueur, for example *amaretto*, which comes from the Italian word *amaro* meaning 'bitter'. And some are named after their ingredients, such as *maraschino* from the Italian *marasca*, 'sour cherry', and *absinthe*, from the Greek word *apsinthion* meaning 'wormwood'. *Advocaat*, however, comes from Dutch *advokaatenborrel* which means 'advocate's dram', as a clearer of the throat.

LANGUAGE

PROVERBS

Proverbs are arranged alphabetically by key words (which are shown in *italic*). In each case the proverb is followed by the century in which it first occurred in print in English in a recognizable form; in many cases related sentiments are attested earlier, often in Greek and Latin, or in medieval French sources. Some of the uses cited here in italics are not in the precise form given here.

Proverb / Date / Notable uses

absence makes the heart grow fonder 19c
actions speak louder than words 17c
all's well that ends well 14c
an *apple* a day keeps the doctor away 19c
don't throw the *baby* out with the bathwater 19c *Thomas Carlyle*
beauty is in the eye of the beholder 18c *David Hume*
beauty is only skin deep 17c
beggars can't be choosers 16c
the early *bird* catches the worm 17c
a *bird* in the hand is worth two in the bush 15c
birds of a feather flock together 16c *Bible, Ecclesiasticus 27*
once *bitten*, twice shy 19c
when the *blind* lead the blind, both shall fall into the ditch 9c *Bible, Matthew 15*
you can't get *blood* from a stone 17c
blood is thicker than water 19c
brevity is the soul of wit 17c *Shakespeare, Hamlet*
you can't make *bricks* without straw 17c *Bible, Exodus 5*
don't cross your *bridges* until you come to them 19c
a new *broom* sweeps clean 16c
you can't have your *cake* and eat it 16c
if the *cap* fits, wear it 18c
when the *cat's* away, the mice will play 17c
a *change* is as good as a rest 19c *Arthur Conan Doyle*
charity begins at home 14c *John Wycliffe*
don't count your *chickens* before they are hatched 16c
clothes make the man 15c
every *cloud* has a silver lining 19c
cut your *coat* according to your cloth 16c
too many *cooks* spoil the broth 16c
curiosity killed the cat 20c
there's none so *deaf* as those that will not hear 16c
needs must when the *devil* drives 15c *Shakespeare, All's Well that Ends Well*
the *devil* finds work for idle hands to do 14c *Geoffrey Chaucer*
the *devil* looks after his own 17c
better the *devil* you know than the devil you don't 16c
discretion is the better part of valour 16c *Shakespeare, Henry IV Part One*
give a *dog* a bad name and hang him 18c
you can't teach an old *dog* new tricks 16c
let sleeping *dogs* lie 14c *Geoffrey Chaucer*
barking *dogs* seldom bite 16c
to *err* is human, to forgive divine 16c
the *exception* proves the rule 17c

Proverb / Date / Notable uses

familiarity breeds contempt 14c
there are as good *fish* in the sea as ever came out of it 16c
a *fool* and his money are soon parted 16c
there's no *fool* like an old fool 16c
fools rush in where angels fear to tread 18c *Alexander Pope*
forewarned is forearmed 15c
a *friend* in need is a friend indeed 11c
those who live in *glass* houses shouldn't throw stones 14c *Geoffrey Chaucer*
all that *glitters* is not gold 13c *Shakespeare, Merchant of Venice, as 'all that glisters ...'*
don't teach your *grandmother* to suck eggs 18c
the *grass* is always greener on the other side of the fence 20c
old *habits* die hard 18c *Benjamin Franklin*
many *hands* make light work 14c
first you catch your *hare* 19c *William Makepeace Thackeray*
more *haste* less speed 14c
he who *hesitates* is lost 18c
there is *honour* among thieves 17c
never look a gift *horse* in the mouth 16c
you may take a *horse* to water but you can't make him drink 12c
hunger is the best sauce 16c
where *ignorance* is bliss, 'tis folly to be wise 18c *Thomas Gray*
strike while the *iron* is hot 14c *Geoffrey Chaucer*
a little *knowledge* is a dangerous thing 18c *Alexander Pope*
better *late* than never 14c
he who *laughs* last, laughs longest 20c
least said, soonest mended 15c
a *leopard* doesn't change its spots 16c *Bible, Jeremiah 13.23*
many a *little* makes a mickle 13c
half a *loaf* is better than no bread 16c
look before you leap 14c
one man's *meat* is another man's poison 16c
it's no use crying over spilt *milk* 17c
a *miss* is as good as a mile 17c
if the *mountain* won't come to Mahomet, Mahomet must go to the mountain 17c *Francis Bacon*
necessity is the mother of invention 16c
no *news* is good news 17c *James I*
don't cut off your *nose* to spite your face 16c
nothing ventured, nothing gained 17c
great *oaks* from little acorns grow 14c *Geoffrey Chaucer*
you can't make an *omelette* without breaking eggs 19c
out of sight, out of mind 13c
the *pen* is mightier than the sword 16c
take care of the *pence* and the pounds will take care of themselves 18c
in for a *penny*, in for a pound 17c
he that pays the *piper* calls the tune 19c
little *pitchers* have large ears 16c
there's no *place* like home 16c
a watched *pot* never boils 19c *Mrs Gaskell*
practice makes perfect 16c
prevention is better than cure 17c

Proverb / Date / Notable uses

pride goes before a fall 14c
procrastination is the thief of time 18c *Bible, Proverbs 16*
the *proof* of the pudding is in the eating 14c
you can't make a silk *purse* out of a sow's ear 16c
it never *rains* but it pours 18c
the *road* to hell is paved with good intentions 16c
spare the *rod* and spoil the child 11c *Bible, Proverbs 13*
Rome was not built in a day 16c
when in *Rome*, do as the Romans do 15c
better *safe* than sorry 19c
there is *safety* in numbers 17c *Bible, Proverbs11, and John Bunyan*
what's *sauce* for the goose is sauce for the gander 17c
as well to be hanged for a *sheep* as a lamb 17c
there's no *smoke* without fire 14c
speech is silver, but silence is golden 19c *Thomas Carlyle*
it's no use shutting the *stable* door after the horse has bolted 14c
a *stitch* in time saves nine 18c
a rolling *stone* gathers no moss 14c
it's the last *straw* that breaks the camel's back 17c
little *strokes* fell great oaks 15c
one *swallow* doesn't make a summer 16c
what you lose on the *swings* you gain on the roundabouts 20c
you can have too much of a good *thing* 15c
little *things* please little minds 16c
time and tide wait for no man 14c *Geoffrey Chaucer, in Latin*
don't put off till *tomorrow* what you can do today 14c *Geoffrey Chaucer*
it's better to *travel* hopefully than to arrive 19c *Robert Louis Stevenson*
the *tree* is known by its fruit 16c *Bible, Matthew 12*
trouble shared is trouble halved 20c *Dorothy L Sayers*
there's many a good *tune* played on an old fiddle 20c *Samuel Butler*
one good *turn* deserves another 15c
variety is the spice of life 18c
all things come to those who *wait* 16c
waste not, want not 8c

Fat Ladies Singing

While some proverbs are thousands of years old, others are more recent arrivals in the language. One modern proverb, 'It ain't over 'til the fat lady sings', is thought to have been coined as recently as 1978 by Dan Cook, a Texan journalist, in the form 'the opera ain't over 'til the fat lady sings'. Although it has been suggested that the phrase was older and was simply popularized by Cook, it has certainly caught on in the public imagination and in collections it is found alongside proverbs coined many centuries before.

SIMILES

A simile is a figure of speech in which a person or thing is described by being explicitly likened to another.

as bald as a coot
as black as ink *or* pitch
as blind as a bat
as blue as the sky
as bold as brass
as bright as a button
as brown as a berry
as calm as a millpond
as clean as a whistle
as clear as a bell *or* as crystal *or (ironically)* as mud
as cold as charity *or* ice

as cool as a cucumber
as cross as two sticks
as daft as a brush
as dead as a dodo *or* a doornail *or* as mutton
as deaf as a post
as different as chalk and cheese
as drunk as a lord *or* a piper
as dry as a bone
as dull as ditchwater
as easy as falling off a log *or* as winking
as fair as a rose
as fit as a fiddle
as flat as a pancake
as free as a bird
as fresh as a daisy *or* as paint
as good as gold
as green as grass
as happy as a lark *or* as a sandboy *or* as Larry *or* as the day is long
as hard as nails
as high as a kite
as innocent as a lamb
as keen as mustard
as large as life
as light as a feather *or* as down
as like as two peas in a pod *or (ironically)* chalk and cheese
as lively as a cricket
as mad as a hatter *or* a March hare
as merry as a grig
as near as a touch
as neat as ninepence
as often as not
as old as Adam *or* Methuselah *or* the hills
as plain as a pikestaff
as pleased as Punch
as poor as a church mouse
as proud as a peacock
as pure as the driven snow
as quick as lightning
as quiet as a mouse
as red as a beetroot
as regular as clockwork
as rich as Croesus
as right as a trivet *or* as rain
as ripe as a cherry
as safe as houses
as sharp as a razor
as sick as a dog *or* a parrot
as silent as the grave
as slippery as an eel
as sober as a judge
as soft as a baby's bottom
as sound as a bell *or* a roach
as steady as a rock
as stiff as a poker
as straight as a die
as strong as a horse
as stubborn as a mule
as sure as a gun *or* as eggs is eggs
as thick *(= conspiratorial)* as thieves
as thick *(=stupid)* as a plank *or* as two short planks
as thin as a rake
as tough as leather *or* old boots
as ugly as sin
as warm as toast
as weak as a kitten
as white as a sheet *or* as snow
as wise as an owl

Common as a Simile

'One thing that literature would be greatly the better for
Would be a more restricted employment by authors of simile and metaphor.'

Ogden Nash, *Many Long Years Ago*, 'Very Like A Whale', 1945.

INTERESTING OLOGIES

An 'ology' is a science whose name ends in *-logy* or *-ology*. This ending comes from the Greek word *logos*, meaning 'word' or 'reason'.

Ology	Study of ...
acarology	mites
agrostology	grasses
aristology	dining
astacology	crayfish
autology	oneself
balneology	bathing and mineral springs
batology	brambles
bryology	mosses
caliology	birds' nests
campanology	bells and bellringing
carcinology	crustaceans
chaology	chaos or chaos theory
chirology	the language of gesture, and the hand
codicology	manuscript volumes
conchology	molluscs and their shells
coprology	the use of obscenity in speech, literature and art
cryptology	codes
cryptozoology	creatures, such as the Loch Ness monster, that are generally regarded as mythical
dactyliology	rings or engraved gems
deltiology	picture postcards
demonology	demons and their ways
garbology	a society's waste materials
graphology	handwriting
hagiology	saints' legends
helminthology	worms, especially parasitic ones
heortology	religious feasts
hepaticology	liverworts
heresiology	heresies
hierology	sacred matters
hippology	horses
hoplology	weapons
hymnology	hymns
hypnology	sleep
irenology	peace
koniology	dust in the air
limacology	slugs
malacology	molluscs
missiology	religious missions
myrmecology	ants
odonatology	dragonflies
oenology	wines
oneirology	dreams
oology	birds' eggs
ophiology	snakes
orchidology	orchids
orology or oreology	mountains
paroemiology	proverbs
phycology	algae
podology	feet
pomology	fruit-growing
pseudology	lying
pteridology	ferns
scatology	excrement
sindonology	the Turin shroud
spectrology	ghosts
speleology	caves
sphygmology	the pulse
storiology	folk tales
thaumatology	miracles
timbrology	stamp collecting
ufology	UFOs
vexillology	flags
xylology	the structure of wood
zymology	the science of fermentation

Mysterious Creatures

One of the more exciting 'ologies' is *cryptozoology*, the study and attempted discovery of creatures that are generally regarded as mythical. The Loch Ness monster, the Bigfoot or sasquatch, the Yeti and numerous other big cats, sea monsters and unexplained beasts – including the unlikely-sounding Mongolian Death Worm – are all the rather elusive targets of cryptozoologists.

ISMS

Most of the words included here denote beliefs and practices. Some, however, denote aspects of discrimination; these include **ageism** and **sexism**. Etymological information is given in parentheses.

ageism	discrimination on the grounds of age
agnosticism	belief in the impossibility of knowing God (Greek *agnostos* unknown, unknowable)
alcoholism	addiction to alcohol
altruism	unselfish concern for the welfare of others (Latin *alteri huic* to this other)
atavism	reversion to an earlier type (Latin *atavus* ancestor)
atheism	belief that God does not exist (Greek *atheos* without god)
barbarism	state of being coarse or uncivilized (Greek *barbaros* foreign, stammering)
behaviourism	basis of psychology in behaviour of people and animals
cannibalism	practice of eating human flesh (Spanish *Canibal* Carib)
capitalism	economic system based on the private ownership of wealth and resources
communism	political and economic system based on collective ownership of wealth and resources
conservatism	inclination to preserve the status quo
consumerism	economic policy of encouraging spending and consuming
cubism	artistic movement using geometrical shapes to represent objects
cynicism	belief in the worst in others (Greek *kynikos* dog-like)
defeatism	belief in the inevitability of defeat
dogmatism	tendency to present statements of opinion as if unquestionable (Greek *dogma* opinion)
dynamism	state of having limitless energy and enthusiasm
egoism	principle that self-interest is the basis of morality (Latin *ego* I)
elitism	belief in the natural superiority of some people (Latin *eligere* to elect)
empiricism	theory that knowledge can only be gained through experiment and observation (Greek *empeiria* experience)
environmentalism	concern to protect the natural environment
escapism	tendency to escape from unpleasant reality into fantasy
evangelism	practice of trying to persuade someone to adopt a particular belief or cause (Greek *evangelion* good news)
exhibitionism	tendency to behave so as to attract attention to oneself
existentialism	philosophy emphasizing freedom of choice and personal responsibility for one's actions
expressionism	artistic movement emphasizing expression of emotions over representation of external reality
extremism	adherence to fanatical or extreme opinions
fanaticism	excessive enthusiasm for something (Latin *fanaticus* filled with a god, frenzied)
favouritism	practice of giving unfair preference to a person or group
feminism	advocacy of equal rights and opportunities for women
feudalism	social system based on tenants' allegiance to a lord
functionalism	theory that the intended use of something should determine its design
hedonism	belief in the importance of pleasure above all else (Greek *hedone* pleasure)
heroism	quality of showing great courage in one's actions
holism	theory that any complex being or system is more than the sum of its parts (Greek *holos* whole)
humanism	philosophy emphasizing human responsibility for moral behaviour

hypnotism	practice of inducing a hypnotic state in others (Greek *hypnos* sleep)
idealism	practice of living according to ideals
imperialism	principle of extending control over other nations' territory (Latin *imperium* sovereignty)
Impressionism	artistic movement emphasizing artists' impressions of nature
individualism	belief in individual freedom and self-reliance
liberalism	belief in tolerance of different opinions or attitudes
magnetism	state of possessing magnetic attraction
mannerism	excessive use of an individual artistic style
Marxism	philosophy that political change is brought about by struggle between social classes
masochism	derivation of pleasure from one's own pain or suffering (named after the Austrian writer Sacher-Masoch)
materialism	excessive interest in material possessions and financial success
monarchism	support of the institution of monarchy
monetarism	economic theory emphasizing the control of a country's money supply
mysticism	practice of gaining direct communication with a deity through prayer and meditation (Greek *mystes* initiate)
narcissism	excessive admiration for oneself or one's appearance
nationalism	advocacy of national unity or independence
naturalism	realistic and non-idealistic representation of objects
nihilism	rejection of moral and religious principles (Latin *nihil* nothing)
objectivism	tendency to emphasize what is objective
opportunism	practice of taking advantage of opportunities regardless of principles
optimism	tendency to expect the best possible outcome (Latin *optimus* best)
pacifism	belief that violence and war are unjustified (Latin *pax* peace, and *facere* to make)
paganism	belief in a religion which worships many gods (Latin *paganus* peasant, civilian)
pantheism	doctrine that equates all natural forces and matter with god (Greek *pas* all, *theos* god)
parochialism	practice of being narrow or provincial in outlook (Latin *parochia* parish)
paternalism	practice of benevolent but over-protective management or government (Latin *pater* father)
patriotism	devotion to one's country (Greek *patriotes* compatriot)
pessimism	tendency to expect the worst possible outcome (Latin *pessimus* worst)
plagiarism	practice of stealing an idea from another's work and presenting it as one's own (Latin *plagiarius* kidnapper)
pluralism	co-existence of several ethnic and religious groups in a society (Latin *plus* more)
pointillism	artistic movement using small dabs of unmixed colour to suggest shapes (French *pointille* dot)
polytheism	belief in more than one god (Greek *polys* many, *theos* god)
pragmatism	a practical, matter-of-fact approach to dealing with problems (Greek *pragma* deed)
professionalism	practice of showing professional competence and conduct
racism *or* **racialism**	discrimination on the grounds of ethnic origin
realism	tendency to present things as they really are
regionalism	devotion to or advocacy of one's own region
sadism	derivation of pleasure from inflicting pain on others (named after the French writer the Marquis de Sade)
Satanism	belief in and worship of the devil

scepticism	tendency to question widely-accepted beliefs (Greek *skeptikos* thoughtful)
sexism	discrimination on the grounds of sex
socialism	doctrine that a country's wealth belongs to the people as a whole
spiritualism	practice of communicating with the spirits of the dead through a medium
stoicism	tendency to accept misfortune or suffering without complaint (Greek *Stoa Poikile* Painted Porch, where Zeno taught)
surrealism	artistic movement emphasizing use of images from the unconscious
symbolism	use of symbols to express ideas or emotions
terrorism	practice of using violence to achieve political ends
Thatcherism	political system based on privatization and monetarism advocated by Margaret Thatcher
tokenism	practice of doing something once or with minimum effort to appear to comply with a law or principle
tourism	practice of travelling to and visiting places for pleasure and relaxation
vandalism	practice of inflicting indiscriminate damage on others' property
vegetarianism	practice of not eating meat or animal products
ventriloquism	practice of making one's voice appear to come from another source (Latin *ventri* belly, *loqui* to speak)
voyeurism	practice of watching private actions of others for pleasure or sexual gratification

PHOBIAS

A phobia is a fear, hatred or extreme dislike of something, especially an irrational one. The term comes from the Greek word *phobos* meaning 'fear'.

Technical term	Everyday term
acerophobia	sourness
achluophobia	darkness
acrophobia	heights
aerophobia	draughts, air
agoraphobia	open spaces
aichmophobia	sharp or pointed objects
aichurophobia	points
ailurophobia	cats
akousticophobia	sound
algophobia	pain
amakaphobia	carriages
amathophobia	dust
androphobia	men
anemophobia	wind or draughts
anginophobia	narrowness
anthropophobia	people or society
antlophobia	flood
apeirophobia	infinity
apiphobia	bees
aquaphobia	water
arachnophobia	spiders
arithmophobia	numbers
asthenophobia	weakness
astraphobia, astrapophobia	lightning
atephobia	ruin
aulophobia	flutes
auroraphobia	Northern Lights
autophobia	being by oneself
bacilliphobia	microbes
barophobia	gravity
basophobia	walking
bathophobia	falling from a high place
batrachophobia	frogs, toads, newts
belonephobia	needles
bibliophobia	books
brontophobia	thunder
cancerphobia, cancerophobia	contracting or having cancer
canophobia	dogs
cheimaphobia	cold
chionophobia	snow
chrometophobia	money
chronophobia	duration
chrystallophobia	crystals
claustrophobia	closed spaces
cnidophobia	stings
cometophobia	comets
cromophobia	colour

Technical term	Everyday term
cyberphobia	computers
cynophobia	dogs
demonophobia	demons
demophobia	crowds
dermatophobia	skin
dikephobia	injustice
doraphobia	fur
dromophobia	crossing streets
dysmorphophobia	personal physical deformity
ecophobia	one's home surroundings
eisoptrophobia	mirrors
electrophobia	electricity
eleutherophobia	freedom
emetophobia	vomiting
entomophobia	insects
eosophobia	dawn
eremophobia	solitude
eretephobia	pins
ereuthrophobia	blushing
ergasiophobia, ergophobia	work
erotophobia	sexual involvement
erythrophobia	blushing
euphobia	good news
genophobia	sex
geumaphobia	taste
graphophobia	writing
gymnophobia	nudity
gynophobia	women
hadephobia	hell
haematophobia	blood
hamartiophobia	sin
haphephobia	touch
harpaxophobia	robbers
hedonophobia	pleasure
helminthophobia	worms
herpetophobia	reptiles
hierophobia	sacred objects
hippophobia	horses
hodophobia	travel
homichlophobia	fog
hormephobia	shock
hydrophobia	water
hypegiaphobia	responsibility
hypnophobia	sleep
ideophobia	ideas
kakorraphiaphobia	failure
katagelophobia	ridicule

Technical term	Everyday term
kenophobia	empty spaces, voids
keraunophobia	thunder
kinesophobia	motion
kleptophobia	stealing
kopophobia	fatigue
kristallophobia	ice
laliophobia	stuttering
linonophobia	string
logophobia	words
lyssophobia	insanity
maniaphobia	insanity
mastigophobia	flogging
mechanophobia	machinery
metallophobia	metals
meteorophobia	meteors
misophobia	contamination
monophobia	one thing, or being alone
musicophobia	music
musophobia	mice
mysophobia	contamination
necrophobia	corpses
nelophobia	glass
neophobia	newness, novelty
nephophobia	clouds
nosophobia	disease
nyctophobia	night or darkness
ochlophobia	crowds
ochophobia	vehicles
odontophobia	teeth
oikophobia	home
olfactophobia	smell
ommatophobia	eyes
oneirophobia	dreams
ophidiophobia, ophiophobia	snakes
ophthalmophobia	being stared at
ornithophobia	birds
ouranophobia	heaven
panphobia, pantophobia	everything
parthenophobia	girls
pathophobia	disease
patroiophobia	heredity
peniaphobia	poverty
phagophobia	eating
phasmophobia	ghosts
phengophobia	daylight
phobophobia	fears
phonophobia	noise or speaking aloud

Technical term	Everyday term	Technical term	Everyday term
photophobia	light	symmetrophobia	symmetry
pnigerophobia	smothering	syphilophobia	syphilis
poinephobia	punishment	tachophobia	speed
polyphobia	many things	taphephobia, taphophobia	being buried alive
potophobia	alcoholic drink	technophobia	technology
pteronophobia	feathers	thaasophobia	sitting
pyrophobia	fire	thalassophobia	sea
rypophobia	soiling	thanatophobia	death
satanophobia	the Devil	theophobia	God
scopophobia, scoptophobia	being looked at	thermophobia	heat
scotophobia	darkness	tonitrophobia	thunder
selaphobia	flashes	toxiphobia, toxicophobia	poison
siderophobia	stars	tremophobia	trembling
sitophobia, sitiophobia	food	triskaidekaphobia, triskaidecaphobia	thirteen
spermaphobia, spermatophobia	germs	xenophobia	strangers, foreigners
stasiphobia	standing	zelophobia	jealousy
stygiophobia	hell	zoophobia	animals

Food Phobias

One infamous, if perhaps medically uncommon, phobia is *arachibutyrophobia* – the fear of peanut butter sticking to the roof of one's mouth. Other food phobias that may or may not have a scientific basis are *ostraconophobia*, fear of shellfish, *lachanophobia*, fear of vegetables and *ichthyophobia*, fear of fish. Fear of food itself is called *sitophobia* or *sitiophobia*.

Everyday term	Technical term	Everyday term	Technical term
alcoholic drink	potophobia	computers	cyberphobia
animals	zoophobia	contamination	misophobia, mysophobia
bees	apiphobia	contracting or having cancer	cancerphobia, cancerophobia
being buried alive	taphephobia, taphophobia	corpses	necrophobia
being by oneself	autophobia	crossing streets	dromophobia
being looked at	scopophobia, scoptophobia	crowds	demophobia, ochlophobia
being stared at	ophthalmophobia	crystals	chrystallophobia
birds	ornithophobia	darkness	achluophobia, scotophobia
blood	haematophobia	dawn	eosophobia
blushing	ereuthrophobia, erythrophobia	daylight	phengophobia
books	bibliophobia	death	thanatophobia
carriages	amakaphobia	demons	demonophobia
cats	ailurophobia	disease	nosophobia, pathophobia
closed spaces	claustrophobia	dogs	canophobia, cynophobia
clouds	nephophobia	draughts, air	aerophobia
cold	cheimaphobia	dreams	oneirophobia
colour	cromophobia		
comets	cometophobia		

Everyday term	Technical term
duration	chronophobia
dust	amathophobia
eating	phagophobia
electricity	electrophobia
empty spaces, voids	kenophobia
everything	panphobia, pantophobia
eyes	ommatophobia
failure	kakorraphiaphobia
falling from a high place	bathophobia
fatigue	kopophobia
fears	phobophobia
feathers	pteronophobia
fire	pyrophobia
flashes	selaphobia
flogging	mastigophobia
flood	antlophobia
flutes	aulophobia
fog	homichlophobia
food	sitophobia, sitiophobia
freedom	eleutherophobia
frogs, toads, newts	batrachophobia
fur	doraphobia
germs	spermaphobia, spermatophobia
ghosts	phasmophobia
girls	parthenophobia
glass	nelophobia
God	theophobia
good news	euphobia
gravity	barophobia
heat	thermophobia
heaven	ouranophobia
heights	acrophobia
hell	stygiophobia, hadephobia
heredity	patroiophobia
home	oikophobia
horses	hippophobia
ice	kristallophobia
ideas	ideophobia
infinity	apeirophobia
injustice	dikephobia
insanity	lyssophobia, maniaphobia
insects	entomophobia
jealousy	zelophobia
light	photophobia
lightning	astraphobia, astrapophobia

Everyday term	Technical term
machinery	mechanophobia
many things	polyphobia
men	androphobia
metals	metallophobia
meteors	meteorophobia
mice	musophobia
microbes	bacilliphobia
mirrors	eisoptrophobia
money	chrometophobia
motion	kinesophobia
music	musicophobia
narrowness	anginophobia
needles	belonephobia
newness, novelty	neophobia
night or darkness	nyctophobia
noise or speaking aloud	phonophobia
Northern Lights	auroraphobia
nudity	gymnophobia
numbers	arithmophobia
one thing, or being alone	monophobia
one's home surroundings	ecophobia
open spaces	agoraphobia
pain	algophobia
people or society	anthropophobia
personal physical deformity	dysmorphophobia
pins	eretephobia
pleasure	hedonophobia
points	aichurophobia
poison	toxiphobia, toxicophobia
poverty	peniaphobia
punishment	poinephobia
reptiles	herpetophobia
responsibility	hypegiaphobia
ridicule	katagelophobia
robbers	harpaxophobia
ruin	atephobia
sacred objects	hierophobia
sea	thalassophobia
sex	genophobia
sexual involvement	erotophobia
sharp or pointed objects	aichmophobia
shock	hormephobia
sin	hamartiophobia
sitting	thaasophobia
skin	dermatophobia

Everyday term	Technical term
sleep	hypnophobia
smell	olfactophobia
smothering	pnigerophobia
snakes	ophidiophobia, ophiophobia
snow	chionophobia
soiling	rypophobia
solitude	eremophobia
sound	akousticophobia
sourness	acerophobia
speed	tachophobia
spiders	arachnophobia
standing	stasiphobia
stars	siderophobia
stealing	kleptophobia
stings	cnidophobia
strangers, foreigners	xenophobia
string	linonophobia
stuttering	laliophobia
symmetry	symmetrophobia
syphilis	syphilophobia
taste	geumaphobia
technology	technophobia
teeth	odontophobia
the Devil	satanophobia
thirteen	triskaidekaphobia, triskaidecaphobia
thunder	brontophobia, keraunophobia, tonitrophobia
touch	haphephobia
travel	hodophobia
trembling	tremophobia
vehicles	ochophobia
vomiting	emetophobia
walking	basophobia
water	aquaphobia, hydrophobia
weakness	asthenophobia
wind or draughts	anemophobia
women	gynophobia
words	logophobia
work	ergasiophobia, ergophobia
worms	helminthophobia
writing	graphophobia

MANIAS

A mania is an abnormal and obsessive desire or inclination, or an extreme enthusiasm, for something. The term comes from the Greek word *mania* meaning 'madness'.

Technical term	Everyday term
ablutomania	personal cleanliness
acronymania	forming acronyms
ailuromania	cats
anthomania	flowers
arithmomania	numbers
balletomania	ballet
bibliomania	books
cleptomania	stealing
cynomania	dogs
demomania	crowds
demonomania	being possessed by devils
dipsomania	alcohol
egomania	oneself
eleutheromania	freedom
ergomania	work
erotomania	sexual passion
etheromania	taking ether
flagellomania	beating and flogging
graphomania	writing
hedonomania	pleasure
hippomania	horses
hydromania	water
infomania	gathering information
kleptomania	stealing
logomania	talking
megalomania	power
melomania	music
methomania	alcohol
metromania	writing verse
monomania	single thought, idea or activity
morphinomania	morphine
mythomania	lying or exaggerating
narcomania	drugs
necromania	dead bodies
nostomania	returning to familiar places
nymphomania	sexual desire
oenomania	alcohol
opsomania	special kind of food
orchidomania	orchids

Technical term	Everyday term
potichomania	imitating Oriental porcelain
pteridomania	ferns
pyromania	fire-raising
technomania	technology
thanatomania	death
theatromania	play-going
theomania	God, religion
tomomania	surgery
toxicomania	poison
trichotillomania	pulling out tufts of one's own hair
tulipomania	tulip-growing
xenomania	foreign things

Everyday term	Technical term
alcohol	dipsomania, methomania, oenomania
ballet	balletomania
beating and flogging	flagellomania
being possessed by devils	demonomania
books	bibliomania
cats	ailuromania
crowds	demomania
dead bodies	necromania
death	thanatomania
dogs	cynomania
drugs	narcomania
ferns	pteridomania
fire-raising	pyromania
flowers	anthomania
foreign things	xenomania
forming acronyms	acronymania
freedom	eleutheromania
gathering information	infomania
God	theomania
horses	hippomania
imitating Oriental porcelain	potichomania
lying or exaggerating	mythomania
morphine	morphinomania
music	melomania
numbers	arithmomania
oneself	egomania
orchids	orchidomania
personal cleanliness	ablutomania
play-going	theatromania
pleasure	hedonomania
poison	toxicomania
power	megalomania
pulling out tufts of one's own hair	trichotillomania
religion	theomania
returning to familiar places	nostomania
sexual desire	nymphomania
sexual passion	erotomania
single thought, idea or activity	monomania
special kind of food	opsomania
stealing	kleptomania, cleptomania
surgery	tomomania
taking ether	etheromania
talking	logomania
technology	technomania
tulip-growing	tulipomania
water	hydromania
work	ergomania
writing	graphomania
writing verse	metromania

COLLECTIVE NAMES FOR ANIMALS

Collective name	Animal
ambush	tigers
army	caterpillars, frogs
bale	turtles
band	gorillas
bask	crocodiles
bed	clams, oysters
bevy	larks, pheasants, quail, swans
bloat	hippopotami
bouquet	pheasants
brace	ducks
brood	chickens, hens
building	rooks
bury	rabbits
busyness	ferrets, flies
cackle	hyenas

COLLECTIVE NAMES FOR ANIMALS

Collective name	Animal
cast	hawks
cete	badgers
charm	finches, goldfinches
chirm	goldfinches
cloud	gnats
clowder	cats
clutch	chickens
colony	ants, bees, penguins, rats
company	parrots
congregation	plovers
convocation	eagles
covey	partridges, quail
crash	rhinoceros
cry	hounds
descent	woodpeckers
dole	doves, turtles
down	hares
draught	fish
dray	squirrels
drift	hogs, swine
drove	cattle, horses, oxen, sheep
erst	bees
exaltation	larks
fall	woodcocks
family	otters
flight	birds
flock	birds, ducks, geese, sheep
gaggle	geese
gam	whales
gang	buffalo, elk
grist	bees
herd	buffalo, cattle, deer, elephants, goats, horses, kangaroos, oxen, seals, whales
hive	bees
horde	gnats
host	sparrows
hover	trout
husk	hares
intrusion	cockroaches
kennel	dogs
kindle	kittens
knot	toads
labour	moles
leap	leopards
leash	foxes
litter	kittens, pigs
mob	kangaroos
murder	crows
murmuration	starlings
muster	peacocks, penguins
mustering	storks
mute	hares, hounds
nest	ants, bees, pheasants, vipers
nid	pheasants
nide	pheasants
nye	pheasants
obstinacy	buffalo
ostentation	peacocks
pace	asses
pack	dogs, grouse, hounds, wolves
paddling	ducks
pandemonium	parrots
parade	elephants
parcel	penguins
parliament	owls, rooks
plague	locusts
pod	seals, whales
pounce	cats
prickle	porcupines
pride	lions
rafter	turkeys
romp	otters
rookery	rooks, seals
rout	wolves
route	wolves
safe	ducks
school	dolphins, fish, porpoises, whales
scurry	squirrels
sedge	cranes
shiver	sharks
shoal	fish
shrewdness	apes
siege	cranes, herons
skein	geese
skulk	foxes
sleuth	bears
sloth	bears
smack	jellyfish
sounder	swine
span	mules
spring	teal
stable	horses
stand	flamingos
stare	owls
streak	tigers
string	horses, ponies

Collective name	Animal
swarm	ants, bees, flies, locusts
team	ducks, horses
tiding	magpies
tittering	magpies
tower	giraffes
tribe	goats
trip	goats, sheep
troop	baboons, kangaroos, monkeys
turmoil	porpoises
turn	turtles
unkindness	ravens
volery	birds
watch	nightingales
wedge	swans
wing	plovers
yoke	oxen
zeal	zebras

Collective Imagination

Some people enjoy inventing new and creative collective nouns for professions or other groups of people. Suggestions have included an *audit* of bookkeepers, a *complex* of psychologists, an *eloquence* of lawyers, a *flush* of plumbers, a *giggle* of girls, an *intrigue* of politicians, a *ponder* of philosophers, a *superfluity* of nuns and a *tedium* of golfers.

ANIMAL ADJECTIVES

Animal	Adjective
ape	simian
ass	asinine
badger	musteline
bear	ursine
bee	apian
bird	avian, avine, volucrine
bull	taurine
butterfly	papilionaceous
calf	vituline
camel	cameline
cat	feline
cattle	bovine
deer	cervine
dog	canine
donkey	asinine
dove	columbine
eagle	aquiline
elephant	elephantine
falcon	falconine
ferret	viverrine
finch	fringilline
fish	piscine, ichthyic
fowl	gallinaceous
fox	vulpine
goat	caprine, hircine
goose	anserine
gull	larine
hare	leporine
hawk	accipitrine
horse	equine, caballine, hippic
lion	leonine
lizard	lacertian, saurian
monkey	simian
mouse	murine
otter	musteline
ox	bovine
parrot	psittacine
pig	porcine, suilline
rattlesnake	crotaline
red deer	elaphine
seal	phocine
sheep	ovine
shrew	soricine
slug	limacine
snake	anguine, colubrine
swallow	hirundine
thrush	turdine
tiger	tigrine
viper	viperine
vulture	vulturine
wasp	vespine
weasel	musteline
wolf	lupine

EATING ADJECTIVES

Adjective	Feeds on ...
anthropophagous	humans (cannibalism)
apivorous	bees
autophagous	itself
baccivorous	berries
carnivorous	flesh
carpophagous	fruit
coprophagous	dung
creophagous	flesh
entomophagous	insects
fructivorous	fruit
frugivorous	fruits or seeds
fucivorous	seaweed
geophagous	soil
graminivorous	grass, cereals, etc
granivorous	seeds, grain
haematophagous	blood
herbivorous	grass or herbage
hippophagous	horses
hylophagous	wood
ichthyophagous	fish
insectivorous	insects
lignivorous	wood
meliphagous	honey
mellivorous	honey
merdivorous	dung
myristicivorous	nutmegs
myrmecophagous	ants
necrophagous	carrion
nucivorous	nuts
omnivorous	both animal and vegetable food
omophagous	raw flesh
ophiophagous	snakes
ossivorous	bones
ostreophagous	oysters
pantophagous	both animal and vegetable food
phyllophagous	leaves
phytophagous	plants
piscivorous	fish
radicivorous	roots
ranivorous	frogs
rhizophagous	roots
sanguivorous, sanguinivorous	blood
saprophagous	decaying organic matter
sarcophagous	flesh
sarcosaprophagous	decaying flesh
scatophagous	dung
theophagous	gods
toxicophagous	poison
vermivorous	worms
xylophagous	wood
zoophagous	animals

Wonderful Words

Often words like *myristicivorous*, meaning feeding on nutmegs, become people's favourite words simply because we don't expect such a word to exist. Other delightful oddities include *callipygous*, having beautiful buttocks, *genethliac*, relating to a birthday, *leiotrichy*, straight-hairedness, *mallemaroking*, the carousing of seamen in icebound ships, *paneity*, the state of being bread, and *pogonotomy*, a wonderful word for shaving.

DIVINATION TECHNIQUES

Divination is seeking to know the future or hidden things by supernatural means, instinctive prevision and prediction.

Term	Divination by ...
aeromancy	atmospheric phenomena
axinomancy	the motions of an axe poised upon a stake, or of an agate placed upon a red-hot axe
belomancy	means of arrows
bibliomancy	opening the bible or other book at random
botanomancy	means of plants, especially the leaves of sage and fig
capnomancy	smoke
cartomancy	playing cards

Term	Divination by ...
ceromancy	dropping melted wax in water
chiromancy	reading the hand
cleromancy	lot
coscinomancy	a sieve and pair of shears
crithomancy	strewing meal over sacrificial animals
crystallomancy	transparent bodies
dactyliomancy	means of a ring
gastromancy	sounds from the belly, or by large-bellied glasses
geomancy	shapes formed, eg when earth is thrown down onto a surface
gyromancy	walking in a circle and falling from giddiness
hepatoscopy	inspection of the livers of animals
hieromancy	observing the objects offered in sacrifice
hydromancy	water
lampadomancy	flame
lithomancy	stones
myomancy	observing the way in which mice move when released from a cage
oenomancy	from the appearance of wine poured out in libations
omoplatoscopy, scapulomancy	observing the cracks appearing in a burning shoulder blade
omphalomancy	the knots in the umbilical cord, to tell the number of future children
oneiromancy	dreams
onychomancy	the fingernails
ornithomancy	means of birds, by observing their flight, etc
pyromancy	fire
rhabdomancy	rod, especially divining for water or ore
sortes	chance opening of the Bible, Homer, Virgil, etc
sortilege	drawing lots
spodomancy	means of ashes
taghairm	lying in a bullock's hide behind a waterfall
tephromancy	ashes, especially those left after a sacrifice
theomancy	means of oracles, or of persons directly inspired immediately by some divinity
tripudium	the hopping of birds feeding, or the dropping of scraps from their bills
zoomancy	observation of animals

COLLECTORS AND ENTHUSIASTS

Devotee	Item or activity
ailurophile, ailourophile	cats
antiquary	antiques
arachnologist	spiders/arachnids
arctophile	teddy bears
audiophile	broadcast sound
balletomane	ballet
bibliophile	books
campanologist	bell-ringing
canophilist, cynophilist	dogs
cartophile, cartophilist	cigarette cards
chirographist	handwriting
chrysophilite	gold
cinephile	cinema

Devotee	Item or activity
conservationist	countryside
Dantophilist	Dante
deltiologist	postcards
discophile	gramophone records
entomologist	insects
environmentalist	the environment
ephemerist	ephemera
ex-librist	bookplates
gastronome	good living
gourmet	good food
hippophile	horses
incunabulist	early printed books
lepidopterist	butterflies
logophile	words
monarchist	the monarchy
neophile	novelty and new things
notaphilist	banknotes, cheques
numismatist	coins/medals
oenophile, oenophilist	wine
ophiophilist	snakes
ornithologist	birds
paroemiographer	proverbs
philatelist, timbrophilist	stamps
phillumenist	matches/matchboxes
philomath	learning
pteridophilist	ferns
scripophile, scripophilist	bond and share certificates
stegophilist	climbing buildings for sport
stigmatophilist	tattooing or body piercing
technophile	technology
tegestologist	beer mats
toxophilite	archery
xenophile	foreigners
zoophile	animals

Curious Collections

People collect almost anything. Guinness World Records® includes people with the largest collections of airsickness bags, autographed drum sticks, beer bottles, belly button fluff, chamber pots, coloured vinyl records, 'do not disturb' signs, four-leaf clovers, garden gnomes, golf balls, hair from historical figures, handcuffs, nail clippers, piggy banks, spoon rests and weighing scales.

FAMOUS LAST WORDS

Prince Albert (1819–61)

'I have had wealth, rank and power, but, if these were all I had, how wretched I should be.'

Attributed.

Augustus (63 BC–AD 14)

'The play is over.'

Attributed.

Béla Bartók (1881–1945)

'The trouble is that I have to go with so much still to say.'

Quoted in David Pickering *Brewer's Twentieth Century Music* (1994).

Ludwig van Beethoven (1770–1827)

'I shall hear in heaven.'

Attributed. Quoted in Ian Crofton and Donald Fraser *A Dictionary of Musical Quotations* (1985).

Julius Caesar (100 or 102–44 BC)
'Et tu, Brute?'
'You too, Brutus?'
Attributed, when struck by his murderers, Cassius and Brutus.

Sir Winston Churchill (1874–1965)
'I am so bored with it all.'
Attributed.

Dame Gladys Cooper (1888–1971)
'If this is what virus pneumonia does to one, I really don't think I shall bother to have it again.'

Bing Crosby (1904–77)
'That was a great game of golf.'
As he finished play at the 18th hole before suffering a heart attack.

Emily Dickinson (1830–86)
'Let us go in; the fog is rising.'
Attributed.

Johann Wolfgang von Goethe (1749–1832)
'More light!'

Henrik Ibsen (1828–1906)
'On the contrary!'
Refuting a nurse's suggestion that he was feeling better.

Lord Horatio Nelson (1758–1805)
'Kiss me, Hardy.'
Attributed, as he lay dying in the cockpit of the *Victory* during the Battle of Trafalgar.

Lawrence Oates (1880–1912)
'I am just going outside and may be some time.'

William Pitt (1759–1806)
'I think that I could eat one of Bellamy's veal pies.'
Attributed.

William Saroyan (1908–81)
'Now what?'

Tom Simpson (1938–67)
'Put me back on my bike.'
He died from heart failure during the Tour de France.

Lytton Strachey (1880–1932)
'If this is dying, then I don't think much of it.'
Attributed.

Dylan Thomas (1914–53)
'I've had 18 straight whiskies. I think that's the record.'
Attributed, before lapsing into his final coma.

Oscar Wilde (1854–1900)
'Either that wallpaper goes or I do.'
Attributed, as he lay dying in a Paris hotel bedroom.

ARABIC ALPHABET

Letter	Name	Usual transliteration
ا	*'alif*	' or *a*
ب	*ba*	*b*
ت	*ta*	*t*
ث	*tha*	*th*
ج	*jim*	*j*
ح	*ha*	*h*
خ	*kha*	*kh*
د	*dal*	*d*
ذ	*dhal*	*dh*
ر	*ra*	*r*
ز	*zay*	*a*
س	*sin*	*s*
ش	*shin*	*sh*
ص	*sad*	*s*
ض	*dad*	*d*
ط	*ta*	*t*
ظ	*za*	*z*
ع	*ʻain*	ʻ or *a*
غ	*ghain*	*gh*
ف	*fa*	*f*
ق	*qaf*	*q*
ك	*kaf*	*k*
ل	*lam*	*l*
م	*mim*	*m*
ن	*nun*	*n*
ه	*ha*	*h*
و	*waw*	*w*, *oo* or *ow*
ي	*ya*	*y*, *ee*, *ay* or *ey*

CYRILLIC ALPHABET

Letter	Usual transliteration
А а	a
Б б	*b*
В в	*v*
Г г	g
Д д	*d*
Е е	e (*ye*)
Ё ё	e (*yö*)
Ж ж	*zh*
З з	z
И и	*i* (*ē*)
Й й	(consonantal *y* sound; only used as the second letter of a diphthong)
К к	*k*
Л л	*l*
М м	*m*
Н н	*n*
О о	*o*
П п	*p*
Р р	*r*
С с	*s*
Т т	*t*
У у	*u*
Ф ф	*f*
Х х	*kh*
Ц ц	*ts*
Ч ч	*ch*
Ш ш	*sh*
Щ щ	*shch* (often pronounced rather as *sh* followed by consonantal *y*)
Ъ ъ	(hard sign; used to separate in pronunciation a following palatalized vowel from a preceding consonant either palatalized or unpalatalized)
Ы ы	*i* (a sound similar to *i*)
Ь ь	(soft sign; used after a consonant to indicate palatalization, a sound like consonantal *y*)
Э э	e (*e*)
Ю ю	*u* (*yoo*)
Я я	*ya* (*yä*)

GREEK ALPHABET

Letter	Name	Usual transliteration	Letter	Name	Usual transliteration
Α α	*alpha*	a	Ν ν	*nū*	*n*
Β β	*bēta*	*b*	Ξ ξ	*xī*	*x*
Γ γ	*gamma*	*g*	Ο ο	*omicron*	*o*
Δ δ	*delta*	*d*	Π π	*pī*	*p*
Ε ε	*epsīlon*	e	Ρ ρ	*rhō*	*r*
Ζ ζ	*zēta*	*z*	Σ σ ς	*sigma*	*s*
Η η	*ēta*	ē	Τ τ	*tau*	*t*
Θ θ	*thēta*	*th*	Υ υ	*upsīlon*	*u* or *y*
Ι ι	*iōta*	*i*	Φ φ	*phī*	*ph*
Κ κ	*kappa*	*k*	Χ χ	*chī*	*kh* or *ch*
Λ λ	*lambda*	*l*	Ψ ψ	*psī*	*ps*
Μ μ	*mū*	*m*	Ω ω	*ōmega*	*ō*

HEBREW ALPHABET

Letter	Name	Usual transliteration	Letter	Name	Usual transliteration
א	*aleph*	’	ל	*lamed*	*l*
ב	*beth*	*b*	ם מ	*mem*	*m*
ג	*gimel*	*g*	ן נ	*nun*	*n*
ד	*daleth*	*d*	ס	*samekh*	*s*
ה	*heh*	*h*	ע	*ayin*	‘
ו	*vav*	*w*	ף פ	*peh*	*p, f*
ז	*zayin*	*z*	ץ צ	*sadhe*	*s*
ח	*cheth*	*h*	ק	*koph*	*q*
ט	*teth*	*t*	ר	*resh*	*r*
י	*yod*	*y, j*	ש	*sin*	*sh, s*
ך כ	*kaph*	*k*	ת	*tav*	*t*

St Cyril's Alphabet

The Cyrillic alphabet is used for Russian, Ukrainian, Serbian and Bulgarian. It is so called because it is traditionally attributed to St Cyril (827–69), a Greek Christian missionary known as the Apostle of the Slavs, who made Slav translations of the Scriptures and whose feast day is still a national holiday in some Eastern European countries. Based on the Greek alphabet, the Cyrillic includes extra symbols to represent Slavic sounds not found in Greek.

RUNIC ALPHABET

The runic alphabet, known as *futhark*, was made up of 24 basic symbols, although there was considerable regional variation in the overall number of symbols and symbol shapes used. Around 4,000 runic inscriptions and a few manuscripts survive, principally made by the early Scandinavians and Anglo-Saxons.

ᚠ	f	ᚷ	g	ᛇ	ï	ᛖ	e
ᚢ	u	ᚹ	w	ᛈ	p	ᛗ	m
ᚦ	þ	ᚻ	h	ᛉ	x	ᛚ	l
ᚩ	o	ᚾ	n	ᛋ	s	ᛝ	ng
ᚱ	r	ᛁ	i	ᛏ	t	ᛟ	œ
ᚴ	k	ᛄ	j	ᛒ	b	ᛞ	d

Pictography

A *pictograph* is a picture used as a symbol for a word or phrase. Pictographs do not relate to the sounds of language, as in most modern writing systems, but represent an abstract idea related to a concrete object, and then the name for that object. In China pictographs developed into a complex system where the written symbol represents a complete word, or part of a word, meaning that in writing modern Chinese a knowledge of 2,000 characters is required, and in Japanese, where the writing system developed from the Chinese one, 1,850 characters are considered essential for everyday use. In contrast, most sound-based alphabets can manage with 30 or fewer symbols.

PHONETIC ALPHABET

The phonetic alphabet, also known as the NATO alphabet, is a system used in international radio communication in which letters of the alphabet are identified by means of code words.

A Alpha
B Bravo
C Charlie
D Delta
E Echo
F Foxtrot
G Golf
H Hotel
I India
J Juliet
K Kilo
L Lima
M Mike
N November
O Oscar
P Papa
Q Quebec
R Romeo
S Sierra
T Tango
U Uniform
V Victor
W Whiskey
X X-ray
Y Yankee
Z Zulu

BRAILLE

Braille is a system of printing for the blind, in which printed characters are represented by raised dots which can be read by touch. Each character is formed by a different combination taken from a basic six-dot matrix. It was invented in 1829 by the Frenchman Louis Braille (1809–52), who was blind from the age of three.

A ⠁	D ⠙	G ⠛	J ⠚	M ⠍	P ⠏	S ⠎	V ⠧	Y ⠽
B ⠃	E ⠑	H ⠓	K ⠅	N ⠝	Q ⠟	T ⠞	W ⠺	Z ⠵
C ⠉	F ⠋	I ⠊	L ⠇	O ⠕	R ⠗	U ⠥	X ⠭	

MORSE CODE

Morse is a method of signalling by a code in which each letter is represented by a combination of dashes and dots or long and short light flashes, sound signals, etc. In the spoken form of Morse code, the word *dah* represents the dash and the word *dit* represents the dot. It was invented by Samuel F B Morse (1791–1872), a US inventor. Morse created one of the first telegraph lines between Washington and Baltimore as an experiment, and developed 'Morse code' (originally called the 'Morse alphabet') for use with it.

A	•—	G	——•	M	——	S	•••	Y	—•——
B	—•••	H	••••	N	—•	T	—	Z	——••
C	—••	I	••	O	———	U	••—		
D	—••	J	•———	P	•——•	V	•••—		
E	•	K	—•—	Q	——•—	W	•——		
F	••—•	L	•—••	R	•—•	X	—••—		

SOS

SOS is an appeal for help or rescue, especially at sea. It is popularly believed to stand for 'Save Our Ship' or even 'Save Our Souls', but the truth is much simpler: it doesn't stand for anything. In fact, it was chosen for ease and clarity of transmission by Morse code (. . . — — — . . .). The signal was adopted internationally in 1908; since 1999 the International Maritime Organization's new Global Maritime Distress and Safety System (GMDSS) for distress calls has led to SOS becoming almost obsolete, on larger ships at least.

SEMAPHORE

Semaphore was widely used in visual telegraphy, especially at sea, before the advent of electricity. Old-style railway signals are a simple form of semaphore, with a single arm having two positions to indicate 'stop' and 'go'.

SIGN LANGUAGE: FINGERSPELLING

Sign language is a means of communication using finger and hand movements, in which signs represent whole words or phrases. Fingerspelling uses the movements to represent letters of the alphabet, enabling words to be spelled letter by letter.

British

Silent Talking

Dactylology is the art of talking with the fingers using sign language. The word comes from an ancient Greek word, *daktylos*, which means 'finger'.

US

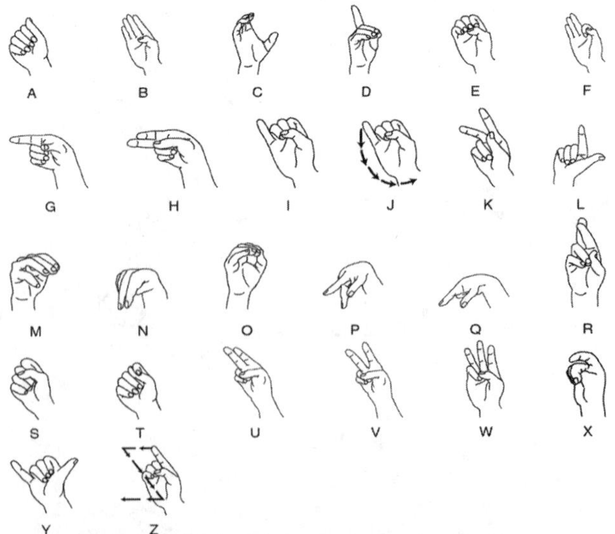

KEYBOARD LAYOUT

The standard arrangement of keys on an English-language computer keyboard is known as *qwerty*, from the letters at the top left-hand side of the keyboard.

Quirky Qwerty

It is widely believed that the arrangement of the letters on the qwerty keyboard was designed to slow typists down. But although it is true that the layout was designed to prevent jamming on the early typewriters, it wasn't achieved by slowing the fingers down. Instead the keys for common letter patterns, such as *sh*, are arranged so as to be far enough apart to prevent the typebars clashing when the keys were hit in rapid succession. An interesting side effect of the qwerty layout is that all the letters for the word *typewriter* are found on the keyboard's top row.

DEWEY DECIMAL CLASSIFICATION

Dewey decimal classification is a system of library classification, based on the division of books into numbered classes, with further subdivision shown by numbers following a decimal point. The system was invented by Melvil Dewey (1851–1931), a US librarian, who designed the system for the Amherst College Library between 1873 and 1876.

000	Generalities	500	Natural sciences and mathematics
100	Philosophy and psychology	600	Technology (applied sciences)
200	Religion	700	The arts
300	Social sciences	800	Literature and rhetoric
400	Language	900	Geography and history

Dewey Worldwide

The Dewey system is used in more than 35 countries. It has been modified and updated many times, has had 22 major editions published and is capable of being infinitely expanded to allow new subject areas to be included. Current topics of concern to librarians using the Dewey system include where to classify books about quidditch, the sport played in the Harry Potter novels by J K Rowling (under 823.914, apparently).

INTERNET SUFFIXES

General suffixes

.ac.uk	UK academic institutions	.asia	organizations in the Asia–Pacific region
.aero	aviation industry		

INTERNET SUFFIXES

.biz	businesses
.cat	Catalan language and culture
.com	commercial sites
.comp	newsgroups about computers
.coop	business co-operatives
.co.uk	UK commercial
.edu	US educational institutions
.gov	US government
.info	general information
.int	international organizations
.jobs	employment-related sites
.mil	US military
.mobi	sites catering for mobile phone/ device
.museum	museums
.name	individuals
.net	major service providers
.org	non-profit organizations
.pro	certain professions
.sci	newsgroups about science
.soc	newsgroups about society
.tel	services connecting telephone and internet
.travel	travel and tourism industry

Geographical suffixes

For suffixes listed by country see the individual entries in the **Countries A–Z** section of **Human Geography**.

.ac	Ascension Island
.ad	Andorra
.ae	United Arab Emirates
.af	Afghanistan
.ag	Antigua and Barbuda
.ai	Anguilla
.al	Albania
.am	Armenia
.an	Netherlands Antilles
.ao	Angola
.aq	Antarctica
.ar	Argentina
.as	American Samoa
.at	Austria
.au	Australia
.aw	Aruba
.ax	Åland
.az	Azerbaijan
.ba	Bosnia and Herzegovina
.bb	Barbados
.bd	Bangladesh
.be	Belgium
.bf	Burkina Faso
.bg	Bulgaria
.bh	Bahrain
.bi	Burundi
.bj	Benin
.bl	St Barthélemy
.bm	Bermuda
.bn	Brunei Darussalam
.bo	Bolivia
.br	Brazil
.bs	The Bahamas
.bt	Bhutan
.bv	Bouvet Island
.bw	Botswana
.by	Belarus
.bz	Belize
.ca	Canada
.cc	Cocos (Keeling) Islands
.cd	Congo, Democratic Republic of the
.cf	Central African Republic
.cg	Congo, Republic of
.ch	Switzerland
.ci	Côte d'Ivoire
.ck	Cook Islands
.cl	Chile
.cm	Cameroon
.cn	China
.co	Colombia
.cr	Costa Rica
.cu	Cuba
.cv	Cape Verde
.cx	Christmas Island
.cy	Cyprus
.cz	Czech Republic
.de	Germany
.dj	Djibouti
.dk	Denmark
.dm	Dominica
.do	Dominican Republic
.dz	Algeria
.ec	Ecuador
.ee	Estonia
.eg	Egypt
.eh	Western Sahara
.er	Eritrea
.es	Spain
.et	Ethiopia
.eu	European Union
.fi	Finland
.fj	Fiji
.fk	Falkland Islands
.fm	Micronesia
.fo	Faroe Islands
.fr	France
.ga	Gabon
.gd	Grenada
.ge	Georgia
.gf	French Guiana
.gg	Guernsey
.gh	Ghana
.gi	Gibraltar
.gl	Greenland
.gm	The Gambia
.gn	Guinea
.gp	Guadeloupe
.gq	Equatorial Guinea
.gr	Greece
.gs	Georgia and the South Sandwich Islands
.gt	Guatemala
.gu	Guam
.gw	Guinea-Bissau
.gy	Guyana
.hk	Hong Kong
.hm	Heard and McDonald Islands
.hn	Honduras
.hr	Croatia
.ht	Haiti
.hu	Hungary
.id	Indonesia
.ie	Ireland
.il	Israel
.im	Isle of Man
.in	India
.io	British Indian Ocean Territory
.iq	Iraq
.ir	Iran
.is	Iceland
.it	Italy

.je	Jersey
.jm	Jamaica
.jo	Jordan
.jp	Japan
.ke	Kenya
.kg	Kyrgyzstan
.kh	Cambodia
.ki	Kiribati
.km	Comoros
.kn	St Kitts and Nevis
.kp	Korea, North
.kr	Korea, South
.kw	Kuwait
.ky	Cayman Islands
.kz	Kazakhstan
.la	Laos
.lb	Lebanon
.lc	St Lucia
.li	Liechtenstein
.lk	Sri Lanka
.lr	Liberia
.ls	Lesotho
.lt	Lithuania
.lu	Luxembourg
.lv	Latvia
.ly	Libya
.ma	Morocco
.mc	Monaco
.md	Moldova
.me	Montenegro
.mf	St Martin
.mg	Madagascar
.mh	Marshall Islands
.mk	Macedonia
.ml	Mali
.mm	Myanmar (Burma)
.mn	Mongolia
.mo	Macau
.mp	Northern Mariana Islands
.mq	Martinique
.mr	Mauritania
.ms	Montserrat
.mt	Malta
.mu	Mauritius
.mv	Maldives
.mw	Malawi
.mx	Mexico
.my	Malaysia
.mz	Mozambique
.na	Namibia
.nc	New Caledonia
.ne	Niger
.nf	Norfolk Island
.ng	Nigeria
.ni	Nicaragua
.nl	The Netherlands
.no	Norway
.np	Nepal
.nr	Nauru
.nu	Niue
.nz	New Zealand
.om	Oman
.pa	Panama
.pe	Peru
.pf	French Polynesia
.pg	Papua New Guinea
.ph	Philippines
.pk	Pakistan
.pl	Poland
.pm	St Pierre and Miquelon
.pn	Pitcairn Islands
.pr	Puerto Rico
.ps	Palestinian Territories
.pt	Portugal
.pw	Palau
.py	Paraguay
.qa	Qatar
.re	Réunion
.ro	Romania
.rs	Serbia
.ru	Russia
.rw	Rwanda
.sa	Saudi Arabia
.sb	Solomon Islands
.sc	Seychelles
.sd	Sudan
.se	Sweden
.sg	Singapore
.sh	St Helena
.si	Slovenia
.sj	Svalbard and Jan Meyen Islands
.sk	Slovakia
.sl	Sierra Leone
.sm	San Marino
.sn	Senegal
.so	Somalia
.sr	Suriname
.st	São Tomé and Príncipe
.sv	El Salvador
.sy	Syria
.sz	Swaziland
.tc	Turks and Caicos Islands
.td	Chad
.tf	French Southern and Antarctic Territories
.tg	Togo
.th	Thailand
.tj	Tajikistan
.tk	Tokelau
.tl	East Timor
.tm	Turkmenistan
.tn	Tunisia
.to	Tonga
.tr	Turkey
.tt	Trinidad and Tobago
.tv	Tuvalu
.tw	Taiwan
.tz	Tanzania
.ua	Ukraine
.ug	Uganda
.uk	United Kingdom
.um	US Minor Outlying Islands
.us	United States
.uy	Uruguay
.uz	Uzbekistan
.va	Vatican
.vc	St Vincent and the Grenadines
.ve	Venezuela
.vg	Virgin Islands (British)
.vi	Virgin Islands (US)
.vn	Vietnam
.vu	Vanuatu
.wf	Wallis and Futuna Islands
.ws	Samoa
.ye	Yemen
.yt	Mayotte
.za	South Africa
.zm	Zambia
.zw	Zimbabwe

Tuvalu TV

The internet domain name .tv is highly desirable to television and media companies. Tuvalu, a small island group in the south-west Pacific Ocean approximately 1,050km/650mi north of Fiji, realized its good fortune and leased the rights to its domain name for $50 million in royalties over a ten-year period.

TRANSPORT

For road and rail bridges and tunnels see **Architecture and Engineering**.

INTERNATIONAL VEHICLE REGISTRATION (IVR) CODES

A	Austria
AFG	Afghanistan
AL	Albania
AM	Armenia
AND	Andorra
AUS	Australia[1]
AX	Åland
AZ	Azerbaijan
B	Belgium
BD	Bangladesh[1]
BDS	Barbados[1]
BF	Burkina Faso
BG	Bulgaria
BIH	Bosnia and Herzegovina
BOL	Bolivia
BR	Brazil
BRN	Bahrain
BRU	Brunei Darussalam[1]
BS	The Bahamas[1]
BUR	Myanmar (Burma)
BW	Botswana[1]
BY	Belarus
BZ	Belize
C	Cuba
CAM	Cameroon
CDN	Canada
CH	Switzerland
CI	Côte d'Ivoire
CL	Sri Lanka[1]
CO	Colombia
CR	Costa Rica
CY	Cyprus[1]
CZ	Czech Republic
D	Germany
DK	Denmark (including Greenland)
DOM	Dominican Republic
DY	Benin
DZ	Algeria
E	Spain
EAK	Kenya[1]
EAT	Tanzania (mainland)[1]
EAU	Uganda[1]
EAZ	Tanzania (Zanzibar)[1]
EC	Ecuador
ER	Eritrea
ES	El Salvador
EST	Estonia
ET	Egypt
ETH	Ethiopia
F	France
FIN	Finland
FJI	Fiji[1]
FL	Liechtenstein
G	Gabon
GB	United Kingdom[1]
GBA	Alderney[1]
GBG	Guernsey[1]
GBJ	Jersey[1]
GBM	Isle of Man[1]
GBZ	Gibraltar
GCA	Guatemala
GE	Georgia
GH	Ghana
GR	Greece
GUY	Guyana[1]
H	Hungary
HKJ	Jordan
HR	Croatia
I	Italy
IL	Israel
IND	India[1]
IR	Iran
IRL	Ireland[1]
IRQ	Iraq
IS	Iceland
J	Japan[1]
JA	Jamaica[1]
K	Cambodia
KS	Kyrgyzstan
KSA	Saudi Arabia
KWT	Kuwait
KZ	Kazakhstan
L	Luxembourg
LAO	Laos
LAR	Libya
LB	Liberia
LS	Lesotho[1]
LT	Lithuania
LV	Latvia
M	Malta[1]
MA	Morocco
MAL	Malaysia[1]
MC	Monaco
MD	Moldova
MEX	Mexico
MGL	Mongolia
MK	Macedonia
MNE	Montenegro
MOC	Mozambique[1]
MS	Mauritius[1]
MW	Malawi[1]
N	Norway
NA	Netherlands Antilles
NAM	Namibia[1]
NAU	Nauru[1]
NEP	Nepal[1]
NGR	Nigeria
NIC	Nicaragua
NL	The Netherlands
NZ	New Zealand[1]
P	Portugal
PA	Panama
PE	Peru
PK	Pakistan[1]
PL	Poland
PNG	Papua New Guinea[1]
PY	Paraguay
Q	Qatar
RA	Argentina
RC	Taiwan
RCA	Central African Republic
RCB	Congo
RCH	Chile
RG	Guinea
RGB	Guinea-Bissau
RH	Haiti
RI	Indonesia[1]
RIM	Mauritania
RL	Lebanon
RM	Madagascar
RMM	Mali
RN	Niger
RO	Romania
ROK	Korea (North)
ROU	Uruguay
RP	Philippines
RSM	San Marino
RU	Burundi
RUS	Russia
RWA	Rwanda
S	Sweden

SD	Swaziland[1]	TG	Togo	WAL	Sierra Leone
SGP	Singapore[1]	TJ	Tajikistan	WD	Dominica[1]
SK	Slovakia	TM	Turkmenistan	WG	Grenada[1]
SLO	Slovenia	TN	Tunisia	WL	St Lucia[1]
SME	Suriname[1]	TR	Turkey	WS	Samoa
SN	Senegal	TT	Trinidad and Tobago[1]	WV	St Vincent and the Grenadines[1]
SO	Somalia	UA	Ukraine	YAR	Yemen
SRB	Serbia	USA	United States of America	YV	Venezuela
SUD	Sudan	UZ	Uzbekistan	Z	Zambia[1]
SY	Seychelles[1]	V	Vatican	ZA	South Africa[1]
SYR	Syria	VN	Vietnam	ZRE	Congo, Democratic Republic of the
T	Thailand[1]	WAG	The Gambia	ZW	Zimbabwe[1]
TCH	Chad				

[1] *In countries so marked, the rule of the road is to drive on the left; in others, vehicles drive on the right.*

Rules of the Road

One theory suggests that driving on the left of the road arose in medieval times. As most people are right-handed, travelling on the left of the road meant that swords or other weapons would be nearest to other travellers. Some people believe that the rise in right-handed driving can be blamed on left-handed French ruler Napoleon I, who reversed the practice in France.

LONDON UNDERGROUND LINES

An underground railway system for London was first proposed in 1843, and construction work began on the Metropolitan Railway in 1860. The line opened between Farringdon and Paddington in 1863 using steam locomotives to pull trains. However, the first electrically-hauled underground line was the City and Southern which opened in 1890, the year in which London's new underground railway first became known as the Tube.

Line	Colour	Line	Colour
Bakerloo	brown	Jubilee	grey
Central	red	Metropolitan	maroon
Circle	yellow	Northern	black
District	green	Piccadilly	navy blue
East London	orange	Victoria	sky blue
Hammersmith and City	pink	Waterloo and City	sea green

Tracing the Tube

The standard London Underground map that we know today was designed by Harry Beck (1903–1974) back in the early 1930s. He abandoned the complicated geographic style of early Tube maps, instead creating a simple plan that was based on electrical circuit diagrams. It clearly showed the various lines (each a different colour) joining the stations. Beck's diagram – with some updates and modifications – is still in use today, more than 70 years after it was first published in 1933.

Rush Hour

The busiest station on the London Underground system is Victoria – London Underground estimate that 76.5 million passengers pass through it annually. Britain's busiest railway station is Clapham Junction, in the London borough of Wandsworth.

MOTORWAYS (MAINLAND UK)

The first British motorway was the M6 Preston Bypass, which opened in Dec 1958. Motorways of 5 miles or longer are shown on the map .

Motorway Madness

The busiest UK motorway is the M25, notably between junctions 14 and 15. The M61 in Greater Manchester has the most lanes, with 17, while 'Spaghetti Junction' on the M6 is officially the most complicated interchange. The highest motorway is the M62 across the Pennines.

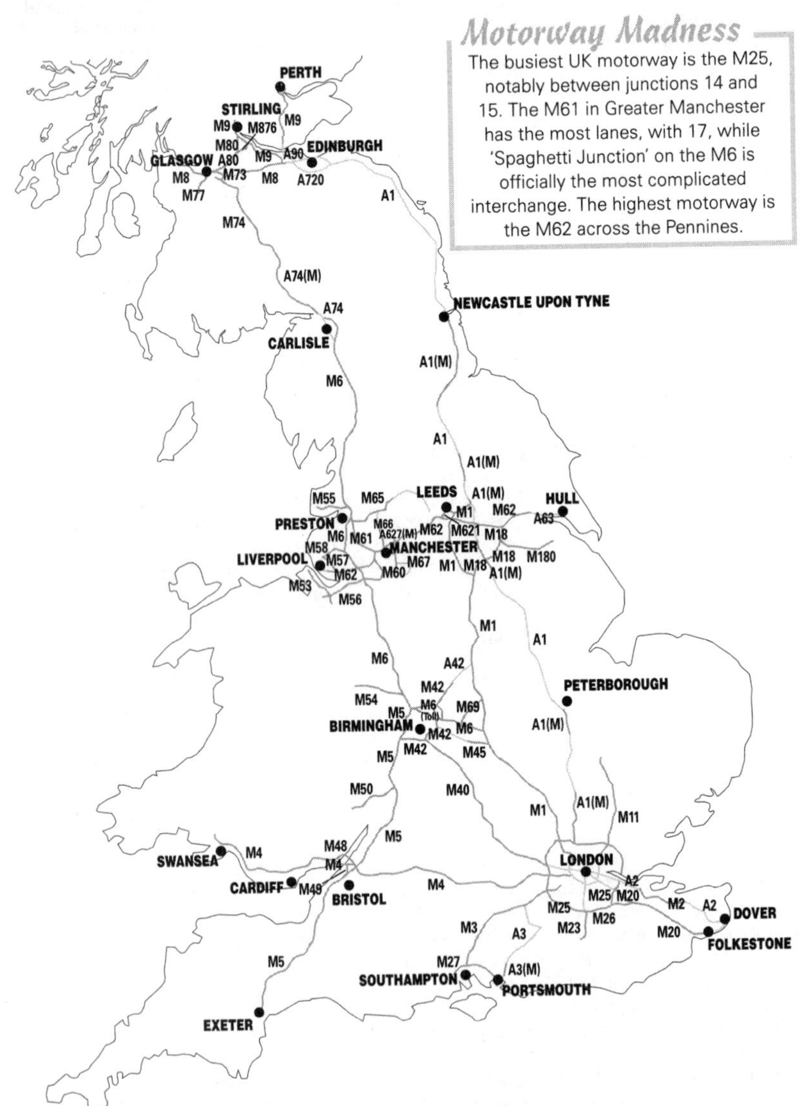

ROAD DISTANCES (UK)

Road distances between British centres are given in statute miles, using routes recommended by the Automobile Association based on the quickest travelling time. *To convert to kilometres, multiply the number given by 1.6093.*

Roman Roads

The first people to construct surfaced roads on a large scale were the Romans. The total distance of the roads built by the Romans has been estimated at a lengthy 85,000km/53,000mi, and their road network covered the whole of the Roman Empire, circling the Mediterranean and extending deep into Asia and northwards across Europe. A traveller in late Roman times could make the entire journey from York to Jerusalem on good, safe roads – something that wasn't possible again until the 20c.

	Birmingham	Bristol	Cambridge	Cardiff	Dover	Edinburgh	Exeter	Glasgow	Holyhead	Hull	Leeds	Liverpool	London	Manchester	Newcastle	Norwich	Nottingham	Penzance	Oxford	Plymouth	Shrewsbury	Southampton	Stranraer	York
Stranraer																								228
Southampton																							447	252
Shrewsbury																						190	287	144
Plymouth																					242	155	502	340
Penzance																				78	315	227	572	406
Oxford																			265	193	113	67	371	185
Nottingham																		104	336	265	85	171	295	86
Norwich																	123	144	407	336	205	192	393	185
Newcastle																258	156	253	477	410	216	319	164	83
Manchester															141	183	71	153	355	281	69	227	226	71
London														199	280	115	128	56	283	215	162	76	419	209
Liverpool													210	34	170	232	107	164	366	294	64	241	234	100
Leeds												72	196	43	91	173	73	171	401	328	116	235	232	24
Hull											59	126	215	97	121	153	92	188	411	341	164	253	259	38
Holyhead										215	163	104	263	123	260	309	174	218	419	347	104	296	332	190
Glasgow									319	245	215	220	402	214	150	379	281	354	559	486	272	436	88	208
Exeter								444	305	297	288	250	170	239	361	295	222	152	112	45	201	114	457	291
Edinburgh							446	45	325	229	205	222	405	218	107	365	268	361	561	488	276	437	130	191
Dover						457	248	490	347	278	265	295	77	283	348	167	202	148	362	290	243	155	503	274
Cardiff					234	395	119	393	209	246	236	200	155	188	311	252	170	109	232	164	110	123	406	241
Cambridge				191	121	337	233	349	246	157	143	195	60	153	224	62	82	82	346	275	142	133	361	153
Bristol			156	45	198	373	81	372	232	227	216	178	119	167	291	217	151	74	195	125	128	75	386	221
Birmingham		85	101	107	202	293	157	291	151	136	115	98	118	88	198	161	59	63	272	199	48	128	307	128
Aberdeen	430	511	468	532	591	130	584	149	457	361	336	361	543	354	239	501	402	497	696	624	412	571	241	325

AIR DISTANCES

Air distances between some major cities, given in statute miles.
To convert to kilometres, multiply the number given by 1.6093.

	Beijing	Buenos Aires	Cairo	Chicago	Delhi	Hong Kong	Honolulu	Istanbul	Johannesburg	Lagos	London	Los Angeles	Mexico City	Montreal	Moscow	Nairobi	Paris	Perth	Rome	Santiago	Sydney	Tokoyo	Washington
Amsterdam	6566	7153	2042	4109	3985	5926	8368	1373	5606	3161	217	5559	5724	3422	1338	4148	261	9118	809	7714	1039	6006	3854
Beijing		12000	6685	7599	2368	1235	6778	4763	10108	8030	5054	6349	7912	7557	3604	8888	5108	4987	5306	13622	5689	1313	7930
Buenos Aires			7468	5587	8340	3124	8693	7783	5725	4832	6985	6140	4592	5640	8382	7427	6892	9734	6931	710	7760	13100	6097
Cairo				6135	2753	5098	9439	764	4012	2443	2187	7589	7730	5431	1790	2203	1995	7766	1329	8029	9196	6362	5859
Chicago					8119	7827	4246	5502	8705	7065	3956	1746	1687	737	5500	8177	4140	11281	4828	5328	9324	6286	590
Delhi						2345	7888	2833	6765	5196	4169	8717	9806	7421	2698	4956	4089	5013	3679	12715	6495	3656	7841
Hong Kong							5543	5998	6728	7541	5979	7231	8794	8564	4839	7301	5987	3752	5773	3733	4586	1807	8385
Honolulu								9547	12892	10367	7252	2553	4116	4923	8802	11498	7463	7115	8150	8147	5078	3831	4822
Istanbul									4776	3207	1552	6994	7255	4795	1089	2967	1394	7846	852	10109	9883	5757	5347
Johannesburg										2854	5640	10443	10070	8322	6280	1809	5422	5564	4802	5738	7601	8535	8199
Lagos											3115	7716	7343	5595	4462	2377	2922	10209	2497	6042	11700	9130	5472
London												5442	5703	3252	1550	4246	220	9246	898	8568	10565	6218	3672
Los Angeles													1563	2482	6992	9688	5633	9535	6340	5594	7498	5451	2294
Mexico City														2307	6700	9949	5714	11098	6601	4168	9061	7014	1871
Montreal															4393	7498	3434	12402	5431	5551	9980	6913	493
Moscow																3951	1540	8355	1478	10118	9425	4668	4884
Nairobi																	4031	7373	3349	7547	9410	8565	7918
Paris																		12587	688	461	10150	6208	3843
Perth																			8309	15129	2037	4925	11829
Rome																				7548	10149	6146	4495
Santiago																					13092	11049	5061
Sydney																						4640	9792
Tokoyo																							6763

Long Haul

The world's longest non-stop commercial flight is operated by Singapore Airlines betwen Singapore and New Jersey, USA. The 15,500km/9,600mi route which was first flown in Jun 2004, takes an exhausting 18.5 hrs.

FAMOUS TRANSPORTATIONS

Argo	The ship that carried Jason and the Argonauts on the quest to bring back the Golden Fleece in Greek mythology.
Ark	The ship that saved Noah, his immediate family and a selection of animals from a widespread flood over the Earth (the Bible, Genesis 6–9).
HMS *Beagle*	The ship on which Charles Darwin (1809–82) sailed as naturalist (from 1831).
Black Bess	The horse that supposedly carried highwayman Dick Turpin (1705–39) on a famous ride to York (18c).
Bluebird	The hydroplane used in Donald Campbell's (1921–67) attempt to become the first man to break 300mph on water (1967).
HMS *Bounty*	The ship on board which there was a mutiny on 28 Apr 1789, led by Fletcher Christian, in which Captain William Bligh (1754–c.1817) and 18 men were cast adrift in an open boat without charts.
Chitty Chitty Bang Bang	The flying car in the film *Chitty Chitty Bang Bang* (1968), based on Ian Fleming's 1964 novel.
Copenhagen	The chestnut stallion that carried the Duke of Wellington (1769–1852) at the Battle of Waterloo (18 Jun 1815).
Discovery	The ship that carried Robert Scott (1868–1912) and his expedition exploring Antarctica (1901–4).
Endurance	The ship that carried Sir Ernest Henry Shackleton (1874–1922) in his Antarctic expeditions but was crushed in the ice on his 1914–16 expedition.
Enola Gay	The US Air Force B-29 Superfortress bomber, piloted by Paul Tibbets (born 1915), that dropped the world's first atomic bomb on Hiroshima, Japan, during World War II on 6 Aug 1945.
Fram	The purpose-built ship for Fridtjof Nansen's (1861–1930) scheme to reach the North Pole by getting frozen into the ice north of Siberia and drifting with currents towards Greenland (1893–5).
Golden Hind	Sir Francis Drake's (c.1540–96) ship in which he circumnavigated the globe (1577–80).
Marengo	The horse that carried Napoleon Bonaparte (1769–1821) at the Battle of Waterloo (18 Jun 1815).
Mayflower	The ship that carried the English religious dissenters the Pilgrim Fathers, who established Plymouth Colony in North America, across the Atlantic in 1620.
Rainbow Warrior	The direct action protest ship operated by environmental charity Greenpeace (original ship 1978–85, current ship from 1989).
Spirit of St Louis	The monoplane in which Charles Lindbergh (1902–74) made the first solo transatlantic flight in 1927, flying from New York, USA, to Paris, France, in 33½ hours.
Victoria	The ship that completed the first circumnavigation of the world (10 Aug 1519–6 Sep 1522), captained by Ferdinand Magellan (c.1480–1521), although Magellan himself was killed in the Philippines.
HMS *Victory*	The ship from which Lord Horatio Nelson (1758–1805) directed the engagement with the French and Spanish fleets at Trafalgar (21 Oct 1805).
Wright Flyer	The first heavier-than-air flying machine that Orville (1871–1948) and Wilbur (1867–1912) Wright flew on 17 Dec 1903 at Kill Devil Hills, Kitty Hawk, North Carolina, USA.

OLYMPIC GAMES

The modern Olympic Games first took place in 1896, and were founded by the French educationist Baron Pierre de Coubertin (1863–1937). In 1894 he helped set up the International Olympic Committee (IOC), which still formulates policy and decides on venues. The Olympics are held every four years; women first competed in 1900; the first separate Winter Games were held in 1924.

Olympic venues

The host city of each Olympic Summer Games and Olympic Winter Games is chosen by the International Olympic Committee (IOC) seven years in advance of the staging.

Olympic Summer Games

1896	Athens, Greece
1900	Paris, France
1904	St Louis, USA
1906[1]	Athens, Greece
1908	London, UK
1912	Stockholm, Sweden
1916	*not held*
1920	Antwerp, Belgium
1924	Paris, France
1928	Amsterdam, The Netherlands
1932	Los Angeles, USA
1936	Berlin, Germany
1940	*not held*
1944	*not held*
1948	London, UK
1952	Helsinki, Finland
1956[2]	Melbourne, Australia
1960	Rome, Italy
1964	Tokyo, Japan
1968	Mexico City, Mexico
1972	Munich, West Germany
1976	Montréal, Canada
1980	Moscow, USSR
1984	Los Angeles, USA
1988	Seoul, South Korea
1992	Barcelona, Spain
1996	Atlanta, USA
2000	Sydney, Australia
2004	Athens, Greece
2008	Beijing, China
2012	London, UK

[1] *Special Olympic Games held to commemorate the tenth anniversary of the birth of the modern Games.*
[2] *The 1956 equestrian events were held at Stockholm, Sweden, owing to quarantine laws in Australia.*

Naked Olympics

According to tradition, the Olympics began in 776 BC, when a festival of athletic competitions began to be held at Olympia, in western Greece, to honour the god Zeus. The festival was held at the end of each period of four years (known as an *Olympiad*), and at its peak attracted entrants from all over the Greek world. Many of the events are still familiar to us today, including boxing, wrestling, long jump, discus and javelin. Others were a little different – for example, a foot race run in full armour and a fiercely competitive chariot race of around 14km/8.7mi. There were separate events for boys and men, who competed naked. The winners were crowned simply with an olive wreath, but would be rewarded by their home city with privileges, money and free food and drink for life. The games were eventually ended by order of the Emperor Theodosius I in AD 393.

Olympic Winter Games

1924	Chamonix, France[1]
1928	St Moritz, Switzerland
1932	Lake Placid, New York, USA
1936	Garmisch-Partenkirchen, Germany
1940	*not held*
1944	*not held*
1948	St Moritz, Switzerland
1952	Oslo, Norway
1956	Cortina, Italy
1960	Squaw Valley, USA
1964	Innsbruck, Austria
1968	Grenoble, France
1972	Sapporo, Japan
1976	Innsbruck, Austria
1980	Lake Placid, New York, USA
1984	Sarajevo, Yugoslavia
1988	Calgary, Canada
1992	Albertville, France
1994[2]	Lillehammer, Norway
1998	Nagano, Japan
2002	Salt Lake City, USA
2006	Turin, Italy
2010	Vancouver, Canada
2014	Sochi, Russia

[1] *Held as the 'International Winter Sports Week'; recognized retrospectively as Olympic Winter Games by the IOC in 1926.*

[2] *In 1994 the Olympic Winter Games celebrations were re-adjusted to take place every four years between the Olympic Summer Games years.*

A Long Wait

Anders Haugen was placed fourth in the skijumping event at the Winter Olympics of 1924. It was only 50 years later, in 1974, that officials realized that a scoring mistake had been made and that Haugen had actually won the bronze medal. The medal was then awarded at a special ceremony in Oslo, Norway, attended by the now-86-year-old skier.

Leading medal winners

Olympic Summer Games

Includes medals won in 2004.

		Gold	Silver	Bronze	Total
1	USA	897	691	605	2193
2	Russia[1]	526	437	410	1373
3	Germany[2]	231	274	304	809
4	Great Britain	189	242	234	665
5	France	183	191	213	587
6	Italy	182	147	164	493
7	Sweden	141	155	173	469
8	Hungary	156	136	156	448
9	East Germany	153	129	127	409
10	Australia	120	126	152	398

[1] *Includes medals won by the former USSR team, and by the Unified Team (Armenia, Azerbaijan, Belarus, Georgia, Kazakhstan, Kyrgyzstan, Moldova, Russia, Tajikistan, Turkmenistan, Ukraine and Uzbekistan) in 1992.*

[2] *Includes medals won as West Germany 1968–88.*

Data source: International Olympic Committee.

Olympic Winter Games

Includes medals won in 2006.

		Gold	Silver	Bronze	Total
1	Russia[1]	121	89	86	296
2	Norway	96	100	84	280
3	Germany[2]	79	80	58	217
4	USA	78	81	58	217
5	Austria	51	64	71	186
6	Finland	41	58	52	151
7	Canada	37	38	44	119
8	Sweden	43	32	43	118
9	Switzerland	38	37	43	118

[1] *Includes medals won by the former USSR team, and by the Unified Team (Armenia, Azerbaijan, Belarus, Georgia, Kazakhstan, Kyrgyzstan, Moldova, Russia, Tajikistan, Turkmenistan, Ukraine and Uzbekistan) in 1992.*
[2] *Includes medals won as West Germany 1968–88.*
Data source: International Olympic Committee.

PARALYMPIC GAMES

An Olympic-style competition for elite athletes with a disability. Summer Games first held in 1952 (solely for competitors from the UK and the Netherlands), then once every four years from 1960; Winter Games first held in 1976, then once every four years until 1992, after which they were held once every four years from 1994, to coincide with the Winter Olympic Games.

Paralympic venues

Since 1988 (Summer Paralympic Games) and 1992 (Winter Paralympic Games) the Paralympics have taken place at the same venue as the Summer and Winter Olympic Games respectively; this is obligatory for Olympic host cities from 2012 onwards.

Paralympic Summer Games

1952	Stoke Mandeville, UK
1960	Rome, Italy
1964	Tokyo, Japan
1968	Tel Aviv, Israel
1972	Heidelberg, West Germany
1976	Toronto, Canada
1980	Arnhem, The Netherlands
1984	Stoke Mandeville, UK, and New York City, USA

Paralympic Winter Games

1976	Örnsköldsvik, Sweden
1980	Geilo, Norway
1984	Innsbruck, Austria
1988	Innsbruck, Austria

Deaflympics

Deaf athletes are not usually involved in the Paralympic Games. Instead, the International Committee of Sports for the Deaf (CISS) holds World Games for the Deaf (known as *Deaflympics*). More than 3,000 athletes from 75 countries took part in the most recent Deaflympic Summer Games in 2005.

Leading medal winners

Totals are for the years 1984–2004.

Paralympic Summer Games

		Gold	Silver	Bronze	Total
1	USA	408	374	403	1185
2	Great Britain	319	335	321	975
3	Germany	293	315	299	907
4	Canada	255	210	222	687
5	France	235	235	217	687
6	Australia	225	229	220	674
7	Spain	171	140	164	475
8	Sweden	153	130	86	369
9	Poland	115	129	101	345
10	China	143	117	83	343

Data source: International Paralympic Committee.

Paralympic Winter Games

		Gold	Silver	Bronze	Total
1	Germany	97	85	83	265
2	Austria	95	80	83	258
3	USA	92	93	64	249
4	Norway	103	75	65	243
5	Russia[1]	52	52	34	138
6	Switzerland	35	54	48	137
7	France	43	41	43	127
8	Finland	54	31	39	124
9	Canada	24	33	38	95
10	Sweden	13	22	23	58

[1] *Includes medals won by the former USSR team, and by the Unified Team (Armenia, Azerbaijan, Belarus, Georgia, Kazakhstan, Kyrgyzstan, Moldova, Russia, Tajikistan, Turkmenistan, Ukraine and Uzbekistan) in 1992.*
Data source: International Paralympic Committee.

The Special Olympics

The Special Olympics are motivational games for people with mental and developmental difficulties. They were first held in Chicago, USA, in 1968. They were inspired by the day camps organized by Eunice Kennedy Shriver (sister of President John F Kennedy and mother-in-law of Arnold Schwarzenegger) in the early 1960s. More than 7,500 competitors took part in the 2007 Special Olympics held in Shanghai, China.

COMMONWEALTH GAMES

Open to competitors from all Commonwealth countries, colonies and dependent or associated territories of a Commonwealth country. First held as the British Empire Games in 1930; take place every four years and between Summer Olympic celebrations; became the British Empire and Commonwealth Games in 1954; known as British Commonwealth Games from 1966 to 1974; current title adopted in 1978.

Commonwealth Games venues

The host city of each Commonwealth Games is chosen by the Commonwealth Games Federation (CGF) seven years in advance.

1930	Hamilton, Canada
1934	London, England
1938	Sydney, Australia
1942	*not held*
1946	*not held*
1950	Auckland, New Zealand
1954	Vancouver, Canada
1958	Cardiff, Wales
1962	Perth, Australia
1966	Kingston, Jamaica
1970	Edinburgh, Scotland
1974	Christchurch, New Zealand
1978	Edmonton, Canada
1982	Brisbane, Australia
1986	Edinburgh, Scotland
1990	Auckland, New Zealand
1994	Victoria, Canada
1998	Kuala Lumpur, Malaysia
2002	Manchester, England
2006	Melbourne, Australia
2010	Delhi, India
2014	Glasgow, Scotland

Leading medal winners

Includes medals won in 2002.

		Gold	Silver	Bronze	Total
1	Australia	730	620	556	1906
2	England	578	553	562	1693
3	Canada	414	442	461	1317
4	New Zealand	124	168	234	526
5	Scotland	82	94	153	329
6	South Africa	92	92	96	280
7	India	102	96	74	272
8	Wales	49	69	96	214
9	Kenya	59	47	56	162
10	Nigeria	39	47	57	143

Growing Games

At the first Commonwealth Games in Hamilton in 1930 (then known as the British Empire Games) there were only around 400 competitors from eleven nations. They had just six sports to choose from – track and field, bowls, boxing, rowing, swimming and diving, and wrestling – and there were 59 events in total. In contrast, the 2006 Commonwealth Games in Melbourne hosted 16 sports with a total of 24 disciplines and 247 events; around 4,500 athletes from 71 Commonwealth countries, territories and regions took part.

SPORTS INTRODUCTION

Sports results are listed for the last 25 years only. Where there are winners in a range of disciplines within one competition (for example Athletics), complete results are given for the last five competitions only. Exceptions exist (for example the FIFA World Cup) where all winners are listed.

Note: For 1992 Summer Olympic events the designation (UT) is given for members of the Unified Team (Armenia, Azerbaijan, Belarus, Georgia, Kazakhstan, Kyrgyzstan, Moldova, Russia, Tajikistan, Turkmenistan, Ukraine and Uzbekistan).

AMERICAN FOOTBALL

Players wear heavy padding and helmets, and passing of the ball by hand, including forward passing, is permitted; played on a rectangular field, divided gridiron-like into segments; object is to score *touchdowns* by moving the ball into the opposing team's *end zone*, but progress has to be made upfield by a series of *plays*: a team must make 9.1m/10yd of ground within four plays, otherwise they lose possession of the ball. Six points are awarded for a touchdown. An extra point can then be gained by kicking the ball between the posts and over the crossbar – the equivalent of a conversion in rugby – or two points can be gained by advancing the ball (through play rather than kicking) from the two-yard line into the end zone in a *two-point conversion*. A goal kicked from anywhere on the field (a *field goal*) is worth three points. Teams consist of more than 40 members, but only eleven are allowed on the field at any one time; special units of players have different roles so they change, eg when the team changes from attacking to defending. First intercollegiate game 1869.

Ruling body (USA): National Football League (NFL)

American football field

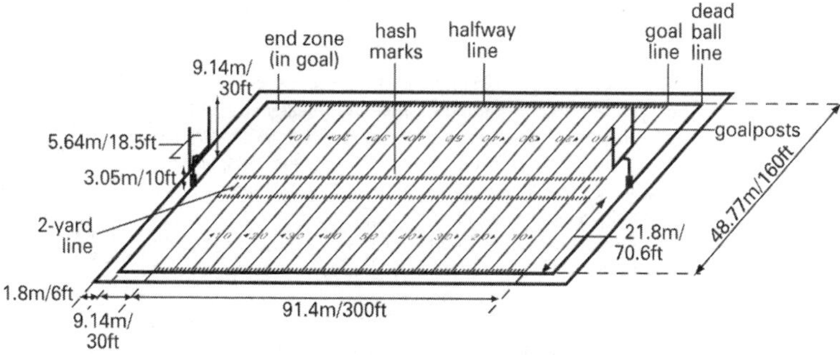

Vikings and Giants

NFL American football teams named after animals: Bears (Chicago), Colts (Indianapolis), Dolphins (Miami), Eagles (Philadelphia), Falcons (Atlanta), Jaguars (Jacksonville), Lions (Detroit), Panthers (Carolina), Rams (St Louis), Ravens (Baltimore) and Seahawks (Seattle).

Other NFL American football teams: Bengals (Cincinnati), Bills (Buffalo), Broncos (Denver), Browns (Cleveland), Buccaneers (Tampa Bay), Cardinals (Arizona), Chargers (San Diego), Chiefs (Kansas City), Cowboys (Dallas), 49ers (San Francisco), Giants (New York), Jets (New York), Packers (Green Bay), Patriots (New England), Raiders (Oakland), Redskins (Washington), Saints (New Orleans), Steelers (Pittsburgh), Texans (Houston), Titans (Tennessee) and Vikings (Minnesota).

AMERICAN FOOTBALL

Super Bowl

First held in 1967; takes place each Jan; an end-of-season meeting between the champions of the National Football Conference (NFC) and the American Football Conference (AFC).

1967	Green Bay Packers (NFC)
1968	Green Bay Packers (NFC)
1969	New York Jets (AFC)
1970	Kansas City Chiefs (AFC)
1971	Baltimore Colts (AFC)
1972	Dallas Cowboys (NFC)
1973	Miami Dolphins (AFC)
1974	Miami Dolphins (AFC)
1975	Pittsburgh Steelers (AFC)
1976	Pittsburgh Steelers (AFC)
1977	Oakland Raiders (AFC)
1978	Dallas Cowboys (NFC)
1979	Pittsburgh Steelers (AFC)
1980	Pittsburgh Steelers (AFC)
1981	Oakland Raiders (AFC)
1982	San Francisco 49ers (NFC)
1983	Washington Redskins (NFC)
1984	Los Angeles Raiders (AFC)
1985	San Francisco 49ers (NFC)
1986	Chicago Bears (NFC)
1987	New York Giants (NFC)
1988	Washington Redskins (NFC)
1989	San Francisco 49ers (NFC)
1990	San Francisco 49ers (NFC)
1991	New York Giants (NFC)
1992	Washington Redskins (NFC)
1993	Dallas Cowboys (NFC)
1994	Dallas Cowboys (NFC)
1995	San Francisco 49ers (NFC)
1996	Dallas Cowboys (NFC)
1997	Green Bay Packers (NFC)
1998	Denver Broncos (AFC)
1999	Denver Broncos (AFC)
2000	St Louis Rams (NFC)
2001	Baltimore Ravens (AFC)
2002	New England Patriots (AFC)
2003	Tampa Bay Buccaneers (NFC)
2004	New England Patriots (AFC)
2005	New England Patriots (AFC)
2006	Pittsburgh Steelers (AFC)
2007	Indianapolis Colts (AFC)

Star-Spangled Super Bowl

The singing of the US National Anthem at the Super Bowl is a time-honoured tradition. While in the early years of the Super Bowl the anthem was often sung by bands or choirs (for example the US Air Force Academy Chorale in 1972 and the Little Angels of Holy Angels Church in 1973), in later years it has usually been the luminaries of US pop music who belt out the Banner. Thus, Super Bowl audiences have been treated to the patriotic warblings of Whitney Houston (1991) and Mariah Carey (2002), the country croonings of Garth Brooks (1993) and the Dixie Chicks (2003), plus the star-spangled likes of Barry Manilow (1984), Cher (1999), the Backstreet Boys (2001) and Beyoncé Knowles (2004). In 2005, however, the Super Bowl returned to its roots with the combined US forces choirs.

ATHLETICS

Tests of running, jumping, throwing and walking skills. The running or track events range from the 100m/328ft sprint to the 42km 195m/26mi 385yd marathon; jumping and throwing or field events consist of high jump, long jump, triple jump and pole vault, and the discus throw, shot put, javelin throw and hammer throw. Multi-event competitions are the decathlon (ten events) for men and the heptathlon (seven events) for women. Athletics dates to c.3800 BC in Egypt; the International Amateur Athletic Federation was founded in 1912.

high jump Field event; competitors attempt to clear a bar without any aids; height increased gradually; three failed attempts means disqualification. The winner clears the greatest height, or has the fewest failures.

long jump Field event; contestant runs up to the take-off mark and leaps into a sandpit; length of the jump measured from front of take-off line to nearest break in the sand made by any part of the competitor's body; also called broad jump in North America.

triple jump Field event; takes place in the same part of the stadium as the long jump, governed by same rules. After the run-up, competitors must take off and hop on the same foot; second phase is a step onto the other foot, followed by a jump; previously called the hop, step and jump.

pole vault Field event; jumping contest for height using fibreglass pole for leverage to clear a bar, which is raised progressively; three attempts may be made to clear the height before attempting a new one.

discus throw Field event; uses a circular disc of wood with metal plates, weighing 2kg/4.4lb for men and 1kg/2.2lb for women. It is thrown with one hand from within the confines of a circle 2.5m/8ft 2in in diameter.

shot put Field event; the shot is a brass or iron sphere weighing 7.26kg/16lb for men and 4kg/8lb 13oz for women. It is propelled, using only one hand, from a starting position under the chin. The thrower must not leave the 2.1m/7ft diameter throwing circle. In competition six throws are allowed.

javelin throw Field event; throwing a spear-like javelin which consists of three parts: pointed metal head, shaft and grip; men's javelin is 2.6–2.7m/8ft 6in–8ft 10in in length and weighs 800g/1.8lb; women's is 2.2–2.3m/7ft 2in–7ft 6in and weighs at least 600g/1.3lb; the competitor runs to a specified mark with the javelin in one hand, and throws it; for throw to count, metal head must touch ground before any other part; first mark made by the head is the point used for measuring the distance achieved.

hammer throw Field event; hammer weighing 7.26kg/16lb is thrown from within the confines of a circle 2.13m/7ft in diameter (protected by a wire cage). Six throws are allowed, the object being to attain the greatest distance.

decathlon Ten-event track-and-field competition held over two days, usually for men: 100m, long jump, shot put, high jump, 400m, 110m hurdles, discus, pole vault, javelin and 1,500m. Points are awarded in each event.

heptathlon Seven-event track-and-field competition held over two days, usually for women: 100m hurdles, shot put, high jump, 200m, long jump, javelin and 800m.

Ruling body: International Association of Athletics Federations (IAAF)

World Championships

First held in 1983; since 1995 every two years.

1999

Men		Women	
100m	Maurice Greene (USA)	100m	Marion Jones (USA)
200m	Maurice Greene (USA)	200m	Inger Miller (USA)
400m	Michael Johnson (USA)	400m	Cathy Freeman (Australia)
800m	Wilson Kipketer (Denmark)	800m	Ludmilla Formanova (Czech Republic)
1500m	Hicham El Guerrouj (Morocco)	1500m	Svetlana Masterkova (Russia)
5000m	Salah Hissou (Morocco)	5000m	Gabriela Szabo (Romania)
10000m	Haile Gebrselassie (Ethiopia)	10000m	Gete Wami (Ethiopia)
marathon	Abel Antón (Spain)	marathon	Jong Song-Ok (North Korea)
3000m steeplechase	Christopher Koskei (Kenya)		
110m hurdles	Colin Jackson (Great Britain)	100m hurdles	Gail Devers (USA)
400m hurdles	Fabrizio Mori (Italy)	400m hurdles	Daimi Pernía (Cuba)
20km walk	Ilya Markov (Russia)	20km walk	Liu Hongyu (China)
50km walk	German Skurygin (Russia)		
4 × 100m relay	USA	4 × 100m relay	The Bahamas
4 × 400m relay	USA	4 × 400m relay	Russia
high jump	Vyacheslav Voronin (Russia)	high jump	Inga Babakova (Ukraine)
long jump	Iván Pedroso (Cuba)	long jump	Niurka Montalvo (Spain)
triple jump	Charles Michael Friedek (Germany)	triple jump	Paraskevi Tsiamita (Greece)
pole vault	Maksim Tarasov (Russia)	pole vault	Stacy Dragila (USA)
shot	C J Hunter (USA)	shot	Astrid Kumbernuss (Germany)
discus	Anthony Washington (USA)	discus	Franka Dietzsch (Germany)
hammer	Karsten Kobs (Germany)	hammer	Michaela Melinte (Romania)
javelin	Aki Parviainen (Finland)	javelin	Mirela Manjani-Tzelili (Greece)
decathlon	Tomás Dvorák (Czech Republic)	heptathlon	Eunice Barber (France)

2001

Men		Women	
100m	Maurice Greene (USA)	100m	Zhanna Pintusevich-Block (Ukraine)
200m	Konstantinos Kederis (Greece)	200m	Marion Jones (USA)
400m	Avard Moncur (Bahamas)	400m	Amy Mbacke Thiam (Senegal)
800m	André Bucher (Switzerland)	800m	Maria Mutola (Mozambique)
1500m	Hicham El Guerrouj (Morocco)	1500m	Gabriela Szabo (Romania)
5000m	Richard Limo (Kenya)	5000m	Olga Yegorova (Russia)
10000m	Charles Kamathi (Kenya)	10000m	Derartu Tulu (Ethiopia)
marathon	Gezahegne Abera (Ethiopia)	marathon	Lidia Simon (Romania)
3000m steeplechase	Reuben Kosgei (Kenya)		
110m hurdles	Allen Johnson (USA)	100m hurdles	Anjanette Kirkland (USA)

Men		Women	
400m hurdles	Félix Sánchez (Dominican Republic)	400m hurdles	Nezha Bidouane (Morocco)
20km walk	Roman Rasskazov (Russia)	20km walk	Olimpiada Ivanova (Russia)
50km walk	Robert Korzeniowski (Poland)		
4 × 100m relay	USA	4 × 100m relay	USA
4 × 400m relay	Jamaica	4 × 400m relay	USA
high jump	Buss Martin (Germany)	high jump	Hestrie Cloete (South Africa)
long jump	Iván Pedroso (Cuba)	long jump	Fiona May (Italy)
triple jump	Jonathan Edwards (Great Britain)	triple jump	Tatyana Lebedeva (Russia)
pole vault	Dmitry Markov (Australia)	pole vault	Stacy Dragila (USA)
shot	John Godina (USA)	shot	Yanina Korolchik (Belarus)
discus	Lars Riedel (Germany)	discus	Natalya Sadova (Russia)
hammer	Szymon Ziółkowski (Poland)	hammer	Yipsi Moreno (Cuba)
javelin	Jan Zelezný (Czech Republic)	javelin	Osleidys Menéndez (Cuba)
decathlon	Tomás Dvorák (Czech Republic)	heptathlon	Yelena Prokhorova (Russia)

2003

Men		Women	
100m	Kim Collins (St Kitts and Nevis)	100m	Torri Edwards[1] (USA)
200m	John Capel (USA)	200m	Anastasia Kapachinskaya[1] (Russia)
400m	Jerome Young (USA)	400m	Ana Guevara (Mexico)
800m	Djabir Saïd-Guerni (Algeria)	800m	Maria Mutola (Mozambique)
1500m	Hicham El Guerrouj (Morocco)	1500m	Tatyana Tomashova (Russia)
5000m	Eliud Kipchoge (Kenya)	5000m	Tirunesh Dibaba (Ethiopia)
10000m	Kenenisa Bekele (Ethiopia)	10000m	Berhane Adere (Ethiopia)
marathon	Jaoud Gharib (Morocco)	marathon	Catherine Ndereba (Kenya)
3000m steeplechase	Saif Saaeed Shaheen (Qatar)		
110m hurdles	Allen Johnson (USA)	100m hurdles	Perdita Felicien (Canada)
400m hurdles	Félix Sánchez (Dominican Republic)	400m hurdles	Jana Pittman (Australia)
20km walk	Jefferson Pérez (Ecuador)	20km walk	Yelena Nikolayeva (Russia)
50km walk	Robert Korzeniowski (Poland)		
4 × 100m relay	USA	4 × 100m relay	France
4 × 400m relay	USA	4 × 400m relay	USA
high jump	Jacques Freitag (South Africa)	high jump	Hestrie Cloete (South Africa)
long jump	Dwight Phillips (USA)	long jump	Eunice Barber (France)
triple jump	Christian Olsson (Sweden)	triple jump	Tatyana Lebedeva (Russia)
pole vault	Giuseppe Gibilisco (Italy)	pole vault	Svetlana Feofanova (Russia)
shot	Andrei Mikhnevich (Belarus)	shot	Svetlana Krivelyova (Russia)
discus	Virgilijus Alekna (Lithuania)	discus	Irina Yatchenko (Belarus)
hammer	Ivan Tikhon (Belarus)	hammer	Yipsi Moreno (Cuba)
javelin	Sergey Makarov (Russia)	javelin	Miréla Manjani (Greece)
decathlon	Tom Pappas (USA)	heptathlon	Carolina Kluft (Sweden)

[1] *Originally won by Kelli White (USA); White was stripped of the medal following a positive drug test.*

Running Records

The world record for the fastest time for the 100m for men was set by the Jamaican athlete Asafa Powell in Rieti, Italy, in Sep 2007. Powell ran the distance – equivalent to 328ft – in just 9.74 seconds. This works out at 37kph, or 23mph. But even the fastest humans are slowcoaches compared with the fastest mammal, the cheetah, which can reach speeds of up to 100kph/62mph in short bursts.

2005

Men		Women	
100m	Justin Gatlin (USA)	100m	Lauryn Williams (USA)
200m	Justin Gatlin (USA)	200m	Allyson Felix (USA)
400m	Jeremy Wariner (USA)	400m	Tonique Williams-Darling (Bahamas)
800m	Rashid Ramzi (Bahrain)	800m	Zulia Calatayud (Cuba)
1 500m	Rashid Ramzi (Bahrain)	1 500m	Tatyana Tomashova (Russia)
5 000m	Benjamin Limo (Kenya)	5 000m	Tirunesh Dibaba (Ethiopia)
10 000m	Kenenisa Bekele (Ethiopia)	10 000m	Tirunesh Dibaba (Ethiopia)
marathon	Jaouad Gharib (Morocco)	marathon	Paula Radcliffe (Great Britain)
3 000m steeplechase	Saif Saaeed Shaheen (Qatar)	3 000m steeplechase	Docus Inzikuru (Uganda)
110m hurdles	Ladji Doucoure (France)	100m hurdles	Michelle Perry (USA)
400m hurdles	Bershawn Jackson (USA)	400m hurdles	Yuliya Pechonkina (Russia)
20km walk	Jefferson Pérez (Ecuador)	20km walk	Olimpiada Ivanova (Russia)
50km walk	Sergey Kirdyapkin (Russia)		
4 × 100m relay	France	4 × 100m relay	USA
4 × 400m relay	USA	4 ××400m relay	Russia
high jump	Yuri Kyrmarenko (Ukraine)	high jump	Kajsa Bergqvist (Sweden)
long jump	Dwight Phillips (USA)	long jump	Tianna Madison (USA)
triple jump	Walter Davis (USA)	triple jump	Trecia Smith (Jamaica)
pole vault	Rens Blom (The Netherlands)	pole vault	Yelena Isinbayeva (Russia)
shot	Adam Nelson (USA)	shot	Nadezhda Ostapchuk (Belarus)
discus	Virgilijus Alekna (Lithuania)	discus	Franka Dietzsch (Germany)
hammer	Ivan Tikhon (Belarus)	hammer	Olga Kuzenkova (Russia)
javelin	Andrus Varnik (Estonia)	javelin	Osleidys Menéndez (Cuba)
decathlon	Bryan Clay (USA)	heptathlon	Carolina Klüft (Sweden)

2007

Men		Women	
100m	Tyson Gay (USA)	100m	Veronica Campbell (Jamaica)
200m	Tyson Gay (USA)	200m	Allyson Felix (USA)
400m	Jeremy Wariner (USA)	400m	Christine Ohuruogu (Great Britain)
800m	Alfred Yego (Kenya)	800m	Janeth Jepkosgei (Kenya)
1 500m	Bernard Lagat (USA)	1 500m	Mariam Jamal (Bahrain)
5 000m	Bernard Lagat (USA)	5 000m	Meseret Defar (Ethiopia)
10 000m	Kenenisa Bekele (Ethiopia)	10 000m	Tirunesh Dibaba (Ethiopia)
marathon	Luke Kibet (Kenya)	marathon	Katherine Ndereba (Kenya)
3 000m steeplechase	Brimin Kipruto (Kenya)		
110m hurdles	Liu Xiang (China)	100m hurdles	Michelle Perry (USA)

Men		Women	
400m hurdles	Kerron Clement (USA)	400m hurdles	Jana Rawlinson (Australia)
20km walk	Jefferson Pérez (Ecuador)	20km walk	Olga Kaniskina (Russia)
50km walk	Nathan Deakes (Australia)		
4 × 100m relay	USA	4 × 100m relay	USA
4 × 400m relay	USA	4 × 400m relay	USA
high jump	Donald Thomas (Bahamas)	high jump	Blanka Vasić (Croatia)
long jump	Irving Saladino (Panama)	long jump	Tatiana Lebedeva (Russia)
triple jump	Nelson Évora (Portugal)	triple jump	Yargelis Savigne (Cuba)
pole vault	Brad Walker (USA)	pole vault	Yelena Isinbayeva (Russia)
shot	Reese Hoffa (USA)	shot	Valerie Vili (New Zealand)
discus	Gerd Kanter (Estonia)	discus	Franka Dietzsch (Germany)
hammer	Ivan Tikhon (Belarus)	hammer	Betty Heidler (Germany)
javelin	Tero Pitkämäki (Finland)	javelin	Barbora Špotáková (Czech Republic)
decathlon	Roman Šebrle (Czech Republic)	heptathlon	Carolina Klüft (Sweden)

AUSTRALIAN RULES FOOTBALL

A handling and kicking game with few rules, a cross between association football and rugby, with 18 players on an oval pitch. The object is to score by kicking the ball between the opponent's goal posts (six points). Smaller posts are positioned either side of the main goal: a ball kicked through that area scores one point; first recorded game played 1858.

Ruling body: Australian Football League (AFL)

Australian Rules football pitch

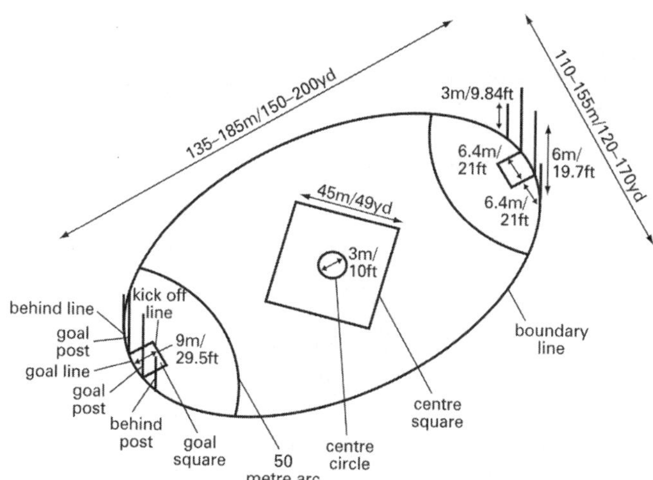

Premiership Trophy

First held in 1897 as the Victorian Football League (1897–1989); inaugural winners were Essendon. The majority of Grand Finals have been played at the MCG in Melbourne.

1983	Hawthorn
1984	Essendon
1985	Essendon
1986	Hawthorn
1987	Carlton
1988	Hawthorn
1989	Hawthorn
1990	Collingwood
1991	Hawthorn
1992	West Coast
1993	Essendon
1994	West Coast
1995	Carlton
1996	North Melbourne
1997	Adelaide
1998	Adelaide
1999	North Melbourne Kangaroos
2000	Essendon
2001	Brisbane Lions
2002	Brisbane Lions
2003	Brisbane Lions
2004	Port Adelaide
2005	Sydney
2006	West Coast
2007	Geelong

Rugby and Rules

The game of Australian Rules football was concocted by Tom Wills, H C A Harrison, W J Hammersley and J B Thompson in the mid-1800s. Wills had been educated in the UK and was football captain at Rugby School. Upon his return to Australia he suggested that cricketers could keep fit during the winter by playing a version of rugby football. Wills worked out the rules for the new game, and the first ever Australian Rules match was held in 1858.

BADMINTON

Indoor game, with two or four players, played on a court using rackets, a shuttlecock (cork or plastic half sphere with 'feathers') and a raised central net; object is to volley the shuttlecock over the net so that the opponent is unable to return it.

Ruling body: International Badminton Federation (IBF)

Badminton court

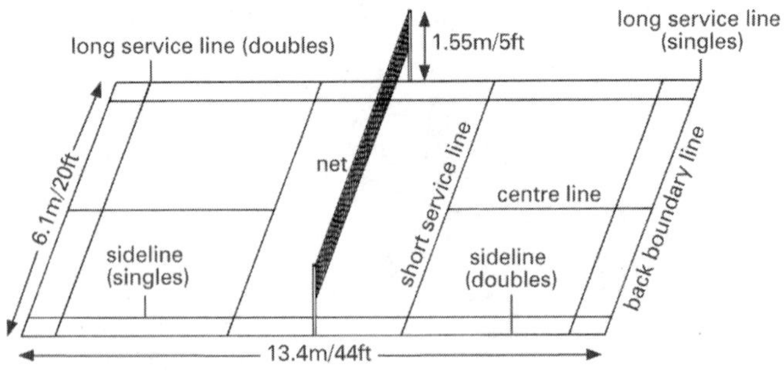

World Championships

First held in 1977; initially took place every three years; since 1983 every two years, and from 2005 annually (except in Olympic years).

	Men	Women
1983	Icuk Sugiarto (Indonesia)	Li Lingwei (China)
1985	Han Jian (China)	Han Aiping (China)
1987	Yang Yang (China)	Han Aiping (China)
1989	Yang Yang (China)	Li Lingwei (China)
1991	Zhao Jianhua (China)	Tang Jiuhong (China)
1993	Joko Suprianto (Indonesia)	Susi Susanti (Indonesia)
1995	Heryanto Arbi (Indonesia)	Ye Zhaoying (China)
1997	Peter Rasmussen (Denmark)	Ye Zhaoying (China)
1999	Sun Jun (China)	Camilla Martin (Denmark)
2001	Hendra Wan (Indonesia)	Gong Ruina (China)
2003	Xia Xuanze (China)	Zhang Ning (China)
2005	Taufik Hidayat (Indonesia)	Xie Xingfang (China)
2006	Lin Dan (China)	Xie Xingfang (China)
2007	Lin Dan (China)	Zhu Lin (China)

Beaufort's Badminton

The name *badminton* derives from Badminton House in Gloucestershire, the seat of the Duke of Beaufort, where the game was played by house guests in the 19c. However, the game actually originated in China over 2,200 years ago.

Thomas Cup

An international team event for men's teams; inaugurated 1949; now held every two years.

1984	Indonesia	1996	Indonesia
1986	China	1998	Indonesia
1988	China	2000	Indonesia
1990	China	2002	Indonesia
1992	Malaysia	2004	China
1994	Indonesia	2006	China

Uber Cup

An international event for women's teams; first held in 1957; now held every two years.

1984	China	1996	Indonesia
1986	China	1998	China
1988	China	2000	China
1990	China	2002	China
1992	China	2004	China
1994	Indonesia	2006	China

All-England Championship

Badminton's premier event prior to the inauguration of the World Championships; first held in 1900.

	Men	Women
1983	Luan Jin (China)	Zhang Ailing (China)
1984	Morten Frost (Denmark)	Li Lingwei (China)
1985	Zhao Jianhua (China)	Han Aiping (China)
1986	Morten Frost (Denmark)	Yun-Ja Kim (Korea)
1987	Morten Frost (Denmark)	Kirsten Larsen (Denmark)
1988	Ib Frederikson (Denmark)	Gu Jiaming (China)
1989	Yang Yang (China)	Li Lingwei (China)
1990	Zhao Jianhua (China)	Susi Susanti (Indonesia)
1991	Ardi Wiranata (Indonesia)	Susi Susanti (Indonesia)
1992	Liu Jun (China)	Tang Jiuhong (China)
1993	Heryanto Arbi (Indonesia)	Susi Susanti (Indonesia)
1994	Heryanto Arbi (Indonesia)	Susi Susanti (Indonesia)
1995	Poul-Erik Hoyer-Larsen (Denmark)	Lim Xiao Qing (Sweden)
1996	Poul-Erik Hoyer-Larsen (Denmark)	Bang Soo Hyun (South Korea)
1997	Dong Jiong (China)	Ye Zhaoying (China)
1998	Sun Jun (China)	Ye Zhaoying (China)
1999	Peter Gade Christensen (Denmark)	Ye Zhaoying (China)
2000	Xia Xuanze (China)	Zichao Gong (China)
2001	Pulella Gopichand (India)	Zichao Gong (China)
2002	Chen Hong (China)	Camilla Martin (Denmark)
2003	Muhammad Hafiz Hashim (Malaysia)	Mi Zhou (China)
2004	Lin Dan (China)	Gong Ruina (China)
2005	Chen Hong (China)	Xie Xingfang (China)
2006	Lin Dan (China)	Xie Xingfang (China)
2007	Lin Dan (China)	Xie Xingfang (China)

BASEBALL

Team game played by two sides of 25 possible players on a diamond-shaped field which has bases at the corners. Essential pieces of equipment are long solid bats, the solid ball *pitched* from the *mound*, and the glove worn by each fielder; team *at bat* tries to score most runs by having its players circle the three bases and touch home plate before being put out by the team *in the field*; players out if their hit is caught, if they are tagged with the ball when *off-base*, if the base is touched by the ball before they arrive at it, or if they *strike out*, ie fail to hit the ball after three pitches have been judged strikes by the umpire; *home run* scored when player hits ball, circles all three bases and crosses home plate; game consists of nine innings; popularly believed to have been invented by Abner Doubleday (1819–93), at Cooperstown, NY, in 1839, but it is now known that a game similar to baseball was played in the USA and England long before Doubleday's time.

Ruling body: International Baseball Federation (IBAF)

Where Have You Gone, Joe DiMaggio?

New York Yankees star Joe DiMaggio (1914–99) was a hit off the field as well as on, marrying actress Marilyn Monroe in 1954. He is also mentioned in the lyrics of Simon and Garfunkel's 1967 hit song *Mrs Robinson*.

Baseball field

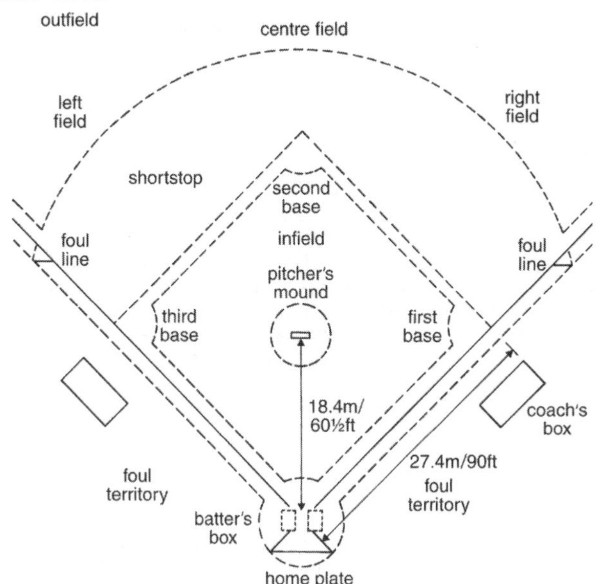

World Series

First held in 1903; takes place each Oct, the best of seven matches; professional baseball's leading event, the end-of-season meeting between the winners of the two major baseball leagues in the USA, the National League (NL) and American League (AL).

1983	Baltimore Orioles (AL)
1984	Detroit Tigers (AL)
1985	Kansas City Royals (AL)
1986	New York Mets (NL)
1987	Minnesota Twins (AL)
1988	Los Angeles Dodgers (NL)
1989	Oakland Athletics (AL)
1990	Cincinnati Reds (NL)
1991	Minnesota Twins (AL)
1992	Toronto Blue Jays (AL)
1993	Toronto Blue Jays (AL)
1994	*not held*
1995	Atlanta Braves (NL)
1996	New York Yankees (AL)
1997	Florida Marlins (NL)
1998	New York Yankees (AL)
1999	New York Yankees (AL)
2000	New York Yankees (AL)
2001	Arizona Diamondbacks (NL)
2002	Anaheim Angels (AL)
2003	Florida Marlins (NL)
2004	Boston Red Sox (AL)
2005	Chicago White Sox (AL)
2006	St Louis Cardinals (NL)
2007	Boston Red Sox (AL)

World Cup

Instituted in 1938; since 2001 held approximately every two years.

1984	Cuba	1998	Cuba
1986	Cuba	2001	Cuba
1988	Cuba	2003	Cuba
1990	Cuba	2005	Cuba
1994	Cuba	2007	USA

Peaches and Sultans

The Iron Horse, the Georgia Peach, Mr October and the Sultan of Swat are just some of the nicknames of major league baseball players (in reality Lou Gehrig (1903–41), Ty Cobb (1886–1961), Reggie Jackson (1946–) and Babe Ruth (1895–1948) respectively). Joe DiMaggio (1914–99) was known as Joltin' Joe and the Yankee Clipper, while Hank Aaron (1934–) was called Hammerin' Hank, Honus Wagner (1874–1955) was the Flying Dutchman and James Hunter (1946–99) was better known as Catfish.

BASKETBALL

Five-a-side team ball game played on a hard surface court with a bottomless basket at each end; object is to move the ball by a series of passing and bouncing moves and throw it through the opponent's basket.

Ruling body: International Basketball Federation (FIBA; Fédération Internationale de Basketball)

Basketball court

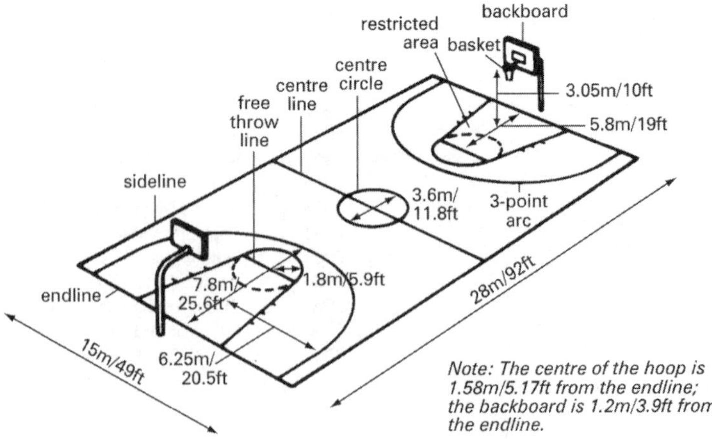

World Championship

First held 1950 for men, 1953 for women; takes place approximately every four years.

	Men	Women
1986	USA	USA
1990	Yugoslavia	USA
1994	USA	Brazil
1998	Yugoslavia	USA
2002	Yugoslavia	USA
2006	Spain	Australia

Basketball's Beginnings

A Canadian, James Naismith (1861–1939), is regarded as being the originator of basketball. He invented the game in 1891 at the YMCA college in Springfield, Massachusetts, USA, using peach baskets on a gym wall. The game was originally designed merely to bridge the gap between the baseball and American football seasons, but it soon became popular in its own right. A similar game is believed to have been played in Mexico in the 10c.

NBA Championship

First held in 1947; the major competition in professional basketball in the USA; an end-of-season play-off involving the champion teams from the Eastern Conference (EC) and Western Conference (WC).

1983	Philadelphia 76ers (EC)
1984	Boston Celtics (EC)
1985	Los Angeles Lakers (WC)
1986	Boston Celtics (EC)
1987	Los Angeles Lakers (WC)
1988	Los Angeles Lakers (WC)
1989	Detroit Pistons (EC)
1990	Detroit Pistons (EC)
1991	Chicago Bulls (EC)
1992	Chicago Bulls (EC)
1993	Chicago Bulls (EC)
1994	Houston Rockets (WC)
1995	Houston Rockets (WC)
1996	Chicago Bulls (EC)
1997	Chicago Bulls (EC)
1998	Chicago Bulls (EC)
1999	San Antonio Spurs (WC)
2000	Los Angeles Lakers (WC)
2001	Los Angeles Lakers (WC)
2002	Los Angeles Lakers (WC)
2003	San Antonio Spurs (WC)
2004	Detroit Pistons (EC)
2005	San Antonio Spurs (WC)
2006	Miami Heat (EC)
2007	San Antonio Spurs (WC)

Magic and Mavericks

NBA basketball teams named after animals: Bobcats (Charlotte), Bucks (Milwaukee), Bulls (Chicago), Grizzlies (Memphis), Hawks (Atlanta), Hornets (New Orleans/Oklahoma City), Raptors (Toronto) and Timberwolves (Minnesota).

Other NBA basketball teams: Cavaliers (Cleveland), Celtics (Boston), Clippers (Los Angeles), Heat (Miami), Jazz (Utah), Kings (Sacramento), Knicks (New York), Lakers (Los Angeles), Magic (Orlando), Mavericks (Dallas), Nets (New Jersey), Nuggets (Denver), Pacers (Indiana), Pistons (Detroit), Rockets (Houston), 76ers (Philadelphia), Spurs (San Antonio), Suns (Phoenix), SuperSonics (Seattle), Trail Blazers (Portland), Warriors (Golden State) and Wizards (Washington).

BOXING

Fistfighting between two people, usually men, in a roped ring 4.3–6.1m/14–20ft square. Professional championship bouts comprise twelve three-minute rounds; amateur bouts three rounds, unless one fighter is knocked out or retires, the referee halts the fight, or a fighter is disqualified. There are 17 weight divisions (see below).

Ruling bodies: International Boxing Federation (IBF), World Boxing Association (WBA), World Boxing Council (WBC), World Boxing Organization (WBO)

Butlers and Butchers

Boxing dates from Greek and Roman times. The first known match in Britain was in 1681 when the Duke of Albemarle organized a bout between his butler and his butcher in New Hall, Essex. The first rules were drawn up in 1743, when each round lasted until one fighter was knocked down; gloves and three-minute rounds were introduced in 1867.

Boxing weight categories

Category	Weight
mini flyweight, minimum weight or strawweight	under 48kg/105 lb
light flyweight or junior flyweight	maximum 49kg/108 lb
flyweight	maximum 51kg/112 lb
super flyweight/junior bantamweight	maximum 52kg/115 lb
bantamweight	maximum 54kg/118 lb
super bantamweight/junior featherweight	maximum 55kg/122 lb
featherweight	maximum 57kg/126 lb
super featherweight/junior lightweight	maximum 59kg/130 lb
lightweight	maximum 61kg/135 lb
super lightweight/junior welterweight	maximum 63.5kg/140 lb
welterweight	maximum 67kg/147 lb
junior middleweight, light middleweight or super welterweight	maximum 70kg/154 lb
middleweight	maximum 73kg/160 lb
super middleweight	maximum 76kg/168 lb
light heavyweight	maximum 79kg/175 lb
cruiserweight	maximum 86kg/190 lb
heavyweight	above 86kg/190 lb

Wilde in the Ring

In 1867 the 8th Marquess of Queensberry, Sir John Douglas (1844–1900), supervised the formulation of new rules to govern boxing, since known as the 'Queensberry Rules'. The same Marquess was unsuccessfully sued for criminal libel by Oscar Wilde in 1895; Queensberry disapproved of Wilde's friendship with his son, Lord Alfred Douglas, and it was Queensberry's allegations of homosexuality that led in turn to Wilde's trial and imprisonment.

World heavyweight champions

The first world heavyweight champion under Queensberry Rules with gloves was James J Corbett in 1892.

1983	Gerrie Coetzee (South Africa)	WBA
1984	Tim Witherspoon (USA)	WBC
1984	Pinklon Thomas (USA)	WBC
1984	Larry Holmes (USA)	IBF
1984	Greg Page (USA)	WBA
1985	Tony Tubbs (USA)	WBA
1985	Pinklon Thomas (USA)	WBC
1985	Michael Spinks (USA)	IBF
1986	Tim Witherspoon (USA)	WBA
1986	Trevor Berbick (Canada)	WBC
1986	Mike Tyson (USA)	WBC
1986	James Smith (USA)	WBA
1987	Tony Tucker (USA)	IBF
1987	Mike Tyson (USA)	WBA/WBC
1987	Mike Tyson (USA)	UND
1989	Francesco Damiani (Italy)	WBO
1990	James (Buster) Douglas (USA)	WBA/WBC/IBF
1990	Evander Holyfield (USA)	WBA/WBC/IBF
1991	Ray Mercer (USA)	WBO
1992	Riddick Bowe (USA)[1]	WBA/WBC/IBF
1992	Michael Moorer (USA)	WBO
1993	Evander Holyfield (USA)	WBA/IBF
1993	Lennox Lewis (UK)	WBC
1993	Tommy Morrison (USA)	WBO
1993	Michael Bentt (USA)	WBO
1994	Herbie Hide (UK)	WBO
1994	Michael Moorer (USA)	WBA/IBF
1994	Oliver McCall (USA)	WBC
1994	George Foreman (USA)[2, 3]	WBA/IBF
1995	Riddick Bowe (USA)	WBO
1995	Bruce Seldon (USA)	WBA
1995	Frank Bruno (UK)	WBC
1995	Frans Botha (South Africa)[4]	IBF
1996	Mike Tyson (USA)[5]	WBA/WBC
1996	Henry Akinwande (UK)	WBO
1996	Michael Moorer (USA)	IBF
1996	Evander Holyfield (USA)	WBA
1997	Evander Holyfield (USA)	WBA/IBF
1997	Lennox Lewis (UK)	WBC
1997	Herbie Hide (UK)	WBO
1999	Vitali Klitschko (Ukraine)	WBO
1999	Lennox Lewis (UK)[6]	UND (WBA/WBC/IBF)
2000	Chris Byrd (USA)	WBO
2000	Evander Holyfield (USA)	WBA
2000	Lennox Lewis (UK)	WBC/IBF
2001	John Ruiz (USA)	WBA
2000	Wladimir Klitschko (Ukraine)	WBO
2001	Hashim Rahman (USA)	WBC/IBF
2001	Lennox Lewis (UK)	WBC/IBF
2002	Lennox Lewis (UK)[7]	IBF
2002	Chris Byrd (USA)	IBF
2003	Roy Jones Jr (USA)	WBA
2003	Corrie Sanders (South Africa)[8]	WBO
2004	John Ruiz (USA)	WBA
2004	Lamon Brewster (USA)	WBO
2004	Vitali Klitschko (Ukraine)	WBC
2005	James Toney[9] (USA)	WBA
2005	John Ruiz (USA)	WBA
2005	Hasim Rahman[10] (USA)	WBC
2005	Nikolay Valuev (Russia)	WBA
2006	Sergei Liakhovich (Belarus)	WBO
2006	Wladimir Klitschko (Ukraine)	IBF
2006	Oleg Maskaev (Russia)	WBC
2006	Shannon Briggs (USA)	WBO
2007	Ruslan Chagaev (Uzbekistan)	WBA
2007	Sultan Ibragimov (Russia)	WBO
2007	Samuel Peter[11] (Nigeria)	WBC

[1] *Stripped of WBC title in 1992.*
[2] *Gave up IBF title in 1995.*
[3] *Stripped of WBA title in 1995.*
[4] *Stripped of IBF title in 1996.*
[5] *Gave up WBC title in 1996.*
[6] *Stripped of WBA title in 2000.*
[7] *Gave up IBF title in 2002*
[8] *Gave up WBO title in 2003*
[9] *Failed drugs test; title returned to John Ruiz.*
[10] *Awarded WBC title upon retirement of Vitali Klitschko.*
[11] *Awarded WBC "interim" title when Oleg Maskaev withdrew from a title fight because of injury.*

IBF International Boxing Federation · *WBA World Boxing Association* · *WBO World Boxing Organization*
UND Undisputed Champion · *WBC World Boxing Council*

CHESS

Game of strategy for two players using chequered board of 64 squares. Each player has 16 pieces: eight pawns, two rooks, two knights, two bishops, queen and king; object is to capture or *checkmate* opponent's king; all pieces have set moves, queen is most versatile.

Ruling body: World Chess Federation (FIDE; Fédération Internationale des Échecs)

World Champions

World Champions have been recognized since 1886; first women's champion recognized in 1927. In 1993 a new Professional Chess Association (PCA) was created as a rival body to FIDE but it collapsed in 1996; replaced by the World Chess Council which also collapsed in 2000.

Men

1975–85	Anatoly Karpov (USSR)
1985–93	Garry Kasparov (USSR)[1]
1993–9	Anatoly Karpov (Russia)
1999	Alexander Khalifman (Russia)
2000–2	Viswanathan Anand (India)
2002–4	Ruslan Ponomariov (Ukraine)
2004–5	Rustam Kasimdzhanov (Uzbekistan)
2005–6	Veselin Topalov (Bulgaria)
2006–7	Vladimir Kramnik (Russia)
2007–	Viswanathan Anand (India)

[1] *Continued as PCA World Champion to 2000.*

Women

1978–91	Maya Chiburdanidze (USSR)
1991–6	Xie Jun (China)
1996–9	Zsuza Polgar (Hungary)
1999–2001	Xie Jun (China)
2001–4	Zhu Chen (China)
2004–6	Antoaneta Stefanova (Bulgaria)
2006–	Xu Yuhua (China)

Chaturanga and Chess

Chess was played in ancient India as *chaturanga*, and the earliest reference to it dates from c.600 AD. The current pieces have existed in standard form for over 500 years.

CRICKET

Bat-and-ball eleven-a-side team game. A wicket consisting of three stumps (wooden sticks) surmounted by a pair of bails (smaller sticks) is placed at each end of a grassy pitch 20.1m/22yd in length. Each team takes it in turn to bat (with long flat-sided wooden bats) and bowl (with a solid ball), the object being to defend the two wickets while trying to score as many runs as possible. A bowler delivers an *over* of six balls to a batsman standing in front of one of the wickets before a different bowler attacks the other wicket. If the batsman hits a ball (and in certain other circumstances), he may exchange places with the other batsman, thus scoring at least one run. A ball reaching the boundary of the field scores four runs automatically, and six if it has not bounced on the way. A batsman can be got out by being *caught* (a fielder catches the ball before it reaches the ground), *bowled* (the ball from the bowler knocks the bails off the stumps), *stumped* (the wicketkeeper knocks the bails off the stumps with the ball while the defending batsman is standing outside his *safe ground* or *crease*), *run out* (the bails on the wicket towards which one of the batsmen is running are knocked off before the safe ground is reached), *leg before wicket* or *lbw* (when the lower part of the batsman's leg prevents the ball from the bowler reaching the wicket) and *hit wicket* (the batsman accidentally knocks the bails off the stumps). Once ten batsmen have been dismissed, the innings comes to a close, but a team can stop its innings or *declare* if it thinks it has made enough runs. In longer games each team has two innings, at the end of which the team with the greater number of runs at the end of the match wins. If both innings are not completed within the permitted time the match is declared a draw. Test matches usually last up to five days; county championship matches four, and limited-over competitions are normally concluded in one day, lasting for a specific number of overs per side.

Ruling bodies: International Cricket Council (ICC), England and Wales Cricket Board (ECB), Marylebone Cricket Club (MCC)

Cricket fielding positions

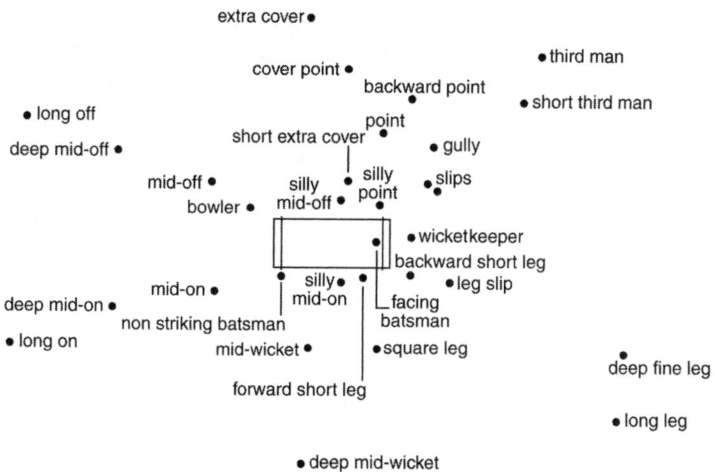

Ashes Series Winners

First played in 1882; held every two years; Australia and England take part.

1982–3	Australia
1985	England
1986–7	England
1989	Australia
1990–1	Australia
1993	Australia
1994–5	Australia
1997	Australia
1998–9	Australia
2001	Australia
2002–3	Australia
2005	England
2006–7	Australia

World Cup

First played in 1975; usually held every four years.

1983	India
1987	Australia
1992	Pakistan
1996	Sri Lanka
1999	Australia
2003	Australia
2007	Australia

Women's World Cup

First played in 1973.

1973	England
1977	Australia
1982	Australia
1988	Australia
1993	England
1997	Australia
2000	New Zealand
2005	Australia

County Championship

The oldest cricket competition in the world; first won by Sussex in 1827; not officially recognized until 1890, when a proper points system was introduced; split into two divisions in 2000.

1983	Essex
1984	Essex
1985	Middlesex
1986	Essex
1987	Nottinghamshire
1988	Worcestershire
1989	Worcestershire
1990	Middlesex
1991	Essex
1992	Essex
1993	Middlesex
1994	Warwickshire
1995	Warwickshire
1996	Leicestershire
1997	Glamorgan
1998	Leicestershire
1999	Surrey
2000	Surrey (Division 2 Northamptonshire)
2001	Yorkshire (Division 2 Sussex)
2002	Surrey (Division 2 Essex)
2003	Sussex (Division 2 Worcestershire)
2004	Warwickshire (Division 2 Nottinghamshire)
2005	Nottinghamshire (Division 2 Lancashire)
2006	Sussex (Division 2 Surrey)
2007	Sussex (Division 2 Somerset)

NatWest Pro40 League

First held in 1969; split into two divisions in 1999; known as the John Player League until 1987, the Refuge Assurance League until 1991, the Axa Equity and Law League until 1999, the CGU League until 2000, the Norwich Union National Cricket League until 2003 and the Totesport National Cricket League until 2005.

1983	Yorkshire
1984	Essex
1985	Essex
1986	Hampshire
1987	Worcestershire
1988	Worcestershire
1989	Lancashire
1990	Derbyshire
1991	Nottinghamshire
1992	Middlesex
1993	Glamorgan
1994	Warwickshire
1995	Kent
1996	Surrey
1997	Warwickshire
1998	Lancashire
1999	Lancashire (Division 2 Sussex)
2000	Gloucestershire (Division 2 Surrey)
2001	Kent (Division 2 Glamorgan)
2002	Glamorgan (Division 2 Gloucestershire)
2003	Surrey (Division 2 Lancashire)
2004	Glamorgan (Division 2 Middlesex)
2005	Essex (Division 2 Sussex)
2006	Essex (Division 2 Gloucestershire)
2007	Worcestershire (Division 2 Durham)

Friends Provident Trophy

First held in 1963; known as the Gillette Cup until 1981, the NatWest Bank Trophy until 2000 and the Cheltenham & Gloucester Trophy until 2007.

1983	Somerset	1992	Northamptonshire	2001	Somerset
1984	Middlesex	1993	Warwickshire	2002	Yorkshire
1985	Essex	1994	Worcestershire	2003	Gloucestershire
1986	Sussex	1995	Warwickshire	2004	Gloucestershire
1987	Nottinghamshire	1996	Lancashire	2005	Hampshire
1988	Middlesex	1997	Essex	2006	Sussex
1989	Warwickshire	1998	Lancashire	2007	Durham
1990	Lancashire	1999	Gloucestershire		
1991	Hampshire	2000	Gloucestershire		

Twenty20 Cup

First held in 2003.

2003	Surrey	2005	Somerset
2004	Leicestershire	2006	Leicestershire
		2007	Kent

Benson and Hedges Cup

Competition ran from 1972 to 2002.

1983	Middlesex	1989	Nottinghamshire	1996	Lancashire
1984	Lancashire	1990	Lancashire	1997	Surrey
1985	Leicestershire	1991	Worcestershire	1998	Essex
1986	Middlesex	1992	Hampshire	1999	Gloucestershire
1987	Yorkshire	1993	Derbyshire	2000	Gloucestershire
1988	Hampshire	1994	Warwickshire	2001	Surrey
		1995	Lancashire	2002	Warwickshire

Pura Cup

Australia's leading domestic competition; contested inter-state since 1892–3; known as the Sheffield Shield until 1999.

1983	New South Wales	1991	Victoria	2000	Queensland
1984	Western Australia	1992	Western Australia	2001	Queensland
1985	New South Wales	1993	New South Wales	2002	Queensland
1986	New South Wales	1994	New South Wales	2003	New South Wales
1987	Western Australia	1995	Queensland	2004	Victoria
1988	Western Australia	1996	South Australia	2005	New South Wales
1989	Western Australia	1997	Queensland	2006	Queensland
1990	New South Wales	1998	Western Australia	2007	Tasmania
		1999	Western Australia		

CROSS-COUNTRY RUNNING

An athletic running event using a predetermined course over natural terrain. The length of race varies; the current race distances are 12km/7.5mi for men's long course races, 8km/5mi for women's long course races and 4km/2.5mi for both short course races. The first recorded international race was in May 1898, and covered a 14.5km/9mi course at Ville D'Avray near Paris, France.

Ruling body: International Association of Athletics Federations (IAAF)

World Championships

First international championship held in 1903, but only included runners from England, Ireland, Scotland and Wales; recognized as an official world championship from 1973; first women's race in 1967.

Individual – Men's long course

1983	Bekele Debele (Ethiopia)
1984–85	Carlos Lopes (Portugal)
1986–89	John Ngugi (Kenya)
1990–91	Khalid Skah (Morocco)
1992	John Ngugi (Kenya)
1993–94	William Sigei (Kenya)
1995–99	Paul Tergat (Kenya)
2000–1	Mohammed Mourhit (Belgium)
2002–6	Kenenisa Bekele (Ethiopia)
2007	Zersenay Tadese (Eritrea)

Individual – Women's long course

1983	Grete Waitz (Norway)
1984	Maricica Puică (Romania)
1985–6	Zola Budd (England)
1987	Annette Sergent (France)
1988	Ingrid Kristiansen (Norway)
1989	Annette Sergent (France)
1990–2	Lynn Jennings (USA)
1993	Albertina Dias (Portugal)
1994	Helen Chepngeno (Kenya)
1995	Derartu Tulu (Ethiopia)
1996	Gete Wami (Ethiopia)
1997	Derartu Tulu (Ethiopia)
1998	Sonia O'Sullivan (Ireland)
1999	Gete Wami (Ethiopia)
2000	Derartu Tulu (Ethiopia)
2001–2	Paula Radcliffe (England)
2003	Werknesh Kidane (Ethiopia)
2004	Benita Johnson (Australia)
2005–6	Tirunesh Dibaba (Ethiopia)
2007	Lornah Kiplagat (The Netherlands)

Team – Men's long course

1982–5	Ethiopia
1986–2003	Kenya
2004–5	Ethiopia
2006–7	Kenya

Team – Women's long course

1983–5	USA
1986	England
1987	USA
1988–90	USSR
1991	Ethiopia *and* Kenya *(shared)*
1992–3	Kenya
1994	Portugal
1995–6	Kenya
1997	Ethiopia
1998	Kenya
1999–2000	Ethiopia
2001	Kenya
2002–7	Ethiopia

CYCLING

Bicycle riding as a sport can take several forms: *time trials* are raced against the clock; *cyclocross* is a mixture of cycling and cross-country running, carrying the bike; *track racing* takes place on purpose-built concrete or wooden velodromes; *criteriums* are races around town or city centres; *road races* are normally in excess of 150km/93mi in length, between two points or several circuits of a predetermined course; *stage races* involve many days' racing over more than 150km/93mi. First cycle race Paris 1868, won by James Moore of England.

Ruling body: International Cycling Union (UCI; Union Cycliste Internationale)

World Road Race Championships

Men's race first held in 1927; first women's race in 1958; takes place annually.

Men

1983	Greg LeMond (USA)
1984	Claude Criquielion (Belgium)
1985	Joop Zoetemelk (The Netherlands)
1986	Moreno Argentin (Italy)
1987	Stephen Roche (Ireland)
1988	Maurizio Fondriest (Italy)
1989	Greg LeMond (USA)
1990	Rudy Dhaenens (Belgium)
1991	Gianni Bugno (Italy)
1992	Gianni Bugno (Italy)
1993	Lance Armstrong (USA)
1994	Luc Leblanc (France)
1995	Abraham Olano (Spain)
1996	Johan Museeuw (Belgium)
1997	Laurent Brochard (France)
1998	Oskar Camenzind (Switzerland)
1999	Óscar Freire Gómez (Spain)
2000	Romans Vainsteins (Latvia)
2001	Óscar Freire Gómez (Spain)
2002	Mario Cipollini (Italy)
2003	Igor Astarloa (Spain)
2004	Óscar Freire Gómez (Spain)
2005	Tom Boonen (Belgium)
2006	Paolo Bettini (Italy)
2007	Paolo Bettini (Italy)

Women

1983	Marianne Berglund (Switzerland)
1984	*not held*
1985	Jeannie Longo (France)
1986	Jeannie Longo (France)
1987	Jeannie Longo (France)
1988	*not held*
1989	Jeannie Longo (France)
1990	Catherine Marsal (France)
1991	Leontien van Moorsel (The Netherlands)
1992	*not held*
1993	Leontien van Moorsel (The Netherlands)
1994	Monica Valvik (Norway)
1995	Jeannie Longo (France)
1996	Barbara Heeb (Switzerland)
1997	Alessandra Cappellotto (Italy)
1998	Diana Ziliute (Lithuania)
1999	Edita Pucinskaite (Lithuania)
2000	Zinaida Stahurskaia (Belarus)
2001	Rosa Polikeviciute (Lithuania)
2002	Susanne Ljungskog (Sweden)
2003	Susanne Ljungskog (Sweden)
2004	Judith Arndt (Germany)
2005	Regina Schleicher (Germany)
2006	Marianne Vos (The Netherlands)
2007	Marta Bastianelli (Italy)

Tour de France

World's premier cycling event; first held in 1903.

1983–4	Laurent Fignon (France)
1985	Bernard Hinault (France)
1986	Greg LeMond (USA)
1987	Stephen Roche (Ireland)
1988	Pedro Delgado (Spain)
1989–90	Greg LeMond (USA)
1991–5	Miguel Indurain (Spain)
1996	Bjarne Riis (Denmark)

1997	Jan Ullrich (Germany)
1998	Marco Pantani (Italy)
1999–2005	Lance Armstrong (USA)
2006	Floyd Landis (USA)
2007	Alberto Contador (Spain)

Yellow Jerseys

The famous *yellow jersey* (or *maillot jaune*) is worn each day of the Tour de France by the race's overall leader. The jersey, which was first worn in 1919, gained its distinctive colour from the yellow pages of *Auto*, the magazine which instituted the Tour in 1903. The Belgian Eddy Merckx holds the record for wearing the jersey, having been yellow-clad for an impressive 96 days. The Tour's cyclists also compete to wear the *green jersey*, since 1953 the reward for the best sprinter, the *red polka-dot jersey*, worn since 1975 by the best mountain climber, and the *white jersey*, first awarded in 1975 to the leading young cyclist under 25 years.

DARTS

Indoor game of throwing three 13cm/5in darts from a distance of 2.37m/7ft 9.25in at a circular board which has its centre 1.73m/5ft 8in from the floor. The standard board is divided into 20 segments numbered 1–20 (not in numerical order); each contains smaller segments which either double or treble that number's score if hit. The centre ring (the *bull*) is worth 50 points, and the area around it (the *outer*) is worth 25 points. Most popular game *501*: players start at that figure and deduct all scores from it, aiming to reduce the starting score exactly to zero; final shot must consist of a double.

Ruling body: British Darts Organization (BDO), World Darts Federation (WDF)

Dartboard

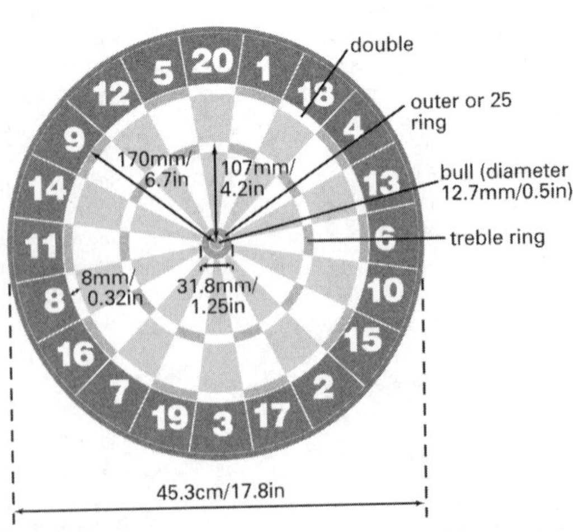

Embassy World Darts Championship

First held at Nottingham in 1978. Women's championship introduced in 2001.

Men

1983	Keith Deller (England)
1984–6	Eric Bristow (England)
1987	John Lowe (England)
1988	Bob Anderson (England)
1989	Jocky Wilson (Scotland)
1990	Phil Taylor (England)
1991	Dennis Priestley (England)
1992	Phil Taylor (England)
1993	John Lowe (England)
1994	John Part (Canada)
1995	Richie Burnett (Wales)
1996	Steve Beaton (England)
1997	Les Wallace (Scotland)
1998–9	Raymond van Barneveld (The Netherlands)
2000	Ted Hankey (England)
2001	John Walton (England)
2002	Tony David (Australia)
2003	Raymond van Barneveld (The Netherlands)
2004	Andy Fordham (England)
2005	Raymond van Barneveld (The Netherlands)
2006	Jelle Klaasen (The Netherlands)
2007	Martin Adams (England)
2008	Mark Webster (Wales)

Women

2001–7	Trina Gulliver (England)
2008	Anastasia Dobromysova (Russia)

Blowin' in the Wind

When Mervyn King lost 5–2 to Raymond van Barneveld in the semifinal of the Embassy World Darts Championship in 2003, the BBC reported that he blamed excessive air-conditioning for blowing his darts off course. Disgruntled King allegedly claimed that the air-conditioning 'was blowing [his] darts all over the shop', and reckoned that Barneveld was not affected because his darts were heavier. King reportedly threatened to boycott subsequent championships and was not swayed by organizers' protests that the air-conditioning had been switched off throughout.

EQUESTRIAN EVENTS

Events in which riders on horseback compete in various disciplines: *dressage*, performance of set manoeuvres signalled by the rider; *three-day event*, a competition in showjumping, cross-country riding and dressage; and *showjumping*, in which competitors take turns to jump a variety of obstacles, often against time; in most competitions, each pair of horse and rider has one attempt at clearing the fences; those that clear the fences and incur no penalty points are then involved in a *jump-off* against the clock, where speed as well as accuracy are important.

Ruling body: International Equestrian Federation (FEI; Fédération Équestre Internationale)

World Equestrian Games

Showjumping championships first held in 1953 (for men) and 1965 (for women); since 1978 men and women have competed together and on equal terms; team competition introduced in 1978; three-day event and dressage championships introduced in 1966; all three now held every four years. Formerly known as the World Championships.

Showjumping

Individual		Team	
1990	Eric Navet (France)/Quito de Baussy	1990	France
1994	Franke Sloothaak (Germany)/S.P. Weihaiwej	1994	Germany
1998	Rodrigo Pessoa (Brazil)/Gandini Lianos	1998	Germany
2002	Dermott Lennon (Ireland)/Liscalgot	2002	France
2006	Joe Lansink (Belgium)/Cavalor Cumano	2006	The Netherlands

Three-day event

Individual		Team	
1990	Blyth Tait (New Zealand)/Messiah	1990	New Zealand
1994	Vaughn Jefferis (New Zealand)/Bounce	1994	Great Britain
1998	Blyth Tait (New Zealand)/Ready Teddy	1998	New Zealand
2002	Jean Teulere (France)/Espoir de la Mare	2002	USA
2006	Zara Phillips (Great Britian)/Toytown	2006	Germany

Dressage

Individual		Team	
1990	Nicole Uphoff (West Germany)/Rembrandt	1990	West Germany
1994	Anky Van Grunsven (The Netherlands)/ Gestion Bonfire; Isabell Werth (Germany)/ Gigolo[1]	1994	Germany
1998	Isabell Werth (Germany)/Gigolo	1998	Germany
2002	Nadine Capellmann (Germany)/Farbenfroh	2002	Germany
2006	Anky Van Grunsven (The Netherlands)/Keltec Salinero; Isabell Werth (Germany)/Satchmo[1]	2006	Germany

[1]In 1994 and 2006 there were separate Freestyle and Special dressage competitions. On both occasions Anky Van Grunsven won the former and Isabell Werth the latter.

FENCING

Sword fighting, using a light *foil*, heavier *épée*, or *sabre* (curved handle, narrow blade). Different target areas exist for each weapon, and protective clothing registers hits electronically.

Ruling body: International Fencing Federation (FIE; Fédération Internationale d'Escrime)

World Championships

Held annually since 1921 (1921–35, known as European Championships). Not held in Olympic years. Women's épée was introduced in 1989 and women's sabre in 1999.

2002

	Men	Women
foil individual	Simone Vanni (Italy)	Svetlana Boiko (Russia)
foil team	Germany	Russia
épée individual	Pavel Kolobkov (Russia)	Hee Hyun (Korea)
épée team	France	Hungary
sabre individual	Stanislav Pozdniakov (Russia)	Tan Xue (China)
sabre team	Russia	Russia

2003

	Men	Women
foil individual	Peter Joppich (Germany)	Valentina Vezzali (Italy)
foil team	Italy	Poland
épée individual	Fabrice Jeannet (France)	Natalia Conrad (Ukraine)
épée team	Russia	Russia
sabre individual	Vladimir Lukashenko (Ukraine)	Dorina Mihai (Romania)
sabre team	Russia	Italy

2005

	Men	Women
foil individual	Salvatore Sanzo (Italy)	Valentina Vezzali (Italy)
foil team	France	South Korea
épée individual	Pavel Kolobkov (Russia)	Danuta Dmowska (Poland)
épée team	France	France
sabre individual	Mihai Covaliu (Romania)	Anne-Lise Touya (France)
sabre team	Russia	USA

2006

	Men	Women
foil individual	Peter Joppich (Germany)	Margherita Granbassi (Italy)
foil team	France	China
épée individual	Wang Lei (China)	Tímea Nagy (Hungary)
épée team	France	Russia
sabre individual	Stanislav Pozdniakov (Russia)	Rebecca Ward (USA)
sabre team	France	France

2007

	Men	Women
foil individual	Peter Joppich (Germany)	Valentina Vezzali (Italy)
foil team	France	Poland
épée individual	Krisztián Kulcsár (Hungary)	Britta Heidemann (Germany)
épée team	France	France
sabre individual	Stanislav Pozdniakov (Russia)	Elena Netchaeva (Russia)
sabre team	Hungary	France

The Language of Fencing

Fencing can be traced back to Egypt in c.1300 BC and was popular in the Middle Ages. It was first practised as a sport in Europe in the 14c–15c, and its many movements were originally named in 1570 by the Frenchman Henri Saint-Didier. Today fencing moves include the *appel*, the *botte*, the *flanconade*, the *imbroccata*, the *stoccado* or *stoccata* and the *tac-au-tac*. Fencing also provides the origin of the term *touché* (claiming or acknowledging a point scored in an argument) which originally referred to a fencing hit by an opponent.

FOOTBALL

A field team game using an inflated ball, formally known as *association football*, and sometimes called *soccer*. An 11-a-side team game played on a grass or synthetic pitch; object is to move the ball around using the foot or head until it can be put into the net, thus scoring a goal. Only the goalkeeper within a specific area is allowed to touch the ball with the hand while it is in play.

Ruling body: Fédération Internationale de Football Association (FIFA), Union of European Football Associations (UEFA), Confederación Sudamericana de Fútbol (CONMEBOL), Football Association (FA), Scottish Football Association (SFA)

Football pitch

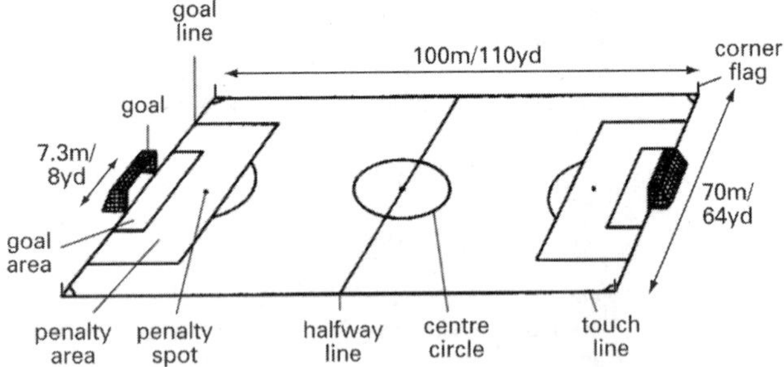

FIFA World Cup

Football's premier event; first contested for the Jules Rimet Trophy in 1930; Brazil won it outright after winning for the third time in 1970; since then teams have competed for the FIFA World Cup; held every four years.

Host countries

1930	Uruguay
1934	Italy
1938	France
1942	*not held*
1946	*not held*
1950	Brazil
1954	Switzerland
1958	Sweden
1962	Chile
1966	England
1970	Mexico
1974	West Germany
1978	Argentina
1982	Spain
1986	Mexico
1990	Italy
1994	USA
1998	France
2002	South Korea/Japan
2006	Germany
2010	South Africa
2014	Brazil

Winners

1930	Uruguay
1934	Italy
1938	Italy
1942	*not held*
1946	*not held*
1950	Uruguay
1954	West Germany
1958	Brazil
1962	Brazil
1966	England
1970	Brazil
1974	West Germany
1978	Argentina
1982	Italy

1986	Argentina	1998	France
1990	West Germany	2002	Brazil
1994	Brazil	2006	Italy

European Championship

Held every four years since 1960; qualifying group matches held over the two years preceding the final.

1960	USSR	1984	France
1964	Spain	1988	Netherlands
1968	Italy	1992	Denmark
1972	West Germany	1996	Germany
1976	Czechoslovakia	2000	France
1980	West Germany	2004	Greece

Copa América

First held in 1916 for South American national sides; there were two tournaments in 1959, won by Argentina and Uruguay; discontinued in 1967, but revived eight years later; from 1987 played every two years, and from 2001 every three.

1983	Uruguay	1997	Brazil
1987	Uruguay	1999	Brazil
1989	Brazil	2001	Colombia
1991	Argentina	2004	Brazil
1993	Argentina	2007	Brazil
1995	Uruguay		

European Champions League

The leading club competition in Europe; open to the leading teams of countries affiliated to the Union of European Football Associations (UEFA), the Cup's ruling body, on a quota basis; commonly known as the 'European Cup'; inaugurated in the 1955–6 season; played annually.

1983	Hamburg (West Germany)	1996	Juventus (Italy)
1984	Liverpool (England)	1997	Borussia Dortmund (Germany)
1985	Juventus (Italy)	1998	Real Madrid (Spain)
1986	Steaua Bucharest (Romania)	1999	Manchester United (England)
1987	FC Porto (Portugal)	2000	Real Madrid (Spain)
1988	PSV Eindhoven (The Netherlands)	2001	Bayern Munich (Germany)
1989	AC Milan (Italy)	2002	Real Madrid (Spain)
1990	AC Milan (Italy)	2003	AC Milan (Italy)
1991	Red Star Belgrade (Yugoslavia)	2004	FC Porto (Portugal)
1992	Barcelona (Spain)	2005	Liverpool (England)
1993	Olympique Marseille[1] (France)	2006	Barcelona (Spain)
1994	AC Milan (Italy)	2007	AC Milan (Italy)
1995	Ajax (The Netherlands)		

[1] *Stripped of title because of match fixing.*

Football Firsts

The Ancient Greeks, Chinese, Egyptians and Romans all played a form of football. It became an organized game in Britain in the 19c, and standard rules were drawn up in 1848. The Football Association (FA) was formed in 1863 and the first FA Cup final was played in 1872; the first World Cup was held in 1930.

UEFA Cup

Held since 1958; originally the Fairs Cup, renamed the UEFA Cup in 1971; open to the runners-up in domestic championships, as well as to the winners of certain other domestic competitions.

1983	Anderlecht (Belgium)
1984	Tottenham Hotspur (England)
1985	Real Madrid (Spain)
1986	Real Madrid (Spain)
1987	IFK Goteborg (Sweden)
1988	Bayer 04 Leverkusen (West Germany)
1989	Napoli (Italy)
1990	Juventus (Italy)
1991	Inter Milan (Italy)
1992	Ajax (The Netherlands)
1993	Juventus (Italy)
1994	Inter Milan (Italy)
1995	Parma (Italy)
1996	Bayern Munich (Germany)
1997	Schalke 04 (Germany)
1998	Inter Milan (Italy)
1999	Parma (Italy)
2000	Galatasaray (Turkey)
2001	Liverpool (England)
2002	Feyenoord (The Netherlands)
2003	FC Porto (Portugal)
2004	Valencia (Spain)
2005	CSKA Moscow (Russia)
2006	Sevilla (Spain)
2007	Sevilla (Spain)

European Cup Winners' Cup

Competititon ran from 1961 to 1999; for winners of European domestic cup competitions.

1983	Aberdeen (Scotland)
1984	Juventus (Italy)
1985	Everton (England)
1986	Dynamo Kiev (USSR)
1987	Ajax (The Netherlands)
1988	Mechelen (Belgium)
1989	Barcelona (Spain)
1990	Sampdoria (Italy)
1991	Manchester United (England)
1992	Werder Bremen (Germany)
1993	Parma (Italy)
1994	Arsenal (England)
1995	Real Zaragoza (Spain)
1996	Paris Saint-Germain (France)
1997	Barcelona (Spain)
1998	Chelsea (England)
1999	Lazio (Italy)

The Other Final

While the World Cup Final was being contested by Germany and Brazil in Jun 2002 in front of more than 69,000 spectators and millions of television viewers worldwide, another final was taking place rather more quietly at the Chlanglimithang Stadium in Thimphu, Bhutan. FIFA's two lowest ranked teams – Bhutan and Montserrat, rated 202 and 203 in the world – had been brought together by a couple of Dutch filmmakers to contest what became known as 'The Other Final' for the sheer love of football. The altitude (2,250m/7,380ft above sea level), stray dogs rambling across the pitch, torrential Himalayan rain and repeated choruses of Montserrat's only worldwide hit song 'Hot Hot Hot' all combined to create a unique match in a nation where the national sport is archery. Despite Montserrat's initial optimism, the end result was 4–0 to Bhutan.

Football Association Challenge Cup (FA Cup)

The world's oldest club knockout competition held annually by the Football Association (FA); first contested in the 1871–2 season; first final at the Kennington Oval on 16 Mar 1872.

1983	Manchester United
1984	Everton
1985	Manchester United
1986	Liverpool
1987	Coventry City
1988	Wimbledon
1989	Liverpool
1990	Manchester United
1991	Tottenham Hotspur
1992	Liverpool
1993	Arsenal
1994	Manchester United
1995	Everton
1996	Manchester United
1997	Chelsea
1998	Arsenal
1999	Manchester United
2000	Chelsea
2001	Chelsea
2002	Arsenal
2003	Arsenal
2004	Manchester United
2005	Arsenal
2006	Liverpool
2007	Chelsea

Football League

The oldest league in the world, and regarded as the toughest; founded in 1888, it has four divisions, with the Premiership (founded in the 1992–3 season) as the top division.

1983	Liverpool
1984	Liverpool
1985	Everton
1986	Liverpool
1987	Everton
1988	Liverpool
1989	Arsenal
1990	Liverpool
1991	Arsenal
1992	Leeds United
1993	Manchester United
1994	Manchester United
1995	Blackburn Rovers
1996	Manchester United
1997	Manchester United
1998	Arsenal
1999	Manchester United
2000	Manchester United
2001	Manchester United
2002	Arsenal
2003	Manchester United
2004	Arsenal
2005	Chelsea
2006	Chelsea
2007	Manchester United

Football League Cup (Carling Cup)

Founded 1961; open to the 92 members of the Football League and the Premiership; formerly known as the Milk Cup, Littlewoods Cup, Rumbelows Cup, Coca-Cola Cup and Worthington Cup.

1983	Liverpool
1984	Liverpool
1985	Norwich City
1986	Oxford United
1987	Arsenal
1988	Luton Town
1989	Nottingham Forest
1990	Nottingham Forest
1991	Sheffield Wednesday
1992	Manchester United
1993	Arsenal
1994	Aston Villa
1995	Liverpool
1996	Aston Villa
1997	Leicester City
1998	Chelsea

1999	Tottenham Hotspur	2004	Middlesbrough
2000	Leicester City	2005	Chelsea
2001	Liverpool	2006	Manchester United
2002	Blackburn Rovers	2007	Chelsea
2003	Liverpool		

Scottish Football League

Organized in various divisions since 1891; in 1998 the top ten teams broke away to form the new independent Scottish Premier League, which was expanded to twelve teams in 2000.

1983	Dundee United	1996	Rangers
1984	Aberdeen	1997	Rangers
1985	Aberdeen	1998	Celtic
1986	Celtic	1999	Rangers
1987	Rangers	2000	Rangers
1988	Celtic	2001	Celtic
1989	Rangers	2002	Celtic
1990	Rangers	2003	Rangers
1991	Rangers	2004	Celtic
1992	Rangers	2005	Rangers
1993	Rangers	2006	Celtic
1994	Rangers	2007	Celtic
1995	Rangers		

Scottish FA Cup

Competition held by the Scottish Football Association (SFA); first contested in the 1873–4 season; first final held in 1874 at Hampden Park.

1983	Aberdeen	1996	Rangers
1984	Aberdeen	1997	Kilmarnock
1985	Celtic	1998	Heart of Midlothian
1986	Aberdeen	1999	Rangers
1987	St Mirren	2000	Rangers
1988	Celtic	2001	Celtic
1989	Celtic	2002	Rangers
1990	Aberdeen	2003	Rangers
1991	Motherwell	2004	Celtic
1992	Rangers	2005	Celtic
1993	Rangers	2006	Heart of Midlothian
1994	Dundee United	2007	Celtic
1995	Celtic		

Scottish League Cup (CIS Insurance Cup)

Founded 1947 and open to the 42 members of the Scottish Football League.

1983	Celtic	1987	Rangers
1984	Rangers	1988	Rangers
1985	Rangers	1989	Rangers
1986	Aberdeen	1990	Aberdeen

1991	Rangers
1992	Hibernian
1993	Rangers
1994	Rangers
1995	Raith Rovers
1996	Aberdeen
1997	Rangers
1998	Celtic
1999	Rangers
2000	Celtic
2001	Celtic
2002	Rangers
2003	Rangers
2004	Livingston
2005	Rangers
2006	Celtic
2007	Hibernian

English Premiership and Football League clubs 2007–8

Club	Stadium	Nickname
Accrington Stanley	Fraser Eagle	The Famous Minnows
Arsenal	Emirates Stadium, Holloway	The Gunners
Aston Villa	Villa Park, Birmingham	The Villans
Barnet	Underhill Stadium	The Bees
Barnsley	Oakwell	The Tykes
Birmingham City	St Andrews	The Blues
Blackburn Rovers	Ewood Park	The Rovers/ The Blue and Whites
Blackpool	Bloomfield Road	The Seasiders
Bolton Wanderers	Reebok Stadium	The Trotters
Bournemouth	Fitness First Stadium	The Cherries
Bradford City	Valley Parade[1]	The Bantams
Brentford	Griffin Park	The Bees
Brighton & Hove Albion	Withdean Stadium	The Seagulls
Bristol City	Ashton Gate	The Robins
Bristol Rovers	Memorial Stadium	The Pirates
Burnley	Turf Moor	The Clarets
Bury	Gigg Lane	The Shakers
Cardiff City	Ninian Park	The Bluebirds
Carlisle United	Brunton Park	The Cumbrians
Charlton Athletic	The Valley	The Addicks
Chelsea	Stamford Bridge	The Blues
Cheltenham Town	Whaddon Road	The Robins
Chester City	Saunders Honda Stadium	The Blues
Chesterfield	Saltergate[2]	The Spireites
Colchester United	Layer Road	The U's
Coventry City	Ricoh Arena	The Sky Blues
Crewe Alexandra	Alexandra Stadium	The Railwaymen
Crystal Palace	Selhurst Park	The Eagles
Dagenham & Redbridge	Victoria Road	the Daggers
Darlington	Reynolds Arena	The Quakers
Derby County	Pride Park Stadium	The Rams
Doncaster Rovers	Belle Vue	The Rovers
Everton	Goodison Park, Liverpool	The Toffees
Fulham	Craven Cottage	The Cottagers
Gillingham	Priestfield Stadium	The Gills
Grimsby Town	Blundell Park	The Mariners
Hartlepool United	Victoria Park	The Pool
Hereford United	Edgar Street	The Bulls
Huddersfield Town	The McAlpine Stadium	The Terriers

Club	Stadium	Nickname
Hull City	Kingston Communications Stadium	The Tigers
Ipswich Town	Portman Road	The Tractor Boys
Leeds United	Elland Road	The Whites
Leicester City	The Walkers Stadium	The Foxes
Leyton Orient	The Matchroom Stadium	The O's
Lincoln City	Sincil Bank Stadium	The Red Imps
Liverpool	Anfield	The Reds
Luton Town	Kenilworth Stadium	The Hatters
Macclesfield Town	The Moss Rose	The Silkmen
Manchester City	City of Manchester Stadium	The Citizens
Manchester United	Old Trafford	The Red Devils
Mansfield Town	Field Mill	The Stags
Middlesbrough	The Riverside Stadium	Boro
Millwall	The New Den	The Lions
Milton Keynes Dons	National Hockey Stadium	The Dons
Morecambe	Christie Park	The Shrimps
Newcastle United	St James' Park	The Magpies
Northampton Town	Sixfields Stadium	The Cobblers
Norwich City	Carrow Road	The Canaries
Nottingham Forest	The City Ground	The Reds
Notts County	Meadow Lane	The Magpies
Oldham Athletic	Boundary Park	The Latics
Peterborough United	London Road	The Posh
Plymouth Argyle	Home Park	The Pilgrims
Portsmouth	Fratton Park	Pompey
Port Vale	Vale Park, Stoke-on-Trent	The Valiants
Preston North End	Deepdale	The Lilywhites
Queen's Park Rangers	Loftus Road, Sheperd's Bush	The R's
Reading	Madejski Stadium	The Royals
Rochdale	Spotland Stadium	The Dale
Rotherham United	Millmoor	The Merry Millers
Scunthorpe United	Glanford Park	The Irons
Sheffield United	Bramall Lane	The Blades
Sheffield Wednesday	Hillsborough	The Owls
Shrewsbury Town	Gay Meadow	The Shrews
Southampton	Friends Provident St Mary's Stadium[3]	The Saints
Southend United	Roots Hall	The Shrimpers
Stockport County	Edgeley Park	The Hatters
Stoke City	The Britannia Stadium, Stoke-on-Trent	The Potters
Sunderland	Stadium of Light	The Black Cats
Swansea City	Vetch Field	The Swans
Swindon Town	County Ground	The Robins
Tottenham Hotspur	White Hart Lane	Spurs
Tranmere Rovers	Prenton Park, Birkenhead	The Rovers
Walsall	Bescot Stadium	The Saddlers
Watford	Vicarage Road	The Hornets
West Bromwich Albion	The Hawthorns	The Baggies

Club	Stadium	Nickname
West Ham United	Upton Park[4]	The Hammers
Wigan Athletic	JJB Stadium	The Latics
Wolverhampton Wanderers	Molineux Stadium	Wolves
Wrexham	The Racecourse Ground	The Robins
Wycombe Wanderers	Causeway Stadium[5]	The Chairboys/The Blues
Yeovil Town	Huish Park	The Glovers

[1] *Officially now The Bradford & Bingley Stadium.*
[2] *Officially The Recreation Ground.*
[3] *Previous home ground was The Dell.*
[4] *Officially Boleyn Ground.*
[5] *Previously known as Adams Park.*

Scottish Premier League and Football League clubs 2007–8

Club	Stadium	Nickname
Aberdeen	Pittodrie Stadium	The Dons
Airdrie United	Excelsior Stadium	The Diamonds
Albion Rovers	Cliftonhill Stadium, Coatbridge	The Wee Rovers
Alloa Athletic	Recreation Park	The Wasps
Arbroath	Gayfield Park	The Red Lichties
Ayr United	Somerset Park	The Honest Men
Berwick Rangers	Shielfield Park	The Borderers
Brechin City	Glebe Park	The City
Celtic	Celtic Park, Glasgow	The Bhoys
Clyde	Broadwood Stadium, Cumbernauld	The Bully Wee
Cowdenbeath	Central Park	The Blue Brazil
Dumbarton	Strathclyde Homes Stadium	The Sons
Dundee	Dens Park	The Dark Blues
Dundee United	Tannadice Park	The Arabs/The Terrors
Dunfermline Athletic	East End Park	The Pars
East Fife	Bayview Stadium, Methil	The Fifers
East Stirlingshire	Firs Park, Falkirk	The Shire
Elgin City	Borough Briggs	City/Black and Whites
Falkirk	Falkirk Stadium	The Bairns
Forfar Athletic	Station Park	The Loons
Greenock Morton	Cappielow Park	The Ton
Gretna	Raydale Park	The Black and Whites
Hamilton Academical	New Douglas Park	The Accies
Heart of Midlothian	Tynecastle Stadium, Edinburgh	The Jam Tarts
Hibernian	Easter Road Stadium, Edinburgh	Hibees
Inverness Caledonian Thistle	Caledonian Stadium	Caley Thistle
Kilmarnock	Rugby Park	Killie
Livingston	Almondvale Stadium	The Livvy Lions
Montrose	Links Park	The Gable Endies
Motherwell	Fir Park Stadium	The Well
Partick Thistle	Firhill Stadium, Glasgow	The Jags
Peterhead	Balmoor Stadium	The Blue Toon
Queen of the South	Palmerston Park, Dumfries	The Doonhamers
Queen's Park	Hampden Park, Glasgow	The Spiders

Club	Stadium	Nickname
Raith Rovers	Stark's Park, Kircaldy	The Rovers
Rangers	Ibrox Stadium, Glasgow	'Gers/Teddy Bears
Ross County	Victoria Park, Dingwall	The County
St Johnstone	McDiarmid Park, Perth	Saints
St Mirren	St Mirren Park, Paisley	The Buddies
Stenhousemuir	Ochilview Park, Stenhousemuir	The Warriors
Stirling Albion	Forthbank Stadium	The Albion/The Reds/The Binos
Stranraer	Stair Park	The Blues

Goals Galore

The record for the most goals scored in a season in the SPL is held by Celtic, who hit the back of the net 105 times in the 2003–4 season. Languishing at the other end of the table is St Johnstone; they scored just 24 times during 2002–3.

Major European football clubs

Belgium

Club	City	Stadium
Anderlecht	Brussels	Constant Vanden Stock Stadium

France

Club	City	Stadium
AS Monaco	Monaco	Stade Louis II
Paris Saint-Germain	Paris	Parc des Princes

Germany

Club	City	Stadium
Bayer 04 Leverkusen	Leverkusen	BayArena
Bayern Munich	Munich	Allianz Arena
Borussia Dortmund	Dortmund	Signal Iduna Park
Borussia Mönchengladbach	Mönchengladbach	Borussia-Park
Eintracht Frankfurt	Frankfurt	Commerzbank-Arena
Hamburg	Hamburg	HSH Nordbank Arena
Schalke 04	Gelsenkirchen	Veltins-Arena

Italy

Club	City	Stadium
AC Milan	Milan	Stadio San Siro
AS Roma	Rome	Stadio Olimpico
Inter Milan	Milan	Stadio Giuseppe Meazza
Juventus	Turin	Stadio Delle Alpi[1]
Lazio	Rome	Stadio Olimpico
Napoli	Naples	Stadio San Paolo
Parma	Parma	Stadio Ennio Tardini

[1] *Juventus are playing in Stadio Olimpico di Torino during the rebuilding of their own stadium.*

The Netherlands

Club	City	Stadium
Ajax	Amsterdam	Amsterdam ArenA
Feyenoord	Rotterdam	Feijenoord Stadion
PSV Eindhoven	Eindhoven	Philips Stadion

Portugal

Club	City	Stadium
Benfica	Lisbon	Estádio da Luz
FC Porto	Porto	Estádio do Dragão
Sporting Portugal	Lisbon	Estádio José Alvalade

Serbia

Club	City	Stadium
Red Star Belgrade	Belgrade	Red Star Stadium ('Marakana')

Spain

Club	City	Stadium
Atletico Madrid	Madrid	Vicente Calderón
Barcelona	Barcelona	Camp Nou
Deportivo la Coruña	La Coruña	Estadio Municipal de Riazor
Real Madrid	Madrid	Santiago Bernabéu
Valencia	Valencia	Mestalla

Turkey

Club	City	Stadium
Fenerbahçe	Istanbul	Şükrü Saracoğlu
Galatasaray	Istanbul	Ali Sami Yen

GAELIC FOOTBALL

Mixture of rugby, soccer and Australian Rules football, played by teams of 15 on a rectangular pitch with goals resembling rugby posts with soccer-style nets attached; points scored by either putting the ball into the goal net (three), or over the crossbar and between the up-rights (one); first game resembling Gaelic football took place 1712 at Slane, Ireland.

Ruling body: Gaelic Athletic Association (GAA)

Gaelic football pitch

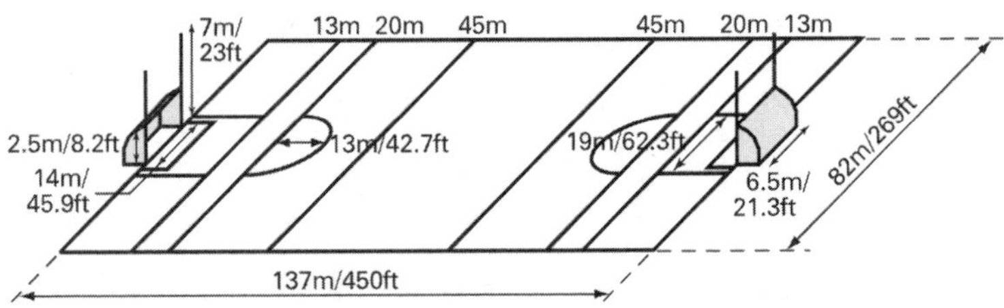

Note: Pitch size is approximate (length minimum 130m/426.5ft, maximum 145m/475.7ft; width minimum 80m/262.5ft, maximum 90m/295.3ft). The goalpost height of 7m/23ft is the minimum permitted.

All-Ireland Championship

First held in 1887, when Limerick won; takes place in Dublin on the third Sunday in Sep each year.

1983	Dublin	1997	Kerry
1984–86	Kerry	1998	Galway
1987–88	Meath	1999	Meath
1989–90	Cork	2000	Kerry
1991	Down	2001	Galway
1992	Donegal	2002	Armagh
1993	Derry	2003	Tyrone
1994	Down	2004	Kerry
1995	Dublin	2005	Tyrone
1996	Meath	2006–7	Kerry

More Than Just Sport

The Gaelic Athletic Association (GAA) was founded to support traditional Irish national sports, including Gaelic football, hurling and camogie, but also to nurture and protect Irish cultural heritage, a role that the GAA is proud to continue today. The GAA's rules state that it 'shall actively support the Irish language, traditional Irish dancing, music, song and other aspects of Irish culture', and through its Scór programmes of cultural competitions it endeavours to 'enrich the culture of the nation and further Gaelic ideals'.

GOLF

Outdoor sport played on a course normally 5,500–7,000m/6,000–7,500yd long, usually with 18 but sometimes nine holes; object is to hit a small ball using a long-handled club from a flat starting point or *tee* along a *fairway* to a hole positioned on an area of smooth grass or *green*; additional hazards: trees, bushes, streams, sand-filled *bunkers* and the *rough*, or uncut grass beside the fairway. In a *strokeplay* competition, the most common, the winner completes the course using the lowest number of strokes. The *par* is the expected number of strokes a good player needs to complete a hole; one stroke above par is called a *bogey*; one stroke below par is a *birdie*; two strokes below an *eagle*; three strokes below an *albatross*; a hole completed in one stroke is a *hole in one*.

Ruling bodies: Royal and Ancient Golf Club of St Andrews (R&A); United States Golf Association (USGA)

The Open Championship

First held at Prestwick in 1860; regarded as the world's leading golf tournament.

1983	Tom Watson (USA)	1996	Tom Lehman (USA)
1984	Severiano Ballesteros (Spain)	1997	Justin Leonard (USA)
1985	Sandy Lyle (Great Britain)	1998	Mark O'Meara (USA)
1986	Greg Norman (Australia)	1999	Paul Lawrie (Great Britain)
1987	Nick Faldo (Great Britain)	2000	Tiger Woods (USA)
1988	Severiano Ballesteros (Spain)	2001	David Duval (USA)
1989	Mark Calcavecchia (USA)	2002	Ernie Els (South Africa)
1990	Nick Faldo (Great Britain)	2003	Ben Curtis (USA)
1991	Ian Baker-Finch (Australia)	2004	Todd Hamilton (USA)
1992	Nick Faldo (Great Britain)	2005	Tiger Woods (USA)
1993	Greg Norman (Australia)	2006	Tiger Woods (USA)
1994	Nick Price (Zimbabwe)	2007	Padraig Harrington (Ireland)
1995	John Daly (USA)		

US Open

First held at Newport, Rhode Island, in 1895.

1983	Larry Nelson (USA)	1996	Steve Jones (USA)
1984	Fuzzy Zoeller (USA)	1997	Ernie Els (South Africa)
1985	Andy North (USA)	1998	Lee Janzen (USA)
1986	Raymond Floyd (USA)	1999	Payne Stewart (USA)
1987	Scott Simpson (USA)	2000	Tiger Woods (USA)
1988	Curtis Strange (USA)	2001	Retief Goosen (South Africa)
1989	Curtis Strange (USA)	2002	Tiger Woods (USA)
1990	Hale Irwin (USA)	2003	Jim Furyk (USA)
1991	Payne Stewart (USA)	2004	Retief Goosen (South Africa)
1992	Tom Kite (USA)	2005	Michael Campbell (New Zealand)
1993	Lee Janzen (USA)	2006	Geoff Ogilvy (Australia)
1994	Ernie Els (South Africa)	2007	Angel Cabrera (Argentina)
1995	Corey Pavin (USA)		

US Masters

First held in 1934; takes place at the Augusta National course in Georgia every Apr.

1983	Severiano Ballesteros (Spain)
1984	Ben Crenshaw (USA)
1985	Bernhard Langer (West Germany)
1986	Jack Nicklaus (USA)
1987	Larry Mize (USA)
1988	Sandy Lyle (Great Britain)
1989	Nick Faldo (Great Britain)
1990	Nick Faldo (Great Britain)
1991	Ian Woosnam (Great Britain)
1992	Fred Couples (USA)
1993	Bernhard Langer (Germany)
1994	José-María Olazábal (Spain)
1995	Ben Crenshaw (USA)
1996	Nick Faldo (Great Britain)
1997	Tiger Woods (USA)
1998	Mark O'Meara (USA)
1999	José-María Olazábal (Spain)
2000	Vijay Singh (Fiji)
2001	Tiger Woods (USA)
2002	Tiger Woods (USA)
2003	Mike Weir (Canada)
2004	Phil Mickelson (USA)
2005	Tiger Woods (USA)
2006	Phil Mickelson (USA)
2007	Zach Johnson (USA)

US PGA Championship

The last of the season's four 'Majors'; first held in 1916, and a matchplay event until 1958.

1983	Hal Sutton (USA)
1984	Lee Trevino (USA)
1985	Hubert Green (USA)
1986	Bob Tway (USA)
1987	Larry Nelson (USA)
1988	Jeff Sluman (USA)
1989	Payne Stewart (USA)
1990	Wayne Grady (Australia)
1991	John Daly (USA)
1992	Nick Price (Zimbabwe)
1993	Paul Azinger (USA)
1994	Nick Price (Zimbabwe)
1995	Steve Elkington (Australia)
1996	Mark Brooks (USA)
1997	Davis Love III (USA)
1998	Vijay Singh (Fiji)
1999	Tiger Woods (USA)
2000	Tiger Woods (USA)
2001	David Toms (USA)
2002	Rich Beem (USA)
2003	Shaun Micheel (USA)
2004	Vijay Singh (Fiji)
2005	Phil Mickelson (USA)
2006	Tiger Woods (USA)
2007	Tiger Woods (USA)

Greenland Golf

Every spring golfers converge from all over the world to compete in the World Ice Golf Championships, held in Uummannaq, Greenland. The green is the 'white', the ball is fluorescent pink or orange, the temperatures drop to –50°C/–58°F and the obstacles are icebergs and polar bears. The shape of the course, which is created anew each year, is dictated by the position of icebergs in the frozen fjord in which the Championships take place; however, the course changes constantly as the pack ice drifts and new icy outcrops are thrown up. It melts completely by May.

Ryder Cup

The leading international team tournament; first held at Worcester, Massachusetts, in 1927; takes place every two years between teams from the USA and Europe (Great Britain 1927–71; Great Britain and Ireland 1973–7).

1983	USA	14½–13½	1995	Europe	14½–13½
1985	Europe	16½–11½	1997	Europe	14½–13½
1987	Europe	15–13	1999	USA	14½–13½
1989	*Drawn*	14–14	2002	Europe	15½–12½
1991	USA	14½–13½	2004	Europe	18½–9½
1993	USA	15–13	2006	Europe	18½–9½

Kolf, Colf, Gouf and Golf

A similar game to golf was played by the Dutch c.1300, and was known as *kolf* or *colf*. *Gouf* was definitely played in Scotland in the 15c, and the world's first golf club, the Gentleman Golfers of Edinburgh, was formed in 1744.

GYMNASTICS

Physical exercises. Men compete on the parallel bars, pommel horse, high bar, rings, horse vault and floor exercise, and women on the asymmetrical bars, beam, horse vault and floor exercise. Judges award marks out of ten, looking for control, suppleness, balance and ingenuity. The ancient Greeks and Romans performed such exercises for health purposes; modern techniques date from late-18c Germany.

Ruling body: International Gymnastics Federation (FIG; Fédération Internationale de Gymnastique)

World Championships

First contested in 1903; women's championships first held in 1934.

Individual

	Men	**Women**
1983	Dmitri Belozerchev (USSR)	Natalia Yurtschenko (USSR)
1985	Yuri Korolev (USSR)	Yelena Shoushounova (USSR) and Oksana Omeliantchuk (USSR)
1987	Dmitri Belozerchev (USSR)	Aurelia Dobre (Romania)
1989	Igor Korobichensky (USSR)	Svetlana Boginskaya (USSR)
1991	Vitaly Scherbo (USSR)	Kim Zmeskal (USA)
1993	Vitaly Scherbo (Belarus)	Shannon Miller (USA)
1994	Ivan Ivankov (Belarus)	Shannon Miller (USA)
1995	Li Xiaoshuang (China)	Lilia Podkopayeva (Ukraine)
1997	Ivan Ivankov (Belarus)	Svetlana Khorkina (Russia)
1999	Nikolay Krukov (Russia)	Maria Olaru (Romania)
2001	Jing Feng (China)	Svetlana Khorkina (Russia)
2003	Paul Hamm (USA)	Svetlana Khorkina (Russia)
2005	Hiroyuki Tomita (Japan)	Chellsie Memmel (USA)
2006	Yang Wei (China)	Vanessa Ferrari (Italy)
2007	Yang Wei (China)	Shawn Johnson (USA)

Team

	Men	Women
1983	China	USSR
1985	USSR	USSR
1987	USSR	Romania
1989	USSR	USSR
1991	USSR	USSR
1993	*no team prize*	*no team prize*
1994	China	Romania
1995	China	Romania
1997	China	Romania
1999	China	Romania
2001	Belarus	Romania
2003	China	USA
2005	*no team prize*	*no team prize*
2006	China	China
2007	China	USA

Perfect Ten

One of the most famous gymnasts of all time is Nadia Comaneci (born 1961) from Romania. At the 1976 Olympic Games, at the age of just 14, Comaneci won gold medals in the parallel bars and beam disciplines, and a bronze in the floor, becoming the first gymnast to obtain a perfect score of 10 for her performance on the bars and beam. She also won a gold medal at the 1978 world championships and gold medals in the 1980 Olympics, later becoming an international judge and coach to the Romanian national team. In 1989 she defected to the USA.

HOCKEY

Stick-and-ball game played by two teams of eleven. The object is to move a hard ball by dribbling or striking it upfield, using a long wooden stick with a curved end, and to score in the opponent's goal. Only the front of the stick can be used to propel the ball. Games are split into two halves of 35 minutes. Also known, especially in North America, as *field hockey*. Originally played on grass, the modern game is more likely to be played on sand-based or water-based artificial surfaces.

Ruling body: International Hockey Federation (FIH; Fédération Internationale de Hockey)

Historic Hockey

The ancient Greeks played a game akin to hockey c.2500 BC, and the ancient Egyptians are believed to have played an early version of it 4,000 years ago. The Romans, ancient Ethiopians and Aztecs are all thought to have played similar games.

Hockey pitch

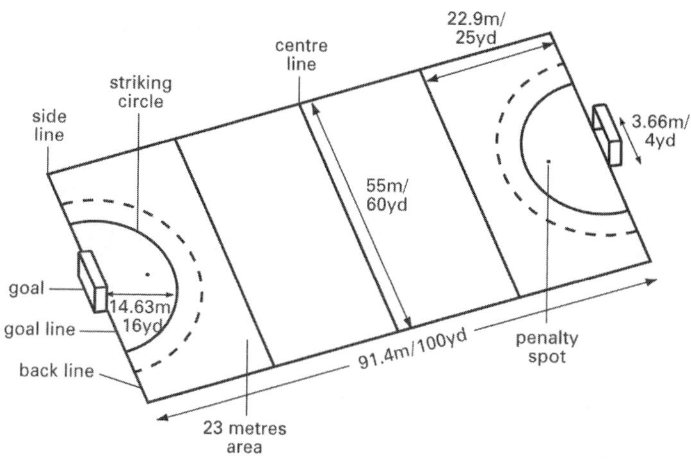

World Cup

Men's tournament first held in 1971, and every four years since 1978; women's tournament first held in 1974, and now takes place every four years.

Men		Women	
1982	Pakistan	1983	The Netherlands
1986	Australia	1986	The Netherlands
1990	The Netherlands	1990	The Netherlands
1994	Pakistan	1994	Australia
1998	The Netherlands	1998	Australia
2002	Germany	2002	Argentina
2006	Germany	2006	The Netherlands

Olympic Games

Regarded as hockey's leading competition; first held in 1908; included at every celebration since 1928; women's competition first held in 1980.

Men		Women	
1984	Pakistan	1984	The Netherlands
1988	Great Britain	1988	Australia
1992	Germany	1992	Spain
1996	The Netherlands	1996	Australia
2000	The Netherlands	2000	Australia
2004	Australia	2004	Germany

HORSE RACING

Racing of horses against one another, each ridden by a jockey. Two categories: flat racing for thoroughbred horses on a flat grass or dirt surface over a predetermined distance from 1–4km/5 furlongs–2.5mi, and national hunt racing in which the horses negotiate either movable hurdles or fixed fences over a distance of up to 6.5km/4.5mi. The ancient Egyptians took part in horse races in c.1200 BC; popularized in 12c England. Most monarchs have supported the sport, hence the name the 'sport of kings'.

Ruling body (UK): British Horseracing Board (BHB)

The Derby

The 'Blue Riband' of the turf; run at Epsom over 1½ miles; first run in 1780.

	Horse (Jockey)		Horse (Jockey)
1983	Teenoso (L Piggott)	1996	Shaamit (M Hills)
1984	Secreto (C Roche)	1997	Benny the Dip (W Ryan)
1985	Slip Anchor (S Cauthen)	1998	High Rise (O Peslier)
1986	Shahrastani (W Swinburn)	1999	Oath (K Fallon)
1987	Reference Point (S Cauthen)	2000	Sinndar (J Murtagh)
1988	Kahyasi (R Cochrane)	2001	Galileo (M Kinane)
1989	Nashwan (W Carson)	2002	High Chaparral (J Murtagh)
1990	Quest For Fame (P Eddery)	2003	Kris Kin (K Fallon)
1991	Generous (A Munro)	2004	North Light (K Fallon)
1992	Dr Devious (J Reid)	2005	Motivator (J Murtagh)
1993	Commander in Chief (M Kinane)	2006	Sir Percy (M Dwyer)
1994	Erhaab (W Carson)	2007	Authorized (F Dettori)
1995	Lammtarra (W Swinburn)		

The Oaks

Run at Epsom over 1½ miles; for fillies only; first run in 1779.

	Horse (Jockey)		Horse (Jockey)
1983	Sun Princess (W Carson)	1996	Lady Carla (P Eddery)
1984	Circus Plume (L Piggott)	1997	Reams of Verse (K Fallon)
1985	Oh So Sharp (S Cauthen)	1998	Shahtoush (M Kinane)
1986	Midway Lady (R Cochrane)	1999	Ramruma (K Fallon)
1987	Unite (W Swinburn)	2000	Love Divine (R Quinn)
1988	Diminuendo (S Cauthen)	2001	Imagine (M Kinane)
1989	Aliysa (W Swinburn)	2002	Kazzia (F Dettori)
1990	Salsabil (W Carson)	2003	Casual Look (M Dwyer)
1991	Jet Ski Lady (C Roche)	2004	Ouija Board (K Fallon)
1992	User Friendly (G Duffield)	2005	Eswarah (R Hills)
1993	Intrepidity (M Roberts)	2006	Alexandrova (K Fallon)
1994	Balanchine (F Dettori)	2007	Light Shift (E Durcan)
1995	Moonshell (F Dettori)		

One Thousand Guineas

Run at Newmarket over 1 mile; for fillies only; first run in 1814.

	Horse (Jockey)
1983	Ma Biche (F Head)
1984	Pebbles (P Robinson)
1985	Oh So Sharp (S Cauthen)
1986	Midway Lady (R Cochrane)
1987	Miesque (F Head)
1988	Ravinella (G Moore)
1989	Musical Bliss (W Swinburn)
1990	Salsabil (W Carson)
1991	Shadayid (W Carson)
1992	Hatoof (W Swinburn)
1993	Sayyedati (W Swinburn)
1994	Las Meninas (J Reid)
1995	Harayir (R Hills)
1996	Bosra Sham (P Eddery)
1997	Sleepytime (K Fallon)
1998	Cape Verdi (F Dettori)
1999	Wince (K Fallon)
2000	Lahan (R Hills)
2001	Ameerat (P Robinson)
2002	Kazzia (F Dettori)
2003	Russian Rhythm (K Fallon)
2004	Attraction (K Darley)
2005	Virginia Waters (K Fallon)
2006	Speciosa (M Fenton)
2007	Finsceal Beo (K Manning)

Charlotte and Wizard

The very first One Thousand Guineas race in 1814 was won by a horse named Charlotte, owned by Christopher Wilson and ridden by Bill Clift. The same team of owner and jockey had also triumphed at the very first Two Thousand Guineas race in 1809 with a horse named Wizard.

Two Thousand Guineas

Run at Newmarket over 1 mile; first run in 1809.

	Horse (Jockey)
1983	Lomond (P Eddery)
1984	El Gran Senor (P Eddery)
1985	Shadeed (L Piggott)
1986	Dancing Brave (G Starkey)
1987	Don't Forget Me (W Carson)
1988	Doyoun (W Swinburn)
1989	Nashwan (W Carson)
1990	Tirol (M Kinane)
1991	Mystiko (M Roberts)
1992	Rodrigo de Traiano (L Piggott)
1993	Zafonic (P Eddery)
1994	Mister Baileys (J Weaver)
1995	Pennekamp (T Jarnet)
1996	Mark of Esteem (F Dettori)
1997	Entrepreneur (M Kinane)
1998	King of Kings (M Kinane)
1999	Island Sands (F Dettori)
2000	King's Best (K Fallon)
2001	Golan (K Fallon)
2002	Rock of Gibraltar (J Murtagh)
2003	Refuse to Bend (P Smullen)
2004	Haafhd (R Hills)
2005	Footstepsinthesand (K Fallon)
2006	George Washington (K Fallon)
2007	Cockney Rebel (O Peslier)

Royal Racing

The One Thousand Guineas and Two Thousand Guineas are raced on the Rowley Mile Racecourse in Newmarket. The course is named after King Charles II (1630–85) – one of whose nicknames was supposedly 'Old Rowley' – who encouraged horse racing in Newmarket in the 17c.

St Leger

The oldest of the five English classics; first run in 1776; run at Doncaster annually over 1 mile 6 furlongs 127 yards.

	Horse (Jockey)
1983	Sun Princess (W Carson)
1984	Commanche Run (L Piggott)
1985	Oh So Sharp (S Cauthen)
1986	Moon Madness (P Eddery)
1987	Reference Point (S Cauthen)
1988	Minster Son (W Carson)
1989	Michelozzo (S Cauthen)
1990	Snurge (R Quinn)
1991	Toulon (P Eddery)
1992	User Friendly (G Duffield)
1993	Bob's Return (P Robinson)
1994	Moonax (P Eddery)
1995	Classic Cliche (F Dettori)
1996	Shantou (F Dettori)
1997	Silver Patriarch (P Eddery)
1998	Nedawi (J Reid)
1999	Mutafaweq (R Hills)
2000	Millenary (R Quinn)
2001	Milan (M Kinane)
2002	Bollin Eric (K Darley)
2003	Brian Boru (J Spencer)
2004	Rule of Law (K McEvoy)
2005	Scorpion (F Dettori)
2006	Sixties Icon (F Dettori)
2007	Lucarno (J Fortune)

Grand National

Steeplechasing's most famous race; first run at Maghull in 1836; at Aintree since 1839; wartime races at Gatwick 1916–18; run over 4½ miles.

	Horse (Jockey)
1983	Corbiere (B de Haan)
1984	Hallo Dandy (N Doughty)
1985	Last Suspect (H Davies)
1986	West Tip (R Dunwoody)
1987	Maori Venture (S Knight)
1988	Rhyme 'N' Reason (B Powell)
1989	Little Polveir (J Frost)
1990	Mr Frisk (M Armytage)
1991	Seagram (N Hawke)
1992	Party Politics (C Llewellyn)
1993	*race declared void* Esha Ness (J White) first past the post
1994	Miinnehoma (R Dunwoody)
1995	Royal Athlete (J Titley)
1996	Rough Quest (M Fitzgerald)
1997	Lord Gyllene (T Dobbin)
1998	Earth Summit (C Llewellyn)
1999	Bobbyjo (P Carberry)
2000	Papillon (R Walsh)
2001	Red Marauder (R Guest)
2002	Bindaree (J Culloty)
2003	Monty's Pass (B Geraghty)
2004	Amberleigh House (G Lee)
2005	Hedgehunter (R Walsh)
2006	Numbersixvalverde (N Madden)
2007	Silver Birch (R Power)

Prix de l'Arc de Triomphe

The leading end-of-season race in Europe; raced over 2,400 metres at Longchamp; first run in 1920.

	Horse (Jockey)
1983	All Along (W Swinburn)
1984	Sagace (Y Saint-Martin)
1985	Rainbow Quest (P Eddery)
1986	Dancing Brave (P Eddery)
1987	Trempolino (P Eddery)
1988	Tony Bin (J Reid)
1989	Caroll House (M Kinane)
1990	Suamarez (G Mosse)
1991	Suave Dancer (C Asmussen)
1992	Subotica (T Jarnet)
1993	Urban Sea (E Saint-Martin)
1994	Carnegie (T Jarnet)

	Horse (Jockey)		Horse (Jockey)
1995	Lammtarra (F Dettori)	2002	Marienbard (F Dettori)
1996	Helissio (O Peslier)	2003	Dalakhani (C Soumillon)
1997	Peintre Celebre (O Peslier)	2004	Bago (T Gillet)
1998	Sagamix (O Peslier)	2005	Hurricane Run (K Fallon)
1999	Montjeu (M Kinane)	2006	Rail Link (S Pasquier)
2000	Sinndar (J Murtagh)	2007	Dylan Thomas (K Fallon)
2001	Sakhee (F Dettori)		

Kentucky Derby

Run at Churchill Downs, Louisville, Kentucky, USA, over 1¼ mile; first run in 1875.

	Horse (Jockey)		Horse (Jockey)
1983	Sunny's Halo (E Delahoussaye)	1996	Grindstone (J Bailey)
1984	Swale (L Pincay, Jr)	1997	Silver Charm (G Stevens)
1985	Spend a Buck (A Cordero, Jr)	1998	Real Quiet (K Desormeaux)
1986	Ferdinand (W Shoemaker)	1999	Charismatic (C Antley)
1987	Alysheba (C McCarron)	2000	Fusaichi Pegasus (K Desormeaux)
1988	Winning Colors (G Stevens)	2001	Monarchos (J Chavez)
1989	Sunday Silence (P Valenzuela)	2002	War Emblem (V Espinoza)
1990	Unbridled (C Perret)	2003	Funny Cide (J Santos)
1991	Strike the Gold (C Antley)	2004	Smarty Jones (S Elliott)
1992	Lil E Tee (P Day)	2005	Giacomo (M Smith)
1993	Sea Hero (J Bailey)	2006	Barbaro (E Prado)
1994	Go for Gin (C McCarron)	2007	Street Sense (C Borel)
1995	Thunder Gulch (G Stevens)		

You Bet

The 2005 Kentucky Derby was the first time that betting had exceeded $100 million on just one race at a US race. The day's big winners were those who had bet on 50–1 outsider Giacomo, who stormed home to win.

Melbourne Cup

Run at Flemington Racecourse, Melbourne, Australia, over 3.2km; first run in 1861.

	Horse (Jockey)		Horse (Jockey)
1983	Kiwi (J Cassidy)	1996	Saintly (D Beadman)
1984	Black Knight (P Cook)	1997	Might And Power (J Cassidy)
1985	What A Nuisance (P Hyland)	1998	Jezabeel (C Munce)
1986	At Talaq (M Clarke)	1999	Rogan Josh (J Marshall)
1987	Kensei (L Olsen)	2000	Brew (K McEvoy)
1988	Empire Rose (A Allen)	2001	Ethereal (S Seamer)
1989	Tawrrific (S Dye)	2002	Media Puzzle (D Oliver)
1990	Kingston Rule (D Beadman)	2003	Makybe Diva (G Boss)
1991	Let's Elope (S King)	2004	Makybe Diva (G Boss)
1992	Subzero (G Hall)	2005	Makybe Diva (G Boss)
1993	Vintage Crop (M Kinane)	2006	Delta Blues (Yasunari Iwata)
1994	Jeune (W Harris)	2007	Efficient (M Rodd)
1995	Doriemus (D Oliver)		

HURLING

Irish 15-a-side field game played with curved sticks (the *hurley* or *camán*) and a ball (the *sliothar*); object to hit ball into opposing team's goal: under the crossbar scores three points; above the crossbar but between the posts scores one.

Ruling body: Gaelic Athletic Association (GAA)

Hurling pitch

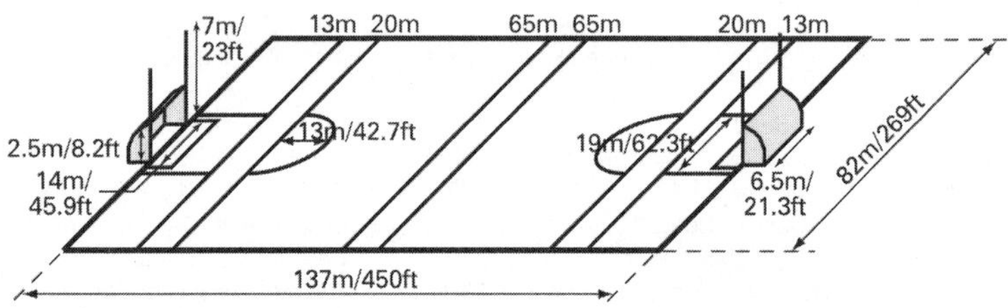

Note: Pitch size is approximate (length minimum 130m/426.5ft, maximum 145m/475.7ft; width minimum 80m/262.5ft, maximum 90m/295.3ft). The goalpost height of 7m/23ft is the minimum permitted.

All-Ireland Senior Championship

First contested in 1887; played on the first Sunday in Sep each year.

1982–83	Kilkenny	1995	Clare
1984	Cork	1996	Wexford
1985	Offaly	1997	Clare
1986	Cork	1998	Offaly
1987–88	Galway	1999	Cork
1989	Tipperary	2000	Kilkenny
1990	Cork	2001	Tipperary
1991	Tipperary	2002–3	Kilkenny
1992–93	Kilkenny	2004–5	Cork
1994	Offaly	2006–7	Kilkenny

Hurling in History

Hurling is thought to be the oldest field game in Europe. The Gaelic Athletic Association believes that it was brought to Ireland by the Celts, and that the game has been part of Irish culture for 2,000 years.

ICE HOCKEY

Fast game played by two teams of six on an ice rink with sticks and a small rubber *puck*; aim is to score goals by using the stick to hit the puck into the opposing team's goal; players wear ice skates and protective clothing; possibly first played in Canada in the 1850s.

Ruling body: International Ice Hockey Federation (IIHF)

Ice hockey rink

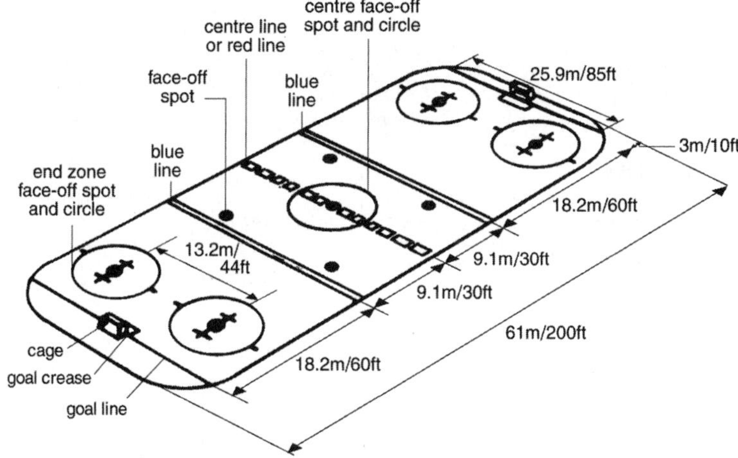

World Championship

First held in 1920; takes place annually (except in the Olympic years 1980, 1984 and 1988); up to 1968 Olympic champions also regarded as world champions.

1983	USSR	1993	Russia	1999–2001	Czech Republic
1985	Czechoslovakia	1994	Canada	2002	Slovakia
1986	USSR	1995	Finland	2003–4	Canada
1987	Sweden	1996	Czech Republic	2005	Czech Republic
1989–90	USSR	1997	Canada	2006	Sweden
1991–2	Sweden	1998	Sweden	2007	Canada

Ouch!

The first ice-hockey goalie to wear a protective mask was one Clint Benedict in 1927. He adopted a leather mask after a shot knocked him unconscious; however, he then couldn't see the game properly, and masks were abandoned until 1959.

Stanley Cup

The most sought-after trophy at club level; the end-of-season meeting between the winners of the two conferences in the National Hockey League (NHL) in the USA and Canada; first held in 1893.

1983	New York Islanders
1984–5	Edmonton Oilers
1986	Montreal Canadiens
1987–8	Edmonton Oilers
1989	Calgary Flames
1990	Edmonton Oilers
1991–2	Pittsburgh Penguins
1993	Montreal Canadiens
1994	New York Rangers
1995	New Jersey Devils
1996	Colorado Avalanche
1997–8	Detroit Red Wings
1999	Dallas Stars
2000	New Jersey Devils
2001	Colorado Avalanche
2002	Detroit Red Wings
2003	New Jersey Devils
2004	Tampa Bay Lightning
2005	*not held — players' strike*
2006	Carolina Hurricanes
2007	Anaheim Ducks

ICE SKATING

Figure skating is artistic dancing on ice for individuals and pairs; first known skating club formed mid-18c London; first artificial rink opened on Baker Street in 1876.

Ruling body: International Skating Union (ISU)

World Championships

First men's championships in 1896; first women's event in 1906; pairs first contested in 1908; Ice Dance officially recognized in 1952.

Men

1983–4	Scott Hamilton (USA)
1985	Alexander Fadeyev (USSR)
1986	Brian Boitano (USA)
1987	Brian Orser (Canada)
1988	Brian Boitano (USA)
1989–91	Kurt Browning (Canada)
1992	Viktor Petrenko (CIS)
1993	Kurt Browning (Canada)
1994–5	Elvis Stojko (Canada)
1996	Todd Eldredge (USA)
1997	Elvis Stojko (Canada)
1998–2000	Alexei Yagudin (Russia)
2001	Evgeny Plushenko (Russia)
2002	Alexei Yagudin (Russia)
2003–4	Evgeny Plushenko (Russia)
2005–6	Stephane Lambiel (Switzerland)
2007	Brian Joubert (France)

Women

1983	Rosalynn Sumners (USA)
1984–5	Katarina Witt (East Germany)
1986	Debbie Thomas (USA)
1987–8	Katarina Witt (East Germany)
1989	Midori Ito (Japan)
1990	Jill Trenary (USA)
1991–2	Kristi Yamaguchi (USA)
1993	Oksana Baiul (Ukraine)
1994	Yuka Sato (Japan)
1995	Lu Chen (China)
1996	Michelle Kwan (USA)
1997	Tara Lipinski (USA)
1998	Michelle Kwan (USA)
1999	Maria Butyrskaya (Russia)
2000–1	Michelle Kwan (USA)
2002	Irina Slutskaya (Russia)
2003	Michelle Kwan (USA)
2004	Shizuka Arakawa (Japan)
2005	Irina Slutskaya (Russia)
2006	Kimmie Meissner (USA)
2007	Miki Ando (Japan)

Pairs

1983	Yelena Valova/Oleg Vasiliev (USSR)
1984	Barbara Underhill/Paul Martini (Canada)
1985	Yelena Valova/Oleg Vasiliev (USSR)
1986–7	Yekaterina Gordeeva/Sergei Grinkov (USSR)
1988	Yelena Valova/Oleg Vasiliev (USSR)
1989–90	Yekaterina Gordeeva/Sergei Grinkov (USSR)
1991–2	Natalya Mishkutienok/Artur Dmtriev (USSR)
1993	Isabelle Brasseu/Lloyd Eisler (Canada)
1994	Evgenia Shiskova/Vadim Naumov (Russia)
1995	Radka Kovarikova/Rene Novotny (Czech Republic)
1996	Marina Eltsova/Andrei Bushkov (Russia)
1997	Mandy Woetzel/Ingo Steuer (Germany)
1998–9	Elena Berezhnay/Anton Sikharulidze (Russia)
2000	Maria Petrova/Alexei Tikhonov (Russia)
2001	Jamie Sale/David Pelletier (Canada)
2002–3	Shen Xue/Zhao Hongbo (China)
2004–5	Tatiana Totmianina/Maxim Marinin (Russia)
2006	Pang Qing/Tong Jian (China)
2007	Shen Xue/Zhao Hongbo (China)

Ice Dance

1983–4	Jayne Torvill/Christopher Dean (Great Britain)
1985–8	Natalya Bestemianova/Andrei Bukin (USSR)
1989–90	Marina Klimova/Sergei Ponomarenko (USSR)
1991	Isabelle and Paul Duchesnay (France)
1992	Marina Klimova/Sergei Ponomarenko (CIS)
1993	Maya Usova/Alexandr Zhulin (Russia)
1994–7	Oksana Gritschuk/Yevgeni Platov (Russia)
1998–9	Anjelika Krylova/Oleg Ovsyannikov (Russia)
2000	Marina Anissina/Gwendal Peizerat (France)
2001	Barbara Fusar-Poli/Maurizio Margaglio (Italy)
2002	Irina Lobacheva/Ilia Averbukh (Russia)
2003	Shae-Lynn Bourne/Victor Kraatz (Canada)
2004–5	Tatiana Navka/Roman Kostomarov (Russia)
2006–7	Albena Denkova/Maxim Stavski (Bulgaria)

Skating or Boxing?

US skater Tonya Harding gained notoriety when she won the US Figure Skating Championships in 1994. The favourite, Nancy Kerrigan, was unable to compete having been clubbed on the knee by a hitman while training, and Harding's ex-husband and her bodyguard were later given prison sentences for their role in the attack. Harding herself was later stripped of her skating title, banned for life from the US Figure Skating Association and fined $100,000 when she was found guilty of withholding information concerning Kerrigan's injury. Harding began a new career as a boxer, but lost her first professional fight – a show bout before a Mike Tyson fight in Memphis, Tennessee, USA, in early 2003 – and retired from the sport the following year, suffering from asthma.

JUDO

Unarmed combat sport of late-19c Japanese origin. Contestants wear a *judogi* or loose-fitting suit and compete on a mat which breaks their falls. When one cannot break a hold, surrender is signalled by slapping the mat; ability is graded from fifth to first Kyu, and then first to 12th Dan – only Dr Jigoro Kano, who devised the sport, has been awarded 12th Dan. Different coloured belts indicate grades; eg white for novice, brown (three degrees) and black (nine degrees).

Ruling body: International Judo Federation (IJF)

World Championships

First held in 1956, now contested every two years; current weight categories established in 1999; women's championship instituted in 1980.

1999

Men		Women	
open class	Shinichi Shinohara (Japan)	open class	Daina Beltran (Cuba)
over 100kg	Shinichi Shinohara (Japan)	over 78kg	Beata Maksymow (Poland)
under 100kg	Kosei Inoue (Japan)	under 78kg	Noriko Anno (Japan)
under 90kg	Hidehiko Yoshida (Japan)	under 70kg	Sibelis Veranes (Cuba)
under 81kg	Graeme Randall (Great Britain)	under 63kg	Keiko Maedo (Japan)
under 73kg	Jimmy Pedro (USA)	under 57kg	Driulis González (Cuba)
under 66kg	Larbi Benboudaoud (France)	under 52kg	Noriko Narasaki (Japan)
under 60kg	Manuelo Poulot (Cuba)	under 48kg	Ryoko Tamura (Japan)

2001

Men		Women	
open class	Aleksandr Michailin (Russia)	open class	Celine Lebrun (France)
over 100kg	Aleksandr Michailin (Russia)	over 78kg	Yuan Hua (China)
under 100kg	Kosei Inoue (Japan)	under 78kg	Noriko Anno (Japan)
under 90kg	Frederic Demontfaucon (France)	under 70kg	Masae Ueno (Japan)
under 81kg	Chul Cho In (South Korea)	under 63kg	Gella van de Cayeve (Belgium)
under 73kg	Vital Makarov (Russia)	under 57kg	Yourisledes Lupety (Cuba)
under 66kg	Arash Miresmaeli (Iran)	under 52kg	Sun Hui Kye (North Korea)
under 60kg	Anis Lounifi (Tunisia)	under 48kg	Ryoko Tamura (Japan)

2003

Men		Women	
open class	Keiji Suzuki (Japan)	open class	Wen Tong (China)
over 100kg	Yauyuki Muneta (Japan)	over 78kg	Fuming Sun (China)
under 100kg	Kosei Inoue (Japan)	under 78kg	Noriko Anno (Japan)
under 90kg	Hee Tae Hwang (South Korea)	under 70kg	Masae Ueno (Japan)
under 81kg	Florian Wanner (Germany)	under 63kg	Daniela Krukower (Argentina)
under 73kg	Won Hee Lee (South Korea)	under 57kg	Sun Hui Kye (North Korea)
under 66kg	Arash Miresmaeli (Iran)	under 52kg	Amarilis Savon (Cuba)
under 60kg	Min Ho Choi (South Korea)	under 48kg	Ryoko Tamura (Japan)

2005

Men		Women	
open class	Dennis van der Geest (The Netherlands)	open class	Midori Shintani (Japan)
over 100kg	Aleksandr Michailin (Russia)	over 78kg	Tong Wen (China)
under 100kg	Keiji Suzuki (Japan)	under 78kg	Yurisel Laborde (Cuba)
under 90kg	Hiroshi Izumi (Japan)	under 70kg	Edith Bosch (The Netherlands)
under 81kg	Guillaume Elmont (The Netherlands)	under 63kg	Lucie Decosse (France)
under 73kg	Akos Braun (Hungary)	under 57kg	Sun Hui Kye (North Korea)
under 66kg	João Derly Junior (Brazil)	under 52kg	Ying Li (China)
under 60kg	Craig Fallon (Great Britain)	under 48kg	Yanet Bermoy (Cuba)

2007

Men		Women	
open class	Yasuyuki Muneta (Japan)	open class	Maki Tsukada (Japan)
over 100kg	Teddy Riner (France)	over 78kg	Tong Wen (China)
under 100kg	Luciano Corrêa (Brazil)	under 78kg	Yurisel Laborde (Cuba)
under 90kg	Irakli Tsirekidze (Georgia)	under 70kg	Gevrise Emane (France)
under 81kg	Tiago Camilo (Brazil)	under 63kg	Driulis González (Cuba)
under 73kg	Wang Ki-Chun (South Korea)	under 57kg	Kye Sun-Hui (North Korea)
under 66kg	João Derly (Brazil)	under 52kg	Shi Junjie (China)
under 60kg	Ruben Houkes (The Netherlands)	under 48kg	Ryoko Tani (Japan)

KARATE

Martial art of unarmed combat, dating from 17c; developed Japan 20c; name adopted 1930s; aim is to be in total control of the body's muscular power, so it can be used with great force and accuracy at any instant. Experts may show their mental and physical training by eg breaking various thicknesses of wood, but in fighting an opponent blows do not actually make contact; levels of prowess symbolized by coloured belts.

Ruling body: World Karate Federation (WKF)

World Championships

First held in Tokyo in 1970; has taken place every two years since 1980; today, there are team competitions plus individual competitions at Kumite and Kata.

Kumite

Men		Women	
1982	Great Britain		
1984	Great Britain		
1986	Great Britain		
1988	Great Britain		
1990	Great Britain		
1992	Spain	1992	Great Britain
1994	France	1994	Spain
1996	France	1996	Great Britain
1998	France	1998	Turkey
2000	France	2000	France
2002	Spain	2002	Spain

Men		Women	
2004	France	2004	Turkey
2006	Spain	2006	Japan

Kata

Men		Women	
1986	Japan	1986	Taiwan
1988	Japan	1988	Japan
1990	Italy	1990	Japan
1992	Japan	1992	Japan
1994	Japan	1994	Japan
1996	Japan	1996	Japan
1998	Japan	1998	Japan
2000	Japan	2000	France
2002	Japan	2002	France
2004	Italy	2004	Japan
2006	Italy	2006	France

Empty Hand

Karate means 'empty hand' in Japanese.

MARATHON

Long-distance running race, normally on open roads, over 42km 195m/26mi 385yd. In the 1980s the half marathon over 21km/13mi 194yd also became popular. For World Championship marathon results see **Athletics**.

Ruling body: International Association of Athletics Federations (IAAF)

London Marathon

First run in 1981, when 6,255 people completed the course of 42km 195m/26mi 385yd. To date, its runners have raised over £350 million for charities.

	Men	Women
1981	Dick Beardsley (USA)/Inge Simonsen (Norway)	Joyce Smith (Great Britain)
1982	Hugh Jones (Great Britain)	Joyce Smith (Great Britain)
1983	Mike Gratton (Great Britain)	Grete Waitz (Norway)
1984	Charlie Spedding (Great Britain)	Ingrid Kristiansen (Norway)
1985	Steve Jones (Great Britain)	Ingrid Kristiansen (Norway)
1986	Toshihiko Seko (Japan)	Grete Waitz (Norway)
1987	Hiromi Taniguchi (Japan)	Ingrid Kristiansen (Norway)
1988	Henrik Jorgensen (Denmark)	Ingrid Kristiansen (Norway)
1989	Douglas Wakiihuri (Kenya)	Veronique Marot (Great Britain)
1990	Allister Hutton (Great Britain)	Wanda Panfil (Poland)
1991	Yakov Tolstikov (Russia)	Rosa Mota (Portugal)
1992	Antonio Pinto (Portugal)	Katrin Dorre (Germany)
1993	Eamonn Martin (Great Britain)	Katrin Dorre (Germany)
1994	Dionicio Ceron (Mexico)	Katrin Dorre (Germany)
1995	Dionicio Ceron (Mexico)	Malgorzata Sobanska (Poland)
1996	Dionicio Ceron (Mexico)	Liz McColgan (Great Britain)

1997	Antonio Pinto (Portugal)	Joyce Chepchumba (Kenya)
1998	Abel Antón (Spain)	Catherina McKiernan (Ireland)
1999	Abdelkader El Mouaziz (Morocco)	Joyce Chepchumba (Kenya)
2000	Antonio Pinto (Portugal)	Tegla Loroupe (Kenya)
2001	Abdelkader El Mouaziz (Morocco)	Derartu Tulu (Ethiopia)
2002	Khalid Khannouchi (USA)	Paula Radcliffe (Great Britain)
2003	Gezahegne Abera (Ethiopia)	Paula Radcliffe (Great Britain)
2004	Evans Rutto (Kenya)	Margaret Okayo (Kenya)
2005	Martin Lel (Kenya)	Paula Radcliffe (Great Britain)
2006	Felix Limo (Kenya)	Deena Kastor (USA)
2007	Martin Lel (Kenya)	Zhou Chunxiu (China)

Deciding Distance

The slightly unusual marathon distance of 42km 195m/26mi 385yd was first used at the London Olympics in 1908, so that competitors would finish exactly in front of the royal box. The race was introduced at the 1896 Olympic Games in Athens, Greece, to commemorate the run of the Greek courier (according to legend, Pheidippides) who ran the c.39km/24mi from Marathon to Athens in 490 BC with the news of a Greek victory over the Persian army.

New York Marathon

The course begins on Staten Island and finishes in Central Park, Manhattan, after passing through all five New York boroughs. The race is held each year in November and was first run in 1970 when it was won by Gary Muhrcke.

	Men	**Women**
1983	Rod Dixon (New Zealand)	Grete Waitz (Norway)
1984	Orlando Pizzolato (Italy)	Grete Waitz (Norway)
1985	Orlando Pizzolato (Italy)	Grete Waitz (Norway)
1986	Gianni Poli (Italy)	Grete Waitz (Norway)
1987	Ibrahim Hussein (Kenya)	Priscilla Welch (Great Britain)
1988	Steve Jones (Great Britain)	Grete Waitz (Norway)
1989	Juma Ikangaa (Tanzania)	Ingrid Kristiansen (Norway)
1990	Douglas Wakiihuri (Kenya)	Wanda Panfil (Poland)
1991	Salvador Garcia (Mexico)	Liz McColgan (Great Britain)
1992	Willie Mtolo (South Africa)	Lisa Ondieki (Australia)
1993	Andres Espinosa (Mexico)	Uta Pippig (Germany)
1994	German Silva (Mexico)	Tegla Loroupe (Kenya)
1995	German Silva (Mexico)	Tegla Loroupe (Kenya)
1996	Giacomo Leone (Italy)	Anuta Catuna (Romania)
1997	John Kagwe (Kenya)	Franziska Rochat-Moser (Switzerland)
1998	John Kagwe (Kenya)	Franca Fiacconi (Italy)
1999	Joseph Chebet (Kenya)	Adriana Fernandez (Mexico)
2000	Abdelkader El Mouaziz (Morocco)	Ludmila Petrova (Russia)
2001	Tesfaye Jifar (Ethiopia)	Margaret Okayo (Kenya)
2002	Rodgers Rop (Kenya)	Joyce Chepchumba (Kenya)
2003	Martin Lel (Kenya)	Margaret Okayo (Kenya)

	Men	Women
2004	Hendrik Ramaala (South Africa)	Paula Radcliffe (Great Britain)
2005	Paul Tergat (Kenya)	Jeļena Prokopčula (Latvia)
2006	Marilson Gomes dos Santos (Brazil)	Jeļena Prokopčula (Latvia)
2007	Martin Lel (Kenya)	Paula Radcliffe (Great Britain)

MOTOR SPORTS

Motor racing: Racing finely-tuned motor cars, either purpose-built or modified production vehicles; season-long (Mar–Nov) *Formula One* world championship involves usually 16–19 races at different venues worldwide; other popular forms include *stock car racing*, *hill climbing*, *sports car racing* and *rallying*; first race 1894, between Paris and Rouen.

Motorcycle racing: Speed competitions for motorcycles which for the annual season-long grand prix are categorized by the engine sizes *80cc*, *125cc*, *250cc*, *500cc*, *Superbike* and *Sidecar*. Other forms include *speedway*, *moto-cross* and *motorcycle trials* riding.

Ruling body: International Automobile Association (FIA; Fédération Internationale d'Automobile), International Motorcycling Federation (FIM; Fédération Internationale de Motocyclisme)

Formula One World Championship

A Formula One drivers' world championship instituted in 1950; constructors' championship instituted in 1958.

	Drivers	Constructors
1983	Nelson Piquet (Brazil; Brabham)	Ferrari
1984	Niki Lauda (Austria; McLaren)	McLaren
1985	Alain Prost (France; McLaren)	McLaren
1986	Alain Prost (France; McLaren)	Williams
1987	Nelson Piquet (Brazil; Williams)	Williams
1988	Ayrton Senna (Brazil; McLaren)	McLaren
1989	Alain Prost (France; McLaren)	McLaren
1990	Ayrton Senna (Brazil; McLaren)	McLaren
1991	Ayrton Senna (Brazil; McLaren)	McLaren
1992	Nigel Mansell (Great Britain; Williams)	Williams
1993	Alain Prost (France; Williams)	Williams
1994	Michael Schumacher (Germany; Benetton)	Williams
1995	Michael Schumacher (Germany; Benetton)	Benetton
1996	Damon Hill (Great Britain; Williams)	Williams
1997	Jacques Villeneuve (Canada; Williams)	Williams
1998	Mika Hakkinen (Finland; McLaren)	McLaren
1999	Mika Hakkinen (Finland; McLaren)	Ferrari
2000	Michael Schumacher (Germany; Ferrari)	Ferrari
2001	Michael Schumacher (Germany; Ferrari)	Ferrari
2002	Michael Schumacher (Germany; Ferrari)	Ferrari
2003	Michael Schumacher (Germany; Ferrari)	Ferrari
2004	Michael Schumacher (Germany; Ferrari)	Ferrari
2005	Fernando Alonso (Spain; Renault)	Renault
2006	Fernando Alonso (Spain; Renault)	Renault
2007	Kimi Raikkonen (Finland; Ferrari)	Ferrari

Le Mans 24-Hour Race

The greatest of all endurance races; first held in 1923.

1983 Al Holbert (USA)
Hurley Haywood (USA)
Vern Schuppan (Australia)
1984 Henri Pescarolo (France
Klaus Ludwig (West Germany)
1985 Klaus Ludwig (West Germany)
John Winter' (West Germany)
Paolo Barilla (Italy)
1986 Hans Stück (West Germany)
Derek Bell (Great Britain)
Al Holbert (USA)
1987 Hans Stück (West Germany)
Derek Bell (Great Britain)
Al Holbert (USA)
1988 Jan Lammers (Holland)
Johnny Dumfries (Great Britain)
Andy Wallace (Great Britain)
1989 Jochen Mass (West Germany)
Manuel Reuter (West Germany)
Stanley Dickens (Sweden)
1990 John Nielsen (Denmark)
Price Cobb (USA)
Martin Brundle (Great Britain)
1991 Volker Weidler (Germany)
Johnny Herbert (Great Britain)
Bertrand Gachot (Belgium)
1992 Derek Warwick (Great Britain)
Mark Blundell (Great Britain)
Yannick Dalmas (France)
1993 Geoff Brabham (Australia)
Christophe Bouchut (France)
Eric Helary (France)
1994 Yannick Dalmas (France)
Hurley Haywood (USA)
Mauro Baldi (Italy)
1995 Yannick Dalmas (France)
J J Lehto (Finland)
Masanori Sekiya (Japan)
1996 Manuel Reuter (Germany)
Davy Jones (USA)
Alexander Würz (Austria)
1997 Michele Alboreto (Italy)
Stefan Johansson (Sweden)
Tom Kristensen (Denmark)
1998 Allan McNish (Great Britain)
Laurent Aiello (France)
Stephane Ortelli (France)
1999 Pierluigi Martini (Italy)
Joachim Winkelhock (Germany)
Yannick Dalmas (France)
2000 Frank Biela (Germany)
Tom Kristensen (Denmark)
Emanuele Pirro (Italy)
2001 Frank Biela (Germany)
Tom Kristensen (Denmark)
Emanuele Pirro (Italy)
2002 Frank Biela (Germany)
Tom Kristensen (Denmark)
Emanuele Pirro (Italy)
2003 Tom Kristensen (Denmark)
Rinaldo Capello (Italy)
Guy Smith (Great Britain)
2004 Tom Kristensen (Denmark)
Rinaldo Capello (Italy)
Seiji Ara (Japan)
2005 Tom Kristensen (Denmark)
J J Lehto (Finland)
Marco Werner (Germany)
2006 Frank Biela (Germany)
Emanuele Pirro (Italy)
Marco Werner (Germany)
2007 Frank Biela (Germany)
Emanuele Pirro (Italy)
Marco Werner (Germany)

Driving into History

With his victory in 2005, Tom Kristensen became the first driver to achieve seven Le Mans wins, surpassing the previous recordholder, the Belgian racing driver Jacky Ickx.

Indianapolis 500

Often known as the Indy 500; first held in 1911; raced over the Indianapolis Raceway as part of the Memorial Day celebrations at the end of May each year.

1983	Tom Sneva (USA)	1996	Buddy Lazier (USA)
1984	Rick Mears (USA)	1997	Arie Luyendyk (The Netherlands)
1985	Danny Sullivan (USA)	1998	Eddie Cheever (USA)
1986	Bobby Rahal (USA)	1999	Kenny Brack (Sweden)
1987	Al Unser (USA)	2000	Juan Montoya (Colombia)
1988	Rick Mears (USA)	2001	Helio Castroneves (Brazil)
1989	Emerson Fittipaldi (Brazil)	2002	Helio Castroneves (Brazil)
1990	Arie Luyendyk (The Netherlands)	2003	Gil de Ferran (Brazil)
1991	Rick Mears (USA)	2004	Buddy Rice (USA)
1992	Al Unser (USA)	2005	Dan Wheldon (Great Britain)
1993	Emerson Fittipaldi (Brazil)	2006	Sam Hornish Jr (USA)
1994	Al Unser (USA)	2007	Dario Franchitti (Great Britain)
1995	Jacques Villeneuve (Canada)		

Winning by a Whisker

Some Indy 500 races have been won by the slenderest of margins. The closest ever finish took place in 1992, when Al Unser beat Scott Goodyear by just 0.043 of a second. Other close races have been in 1982 (0.16 of a second separating the winner from the runner up), 1997 (0.57 of a second) and 1996 (0.695 of a second).

World Rally Championship

First held in 1979; comprises a series of races in 16 different countries over a variety of terrains, between Jan and Nov.

1983	Hannu Mikkola (Finland)	1996	Tommi Makinen (Finland)
1984	Stig Blomqvist (Sweden)	1997	Tommi Makinen (Finland)
1985	Timo Salonen (Finland)	1998	Tommi Makinen (Finland)
1986	Juha Kankkunen (Finland)	1999	Tommi Makinen (Finland)
1987	Juha Kankkunen (Finland)	2000	Marcus Gronholm (Finland)
1988	Miki Biasion (Italy)	2001	Richard Burns (Great Britain)
1989	Miki Biasion (Italy)	2002	Marcus Gronholm (Finland)
1990	Carlos Sainz (Spain)	2003	Petter Solberg (Norway)
1991	Juha Kankkunen (Finland)	2004	Sébastien Loeb (France)
1992	Carlos Sainz (Spain)	2005	Sébastien Loeb (France)
1993	Juha Kankkunen (Finland)	2006	Sébastien Loeb (France)
1994	Didier Auriol (France)	2007	Sébastien Loeb (France)
1995	Colin McRae (Great Britain)		

Motorcycling World Championships

First organized in 1949; current titles for Superbike, 500cc, 250cc, 125cc, 80cc and Sidecar; Formula One and Endurance world championships also held annually; the most prestigious title is the 500cc category, known as MotoGP.

500cc

1983	Freddie Spencer (USA)	1996	Michael Doohan (Australia)
1984	Eddie Lawson (USA)	1997	Michael Doohan (Australia)
1985	Freddie Spencer (USA)	1998	Michael Doohan (Australia)
1986	Eddie Lawson (USA)	1999	Alex Criville (Spain)
1987	Wayne Gardner (Australia)	2000	Kenny Roberts (USA)
1988	Eddie Lawson (USA)	2001	Valentino Rossi (Italy)
1989	Eddie Lawson (USA)	2002	Valentino Rossi (Italy)
1990	Wayne Rainey (USA)	2003	Valentino Rossi (Italy)
1991	Wayne Rainey (USA)	2004	Valentino Rossi (Italy)
1992	Wayne Rainey (USA)	2005	Valentino Rossi (Italy)
1993	Kevin Schwantz (USA)	2006	Nicky Hayden (USA)
1994	Michael Doohan (Australia)	2007	Casey Stoner (Australia)
1995	Michael Doohan (Australia)		

Isle of Man TT Races

The most famous of all motorcycle races; take place each Jun; first held 1907; principal race is the Senior TT.

Senior TT

1983	Rob McElnea (Great Britain)	1996	Phil McCallen (Northern Ireland)
1984	Rob McElnea (Great Britain)	1997	Phil McCallen (Northern Ireland)
1985	Joey Dunlop (Northern Ireland)	1998	Ian Simpson (Great Britain)
1986	Roger Burnett (Great Britain)	1999	David Jefferies (Great Britain)
1987	Joey Dunlop (Northern Ireland)	2000	David Jefferies (Great Britain)
1988	Joey Dunlop (Northern Ireland)	2001	*not held*
1989	Steve Hislop (Great Britain)	2002	David Jefferies (Great Britain)
1990	Carl Fogarty (Great Britain)	2003	Adrian Archibald (Northern Ireland)
1991	Steve Hislop (Great Britain)	2004	Adrian Archibald (Northern Ireland)
1992	Steve Hislop (Great Britain)	2005	John McGuinness (Great Britain)
1993	Phil McCallen (Northern Ireland)	2006	John McGuinness (Great Britain)
1994	Steve Hislop (Great Britain)	2007	John McGuinness (Great Britain)
1995	Joey Dunlop (Northern Ireland)		

Road Racing

The TT takes place over temporarily closed public roads in the Isle of Man. The island became the home of road racing in the early 1900s, when racing on public roads in the UK was forbidden by an Act of Parliament, and a strict 20mph/32kph speed limit was enforced. However, the ban did not apply to the Isle of Man, and after a little persuasion by early racing enthusiasts, Tynwald – the island's Parliament – passed a Bill allowing road racing in 1904.

ROWING

Propulsion of a boat by oars; involves two or more rowers, each with an oar, and often with a coxswain; sculling involves rowers with two oars; rowing as an organized sport dates from 1715 (first rowing of the Doggett's Coat and Badge race on the River Thames, London).

Ruling body: International Rowing Federation (FISA; Fédération Internationale des Sociétés d'Aviron)

World Championships

First held for men in 1962 and for women in 1974; Olympic champions assume the role of world champion in Olympic years; principal event is the single sculls.

	Single sculls – Men	**Single sculls – Women**
1983	Peter Michael Kolbe (West Germany)	Jutta Hampe (East Germany)
1984	Pertti Karppinen (Finland)	Valeria Racila (Romania)
1985	Pertti Karppinen (Finland)	Cornelia Linse (East Germany)
1986	Peter Michael Kolbe (West Germany)	Jutta Hampe (East Germany)
1987	Thomas Lange (East Germany)	Magdelena Georgieva (Bulgaria)
1988	Thomas Lange (East Germany)	Jutta Behrendt (East Germany)
1989	Thomas Lange (East Germany)	Elisabeta Lipa (Romania)
1990	Yuri Janson (USSR)	Brigit Peter (East Germany)
1991	Thomas Lange (Germany)	Silke Laumann (Canada)
1992	Thomas Lange (Germany)	Elisabeta Lipa (Romania)
1993	Derek Porter (Canada)	Jana Phieme (Germany)
1994	Andre Wilms (Germany)	Trine Hansen (Denmark)
1995	Iztok Cop (Slovenia)	Maria Brandin (Sweden)
1996	Xeno Müller (Switzerland)	Ekaterina Khodotovich (Belarus)
1997	Jamie Koven (USA)	Ekaterina Khodotovich (Belarus)
1998	Rob Waddell (New Zealand)	Irina Fedotova (Russia)
1999	Rob Waddell (New Zealand)	Ekaterina Karsten-Khodotovich (Belarus)
2000	Rob Waddell (New Zealand)	Ekaterina Karsten-Khodotovich (Belarus)
2001	Olaf Tufte (Norway)	Katrin Rutschow-Stomporowski (Germany)
2002	Marcel Hacker (Germany)	Rumyana Neykova (Bulgaria)
2003	Olaf Tufte (Norway)	Rumyana Neykova (Bulgaria)
2004	Olaf Tufte (Norway)	Katrin Rutschow-Stomporowski (Germany)
2005	Mahe Drysdale (New Zealand)	Ekaterina Karsten-Khodotovich (Belarus)
2006	Mahe Drysdale (New Zealand)	Ekaterina Karsten-Khodotovich (Belarus)
2007	Mahe Drysdale (New Zealand)	Ekaterina Karsten-Khodotovich (Belarus)

University Boat Race

An annual contest between the crews from the Oxford and Cambridge University rowing clubs; first contested in 1829; not held in some years in the early history of the race; held twice in 1849 (Mar/Dec); the current course is from Putney to Mortlake.

1829	Oxford	1852, 1854	Oxford	1870–4	Cambridge
1836	Cambridge	1856	Cambridge	1875	Oxford
1839–41	Cambridge	1857	Oxford	1876	Cambridge
1842	Oxford	1858	Cambridge	1877	*dead heat*
1845–6	Cambridge	1859	Oxford	1878	Oxford
1849 (Mar)	Cambridge	1860	Cambridge	1879	Cambridge
1849 (Dec)	Oxford	1861–9	Oxford	1880–3	Oxford

1884	Cambridge	1924–36	Cambridge	1965–7	Oxford
1885	Oxford	1937–8	Oxford	1968–73	Cambridge
1886–9	Cambridge	1939	Cambridge	1974	Oxford
1890–8	Oxford	1940–5	*not held*	1975	Cambridge
1899–1900	Cambridge	1946	Oxford	1976–85	Oxford
1901	Oxford	1947–51	Cambridge	1986	Cambridge
1902–4	Cambridge	1952	Oxford	1987–92	Oxford
1905	Oxford	1953	Cambridge	1993–9	Cambridge
1906–8	Cambridge	1954	Oxford	2000	Oxford
1909–13	Oxford	1955–8	Cambridge	2001	Cambridge
1914	Cambridge	1959–60	Oxford	2002–3	Oxford
1915–19	*not held*	1961–2	Cambridge	2004	Cambridge
1920–2	Cambridge	1963	Oxford	2005–6	Oxford
1923	Oxford	1964	Cambridge	2007	Cambridge

RUGBY LEAGUE

Team ball game played with oval ball; developed 1823 from football (supposedly when William Webb Ellis of Rugby school picked up the ball and ran with it); Rugby League was formed by the breakaway Northern Union after a dispute with the Rugby Football Union about pay in 1895; object is to score a *try* by grounding ball in opposing team's scoring area behind goal line. The 13-a-side Rugby League game is now a professional game; scoring: try 4 points, conversion 2 points, penalty 2 points, drop goal 1 point.

Ruling bodies: Rugby Football League (RFL), Rugby League International Federation (RLIF)

Rugby League pitch

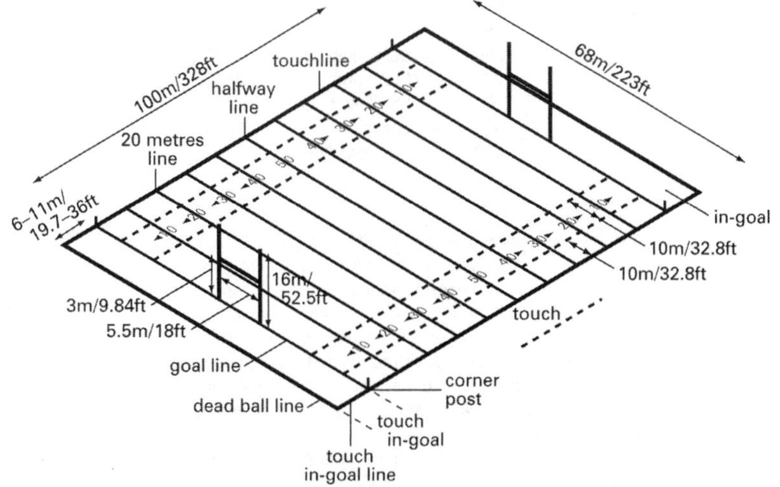

RUGBY LEAGUE

World Cup

First held in 1954 between Great Britain, France, Australia and New Zealand; played intermittently since; will next be held in 2008.

1954	Great Britain	1970	Australia	1988	Australia
1957	Australia	1972	Great Britain	1992	Australia
1960	Great Britain	1975	Australia	1995	Australia
1968	Australia	1977	Australia	2000	Australia

Engage Super League

First held in 1996. The top six teams in the league at the end of the season play off for the title; known as the JJB Super League from 1996 to 1999 and the Tetley's Super League 2000–2004.

1996	St Helens	2000	St Helens	2004	Leeds Rhinos
1997	Bradford	2001	Bradford Bulls	2005	Bradford Bulls
1998	Wigan Warriors	2002	St Helens	2006	St Helens
1999	St Helens	2003	Bradford Bulls	2007	Leeds Rhinos

Challenge Cup

First contested in 1897 and won by Batley; first final at Wembley Stadium in 1929.

1983	Featherstone	1992	Wigan	2001	St Helens
1984	Widnes	1993	Wigan	2002	Wigan Warriors
1985	Wigan	1994	Wigan	2003	Bradford Bulls
1986	Castleford	1995	Wigan	2004	St Helens
1987	Halifax	1996	St Helens	2005	Hull
1988	Wigan	1997	St Helens	2006	St Helens
1989	Wigan	1998	Sheffield Eagles	2007	St Helens
1990	Wigan	1999	Leeds Rhinos		
1991	Wigan	2000	Bradford Bulls		

Poor Lad

The most memorable of all Challenge Cup finals was the 1968 match, in which Wakefield Trinity scored a try in the last minute to narrow the score to 11–10 and leave Don Fox with the apparently simple task of kicking a conversion from in front of the posts to secure victory. However, the pitch was saturated, and Fox managed to miss the kick, meaning that Wakefield lost the game. Commentator Eddie Waring could only feel sympathy for the kicker, repeating the words 'Poor lad' as Fox slumped down in the Wembley mud, never to play rugby again.

RUGBY UNION

Team ball game played with oval ball; developed 1823 from football (supposedly when William Webb Ellis of Rugby school picked up the ball and ran with it); object is to score a *try* by grounding ball in opposing team's scoring area behind goal line. The 15-a-side Rugby Union game is now a professional game; scoring: try 5 points, conversion 2 points, penalty 3 points, drop goal 3 points.

Ruling body: Rugby Football Union (RFU), International Rugby Board (IRB)

Rugby Union pitch

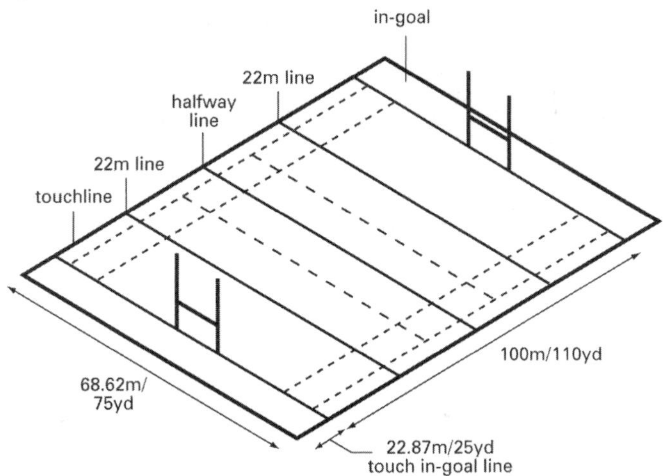

World Cup

The first Rugby Union World Cup was staged in 1987 and now takes place every four years.

1987	New Zealand	1995	South Africa	2003	England
1991	Australia	1999	Australia	2007	South Africa

Whipping Boys

The World Cup can be an opportunity for the smaller rugby-playing nations to take on the big boys. Sometimes, however, this results in very one-sided games. In the 1995 game against Japan, New Zealand racked up 145 points (including 21 tries, a record 45 points from Simon Culhane, and a record six tries from Marc Ellis), while their opponents scored just 17.

Six Nations Championship

A round robin competition involving England, Ireland, Scotland, Wales, France and, from 2000, Italy; first contested in 1882.

1983	France and Ireland	1985	Ireland	1987	France
1984	Scotland	1986	France and Scotland	1988	France and Wales

1989	France	1996	England	2003	England
1990	Scotland	1997	France	2004	France
1991	England	1998	France	2005	Wales
1992	England	1999	Scotland	2006	France
1993	France	2000	England	2007	France
1994	Wales	2001	England		
1995	England	2002	France		

County Championship

First held in 1889. Since 2007 the winners have been awarded the Bill Beaumont Cup.

1983	Gloucestershire	1992	Lancashire	2001	*not held*
1984	Gloucestershire	1993	Lancashire	2002	Gloucestershire
1985	Middlesex	1994	Yorkshire	2003	Lancashire
1986	Warwickshire	1995	Warwickshire	2004	Devon
1987	Yorkshire	1996	Gloucestershire	2005	Devon
1988	Lancashire	1997	Cumbria	2006	Lancashire
1989	Durham	1998	Cheshire	2007	Devon
1990	Lancashire	1999	Cornwall		
1991	Cornwall	2000	Yorkshire		

EDF Cup

An annual knockout competition for English club sides; first held in the 1971–2 season; known as the John Player Special Cup until 1988, the Pilkington Cup until 1997, the Tetley's Bitter Cup until 2000, and the Powergen Cup until 2006.

1983	Bristol	1992	Bath	2001	Newcastle Falcons
1984	Bath	1993	Leicester	2002	London Irish
1985	Bath	1994	Bath	2003	Gloucester
1986	Bath	1995	Bath	2004	Newcastle Falcons
1987	Bath	1996	Bath	2005	Leeds Tykes
1988	Harlequins	1997	Leicester	2006	London Wasps
1989	Bath	1998	Saracens	2007	Leicester Tigers
1990	Bath	1999	London Wasps		
1991	Harlequins	2000	London Wasps		

English League (Guinness Premiership)

Known as the Courage League until 1997, the Allied Dunbar Premier League between 1998 and 2000, and the Zurich Premiership until 2005.

1988	Leicester	1995	Leicester	2002	Leicester Tigers
1989	Bath	1996	Bath	2003	London Wasps
1990	Wasps	1997	Wasps	2004	London Wasps
1991	Bath	1998	Newcastle Falcons	2005	London Wasps
1992	Bath	1999	Leicester Tigers	2006	Sale Sharks
1993	Bath	2000	Leicester Tigers	2007	Leicester Tigers
1994	Bath	2001	Leicester Tigers		

Welsh Rugby Union Challenge Cup (Konica Minolta)

The knockout tournament for Welsh clubs; first held in 1971–2; formerly known as the Schweppes Welsh Cup, the Swalec Cup and the Principality Cup.

1983	Pontypool	1992	Llanelli	2001	Newport
1984	Cardiff	1993	Llanelli	2002	Pontypridd
1985	Llanelli	1994	Cardiff	2003	Llanelli
1986	Cardiff	1995	Swansea	2004	Neath
1987	Cardiff	1996	Pontypridd	2005	Llanelli
1988	Llanelli	1997	Cardiff	2006	Pontypridd
1989	Neath	1998	Llanelli	2007	Llandovery
1990	Neath	1999	Swansea		
1991	Llanelli	2000	Llanelli		

Welsh Premiership (Principality Premiership)

Premiership begun in 1991 and revived in 1998; from 1992 to 1997 the title was taken by the Division 1 Welsh League champions.

1993	Llanelli	1998	Swansea	2003	Bridgend
1994	Swansea	1999	Llanelli	2004	Newport
1995	Cardiff	2000	Cardiff	2005	Neath
1996	Neath	2001	Swansea	2006	Neath
1997	Pontypridd	2002	Llanelli	2007	Neath

Scottish Club Championship (BT Premiership)

First held in 1973–4.

1983	Gala	1992	Melrose	2001	Hawick
1984	Hawick	1993	Melrose	2002	Hawick
1985	Hawick	1994	Melrose	2003	Boroughmuir
1986	Hawick	1995	Stirling County	2004	Glasgow Hawks
1987	Hawick	1996	Melrose	2005	Glasgow Hawks
1988	Kelso	1997	Melrose	2006	Glasgow Hawks
1989	Kelso	1998	Watsonians	2007	Currie
1990	Melrose	1999	Heriot's FP		
1991	Boroughmuir	2000	Heriot's FP		

A Gentleman's Game

Because of rugby's public school origins, class is often mentioned in connection with the sport, especially in the UK. Two well-known descriptions of the game emphasize this: 'a game played by gentlemen with odd-shaped balls' and 'a game for hooligans played by gentlemen' (soccer being vice versa).

SAILING

Travelling over water in a suitable craft, usually a small single or double-sided dinghy, often with outboard motor or auxiliary engine for use in no wind; sailing involves racing small, light sailing vessels with crews of one, two or three; large ocean-going yachts may be 25m/80ft or more in length; several classes of racing yacht in Olympic and international competitions – eg the Admiral's Cup and America's Cup.

Ruling body: International Sailing Federation (ISAF); Royal Ocean Racing Club (RORC)

America's Cup

One of sport's famous trophies; first won by the schooner *Magic* in 1870; now held approximately every four years, when challengers compete in a series of races to find which of them races against the holder; all 25 winners up to 1983 were from the USA.

	Winning Yacht (Nation) (Skipper)
1983	*Australia II* (Australia) (John Bertrand)
1987	*Stars & Stripes* (USA) (Dennis Conner)
1988	*Stars & Stripes* (USA) (Dennis Conner)[1]
1992	*America* (USA) (Bill Koch)
1995	*Black Magic* (New Zealand) (Russell Coutts)
2000	*Black Magic* (New Zealand) (Russell Coutts)
2003	*Alinghi* (Switzerland) (Russell Coutts)
2007	*Alinghi* (Switzerland) (Brad Butterworth)

[1] Stars & Stripes *won a special challenge match but on appeal the race was awarded to the New Zealand boat. However, the decision was reversed by the New York Appeals Court in 1989.*

The Auld Mug

Europe secured its first America's Cup victory in 2003 with a win for Switzerland, a landlocked country not usually known for its sailing prowess. However, the win is less surprising given that Alinghi's skipper was Russell Coutts, a Kiwi who had defected to the Swiss attempt with several key New Zealand team members. The America's Cup is affectionately known by those in the business as the 'Auld Mug'.

Admiral's Cup

A two-yearly series of races, originally held in the English Channel, around Fastnet Rock and at Cowes; originally four national teams of three boats per team, now nine teams of three boats per team; first held in 1957.

1983	West Germany
1985	West Germany
1987	New Zealand
1989	Great Britain
1991	France
1993	Germany
1995	Italy
1997	USA
1999	The Netherlands
2001	*not held*
2003	Australia
2005	*not held*
2007	*not held*

SKIING

Propelling oneself along snow while standing on skis, aided by poles; named from Norwegian *ski*, 'snowshoe'; two forms of competition skiing: *alpine skiing*, consisting of the *downhill*, *slalom* (zigzag courses through markers), *giant slalom* (over a longer course), *Super-G* or *super-giant slalom*, and *Nordic skiing* or *langlaufing* (on narrower skis to which only the toe is attached), incorporating *ski jumping*, cross-country skiing and the biathlon.

Ruling body: International Ski Federation (FIS; Fédération Internationale de Ski)

World Cup

A season-long competition first organized in 1967; champions are declared in downhill, slalom, giant slalom and super-giant slalom, as well as the overall champion; points are obtained for performances in each category.

Overall winners

	Men	Women
1983	Phil Mahre (USA)	Tamara McKinney (USA)
1984	Pirmin Zurbriggen (Switzerland)	Erika Hess (Switzerland)
1985	Marc Girardelli (Luxembourg)	Michela Figini (Switzerland)
1986	Marc Girardelli (Luxembourg)	Maria Walliser (Switzerland)
1987	Pirmin Zurbriggen (Switzerland)	Maria Walliser (Switzerland)
1988	Pirmin Zurbriggen (Switzerland)	Michela Figini (Switzerland)
1989	Marc Girardelli (Luxembourg)	Vreni Schneider (Switzerland)
1990	Pirmin Zurbriggen (Switzerland)	Petra Kronberger (Austria)
1991	Marc Girardelli (Luxembourg)	Petra Kronberger (Austria)
1992	Paul Accola (Switzerland)	Petra Kronberger (Austria)
1993	Marc Girardelli (Luxembourg)	Anita Wachter (Austria)
1994	Kjetil-Andre Aamodt (Norway)	Vreni Schneider (Switzerland)
1995	Alberto Tomba (Italy)	Vreni Schneider (Switzerland)
1996	Lasse Kjus (Norway)	Katja Seizinger (Germany)
1997	Luc Alphand (France)	Pernilla Wiberg (Sweden)
1998	Hermann Maier (Austria)	Katja Seizinger (Germany)
1999	Lasse Kjus (Norway)	Alexandra Meissnitzer (Austria)
2000	Hermann Maier (Austria)	Renate Götschl (Austria)
2001	Hermann Maier (Austria)	Janica Kostelic (Croatia)
2002	Stephan Eberharter (Austria)	Michaela Dorfmeister (Austria)
2003	Stephan Eberharter (Austria)	Janica Kostelic (Croatia)
2004	Hermann Maier (Austria)	Anja Paerson (Sweden)
2005	Bode Miller (USA)	Anja Paerson (Sweden)
2006	Benjamin Raich (Austria)	Janica Kostelic (Croatia)
2007	Aksel Lund Svindal (Norway)	Nicole Hosp (Austria)

SNOOKER

Indoor game played on a standard billiard table by two (or occasionally four) players; aim is to *pot* the 21 coloured balls (arranged on the table at the start) by hitting them with the white *cue ball*, itself hit using a tapered pole or *cue*. Fifteen of the balls are red; these must be potted alternately with the coloured ones. This sequence is called a *break* and continues until a mistake is made; reds remain in the pockets but coloured balls are returned to their designated *spots* on the table until no reds are left, when they are potted in ascending order; game ends when the black is finally potted. Points 1–7 relate to the colours, in order: red, yellow, green, brown, blue, pink, black. The maximum break possible is 147.

Ruling body: International Billiards and Snooker Federation (IBSF), World Professional Billiards and Snooker Association (WPBSA)

Snooker table

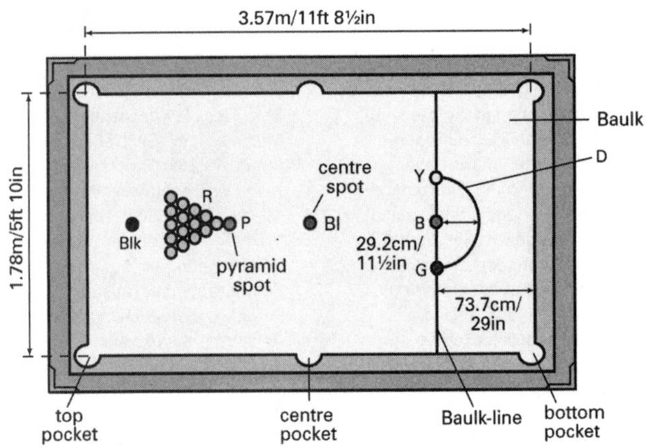

Note: The snooker table is 85–88cm/2ft 9½in–2ft 10½in high.

Y	yellow	P	pink
G	green	R	red
B	brown	Blk	black
Bl	blue		

Breaking the Bank

Ronnie O'Sullivan made the fastest ever 147 break (at the 1997 World Championship), pocketing not only the balls but also £165,000 in bonus money. His maximum break took just 5 minutes and 20 seconds – working out at a cool £515 per second!

World Professional Championships

First played in 1927 season; a knockout competition open to professional players who are members of the World Professional Billiards and Snooker Association; played at the Crucible Theatre, Sheffield, since 1977.

1983	Steve Davis	(England)
1984	Steve Davis	(England)
1985	Dennis Taylor	(Northern Ireland)
1986	Joe Johnson	(England)
1987	Steve Davis	(England)
1988	Steve Davis	(England)
1989	Steve Davis	(England)
1990	Stephen Hendry	(Scotland)
1991	John Parrott	(England)
1992	Stephen Hendry	(Scotland)
1993	Stephen Hendry	(Scotland)
1994	Stephen Hendry	(Scotland)
1995	Stephen Hendry	(Scotland)
1996	Stephen Hendry	(Scotland)
1997	Ken Doherty	(Ireland)
1998	John Higgins	(Scotland)
1999	Stephen Hendry	(Scotland)
2000	Mark Williams	(Wales)
2001	Ronnie O'Sullivan	(England)
2002	Peter Ebdon	(England)
2003	Mark Williams	(Wales)
2004	Ronnie O'Sullivan	(England)
2005	Shaun Murphy	(England)
2006	Graeme Dott	(Scotland)
2007	John Higgins	(Scotland)

Sinistral Snooker

Lefties everywhere rejoiced when Mark Williams won the Championship in 2000, the first left-hander ever to do so.

SQUASH

Strenuous indoor racket-and-ball game played (in English singles) on an enclosed court; small rubber ball is hit alternately by players against the front wall; object is to play so that the ball cannot be returned; developed 1817 from rackets at Harrow school. Also sometimes known as *squash rackets*.

Ruling body: World Squash Federation (WSF)

Squash Worldwide

The World Squash Federation keeps records of the number of squash courts worldwide; they estimate that there are more than 47,000 courts around the globe. They calculate that there are 6,136 courts in Africa, 6,436 in Asia, 22,973 in Europe, 7,339 in the Americas and 4,443 in Oceania. Squash-playing nations include Antigua (2 courts), Bhutan (1 court), Republic of Congo (2 courts), Kyrgyzstan (2 courts), Moldova (1 court) and Vanuatu (2 courts). Somewhat surprisingly, Papua New Guinea has no fewer than 48 courts.

SQUASH

Squash court

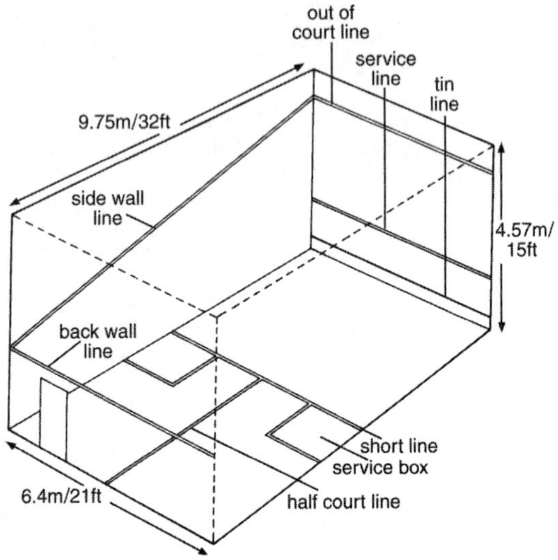

World Open Championship

First held in 1976; takes place annually for men and women; women's event first held 1979; every two years for women until 1989.

Men

1983	Jahangir Khan (Pakistan)	1996	Jansher Khan (Pakistan)
1984	Jahangir Khan (Pakistan)	1997	Rodney Eyles (Australia)
1985	Jahangir Khan (Pakistan)	1998	Jonathon Power (Canada)
1986	Ross Norman (New Zealand)	1999	Peter Nicol (Great Britain)
1987	Jansher Khan (Pakistan)	2000	*not held*
1988	Jahangir Khan (Pakistan)	2001	*not held*
1989	Jansher Khan (Pakistan)	2002	David Palmer (Australia)
1990	Jansher Khan (Pakistan)	2003	Amr Shabana (Egypt)
1991	Rodney Martin (Australia)	2004	Thierry Lincou (France)
1992	Jansher Khan (Pakistan)	2005	Amr Shabana (Egypt)
1993	Jansher Khan (Pakistan)	2006	David Palmer (Australia)
1994	Jansher Khan (Pakistan)	2007	Amr Shabana (Egypt)
1995	Jansher Khan (Pakistan)		

Women

1983	Vicki Cardwell (Australia)	1992	Sue Devoy (New Zealand)
1985	Sue Devoy (New Zealand)	1993	Michelle Martin (Australia)
1987	Sue Devoy (New Zealand)	1994	Michelle Martin (Australia)
1989	Martine Le Moignan (Great Britain)	1995	Michelle Martin (Australia)
1990	Sue Devoy (New Zealand)	1996	Sarah Fitz-Gerald (Australia)
1991	*not held*	1997	Sarah Fitz-Gerald (Australia)

1998	Sarah Fitz-Gerald (Australia)	2004	Vanessa Atkinson (The Netherlands)
1999	Cassie Campion (Great Britain)	2005	Nicol David (Malaysia)
2000	Carol Owens (Australia)	2006	Nicol David (Malaysia)
2001	Sarah Fitz-Gerald (Australia)	2007	Rachael Grinham (Australia)
2002	Sarah Fitz-Gerald (Australia)		
2003	Carol Owens (New Zealand)		

SWIMMING AND DIVING

Swimming: Propelling oneself through water without mechanical aids. Four strokes: *breaststroke*, the slowest stroke, developed in the 16c; *front crawl* or *freestyle*, the fastest stroke; *backstroke*; and *butterfly*, developed in the USA in the 20c. In competitions there are also relays, involving four swimmers, and medley races, combining all four strokes. Olympic-size pool is 50m/55yd long, with eight lanes; race lengths from 50m/55yd to 1,500m/1,640yd; earliest reference to swimming as a sport is 36 BC Japan.

Diving: Jumping from an elevated rigid or sprung board into a swimming pool, often performing a variety of twists and somersaults. Style gains marks, as does successfully completing the dive, based on the level of difficulty of each attempt (which is used as a multiplying factor). Springboard events take place from a board 3m/9ft 10in above the water; platform diving from a rigid base 10m/32ft 10in above the water.

Ruling body: International Swimming Federation (FINA; Fédération Internationale de Natation)

World Championships

First held in 1973 and again in 1975; from 1978 held approximately every four years; since 2001 held every two years.

1998

Men

50m freestyle	Bill Pilczuk (USA)
100m freestyle	Alexander Popov (Russia)
200m freestyle	Michael Klim (Australia)
400m freestyle	Ian Thorpe (Australia)
1 500m freestyle	Grant Hackett (Australia)
100m backstroke	Lenny Krayzelburg (USA)
200m backstroke	Lenny Krayzelburg (USA)
100m breaststroke	Fred Deburghgraeve (Belgium)
200m breaststroke	Kurt Grote (USA)
100m butterfly	Michael Klim (Australia)
200m butterfly	Denys Sylantyev (Ukraine)
200m individual medley	Marcel Wouda (The Netherlands)
400m individual medley	Tom Dolan (USA)
4 × 100m freestyle relay	USA
4 × 200m freestyle relay	Australia
4 × 100m medley relay	Australia
1m springboard diving	Yu Zhuocheng (China)
3m springboard diving	Dimitri Sautin (Russia)
10m platform diving	Dimitri Sautin (Russia)

Women

50m freestyle	Amy Van Dyken (USA)
100m freestyle	Jenny Thompson (USA)

Women

200m freestyle	Claudia Poll (Costa Rica)
400m freestyle	Yan Chen (China)
800m freestyle	Brooke Bennett (USA)
100m backstroke	Lea Maurer (USA)
200m backstroke	Roxanna Maracineanu (France)
100m breaststroke	Kristy Kowal (USA)
200m breaststroke	Agnes Kovacs (Hungary)
100m butterfly	Jenny Thompson (USA)
200m butterfly	Susie O'Neill (Australia)
200m individual medley	Wu Yanyan (China)
400m individual medley	Yan Chen (China)
4 × 100m freestyle relay	USA
4 × 200m freestyle relay	Germany
4 × 100m medley relay	USA
1m springboard diving	Irina Lashko (Russia)
3m springboard diving	Yulia Pakhalina (Russia)
10m platform diving	Olena Zhupyna (Ukraine)

2001

Men

50m freestyle	Anthony Ervin (USA)
100m freestyle	Anthony Ervin (USA)
200m freestyle	Ian Thorpe (Australia)
400m freestyle	Ian Thorpe (Australia)
1500m freestyle	Grant Hackett (Australia)
100m backstroke	Matt Welsh (Australia)
200m backstroke	Aaron Peirsol (USA)
50m breaststroke	Oleg Lisogor (Ukraine)
100m breaststroke	Roman Sloudnov (Russia)
200m breaststroke	Brendan Hansen (USA)
50m butterfly	Geoff Huegill (Australia)
100m butterfly	Lars Frolander (Sweden)
200m butterfly	Michael Phelps (USA)
200m individual medley	Massimiliano Rosolini (Italy)
400m individual medley	Alessio Boggiatto (Italy)
4 × 100m freestyle relay	Australia
4 × 200m freestyle relay	Australia
4 × 100m medley relay	Australia
1m springboard diving	Feng Wang (China)
3m springboard diving	Dimitri Sautin (Russia)
10m platform diving	Tian Liang (China)

Women

50m freestyle	Inge de Bruijn (The Netherlands)
100m freestyle	Inge de Bruijn (The Netherlands)
200m freestyle	Giaan Rooney (Australia)
400m freestyle	Yana Klochova (Ukraine)
800m freestyle	Hannah Stockbauer (Germany)
1500m freestyle	Hannah Stockbauer (Germany)
50m backstroke	Haley Cope (USA)
100m backstroke	Natalie Coughlin (USA)

Women

200m backstroke	Diana Iuliana Mocanu (Romania)
50m breaststroke	Luo Xuejuan (China)
100m breaststroke	Luo Xuejuan (China)
200m breaststroke	Agnes Kovacs (Hungary)
50m butterfly	Inge de Bruijn (The Netherlands)
100m butterfly	Petria Thomas (Australia)
200m butterfly	Petria Thomas (Australia)
200m individual medley	Martha Bowen (USA)
400m individual medley	Yana Klochova (Ukraine)
4 × 100m freestyle relay	Germany
4 × 200m freestyle relay	Great Britain
4 × 100m medley relay	Australia
1m springboard diving	Blythe Hartley (Canada)
3m springboard diving	Guo Jingjing (China)
10m platform diving	Mian Xu (China)

2003

Men

50m freestyle	Alexander Popov (Russia)
100m freestyle	Alexander Popov (Russia)
200m freestyle	Ian Thorpe (Australia)
400m freestyle	Ian Thorpe (Australia)
1 500m freestyle	Grant Hackett (Australia)
100m backstroke	Aaron Peirsol (USA)
200m backstroke	Aaron Peirsol (USA)
50m breaststroke	James Gibson (Great Britain)
100m breaststroke	Kosuke Kitajima (Japan)
200m breaststroke	Kosuke Kitajima (Japan)
50m butterfly	Matthew Welsh (Australia)
100m butterfly	Ian Crocker (USA)
200m butterfly	Michael Phelps (USA)
200m individual medley	Michael Phelps (USA)
400m individual medley	Michael Phelps (USA)
4 × 100m freestyle relay	Russia
4 × 200m freestyle relay	Australia
4 × 100m medley relay	USA
1m springboard diving	Xiang Xu (China)
3m springboard diving	Alexander Dobrosok (Russia)
10m platform diving	Alexandre Despatie (Canada)

Women

50m freestyle	Inge de Bruijn (The Netherlands)
100m freestyle	Hanna-Maria Seppälä (Finland)
200m freestyle	Alena Popchanka (Bulgaria)
400m freestyle	Hannah Stockbauer (Germany)
800m freestyle	Hannah Stockbauer (Germany)
1 500m freestyle	Hannah Stockbauer (Germany)
50m backstroke	Nina Zhivanevskaya (Spain)
100m backstroke	Antje Buschschulte (Germany)
200m backstroke	Katy Sexton (Great Britain)
50m breaststroke	Luo Xuejuan (China)

Women

100m breaststroke	Luo Xuejuan (China)
200m breaststroke	Amanda Beard (USA)
50m butterfly	Inge de Bruijn (The Netherlands)
100m butterfly	Jenny Thompson (USA)
200m butterfly	Otylia Jedrzejczak (Poland)
200m individual medley	Yana Klochova (Ukraine)
400m individual medley	Yana Klochova (Ukraine)
4 × 100m freestyle relay	USA
4 × 200m freestyle relay	USA
4 × 100m medley relay	China
1m springboard diving	Irina Lashko (Australia)
3m springboard diving	Guo Jingjing (China)
10m platform diving	Emilie Heymans (Canada)

2005

Men

50m freestyle	Roland Schoeman (South Africa)
100m freestyle	Filippo Magnini (Italy)
200m freestyle	Michael Phelps (USA)
400m freestyle	Grant Hackett (Australia)
800m freestyle	Grant Hackett (Australia)
1 500m freestyle	Grant Hackett (Australia)
50m backstroke	Aristeidis Grigoriadis (Greece)
100m backstroke	Aaron Peirsol (USA)
200m backstroke	Aaron Peirsol (USA)
50m breaststroke	Mark Warnecke (Germany)
100m breaststroke	Brendan Hansen (USA)
200m breaststroke	Brendan Hansen (USA)
50m butterfly	Roland Schoeman (South Africa)
100m butterfly	Ian Crocker (USA)
200m butterfly	Pawel Korzeniowski (Poland)
200m individual medley	Michael Phelps (USA)
400m individual medley	Laszlo Cseh (Hungary)
4x100m freestyle relay	USA
4x200m freestyle relay	USA
4x100m medley relay	USA
1m springboard diving	Alexandre Despatie (Canada)
3m springboard diving	Alexandre Despatie (Canada)
10m platform diving	Hu Jia (China)
3m springboard synchronized	Wang Feng/He Chong (China)
10m platform synchronized	Dmitry Dobrosok/Gleb Galperin (Russia)

Women

50m freestyle	Lisbeth Lenton (Australia)
100m freestyle	Jodie Henry (Australia)
200m freestyle	Solenne Figues (France)
400m freestyle	Laure Manaudou (France)
800m freestyle	Kate Ziegler (USA)
1 500m freestyle	Kate Ziegler (USA)
50m backstroke	Giaan Rooney (Australia)
100m backstroke	Kirsty Coventry (Zimbabwe)

Women

200m backstroke	Kirsty Coventry (Zimbabwe)
50m breaststroke	Jade Edmistone (Australia)
100m breaststroke	Leisel Jones (Australia)
200m breaststroke	Leisel Jones (Australia)
50m butterfly	Danni Miatke (Australia)
100m butterfly	Jessicah Schipper (Australia)
200m butterfly	Otylia Jedrzejczak (Poland)
200m individual medley	Katie Hoff (USA)
400m individual medley	Katie Hoff (USA)
4 × 100m freestyle relay	Australia
4 × 200m freestyle relay	USA
4 × 100m medley relay	Australia
1m springboard diving	Blythe Hartley (Canada)
3m springboard diving	Guo Jingjing (China)
10m platform diving	Laura Ann Wilkinson (USA)
3m springboard synchronized	Li Ting/Guo Jingjing (China)
10m platform synchronized	Jia Tong/Pei Lin Yuan (China)

2007

Men

50m freestyle	Benjamin Wildman-Tobriner (USA)
100m freestyle	Filippo Magnini (Italy)/Brent Hayden (Canada)
200m freestyle	Michael Phelps (USA)
400m freestyle	Tae Hwan Park (South Korea)
800m freestyle	Oussama Mellouli (Tunisia)
1500m freestyle	Mateusz Sawrymowicz (Poland)
50m backstroke	Gerhard Zandberg (South Africa)
100m backstroke	Aaron Peirsol (USA)
200m backstroke	Ryan Lochte (USA)
50m breaststroke	Oleg Lisogor (Ukraine)
100m breaststroke	Brendan Hansen (USA)
200m breaststroke	Kosuke Kitajima (Japan)
50m butterfly	Roland Schoeman (South Africa)
100m butterfly	Michael Phelps (USA)
200m butterfly	Michael Phelps (USA)
200m individual medley	Michael Phelps (USA)
400m individual medley	Michael Phelps (USA)
4 × 100m freestyle relay	USA
4 × 200m freestyle relay	USA
4 × 100m medley relay	Australia
1m springboard diving	Luo Yutong (China)
3m springboard diving	Qin Kai (China)
10m platform diving	Gleb Galperin (Russia)
3m springboard synchronized	Qin Kai/Wang Feng (China)
10m platform synchronized	Lin Yue/Huo Liang (China)

Women

50m freestyle	Libby Lenton (Australia)
100m freestyle	Libby Lenton (Australia)
200m freestyle	Laure Manaudou (France)
400m freestyle	Laure Manaudou (France)

Women

800m freestyle	Kate Ziegler (USA)
1500m freestyle	Kate Ziegler (USA)
50m backstroke	Leila Vaziri (USA)
100m backstroke	Natalie Coughlin (USA)
200m backstroke	Margaret Hoelzer (USA)
50m breaststroke	Jessica Hardy (USA)
100m breaststroke	Leisel Jones (Australia)
200m breaststroke	Leisel Jones (Australia)
50m butterfly	Therese Alshammar (Sweden)
100m butterfly	Libby Lenton (Australia)
200m butterfly	Jessicah Schipper (Australia)
200m individual medley	Katie Hoff (USA)
400m individual medley	Katie Hoff (USA)
4 × 100m freestyle relay	Australia
4 × 200m freestyle relay	USA
4 × 100m medley relay	Australia
1m springboard diving	He Zi (China)
3m springboard diving	Guo Jingjing (China)
10m platform diving	Wang Xin (China)
3m springboard synchronized	Guo Jingjing/Wu Minxia (China)
10m platform synchronized	Jia Tong/Chen Ruolin (China)

TENNIS

Properly lawn tennis. Racket-and-ball game for two or four players; net is stretched across centre; rackets have oval heads strung with nylon or gut; playing surface can be grass, clay, shale, concrete, wood, or other man-made materials; object is to play unreturnable strokes, thus scoring points; progression of scoring is 15, 30, 40, deuce if both reach 40, and game; set won by winning six games with a two game lead (or one in a 'short' set); a very close set can be decided using a tie-break. In doubles, players may hit the ball in any order, but must serve in rotation.

Ruling bodies: International Tennis Federation (ITF), Lawn Tennis Association (LTA)

Tennis court

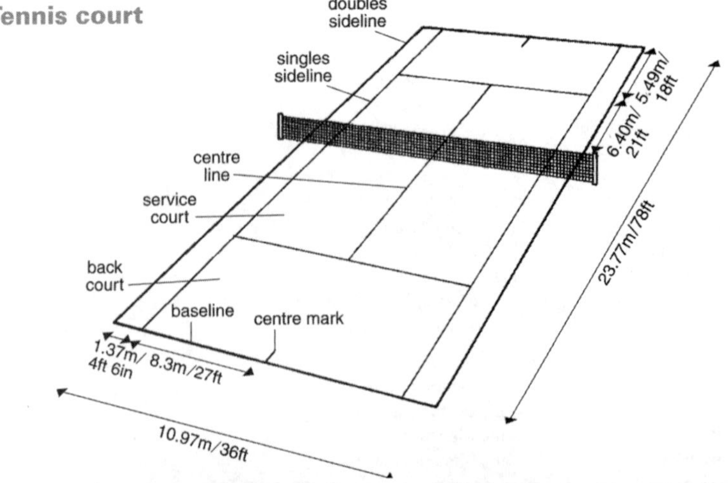

All-England Championships at Wimbledon

The All-England Championships at Wimbledon are lawn tennis's most prestigious championships; first held in 1877.

	Men's singles	Women's singles
1983	John McEnroe (USA)	Martina Navratilova (USA)
1984	John McEnroe (USA)	Martina Navratilova (USA)
1985	Boris Becker (West Germany)	Martina Navratilova (USA)
1986	Boris Becker (West Germany)	Martina Navratilova (USA)
1987	Pat Cash (Australia)	Martina Navratilova (USA)
1988	Stefan Edberg (Sweden)	Steffi Graf (West Germany)
1989	Boris Becker (West Germany)	Steffi Graf (West Germany)
1990	Stefan Edberg (Sweden)	Martina Navratilova (USA)
1991	Michael Stich (Germany)	Steffi Graf (Germany)
1992	André Agassi (USA)	Steffi Graf (Germany)
1993	Pete Sampras (USA)	Steffi Graf (Germany)
1994	Pete Sampras (USA)	Conchita Martínez (Spain)
1995	Pete Sampras (USA)	Steffi Graf (Germany)
1996	Richard Krajicek (The Netherlands)	Steffi Graf (Germany)
1997	Pete Sampras (USA)	Martina Hingis (Switzerland)
1998	Pete Sampras (USA)	Jana Novotna (Czech Republic)
1999	Pete Sampras (USA)	Lindsay Davenport (USA)
2000	Pete Sampras (USA)	Venus Williams (USA)
2001	Goran Ivanisevic (Croatia)	Venus Williams (USA)
2002	Lleyton Hewitt (Australia)	Serena Williams (USA)
2003	Roger Federer (Switzerland)	Serena Williams (USA)
2004	Roger Federer (Switzerland)	Maria Sharapova (Russia)
2005	Roger Federer (Switzerland)	Venus Williams (USA)
2006	Roger Federer (Switzerland)	Amélie Mauresmo (France)
2007	Roger Federer (Switzerland)	Venus Williams (USA)

Men's doubles

1983	Peter Fleming/John McEnroe (USA)
1984	Peter Fleming/John McEnroe (USA)
1985	Heinz Gunthardt (Switzerland)/Balazs Taroczy (Hungary)
1986	Joakim Nystrom/Mats Wilander (Sweden)
1987	Ken Flach/Robert Seguso (USA)
1988	Ken Flach/Robert Seguso (USA)
1989	John Fitzgerald (Australia)/Anders Jarryd (Sweden)
1990	Rick Leach/Jim Pugh (USA)
1991	John Fitzgerald (Australia)/Anders Jarryd (Sweden)
1992	John McEnroe (USA)/Michael Stich (Germany)
1993	Todd Woodbridge/Mark Woodforde (Australia)
1994	Todd Woodbridge/Mark Woodforde (Australia)
1995	Todd Woodbridge/Mark Woodforde (Australia)
1996	Todd Woodbridge/Mark Woodforde (Australia)
1997	Todd Woodbridge/Mark Woodforde (Australia)
1998	Jacco Eltingh/Paul Haarhuis (The Netherlands)
1999	Mahesh Bhupathi/Leander Paes (India)
2000	Todd Woodbridge/Mark Woodforde (Australia)
2001	Donald Johnson/Jared Palmer (USA)

Men's doubles

2002 Todd Woodbridge (Australia)/Jonas Bjorkman (Sweden)
2003 Todd Woodbridge (Australia)/Jonas Bjorkman (Sweden)
2004 Todd Woodbridge (Australia)/Jonas Bjorkman (Sweden)
2005 Stephen Huss (Australia)/Wesley Moodie (South Africa)
2006 Bob Bryan/Mike Bryan (USA)
2007 Arnaud Clement/Michaël Llodra (France)

Women's doubles

1983 Martina Navratilova/Pam Shriver (USA)
1984 Martina Navratilova/Pam Shriver (USA)
1985 Kathy Jordan/Elizabeth Smylie (Australia)
1986 Martina Navratilova/Pam Shriver (USA)
1987 Claudia Kohde-Kilsch (West Germany)/Helena Sukova (Czechoslovakia)
1988 Steffi Graf (West Germany)/Gabriela Sabatini (Argentina)
1989 Jana Novotna/Helena Sukova (Czechoslovakia)
1990 Jana Novotna/Helena Sukova (Czechoslovakia)
1991 Natalya Zvereva/Larissa Savchenko (USSR)
1992 Gigi Fernandez (USA)/Natalya Zvereva (CIS)
1993 Gigi Fernandez (USA)/Natalya Zvereva (CIS)
1994 Gigi Fernandez (USA)/Natalya Zvereva (CIS)
1995 Arantxa Sanchez Vicario (Spain)/Jana Novotna (Czech Republic)
1996 Helena Sukova (Czech Republic)/Martina Hingis (Switzerland)
1997 Gigi Fernandez (USA)/Natalya Zvereva (Belarus)
1998 Jana Novotna (Czech Republic)/Martina Hingis (Switzerland)
1999 Lindsay Davenport/Corina Morariu (USA)
2000 Serena Williams/Venus Williams (USA)
2001 Lisa Raymond (USA)/Rennae Stubbs (Australia)
2002 Serena Williams/Venus Williams (USA)
2003 Kim Clijsters (Belgium)/Ai Sugiyama (Japan)
2004 Cara Black (Zimbabwe)/Rennae Stubbs (Australia)
2005 Cara Black (Zimbabwe)/Liezel Huber (South Africa)
2006 Zi Yan/Jie Zheng (China)
2007 Cara Black (Zimbabwe)/Liezel Huber (South Africa)

Mixed doubles

1983 Wendy Turnbull (Australia)/John Lloyd (Great Britain)
1984 Wendy Turnbull (Australia)/John Lloyd (Great Britain)
1985 Martina Navratilova (USA)/Paul McNamee (Australia)
1986 Kathy Jordan/Ken Flach (USA)
1987 Jo Durie/Jeremy Bates (Great Britain)
1988 Zina Garrison/Sherwood Stewart (USA)
1989 Jana Novotna (Czechoslovakia)/Jim Pugh (USA)
1990 Zina Garrison/Rick Leach (USA)
1991 Elizabeth Smylie/John Fitzgerald (Australia)
1992 Larissa Savchenko-Neiland (Latvia)/Cyril Suk (Czechoslovakia)
1993 Martina Navratilova (USA)/Mark Woodforde (Australia)
1994 Helena Sukova (Czech Republic)/Todd Woodbridge (Australia)
1995 Martina Navratilova/Jonathan Stark (USA)
1996 Helena Sukova/Cyril Suk (Czech Republic)
1997 Helena Sukova/Cyril Suk (Czech Republic)
1998 Serena Williams (USA)/Max Mirnyi (Belarus)

Mixed doubles

1999	Lisa Raymond (USA)/Leander Paes (India)
2000	Kimberly Po/Donald Johnson (USA)
2001	Daniela Hantuchova (Slovakia)/Leos Friedl (Czech Republic)
2002	Elena Likhovtseva (Russia)/Mahesh Bhupathi (India)
2003	Martina Navratilova (USA)/Leander Paes (India)
2004	Cara Black/Wayne Black (Zimbabwe)
2005	Mary Pierce (France)/Mahesh Bhupathi (India)
2006	Vera Zvonareva (Russia)/Andy Ram (Israel)
2007	Jelena Janković (Serbia)/Jamie Murray (Great Britain)

US Open

First held in 1891 as the United States Championship; became the United States Open in 1968.

	Men's singles	**Women's singles**
1983	Jimmy Connors (USA)	Martina Navratilova (USA)
1984	John McEnroe (USA)	Martina Navratilova (USA)
1985	Ivan Lendl (Czechoslovakia)	Hana Mandlikova (Czechoslovakia)
1986	Ivan Lendl (Czechoslovakia)	Martina Navratilova (USA)
1987	Ivan Lendl (Czechoslovakia)	Martina Navratilova (USA)
1988	Mats Wilander (Sweden)	Steffi Graf (West Germany)
1989	Boris Becker (West Germany)	Steffi Graf (West Germany)
1990	Pete Sampras (USA)	Gabriela Sabatini (Argentina)
1991	Stefan Edberg (Sweden)	Monica Seles (Yugoslavia)
1992	Stefan Edberg (Sweden)	Monica Seles (Yugoslavia)
1993	Pete Sampras (USA)	Steffi Graf (Germany)
1994	André Agassi (USA)	Arantxa Sanchez Vicario (Spain)
1995	Pete Sampras (USA)	Steffi Graf (Germany)
1996	Pete Sampras (USA)	Steffi Graf (Germany)
1997	Pat Rafter (Australia)	Martina Hingis (Switzerland)
1998	Pat Rafter (Australia)	Lindsay Davenport (USA)
1999	André Agassi (USA)	Serena Williams (USA)
2000	Marat Safin (Russia)	Venus Williams (USA)
2001	Lleyton Hewitt (Australia)	Venus Williams (USA)
2002	Pete Sampras (USA)	Serena Williams (USA)
2003	Andy Roddick (USA)	Justine Henin-Hardenne (Belgium)
2004	Roger Federer (Switzerland)	Svetlana Kuznetsova (Russia)
2005	Roger Federer (Switzerland)	Kim Clijsters (Belgium)
2006	Roger Federer (Switzerland)	Maria Sharapova (Russia)
2007	Roger Federer (Switzerland)	Justine Henin (Belgium)

Anyone for Sphairistike?

'Field tennis' was played in the 18c, but a game similar to the modern game was invented in Wales in 1873 by Walter Wingfield, who christened the new game *sphairistike*. He patented the game and it was quite widely known for a time by this name, which comes from the Greek *sphairistike techne* 'the art of playing ball', from *sphaira* 'ball'. The simpler term *tennis* is thought to come from the French word *tenez*, the imperative of *tenir* meaning 'to take or receive'.

French Open

First held in 1891 as the French Championships, became an international competition in 1925, and was renamed the French Open in 1968 when professionals were first allowed to enter.

	Men's singles	Women's singles
1983	Yannick Noah (France)	Chris Evert Lloyd (USA)
1984	Ivan Lendl (Czechoslovakia)	Martina Navratilova (USA)
1985	Mats Wilander (Sweden)	Chris Evert Lloyd (USA)
1986	Ivan Lendl (Czechoslovakia)	Chris Evert Lloyd (USA)
1987	Ivan Lendl (Czechoslovakia)	Steffi Graf (West Germany)
1988	Mats Wilander (Sweden)	Steffi Graf (West Germany)
1989	Michael Chang (USA)	Arantxa Sanchez Vicario (Spain)
1990	Andres Gomez (Ecuador)	Monica Seles (Yugoslavia)
1991	Jim Courier (USA)	Monica Seles (Yugoslavia)
1992	Jim Courier (USA)	Monica Seles (Yugoslavia)
1993	Sergi Bruguera (Spain)	Steffi Graf (Germany)
1994	Sergi Bruguera (Spain)	Arantxa Sanchez Vicario (Spain)
1995	Thomas Muster (Austria)	Steffi Graf (Germany)
1996	Yevgeny Kafelnikov (Russia)	Iva Majoli (Croatia)
1997	Gustavo Kuerten (Brazil)	Steffi Graf (Germany)
1998	Carlos Moya (Spain)	Arantxa Sanchez Vicario (Spain)
1999	André Agassi (USA)	Steffi Graf (Germany)
2000	Gustavo Kuerten (Brazil)	Mary Pierce (France)
2001	Gustavo Kuerten (Brazil)	Jennifer Capriati (USA)
2002	Albert Costa (Spain)	Serena Williams (USA)
2003	Juan Carlos Ferrero (Spain)	Justine Henin-Hardenne (Belgium)
2004	Gaston Gaudio (Argentina)	Anastasia Myskina (Russia)
2005	Rafael Nadal (Spain)	Justine Henin-Hardenne (Belgium)
2006	Rafael Nadal (Spain)	Justine Henin-Hardenne (Belgium)
2007	Rafael Nadal (Spain)	Justine Henin (Belgium)

Australian Open

First held in 1905 as the Australasian Tennis Championships; became the Australian Championships in 1927.

	Men's singles	Women's singles
1983	Mats Wilander (Sweden)	Martina Navratilova (USA)
1984	Mats Wilander (Sweden)	Chris Evert Lloyd (USA)
1985	Stefan Edberg (Sweden)	Martina Navratilova (USA)
1986	*not held*	*not held*
1987	Stefan Edberg (Sweden)	Hana Mandlikova (Czechoslovakia)
1988	Mats Wilander (Sweden)	Steffi Graf (West Germany)
1989	Ivan Lendl (Czechoslovakia)	Steffi Graf (West Germany)
1990	Ivan Lendl (Czechoslovakia)	Steffi Graf (Germany)
1991	Boris Becker (Germany)	Monica Seles (Yugoslavia)
1992	Jim Courier (USA)	Monica Seles (Yugoslavia)
1993	Jim Courier (USA)	Monica Seles (Yugoslavia)
1994	Pete Sampras (USA)	Steffi Graf (Germany)
1995	André Agassi (USA)	Mary Pierce (France)
1996	Boris Becker (Germany)	Monica Seles (USA)

	Men's singles	Women's singles
1997	Pete Sampras (USA)	Martina Hingis (Switzerland)
1998	Petr Korda (Czech Republic)	Martina Hingis (Switzerland)
1999	Yevgeny Kafelnikov (Russia)	Martina Hingis (Switzerland)
2000	André Agassi (USA)	Lindsay Davenport (USA)
2001	André Agassi (USA)	Jennifer Capriati (USA)
2002	Thomas Johansson (Sweden)	Jennifer Capriati (USA)
2003	André Agassi (USA)	Serena Williams (USA)
2004	Roger Federer (Switzerland)	Justine Henin-Hardenne (Belgium)
2005	Marat Safin (Russia)	Serena Williams (USA)
2006	Roger Federer (Switzerland)	Amélie Mauresmo (France)
2007	Roger Federer (Switzerland)	Serena Williams (USA)

Davis Cup

International men's team competition organized on a knockout basis; first held in 1900; contested on a challenge basis until 1972.

1983	Australia	1992	USA	2001	France
1984	Sweden	1993	Germany	2002	Russia
1985	Sweden	1994	Sweden	2003	Australia
1986	Australia	1995	USA	2004	Spain
1987	Sweden	1996	France	2005	Croatia
1988	West Germany	1997	Sweden	2006	Russia
1989	West Germany	1998	Sweden	2007	USA
1990	USA	1999	Australia		
1991	France	2000	Spain		

Grand Slam winners (singles)

Players who have won the Australian Open, the French Open, Wimbledon and the US Open in the same calendar year.

Men		Women	
1938	Don Budge (USA)	1953	Maureen Connolly (USA)
1962	Rod Laver (Australia)	1970	Margaret Court (Australia)
1969	Rod Laver (Australia)	1988	Steffi Graf (West Germany)

Watching the Clock

The scoring system in tennis may be inspired by the presence of a clock face at the head of early courts. As players won points, the appropriate hand was moved to reflect this. The first point was therefore fifteen (minutes), the second thirty, the third forty-five and finally, when the hour was reached, game. Forty-five was later shortened to forty as it took less time to call out.

VOLLEYBALL

Indoor court game; two teams of six play on a court which has a raised net stretched across the centre; aim is to score points by grounding the inflated ball on opponent's side after hitting it over net with the arms or hands; ball may not be hit more than three times on one team's side of the net.

Ruling body: International Volleyball Federation (FIVB; Fédération Internationale de Volleyball)

Volleyball court

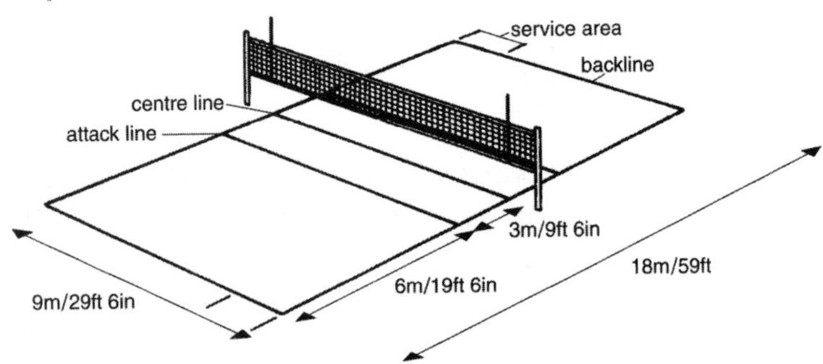

World Championships

Inaugurated in 1949; first women's championships in 1952; now held every four years, but Olympic champions are also world champions in Olympic years.

	Men	Women
1986	USA	China
1988	USA	USSR
1990	Italy	USSR
1992	Brazil	Cuba
1994	Italy	Cuba
1996	The Netherlands	Cuba
1998	Italy	Cuba
2000	Yugoslavia	Cuba
2002	Brazil	Italy
2004	Brazil	China
2006	Brazil	Russia

A Whole New Ball Game

Volleyball was invented in 1895 by William G Morgan of Springfield College, Holyoke, Massachusetts, who named the game 'mintonette'. It was intended as a less strenuous version of basketball, invented just a few years previously at the same college.

WEIGHTLIFTING

Test of strength by lifting weights attached to both ends of a metal pole or *barbell*. Competitors have to make two successful lifts: the *snatch*, taking the bar to an outstretched position above the head in one movement (held for two seconds), and the *clean and jerk* or *jerk* which is achieved in two movements, first onto the chest, then above the head with outstretched arms; aggregate weight of the two lifts gives a competitor's total, and the weights are gradually increased. Another form is *powerlifting*, which calls for sheer strength rather than technique, and takes three forms: the *squat*, *dead lift* and *bench press*. Weightlifting was part of ancient Olympic Games; introduced as sport c.1850.

Ruling body: International Weightlifting Federation (IWF)

World Championships

First held in 1891; 11 weight divisions; the most prestigious is the 105kg-plus category (formerly known as Super Heavyweight, then 110kg-plus; in 1993 changed to 108kg-plus; in 1998 reduced to current weight); Olympic champions are automatically world champions in Olympic years. Women's World Championships instituted in 1987; the most prestigious of 7 weight divisions is the 75kg-plus category (formerly 82.5kg-plus; in 1993 changed to 83kg-plus; in 1998 reduced to current weight).

	Men 105kg-plus	**Women 75kg-plus**
1983	Anatoli Pisarenko (USSR)	
1984	Dean Lukin (Australia)	
1985	Antonio Krastev (Bulgaria)	
1986	Antonio Krastev (Bulgaria)	
1987	Aleksandr Kurlovich (USSR)	Han Changmei (China)
1988	Aleksandr Kurlovich (USSR)	Han Changmei (China)
1989	Stefan Botev (Bulgaria)	Han Changmei (China)
1990	Stefan Botev (Bulgaria)	Li Yajuan (China)
1991	Aleksandr Kurlovich (USSR)	Li Yajuan (China)
1992	Aleksandr Kurlovich (UT)	Li Yajuan (China)
1993	Ronnie Weller (Germany)	Li Yajuan (China)
1994	Aleksandr Kurlovich (Belarus)	Karolina Lundahl (Finland)
1995	Andrey Chemerkin (Russia)	Erika Takacs (Hungary)
1996	Andrey Chemerkin (Russia)	Ni Wan (China)
1997	Andrey Chemerkin (Russia)	Ma Runmei (China)
1998	Andrey Chemerkin (Russia)	Tang Gonghong (China)
1999	Andrey Chemerkin (Russia)	Ding Meiyuan (China)
2000	Hossein Reza Zadeh (Iran)	Ding Meiyuan (China)
2001	Saeed Salem Jaber (Qatar)	Albina Khomich (Russia)
2002	Hossein Reza Zadeh (Iran)	Agata Wrobel (Poland)
2003	Hossein Reza Zadeh (Iran)	Ding Meiyuan (China)
2004	Hossein Reza Zadeh (Iran)	Tang Gonghong (China)
2005	Hossein Reza Zadeh (Iran)	Jang Mi-Ran (South Korea)
2006	Hossein Reza Zadeh (Iran)	Jang Mi-Ran (South Korea)
2007	Viktors Scerbatihs (Latvia)	Jang Mi-Ran (South Korea)

WRESTLING

Fighting person to person without using fists; aim is to throw opponent to the ground; most popular forms are *freestyle*, where the legs can be used to hold and trip, and *Graeco-Roman* where holds below the waist are not allowed. Ten weight divisions, from 55kg to 120kg.

Ruling body: International Federation of Associated Wrestling Styles (FILA; Fédération Internationale de Lutte Amateur)

World Championships

Graeco-Roman world championships first held in 1921; first freestyle championships in 1951; each style contests 10 weight divisions, the heaviest being the 120kg (formerly over 100kg and, until Dec 2001, 130kg) category; Olympic champions become world champions in Olympic years.

Super-heavyweight/120kg

	Freestyle	Graeco-Roman
1983	Salman Khasimikov (USSR)	Jewgeni Artjuchin (Russia)
1984	Bruce Baumgartner (USA)	Jeffrey Blatnick (USA)
1985	David Gobedzhishvilli (USSR)	Igor Rostorotzki (USSR)
1986	Bruce Baumgartner (USA)	Thomas Johansson (Sweden)
1987	Aslam Khadartsev (USSR)	Igor Rostorotzki (USSR)
1988	David Gobedzhishvilli (USSR)	Aleksandr Karelin (USSR)
1989	Ali Reiza Soleimani (Iran)	Aleksandr Karelin (USSR)
1990	David Gobedzhishvilli (USSR)	Aleksandr Karelin (USSR)
1991	Andreas Schroder (Germany)	Aleksandr Karelin (USSR)
1992	Bruce Baumgartner (USA)	Aleksandr Karelin (UT)
1993	Bruce Baumgartner (USA)	Aleksandr Karelin (Russia)
1994	Mahmut Demir (Turkey)	Aleksandr Karelin (Russia)
1995	Bruce Baumgartner (USA)	Aleksandr Karelin (Russia)
1996	Mahmut Demir (Turkey)	Aleksandr Karelin (Russia)
1997	Zekeriya Güclü (Turkey)	Aleksandr Karelin (Russia)
1998	Alexis Rodriguez (Cuba)	Aleksandr Karelin (Russia)
1999	Stephen Neal (USA)	Aleksandr Karelin (Russia)
2000	David Moussoulbes (Russia)	Rulon Gardner (USA)
2001	David Moussoulbes (Russia)	Rulon Gardner (USA)
2002	David Moussoulbes (Russia)	Dremiel Byers (USA)
2003	Artur Taymazov (Uzbekistan)	Khassan Baroev (Russia)
2004	Artur Taymazov (Uzbekistan)	Khassan Baroev (Russia)
2005	Aydin Polatci (Turkey)	Mijail López Núñez (Cuba)
2006	Artur Taymazov (Uzbekistan)	Khassan Baroev (Russia)
2007	Bilyal Makhov (Russia)	Mijail López Núñez (Cuba)

Wrestling Around the World

Other forms of wrestling include *sumo*, the national sport in Japan; *sambo* in Russia; *kushti* in Iran; *glima* in Iceland; *Schwingen* in Switzerland; and *yagli*, the national sport in Turkey. There are also variations within the UK, such as *Devon and Cornwall* wrestling and *Cumberland and Westmoreland* wrestling.

CRUFTS WINNERS

Crufts is the world's largest dog show. It is held annually under the auspices of the Kennel Club UK. Named after the show's founder, Charles Cruft (1852–1938); first held in 1891.

Year	Name	Breed
1983	Ch Montravia Kaskarak Hitari	Afghan Hound
1984	Ch Saxonsprings Hackensack	Lhasa Apso
1985	Ch Montravia Tommy-Gun	Standard Poodle
1986	Ch Ginger Xmas Carol	Airedale Terrier
1987	Ch Viscount Grant	Afghan Hound
1988	Sh Ch Starlite Express at Valsett	English Setter
1989	Ch Potterdale Classic of Moonhill	Bearded Collie
1990	Ch Olac Moon Pilot	West Highland White Terrier
1991	Sh Ch Raycrofts Socialite	Clumber Spaniel
1992	Ch Pencloe Dutch Gold	Whippet
1993	Sh Ch Danaway Debonair	Irish Setter
1994	Ch Purston Hit	Welsh Terrier
1995	Ch Starchelle Chicago Bear	Irish Setter
1996	Sh Ch Canigou Cambrai	Cocker Spaniel
1997	Ch Ozmilion Mystification	Yorkshire Terrier
1998	Ch Saredon Forever Young	Welsh Terrier
1999	Sh Ch Caspians Intrepid	Irish Setter
2000	Ch Torums Scarf Michael	Kerry Blue Terrier
2001	Ch Jethard Cidevant	Basenji
2002	Nord Ch Topscore Contradiction	Standard Poodle
2003	Ch Yakee A Dangerous Liaison	Pekingese
2004	Ch Cobyco Call The Tune	Whippet
2005	Am Ch/Ch Cracknor Cause Celebre	Norfolk Terrier
2006	Am Ch Caitland Isle Take a Chance	Australian Shepherd
2007	Ch/Am Ch Araki Fabulous Willy	Tibetan Terrier

Note: In the names of pedigree dogs, Ch stands for Champion, Am Ch for American Champion, Nord Ch for Nordic Champion and Sh Ch for Show Champion.

MONOPOLY® PROPERTY VALUES

Property values shown are for the standard British edition of the game.

Property	Value	Colour	Property	Value	Colour
Old Kent Road	£60	brown	Bow Street	£180	orange
Whitechapel Road	£60	brown	Marlborough Street	£180	orange
King's Cross Station	£200	—	Vine Street	£200	orange
The Angel Islington	£100	light blue	Strand	£220	red
Euston Road	£100	light blue	Fleet Street	£220	red
Pentonville Road	£120	light blue	Trafalgar Square	£240	red
Pall Mall	£140	pink	Fenchurch Street Station	£200	—
Electric Company	£150	—	Leicester Square	£260	yellow
Whitehall	£140	pink	Coventry Street	£260	yellow
Northumberland Avenue	£160	pink	Water Works	£150	—
Marylebone Station	£200	—	Piccadilly	£280	yellow

Property	Value	Colour	Property	Value	Colour
Regent Street	£300	green	Park Lane	£350	navy blue/ purple
Oxford Street	£300	green			
Bond Street	£320	green	Mayfair	£400	navy blue/ purple
Liverpool Street Station	£200	—			

More than a Game ...

When Monopoly® games were sent to prisoner-of-war camps during World War II, the prisoners were getting more than an evening's entertainment. The UK manufacturers of the time, Waddingtons, came up with ingenious ways to conceal maps, compasses and other escape equipment inside the board and pieces, and real bank notes were also hidden amongst the game's currency.

BINGO CALLS

A selection of traditional bingo calls is given.

1 Kelly's eye *or* Buttered scone *or* At the beginning
2 One little duck *or* Me and you *or* Little boy blue
3 Cup of tea *or* You and me
4 Knock at the door
5 Man alive
6 Half a dozen *or* Tom's tricks
7 Lucky
8 Garden Gate *or* One fat lady
9 Doctor's orders
10 Gordon's Den[1]
11 Legs eleven
12 One dozen
13 Unlucky for some *or* Baker's dozen
14 Valentine's Day
15 Young and keen *or* Rugby Team
16 Sweet sixteen *or* Never been kissed
17 Dancing queen
18 Coming of age *or* Now you can vote
19 Goodbye teens
20 One score
21 Key of the door
22 Two little ducks *or* All the twos
23 Thee and me *or* The Lord's My Shepherd
24 Two dozen
25 Duck and dive
30 Dirty Gertie
40 Naughty forty
50 Half a century
60 Five dozen
70 Three score and ten
80 Eight and blank
90 Top of the shop

[1] *Name changes with the incumbent prime minister; for example, during Margaret Thatcher's time in office it would have been Maggie's Den.*

Bingo Lingo

Other classic bingo calls include *Tweak of the thumb* (51), *Heinz varieties* (57), *Brighton line* (59), *Old age pension* (65), *Clickety click* (66), *Danny la Rue* (72), *Trombones* (76), *Torquay in Devon* (87), *Two fat ladies* (88) and *Nearly there* (89). However, holiday camp operator Butlins have been trying out some more modern versions: *Buckle my Shoe* (32) has become *Jimmy Choo* and *Bang on the Drum* (71) has been dropped in favour of *J-Lo's Bum*!

INDEX

A

B

D

E

F

G

H

I

L

N

O

P

Q

R

S

U

V

W

Y

Z